Lecture Notes in Computer Science 16082

Founding Editors

Gerhard Goos
Juris Hartmanis

AF173219

The series Lecture Notes in Computer Science (LNCS), including its subseries Lecture Notes in Artificial Intelligence (LNAI) and Lecture Notes in Bioinformatics (LNBI), has established itself as a medium for the publication of new developments in computer science and information technology research, teaching, and education.

LNCS enjoys close cooperation with the computer science R & D community, the series counts many renowned academics among its volume editors and paper authors, and collaborates with prestigious societies. Its mission is to serve this international community by providing an invaluable service, mainly focused on the publication of conference and workshop proceedings and postproceedings. LNCS commenced publication in 1973.

Davide Taibi · Darja Smite
Editors

Software Engineering and Advanced Applications

51st Euromicro Conference, SEAA 2025
Salerno, Italy, September 10–12, 2025
Proceedings, Part II

 Springer

Editors
Davide Taibi ⓘ
University of Oulu
Oulu, Finland

Darja Smite ⓘ
Blekinge Institute of Technology
Karlskrona, Sweden

ISSN 0302-9743   ISSN 1611-3349 (electronic)
Lecture Notes in Computer Science
ISBN 978-3-032-04199-9   ISBN 978-3-032-04200-2 (eBook)
https://doi.org/10.1007/978-3-032-04200-2

This Springer imprint is published by the registered company Springer Nature Switzerland AG
The registered company address is: Gewerbestrasse 11, 6330 Cham, Switzerland

If disposing of this product, please recycle the paper.

Preface

These three LNCS volumes contain the papers presented at SEAA 2025, the *51st Euromicro Conference Series on Software Engineering and Advanced Applications*, held on September 10–12, 2025, in Salerno, Italy.

SEAA serves as a long-standing international forum for researchers, practitioners, and students to share and discuss the latest innovations, emerging trends, practical experiences, and ongoing challenges and concerns in the field of software engineering and advanced information technology applications for software-intensive systems.

To address this mission, the 2025 edition of SEAA once again brought together a vibrant community through a diverse program. This year, the conference featured nine specialized tracks, each led by a team of co-chairs. These tracks spanned a wide range of topics and reflected the truly multidisciplinary nature of software engineering research and practice.

This year, SEAA received a record high number of 177 research submissions over nine thematic tracks. Each submission underwent a rigorous single-blinded peer-review process. Every paper was assigned to at least three and up to five independent reviewers, selected based on topic expertise. Reviewers were each asked to evaluate 2–3 papers. They assessed submissions according to criteria such as scientific soundness, originality, relevance to the SEAA community and the track theme, clarity of presentation, and contribution to the field. In cases where reviews yielded divergent scores or conflicting recommendations, track chairs actively moderated discussions to facilitate consensus. Conflicts of interest with the track chairs were further handled by the PC Chairs.

Following this process, a total of 62 full papers (including two vision papers) and 20 short papers were selected for inclusion in the proceedings. The diverse set of contributions reflects the high quality and breadth of work being conducted in the SEAA community.

The final program would not have been possible to complete without the effort, commitment, and invaluable contribution of the track chairs. From managing submissions and overseeing the peer-review process, to assisting in completing the exciting program, the track chairs were central to SEAA 2025's quality and relevance. We express our sincere appreciation to the track chairs as listed below.

1. **Cyber-Physical Systems** (CPS): V. Klös (Carl von Ossietzky University of Oldenburg, Germany), and S. Mubeen (Mälardalen University, Sweden)
2. **Data-and AI-Driven Engineering** (DAIDE): J. Bosch (Chalmers & Gothenburg University, Sweden), and H. Holmström Olsson (Malmö University, Sweden)
3. **Emerging Computing Technologies** (ECT): R. Abreu (University of Porto and Meta Inc., Portugal), A. Janes (Free University of Bozen-Bolzano, Italy), V. Lenarduzzi (University of Oulu, Finland), and S. Ali (Simula Research Laboratory, Oslo, Norway)
4. **Model-Driven Engineering and Modeling Languages** (MDEML): A. Bucaioni (Mälardalen University, Sweden), F. Ciccozzi (Mälardalen University, Sweden), and A. Wortmann (Stuttgart University, Germany)

5. **Software Management: Measurement, Peopleware, and Innovation** (SM): O. Demirors (Izmir Institute of Technology, Turkey), and V. Pontillo (Vrije Universiteit Brussel, Belgium)

6. **Systematic Literature Reviews and Mapping Studies in Software Engineering** (SMSE): S. Swift (Brunel University London, UK), and Mahir Arzoky (Brunel University London, UK)

7. **Software Process and Product Improvement** (SPPI): S. Biffl (Vienna University of Technology, Austria), R. Rabiser (Johannes Kepler University Linz, Austria), and D. Winkler (Vienna University of Technology, Austria)

8. **Software Analytics: Mining Software Open Datasets and Repositories** (STREAM): A. Ampatzoglou (University of Macedonia, Greece), and E.M. Arvanitou (University of Macedonia, Greece)

9. **Practical Aspects of Software Engineering** (KKIO): L. Madeyski, (Wrocław University of Science and Technology, Poland), M. Ochodek (Poznań University of Technology, Poland), M. Staron (University of Gothenburg, Sweden), and A. Zalewski (Warsaw University of Technology, Poland)

We extend our gratitude to the SEAA 2025 keynote speakers—Henry Muccini from FrAmeLab, University of L'Aquila, and Alberto Brandolini from Avanscoperta—for sharing their thought-provoking insights and helping to spark discussions throughout the event. Their talks on LLM-Agent Architectures and the Pitfalls of Remote Work were true highlights of the program.

Finally, we would also like to thank SEAA Steering Committee members for their continued guidance and valuable advice throughout the organization of the conference.

We hope you thoroughly enjoyed Euromicro SEAA 2025 and found it inspiring, insightful, and engaging.

July 2025

Davide Taibi
Darja Šmite

Organization

Program Committee Chairs

Davide Taibi   University of Oulu, Finland
Darja Šmite   Blekinge Institute of Technology, Sweden

General Chairs

Gemma Catolino   University of Salerno, Italy
Carmine Gravino   University of Salerno, Italy

Publicity Chair

Matteo Esposito   University of Oulu, Finland

Proceedings Chairs

Ashley van Can   Utrecht University, Netherlands
Julian Frattini   Chalmers University of Technology and
                                   University of Gothenburg, Sweden

Finance Chair

Francesco Leporati   University of Pavia, Italy

Steering Committee

Stefan Biffl   Technische Universität Wien, Austria
Michel Chaudron   Eindhoven University of Technology, Netherlands
Onur Demirors   IzTech, Turkey
Carmine Gravino   University of Salerno, Italy

| Helena Holmström Olsson | Malmö University, Sweden |
| Andreas Wortmann | Stuttgart University, Germany |

Program Committee

Alain Abran	École de Technologie Supérieure, Canada
Shaukat Ali	Simula Research Laboratory, Norway
Rami Almwari	Brunel University London, UK
Mohammad Alshayeb	King Fahd University of PetroleumMinerals, Saudi Arabia
Ahmad Altarawneh	Brunel University London, UK
Sousuke Amasaki	Nanzan University, Japan
Apostolos Ampatzoglou	University of Macedonia, Greece
Areti Ampatzoglou	Aristotle University of Thessaloniki, Greece
Vasilios Andrikopoulos	University of Groningen, the Netherlands
Lefteris Angelis	Aristotle University of Thessaloniki, Greece
Paolo Arcaini	National Institute of Informatics, Japan
Ove Armbrust	Apple, USA
Elvira-Maria Arvanitou	University of Macedonia, Greece
Mahir Arzoky	Brunel University London, UK
Vaibhav Kumar Bajpai	Microsoft, USA
Francesco Basciani	Gran Sasso Science Institute, Italy
Steffen Becker	University of Stuttgart, Germany
Christian Berger	University of Gothenburg, Sweden
Stamatia Bibi	University of Western Macedonia, Greece
Stefan Biffl	TU Wien, Austria
Ilona Bluemke	Warsaw University of Technology, Poland
Florian Bock	Friedrich-Alexander Universität Erlangen, Germany
Marek Bolanowski	Rzeszów University of Technology, Poland
Matthias Book	University of Iceland, Iceland
Jan Bosch	Chalmers University of Technology, Sweden
Ruth Breu	University of Innsbruck, Austria
Alessio Bucaioni	Mälardalen University, Sweden
Alena Buchalcevova	Prague University of Economics and Business, Czechia
Daniel Bujosa	Mälardalen University, Sweden
Piotr Błaszyński	West Pomeranian University of Technology, Poland
Matteo Camilli	Politecnico di Milano, Italy
Jose Campos	University of Porto, Portugal

Gustavo Carvalho	Universidade Federal de Pernambuco, Brazil
Theodore Chaikalis	University of Macedonia, Greece
Panagiota Chatzipetrou	Örebro University, Sweden
Michel Chaudron	Eindhoven University of Technology, The Netherlands
Sophie Chaveli	Brunel University London, UK
Antonio Cicchetti	Mälardalen University, Sweden
Federico Ciccozzi	Mälardalen University, Sweden
Steve Counsell	Brunel University London, UK
Tommaso Cucinotta	Scuola Superiore Sant'Anna, Italy
Wlodzimierz Dabrowski	Warsaw University of Technology, Poland
Maya Daneva	University of Twente, the Netherlands
Juan de Lara	Universidad Autónoma de Madrid, Spain
Onur Demirors	İzmir Institute of Technology, Turkey
Anna Derezinska	Warsaw University of Technology, Poland
Giuseppe Destefanis	Brunel University London, UK
Dario Di Dario	University of Salerno, Italy
Davide Di Ruscio	University of L'Aquila, Italy
Amleto Di Salle	Gran Sasso Science Institute, Italy
Pedro Diniz	University of Porto, Portugal
Arpita Dutta	National University of Singapore, Singapore
Frank Elberzhager	Fraunhofer IESE, Germany
Traecy Elezi	Brunel University London, UK
Christoph Elsner	Siemens AG, Germany
Matteo Esposito	University of Oulu, Finland
Aleksander Fabijan	Microsoft, USA
Daniel Feitosa	University of Groningen, The Netherlands
Sebastian Feld	Delft University of Technology, The Netherlands
Michael Felderer	German Aerospace Center (DLR), Germany and University of Cologne, Germany
Filomena Ferrucci	University of Salerno, Italy
Mariusz Flasinski	Jagiellonian University, Poland
Vahid Garousi	Queen's University Belfast, UK
Marcela Genero	University of Castilla-La Mancha, Spain
Simos Gerasimou	University of York, UK
Christopher Gerking	Karlsruhe Institute of Technology, Germany
Fabian Gilson	University of Canterbury, New Zealand
Görkem Giray	Independent Researcher, Turkey
Krzysztof Goczyła	Gdańsk University of Technology, Poland
Thomas Goldschmidt	Avalara, Germany
Raffaela Groner	Chalmers University of Technology, Sweden and University of Gothenburg, Sweden

Volker Gruhn	University of Duisburg-Essen, Germany
Rong Gu	Mälardalen University, Sweden
Sebastian Götz	Dresden University of Technology, Germany
Tuna Hacaloglu	Atilim University, Turkey and École de Technologie Superieure, Canada
Simon Hacks	Stockholm University, Sweden
Philipp Haindl	St. Pölten University of Applied Sciences, Austria
David Halasz	Microsoft, Czechia
Rachel Harrison	Oxford Brookes University, UK
Sara Hassan	Birmingham City University, UK
Petra Heck	Fontys University of Applied Sciences, The Netherlands
Jens Heidrich	Fraunhofer IESE, Germany
Paula Herber	University of Münster, Germany
Sebastian Herold	Karlstad University, Sweden
Hans-Martin Heyn	Chalmers University of Technology, Sweden and University of Gothenburg, Sweden
Bogumila Hnatkowska	Wrocław University of Technology, Poland
Petr Hnetynka	Charles University, Czechia
Helena Holmström Olsson	Malmö University, Sweden
Frank Houdek	Mercedes-Benz AG, Germany
Zbigniew Huzar	Wrocław University of Technology, Poland
Sami Hyrynsalmi	LUT University, Finland
Martin Höst	Malmö University, Sweden
Zear Ibrahim	Brunel University London, UK
Andrea Janes	Free University of Bozen-Bolzano, Italy
Aleksander Jarzebowicz	Gdańsk University of Technology, Poland
Frank Johnsen	Norwegian Defence Research Establishment (FFI), Norway
Robbert Jongeling	Mälardalen University, Sweden
Marija Katic	University of London, UK
Wiem Khlif	University of Sfax, Tunisia
Michael Klaes	Fraunhofer IESE, Germany
Verena Klös	Universität Oldenburg, Germany
Ayça Kolukısa Tarhan	Hacettepe University, Turkey
Sylwia Kopczynska	Poznań University of Technology, Poland
Piotr Kosiuczenko	Military University of Technology, Poland
Marek Kretowski	Bialystok University of Technology, Poland
Marco Kuhrmann	Reutlingen University, Germany
Supriya Lal	Yelp Inc., USA
Malvina Latifaj	Mälardalen University, Sweden
Valentina Lenarduzzi	University of Oulu, Finland

Zengyang Li	Central China Normal University, China
Peng Liang	Wuhan University, China
Sherlock Licorish	University of Otago, New Zealand
Lech Madeyski	Wrocław University of Science and Technology, Poland
Nazim Madhavji	University of Western Ontario, Canada
Ashley Mann	Brunel University of London, UK
Faisal Maramazi	Brunel University of London, UK
Rui Maranhao	University of Porto, Portugal
Bartosz Marcinkowski	University of Gdansk, Poland
Antonio Martini	University of Oslo, Norway
Jacopo Mauro	University of Southern Denmark, Denmark
Alistair Mcewan	University of Derby, UK
Jorge Melegati	Free University of Bozen-Bolzano, Italy
Emilia Mendes	Aarhus University, Denmark
Andreas Metzger	Paluno and University of Duisburg-Essen, Germany
Judith Michael	RWTH Aachen University, Germany
Jakub Miler	Gdansk University of Technology, Poland
Yoshiki Mitani	SEC and IPA, Japan
Milko Monecke	Technische Universität Berlin, Germany
Maurizio Morisio	Politecnico di Torino, Italy
Saad Mubeen	Mälardalens University, Sweden
Henry Muccini	University of L'Aquila, Italy
Tomi Männistö	University of Helsinki, Finland
Jürgen Münch	Reutlingen University, Germany
Elisa Yumi Nakagawa	University of São Paulo, Brazil
Jerzy Nawrocki	Poznań University of Technology, Poland
Erika Nazaruka	Riga Technical University, Latvia
Michael Neumann	Hochschule Hannover, Germany
Yen Ying Ng	Nicolaus Copernicus University, Poland
Arne Noyer	Ostfalia University of Applied Sciences, Germany
Mirosław Ochodek	Poznań University of Technology, Poland
Marco Ortu	University of Cagliari, Italy
Necmettin Ozkan	Gebze Technical University, Turkey
Claus Pahl	Free University of Bozen-Bolzano, Italy
Oscar Pastor	Universidad Politécnica de Valencia, Spain
Andrzej Paszkiewicz	Rzeszów University of Technology, Poland
Fabiano Pecorelli	Pegaso University, Italy
Rui Humberto Pereira	Instituto Superior de Contabilidade e Administração do Porto, Portugal
Manuela Petrescu	Babeş-Bolyai University Cluj-Napoca, Romania

Daniel Strüber	Chalmers University of Technology and University of Gothenburg, Sweden, and Radboud University Nijmegen, Netherlands
Jacek Stój	Silesian University of Technology, Poland
Dan Mircea Suciu	Babeş-Bolyai University Cluj-Napoca, Romania
Jakub Swacha	University of Szczecin, Poland
Stephen Swift	Brunel University of London, UK
Kari Systä	Tampere University of Technology, Finland
Tomasz Szmuc	AGH University of Science and Technology, Poland
Marcin Szpyrka	AGH University of Science and Technology, Poland
Davide Taibi	University of Oulu, Finland
Matthias Tichy	Ulm University, Germany
Juha-Pekka Tolvanen	MetaCase, Finland, and University of Jyväskylä, Finland
Adam Trendowicz	Fraunhofer IESE, Germany
Dimitri Van Landuyt	Katholieke Universiteit Leuven, Belgium
Anita Walkowiak	Wrocław University of Science and Technology, Poland
Bartosz Walter	Poznań University of Technology, Poland
Jörg Walter	OFFIS Institute for Information Technology, Germany
Xiaofeng Wang	Free University of Bozen-Bolzano, Italy
Bianca Wiesmayr	Johannes Kepler University Linz, Austria
Dietmar Winkler	Vienna University of Technology, Austria
Emily Winter	Lancaster University, UK
Andreas Wortmann	University of Stuttgart, Germany
Konrad Wrona	NATO Communications and Information Agency, The Netherlands
Włodzimierz Wysocki	West Pomeranian University of Technology, Poland
Andrzej Zalewski	Warsaw University of Technology, Poland
Janusz Zalewski	Florida Gulf Coast University, USA
Jianjun Zhao	Kyushu University, Japan
Zbigniew Zielinski	Military University of Technology, Poland
Darja Šmite	Blekinge Institute of Technology, Sweden

Sponsors

Contents – Part II

**Systematic Literature Reviews and Mapping Studies in Software
Engineering**

Practical Aspects of Software Engineering

Unmasking Out Code Smells: A Multiphase Framework for Accurate and Scalable Detection

Bruno Monteiro, Kouamana Bousson, and Nuno Pombo$^{(\boxtimes)}$

Universidade da Beira Interior, Covilhã, Portugal
{bruno.miguel.monteiro,bousson,ngpombo}@ubi.pt

Abstract. Detecting code smells is crucial for maintaining software quality and mitigating technical debt, as these subtle design issues complicate software maintainability and evolution. Existing heuristic-based tools and static analysis frameworks often struggle with the complexity of modern systems, yielding inconsistent and unscalable results. This research introduces a multiphase framework for code smell detection, integrating Modified Fuzzy C-Means with supervision (MFCMS) and Principal Component Analysis (PCA) to improve feature selection, reduce dimensionality, and enhance detection accuracy while ensuring scalability.

The framework leverages MFCMS to address feature uncertainty and PCA to mitigate feature correlation, enabling efficient, interpretable feature selection that preserves essential data for accurate classification. Although the framework shows promise, challenges in generalizability to diverse datasets and code smells, as well as dataset imbalance, are acknowledged, offering directions for future research. This work advances the state of the art by providing a robust, scalable, and practical methodology for automated code smell detection, integral to modern software quality assurance practices.

Keywords: Code Smells · Machine Learning in Software · Engineering · Software Quality · Modified Fuzzy C-Means Algorithm (MFCMS)

1 Introduction

1.1 Motivation

The quality of software systems is critical for ensuring their maintainability, scalability, and long-term success. Code smells, subtle indicators of potential design issues, negatively impact software quality by increasing technical debt and complicating system evolution [3]. Detecting and addressing code smells early in the development lifecycle is essential to minimize maintenance costs and ensure robust, high-quality software.

Despite the availability of static analysis tools and traditional approaches for code smell detection, these methods often fall short in providing reliable results. They tend to rely on rigid heuristics, which are prone to generating high false positive and false negative rates, making their outcomes inconsistent [13]. Furthermore, the growing complexity of modern software systems introduces challenges in handling large datasets, overlapping feature spaces, and the evolving nature of software metrics [19].

© The Author(s), under exclusive license to Springer Nature Switzerland AG 2026
D. Taibi and D. Smite (Eds.): SEAA 2025, LNCS 16082, pp. 3–22, 2026.
https://doi.org/10.1007/978-3-032-04200-2_1

Recent advancements in machine learning offer a promising direction for addressing these challenges. By leveraging intelligent models capable of extracting complex patterns from data, machine learning provides opportunities to enhance the accuracy, scalability, and adaptability of code smell detection frameworks. The integration of advanced techniques in feature selection and dimensionality reduction has further enabled the creation of efficient and generalizable solutions to tackle high-dimensional data and improve detection performance.

1.2 Research Gap

Despite significant advancements in automated code smell detection, several challenges and gaps remain unaddressed. Traditional approaches, such as heuristic-based static analysis tools (e.g., SonarQube [4]), often suffer from limited flexibility, high false positive rates, and an inability to generalize across diverse software systems. These limitations highlight the need for more adaptable and scalable solutions.

Machine learning techniques have shown promise in improving detection accuracy; however, their effectiveness is often hindered by high-dimensional datasets and feature redundancy [1]. Existing feature selection methods, while useful, frequently fail to handle the overlapping and uncertain relationships inherent in software metrics. This gap is particularly evident in the limited use of advanced fuzzy logic systems, which can provide a more nuanced approach to dealing with uncertainty in software data.

Another notable gap lies in the generalizability and quality of detection frameworks. On the one hand, datasets used in this area are often not publicly accessible or are created without the involvement of expert software developers. Additionally, limited attention has been paid to the interpretability of results, which is critical for actionable quality assurance. Without clear and interpretable outputs, even advanced models may face resistance in real-world adoption, undermining their practical value.

These gaps underline the necessity for a multiphase methodology that combines robust feature selection, scalable machine learning models, and interpretable results. Such methodologies must also consider the integration of real-time detection capabilities to support modern continuous integration and delivery pipelines. This study addresses these challenges by integrating Modified Fuzzy C-Means with supervision (MFCMS) and Principal Component Analysis (PCA) to improve the accuracy, efficiency, and scalability of code smell detection frameworks.

1.3 Research Questions

This study aims to address the following research questions:

- RQ1: How effective is the proposed multiphase methodology in improving the accuracy and reliability of detecting code smells, specifically the Long Method smell, compared to existing approaches?
- RQ2: What is the impact of using the Modified Fuzzy C-Means algorithm with supervision (MFCMS) for feature selection on the overall model performance?
- RQ3: How does the integration of Principal Component Analysis (PCA) affect the dimensionality reduction and classification accuracy?

- RQ4: What are the trade-offs in computational cost versus detection performance when applying the proposed feature selection techniques?
- RQ5: How does the proposed methodology perform across different datasets and software systems, in terms of generalizability and robustness?
- RQ6: How do the results vary between the experimental setups using only MFCMS and the combination of MFCMS and PCA?

1.4 Contributions

1. Development of a Multiphase Methodology for Code Smell Detection: The integration of MFCMS and PCA provides a novel approach to feature selection, reducing dimensionality while preserving critical information for accurate classification. This methodology effectively combines fuzzy logic with advanced statistical techniques, offering a robust and scalable solution for code smell detection.
2. Application of Fuzzy Logic for Handling Uncertainty in Feature Selection: The use of MFCMS demonstrates the capability of fuzzy logic to address the overlapping and uncertain nature of software metrics. This contribution highlights the potential of fuzzy systems to improve machine learning applications in software engineering.
3. Scalability and Generalizability of the Framework: By addressing high-dimensionality challenges and reducing computational overhead, the methodology is adapt able to diverse datasets and other types of code smells, demonstrating its potential for broader applications in software quality assurance

These contributions collectively push the boundaries of automated code smell detection, making substantial advancements in accuracy, efficiency, and applicability.

2 Background

Detecting and mitigating code smells is a critical aspect of software quality assurance, with numerous approaches proposed in recent years. This section provides an overview of existing methods, highlighting their strengths, limitations, and the gaps addressed by the proposed methodology.

2.1 Code Smells and Their Impact on Software Quality

Code smells are indicators of potential design flaws or coding practices that may not directly cause errors but make a codebase harder to maintain, extend, and understand. They often signify deeper structural issues, such as poor modularization, excessive complexity, or violations of best practices [18]. Common examples include the Long Method, God Class, and Data Clump. While code smells are not inherently bugs, they correlate strongly with decreased readability, higher maintenance costs, and increased technical debt—hidden costs accumulated from suboptimal decisions that hinder future development. As technical debt grows, teams may face challenges such as slower development cycles and higher defect rates, making code smell detection and resolution a critical task [19].

The automation of code smell detection has become increasingly significant in modern software development practices. With the growing size and complexity of software systems, relying solely on manual reviews or heuristic-based tools is no longer sufficient. Automated detection tools can systematically identify smells across large codebases, enabling teams to address issues early in the development lifecycle. By integrating automated code smell detection into continuous integration pipelines, organizations can ensure that code quality remains high, reducing long-term costs and improving software reliability [5]. Furthermore, automated tools enhance collaboration by providing objective insights, helping developers prioritize and resolve smells effectively.

Despite its importance, detecting code smells presents several challenges. First, the subjective nature of code smells leads to inconsistencies in definitions and thresholds [2, 10]. For example, what constitutes a Long Method may vary between projects and teams. Second, the availability and quality of datasets for training detection models are often limited, with many datasets focusing on specific smells or programming languages. Finally, the computational complexity of analyzing large codebases and high-dimensional feature spaces can hinder scalability. Advanced techniques in machine learning and feature selection are crucial for overcoming these challenges, enabling more accurate, scalable, and adaptable detection frameworks. These challenges underline the need for innovative methodologies that balance precision, scalability, and interpretability in code smell detection.

2.2 Static Analysis Tools

Static analysis tools, such as SonarQube, and Checkstyle[1], have been the foundation for code smell detection in software development. These tools rely on heuristic-based rules to identify potential design flaws by matching code against predefined patterns. Their ease of use and ability to quickly scan large code-bases make them popular among development teams. However, their rigidity poses significant limitations. Heuristic rules often fail to adapt to varying contexts, leading to high rates of false positives or false negatives.

This inflexibility makes these tools less effective for projects with unique coding standards or complex architectural designs. Furthermore, static tools generally focus on syntactic patterns and struggle to analyze deeper semantic relationships in the code, limiting their capability to detect nuanced code smells.

2.3 Machine Learning-Based Methods

In response to the limitations of heuristic-based tools, machine learning approaches have gained traction for code smell detection [1, 9]. Supervised methods, such as decision trees, support vector machines (SVM), and ensemble techniques like random forests, leverage labeled datasets to classify code smells with greater accuracy [21]. Unsupervised methods, including clustering algorithms, identify patterns in unlabeled data, making them suitable for exploratory analysis. Machine learning models offer the advantage of learning from data, enabling them to adapt to different contexts and improve detection

---

[1] https://github.com/checkstyle/checkstyle.

over time. However, these approaches are not without challenges. Many machine learning models require high-dimensional datasets, which can lead to overfitting, particularly when training data is limited [17]. Additionally, the results produced by these models are often difficult to interpret, making it challenging for developers to trust and act on the findings.

2.4   Feature Selection Techniques

Feature selection is a critical step in machine learning workflows for code smell detection, as it directly impacts the accuracy and efficiency of the models. Techniques such as PCA, mutual information, and clustering-based approaches are commonly used to reduce dataset dimensionality [15]. PCA, for example, transforms features into uncorrelated principal components, mitigating multicollinearity and enhancing model performance. Mutual information identifies the most relevant features by measuring their dependency on the target variable. Clustering methods group similar features, allowing irrelevant or redundant ones to be excluded. Despite their benefits, feature selection techniques face challenges in retaining all essential information while reducing complexity. Over-reduction can lead to loss of key features, negatively impacting detection accuracy, while insufficient reduction can increase computational costs, particularly for large-scale systems.

2.5   Integrating and Advancing Detection Approaches

The combination of static analysis, machine learning, and feature selection techniques represents a growing trend in code smell detection [7]. Hybrid approaches aim to leverage the simplicity of heuristic-based tools with the adaptability and accuracy of machine learning models. For instance, static tools can provide initial rule-based detections that are refined using machine learning and optimized feature sets. This layered approach addresses the shortcomings of individual techniques, improving detection reliability and scalability. However, integrating these methods introduces additional complexity, such as ensuring seamless interoperability between tools and managing the trade-offs between performance and interpretability. Despite these challenges, hybrid and advanced approaches show promise for creating robust frameworks capable of detecting code smells in diverse software contexts, paving the way for more maintainable and high-quality codebases.

The integration of static analysis, machine learning, and feature selection techniques for code smell detection introduces several significant challenges that must be addressed to ensure effective and scalable solutions. First, data limitations, such as the lack of high-quality and diverse datasets, inconsistent labeling, and class imbalance, hinder the development and generalization of machine learning models across varied software systems and contexts. Algorithmic challenges, including overfitting in high-dimensional datasets, feature redundancy, and the interpretability of black-box models, further complicate the detection process.

Furthermore, the seamless integration of these methods into a unified framework poses practical difficulties, as differences in data formats, processing needs, and outputs create interoperability issues. Balancing performance and scalability is particularly critical for large-scale codebases, as hybrid methods often increase computational overhead [16]. Moreover, embedding these approaches into realworld development workflows requires consideration of software diversity, ensuring that methods are adaptable to varying coding standards, architectures, and domain-specific requirements [11]. The need for real-time analysis in continuous integration and delivery pipelines adds further complexity, as does potential resistance from developers who may view these advanced techniques as overly complex or intrusive.

2.6 The Role of Fuzzy Logic in Software Engineering

Fuzzy logic [20], introduced as a mathematical framework for representing uncertainty and imprecision, has become an essential tool in various domains, including software engineering. Unlike classical logic systems that rely on binary decisions, fuzzy logic enables reasoning with degrees of truth, making it particularly well-suited for addressing subjective and ambiguous scenarios. In software engineering, many problems, such as code smell detection, involve inherently imprecise and overlapping definitions. For instance, determining whether a method is "too long" or a class is "too complex" often depends on subjective thresholds or vague criteria. Fuzzy logic provides a mechanism to formalize these uncertainties, allowing for more nuanced and flexible analysis that aligns with the complex nature of software systems.

In the context of feature selection and clustering, fuzzy logic has demonstrated significant utility, particularly for handling high-dimensional and noisy datasets. Feature selection methods leveraging fuzzy logic can evaluate the relevance of features by assigning them degrees of membership to clusters, thereby retaining critical attributes while filtering out redundant or irrelevant ones. For example, in code smell detection, fuzzy clustering can identify groups of software metrics that are most indicative of specific smells, such as cyclomatic complexity for Long Method or coupling metrics for God Class [14]. Beyond code smells, fuzzy logic has also been employed in software fault prediction, test case prioritization, and project risk assessment, showcasing its versatility in solving multifaceted software engineering problems.

Fuzzy clustering methods, such as the MFCM, offer distinct advantages over traditional clustering techniques. Unlike hard clustering methods, where each data point belongs to only one cluster, fuzzy clustering assigns membership values to multiple clusters, capturing the overlap and ambiguity inherent in software metric datasets. This flexibility is particularly beneficial for code smell detection, where metrics often exhibit partial or conflicting correlations with multiple smells. The MFCM improves upon classical fuzzy clustering by incorporating additional supervisory signals or constraints, enhancing the accuracy and relevance of cluster formation. These capabilities make fuzzy logic-based approaches a powerful complement to traditional machine learning methods, offering a robust solution for handling the uncertainty and complexity of software engineering tasks.

2.7 Advancements in Multiphase Detection Methodologies

The detection of code smells has increasingly benefited from multiphase methodologies that combine multiple techniques, such as clustering, dimensionality reduction, and machine learning models [6]. These hybrid approaches aim to leverage the strengths of individual techniques to enhance overall detection performance. For example, clustering methods can group related features or software metrics, while PCA reduces dimensionality and mitigates multicollinearity. Machine learning models, trained on these refined datasets, can then provide more accurate and generalizable predictions. Such combinations address the limitations of single-method approaches, improving both scalability and reliability in code smell detection. The integration of these techniques has proven effective in enhancing performance by managing high-dimensional data and uncovering subtle patterns within complex software systems [7].

Despite their promise, hybrid methods also reveal gaps and challenges. A widely adopted approach combines feature selection with classification; however, this integration often compromises model interpretability and overlooks the computational overhead associated with using multiple techniques. Research shows that while dimensionality reduction techniques like PCA are effective in improving efficiency, they may obscure the relationships between features, complicating the understanding of code smell indicators.

Furthermore, achieving a balance between computational efficiency, detection accuracy, and model interpretability remains a critical challenge. Addressing these gaps requires the development of methodologies that not only integrate techniques seamlessly but also provide interpretable results and operate efficiently in real-world software development environments.

These advancements point toward a promising future for scalable and actionable code smell detection frameworks.

3   Methods

This section outlines the methodology employed to develop and validate a robust framework for detecting code smells using a multiphase approach that integrates feature selection and machine learning techniques. The proposed methodology leverages fuzzy systems, specifically a modified version of the Fuzzy C-Means (FCM) algorithm, to optimize feature reduction and improve classification performance in detecting code smells. The focus is on the Long Method smell as a representative case study, though the framework is adaptable to other types of code smells.

3.1   Overview of the Proposed Approach

The methodology consists of the following main phases:

1. **Data Preprocessing**: Prepare the dataset by cleaning, normalizing, and splitting it into training and testing subsets.
2. **Feature Selection**: Use the MFCMS to reduce data dimensionality and extract the most relevant features.
3. **Model Training and Optimization**: Train machine learning models, optimizing hyperparameters to achieve high predictive accuracy.
4. **Evaluation and Validation**: Assess the effectiveness of the models using performance metrics such as accuracy, precision, recall, F1-score, and Area Under the Curve (AUC).

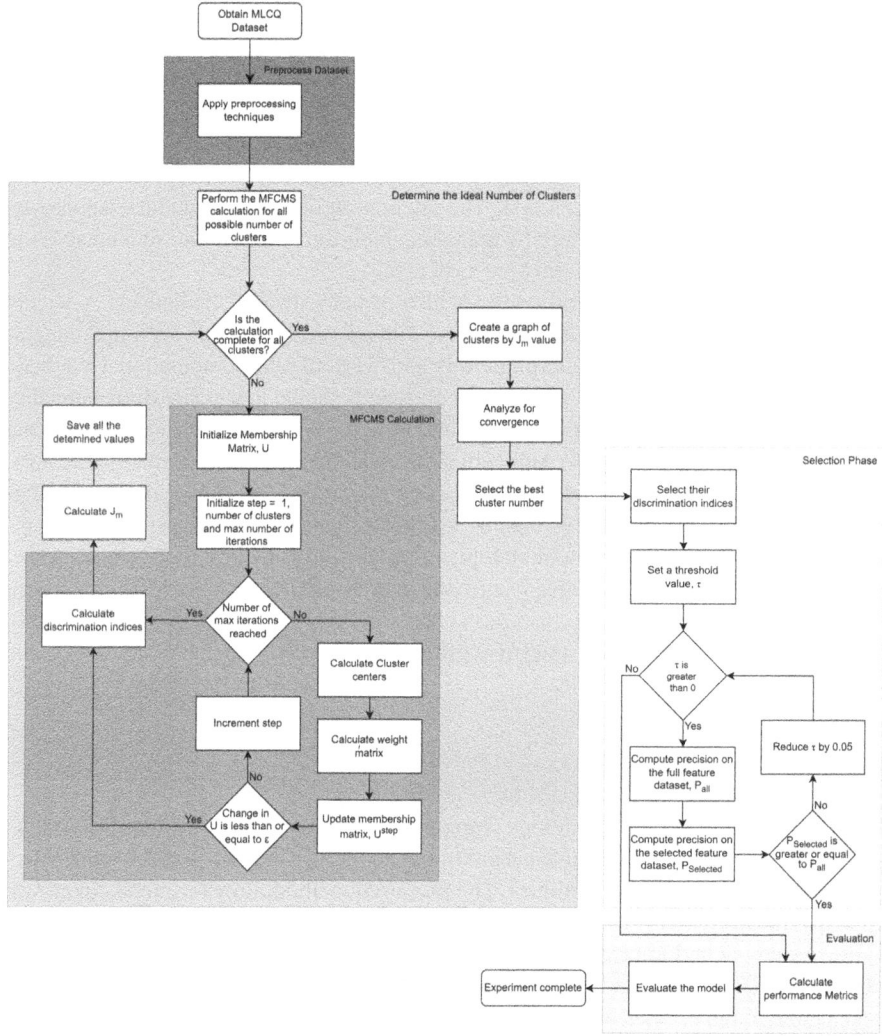

Fig. 1. Multiphase Methodology.

Figure 1 provides a visual overview of the multiphase methodology implemented for code smell detection. The flowchart begins with the dataset preprocessing phase, emphasizing the need for normalization and preparation of the software metrics for analysis. This step ensures consistency and scalability of the subsequent processes. The next phase involves feature selection, where clustering techniques iteratively refine the dataset by identifying and retaining the most relevant features. This phase is pivotal in reducing dimensionality and computational overhead while preserving critical information necessary for effective code smell detection.

The final stages of the methodology include machine learning model implementation and evaluation. In these phases, the refined dataset is used to train and optimize the classification model, with hyperparameter tuning ensuring optimal performance. The results are rigorously evaluated using metrics like accuracy, precision, recall, F1-score, and AUC to assess the methodology's effectiveness. The flowchart effectively conveys the structured, iterative nature of the approach, highlighting how each step integrates seamlessly to enhance detection performance and interpretability.

3.2 Dataset Preparation

The dataset used for this research was the Madeyski Lewowski Code Quest (MLCQ), which contains annotated examples of industrially relevant software projects exhibiting various code smells. For this study, we focused on instances highlighting the presence or absence of the Long Method smell. Additionally, we utilized the software metrics extracted by Kovačević et al., as extracting these metrics independently is time-consuming and requires specialized tools [8].

   The dataset was preprocessed as follows, according to each experiment:

- **Experiment 1**: The dataset was preprocessed using MinMax normalization to ensure that all features were scaled to the range [0, 1] , reducing the risk of bias due to differing feature scales. The dataset was also divided into training (70%) and testing (30%) sets;
- **Experiment 2**: For this experiment, the dataset was transformed using PCA without reducing the number of features. This transformation was performed to decorrelate the dataset's features and mitigate potential issues caused by highly correlated features. After applying PCA, the same normalization method used in Experiment 1 was applied. Additionally, the dataset was partitioned in the same way as in Experiment 1.

3.3 Feature Selection with MFCMS

Feature selection is a critical component for reducing dimensionality and enhancing the model's efficiency. A three-step feature selection process was applied:

1. **MFCMS:**

   - The MFCMS algorithm operates similarly to the traditional FCM algorithm by optimizing its objective function. However, it stands out by integrating both supervised and unsupervised components, enabling more effective cluster modeling;
   - For each feature, its discriminative power between clusters is assessed. These values indicate how effectively a feature distinguishes between clusters. A higher value signifies that the feature plays a more significant role in cluster separation, as it contributes more to differentiating between clusters.

2. **Determining the Ideal Number of Clusters:**

   - Determining the ideal number of clusters for the MFCMS algorithm is essential for effective feature selection, as it ensures that the clusters accurately capture meaningful patterns in the data. This was achieved by analyzing the value of the algorithm's objective function while excluding the supervised component of the formula.

By doing so, the final value reflects the natural structure of the data, free from any potential bias introduced by the supervised component;

– To find the ideal value, we applied the Cauchy convergence criterion, which states that the algorithm converges when the changes in cluster centers between successive iterations become negligibly small.

Specifically, this criterion ensures that the differences in cluster centers fall below a predefined threshold, signaling stability in the clustering process.

3. **Selection Phase:**

– This phase is dedicated to selecting the most important features in the dataset that will positively impact the overall performance of the learning model;
– The core idea is to identify the features that most significantly improve the model's outcome. This is accomplished by analyzing the discrimination indices of each feature across all clusters;
– The implementation of this process follows the same reasoning outlined by the authors in [12].

3.4   Machine Learning Model Development

The selected features were used to train a Random Forest classifier, a robust ensemble learning method known for its high accuracy and resilience against overfitting. The following steps were followed:

1. **Hyperparameter Optimization:**

– A Grid Search approach was employed to determine the optimal hyperparameters, including the number of trees, maximum tree depth, and minimum number of samples required to split a node;
– Cross-validation ensured that the chosen hyperparameters generalized well to unseen data.

2. **Training:**

– Ten-fold cross-validation was conducted during training to evaluate the model's ability to generalize to unseen data and to mitigate the risk of overfitting;
– The Random Forest classifier was trained on the preprocessed and featurere-duced dataset to allow comparison and to evaluate the effectiveness of the feature selection procedure.

3.5   Evaluation Metrics

The trained model was evaluated on a test set comprising unseen data, using a comprehensive set of performance metrics derived from the confusion matrix. These metrics included:

– **Accuracy**: Overall correctness of the predictions;
– **Precision**: Proportion of true positive predictions among all positive predictions;

- **Recall (Sensitivity)**: Ability of the model to identify all true positive instances;
- **F1-Score**: Harmonic mean of precision and recall, emphasizing the balance between the two;
- **Area Under the Curve (AUC) Score**: Ability of the model to distinguish between classes at varying threshold levels.

3.6 Experimental Validation

To ensure the generalizability and reliability of the approach, the following steps were taken:

1. **Experimentation**: Two experiments were conducted to evaluate the impact of different approaches to preprocessing the dataset on both the model's performance and the effectiveness of the feature selection process:

   - **Experiment 1**: The model was trained using the preprocessed dataset combined with the feature selection process based on MFCMS;
   - **Experiment 2**: The model was trained using the preprocessed dataset enhanced by PCA for feature decorrelation, in combination with the feature selection process based on MFCMS.

2. **Performance Comparison**: The results from both experiments were analyzed to assess the impact of dimensionality reduction on the model's performance. Specific performance metrics, derived from the confusion matrix and other evaluation methods, were used for this analysis. Additionally, the effectiveness of dataset reduction was evaluated in each experiment to derive meaningful conclusions about its influence on the model's accuracy, computational efficiency, and predictive reliability.

3.7 Implementation Environment

The experiments were conducted on a computing environment with the following specifications:

- **Processor**: AMD Ryzen 5 7600X;
- **RAM**: 32 GB;
- **GPU**: NVIDIA GeForce RTX 3060 12GB;
- **Software**: Python 3.10.12, Scikit-learn, NumPy, Pandas, and Matplotlib;
- **Operating System**: Windows 10 Pro with Windows Subsystem for Linux 2 (WSL2).

4 Results

This section presents the results of the experiments conducted to evaluate the proposed methodology for detecting code smells, with a particular focus on the Long Method smell. The evaluation emphasizes the effectiveness of the feature selection techniques and the overall performance of the machine learning model in identifying code smells.

As shown in Fig. 2, for Experiment 1, the ideal number of clusters was determined to be approximately $c = 10$. At this point, the curve flattens significantly, suggesting that the algorithm has likely converged, as per Cauchy's convergence criterion. Adding

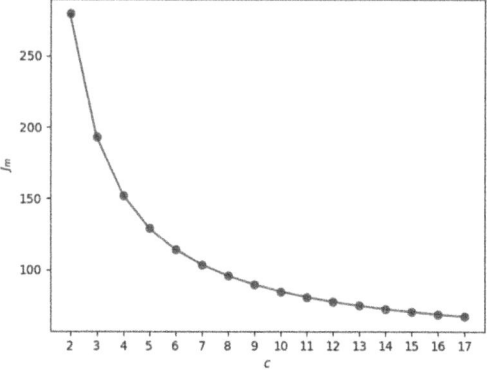

Fig. 2. Analysis of Jm against cluster number for Experiment 1.

Table 1. Number of features selected for the best threshold value τ in Experiment 1.

τ	Total Number of Features	Number of Features Selected
0.9999	26	24

more clusters beyond this threshold would not substantially improve the quality of the clustering. Therefore, the MFCMS algorithm for this experiment was executed with 10 clusters.

As shown in Table 1, with a threshold of $\tau = 0.9999$, 24 features were selected from the original 26. This result demonstrates the potential of MFCMS for dimensionality reduction. However, the reduction achieved in this experiment was not particularly significant.

Table 2. Results for the test set in the Experiment 1.

Metrics	Results without Feature Selection	Results with Feature Selection
Accuracy	92.9%	93.3%
Precision	75.0%	78.9%
AUC	0.76	0.77
F1-Score	63.8%	65.2%
Recall	55.5%	55.5%

The model trained with these selected features demonstrated satisfactory performance, achieving an accuracy of 93.3%, a precision of 78.9%, a recall of 55.5%, an F1-score of 65.2%, and an AUC of 0.77. These results represent an improvement over the baseline model, where feature selection was not applied, as shown in Table 2.

However, a closer examination of Table 3, which provides a detailed classification report, reveals that while the model performs well in predicting negative instances, it still struggles with a high number of misclassified instances where the targeted code smell is present. This highlights a need for further refinement to enhance the model's ability to detect the Long Method smell.

Table 3. Classification report in the method with feature selection in Experiment 1

Long Method	Precision	Recall	F1-Score	Support
Absence	0.95	0.98	0.96	428
Presence	0.79	0.56	0.65	54
accuracy			0.93	482
macro avg	0.87	0.77	0.81	482
weighted avg	0.93	0.93	0.93	482

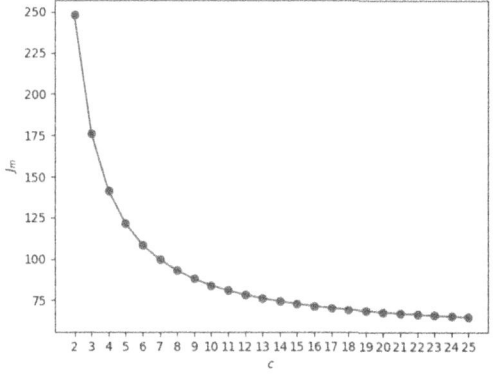

Fig. 3. Analysis of Jm against cluster number for Experiment 2.

In the second experiment, an analysis of Fig. 3 revealed that the curve begins to flatten significantly around $c = 8$. Therefore, consistent with the reasoning applied in Experiment 1, the MFCMS algorithm for Experiment 2 was executed using this cluster count.

As shown in Table 4, using a threshold of $\tau = 0.6999$, the algorithm selected 20 features from the original 26. This represents a more substantial reduction compared to the outcome of Experiment 1, highlighting improved dimensionality reduction in this case.

In the second experiment, PCA was applied to further improve the feature selection process based on MFCMS. The use of PCA resulted in a smaller feature set while preserving critical information for classification. This integration resulted in improved model performance across all metrics, with the model achieving an accuracy of 93.1%,

Table 4. Number of features selected for the best threshold value τ in Experiment 2.

τ	Total Number of Features	Number of Features Selected
0.6999	26	20

precision of 75.6%, recall of 57.4%, F1-score of 65.3%, and an AUC of 0.78, as stated by Table 5. These results confirm that integrating PCA not only reduced the feature set but also improved the model's generalization ability, enabling it to outperform the baseline model despite using fewer features.

Table 5. Results for the test set in the Experiment 2.

Metrics	Results without Feature Selection	Results with Feature Selection
Accuracy	92.9%	93.1%
Precision	75.0%	75.6%
AUC	0.76	0.78
F1-Score	63.8%	65.3%
Recall	55.5%	57.4%

Table 6 provides a detailed summary of the model's classification performance for each class. Similar to the findings from the previous experiment, the model exhibited strong performance in identifying the absence of the long method smell. However, it continues to face challenges in accurately detecting the presence of the long method smell.

A comparative analysis of the two experiments revealed that the approach incorporating PCA consistently outperformed the alternative in terms of dimensionality reduction. This suggests that Experiment 1 was hindered by the presence of correlations between features, whereas Experiment 2 benefited from the use of uncorrelated components.

Table 6. Classification report in the method with feature selection in Experiment 2

Long Method	Precision	Recall	F1-Score	Support
Absence	0.95	0.98	0.96	428
Presence	0.76	0.57	0.65	54
accuracy			0.93	482
macro avg	0.85	0.78	0.81	482
weighted avg	0.93	0.93	0.93	482

In terms of performance metrics, Experiment 1 demonstrated higher accuracy and precision. However, when considering additional metrics, Experiment 2 delivered slightly better overall performance, highlighting its balanced effectiveness across various evaluation criteria.

Both experiments, however, exhibited poor classification performance in detecting the presence of the long method smell, as reflected in the low recall and F1-scores. This shortcoming is likely attributable to the dataset's imbalanced nature, where positive instances are significantly fewer than negative ones. Addressing this imbalance will be crucial in future work, although it presents significant challenges.

Undersampling could lead to overfitting by drastically reducing the dataset size, thereby limiting the model's ability to generalize effectively. On the other hand, over-sampling techniques risk introducing noise or bias by generating synthetic instances that may not accurately represent real-world scenarios involving the long method smell. To overcome these challenges, developing a well-balanced dataset will be critical. Such efforts could improve the model's accuracy, precision, recall, and overall AUC, ultimately enhancing its reliability in detecting this code smell.

5   Discussion

This section discusses the experimental findings in the context of the research questions posed earlier. The discussion explores how the results address these questions and highlights their implications for detecting code smells, particularly the Long Method smell, using the proposed methodology.

RQ1: How Effective is the Proposed Multiphase Methodology in Improving the Accuracy and Reliability of Detecting Code Smells, Specifically the Long Method Smell, Compared to Existing Approaches?
The results highlight the effectiveness of the proposed methodology in detecting code smells. Both experiments delivered strong performance across multiple metrics. Notably, the experiment incorporating PCA during preprocessing outperformed the one without it, especially in terms of feature reduction capability. By reducing feature correlations and enhancing the clarity of the underlying data structure, PCA played a key role in achieving these outcomes. However, Experiment 1 reveled a slightly better improvement over the Experiment 2 in terms of accuracy and precision.

Nonetheless, these results confirm that integrating advanced feature selection techniques into the detection pipeline enhances the model's ability to identify code smells effectively and consistently.

RQ2: What is the Impact of Using the Modified Fuzzy C-Means Algorithm with Supervision (MFCMS) for Feature Selection on the Overall Model Performance?
The standalone use of MFCMS reduced the dimensionality of the dataset while maintaining relevant features for classification. This reduction in feature space resulted in improved computational efficiency and strong classification performance, as reflected in Experiment 1. However, the model still struggled with some misclassifications, particularly regarding the presence of the studied code smell. These findings highlight the

strength of MFCMS as a feature selection tool, though further refinement is beneficial to improve the overall classification of the approach.

RQ3: How Does the Integration of Principal Component Analysis (PCA) Affect the Dimensionality Reduction and Classification Accuracy?

The integration of PCA produced a smaller, more efficient feature set by effectively reducing multicollinearity and correlations among features. This combination enhances the ability to identify and focus on the most relevant features. However, while the Experiment with PCA improved dimensionality reduction, it did not result in a significant improvement in classification accuracy and precision. Nevertheless, PCA contributed to improvements in other metrics, such as recall, F1-Score and AUC, suggesting that it helped the model capture relevant patterns and enhance the overall performance, despite the trade-off in accuracy and precision. These findings highlight the critical role of PCA in dataset preprocessing and the effectiveness of MFCMS-based feature selection in optimizing feature sets, particularly for complex datasets with highly correlated features.

RQ4: What are the Trade-offs in Computational Cost Versus Detection Performance When Applying the Proposed Feature Selection Techniques?

The integration of PCA with MFCMS achieved a substantial reduction in the number of features, decreasing the computational complexity of the classification task. Although the addition of PCA introduces some overhead during the preprocessing stage, the overall gains in model efficiency and performance outweigh these costs.

Performing the MFCMS algorithm involves a certain computational cost, as the algorithm requires convergence, meaning the objective function must be minimized. Additionally, determining the ideal number of clusters adds another layer of computational overhead, as it requires evaluating different cluster configurations. While this process can be computationally expensive, it is crucial for ensuring that the feature selection process is optimized. The trade-off between computational cost and detection performance becomes apparent, as the need for convergence and cluster optimization may slow down the process but ultimately leads to better feature selection and, in some cases, improved detection accuracy. Balancing these factors is essential for maximizing the benefits of the feature selection techniques without overwhelming computational resources.

RQ5: How Does the Proposed Methodology Perform Across Different Datasets and Software Systems, in Terms of Generalizability and Robustness?

While this study focused on the Madeyski Lewowski Code Quest (MLCQ) dataset, the results suggest that the methodology is robust and generalizable. The consistent improvements in performance across experiments indicate that the approach effectively captures key patterns relevant to code smell detection. However, further validation on diverse datasets with varying characteristics is necessary to confirm the generalizability of the findings.

RQ6: How Do the Results Vary Between the Experimental Setups Using Only MFCMS and the Combination of MFCMS and PCA?

The comparative analysis of the experiments revealed that the combination of MFCMS and PCA consistently outperformed the standalone MFCMS approach in terms of dimensionality reduction. By selecting fewer features, the combined approach maintained performance while reducing complexity, compared to the baseline model that did not employ feature selection. Although the experiment using only MFCMS achieved slightly better accuracy and precision, the combination of MFCMS and PCA showed marginal improvements in other metrics, such as recall, F1-score, and AUC. This indicates that while the standalone MFCMS approach excels in certain areas, the integration with PCA provides a more balanced overall performance across a wider range of evaluation metrics. Additionally, PCA addressed the limitations of the first experiment, particularly in managing correlated features, contributing to better performance in these other metrics.

Implications and Future Directions. The findings of this study have important implications for the field of software engineering. The proposed methodology offers a scalable and efficient solution for automating the detection of code smells, reducing reliance on subjective human judgment. By integrating advanced feature selection techniques, the approach addresses key challenges in dimensionality reduction and classification accuracy. Future research could extend this methodology to other types of code smells, further validate its effectiveness on diverse datasets, and explore additional techniques for addressing imbalanced datasets. Moreover, integrating this approach into real-world software development workflows could provide valuable insights into its practical applicability and impact on code maintainability.

6   Threats for Validation

This section addresses potential threats to the validity of the findings, categorized as internal, external, construct, and conclusion validity.

6.1   Internal Validity

The main threat to internal validity is the dependency on the dataset's quality and preprocessing. Errors in data normalization, feature engineering, or labeling could affect results. This was mitigated through consistent preprocessing techniques like MinMax normalization. Hyperparameter optimization was another concern, addressed using grid search and cross-validation to ensure optimal model training.

6.2   External Validity

External validity relates to generalizing the results to other datasets or code smells. The study focused on the Madeyski Lewowski Code Quest (MLCQ) dataset and the Long Method smell, limiting direct application to other datasets or smells like Feature Envy. While adaptable, further experiments on diverse datasets are needed to confirm broader applicability.

6.3 Construct Validity

Construct validity examines whether the evaluation measures are appropriate. Metrics like accuracy, precision, recall, F1-score, and AUC are standard but may not capture all dimensions, such as maintainability impact. While feature importance analysis improved interpretability, the definition of Long Method based on thresholds could introduce biases, necessitating refinement through empirical studies.

6.4 Conclusion Validity

Conclusion validity addresses result reliability. The relatively small dataset and potential class imbalances could affect reliability, despite the use of feature selection and optimization. Overfitting risks were mitigated through cross-validation and dimensionality reduction techniques, enhancing model generalizability.

7 Conclusions

This study presented a novel multiphase methodology for detecting code smells, particularly the Long Method smell, by integrating the MFCMS and PCA. The results demonstrated that the proposed methodology significantly improves the accuracy, precision, recall, and overall reliability of detecting code smells compared to existing approaches. The enhanced feature selection process reduced dimensionality while preserving critical information, enabling more efficient and effective classification.

The combination of MFCMS and PCA consistently outperformed standalone MFCMS in dimensionality reduction, highlighting the importance of addressing feature redundancy and correlation within the dataset.

This integration not only improved the model's generalization ability but also reduced computational overhead, enhancing the scalability of the methodology for larger datasets. By streamlining feature selection and improving performance, the approach offers a more efficient and effective solution for handling complex, high-dimensional data.

Despite the promising results, several threats to validity were identified. The dependency on a single dataset (Madeyski Lewowski Code Quest) and the focus on a single code smell (Long Method) limit the generalizability of the findings. Additional experiments on diverse datasets and code smells are necessary to validate the robustness of the methodology. Furthermore, addressing potential biases in the dataset and refining the criteria for code smells will enhance the applicability and reliability of the proposed approach.

Acknowledgment. This work is funded by FCT/MCTES through national funds and when applicable co-funded by FEDER—PT2020 partnership agreement under the project UIDB/EEA/50008/2020.

References

1. Azeem, M.I., Palomba, F., Shi, L., Wang, Q.: Machine learning techniques for code smell detection: a systematic literature review and meta-analysis. Inform. Softw. Technol. **108**, 115–138 (2019). https://doi.org/10.1016/j.infsof.2018.12.009, https://www.sciencedirect.com/science/article/pii/S0950584918302623

2. Bavota, G., De Lucia, A., Oliveto, R.: Identifying extract class refactoring opportunities using structural and semantic cohesion measures. J. Syst. Softw. **84**(3), 397–414 (2011). https://doi.org/10.1016/j.jss.2010.11.918, https://www.sciencedirect.com/science/article/pii/S0164121210003195

3. Bertolino, A.: Software testing research: achievements, challenges, dreams. In: Future of Software Engineering (FOSE '07), pp. 85–103 (2007). https://doi.org/10.1109/FOSE.2007.25

4. Campbell, G.A., Papapetrou, P.P.: SonarQube in action. Manning Publications (2013)

5. Candea, G., Bucur, S., Zamfir, C.: Automated software testing as a service. In: Proceedings of the 1st ACM Symposium on Cloud Computting, pp. 155–160. SoCC '10, Association for Computing Machinery, New York, NY, USA (2010). https://doi.org/10.1145/1807128.1807153

6. Hamouda, E., El-Korany, A., Makady, S.: Smell-ml: a machine learning framework for detecting rarely studied code smells. IEEE Access **13**, 12966–12980 (2025). https://doi.org/10.1109/ACCESS.2025.3530927

7. Jain, S., Saha, A.: Improving performance with hybrid feature selection and ensemble machine learning techniques for code smell detection. Sci. Comput. Program. **212**, 102713 (2021). https://doi.org/10.1016/j.scico.2021.102713

8. Kovačević, A., et al.: Automatic detection of long method and god class code smells through neural source code embeddings. Expert Syst. Appl. **204**, 117607 (2022). https://doi.org/10.1016/j.eswa.2022.117607. https://www.sciencedirect.com/science/article/pii/S0957417422009186

9. Liu, H., Jin, J., Xu, Z., Zou, Y., Bu, Y., Zhang, L.: Deep learning based code smell detection. IEEE Trans. Software Eng. **47**(9), 1811–1837 (2021). https://doi.org/10.1109/TSE.2019.2936376

10. Liu, H., Liu, Q., Niu, Z., Liu, Y.: Dynamic and automatic feedback-based threshold adaptation for code smell detection. IEEE Trans. Software Eng. **42**(6), 544–558 (2016). https://doi.org/10.1109/TSE.2015.2503740

11. Magalhães, M., Morgado, , Jesus, H., Pombo, N.: Unlocking the potential of dynamic languages: An exploration of automated unit test generation techniques. In: 2023 IEEE International Conference On Artificial Intelligence Testing (AITest), pp. 122–126 (2023). https://doi.org/10.1109/AITest58265.2023.00027

12. Marcelloni, F.: Feature selection based on a modified fuzzy c-means algorithm with supervision. Inform. Sci. **151**, 201–226 (2003). https://doi.org/10.1016/S0020-0255(02)00402-4

13. Mens, T., Tourwe, T.: A survey of software refactoring. IEEE Trans. Software Eng. **30**(2), 126–139 (2004). https://doi.org/10.1109/TSE.2004.1265817

14. Panda, R.R., Nagwani, N.K.: Multi-label software bug categorisation based on fuzzy similarity. Int. J. Comput. Sci. Eng. **24**(3), 244–258 (2021). https://doi.org/10.1504/ijcse.2021.115645

15. Pinho, A., Pombo, N., Silva, B.M., Bousson, K., Garcia, N.: Towards an accurate sleep apnea detection based on ECG signal: the quintessential of a wise feature selection. Appl. Soft Comput. **83**, 105568 (2019). https://doi.org/10.1016/j.asoc.2019.105568, https://www.sciencedirect.com/science/article/pii/S1568494619303485

16. Pombo, N., Teixeira, R.: Contribution of temporal sequence activities to predict bug fixing time. In: 2020 IEEE 14th International Conference on Application of Information and Communication Technologies (AICT), pp. 1–6 (2020). https://doi.org/10.1109/AICT50176.2020.9368603

17. Sarker, I.H.: Machine learning: Algorithms, real-world applications and research directions. SN Comput. Sci. **2**(3) (2021).https://doi.org/10.1007/s42979-021-00592-x

18. Tufano, M., et al.: When and why your code starts to smell bad (and whether the smells go away). IEEE Trans. Software Eng. **43**(11), 1063–1088 (2017). https://doi.org/10.1109/TSE.2017.2653105

19. Wu, H., Yin, R., Gao, J., Huang, Z., Huang, H.: To what extent can code quality be improved by eliminating test smells? In: 2022 International Conference on Code Quality (ICCQ), pp. 19–26 (2022). https://doi.org/10.1109/ICCQ53703.2022.9763153

20. Zadeh, L.: Fuzzy sets. Inform. Control **8**(3), 338–353 (1965). https://doi.org/10.1016/S0019-9958(65)90241-X, https://www.sciencedirect.com/science/article/pii/S001999586590241X

21. Zhang, Y., Ge, C., Liu, H., Zheng, K.: Code smell detection based on supervised learning models: a survey. Neurocomputing **565**, 127014 (2024). https://doi.org/10.1016/j.neucom.2023.127014, https://www.sciencedirect.com/science/article/pii/S0925231223011372

Mocking Classes in Kotlin with Mockative

Kristian Degn Abrahamsen[1] and Jacopo Mauro[2(✉)]

[1] Cardlay, Odense, Denmark
[2] University of Southern Denmark, Odense, Denmark
mauro@imada.sdu.dk

Abstract. Unit testing is instrumental in enhancing code quality, documenting system behavior, and preventing regressions in contemporary software development. One of the current limitations of the most popular existing unit-testing frameworks for the Kotlin language (e.g., MockK and Mockito) is that they are inherently tied to the Java Virtual Machine (JVM), restricting their use to JVM-compatible environments.

To overcome this limitation, in this paper we present an extended version of Mockative, a Kotlin-specific mocking framework designed to operate across multiple platforms beyond the JVM. While originally Mockative was limited to interface mocking, we have enhanced it to support class mocking and spying through the utilization of Kotlin Symbol Processing (KSP) and KotlinPoet libraries. We show that Mockative is a viable alternative to traditional JVM-bound frameworks, particularly in Kotlin/Native environments. Our extension can mock simple classes up to four times faster than MockK and Mockito, although it exhibits a marginal performance decline in scenarios involving classes with extensive method definitions.

Keywords: Unit Testing · Mock · Kotlin

1 Introduction

Testing is a big part of software development, used to ensure that the product developed works as expected with fewer unforeseen errors and failures [4].

Unit testing is part of the testing process, where individual units of code are tested in isolation. Different benefits of unit testing include better documentation, increases in code quality, more modular code, catching of regressions, etc. The unit tests in the test suite are usually written in the programming language of the code base, and the tested logic uses the compiled code of the code base. Tools are used to facilitate the development and execution of unit tests, decoupling the system under test from its dependencies thus making it easier to maintain the unit tests suite [13].

This work was supported by the Independent Research Fund Denmark under grant number 10.46540/4283-00007B.

D. Taibi and D. Smite (Eds.): SEAA 2025, LNCS 16082, pp. 23–31, 2026.
https://doi.org/10.1007/978-3-032-04200-2_2

In this work, we focus on tools to create mocks and spies, i.e., simulated objects that mimic the behavior of real components in controlled ways for the programming language Kotlin. Kotlin is a modern, statically typed, object-oriented programming language, designed to be fully interoperable with Java [8]. This is achieved by compiling Kotlin code to Java bytecode, which can be run on the Java Virtual Machine (JVM). This constraint introduced a tight coupling between Kotlin and the JVM, making the language highly optimized for the JVM. This coupling can be seen in the popular unit-testing frameworks used in Kotlin: *MockK* [16] and *Mockito* [15], which are both built for the JVM.

Kotlin, however, has been extended to be able to compile to other platforms, such as JavaScript and native code [10]. This allows for the use of Kotlin in a wider range of environments that do not support the JVM. This also has implications for unit testing tools in Kotlin, as the unit testing frameworks that are built for the JVM will not work on other platforms. Validating the behavior of Kotlin applications on the actual target platform is crucial since certain features (e.g., multithreading in iOS) can exhibit differences compared to the JVM or the target devices may lack the computational power and resources available on the JVM, potentially leading to unexpected behavior not observable in a JVM environment. For this reason, a new testing framework called *Mockative* [14] has been developed, which is built for Kotlin. This means that using this tool, Kotlin code compiled to native binaries becomes unit-testable.

Mockative was initially developed by Nicklas Jensen, a developer at Cardlay, in 2021 and supported only interface mocking. In this work, we present the extension of Mockative to support class mocking and spies. The main modification was to alter the structure of the generated code to allow subclassing of the classes to be mocked, relying on the Kotlin Symbol Processing (KSP) tool developed by Google [11] used to identify all classes for which mocks should be generated through the use of annotations, and KotlinPoet, an object-oriented library developed by Square. For spies, we simply allow the passing of real instances to the generated mock class. During runtime, Mockative checks whether a fallback spy instance is provided and, if so, it invokes the real method when no specific mock behavior is configured. These extensions expand Mockative's functionality and align it with the capabilities of mature mocking frameworks for the JVM, enhancing its utility in simplifying the unit testing process.

We compare Mockative with Mockito and MockK, the two most used mocking frameworks for Kotlin. Results show that although Mockative supports multiple platforms beyond those accommodated by Mockito and MockK, it still performs comparably well on the JVM. Mockative in particular excels in an incremental scenario in which only part of the mocks need to be regenerated.

2   Preliminaries

In this Section, we briefly recall the general concepts of unit testing and then provide an overview of the most popular Mocking frameworks for Kotlin.

Mocks and Spies. Unit testing relies on the concept of *test doubles* [13], i.e., objects that are used to stand in for real objects in the System Under Test (SUT). The test doubles can be used to isolate the SUT from its dependencies, which can make the tests more readable, easier to write and maintain, and faster to run. In this context, the terms *mocks* and *spies* refer to two different types of test doubles used to simulate the behavior of real objects. Mocks are objects that simulate the behavior of real components in a controlled way. They are pre-programmed with expectations about how they should be used during the test. This includes specifying which methods should be called, with what parameters, and what the return values should be. Mocks are primarily used to verify that certain interactions occur between the code under test and its dependencies. Spies, on the other hand, are similar to mocks but with a key difference: they wrap real objects instead of entirely replacing them. Spies allow the real object to perform its actual behavior while also recording the interactions. Mocks are usually automatically generated, while writing *spies* requires some form of developer intervention since they can be configured to return real responses when no specific behavior is set.

MockK. MockK [16] is an open-source mocking framework supporting mocking for Android and the JVM. It is quite a popular tool with 5k stars on GitHub and actively developed by 3 main developers and 100+ contributors.

In MockK, generating a mock is done via calling the method io.mockk.mockk or via annotations when using JUnit. Overall, MockK supports features such as verification of mocks and spies, unmocking mocks, more than 40 argument-matchers, and 23 ways of making answers to stubs.

Mockito. Mockito [15] is an open-source mocking framework that supports mocking for Android and JVM. It brands itself as the most used mocking framework for Java having more than 10k stars on GitHub and 250+ contributors.

Mockito offers similar features to MockK. Being written in Java, however, it does not support languages null-safety features (present instead in MockK and Mockative since they are written in Kotlin).

Mockative. Mockative is an open-source mocking framework developed due to the lack of mocking frameworks for Kotlin/Native and Kotlin Multiplatform. The native platforms include: macOS, iOS, tvOS, watchOS, Linux, Windows, and Android NDK [9]. Kotlin Multiplatform allows for sharing a code base between all of these native targets, such as sharing business logic to avoid duplicating logic in all the platforms (e.g., it can support mocking the development of an iOS-app and an Android-app using a shared backend).

Making a mocking framework for Kotlin Multiplatform requires code generation since in the current settings there is a complete lack of runtime reflection and dynamic code constructs.[1] Instead of injecting code at runtime into already compiled classes, Mockative generates code. The generated code is either a subclass of a provided class that the user wants to mock, or it is an implementation of an abstract class or interface. This is done using symbol processing by relying on Kotlin Symbol Processing (KSP), i.e., a lightweight, efficient tool for parsing and generating code during the build process.

Mockito, similarly to MockK, heavily rely on the ByteBuddy [3] for bytecode manipulation. The most commonly used methods in Mockito involve retransforming classes, injecting code into class files at runtime, and subclassing classes to create instances of abstract classes or interfaces. ByteBuddy's API employs the builder software design pattern [5], which allows users to build the desired subclass layer by layer, specifying methods to intercept and their implementations. Mockito, similarly to MockK, use the proxy pattern in their implementations, i.e., a proxy is used to add code that is executed before the actual implementation call [6]. ByteBuddy is used for method interception to easily insert logic at the beginning and end of functions.

The generation of code is simply writing text to files. To increase the readability and scalability libraries like KotlinPoet [12] are used to simplify the code generation process for .kt source files.

When creating a mock in Mockative, the function used is mock as follows.

```
1 fun <T : Any> mock(type: KClass<T>): T =
2     throw NoSuchMockException(type)
```

This seems to just throw an exception whenever it is called. However, as a consequence of generating code at compile time, this function is never called when Mockative is used correctly, because Mockative KSP will generate a more specific function overloading the mock function. The generated function is in the same package, while being more specific, hence, compiler will use the generated function instead.

The generation of a mock is done via annotating a property in the test class with a provided annotation from Mockative, which will be processed by the KSP implementation in the published mockative-processor module.

```
1 @io.mockative.Mock val mock1: HelloClass =
2         io.mockative.mock(io.mockative.classOf<HelloClass>())
```

3   Implementation

In Mockative, the generated mocked classes extended Mockable, which contained the logic for mocking. To support class mocking, this was changed because a class in Kotlin is not allowed to have more than one superclass to avoid the well-known diamond problem of inheritance in object-oriented programming [7].

---

[1] Kotlin/Native has very limited support for reflection. Using Kotlin/Native reflection, one only has access to qualifiedName and simpleName on a kotlin.reflect.KClass, which corresponds to the java.lang.Class but with much less functionality.

The generated mocked class indeed must be usable wherever the original class is used, which necessitates that the mock class subclasses the targeted class. Previously, this issue did not arise as Mockative only supported mocking of interfaces, where multiple interfaces can be implemented simultaneously, but a class can only extend one superclass.

The implementation ensures that no race conditions occur between tests. The code generation for functions has transitioned from

```
override fun myFunc(
        arg1: Type, arg2: Type, ...
) = invoke(Invocation.Function("myFunc", listOf(arg1, arg2)),
        returnsUnit=false)
```

to the following static function invocation.

```
override fun myFunc(
    arg1: Type, arg2: Type, ...
) = Mockable.invoke(
    Invocation.Function(this, "myFunc", listOf(arg1, arg2)),
        returnsUnit=false
)
```

Looking into the code changes for mocking classes, KSP and KotlinPoet are heavily used. Since KSP supports incremental builds, to exploit this feature we instruct KSP on which files to consider for searching for dirty files. Indeed, we only want to generate mock classes for classes that are marked to be mocked. Therefore, we add the containing file of the class to mock to the list of processed files, such that when asking KSP for files to process in the next round, the file is only given if its signature has changed.

When all the information was acquired for the class to mock, KotlinPoet was used for the code generation. From a technical point of view, the class declaration is accessed to determine its class kind to establish whether it is an interface or a class. For interfaces, the process is straightforward, involving only the addition of functions and properties. For classes, the correct parameters must be passed to the selected constructor of the superclass.

During the code generation, we had to solve issues arising from the declaration-site variance of Kotlin. Different from Java, Kotlin allows the specification of variance directly at the point where a generic class or interface is declared, rather than at the point of its use. This is done using the out and in keywords to indicate covariance and contravariance, respectively. To manage this problem we implemented the method applySafeAnnotations that ensures that appropriate annotations are applied to manage variance conflicts safely.

As far as spies are concerned, to generate them, a function needs to be created as follows.

```
fun <T : Any> spy(type: KClass<T>, instance: T) : T =
    throw NoSuchMockException(type)
```

This has mostly the same signature as the mock function, but now it has an instance passed to it as argument. This argument should be of the same type as the class for which the mock is generated. Since spies and mocks function similarly, the class implementation is reused. However, an additional fallback function is added for cases where no stubbings are found. The fallback functions for overriding the superclass' functions look like the following

```
{ @Suppress("DEPRECATION_ERROR")spyInstance!!.foo('arg1') }
```

which, when invoked, will call the specified method on the provided instance instead of the one of the generated mock class. Here, we use the !! operator on the spyInstance because the function block is only executed when the mock is a spy. The !! operator asserts that spyInstance is not null, bypassing Kotlin's null safety checks when you're certain (or want to enforce) that the value is non-null. The necessity to add the @Suppress("DEPRECATION_ERROR") arises instead from the fact that when working with KSP, we sometimes need to call methods that have been deprecated with DeprecationLevel.ERROR and KSP does not consistently retrieve all annotations on functions.

4   Evaluation

In this section we present the performance comparisons between the various mocking frameworks. We simply generate a given number of mocks and measure the time taken by the tool to build them and the overall time taken to stub and invoke the mocks. Since MockK and Mockito run only on the JVM, we compare the performance of Mockative with these two frameworks on the JVM platform.

We created a first benchmark, dubbed *one-method*, by generating respectively 32, 64, 128, 256 and 512 classes to mock, using the following class as template.

```
@MockativeMockable
class HelloClass: HelloClassX {
        override fun sayHello(name: String): String {
                return "Hello, World! from $name"
        }
}
```

We then generated the instances of the mocks for these classes, using the approach prescribed by their respective frameworks. For example, the first mock in Mockito is generated as follows.

```
@io.mockative.Mock val mock1: HelloClass1 =
    io.mockative.mock(io.mockative.classOf<HelloClass1>())
val mock1: HelloClass1 = io.mockk.mockk()
val mock1: HelloClass1 =
    org.mockito.Mockito.mock(HelloClass1::class.java)
```

To test the impact of function quantity within a class, we created another benchmark dubbed *method-heavy* by generating the same classes but adding 100 different sayHello methods instead of only one.

For the building time, we measured the average time taken to build a list of the mocks for the classes and the method-heavy classes. The timing recorded spans from the start of the build to the completion of the list of the mocks, but not the end of compilation. This is because MockK and Mockito inject code at runtime and tacking the time at the end of compilation would penalize these frameworks since the compiler would likely optimize the mocks away if their variables are not used and considered dead code. The averages are based on 10 runs on warmed-up code. Specifically, 15 tests were conducted, with the initial 5 discarded to ensure the system's cache, branch predictions, and JVM are adequately prepared for the code being run. The tests were done by running `gradle clean` before each test, except for the case in which we tested the incremental process of Mockative. The tests were executed on an apple M2 air chip with 16 GB of memory and using Kotlin 1.9.22.

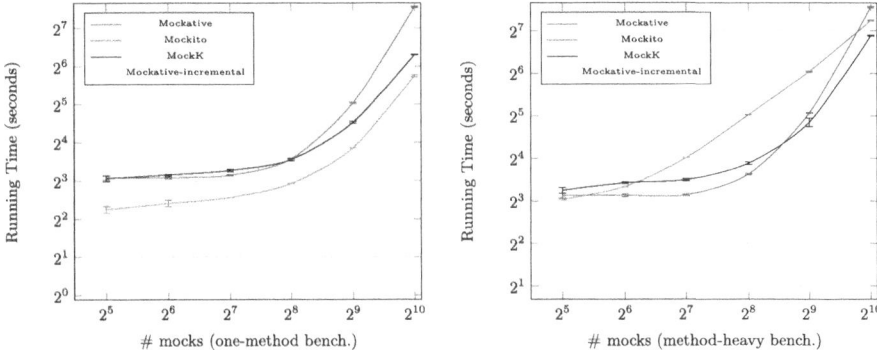

Fig. 1. Average running times for stubbing one method in Mockative (with normal and incremental builds), MockK, Mockito. *one-method* on the left, `method-heavy` on the right.

Figure 1 presents the average running times for the three frameworks considering the build time to create the mocks and the time to run them. For the one-method benchmark it is evident that Mockito has the longest runtime, being more than twice as slow as Mockative, with MockK positioned between the two. Mockative demonstrates a faster runtime, and its growth in seconds relative to the number of stubbings increases more slowly than that of MockK and Mockito. When incremental builds are enabled, it is even more apparent that Mockative significantly outperforms MockK and Mockito, being up to four times faster than Mockito and 2.8 times faster than MockK.

When stubbing a single method in classes containing 100 methods, for mocking fewer than 256 classes, Mockative is faster than both MockK and Mockito, with MockK generally showing the worst performance. However, as the number of methods increases, Mockative's performance declines. The generation of method-heavy classes affects Mockative more than the other frameworks, even though incremental builds for Mockative significantly reduce the impact.

As far as spies are concerned, they exhibit a similar build and stubbing time since the primary difference is the addition of a fallback to a real implementation. Due to this similarity, we avoid presenting the same experiments.

We conclude this section by presenting the performance of Mockative across various Kotlin multiplatform targets. These tests were done by specifying the

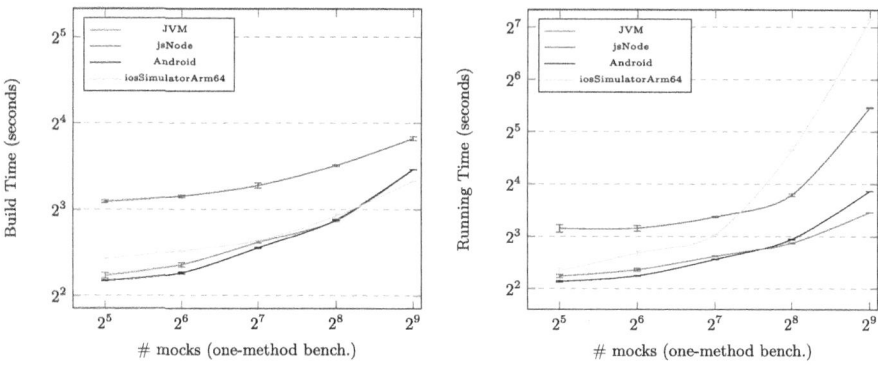

Fig. 2. Average Mockative running times for build and stubbing in various platforms.

target platform in the `build.gradle` file and running the tests on the respective platforms. Figure 2 present the built time and the run time for stubbing a mock using the one-method benchmark. It is possible to see that Android benchmarks are closely aligned with the JVM benchmarks. This is not surprising since they are conducted on the JVM [1]. As far as the jsNode and ios platforms are concerned, both build times and runtimes show lower performance than when targeting Android and JVM. It is possible to see that Android benchmarks are closely aligned with the JVM benchmarks. This is not surprising since they are conducted on the JVM [1]. As far as the jsNode and ios platforms are concerned, both build times and runtimes show lower performance than Android and JVM.

For reproducibility purposes, the code for the tests is available within the Mockative fork on the *compare-frameworks* available at https://github.com/kris098e/mockative-fork/tree/compare-frameworks.

5   Conclusion

In this paper, we have presented an extension of Mockative to support class mocking and spies. Mockative is designed to simplify the process of creating mocks for unit tests in KMM projects and generate mock implementations at compile time. We have demonstrated the capabilities of Mockative through a series of benchmarks comparing its performance to that of MockK and Mockito, two popular mocking frameworks for Kotlin that are bound to the JVM.

The only other mocking framework for Kotlin native we are aware of is mocKMP [17]. MocKMP is similar to Mockative but slightly less popular and, different from our extension, it does not support the mocking of classes and spies.

As future work, we plan to investigate how the newly released Kotlin 2 compiler could impact Mockative. While our initial performance analysis using Kotlin 2.1 suggests that there are no significant deviations in benchmark results compared to the more mature 1.9 version, leveraging new compiler features could lead to further optimizations. In particular, we aim to explore how Mockative can be enhanced by getting inspiration from promising new compiler plugins such as Mokkery [2].

References

1. Android Developers: Local Unit Tests (2024). https://developer.android.com/training/testing/local-tests
2. Baczyński, D.: Mokkery: mocking library for Kotlin Multiplatform, compiler plugin driven (2024). https://github.com/lupuuss/Mokkery
3. Byte Buddy Contributors: Byte Buddy - Runtime Code Generation for the Java Virtual Machine (2024). https://github.com/raphw/byte-buddy/tree/master
4. Crispin, L., Gregory, J.: Agile Testing: A Practical Guide for Testers and Agile Teams. Addison-Wesley (2009)
5. DigitalOcean: Builder Design Pattern in Java (2022). https://www.digitalocean.com/community/tutorials/builder-design-pattern-in-java
6. DigitalOcean: Proxy Design Pattern Tutorial (2022). https://www.digitalocean.com/community/tutorials/proxy-design-pattern
7. Gabbrielli, M., Martini, S., Giallorenzo, S.: Programming Languages: Principles and Paradigms, Second Edition. Undergraduate Topics in Computer Science. Springer, Heidelberg (2023). https://doi.org/10.1007/978-3-031-34144-1
8. JetBrains: Kotlin 1.0 Released: Pragmatic Language for JVM and Android (2016). https://blog.jetbrains.com/kotlin/2016/02/kotlin-1-0-released-pragmatic-language-for-jvm-and-android/
9. JetBrains: Kotlin/Native Overview (2023). https://kotlinlang.org/docs/native-overview.html
10. JetBrains: Getting started with kotlin multiplatform (2024). https://www.jetbrains.com/help/kotlin-multiplatform-dev/multiplatform-getting-started.html
11. JetBrains: Kotlin Symbol Processing (KSP) Overview (2024). https://kotlinlang.org/docs/ksp-overview.html
12. KotlinPoet Contributors: KotlinPoet - A Kotlin API for generating .kt source files (2024). https://square.github.io/kotlinpoet/
13. Microsoft: Unit Testing: Mocking (2024). https://microsoft.github.io/code-with-engineering-playbook/automated-testing/unit-testing/mocking/
14. Mockative: A mocking library for kotlin (2024). https://github.com/mockative/mockative
15. Mockito Contributors: Mockito: mocking framework for unit tests in java (2024). https://github.com/mockito/mockito
16. MockK Contributors: MockK: mocking library for Kotlin (2024). https://github.com/mockk/mockk
17. MocKMP Contributors: MocKMP: A Kotlin Multiplatform library for mocking (2024). https://github.com/kosi-libs/MocKMP

ESCOPlus: A Framework for Enriching the ESCO Taxonomy with Digital Skills from Stack Overflow

Dimitrios Christos Kavargyris[1]([✉]), Konstantinos Georgiou[1], Iosifina Maraki[1], Nikolaos Mittas[2], and Lefteris Angelis[1]

[1] School of Informatics, Aristotle University of Thessaloniki, Thessaloniki, Greece
dakavrgy@csd.auth.gr
[2] Department of Chemistry, School of Science, Democritus University of Thrace, Kavala, Greece

Abstract. The recruitment process in IT companies is increasingly informed by standardized taxonomies such as European Skills, Competences, Qualifications, and Occupations (ESCO), which aim to structure and harmonize skill definitions across Europe. However, to remain effective in the rapidly evolving digital landscape, these taxonomies require continuous updates—particularly in areas like programming languages, frameworks, and specialized software development—a gap this study aims to address. We introduce ESCOPlus, a non-proprietary and open-source framework that enhances ESCO by integrating user-generated content from Stack Overflow (SO). Our approach extracts digital skills from the tags used by SO users in the European Union (EU) between 2020 and 2024, analyzes their co-occurrence with the ESCO taxonomy, and applies association rule mining to uncover strong relationships. Additionally, textual similarity measures identify alternative labels (closely related names to existing ESCO skills) to improve taxonomy completeness. As a final outcome, the ESCOPlus framework extended the taxonomy with 44 new digital skills. The extension of the ESCO taxonomy introduces a dynamic, data-driven methodology for taxonomy enrichment, enhancing skill classification in recruitment, HR analytics, and curriculum design to better align with evolving industry needs.

Keywords: Digital skills · Skills supply · ESCO · StackOverflow · Association rules graph · Data mining

1 Introduction

Software engineering is constantly evolving, with new technologies, frameworks, and programming languages emerging at a rapid pace [1]. Developers must continuously adapt, and even experienced professionals often struggle to keep up [2]. This dynamic environment has created a widening gap between the skills demanded by employers and those available in the workforce. Reports indicate

D. Taibi and D. Smite (Eds.): SEAA 2025, LNCS 16082, pp. 32–48, 2026.
https://doi.org/10.1007/978-3-032-04200-2_3

that over 40% of employers face difficulties in finding candidates [3] with the right technical skills, particularly in software development and emerging technologies[1]. The World Economic Forum highlights that 50% of all employees will require reskilling by 2025[2], emphasizing the need for continuously updated skill frameworks.

At the European policy level, digital skills are a strategic priority, essential for employability, inclusion, and the EU's global competitiveness. To support this, the European Commission introduced the *Digital Competence Framework for Citizens (DigComp)*[3], defining the competences needed for employment, learning, and participation. DigComp was later mapped to the European Skills, Competences, Qualifications, and Occupations (ESCO) taxonomy[4] to facilitate digital skill analysis in job ads and enhance labor market transparency. However, fast-evolving domains—such as programming libraries and frameworks—remain underrepresented in ESCO. Leveraging Stack Overflow (SO) as a data source [4] offers a way to bridge this gap between formal taxonomies and real-world skill needs. Alternative data sources such as Online Job Advertisements (OJAs) provide timely insights into labor market trends, making them valuable for policymakers and training institutions. However, extracting accurate skill information remains challenging, especially in fast-evolving sectors like IT, where outdated taxonomies and limited annotated datasets hinder semantic methods.

To address the persistent gap between existing skill taxonomies and the actual skills demanded by the labor market, an EU Horizon research project named SKILLAB[5] [5], aims to design a comprehensive framework for dynamic skills identification and forecasting, grounded in real-time labor market data, and also to bridge this divide by integrating the ESCO taxonomy with real-time labor market monitoring tools [6]. Central to this effort is the development of an Intelligent Agent, a state-of-the-art recommendation system designed to propose new skills based on ESCO information. This system is designed to manage the complexity of aligning individual skill profiles with organizational needs, particularly in the context of HR planning and strategic reskilling initiatives.

In this context, this study introduces ESCOPlus, a non-proprietary and open-source framework designed to enhance ESCO by integrating real-world, user-generated skills from SO. ESCOPlus incorporates non-ESCO digital skills, including emerging technologies (e.g., Node.js, Flask, ReactJS) and alternative labels—terms closely related to existing ESCO skills but not explicitly represented, such as JavaFX, Java 8, and PyTorch. These additions support both professionals and organizations by reflecting the current EU labour market [7]. High-confidence links between ESCO and non-ESCO skills are derived using association rule mining and textual similarity. ESCOPlus supports IT profes-

---

[1] https://go.manpowergroup.com/talent-shortage.
[2] https://www.weforum.org/publications/the-future-of-jobs-report-2023.
[3] https://esco.ec.europa.eu/en/about-esco/publications/publication/mapping-digcomp-digital-competences-esco-skills-framework.
[4] https://ec.europa.eu/esco.
[5] https://cordis.europa.eu/project/id/101132663.

sionals seeking to reskill, recruiters aiming to improve job matching, and educators updating curricula with real-world technologies [8]. Motivated by the need to align formal taxonomies with rapidly evolving digital skills, the research *goals* of this paper are presented below:

– *(g1)* Enhance the ESCO skills taxonomy by integrating real-world, user-generated skills from SO.
– *(g2)* Contribute to the global labor market by improving skill classification systems, ensuring better alignment between workforce skills and industry needs.

The rest of the paper is structured as follows: Sect. 2 reviews related work on skill analysis, SO as a skill network, and the value of user-generated content. Section 3 outlines the ESCOPlus framework architecture and its core components. In Sect. 4, we present results from association rule mining and textual similarity. Section 5 discusses key findings and threats to validity. Finally, Sect. 6 concludes with recommendations for integrating ESCOPlus into practice and enriching the ESCO taxonomy.

2 Related Work

In recent years, the intersection of user-generated platforms like SO [9] and labor market intelligence [10] has drawn increasing attention for its potential to enrich traditional skills taxonomies. As highlighted by Seredko [11], incorporating such sources into labor market intelligence enables a more responsive and data-driven approach to skills monitoring, taxonomy enrichment, and educational alignment. While formal frameworks such as ESCO [12] and O*NET [13] provide structured descriptions of occupational and skill classifications, they often lack the agility to capture rapidly emerging technical competencies. On the other hand, platforms like SO serve as real-time, community-driven repositories of specialized knowledge, offering granular insights into contemporary programming languages, frameworks, and tools.

In previous research, while the automatic construction of taxonomies has garnered significant attention, the augmentation of existing hierarchies remains less explored [14]. Many automated taxonomy enrichment efforts heavily depend on domain-specific knowledge or leverage lexical structures unique to existing resources, such as WordNet synsets or Wikipedia categories. Recent advancements have introduced methodologies aiming to enrich generic taxonomies automatically. Wang et al. [15] utilized a hierarchical Dirichlet model to complete hierarchies with missing categories and subsequently classified corpus elements under the enhanced taxonomy. However, their approach modifies the taxonomy's structure and does not incorporate new entities into hierarchical categories, differing from our objective of preserving the ESCO framework while updating it with new skills.

SO has emerged as a valuable resource for extracting real-time insights into developer practices, tool usage, and emerging technologies. Its large-scale, user-generated content provides a dynamic snapshot of industry-relevant skills, making it an ideal complement to more static sources like ESCO. SO has emerged as a valuable resource for extracting real-time insights into developer practices, tool usage, and emerging technologies. Its large-scale, user-generated content provides a dynamic snapshot of industry-relevant skills, making it an ideal complement to more static sources like ESCO. Several studies [16–19] have leveraged SO tags, posts, and co-occurrence patterns to uncover trends in programming languages and frameworks. In this work, we use SO not only as a skill signal source, but also as a means of identifying alternative labels and validating emerging technical competencies that are often absent from formal taxonomies.

3   ESCOPlus Framework

In this section, we present the ESCOPlus framework, organized into a three-phase methodology (Fig. 1). The *Vision* phase defines ESCO as the reference taxonomy for skill enrichment. In the *Action* phase, user-generated tags from SO N are collected, processed, and matched to ESCO skills. Association rule mining and textual similarity are applied to identify new skills and alternative labels. The *Plan* phase finalizes the selection of skills to be incorporated into the enhanced taxonomy, aiming to improve its relevance to evolving industry needs.

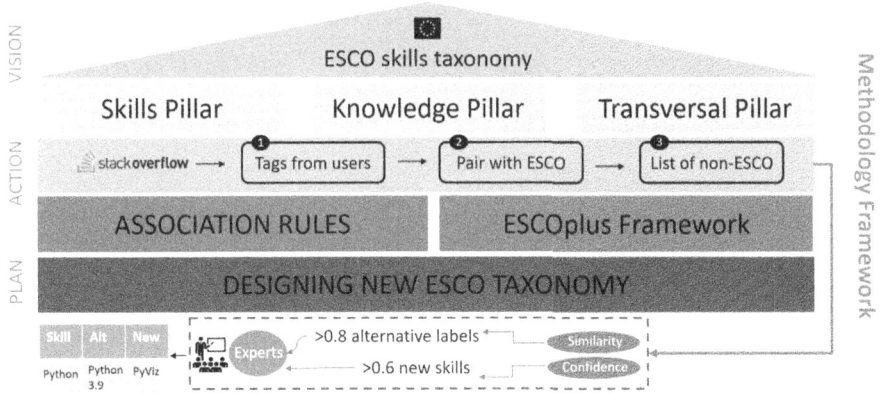

Fig. 1. ESCOPlus architecture

3.1   VISION Phase

In the *Vision* phase of the ESCOPlus framework, we use the ESCO taxonomy as the main reference for skill comparison and enrichment. Developed by the

European Commission, ESCO supports labor market transparency and mobility across Europe. Its Skills and Competences Pillar includes categories for Knowledge (theoretical subjects), Skills (practical abilities), and Transversal Skills (e.g., critical thinking, teamwork). Language skills were excluded from this study due to their limited relevance for technical competencies. All data were retrieved throughrough the official ESCO API[6] and structured for analysis.

3.2   ACTION Phase

Data Collection. The first phase of the *Action* involves data collection and preprocessing through a customized, semi-automated retrieval system using a Python-based web scraper. This scraper dynamically queries SO based on user-constructed search criteria, ensuring adaptability to SO's evolving structure. The focus was on user profiles from SO, specifically extracting user-generated tags that reflect their skills. Geographical filtering limited the dataset to users associated with EU countries. As shown in Fig. 2, most tagged contributions originated from Germany, France, Italy, and Spain. To ensure data integrity, we applied a deduplication step, resulting in a final dataset of 100,000 unique user profiles and their corresponding skills.

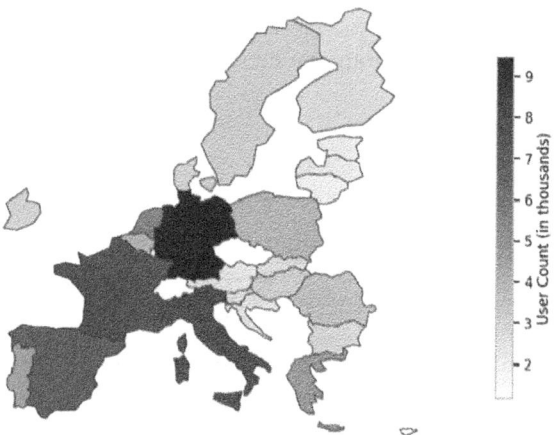

Fig. 2. ESCOPlus users

Data Preprocessing. Once the dataset was finalized, the next step was data preprocessing to align the extracted skills with the ESCO taxonomy. Initially, all user-generated tags were collected from SO profiles. These tags were then systematically mapped to the corresponding ESCO skill names wherever possible. If an exact match was found, the ESCO skill name was assigned; otherwise, the

---

[6] https://ec.europa.eu/esco/api.

entry was marked as null, indicating that the skill was not present in ESCO. For instance, if a user had the tag "python", it was mapped to "python (programming Language)" in ESCO. Following manual validation, this ESCO skill was incorporated into the dataset. The final structured dataset was represented in a binary format, where each skill was assigned 1 if it had a corresponding ESCO entry and 0 if no match was found.

ESCO and Non-ESCO Skills. In order to create the knowledge base used in our work we define:

ESCO Skills: These are well-defined terms aligned with ESCO. However, during our analysis, we identified 1,120 ESCO skills within user-generated tags, highlighting the need for a more abstract and structured skill representation. To address this, we incorporated an additional layer of classification by selecting the most popular technologies from a recently published SO report[7], ensuring that our taxonomy reflects current industry trends and widely used tools (Table 1). While the report served as a reference for validating relevance, the actual tags were extracted from individual user profiles to enable fine-grained skill matching with the ESCO taxonomy.

Non-ESCO Skills: These terms refer to skills that were not identified during the matching process when leveraging the ESCO taxonomy. They primarily encompass technical skills, programming languages, and hard skills that are widely recognized in industry but are either missing or not explicitly defined within ESCO (Table 2). The most commonly used foundation for building web pages and applications is *bash*, which appears most frequently in the dataset. Additionally, *bash* and *node.js* are widely used in backend web development, playing a crucial role in scripting and server-side programming. Including these skills in the ESCO taxonomy would better reflect modern web development practices and industry needs.

Association Rule Mining. The next step in the *Action phase* analyzes associations between ESCO and non-ESCO skills using Association Rules Graphs (ARG), following the method of Fan et al. [21]. Since each SO post may include multiple skill tags, ARG helps visualize co-occurrence patterns and potential relationships between skills. ARG is modeled as a directed graph $G = (V, E)$, where nodes (V) represent skill tags and edges (E) denote their co-occurrence, weighted by confidence scores. The confidence score reflects how likely it is for a skill tag_j to appear given the presence of another skill tag_i, and is defined as:

$$\text{conf}(\text{tag}_i \to \text{tag}_j) = \frac{\text{supp}(\text{tag}_i, \text{tag}_j)}{\text{freq}(\text{tag}_i)} \tag{1}$$

Here, *support* refers to the number of times two tags co-occur within the same user-generated tag set, and *frequency* is the number of tag sets in which tag_i

---

[7] https://survey.stackoverflow.co/2024/.

Table 1. ESCO Skills

Skill	Frequency	Percentage
java	661	3.8
python (computer programming)	608	3.5
javascript	529	3.0
c#	509	2.9
android (mobile operating systems)	470	2.7
php	364	2.1
microsoft visual c++	292	1.70
mysql	242	1.4
asp.net	235	1.3
css	158	0.92
kali linux	137	0.80
angular	136	0.79
xquery	135	0.78
ajax framework	107	0.62
swift (computer programming)	107	0.62
use scripting programming	104	0.60
typescript	93	0.54
postgresql	83	0.48
ruby (computer programming)	79	0.46
eclipse (integrated development environment software)	76	0.44
objective-c	60	0.35
apache maven	58	0.33
hardware platforms	58	0.33
prolog (computer programming)	57	0.33
hadoop	53	0.30
xcode	53	0.30
haskell	47	0.27
Total ESCO Skills = 1120		**100.0%**

appears. The resulting *confidence score* quantifies the strength of the directional association between two skills based on their co-occurrence in user-tagged data.

The average confidence score across all skill associations is 0.49, with only those exceeding the 0.6 threshold (Table 3) considered for integration into ESCOPlus. This filtering ensures that only strong, meaningful relationships are included, maintaining the relevance of the taxonomy and highlighting the need for careful validation of new skill entries. Figure 3 presents the ARG, illustrating the interconnections within the ESCOnon-ESCO ecosystem. Due to the high density of connections between the two key skill categories, the graph initially

Table 2. Non-ESCO Skills

Skill	Frequency	Percentage
bash	61	3.562
node.js	60	3.504
jquery (library)	55	3.212
regex (nlp techinque)	51	2.978
json	50	2.920
reactjs (framework)	47	2.745
ruby-on-rails (web-app framework)	47	2.745
python-3.10 (version of programming language)	43	2.511
docker (open source tool)	40	2.336
qt (software)	34	1.986
django-rest-framework	34	1.986
visual-studio-code (text editor)	32	1.869
pandas (library)	31	1.810
delphi (programming language)	31	1.810
scikit-learn (python library)	30	1.752
vue.js (JavaScript library)	30	1.752
numpy (python library)	30	1.752
matplotlib (python library)	30	1.752
flask (Python api)	29	1.694
laravel-5.0 (framework)	29	1.694
phpstorm (software)	29	1.694
wpf (windows presentation foundation)	28	1.635
symfony (framework)	28	1.635
jpa (Java api)	28	1.635
spring-boot (framework)	26	1.518
Total Non-ESCO Skills = 303		**100.0%**

appeared overly cluttered, making it difficult to interpret meaningful relationships. To address this, we applied the Leiden community detection [20] algorithm to decompose the network into distinct communities, each representing a cohesive subset of interconnected skills.

The ESCOPlus framework enhances the ESCO taxonomy by integrating non-ESCO skills that show high-confidence associations with existing ESCO-defined skills. Only skills with a confidence score above *0.6* were considered, reflecting strong co-occurrence with established skills. For example, *android-fragments* and *android-layout* are closely linked to *android* (0.93 and 0.77), while *matplotlib*, *scikit-learn*, and *numpy* align with *python* (0.78, 0.76, and 0.70), underscoring their role in data science. In the network visualization, font size reflects

Table 3. Confidence Scores of Skill Associations

non-ESCO skills	ESCO skills	Confidence
android-fragments	android	0.9318
ggplot2	r	0.8361
xaml	c#	0.8333
matplotlib	python	0.7802
laravel-5	php	0.7755
android-layout	android	0.7717
scikit-learn	python	0.7647
python-2.7	python	0.7636
flask	python	0.7500
android-recyclerview	android	0.7451
jpa	java	0.7358
pandas	python	0.7280
hibernate	java	0.7241
numpy	python	0.7048
django	python	0.6897
entity-framework	c#	0.6824
asp.net-core	c#	0.6807
symfony	php	0.6760
doctrine-orm	php	0.6750
Average Confidence:		**0.49**

skill frequency, while edge thickness and direction encode the confidence metric $\text{conf}(\text{tag}_i \rightarrow \text{tag}_j)$. Based on these associations, the network was clustered into seven communities—*Java, JavaScript, Python, Android, PHP, C#*, and *Microsoft Visual C++*—representing distinct technical domains (Fig. 3). This association rule graph (ARG) forms the structural basis of ESCOPlus enrichment.

Textual Similarity. To enhance the ESCO taxonomy with alternative labels, we applied textual similarity between ESCO and non-ESCO skill terms using cosine similarity [22] over TF-IDF vectors, represent text by assigning weights to words based on how important they are. This approach computes similarity based on the lexical overlap and frequency of terms, representing each skill as a sparse vector in a shared feature space. For example, the terms *"Python"* and *"Python3.10"* yield a high similarity score due to their strong textual resemblance. We used a threshold of 0.8 to retain only highly similar term pairs. Table 4 presents the top 15 non-ESCO skills proposed as alternative labels to existing ESCO entries.

Table 4. Top 15 Non-ESCO Skills Proposed for ESCO Enhancement

ESCO Skill	Non-ESCO Skill	Similarity Score
mysql	mysql-5.7	1.000000
drupal	drupal-7	1.000000
python	python3.10	1.000000
java	java-8	1.000000
php	php-5.2	1.000000
java	java-stream	0.987234
broadcast	android-broadcast	0.898266
asp.net	asp.net-core	0.878266
linux	linux-kernel	0.858266
layout	android-layout	0.848237
build	android-build	0.834564
console	google-play-console	0.818237
eclipse	eclipse-marketplace	0.808237
angular	angular-services	0.768237
typescript	typescript-generics	0.707123
Average Similarity Score:		**0.44**

3.3   PLAN Phase

The *Plan Phase* is the final step in our methodology, and involves validating the previously identified non-ESCO skills and integrating them into the extended ESCOPlus taxonomy. This process ensures that the findings contribute meaningfully to labor market intelligence, curriculum development, and HR practices. The validation process involved an internal structured review, where the research team evaluated 1,120 ESCO skills and 303 non-ESCO skills to determine their relevance and inclusion in the ESCOPlus framework. To ensure accuracy and relevance, the internal validation process involved a panel of two domain experts in software engineering and labor market analytics, specifically the last two authors of this study. Each proposed skill (ESCO and non-ESCO) was independently reviewed by both researchers. In cases where both reviewers agreed (over 85% of cases), the decision was accepted directly. For the remaining items, a consensus meeting was held to discuss and resolve disagreements. In this context, skills were added to the taxonomy only if they met the following conditions:

– **Confidence level** among with internal review ≥ 0.6
– **Similarity threshold** with existing ESCO skills (alternative labels) ≥ 0.8

These threshold values were selected to balance precision and relevance. A confidence level of ≥ 0.6 is commonly used in association rule mining to indicate strong co-occurrence relationships without introducing excessive noise. Similarly,

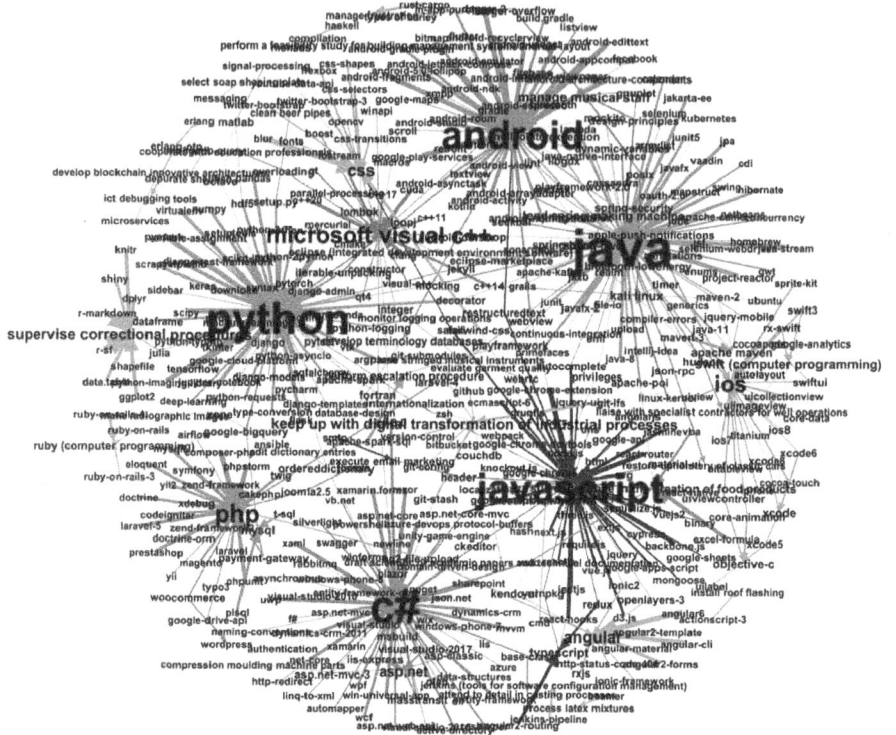

Fig. 3. ARG for ESCOPlus communities

a similarity threshold of ≥ 0.8 in cosine-based textual similarity ensures high lexical proximity between proposed and existing ESCO terms, minimizing semantic ambiguity. Both thresholds were validated during the manual review process to maintain alignment with the ESCO taxonomy's standards and naming conventions. Once validated, the enriched taxonomy was structured to enable mapping with emerging job vacancies and guide the development of future-oriented curricula, although this integration remains a subject for future implementation and evaluation.

4   The Proposed ESCO Extensions

The final outcome of the ESCOPlus framework, aligned with *(g1)*, is the extension of the existing ESCO taxonomy with carefully validated non-ESCO skills that reflect current technological developments, industry needs, and user-generated expertise. These proposed extensions aim to improve the coverage of modern digital competencies and bridge the gap between formal skills taxonomies and real-world labor market signals. To support this enrichment process, we leveraged association patterns visualized in Fig. 3, which highlights key

Table 5. Proposed New Skills and Alternative Skills for ESCOPlus

Cluster	Non-ESCO Skill	Label	Confidence Score	Similarity Score
Java	java-8	A	–	1.000
	jpa	N	0.7358	–
	intellij-idea	N	0.6358	–
	kubernetes	N	0.6958	–
	java-stream	A	–	0.8354
	rx-java	A	–	0.7954
JavaScript	facebook-javascript-sdk	A	–	0.754
	vue.js	N	0.6345	–
	reactjs	N	0.6554	–
	react-native	N	0.7445	–
	jquery	N	0.6134	–
	d3.js	N	0.6934	–
Python	python-jira	A/N	0.9012	0.77
	python-3.10	A/N	0.8543	0.70
	pandas	N	0.7280	–
	flask	N	0.7500	–
	python-logging	A/N	0.6334	0.7546
	django-rest-framework	N	0.8334	–
	pytest	N	0.7869	–
Android	realm	N	0.5543	–
	playframework-2.0	N	0.5434	–
	mockito	N	0.6434	–
	libgdx	N	0.7434	–
	android-studio-import	A	–	0.70
	android-permissions	A	0.8543	0.8340
PHP	php-7	A	–	1.00
	composer-php	A/N	1.000	0.8076
	phpstorm	A/N	0.875	0.8076
	zend-framework2	N	0.825	–
	phpunit	N	0.825	–
	laravel5.0	N	0.725	–
C#	xaml	N	0.8333	–
	entiny-framework	N	0.6824	–
	asp.net-core	N	0.6807	–
	c#-8.0	A/N	0.6807	0.8078
Microsoft Visual c++	c++-11.0	A	–	0.7078
	qt (software)	N	0.5456	–
	iostream	N	0.5956	–
	cmake (software)	N	0.6956	–
Summary	Total Alternative Skills (**A**)	**8**		
	Total New Skills (**N**)	**30**		
	Total Hybrid (**A/N**) Skills	**6**		

connections between ESCO and non-ESCO skills. This analysis enabled us to identify central ESCO skills that frequently co-occur with multiple emerging non-ESCO skills, supporting their inclusion as alternative or preffered labels.

Table 5 presents a structured overview of the recommended additions, categorized into distinct technology clusters: Java, JavaScript, Python, Android, PHP, C#, and Microsoft Visual C++. Each cluster includes skills that have either been identified as Alternative labels (A), which semantically align with existing ESCO skills, or as New skills (N) that are not currently represented in ESCO but emerged from the analysis of community practices and domain-specific usage. Additionally, some skills are marked as Hybrid (A/N), indicating a dual nature where they may serve both as alternative identifiers and as potential new entries depending on expert judgment.

From the analysis, a total of 8 alternative skills, 30 new skills, and 6 hybrid skills have been proposed for inclusion. These numbers illustrate a substantial opportunity to enrich ESCO's taxonomy, especially in domains like Python, PHP, and JavaScript, where dynamic open-source ecosystems and evolving developer tools introduce frequent innovation. For instance, tools like pytest, Django REST framework, and Vue.js are not merely language add-ons but represent ecosystem-defining competencies. Moreover, the presence of popular frameworks, exemplified by ReactJS, Kubernetes, and Android permissions, highlights the growing need for taxonomies to capture not only language fundamentals but also ecosystem fluency and deployment-related skills. The identification of these skills was backed by confidence scores and semantic similarity values derived from expert feedback and vector similarity analysis, ensuring both relevance and accuracy.

The ESCOPlus Framework (Fig. 4), is built via Python backend[8], provides a structured interface for exploring skills and their extensions within the ESCO taxonomy. The interface presents skill details in a clear, hierarchical manner, with the a skill category (e.g., Python) displayed alongside its description, outlining its core principles and applications. Below this, the system categorizes skills into Alternative Labels, which represent closely related terminology, and New Skills, highlighting emerging competencies recognized through data-driven analysis. The navigation bar at the top offers quick access to key sections, including the ESCOPlus Hub, Trends, and New Skills.

5   Discussion and Threats

In this section, we present key findings and their implications for stakeholders, aligned with the *(g2)* goal of the ESCOPlus framework. The target groups—IT professionals, HR specialists, and educational institutions—interact directly with skill taxonomies in real-world contexts. IT professionals align their profiles with job requirements, HR teams use taxonomies for candidate screening, and educators design training based on labor market needs. As primary stakeholders

---

[8] https://github.com/dkavargy/ESCOPlus.

impacted by digital skill shifts, these groups are central to taxonomy enrichment efforts.

5.1   IT Professionals and Job Seekers

The ESCOPlus framework supports IT professionals and job seekers by iden-tifying emerging skills and alternative labels aligned with evolving industry demands. Key additions such as Python logging, Django REST framework, Kubernetes, and Vue.js reflect the growing emphasis on automation, cloud deployment, and full-stack development. The inclusion of version-specific skills like Python 3.10, Java Stream, and Java 8 underscores the importance of rec-ognizing terminology variations, especially in contexts involving legacy systems. By capturing both general and specific technologies, ESCOPlus enables profes-sionals to stay aligned with current trends and market needs.

5.2   Recruiters and HR Specialists

For recruiters and HR specialists, the findings highlight the need to update job descriptions and hiring criteria to reflect evolving digital skill sets. The emergence of hybrid skills (e.g., Python-Jira, C# 8.0, Composer-PHP) underscores the importance of flexibility in recruitment strategies. Updating internal taxonomies in applicant tracking systems and broadening keyword searches can improve candidate matching by capturing alternative skill labels.

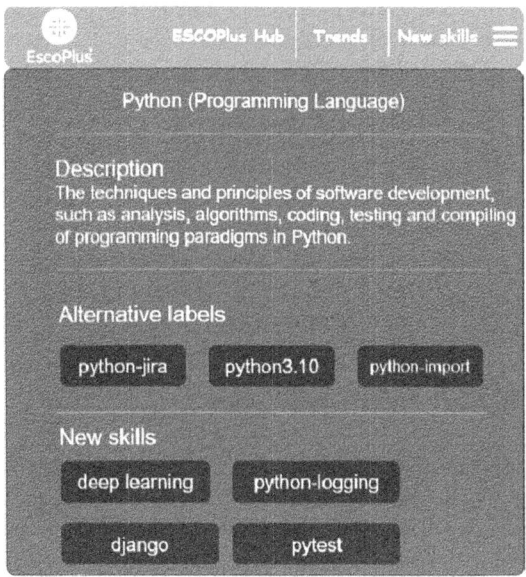

Fig. 4. ESCOPlus GUI

5.3   Educational Institutions and Training Providers

The integration of emerging and alternative skills in the ESCOPlus framework offers not only a broader understanding of current labor market dynamics, but also provides educational stakeholders—such as curriculum designers, training providers, and upskilling platforms—with a structured roadmap for aligning learning content with evolving digital demands. The increasing presence of DevOps-related technologies (e.g., Kubernetes, Ansible), front-end frameworks (Vue.js, ReactJS), and software testing tools (Pytest, PHPUnit) underscores the need to incorporate these skills into IT programs and certifications. Furthermore, educational institutions should consider developing micro-credential programs that cater to the demand for highly specialized technical competencies, ensuring that graduates are well-prepared for the evolving job market.

5.4   Threats to Validity

While the ESCOPlus framework offers a strong foundation, several limitations may affect the generalizability of its findings. The identification of new and alternative skills is based on co-occurrence patterns and expert validation, potentially introducing bias due to dataset composition and temporal trends. Additionally, reliance on similarity thresholds and confidence scores may overlook contextual nuances, leading to misclassification. The framework currently focuses on the IT domain, where skills evolve rapidly; however, its applicability to other sectors like marketing, healthcare, and engineering remains to be explored. Another constraint is that skill matching was performed using only ESCO's preferred labels, excluding alternative labels to maintain consistency. Lastly, while ESCOPlus emphasizes technical skills due to their prevalence on SO, future work will aim to incorporate GenAI and soft skills as part of a broader taxonomy expansion. Furthermore, we explicitly highlight the dynamic and evolving nature of digital skills and argue that the method should be applied periodically—for example, annually or biannually—to ensure that the taxonomy remains aligned with real-world skill demands. Since the tool relies on publicly available and regularly updated data from platforms like SO, it can be re-run at predefined intervals, allowing policymakers and practitioners to monitor emerging technologies and maintain the relevance of the ESCO taxonomy over time.

6   Conclusion and Future Works

The development and implementation of the ESCOPlus Framework contributes to the enrichment of the ESCO taxonomy with emerging, non-standard, and user-generated skills. By leveraging data from developer communities and combining it with standardized taxonomies, the framework can serve as a proxy for identifying the dynamic supply of digital competencies. Such insights are particularly relevant in contexts where official taxonomies fall short in capturing fast-evolving trends, making ESCOPlus a valuable tool for detecting underrepresented or uprising skillsets. Finally, the main conclusions are as follows:

- ESCOPlus successfully enriched the taxonomy with 30 new, 8 alternative, and 6 hybrid digital skills, including widely used technologies like Vue.js, Kubernetes, and Django REST.
- High-confidence associations and similarity measures ensured the addition of relevant tools including Java 8, Python 3.10, and ReactJS.

Looking ahead, ESCOPlus can contribute to a more structured alignment between occupations and domain-specific competencies through the classification of skills by scientific domain. These outcomes can inform evidence-based decisions in workforce planning and digital transformation strategies. Finally, the skill identification method presented here may serve as a proxy for digital skill supply, reflecting the self-reported expertise of developers and supporting better alignment with labor market demands. While the enhancements proposed by ESCOPlus are not yet incorporated into the current official version of the ESCO taxonomy, ESCO is a dynamic and evolving resource. The results of this study are intended to inform and support future updates of the taxonomy. To that end, the ESCOPlus framework is modular and re-executable, allowing it to be rerun periodically (e.g., semi-annually) to detect emerging skills using real-time data from SO. Future iterations will support incremental updates and dashboards to highlight fast-evolving technologies, enabling continuous enrichment of the ESCO taxonomy with minimal manual effort.

Acknowledgements. The authors acknowledge the funding received from the EUn's Horizon Europe Framework Programme SKILLAB under grant agreement No. 101132663. Also we wish to thank the anonymous reviewers for their valuable comments, which helped us to improve the paper.

References

1. Cico, O., Jaccheri, L., Nguyen-Duc, A., Zhang, H.: Exploring the intersection between software industry and software engineering education-a systematic mapping of software engineering trends. J. Syst. Softw. **172**, 110736 (2021)
2. Giabelli, A., Malandri, L., Mercorio, F., Mezzanzanica, M., Seveso, A.: NEO: a tool for taxonomy enrichment with new emerging occupations. In: Pan, J.Z., et al. (eds.) ISWC 2020. LNCS, vol. 12507, pp. 568–584. Springer, Cham (2020). https://doi.org/10.1007/978-3-030-62466-8_35
3. Peltokorpi, V.: In search of 'low-hanging fruits' or 'ideal' candidates? Understanding headhunters' candidate search activities. Hum. Resour. Manag. J. **31**(3), 639–657 (2021)
4. Wang, L., Zhou, Y., Sanders, K., Marler, J.H., Zou, Y.: Determinants of effective HR analytics implementation: an in-depth review and a dynamic framework for future research. J. Bus. Res. **170**, 114312 (2024)
5. Aluas, M., et al.: SKILLAB: skills matter. In: 2024 50th Euromicro Conference on Software Engineering and Advanced Applications (SEAA), pp. 491–498. IEEE (2024)

6. Kavargyris, D.C., Georgiou, K., Papaioannou, E., Petrakis, K., Mittas, N., Angelis, L.: ESCOX: a tool for skill and occupation extraction using LLMs from unstructured text. Softw. Impacts 100772 (2025)

7. Panzaru, C., Grama, A.: Towards explicit soft skills labelling in ESCO through semantic NLP analysis (2024)

8. Minor, K., McLoughlin, E., Carlisle, S.: The digital skills gap–is it time to rethink the needs of tourism and hospitality organizations in the UK? J. Hosp. Tourism Educ. 1–12 (2024)

9. Papoutsoglou, M., Rigas, E.S., Kapitsaki, G.M., Angelis, L., Wachs, J.: Online labour market analytics for the green economy: the case of electric vehicles. Technol. Forecast. Soc. Chang. **177**, 121517 (2022)

10. Boselli, R., et al.: WoLMIS: a labor market intelligence system for classifying web job vacancies. J. Intell. Inf. Syst. **51**, 477–502 (2018)

11. Seredko, A.: Doing Knowledge@ Scale: Sociomaterial Practices and Professional Learning of Software Developers on SO (2024)

12. Zhang, M.: Computational Job Market Analysis with Natural Language Processing. arXiv preprint arXiv:2404.18977 (2024)

13. Vankevich, A., Kalinouskaya, I.: Better understanding of the labour market using Big Data. Ekonomia i prawo. Econ. law **20**(3), 677–692 (2021)

14. Wang, C., He, X., Zhou, A.: A short survey on taxonomy learning from text corpora: issues, resources and recent advances. In: EMLP, pp. 1190–1203 (2017)

15. Wang, J., Kang, C., Chang, Y., Han, J.: A hierarchical dirichlet model for taxonomy expansion for search engines. In: WWW, pp. 961–970 (2014)

16. He, J., et al.: PTM4Tag+: tag recommendation of SO posts with pre-trained models. Empir. Softw. Eng. **30**(1), 1–41 (2025)

17. Deeprom, R., Yang, S., Higo, Y., Choetkiertikul, M., Ragkhitwetsagul, C.: Challenges in adopting LLaMA: an empirical study of discussions on SO. In: CEUR Workshop Proceedings, vol. 3864, pp. 35–42. CEUR-WS (2024)

18. Allamanis, M., Sutton, C.: Mining source code repositories at massive scale using language modeling. In: 2013 10th Working Conference on Mining Software Repositories (MSR), pp. 207–216. IEEE (2013)

19. Chehreh, I., Ansari, E., Bigham, B.S.: Advanced automated tagging for SO: a multi-stage approach using deep learning and NLP techniques. In: 2024 20th CSI International Symposium on Artificial Intelligence and Signal Processing (AISP), pp. 1–6. IEEE (2024)

20. Traag, V.A., Waltman, L., Van Eck, N.J.: From Louvain to Leiden: guaranteeing well-connected communities. Sci. Rep. **9**(1), 1–12 (2019)

21. Fan, W., Wang, X., Wu, Y., Xu, J.: Association rules with graph patterns. Proc. VLDB Endow. (PVLDB) **8**(12), 1502–1513 (2015)

22. Xia, P., Zhang, L., Li, F.: Learning similarity with textual similarity ensemble. Inf. Sci. **307**, 39–52 (2015)

23. Napierała, J.: Enhancing taxonomy-based extraction: leveraging information from online community platforms for digital skills demand identification in job ads. Stat. J. IAOS **40**(3), 591–602 (2024)

Experiment Evaluating Configurations of AWS Lambda Functions

Ilona Bluemke[iD] and Arkadiusz Zdanowski[✉]

Warsaw University of Technology, Institute of Computer Science, Nowowiejska 15/19, 00-665 Warsaw, Poland
{Ilona.Bluemke,arkadiusz.zdanowski.stud}@pw.edu.pl

Abstract. Serverless computing has emerged as a significant paradigm in cloud computing, enabling scalable and cost-efficient execution of event-driven workloads, known as Function-as-a-Service (FaaS). Among the leading FaaS platforms, AWS Lambda is the most widely used. Optimizing it for performance and cost is challenging, due to numerous configuration parameters. We developed a tool which we used in experiments examining different configurations and processors architectures for several algorithms. In this paper one of such experiments is presented in details.

Keywords: Serverless Computing · Function-as-a-Service · Amazon Web Services · AWS Lambda Component

1 Introduction

Cloud computing has revolutionized the way applications are developed and deployed by providing access to computing resources. Serverless computing [1] extends this model by eliminating infrastructure management, allowing developers to focus solely on writing and executing code. Among serverless platforms, AWS Lambda [2] is one of the most widely used implementations of the Function as a Service (FaaS) model [3], enabling automatic scaling and event-driven execution of functions. FaaS functions (self-contained, stateless units of execution, which may contain several programming-level functions [4]) are designed to operate independently and are triggered by external events, such as HTTP requests, database updates, or scheduled tasks. Basic information on FaaS and AWS Lambda functions are given in Sect. 2.

Despite its advantages, optimizing AWS Lambda functions for cost and performance remains challenging. Users can configure memory size and processor architecture, but the impact of these parameters on execution efficiency is not well-documented. Existing benchmarking tools (listed in Sect. 3.2) provide limited configuration choices or lack comprehensive statistical analysis, making it difficult to compare different configurations systematically. At the Institute of Computer Science, Warsaw University of Technology a tool - LambdaLab [5], that examines AWS Lambda performance with a range of configurations, including x86_64 and arm64 processor architectures was designed and implemented.

D. Taibi and D. Smite (Eds.): SEAA 2025, LNCS 16082, pp. 49–62, 2026.
https://doi.org/10.1007/978-3-032-04200-2_4

This tool was used to conduct a series of experiments analyzing CPU-intensive workloads on AWS Lambda. The results provide valuable insights into performance trade-offs, highlighting the impact of memory size and processor architecture on execution cost. In Sect. 2 a brief theoretical background on serverless architectures is given. Various benchmarking approaches and tools used in performance evaluation are presented in Sect. 3.

Some of experimental results obtained with our tool LambdaLab are presented in Sect. 4. Various workloads were used to measure execution time, cost, and performance efficiency. The results illustrate significant differences between processor architectures and demonstrate how memory allocation impacts execution cost.

In last section a summary of key findings is provided, potential directions for future research are also given. The effectiveness of the benchmarking tool is assessed. By addressing the gaps in existing serverless benchmarking tools, this work contributes to a better understanding of AWS Lambda cost and performance optimization and provides a practical solution for developers and researchers.

2 Theoretical Background

FaaS functions are designed to operate independently and are triggered by external events, such as HTTP requests, database updates, or scheduled tasks. Once the event arrives, it is passed to a controller for validation. If the event is valid, the controller initiates a function container. A container in serverless computing is a lightweight, isolated environment where the function code is executed. It is designed specifically to start quickly, ensuring minimal latency when a function is invoked. The container includes the runtime environment (the chosen programming language engine, libraries and frameworks) and the function's source code.

AWS Lambda is a widely used serverless compute service that executes code in response to events and automatically manages the underlying resources. Lambda integrates with many AWS services, which provide Backend as a Service (BaaS) capabilities. AWS Lambda offers two processor architecture options for running functions: x86_64 (CISC) and arm64 (RISC).

3 Related Work

In the rapidly evolving landscape of cloud computing, serverless architectures have gained popularity due to their scalability, cost-effectiveness, and ease of deployment. Optimizing serverless workloads for performance and cost remains a challenging task. Determining the optimal settings for the lowest cost or execution time is not straightforward due to the wide range of configuration options, performance variations between processor architectures, and the workload-dependent nature of function execution efficiency.

Systematic benchmarking is essential to make justified decisions and achieve the best performance-cost balance. By analyzing execution times, resource utilization, and pricing models in different configurations, benchmarking provides valuable insights that help developers optimize their serverless applications.

The performance evaluation of Function-as-a-Service (FaaS) platforms, such as AWS Lambda, has been an active area of research. Scheuner and Leitner [6] conducted a literature review covering 112 studies from both academic (51) and other (61) literature sources. Their findings indicate that AWS Lambda is the most frequently studied platform, followed by Azure Functions, Google Cloud Functions, and IBM Cloud Functions.

The majority of research has focused on micro-benchmarks measuring CPU speed and platform overhead, such as cold start latency. The study identified a difference between academic and industrial benchmarking approaches, particularly regarding the configurations tested and the transparency of experimental setups.

While many studies focus on simple function executions, there is limited research on complex workloads and function triggers, such as message queues, streams, and workflow integrations.

3.1 Benchmarking Tools

Numerous benchmarking tools have been developed to optimize memory allocation and execution time for serverless computing engines, each with unique strengths and limitations. Some tools focus on performance analysis of runtimes, while others provide visual tuning recommendations. Most tools share common drawbacks, such as limited configurability, lack of statistical analysis, and absence of explicit cross-architecture comparison.

The **AWS Lambda Benchmark Tool** [7] allows users to run concurrent executions and analyze latency, cold starts, memory usage, and cost efficiency. It does not offer many configuration options, which limits its range of use, and it does not support comparative cross-architecture benchmarking.

The **AWS Lambda Benchmark** [8] repository provides implementations for multiple runtimes (Node.js, Haskell, Python, Go, Rust, and Java) to compare execution time and cost efficiency. While useful for language comparisons, it suffers from the lack of updates (the last commit was pushed in 2019), which may lead to compatibility issues with newer AWS Lambda features. Additionally, it lacks advanced statistical methods to analyze performance variability.

ServerlessBench [9] is a comprehensive benchmarking framework for analyzing serverless computing performance of cloud providers. It enables systematic testing of factors like execution time, resource allocation, and cold start effects. Its complex setup can be a barrier for users without advanced technical expertise, and limited documentation further complicates its usability.

FaaSdom [10] is a benchmark suite that focuses on application-level benchmarking rather than simple micro-benchmarks, making it a valuable tool for evaluating real-world workloads. Its scope is limited since it does not cover all workload types, and resource-intensive benchmarking can result in high computational costs.

ServerlessBenchmark [11] is a command-line tool designed to benchmark major serverless platforms, including AWS Lambda, Google Cloud Functions, Azure Functions, and IBM Cloud Functions. While useful for cross-provider comparisons, it lacks customization options for user-defined workloads, and it has seen limited development activity, due to the lack of active contributors on GitHub, potentially impacting its relevance.

One of the most widely used tools, and the one recommended by AWS is AWS **Lambda Power Tuning** [12], which provides a visual tool for fine-tuning memory and execution configuration. It plots execution time and cost against allocated memory, supporting developers in the selection of an appropriate configuration, but its predefined memory steps may not always capture the best option, and it does not support cross-architecture comparisons.

3.2 Benchmarking Experiments

Several benchmarking experiments have been conducted to evaluate AWS Lambda's performance of programming languages and runtimes. While benchmarking tools provide a framework for running and analyzing tests, benchmarking experiments are conducted by researchers and organizations to evaluate the real-world performance of serverless computing. These experiments either utilize the tools described in Section A or employ custom, undisclosed methodologies, often suffering from limited transparency, lack of statistical rigor, and insufficient reproducibility. Despite providing valuable insights, many of these experiments fail to follow rigorous benchmarking principles. As noted by Scheuner and Leitner [6] common issues include:

- Reliance on mean values without confidence intervals or variance analysis.
- Lack of source code, as the source code and configurations are rarely disclosed.
- Potential biases in experiments conducted by cloud providers, where independent verification is impossible.

In AWS Lambda Benchmarking Study [13], Xebia conducted a benchmark comparing the performance of Rust, Scala, Python, and TypeScript in AWS Lambda. The study focused on real-world use cases and aimed to provide insights for developers. The implementations followed common algorithms and standard practices, using official AWS SDKs. The results showed that in terms of execution time and cost efficiency, Rust outperformed the other languages. Python followed closely in second place, while Scala, surprisingly, was the worst. Furthermore, the study did not provide detailed statistical analyses, such as confidence intervals or hypothesis testing, to reliably assess the execution cost variability.

In Benchmarking of Serverless Computing Platforms [14], Martins, Araujo, and Da Cunha conducted a comprehensive benchmarking study of various serverless computing platforms, including AWS Lambda. The study evaluated performance metrics such as cold start latency, execution time, and scalability in different programming languages and configurations. While the study provided valuable insights into the performance characteristics of serverless platforms, it mainly reported average values without employing rigorous statistical methods to measure variability or determine statistical significance.

In Performance and Usability Benchmarking [15], Sadaqat, Sánchez-Gordón, and Colomo-Palacios conducted a benchmarking study focusing on the performance and usability of serverless computing platforms. The study examined execution time, memory usage, and developer experience for different platforms and languages. While it provided a broad evaluation, it lacked detailed statistical analyses to measure performance variability and did not include the experimental configurations, which limits its reproducibility. Additionally, the study relied on subjective evaluations from an unspecified group of developers rather than a formal testing structure.

In SuperFlow: Performance Testing for Serverless Computing [16], Wen, Chen, Sarro, and Liu introduced SuperFlow, a performance testing framework for serverless computing. Their study evaluated AWS Lambda's performance under various workloads, focusing on factors such as execution time, resource utilization, and scalability. While the framework aimed to provide a systematic approach to performance testing, this study did not discuss the statistical methods used to analyze the results, leaving questions about the robustness of the findings.

In Comparison of AWS Lambda Arm vs. x86 Performance and Cost [17], AWS, in collaboration with its partner, Cascadeo, conducted experiments evaluating the performance and cost efficiency of AWS Lambda functions running on Arm-based Graviton2 processors versus traditional x86 processors.

In Evaluation of ARM vs. x86 in Serverless Functions [18], Chen conducted an independent study evaluating the performance of ARM64 architecture compared to x86 in serverless functions. Out of 18 functions tested, ARM provided faster runtime while x86 in only 7 functions. The research indicated that ARM64 could offer better cost efficiency for certain workloads. In this study, mean values were primarily reported, and no rigorous statistical analyses were conducted to determine the significance of the performance differences.

In summary, while these benchmarking experiments provide valuable insights into AWS Lambda's performance in various languages and architectures, they often lack transparency and rigorous statistical analysis. The absence of detailed experimental setups and comprehensive statistical evaluations limits the reproducibility and validity of the findings. Future research should focus on improving the mentioned drawbacks.

4 Experiment

At the Institute of Computer Science, Warsaw University of Technology a tool - LambdaLab (details in [5]) was designed and implemented. This tool evaluates the performance of AWS Lambda with various processor architectures and memory configurations for provided workload. It was used to experiment with different configurations in AWS Lambda.

4.1 LambdaLab Tool

LambdaLab tool collects detailed execution data, generates performance graphs, and provides rankings of all configurations under test, enabling users to identify the most optimal setups for workloads. It enables comparisons of processor architectures and measures the workload execution time with high precision, isolating it from the initialization and runtime overhead delay. Furthermore, it employs statistical methods of confidence intervals and mean values to provide the most probable range of values, based on multiple repeated runs of the workflow.

While similar tools exist, e.g. AWS Lambda Power Tuning [12, 13] LambdaLab introduces key improvements, including:

- Multi-architecture benchmarking, allowing direct comparison between x86_64 and arm64.
- Unrestricted configuration testing, enabling evaluations of all available memory sizes.
- Robust statistical analysis, including confidence intervals to improve result reliability.
- Automated data visualization and ranking, assisting users in selecting the optimal configuration.

By incorporating these features, LambdaLab is more flexible than the other tools.

4.2 Experiment with Fibonacci Numbers

An iterative approach to calculate Fibonacci numbers was chosen for the first experiment. This is "LINEAR_FIB" algorithm which can be found in [19]. It was chosen because it ensures deterministic CPU utilization, making it a reliable, repeatable benchmark. Furthermore, it is often used in related works mentioned in Sect. 2. The function, computing the nth Fibonacci number was implemented in Python. This algorithm is a reliable CPU benchmark because it focuses on computation using simple arithmetic operations, while avoiding memory-dependent operations, such as recursive function calls or large data structures. The algorithm's memory complexity is $O(1)$, as only two variables are used to store the intermediate results. Its time complexity is $O(n)$, since each Fibonacci number is computed only once.

Our tool LambdaLab was used in the experiment. Workload code (Fibonacci numbers) was executed for n = 90000. To ensure statistically meaningful results, the execution was repeated 10 times for each combination of memory size and processor architecture. The runtime environment used was Python 3.13.

The experiment tested 27 memory sizes, in the range from 128 to 3008 (128, 192, 256, 320, 384, 448, 512, 576, 640, 704, 768, 832, 896, 960, 1024, 1152, 1280, 1408, 1536, 1664, 1792, 1920, 2048, 2304, 2560, 2816, 3008). The experiment was performed on both arm64 and x86_64 processor architectures. Therefore, in total, there were 56 unique configurations. The invocation of the workload code was repeated 10 times for every configuration, resulting in 560 individual executions. The LambdaLab was also used to aggregate and analyze results producing Fig. 1. The results demonstrate that each configuration produced consistent execution times in repeated runs, which indicates high repeatability. This consistency ensures statistical reliability for further analysis, where data is aggregated using mean values.

Furthermore, Fig. 1 illustrates the general trend that if the allocated memory size increases, the corresponding execution time decreases significantly, particularly in the lower memory range. Notably, as memory size exceeds approximately 1000 MB, the performance improvements diminish, which results in an asymptotic behavior at around 100 ms, which reflects that the maximum processing speed is achieved and the execution time is stabilized.

Additionally, it can be observed that x86_64 consistently achieves shorter execution times compared to arm64, but the gap between the two architectures narrows down as the memory size increases. The arm64 architecture benefits from a lower cost per GB-second than x86_64. This raises an intriguing question whether arm64's cost advantage can compensate for its longer execution times. Deeper insights into this trade-off can be seen in Fig. 1.

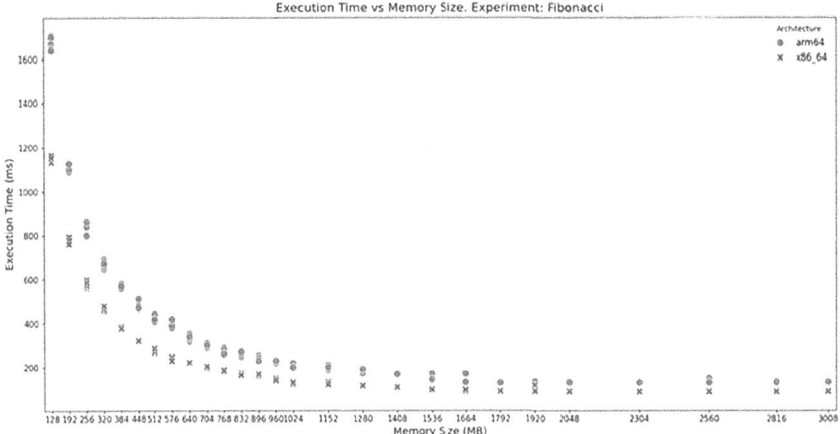

Fig. 1. Execution time vs memory size

To compare execution cost formula (1) is used:

$$BenchExCost = \left(\frac{ExTime(ms)}{1000} \right) * \left(\frac{MemSize(MB)}{1024} \right) * CostGBSec \qquad (1)$$

In Fig. 2 the execution cost associated with the execution time are shown. Both time and cost dimensions are aggregated for the repeated runs for every memory configuration. The data is presented by points connected with solid lines, representing the average values, with shaded regions around each line indicating the 95% confidence intervals. Architectures are color-coded: x86_64 is represented in blue, while arm64 is depicted in green. Both time and cost dimensions are shown together, as a dual-axis representation, which allows for a direct comparison of execution time (on the left y-axis, milliseconds) and cost (on the right y-axis), on different configurations.

The time trends in Fig. 2 confirm the earlier observations from Fig. 1: x86_64 achieves consistently lower execution times than arm64, with a significant time performance difference of around 40%. For example, for 256 MB, x86_64 achieves 576 ms, while arm64 achieves 841 ms. The detailed comparison, including the percentage values, is presented in Fig. 3.

The confidence intervals (denoted as CI) provide valuable information into the repeatability of the execution. For x86_64 we can observe a very small CI, except for the memory size of 1920 MB, where a large CI is observed. This indicates that some underlying hardware or runtime change is happening between 1792 MB and 1920 MB memory range. On the other hand, for arm64, the overall CI is larger than x86_64, with the worst consistency at memory sizes of 1280 MB, 1536 MB, 1664 MB, 2560 MB. Interestingly, arm64 is stable at 1920 MB, unlike x86_64. Overall, the CI indicate that both for majority of the configurations both processor architectures achieve stable results, with a slight edge for x86_64, but for both of them, there are some specific configurations which produce unstable execution environments.

Interestingly, the most inefficient configurations can be found by locating the local maxima in the cost curves. In such configurations, the reduction in time was not sufficient

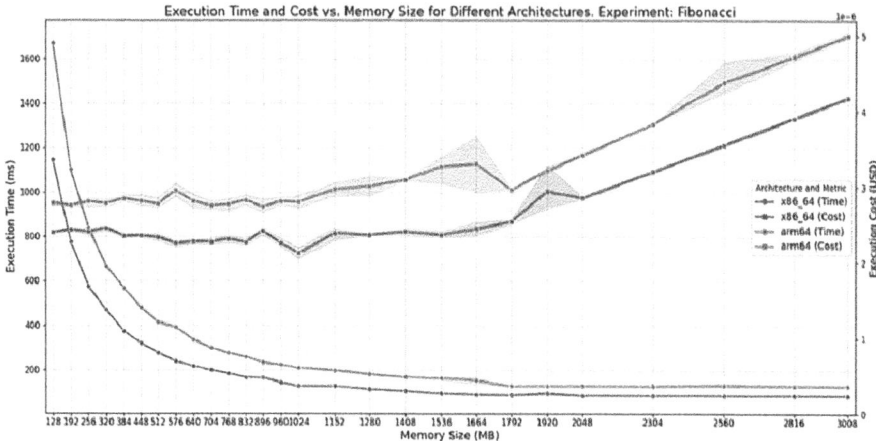

Fig. 2. Average execution time and cost vs memory size

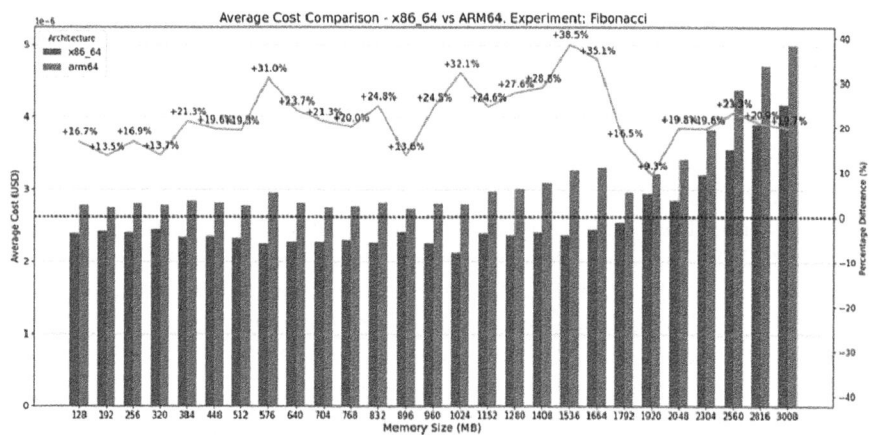

Fig. 3. Average cost comparison

to offset the cost increase associated with higher memory size increase. For example, the {x86_64, 192} configuration shows this imbalance: the memory size increases from 128 to 192 (by 50%), the time decreases from 1146 ms to 776 ms (by only 47%), which results in cost increase by 1.6%.

Overall, for this specific workload, the x86_64 configuration proves cheaper than ARM for all memory sizes. Despite ARM's lower price per GB-second, its slower execution time offsets the cost advantage. This cost discrepancy raises an important question about whether there is a systematic relationship between cost and memory size or if the observed cost differences are influenced by other factors and appear randomly distributed. This dilemma can be further explored by examining Fig. 3.

In Fig. 3 detailed cost comparison for both processor architectures is presented. The blue bars represent the x86_64 architecture, while the green bars are for the arm64. Each bar's height reflects the average cost in USD. Notably, the cost axis is scaled by a factor of 10–6. Above the bars, the orange line shows the percentage cost difference between the architectures, for each memory size. The black dashed line provides a 0% reference point for the orange line, indicating where the cost would be equal for both architectures.

Figure 3 confirms that arm64 is consistently more expensive than x86_64, and reveals that the relative cost difference ranges from 9.3% to 38.5%. The largest cost disparity occurs at the memory size of 1536 MB, highlighting a notable inefficiency of arm64 in this configuration. Conversely, the smallest cost difference is observed at 1920 MB, which may be caused by the instability of x86_64's execution cost, as highlighted in Fig. 2.

For lower memory sizes, up to 320 MB, the cost difference remains relatively stable averaging approximately 15 ± 2%, however, at 576, the disparity escalates to 31%, before gradually declining to 13.6% at 896 MB. From there, the difference rises again, reaching its peak of 38.5% at 1536. Following the maximum, the cost disparity drops to its minimum of 9.3% at 1920 MB, after which it begins to increase once more.

This variability underscores the importance of identifying optimal configurations for specific workloads, as even small changes in memory size can have a disproportionate and unpredictable impact on cost. Such optimization is crucial for ensuring cost efficiency, particularly when deploying workloads at scale. The time and cost rankings, which are useful for selecting optimal configurations, are presented in Tables 1 and 2 respectively.

The Tables 1 and 2 present the rankings of configurations based on normalized execution cost and time. These rankings are calculated using (2) and (3) which allow fair and meaningful comparisons between configurations.

$$NormalizedExTime = \frac{ExTimeCurrentConfig - FastestExTime}{SlowestExTime - FastestExTime} \tag{2}$$

$$NormalizedExCost = \frac{ExCostCurrentConfig - CheapestExCost}{MostExpensiveExCost - CheapestExnCost} \tag{3}$$

Each table highlights only the top 10% of the range, defined as configurations with the normalized metric value of at most 0.1.

Table 1 ranks configurations by their execution cost. The results highlight the dominance of x86_64 architecture in the cost ranking. The top 17 configurations, which represent the top 10% of the normalized execution cost rankings, are exclusively occupied by x86_64 configurations. This dominance indicates that, in all tested memory sizes, arm64 configurations consistently generated higher cost.

Interestingly, the absolute differences of cost among the top configurations remain within a small range of 0.29$ per 1 million invocations. This level of consistency highlights the stability of x86_64 configurations for varying memory sizes. This observation starts further examination of whether a similar pattern is evident in the execution time domain.

In Table 2 the configurations are ranked by execution time, with the fastest configurations listed first. The ranking is based on the Normalized Execution Time column. Similarly to the cost ranking in Table 1, the time ranking in Table 2 includes only the top 10% of results, defined as the configurations with normalized execution time of at most 0.1.

Table 1. Ranking by normalized execution cost.

Cost rank	Architecture	Memory size (MB)	Cost per 1,000,000 Invocations (USD)	Normalized Execution Cost
1	x86_64	1024	2.12	0.00
2	x86_64	576	2.25	0.05
3	x86_64	960	2.26	0.05
4	x86_64	832	2.27	0.05
5	x86_64	704	2.27	0.05
6	x86_64	640	2.27	0.05
7	x86_64	768	2.31	0.07
8	x86_64	512	2.33	0.07
9	x86_64	384	2.35	0.08
10	x86_64	448	2.35	0.08
11	x86_64	1280	2.36	0.08
12	x86_64	1536	2.36	0.08
13	x86_64	1152	2.38	0.09
14	x86_64	128	2.39	0.09
15	x86_64	256	2.40	0.10
16	x86_64	1408	2.40	0.10
17	x86_64	896	2.41	0.10

The fastest configuration is x86_64 with 2816 MB, achieving an average execution time of 85.25 ms, followed closely by other x86_64 configurations with similar memory sizes (2560 MB, 2304 MB, 3008 MB, 2048 MB, 1792 MB, 1664MB). All these configurations have an exceptionally low value of Normalized Execution Time, around the absolute minimum of 0.00, which indicates high stability and efficiency of x86_64 in handling the experiment workload. The fastest arm64 configuration with 1792 MB ranks only 12th overall, achieving an average execution time of 127.03 ms, which is 49% slower than the fastest x86_64 configuration. This result emphasizes the substantial time advantage of x86_64 over arm64 in all tested configurations.

Table 2. Ranking by execution time

Time rank	Architecture	Memory size (MB)	Average Execution Time (ms)	Normalized Execution Time
1	x86_64	2816	85.25	0.00
2	x86_64	2560	85.28	0.00
3	x86_64	2304	85.32	0.00

(*continued*)

Table 2. (*continued*)

Time rank	Architecture	Memory size (MB)	Average Execution Time (ms)	Normalized Execution Time
4	x86_64	3008	85.36	0.00
5	x86_64	2048	85.68	0.00
6	x86_64	1792	87.23	0.00
7	x86_64	1664	90.28	0.00
8	x86_64	1920	94.11	0.01
9	x86_64	1536	94.41	0.01
10	x86_64	1408	104.73	0.01
11	x86_64	1280	113.21	0.02
12	arm64	1792	127.03	0.03
13	x86_64	1152	127.06	0.03
14	x86_64	1024	127.1	0.03
15	arm64	2304	127.61	0.03
16	arm64	3008	127.72	0.03
17	arm64	2048	128.25	0.03
18	arm64	1920	128.56	0.03
19	arm64	2816	128.78	0.03
20	arm64	2560	131.47	0.03
21	x86_64	960	144.34	0.04
22	arm64	166	152.45	0.04
23	arm64	1536	163.49	0.05
24	x86_64	896	165.16	0.05
25	x86_64	832	167.16	0.05
26	arm64	1408	168.66	0.05
27	arm64	1280	180.62	0.06
28	x86_64	768	184.66	0.06
29	arm64	1152	197.87	0.07
30	x86_64	704	198.23	0.07
31	arm64	1024	209.88	0.08
32	x86_64	640	218.15	0.08
33	arm64	960	224.72	0.09
34	arm64	896	234.46	0.09
35	x86_64	576	240.04	0.10

4.3 Summary of Experiment

The results of experiment with the Fibonacci workload show significant differences between the x86_64 and arm64 architectures in terms of execution time and cost efficiency especially regarding the following aspects:

Execution Time: The x86_64 configurations consistently outperform arm64 in execution time, with the fastest arm64 configuration being approximately 49% slower than the fastest x86_64 configuration, as shown in Table 2. This trend is confirmed for all tested memory sizes, as seen in the Figs. 1 and 2.

Execution Cost: The x86_64 configurations dominate the cost rankings, taking all positions in the top 10% of results, as in Table 1. Despite arm64's lower cost per GB-second, its slower execution times lead to higher overall costs compared to x86_64, as visualized in Figs. 2 and 3.

Consistency: Confidence intervals in Fig. 2 highlight that x86_64 presents greater consistency in all configurations, with narrow intervals for both time and cost metrics. Arm64 generally exhibits higher variability in most configurations.

Optimization Potential: Numerous local inefficiencies, such as cost maxima, underline the importance of identifying optimal configurations tailored to specific workloads. Small changes in memory size can result in disproportionate impacts on cost and performance, reinforcing the need for detailed benchmarking.

Best Configurations: Among the analyzed configurations, two stand out: x86_64 at 2816 MB and 1024 MB. The 2816 MB configuration achieves the fastest execution time of 85.25 ms, which is 33% faster than the 1024 MB configuration's time of 127.1 ms, however, the 1024 MB configuration is the most cost-efficient, with a cost of 2.12 USD per 1,000,000 invocations, compared to 2.41 USD for the 2816 MB configuration, a 12% cost reduction.

Concluding, x86_64 proved superior for the experiment single-threaded, CPU-intensive workload, providing better performance, cost efficiency, and consistency for all configurations. Users must consider a trade-off between speed and cost efficiency, as shown by the contrast between the fastest configuration (2816 MB) and the most cost-efficient configuration (1024 MB). Tools like LambdaLab are essential for uncovering such insights and enabling informed decisions tailored to workload. Nonetheless, these configurations must be reassessed periodically, as updates to runtimes and processor architectures may impact performance and cost dynamics over time.

5 Conclusions

The primary goal of this work was to examine how processor architecture impacts execution time and cost efficiency for different workloads, using LambdaLab to conduct systematic experiments. In this paper an experiment with single-threaded CPU-intensive iterative workload (Fibonacci computation) was described. We also conducted other experiments with single- and multi - threaded cryptographic workload (SHA-256 hashing). This experiment is presented in [20]. These experiments were chosen to verify the AWS and partners' benchmarking study [17], which claims that arm64 is the superior architecture in all scenarios. Our experiment was chosen to challenge the arm64's universal superiority. The results clearly demonstrated that without hardware-level optimizations, x86_64 outperforms arm64 in both execution time and cost. This distinction is crucial because it shows that performance advantages are not inherent to an architecture but are highly dependent on workload characteristics and the presence (or absence) of specialized hardware optimizations.

In future, using LambdaLab tool, experiments with other workloads can be conducted e.g. memory-intensive workloads - to evaluate how architectures handle memory allocation and garbage collection, multi-threading and multiprocessing and I/O-heavy workloads - which may reveal differences in how architectures manage network and disk operations. The tool also can be improved by adding new functions.

Our work demonstrates the importance of systematic benchmarking in serverless computing. LambdaLab provides a structured and repeatable environment for evaluating AWS Lambda configurations, ensuring that developers and researchers can make justified decisions based on statistically correct data. The results confirm that selecting the right architecture and memory configuration can lead to substantial cost savings, and benchmarking tools like LambdaLab are essential for uncovering these insights.

References

1. Li, Z., et al.: The serverless computing survey: a technical primer for design architecture. ACM Comput. Surv. **10**(54), 1–34 (2022). https://doi.org/10.1145/3508360
2. What is AWS Lambda?-AWS Lambda. https://docs.aws.amazon.com/lambda/latest/dg/welcome.html. Accessed 1 Jan 2025
3. What Is Function as a Service (FaaS)? IBM. https://www.ibm.com/think/topics/faas. Accessed 1 Feb 2025
4. Harper, R.: Practical foundations for programming languages, 2nd edn. Cambridge University Press (2016), https://doi.org/10.1017/CBO9781316576892
5. Zdanowski, A.: LambdaLab: a tool for performance evaluation and configuration optimization of AWS Lambda functions, Bachelor's Thesis, Institute of Computer Science Warsaw University of Technology (2025/3)
6. Scheuner, J., Leitner, P.: Function-as-a-service performance evaluation: a multivocal literature review. J. Syst. Softw. (170), 110708 (2020). https://doi.org/10.1016/j.jss.2020.110708
7. Ayala, B.: Bryan-0/aws-lambda-benchmark-tool (2024). https://github.com/Bryan-0/aws-lambda-benchmark-tool, Python. Accessed 4 Feb (2025)
8. theam/aws-lambda-benchmark (2024). https://github.com/theam/aws-lambda-benchmark. The Agile Monkeys. Accessed 4 Dec 2025
9. Yu, T., et al.: Characterizing serverless platforms with serverless bench. In: Proceedings of the 11th ACM Symposium on Cloud Computing, pp. 30–44. ACM, Virtual Event USA (2020). https://doi.org/10.1145/3419111.3421280
10. Maissen, P., Felber, P. Kropf, P., Schiavoni ,V.: FaaSdom: a benchmark suite for serverless computing. In: Proceedings of the 14th ACM International Conference on Distributed and Event-based Systems, pp. 73–84. ACM, Montreal Quebec Canada (2020) https://doi.org/10.1145/3401025.3401738
11. hjmart93, hjmart93/ServerlessBenchmark (2023). https://github.com/hjmart93/ServerlessBenchmark. Python. Accessed 24 Feb (2025)

12. Casalboni A.: alexcasalboni/aws-lambda-power-tuning. https://github.com/alexcasalboni/aws-lambda-power-tuning, JavaScript. Accessed 4 Feb (2025)
13. AWS Lambda Benchmarking: Rust, Scala, Python, TypeScript – Xebia, https://xebia.com/blog/aws-lambda-benchmarking/, last accessed (2025/02/04)
14. Martins, H., Araujo, F., Da Cunha, P.R.: Benchmarking serverless computing platforms. J. Grid Comput. 4(18), 691–709 (2020). https://doi.org/10.1007/s10723-020-09523-1
15. Sadaqat, M., Sánchez-Gordón, M., Colomo-Palacios, R.: Benchmarking serverless computing: performance and usability. J. Inf. Technol. Res. 1(15), 1–17 (2022). https://doi.org/10.4018/JITR.299374
16. Wen J., Chen Z., Sarro F., Liu X.: SuperFlow: performance testing for serverless computing(2023). http://arxiv.org/abs/2306.01620, arXiv: arXiv:2306.01620. Accessed 9 Oct (2024)
17. Comparing AWS Lambda Arm vs. x86 Performance, Cost, and Analysis AWS Partner Network (APN) Blog. https://aws.amazon.com/blogs/apn/comparing-aws-lambda-arm-vs-x86-performance-cost-and-analysis-2/. Accessed 17 Jan (2025)
18. Chen, X., Hung, L.-H., Cordingly, R., Lloyd, W.: X86 vs. ARM64: an investigation of factors influencing serverless performance. In: Proceedings of the 9th Int. Workshop on Serverless Computing, pp. 7–12, Bologna Italy (2023). https://doi.org/10.1145/3631295.3631394
19. Farooq, S.M., Basha, S.H.S.: A study on Fibonacci series generation algorithms. In: 3rd Int. Conference on Advanced Computing and Communication Systems (ICACC), pp. 1–5. IEEE, Coimbatore, India (2016). https://doi.org/10.1109/ICACCS.2016.7586379
20. Bluemke, I., Zdanowski, A. : Evaluation of configurations of AWS Lambda functions. Int. J. Electron. Telecommun 3(71) (2025)

Intelligent Defect Detection for Manufacturing: The Kitchen Cabinets Industrial Case

Sadhana Lakshminarayanan[1] and Romina Spalazzese[1,2](✉) (iD)

[1] Department of Computer Science and Media Technology, Malmö University, Malmö, Sweden
[2] Sustainable Digitalisation Research Centre, Malmö University, Malmö, Sweden
romina.spalazzese@mau.se

Abstract. In modern Industry, I4.0, artificial intelligence technology like Machine Learning (ML) and Deep Learning (DL) are increasingly used to fully realize the digital transformation. And is no news that Sustainability and Sustainable Digitalization are key. To this end, automatic anomaly detection is a concrete area for improvement in production lines, focusing on processes. In this paper, we investigate how to build an optimal Intelligent Defect Detection (IDD) model for furniture manufacturing, by taking the case of kitchen cabinets. We study (ML) Support Vector Machine, K-Neighbour Network, and (DL) YOLO models on different datasets and by analyzing training time, accuracy, precision, recall, F1-score, and robustness to lighting conditions. We contribute with an optimal IDD and a critical discussion. Our conclusions are based on the experiments conducted on the real world industrial manufacturing of kitchen cabinets.

Keywords: Anomaly detection · Defect detection · Machine Learning · Deep Learning · Industrial Internet of Things · Sustainability · ML · DL · SVM · KNN · YOLO · IIoT · I4.0

1 Introduction

In recent years we have been experiencing the fourth industrial revolution, i.e., Industry 4.0 (I4.0), that led to the transformation of many companies going from legacy into more modern and flexible ones. The transformation includes new hardware, software, data, processes to better respond to the market requests for fast changes and adaptation. Furniture manufacturing is an example of such industry making the transition happen. In addition, more recently Industry is also heavily investing on research and adoption of promising technologies like Machine Learning (ML) and Deep Learning (DL) into their processes and production lines towards improved and more automated ones. As part of the digital transformation, a key concern for complex I4.0 digital production systems is sustainability. In particular, Sustainable Digitalization involving both realizing the digitalization in a sustainable way and creating support/benefits for society through digitalization. This involves all of the four sustainable digitalization pillars namely: environmental, social, economic, and technological.

D. Taibi and D. Smite (Eds.): SEAA 2025, LNCS 16082, pp. 63–79, 2026.
https://doi.org/10.1007/978-3-032-04200-2_5

Within sustainable digitalization, concrete core issues in I4.0 is anomaly detection. More specifically, there is a need for detecting defects (i) automatically, (ii) early in the production line so to: a) higher the product(ion) quality, b) lower costs, c) avoid human health issues, d) minimize wastage, and e) make technology more suited and adaptable for long term use and evolution in environments that continuously change.

Anomaly detection, researched for almost 60 years, plays an important role in many communities including, e.g., data mining, machine learning, computer vision, and statistics [11]. Traditionally, anomaly detection tasks have predominantly relied on human intervention, a practice that presents several drawbacks: human fatigue, false positives, health risks, operational costs [9]. To overcome these and more pitfalls, automatic visual (or vision) inspection entails utilizing a sensor such like a camera to generate image data and employing techniques from image processing and pattern recognition to assess and interpret imaged objects. The advantages of automatic visual inspection, in addition to avoiding human health issues, encompass enhanced accuracy, reliability, repeatability, and overall quality assurance achieved at a faster pace, lower cost and minimized wastage compared to manual labor [4]. Due to such advantages, some research investigated anomaly detection systems using ML/DL towards maximum quality assurance [12].

In this work, in collaboration with an external stakeholder involved in furniture manufacturing in South Sweden[1], we thus investigate the following **overarching research question** (RQ): *How can we build an optimal intelligent defect detection model for kitchen cabinets manufacturing?*

With Intelligent Defect Detection (IDD) we refer to an automatic visual inspection system using computer vision and ML/DL. With optimal model we mean the ML/DL model, i.e., minimizing training time, and maximizing accuracy and robustness w.r.t. different environment lighting conditions.

Our main contributions are an optimal IDD for detecting defects on kitchen cabinets during manufacturing as well as a critical discussion about it.

The Kitchen Cabinet Industrial Case. Figure 1 shows the steps in the production of kitchen cabinets of our external stakeholder in South Sweden and at which point in the process we aim to inspect the quality (see magnifier symbol).

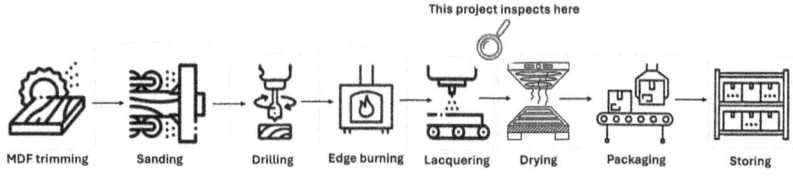

Fig. 1. Production steps in the manufacturing of kitchen cabinet

---

[1] Due to non-disclosure agreement, we cannot share more information.

When we started this study, our partner stakeholder performed quality control at the end of the production line, before packaging. However, the company finds that a lot of defects are typically detected on the back side of kitchen cabinet (B side) on the lacquering line. The time between the lacquering of the B side and the end of the line is 3 to 5 days. Since typically the number of products produced in that time frame is in thousands, implementing an IDD for early detection of defects on the B side on the lacquering line becomes essential. This would mean that defective samples can be identified while the lacquer is wet and sent to rework (which is impossible after drying making the cabinets becomes wastage). Detection at an early stage would thus result in a more sustainable and quality manufacturing.

The goal of this work is to identify an optimal IDD model ahead in the production line (after lacquering) to automatically classify various defects on kitchen cabinet boards. The company identified surface irregularities (cavity) and lacquering issues (roller-stripe) as the defects causing major wastage of resources in production; so, this study focuses on these two defects and aims to use image processing in combination with ML/DL techniques to balance training time and performances while reliably functioning under diverse lighting conditions.

The reminder of this paper is organized as follows. Section 2 summarizes related work. Section 3 describes our approach while Sect. 4 reports about the experiments we conducted. A critical discussion is provided in Sect. 5 while conclusions and future directions are drawn in Sect. 6.

2   Related Work

Image Processing Techniques and ML. Traditional image processing techniques are, e.g., thresholding, edge detection, texture-based image processing, and segmentation. Based on a survey of defect detection and classification approaches used in the industry ([3]), there remains a significant demand for the development of general defect detection methods using image processing that can handle any type of defect on any material. Texture is a crucial attribute largely used for image processing and segmentation, commonly known as texture segmentation. Within industrial environments, many uncertainties exist, spanning from the intensity of defects to their shapes and sizes. Hence, it becomes imperative to devise methods capable of adapting to such extensive variations. Learning-based approaches emerge as best alternatives to pre-programmed feature-detection techniques due to their inherent robustness in handling variations. Iivarinen evaluates the effectiveness of two histogram-based texture analysis techniques for detecting surface defects [8]. The examined techniques, Gray Level Co-occurrence Matrix (GLCM) and Local Binary Pattern (LBP), generate texture features from small image windows. Despite GLCM is one of the most efficient texture analysis methods, under varying lighting conditions, and depending on the clarity of the image, it might have some drawbacks and not always give the best results. One such drawback is that GLCM is often less accurate near the class borders. Gabor filter is another commonly used technique to extract textures from an image which can overcome this drawback of GLCM

[10]. Other ML algorithms like decision trees and K-Nearest Neighbors are used in surface defects as traditional solutions. However, it is challenging to implement robust models since can be domain specific and require defect patterns on surfaces to exhibit consistent contrast with the background.

Deep Learning. Convolutional Neural Networks (CNN) became one of the fastest-growing fields with n need of explicit feature extraction as in ML thus improving the challenges with lighting or complex data [3]. Cha et al. in [2] introduced the use of CNNs for assessing concrete cracks achieving an accuracy of approximately 98%. This CNN-based approach can also be expanded to classify additional types of damage, such as steel delamination, by incorporating these categories into its training dataset. Faster Region-based CNN (Faster-RCNN) [6] achieved better accuracy and speed compared to its predecessor RCNN. Other DL models have demonstrated impressive results in recent years with regard to various defect detection problems, e.g., Visual Geometry Group network (VGGNet) for ceramic sanitary ware defect detection [15]. Since its debut, the YOLO (You Only Look Once) series of object detectors has advanced swiftly. The survey in [7] shows that YOLO-v8 is suuitable to meet industrial needs, e.g., for automated quality inspection in industrial surface defect detection, being designed to deliver real-time performance and high classification accuracy while being computationally efficient. A study conducted at Microsoft by Kaiming He and Jian Sun [5], addresses how constrained time cost often presents challenges for engineers and developers in both industrial and commercial scenarios.

Despite the advanced developments of CNN architectures, the black-box nature of deep learning models makes it challenging to comprehend the automatic feature extraction process, making it less reliable. Besides, it requires a substantial amount of training data to ensure robustness. This may lead to high computation and training time making retraining of the models expensive in an industrial setup especially involving constrained time cost. Conversely, explicit feature extraction and traditional image processing are more reliable but highly tailored to the specific application and are not robust to variation in environmental factors. Therefore, achieving an optimal balance between manually crafted feature detection rules and automated feature extraction methods could create a complementary approach. Bhatt. et al., in [1], suggest techniques like Sobel filtering, Laplacian filtering, Canny edge detection, morphological operations, and thresholding can identify distinctive features during the pre-processing phase. These identified features can be fed into a deep-learning network. The network, through a convolutional neural network (CNN) layer, can then automatically extract additional features. This hybrid approach leverages the advantages of both methods and could lead to an efficient detection system [14].

Additionally, DL models can eliminate the need for such image processing due to their automatic feature extraction capabilities. To the best of our knowledge, no previous research examined the application of exclusive image processing alongside DL models to study the impact on performance and training time. Image processing methods, such as enhancement or segmentation of the Region of Interest (ROI) are employed to highlight defects which are then trained with the models. This approach aims at enabling reliable training of DL models with reduced training time and good robustness making them more suitable for industrial applications especially beneficial under constrained time cost scenarios.

3   Our Approach

Our work focuses on identifying and implementing an IDD for kitchen cabinets manufacturing within an industrial production setting with minimal training time and high performance under varying lighting conditions. The primary focus is on detecting defects within the lacquering section of the production line. The defects of interest are two: surface irregularities like cavities and lacquering issues like roller-stripe defects.

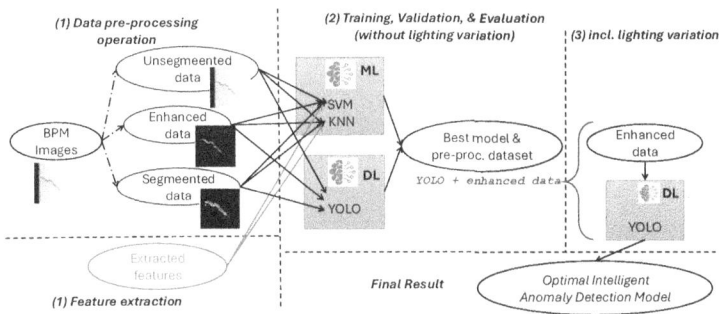

Fig. 2. Our approach

Figure 2 shows the core of our approach, where digital image processing, a.k.a. traditional image processing, is adopted to achieve the enhancement/segmentation of the defects. The approach takes as input images in Bitmap (BMP) format of varying brightness and resolution and (1) the data pre-processing operations described below are performed. In this work we use a low-level process, which involves contrast enhancement, and a mid-level process involving segmentation. For defect enhancement, the Gabor filter is used which highlights the defects from the neighboring pixels. The resulting dataset to this process is referred to as '**enhanced data**'. Instead, to segment defects from the background (kitchen cabinet and conveyor belt), a combination of digital image processing techniques is applied sequentially—Gaussian blur, Gabor filter, erosion, and adaptive thresholding with mean. This segmentation method is tailored to accommodate all relevant **defect classes**, including **cavities, roller stripes**, and **non-defective** areas, resulting in the isolation of the defects as the object of interest. The resulting dataset to this process is referred to as '**segmented data**' throughout this work. The dataset that does not undergo the image processing techniques described above (it is used as is) is referred to as '**unsegmented data**'. Subsequently, (2) in Fig. 2, classification is implemented using suitable

ML (Support Vector Machine (SVM), K-Nearest Neighbors (KNN)) and DL (YOLO) models. To identify the best performing ML/DL model we study for all of them the training time, accuracy, precision, recall, and F1 score (both with and without digital image processing-enhancement/segmentation). Please note that for SVM and KNN, previously extracted features (1) are also provided as input. This leads us to identify the best model and pre-processed dataset i.e., YOLO and enhanced data. These latter are then used again to evaluate the model against varying lighting conditions too (3). At the end of this process we obtain the optimal IDD model.

To summarize, we investigate the following sub research questions. By considering as intelligent defect detection models a DL model YOLOv8n and an SVM and a KNN as ML models:

SRQ1: *How does enhancing/segmenting the defects prior to training the DL/ML model impact the performance and training time of the model?*

SRQ2: *How do the ML and DL model in terms of performance and training time when enhancing, segmenting, or not pre-processing the defects?*

SRQ3: *How robust is the best-performing model with respect to varied lighting conditions?* SVM, KNN, and YOLO were chosen since they balance accuracy, interpretability, and real-world applicability and allow for a comparison between traditional feature-based methods and end-to-end learning-based approaches.

3.1   Data Collection

The data we used is provided by our external stakeholder from their production line in the manufacturing unit. Collected using a Cognex camera within a light-controlled chamber, situated along the conveyor belt route, the data encompasses images of cabinets before packaging. Illuminated adequately to eliminate shadows, the chamber ensures optimal image capture conditions. These images, both defective and non-defective including various cabinet sizes with(out) mounting holes, are obtained from the camera connected to a computer. Images are stored in BMP format. BMP files are typically uncompressed, i.e., store raw image data without any compression. This results in preserving all the necessary information of the image without loss of quality.

3.2   Types of Defects and Data Pre-Processing

In this work, we consider three classes of images - two classes being defective and one non-defective. The two considered defective classes are cavities and roller stripe defects. While the cavity represents the defects on the Medium Density Fiberboard (MDF) itself such as dents, bumps and scratches, the roller stripe defect is caused during the process of lacquering. A roller dipped in a tub of lacquer is rolled over the cabinet boards. In some cases, this rolling procedure leaves an extra layer of lacquer in the form of stripes on the surface. Hence named roller stripe. Figure 3 show some of the defective and non-defective image classes used in this work. The collected BMP images are cleaned and separated based on the defects and stored in separate folders with defect names as labels. The images with lighting issues and shadows are removed as a part of data cleaning. The used data images are of two types: cropped images focusing on the area of defects and images of the entire cabinet. The aim of incorporating the two image types is to improve the learning of the algorithms, and to achieve a good generalization and capability to differentiate the defects from regular cabinets' features. For instance, the cropped candidates help the model in learning the details of various defects representing more focused information. On the other hand, using the entire cabinet images help the model learn the other aspects and can provide context and additional information like the design, shape, size, types and placement of mounting holes. At this stage the balanced 'unsegmented data' contained 3578 images (of which 1294 in the cavity class, 1180 in the roller stripe class, and 1104 in the normal class).

Cavity   Roller Stripe   Normal

Fig. 3. Examples of cavity and roller stripe defects, and non-defective surface

Various digital image processing techniques are then applied to form two additional datasets ('segmented data' and 'enhanced data'). To segment defects from the background (kitchen cabinet and conveyor belt), we sequentially applied Gaussian blur, Gabor filter, erosion, and adaptive thresholding with mean. This segmentation method is customized to accommodate all relevant defect classes, such as cavities, roller stripes, and non-defective areas, effectively isolating the defects as the object of interest. Instead, for defect enhancement only the Gabor filter is used which accentuates defects from the surrounding pixels. Then, the different ML and DL models are trained by using the three datasets (unsegmented data, enhanced data, and segmented data).

3.3   Feature Extraction

GLCM texture analysis method helps quantifying the spatial relationships between pairs of pixels in an image by calculating how often pairs of pixel intensity values occur at specific spatial offsets or distances [13]. GLCM provides statistical information about the texture patterns present in an image which can be used for classification. The GLCM matrices are obtained with five different combinations of distance and angle on each of the datasets - unsegmented, enhanced and segmented. Five statistical features dissimilarity, correlation, homogeneity, energy, and contrast are then computed for each of the matrices. In the end, a total of 25 features are extracted which are stored in a CSV file format along with label to be trained. This CSV serves as input to the machine learning models for classification.

3.4   Model Training, Validation and Evaluation

Owing to their popularity and effectiveness in surface detection in the existing works, traditional ML models, SVM and KNN, are implemented. The data is split into 80-20 for training and validation, respectively. Unlike the ML models, DL models are directly fed with images without feature extraction, but the input dataset is varied to include images where defects are segmented, unsegmented or enhanced. The DL model is then trained with suitable parameters and is validated on unseen data. After evaluating both ML and DL models, the best model in terms of training time and performance metrics is chosen to be used for the defect detection task with the additional consideration for robustness with respect to lighting variations. To check the robustness, the lighting of the images, of the best dataset identified during the previous step, is varied by gamma correction. Four different gamma values–0.25, 0.5, 1.5, and 2.5 are chosen to create four different datasets with different lighting conditions to test the defect detection model.

4   Experimental Setup and Results

The experiments are run in HP desktop Z4 with Nvidia RTX 4500 ad-a-generation. The system is equipped with a powerful Intel(R) Xeon(R) w5-2465X 3–10 GHz, 64 GB of RAM, and 1 TB solid-state drive. Sci-kit learn library is used to implement both the ML classifiers–SVM and KNN and ultralytics is used to implement the DL model–YOLOv8n-cls.

4.1   GLCM Patch Analysis

To determine the parameters of the GLCM i.e., distance (d) and angle (θ), four image patches of size 35×35 were extracted from both the clean area i.e., the non-defective area of the cabinet, and four patches from the cavity area i.e., the defective area of the cabinet. For each of these eight extracted patches, a eight GLCM matrix was computed with a different combination of distance and angle. From the obtained matrices, statistical features such as dissimilarity, correlation, homogeneity, energy, and contrast were deducted. The features were plotted in various combinations to visualize how the set values for the distance and angle affect the plot. Based on how the features for different regions cluster, the parameter values are chosen. The idea here is that the regions cluster better for the right parameters. After experimenting with different combinations, it was found that the feature clusters were better for smaller d. Figure 4 shows a sample image with extracted patches and the corresponding plots for various feature combinations. It can be noted how the defective and non-defective regions form distinct clusters. Based on the insights from this experiment, five different GLCM matrices were generated using the following pixel distance (d) and angle (θ) combinations: (d = 1, θ = 0°), (d = 2, θ = 0°), (d = 5, θ = 135°), (d = 2, θ = 45°), and (d = 5, θ = 90°). For each GLCM, five statistical features—dissimilarity, correlation, homogeneity, energy, and contrast—were extracted, resulting in a total of 25 features along with the labels to be trained. The 25 features were saved in CSV format to be used for classification in ML algorithms.

4.2   Defect Enhancement and Defect Segmentation

Defect Enhancement. The preprocessed images are initially subjected to a band-pass filter using a Gabor filter to remove unnecessary information and enhance the defects. The parameters for the filters are determined through trial and error, taking into account the nature of the defects and the specific information that needs to be highlighted by the filter. The chosen parameter values are as follows: Kernel size (x, y)–(5, 5) since the defects are very small. Setting larger values leads to picking up unnecessary information besides just the defects. λ–36°; smaller value detects small features while larger values detect global features Θ–90°; setting the filter direction to be horizontal ϕ–90°; phase offset by trial and error σ–10; setting a large standard deviation misses the small defective features γ–0.5; setting 1 represents a spherical shape of the filter while a value closer to 0 represents the elliptical shape of the filter. Figure 5 shows examples of images from our industrial dataset before and after the Gabor filter application.

The Gabor filter helps in highlighting the necessary defective information for the models to learn the pattern better. These enhanced defect images will be used to train the ML and DL models to measure the impact of defect enhancement. The results obtained from this operation are referred to as enhanced data, while the input given in this section are referred to as unsegmented data.

Defect Segmenetation. In this case, the pre-processed images undergo a series of image processing techniques in the following sequence–Image blurring is applied to the grayscale image with a 7 × 7 Gaussian kernel with a standard deviation of 5 resulting in a smoothened image. The blurred image is then passed into the Gabor filter with the same parameter values as above, in Sect. 4.2 except for the change in λ which is now set to 30°. The resultant image from the Gabor filter is then put through the morphological operation of erosion with a 3 × 3 kernel to get rid of the other texture information surrounding the ROI while holding the defective information. Adaptive mean thresholding is then used with a binary inverse threshold by choosing a neighborhood of 9 × 9 thus resulting in an image that is left just with the defective region segmented from the original image.

Support Vector Machine. The extracted 25 features from the GLCM along with the labels for training, are saved in a CSV file. The file is used to train and test the SVM model, and the metrics such as accuracy, precision, recall, and F1-score are used to evaluate the model. For this multi-class classification, one

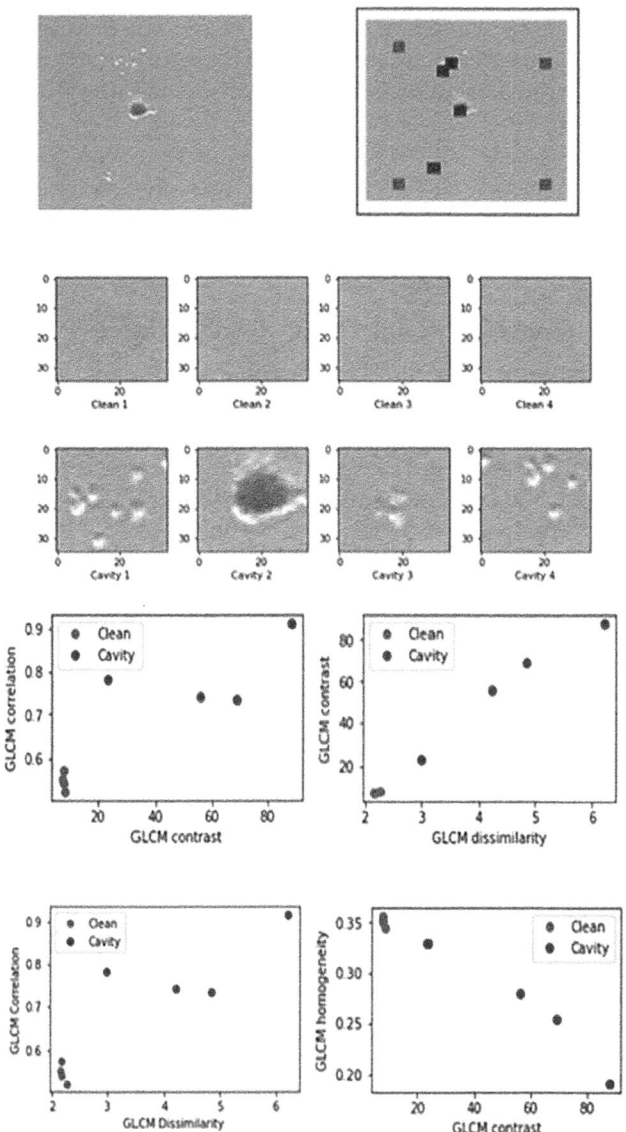

Fig. 4. Patch extraction of a sample image

versus rest (OvR) is used. In the experiments, soft margin SVM is adopted by setting the c value to 1; RBF kernel is used by trial and error as it is classified the best compared to the rest of the kernels. SVM was run on unsegmented, enhanced, and segmented data. Table 1 shows experimental results.

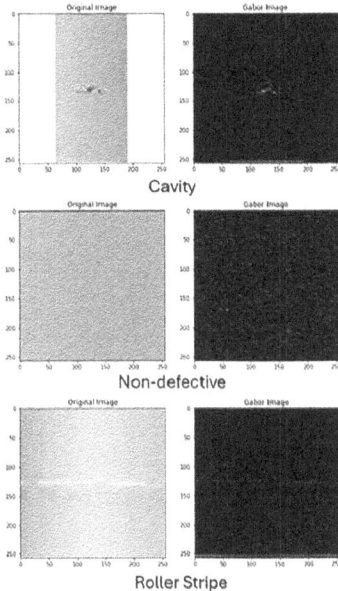

Fig. 5. Defect enhancement with Gabor filter

K-Nearest Neighbors. The same CSV file with 25 features that are used for SVM is now used as input to the KNN. Before training the algorithm, the optimal k-value is found by $\sqrt{N}$, where N is the number of samples. With k = 59, the algorithm was run on unsegmented data, enhanced data, and segmented data. Performances for each dataset is in Table 1.

Table 1. Comparison of SVM and KNN on different input datasets

Models and Input	Accuracy	Precision	Recall	F1 score	Training time
SVM (Unsegmented data)	67.69	73.23	67.66	67.00	21.2 s
SVM (Segmented data)	87.74	87.54	87.47	87.41	19.8 s
SVM (Enhanced data)	88.58	88.93	88.68	88.63	23.5 s
KNN (Unsegmented data)	80.36	80.75	80.14	80.07	28.2 s
KNN (Segmented data)	83.42	83.05	83.16	83.08	16.2 s
KNN (Enhanced data)	87.04	86.76	86.80	86.70	16.4 s

4.3   DL Model Training, Validation, and Evaluation

For Deep Learning, YOLOv8n-cls is chosen in this work to classify the defects owing to its less computation and high speed [53]. The YOLOv8 nano-classification (YOLOv8n-cls) model is trained on 3 different datasets similar

Table 2. Comparison of YOLOv8n on different inputs

Input	Epochs	Accuracy	Precision	Recall	F1 score	Training time
Unsegmented data	50	98.20	98.88	98.94	98.86	824 s
Segmented data	20	97.40	96.02	96.04	96.03	391 s
Enhanced data	20	98.10	97.02	97.33	97.17	414 s

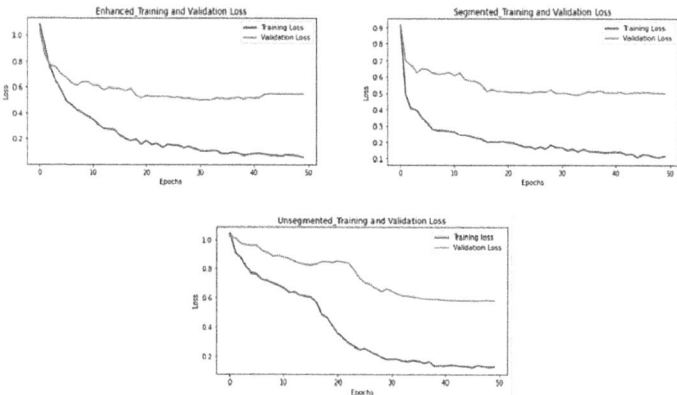

Fig. 6. Training vs Validation loss for the 3 models

to the ML models i.e., unsegmented, segmented, and enhanced. The model is trained with a single GPU setting and a batch size of 32 for 50 epochs. The model is trained from scratch using yaml file with Adam optimizer, cross-entropy loss, and cosine learning rate scheduler which helps in managing the learning rate for better convergence. The default augmentation hyperparameters are not utilized owing to manual augmentation implemented to ensure a fair comparison between ML and DL models. The performance of these 3 models is shown in Table 2 concerning 50 epochs and the performance of the model trained on segmented and enhanced data with 20 epochs respectively. Figure 6 illustrates the train versus validation loss trends across 50 epochs for models trained on enhanced, segmented, and unsegmented data. In the case of unsegmented data, the validation and training loss consistently decreases throughout the 50 epochs. However, for models trained on segmented and enhanced data, the validation loss plateaus around the 20th epoch and then shows no further decrease. However, the train loss continues to decrease constantly indicating overfitting behavior. This suggests that training should ideally halt around the convergence point, typically observed at the 17th epoch, to prevent overfitting. Hence, the training is stopped for enhanced and segmented data at epoch 20. The plot in Fig. 7 shows the training loss for each epoch for YOLOv8n-cls for all the 3 data inputsâĂŞ unsegmented, segmented, and enhanced datasets. It can be seen how the convergence rate for each model varies and at any given point on the y-axis, the training curve for unsegmented data lags the segmented and enhanced data.

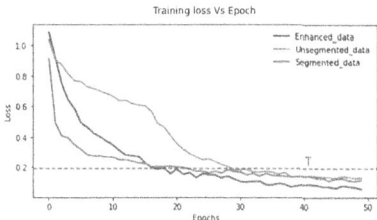

Fig. 7. Training loss of the 3 DL models with different input data

4.4 Robustness of DL Model to Lighting Variation

The robustness of the YOLOv8n-cls model trained on enhanced data, showing both optimal performance and convergence time, is checked for varying lighting. The robustness of such model trained for 20 epochs is checked against the perturbed data with various gamma values as described in Sect. 3.4. The performance metrics accuracy, precision, recall and F1 score are used for evaluation and results are shown in Table 3. The averaage inference time per image is 3 ms.

Table 3. Performances for varying Gamma of the DL model with enhanced input

Gamma	Accuracy	Precision	Recall	F1 score
0.25	92.75	92.68	93.06	92.70
0.5	95.26	95.17	95.59	95.52
1 (No variation)	98.10	97.02	97.33	97.17
1.5	97.49	97.40	97.55	97.45
2.5	89.13	88.67	90.78	88.61

5   Analysis and Discussion

In the studied ML algorithms, there's a noticeable difference in performance metrics of SVM and KNN when comparing segmented/ enhanced data to unsegmented data. For SVM, accuracy is notably higher with enhanced data (88.58%)

and segmented (87.74%) compared to unsegmented data (67.69%). Also, for KNN, a notable difference in the accuracy of enhanced data (87.04%) compared to unsegmented data (80.36%) is inferred. Precision, recall, and F1 score follows a similar trend across datasets for both SVM and KNN as shown in Table 1. This increase in performance can be attributed to the feature extraction method employed for ML in this study—GLCM, an intensity-based texture analysis technique. Performing segmentation or enhancement of defects naturally intensifies the desired regions of the image, thereby enhancing performance. Although there is a significant increase in the performance of ML models in terms of the chosen metrics for enhanced and segmented input, there seems to be not much difference in the training time. This is understandable owing to the feature extraction method performed as ML is eventually trained on the same amount of data in the form of a CSV file irrespective of the input.

For the DL model i.e., YOLOv8n-cls used in this work, there seems to be no notable change in performance as seen from Table 2. It can be seen that the enhanced dataset achieves an accuracy of 98% and a precision of 97% with only 20 epochs as opposed to training the model with unsegmented data for 50 epochs to achieve similar accuracy and precision (Table 2). It can be inferred that for the DL model, the difference in performance with respect to chosen metrics is not as significant as it was in ML models at the expense of more epochs. However, based on the plot in Fig. 7, it can be seen how the decrease in loss over 50 epochs varies and reaches convergence. Visually, *the models with enhanced (blue) and segmented (green) data input reach convergence much earlier than that of the model with unsegmented data (orange). The faster the convergence, the lesser the training time of the model* **thus, answering SRQ1.** To find the difference in the rate of convergence, a threshold (T) is set at the convergence point. The threshold is chosen based on the train vs validation loss plots from Fig. 6 for segmented and enhanced data. Since the validation loss for these 2 datasets stops improving at epoch 17, it hints at convergence. So, the threshold line was set at this point. As seen from the plot in Fig. 7, the training loss for the segmented and enhanced data reaches the threshold at as early as epoch 17 while the training loss for the unsegmented data reaches the said threshold at epoch 30. Based on the formula below, the rate of difference in convergence rate between the segmented/ enhanced data and unsegmented data are found.

$$\frac{\text{Time to reach T by model with unsegmented input} - \text{Time to reach T with enhanced or segmented input}}{\text{Time to reach T by model with enhanced or segmented input}} \quad (1)$$

$$\text{Time to reach T} = \text{Number of epochs to reach T} * \text{Average time per epoch} \quad (2)$$

With respect to segmented data, convergence rate difference is: $(30*16.9-17*19.55)/17*19.55 = (507-332.35)/332.35 = 0.5255 = 52.55\%$. With respect to enhanced data, convergence rate difference is $(30*16.9-17*20.7)/17*20.7 = (507-351.9)/351.9 = 0.4407 = 44.07\%$. From the above discussion, it can be inferred that the performance of ML models significantly varies depending on whether the input data undergoes enhancement/ segmentation, although there is no difference in training time. However, for the DL model chosen, there is no significant difference in performance metrics based on varying input data, but the convergence time is lower for enhanced and segmented input. **This addresses SRQ2**, comparing the impact of data enhancement and segmentation with respect to the performance of ML and DL models. By comparing all constructed models, it is evident that the DL model *YOLOv8n-cls, trained on the enhanced dataset, exhibits optimal performance metrics and training time* -it demonstrates an improved convergence rate w.r.t the unsegmented dataset. Although segmented data shows a better convergence rate than enhanced data, the latter achieves the highest accuracy and performance metrics. So this model is tested for robustness against lighting conditions. Table 3 illustrates that *for gamma variation between 0.5 and 1.5, the models exhibit good performance similar to the YOLOv8n-cls model with no light variation*. However, for gamma = 0.25 and gamma = 2.5, although the models give a reasonably good performance, a significant decrease can be seen. **This addresses SRQ3.** Finally we can **answer the overarching research question** about an optimal intelligent defect detection model for kitchen cabinets manufacturing. *The combination of YOLOv8n-cls with enhanced data yields optimal performance, training time and is robust to lighting variations* - with an average inference time of 3ms per image. As additional remark, we realized an enhancement and segmentation pipeline tailored to the specific characteristics of the defects encountered. For example, a horizontal Gabor filter is employed due to the horizontal nature of the roller stripe defect. With slight adjustments to filter parameters, similar results can be achieved for different defects across various domains, provided their characteristics are not markedly different. It's worth noting that while the pipeline utilized in this study effectively enhances and segments defects, it's not the sole approach to achieving the objective; alternative combinations of image processing steps may also prove effective. It is also important to note that the applied manual augmentation is intended to ensure a fair comparison between the ML and DL models in this work. This approach would not impact the manufacturer's decision to deploy the same pipeline used in this work, where manual augmentation is applied and YOLOv8's default augmentations are not used. However, it is efficient to use YOLOv8's default augmentations, as the manual augmentation was solely implemented to facilitate a fair comparison between ML and DL models in this study. Finally, while the obtained results are promising, when deploying the model in production there might be a reduction in accuracy and retraining the model with pre-drying data might be needed. The training data were collected before the packaging stage while the visual appearance of the board surface before the drying of the lacquer stage may differ in texture and reflectance. However, we believe that YOLOv8's deep feature learning would still offer a better performance compared to traditional manual feature extraction methods.

6   Conclusion and Future Directions

Industry 4.0 manufacturing represents a fertile area to contribute to a more sustainable development. Towards less resource wastage, we investigated an optimal intelligent defect detection model for surface defect detection in the manufacturing of kitchen cabinets. The implementation and experiments used ML (SVN,

KNN) and DL (YOLO) models, computer vision, and a real world dataset from our external industrial stakeholder. We studied the impact of segmentation and enhancement of defects on both performance and training time of ML and DL models and compared it with the unsegmented data. Overall, the combination of YOLOv8n-cls with enhanced data yields optimal performance, training time and robustness to variations in lighting conditions. This emphasizes the importance not only of the choice of model but also the choice of right image pre-processing of the input image data. It is evident that applying defect enhancement or segmentation also increases the reliability of the DL model, serving as a prompt for the model to learn the correct characteristics from the input data, contributing to reliability in training and consequently in prediction phase.

Overall, the findings of this study suggest that a suitable image processing for defect enhancement or segmentation, coupled with appropriate model selection, can yield significant improvements in defect classification tasks with improved training time. In other words, deploying the most effective defect detection model in the lacquering section would enable the company to identify defects ahead in the production line while the lacquer is still wet. This enables rework of defective cabinets thereby enhancing the quality of the manufactured cabinets and reducing resource wastage in terms of energy and raw materials. This implementation would result in a more sustainable, reliable, and robust quality control system with high inference speed and short training time.

As future work, it would be interesting to apply our defect detection workflow and training pipeline, especially the approach of training deep learning models with feature highlighting, in different domains such as steel, fabric, and glassware. Comparable results may be achieved with minor adjustments to filter parameters, provided that there is no substantial variation in defect characteristics in production. Naturally, this would require domain-specific datasets, appropriate defect pre-processing, and retraining of the model.

The adaptability of the employed techniques highlights the potential for broader applicability across different datasets and defect types. These insights contribute to advancing the field of automated defect detection and hold promise for enhancing quality control processes across various industries, enabling reduced retraining expenses and increased reliability. A final relevant future work could be the investigation of the adaptability of the proposed techniques across other defect types and datasets. Experimenting with alternative pipelines may reveal novel approaches for enhancing defect detection performance.

Acknowledgements. This work is partially funded by KKS, the Swedish Knowledge Foundation, through the project "Intelligent and Trustworthy IoT Systems" (grant n. 20220087).

Disclosure of Interests. The authors have no competing interests to declare that are relevant to the content of this article.

References

1. Bhatt, P.M., et al.: Image-based surface defect detection using deep learning: a review. J. Comput. Inf. Sci. Eng. **21**(4), 040801 (2021). https://doi.org/10.1115/1.4049535
2. Cha, Y.J., Choi, W., Büyüköztürk, O.: Deep learning-based crack damage detection using convolutional neural networks. Comput.-Aided Civ. Infrastruct. Eng. **32**(5), 361–378 (2017). https://doi.org/10.1111/mice.12263
3. Czimmermann, T., et al.: Visual-based defect detection and classification approaches for industrial applications—a survey. Sensors **20**(5) (2020). https://doi.org/10.3390/s20051459
4. Haralick, R.M., Shapiro, L.G.: Glossary of computer vision terms. Pattern Recogn. **24**(1), 69–93 (1990). https://doi.org/10.1016/0031-3203(91)90117-N
5. He, K., Sun, J.: Convolutional neural networks at constrained time cost. In: 2015 IEEE Conference on Computer Vision and Pattern Recognition (CVPR), pp. 5353–5360 (2015). https://doi.org/10.1109/CVPR.2015.7299173
6. Hmidani, O., Alaoui, E.M.I.: A comprehensive survey of the r-cnn family for object detection. In: 2022 5th International Conference on Advanced Communication Technologies and Networking (CommNet), pp. 1–6 (2022)
7. Hussain, M.: Yolo-v1 to yolo-v8, the rise of yolo and its complementary nature toward digital manufacturing and industrial defect detection. Machines **11**(7) (2023). https://doi.org/10.3390/machines11070677
8. Iivarinen, J.: Surface defect detection with histogram-based texture features. In: Casasent, D.P. (ed.) Intelligent Robots and Computer Vision XIX: Algorithms, Techniques, and Active Vision, vol. 4197, pp. 140 – 145. International Society for Optics and Photonics, SPIE (2000). https://doi.org/10.1117/12.403757
9. Liu, J., Xie, G., Wang, J., Li, S., Wang, C., Zheng, F., Jin, Y.: Deep industrial image anomaly detection: a survey. Mach. Intell. Res. **21**(1), 104–135 (2024). https://doi.org/10.1007/s11633-023-1459-z
10. Mirzapour, F., Ghassemian, H.: Using glcm and gabor filters for classification of pan images. In: 2013 21st Iranian Conference on Electrical Engineering (ICEE), pp. 1–6 (2013). https://doi.org/10.1109/IranianCEE.2013.6599565
11. Pang, G., Shen, C., Cao, L., Hengel, A.V.D.: Deep learning for anomaly detection: a review. ACM Comput. Surv. **54**(2) (2021). https://doi.org/10.1145/3439950
12. Psarommatis, F., May, G., Dreyfus, P.A., Kiritsis, D.: Zero defect manufacturing: state-of-the-art review, shortcomings and future directions in research. Int. J. Prod. Res. **58**(1), 1–17 (2020). https://doi.org/10.1080/00207543.2019.1605228
13. Salem, Y.B., Abdelkrim, M.N.: Texture classification of fabric defects using machine learning. Int. J. Electr. Comput. Eng. (IJECE) **10**(4) (2020). https://doi.org/10.11591/ijece.v10i4.pp4390-4399
14. Sarkar, A., Dutta, T., Roy, B.K.: Fault identification on cigarette packets - an image processing approach. In: 2014 Annual IEEE India Conference (INDICON), pp. 1–6 (2014). https://doi.org/10.1109/INDICON.2014.7030591
15. Teng, B., Zhao, H., Jia, P., Yuan, J., Tian, C.: Research on ceramic sanitary ware defect detection method based on improved vgg network. J. Phys. Conf. Ser. **1650**(2), 022084 (2020). https://doi.org/10.1088/1742-6596/1650/2/022084

"To Measure Is to Know", but Not in Software Engineering. A Call for Operational Definitions of Code Metrics

Adam Roman[✉][iD], Michał Mnich[iD], and Jarosław Hryszko[iD]

Jagiellonian University, Kraków, Poland
{adam.roman,michal.mnich,jaroslaw.hryszko}@uj.edu.pl

Abstract. Measurement is crucial in software engineering. Based on the results of measurement, critical software business decisions are made. Therefore, software metrics should have precise operational definitions describing how the measurement should be made. We examine this issue in the context of two well-known metrics, LOC and number of branches, as well as related test coverage metrics. We also show significant differences in how measurement tools understand the same metrics. We analyze the reasons for these differences and propose a unified approach to defining software metrics based on formal grammars.

Keywords: software metric · software measurement · formal grammar · abstract syntax tree · parse tree · LOC · statement coverage · branch · branch coverage

1 Introduction

Software measurement is vital in software engineering, supporting quality evaluation, defect prediction, cost estimation, and progress tracking. Empirical studies confirm correlations between metrics (e.g., lines of code, cyclomatic complexity) and defect rates in various prediction models [12,15,21,33]. Reliable measurement requires precise *operational definitions*, yet standardized definitions for code metrics remain lacking [19,25,31]. This absence contributes to measurement's marginalization in the field. Fenton [14] notes that measurement is often seen as a luxury. Many metrics are poorly defined, such as Halstead's metrics [16], branch coverage, and NPATH [11,26], which is implemented incorrectly in popular tools like Checkstyle and pdepend [2,3].

Consequently, tools often yield inconsistent results for the same metric – an issue embarrassing for a field that calls itself *engineering*. Despite huge advances in IT (e.g., ML, LLMs), we still lack consistency in basic tasks like counting lines of code. Some argue that metric ambiguity causes only systematic error or negligible differences. However, this overlooks key issues: tools vary widely; users often don't know what is being measured; and models using metrics (e.g., for defect or cost prediction) may fail if input metrics differ from those used during training. Without standardization, such models risk producing invalid results.

© The Author(s), under exclusive license to Springer Nature Switzerland AG 2026
D. Taibi and D. Smite (Eds.): SEAA 2025, LNCS 16082, pp. 80–89, 2026.
https://doi.org/10.1007/978-3-032-04200-2_6

Therefore, we propose a framework for creating operational definitions of code metrics based on precise criteria, based on the theory of formal grammars. The choice of a method based on formal grammars is natural since the code is subject to parsing, resulting in a parse tree built according to the strict rules of the grammar of a given language.

There exist models and standards for software measurement (cf. [18,19,24]), but they assume that base measures are well-defined, which in practice is not always the case (see Sect. 3). Notice that our model is not intended to provide a measurement framework, but a framework for creating operational definitions of metrics that ensure consistency in measurements within a single tool and between different tools.

It is enough to consider only base measures in our framework. Once they are well-defined, the derived measures (e.g., coverage metrics) will also be well-defined, as they can be expressed as precisely defined functions of base measures.

2   A Case Study: Lines of Code and Branch Coverage

Lines of Code (LOC) and branch coverage well illustrate the ambiguity of software metrics. Despite their popularity, there is no universally accepted definition of a "statement," "line of code," or "branch." LOC may or may not include comments, blank lines, compiler directives, or structural elements like braces. Expressions like x > 0 ? y = 1 : y = 2 could count as one or three LOCs.

Branches are similarly ambiguous. They can be defined as decision points or "DD-paths" [6], or as control transfers between statements [20], depending on how statements are defined. Many papers using branch coverage omit definitions entirely (e.g., [27,30]), or conflate branch coverage with decision coverage [28]. Others vaguely refer to "code coverage" [10].

Three important points should be noted when discussing the concepts of statements, branches, and test coverage metrics related to them.

1) **Statement and branch are code-level concepts**. They reflect the source code structure and should be measured directly on the code, not on models (as in [20]). Similar model-based concepts, such as node, edge, or transition coverage, exist [4,9], but they are distinct. For instance, a branch (code-based) differs from an edge (model-based), though often used interchangeably [23,32]. Model types also affect coverage relationships. Rechtberger et al. [29] show that prime path coverage doesn't subsume edge-pair coverage in FSMs unless self-loops are excluded—an assumption valid for CFGs but not FSMs.

2) **A branch should be an atomic control flow step**. Branch coverage should reflect transitions between adjacent instructions. Otherwise, tools may report misleading coverage, e.g., when an exception occurs in the middle of a "linear" code sequence.

3) **Test coverage must clarify what is actually covered**. Coverage assumes atomic test items, fully covered or not. However, coverage can be partial due to constructs like exceptions or short-circuiting.

3 Experiment

The ambiguity in metric definitions leads to discrepancies across code coverage tools. Horvath et al. [17] show that bytecode vs. source-level instrumentation produces significantly different method-level coverage results. Alemerien [8] provides statistical evidence of inconsistencies in branch, line, statement, and method coverage across tools. Li [22] observes that despite standard textbook definitions, tools implement branch coverage differently – one tool's "branch coverage" actually aligns with clause coverage.

In our study, we evaluated five tools. VS Coverage[1] and Dot Cover[2] report statement coverage; Fine Code Coverage[3], Coverlet[4], and Open Cover[5] also report branch coverage. CS Coverage instruments source code, while others use bytecode. We tested these tools on four open-source C projects (see Table 1); our experimental data is available at [7].

Table 1. Selected projects

Name	Version	# classes	GitHub stars	Reference
WinSW	2.12.0	51	11712	github.com/winsw/winsw
Ulid	1.3.4	8	1204	github.com/Cysharp/Ulid
ScreenToGif	2.41	313	23220	github.com/NickeManarin/ScreenToGif
Terminal.GUI	1.17.1	290	9453	github.com/gui-cs/Terminal.Gui

We selected popular GitHub projects based on star count. As shown in Table 2, all tools reported noticeably different results for the number of statements, branches, and their respective coverage. Dashes indicate metrics the tool could not compute.

Differences in the number of statements and branches and different ways of interpreting the coverage lead to significant differences in statement and branch coverage metrics. These results are shown in Table 3. In the extreme case, the spread in reported metrics ranges from 18.61% to 75.31% (!).

We investigated some of these discrepancies. For example, some tools do not cover variable declarations and the `#if NET` debug clause; they treat the concept of statement differently (probably due to source code vs. bytecode calculations), and some seem not to include coverage for asynchronous methods. Some tools do not report the coverage of abstract classes or methods, while others do. Finally, sometimes the tools report non-covered code as covered in an unwarranted manner.

---

[1] https://learn.microsoft.com/en-us/visualstudio/test/using-code-coverage-to-determine-how-much-code-is-being-tested?view=vs-2022&tabs=csharp.

[2] www.jetbrains.com/dotcover.

[3] marketplace.visualstudio.com.

[4] github.com/coverlet-coverage/coverlet.

[5] github.com/OpenCover/opencover.

Table 2. Reported metric values (statements, branches, and their coverage)

Project Fine Code	VS Coverlet	Fine Code Open Cover	Coverlet	Open Cover	Dot Cover
	# of covered statements/total # of statements				
WinSW	854/3294	901/3414	901/3414	227/3332	801/3136
Ulid	424/575	421/575	221/575	155/575	305/589
ScreenToGif	132/10932	119/9631	119/10065	1514/11218	120/9879
Terminal.GUI	−/−	35034/46517	35034/46517	8652/46485	−/−
	# of covered branches/total # of branches				
WinSW		181/865	169/853	18/739	
Ulid		94/158	36/158	11/150	
ScreenToGif		80/2940	80/3284	294/2813	
Terminal.GUI		12098/17481	12098/17481	2093/15492	

Table 3. Variance in achieved coverage

Project	Statement coverage		Branch coverage	
	min	max	min	max
WinSW	6.81%	28.41%	2.43%	20.92%
Ulid	26.95%	73.73%	7.33%	59.49%
ScreenToGif	1.18%	13.49%	2.43%	10.45%
Terminal.GUI	18.61%	75.31%	13.51%	69.21%

The results of our experiments are consistent with those of [8] and [17]. The authors of the former believe that the reasons behind the differences in measurements may relate to factors such as instrumentation (the tools instrument the object programs in different ways), variety of code analysis, size and complexity of programs (larger and more complex programs use complex programming structures), and definitions of code coverage metrics.

The last-mentioned factor agrees with our observations. The primary reason for measurement inconsistency problems is the definition of coverage metrics. These definitions are often written vaguely or refer to overly general concepts. For example, consider the following three definitions of statement coverage metric found in the documentation of two measurement tools and in the DO-178C standard [1,8,13]: 1) "A code coverage metric that measures which statements in a body of code have been executed through a test run, and which statements have not."; 2) "The number of statements in basic blocks that were executed at least once, divided by the total number of statements."; 3) "Statement Coverage: Every statement in the program has been invoked at least once." All three definitions use the vague notions of a statement and its execution. The second one also relates statements to basic blocks, which is unnecessary. We did not find a precise *operational* definition of statement coverage or branch coverage in the documentation of any of the tools used. Most tools in their documentation do not provide *any* definition of the metrics they measure.

4   A Framework for Creating Operational Definitions of Metrics

The proposed framework defines how to measure metrics precisely, using a reference grammar and parse tree operations. While demonstrated for source code instrumentation, it can be adapted for bytecode. The key idea is to use a formal grammar and tree traversal (e.g., via the Visitor pattern) to compute metrics. A reference grammar is necessary to ensure unambiguous parse tree operations. Metrics are defined operationally as actions (e.g., variable updates) tied to grammar rules during the parsing process.

The framework assumes the existence of a *reference grammar* $G = (N, T, P, S)$ for a given programming language, where N is a finite set of nonterminals, T is a finite set of terminals, $N \cap T = \emptyset$, $P \subset (N \cup T)^+ \times (N \cup T)^*$ is a finite set of productions, and $S \in N$ is a start symbol. We assume that for each grammar rule of the form $X := Y$, where $X \in N, Y \in (N \cup T)^*$, we have a suitable method to access the rule context objects (parse tree nodes) associated with X and Y and to perform a suitable set of actions when parsing X. For example, for a rule defining a comparison between two expressions

```
<comp> := <expr> EXPR_OPER <expr>
```

we assume to have a method that performs actions corresponding to the nonterminal <comp>, as well as methods that allow to recursively visit the subtree for <comp>, e.g., visitComp() function can invoke functions such as visit.left(), visit.right(), and visit.operator(). The operational definition of a metric is simply a set of rules defined in methods corresponding to rule elements, described in classes corresponding to each rule.

Let us consider a toy example of a simple language with its reference grammar defined as shown in Fig. 1a. Terms in parentheses indicate nonterminals, and terms in capital letters indicate terminals. Suppose we have a Visitor class, which has defined functions for all nonterminal and terminal symbols:

```
class Visitor  {
  int LOC; // fields representing
  int CC;  // metric values
  int branches;
  ...
  public Visitor() {  // constructor
    LOC=0; CC=1; branches=0;  ... }
  public code() { ... }
  public prog() { ... }
  public stmt() { ... }
  ...
}
```

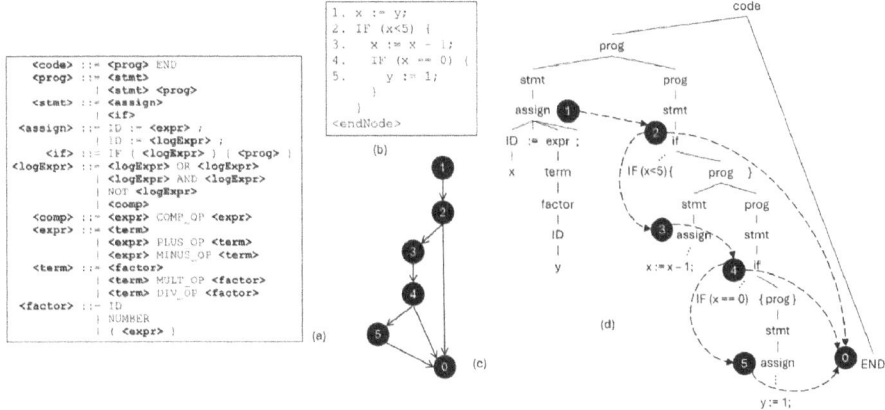

Fig. 1. A sample grammar, a code, its CFG, and its parse tree

We assume that the parse tree is traversed in a pre-order manner and that each method is invoked every time the visitor enters a corresponding symbol for the first time during the parsing of the tree.

We will now give three simple examples of operational definitions for some code metrics. The role of these examples is to demonstrate the advantages of the proposed approach – precision and consistency. Let us start with the Lines of Code metric for a programming language L. It could be defined as "the number of occurrences of the nonterminal <stmt> in a parse tree derived from a reference grammar for L". The corresponding code in the Visitor class for calculating it could look as follows:

```
public stmt()  { LOC++ }
```

After parsing the whole tree, LOC is the value of the Lines of Code metric. The metric's operational definition is included in the code rules in stmt(). It counts the number of nonterminals stmt in the parse tree. Notice that instead of using a vague notion of "statement", we define it precisely, as any part of code that can be generated in a parse tree from a concrete nonterminal symbol <stmt>. This way, we were able to define the LOC metric precisely. This example is simple, but in actual grammars, such as Java grammar [5], many different nonterminals could be taken into account when calculating the Lines of Code, e.g., importDeclaration, emptyStatement_, etc.

The framework's advantage is that forcing the definition of metrics in the precise terms of a formal grammar reveals what *exactly* is being counted. We show this with the example of another metric, cyclomatic complexity (CC). Its standard definition, by McCabe, is "the number of linearly independent paths through a program's source code". This metric uses the vague notion of "path". Suppose the metric is defined within our framework as follows:

```
public logExpr()  {
    CC=CC+count.children(['OR', 'AND'])
}
public if()  {
    CC++
}
```

We assume that count.children() function counts the number of terminals from the list that are children of a given <logExpr> nonterminal in a parse tree.

The above definition of CC reveals that to calculate the cyclomatic complexity, we count not only the number of decision points (IF statements) but also all the OR and AND operators in both IF predicates and assignment statements. This is because even a single assignment instruction can be transformed by a compiler into a set of instructions with decision points due to the short-circuiting. For example, "x = A OR B" will be transformed to "if (A) x = A else x = B". Some tools calculate the cyclomatic complexity precisely this way. In contrast, others count only the decision points in the source code, treating all compound predicates in decision statements as 'atomic" decision points.

Notice that if we want to treat statements as "atomic" parts of instructions, such as logical statements that can be executed partially with a short-circuiting mechanism, we could define the LOC using a similar concept, as the number of stmt nonterminals plus the number of terminals OR and AND.

Let us now consider the number of branches metric. Suppose we intend to define a branch as a direct control flow from one statement to another, i.e., all the possible direct control flows between IF and ASSIGN statements. Each ASSIGN instruction begins one unconditional transfer flow, and each IF instruction begins two conditional transfer flows, depending on the decision outcome. The operational definition of such a branch coverage metric might be as follows:

```
assign() { branches = branches + 1 }
if() { branches = branches + 2 }
```

The idea of this definition is shown in Fig. 1b–d. On the parse tree (d), we marked the nodes corresponding to the source code statements (b); the dashed edges represent the branches. When we apply the rules from the above-mentioned operational definition of branch coverage and count the number of appropriate edges between graph nodes, we obtain exactly the number of edges in the code's Control Flow Graph (c).

A reference grammar allows us to systematically review all the grammar rules and decide if they need to be processed for a given metric to be calculated. For example, if we decide that branches should also be considered in case of constructs like the previously mentioned "? :" operator, equivalent to the IF statement, we can handle it by considering a specific code for a grammar rule that defines this concept. In other words, relating the operational definition of a metric to grammar rules allows us to define precisely which constructs should be taken into account and which should not.

5 Conclusions and Future Work

We demonstrated that different tools may interpret and measure the same code differently, and we proposed a formal, grammar-based framework for designing precise and consistent operational definitions of metrics, which enables the avoidance of ambiguities. When it comes to code metrics definition, many complex issues need to be addressed (e.g., different strategies for code evaluation, semantics preserving code transformation, program execution principles, etc.). Our approach addresses this issue by relying on a parse tree based on a reference grammar, which ensures the measurement process is unambiguous.

We advocate the creation of a publicly available repository containing operational definitions of metrics based on the framework proposed in this paper. The definitions can be provided as a ready-made source code that exercises a parse tree and calculates metric values. Measurement tool manufacturers could consistently use these ready-made code fragments (or precise definitions of operations performed on elements of parse trees) in their products.

Using a formal grammar-based approach has several advantages:

- it is a universal approach since a formal grammar must exist for every language for parsing to be possible
- the grammar depends on the programming language, so each language can have its own set of metrics defined, taking into account the different characteristics of specific languages (e.g., certain metrics may be interpreted differently in object-oriented languages than in functional languages)
- formal grammars are, by definition, formal, so defining operational metrics using them can be done in a precise way; this ensures consistency of measurement regardless of the tool used, and there is no measurement error.

Future work should focus on developing standardized definitions and measurement procedures for code and test coverage metrics for different programming languages. This involves formalizing the operational definitions to ensure consistency and comparability across various tools and environments. An in-depth analysis of a broader range of coverage tools could provide more insights into the sources of discrepancies. This analysis should include widely used and emerging tools to cover a comprehensive spectrum of instrumentation techniques and measurement approaches.

Although a database of metrics definitions could be created independently for each programming language, another approach could be to use a database of metrics definitions for an indirect representation of code, as used in LLVM, for example. Frontend compilers translate source code from any language into LLVM intermediate representation (IR). This separation means that LLVM can support any language capable of being compiled into its IR. However, due to the low-level nature of the LLVM language, defining the operational definitions of some metrics may be challenging.

References

1. RTCA/DO-178C – Software Considerations in Airborne Systems and Equipment Certification. https://my.rtca.org/productdetails?id=a1B36000001IcmqEAC. Accessed 26 July 2024

2. pdepend tool (2023). https://github.com/pdepend/pdepend. Accessed 29 Dec 2024

3. Checkstyle tool (2024). https://checkstyle.sourceforge.io/. Accessed 29 Dec 2024

4. ISTQB Certified Tester – Foundation Level Syllabus. Technical report, International Software Testing Qualifications Board (2024). https://www.istqb.org

5. Java grammar (2024). https://github.com/antlr/grammars-v4/blob/master/java/java20/Java20Parser.g4. Accessed 26 July 2024

6. Software and Systems Engineering Vocabulary (SE VOCAB) (2024). https://pascal.computer.org/. Accessed 26 July 2024

7. Source data for experiment (2024). https://www.ii.uj.edu.pl/~roman/results.xlsx

8. Alemerien, K., Kenneth, M.: Examining the effectiveness of testing coverage tools: an empirical study. Int. J. Softw. Eng. Appl. **8**, 139–162 (2014). https://doi.org/10.14257/ijseia.2014.8.5.12

9. Ammann, P., Offutt, J.: Introduction to Software Testing. Cambridge University Press, Cambridge (2006)

10. Avadhani, B., Giri, S.R., Pulipati, V.R.: The mechanism of generating the automated Java unit test cases by achieving maximum code coverage. In: Kiran Mai, C., Kiranmayee, B.V., Favorskaya, M.N., Chandra Satapathy, S., Raju, K.S. (eds.) Proceedings of International Conference on Advances in Computer Engineering and Communication Systems. LAIS, vol. 20, pp. 41–56. Springer, Singapore (2021). https://doi.org/10.1007/978-981-15-9293-5_4

11. Bagnara, R., Bagnara, A., Benedetti, A., Hill, P.M.: The ACPATH metric: precise estimation of the number of acyclic paths in C-like languages. arXiv abs/1610.07914 (2016). https://api.semanticscholar.org/CorpusID:2031964

12. Begoug, M., Chouchen, M., Ouni, A., Abdullah Alomar, E., Mkaouer, M.W.: Fine-grained just-in-time defect prediction at the block level in infrastructure-as-code (IAC). In: Proceedings of the 21st International Conference on Mining Software Repositories, MSR 2024, pp. 100–112. Association for Computing Machinery, New York (2024). https://doi.org/10.1145/3643991.3644934

13. Chen, S.: Research on software test coverage analysis methods under DO-178C. In: Proceedings of the 3rd International Conference on Digital Economy and Computer Application (DECA 2023), pp. 265–276. Atlantis Press (2023)

14. Fenton, N., Bieman, J.: Software Metrics: A Rigorous and Practical Approach, 3rd edn. CRC Press, Inc. (2014)

15. Giray, G., Bennin, K.E., Köksal, Ö., Babur, Ö., Tekinerdogan, B.: On the use of deep learning in software defect prediction. J. Syst. Softw. **195**, 111537 (2023)

16. Halstead, M.: Elements of Software Science. Elsevier, New York (1977)

17. Horváth, F., Gergely, T., Beszédes, A., Tengeri, D., Balogh, G., Gyimóthy, T.: Code coverage differences of Java bytecode and source code instrumentation tools. Softw. Qual. J. **27**, 79–123 (2019)

18. ISO: ISO/IEC 15939:2017, Systems and software engineering – Measurement process (2017)

19. ISO: ISO/IEC 25020:2019, Software Engineering - Software Product Quality Requirements and Evaluation (SQuaRE) - Quality measurement framework (2019)

20. ISO: ISO/IEC/IEEE 29119-4 – Software and systems engineering – Software testing – Part 4: Test techniques (2021)

21. Kamei, Y., et al.: A large-scale empirical study of just-in-time quality assurance. IEEE Trans. Softw. Eng. **39**(06), 757–773 (2013)
22. Li, N., Meng, X., Offutt, J., Deng, L.: Is bytecode instrumentation as good as source code instrumentation: an empirical study with industrial tools (experience report). In: 2013 IEEE 24th International Symposium on Software Reliability Engineering (ISSRE), pp. 380–389 (2013). https://doi.org/10.1109/ISSRE.2013.6698891
23. Masri, W., Zaraket, F.: Coverage-based software testing: beyond basic test requirements. In: Advances in Computers, vol. 103, pp. 79–142. Elsevier (2016)
24. McGarry, J.: PSM – Practical Software Measurement: Objective Information for Decision Makers. Addison Wesley (2001)
25. McGarry, J., Card, D.N., Peasant, J.: Software measurement process - standardization and application. In: Proceedings of the 4th IEEE International Symposium and Forum on Software Engineering Standards, ISESS 1999, p. 258. IEEE Computer Society, USA (1999)
26. Nejmeh, B.A.: NPATH: a measure of execution path complexity and its applications. Commun. ACM **31**, 188–200 (1988)
27. Nilizadeh, A., Leavens, G.T., Păsăreanu, C.S.: Using a guided fuzzer and preconditions to achieve branch coverage with valid inputs. In: Loulergue, F., Wotawa, F. (eds.) TAP 2021. LNCS, vol. 12740, pp. 72–84. Springer, Cham (2021). https://doi.org/10.1007/978-3-030-79379-1_5
28. Nilizadeh, A., Leavens, G.T., Pasareanu, C.S., Le, X.B.D., Cok, D.R.: Does going beyond branch coverage make program repair tools more reliable? In: International Conference on Software Testing (2024)
29. Rechtberger, V., Bures, M., Ahmed, B.S.: Overview of test coverage criteria for test case generation from finite state machines modelled as directed graphs. In: 2022 IEEE International Conference on Software Testing, Verification and Validation Workshops (ICSTW), pp. 207–214. IEEE Computer Society, Los Alamitos, CA, USA (2022). https://doi.org/10.1109/ICSTW55395.2022.00044. https://doi.ieeecomputersociety.org/10.1109/ICSTW55395.2022.00044
30. Ryan, G., et al.: Code-aware prompting: a study of coverage-guided test generation in regression setting using LLM. Proc. ACM Softw. Eng. **1**(FSE) (2024)
31. Staron, M., Meding, W., Nilsson, C.: A framework for developing measurement systems and its industrial evaluation. Inf. Softw. Technol. **51**(4), 721–737 (2009)
32. Wang, Y., et al.: Not all coverage measurements are equal: Fuzzing by coverage accounting for input prioritization. In: 27th Annual Network and Distributed System Security Symposium, NDSS 2020. The Internet Society (2020)
33. Zhao, Y., Damevski, K., Chen, H.: A systematic survey of just-in-time software defect prediction. ACM Comput. Surv. **55**(10) (2023)

Unlocking the OKR Framework: Insights into Benefits and Barriers for an Effective Implementation in Practice

Jonathan Misslisch[1], Tim Bauer[1], Florian Eibl[1], Michael Neumann[1(✉)],
Julia Spanke[2], Eva-Maria Schön[3], and Adam Przybyłek[4]

[1] University of Applied Sciences and Arts Hannover, Hannover, Germany
michael.neumann@hs-hannover.de
[2] Mecklenburgische Versicherungs-Gesellschaft a.G., Hannover, Germany
[3] University of Applied Sciences Emden/Leer, Emden/Leer, Germany
[4] Gdańsk University of Technology, Gdńask, Poland

Abstract. *Context:* The Objectives and Key Results (OKR) framework provides a structured but flexible approach for defining and measuring strategic and operational objectives. Despite its widespread use and associated benefits, such as increased transparency and improved communication for goal setting, there are numerous challenges in implementing the framework. *Objective:* This study aims to present the current state of OKR practice and identify the main barriers and benefits of OKR implementation in practice. *Method:* We employed a mixed-methods approach, starting with a web-content analysis of practitioner insights sourced from Google News, LinkedIn, and Reddit. This was followed by a multiple case study comprising two German companies. *Results:* Our findings reveal that OKR implementation yields significant benefits while also encountering some barriers. The main benefits identified include improved alignment with the strategic objectives of the management level, enhanced cross-departmental coordination, and bidirectional communication effects that strengthen employee engagement. Conversely, the primary barriers involve inconsistent understanding of objectives within the organization, and insufficient organizational maturity and support. This nuanced interplay highlights the need for tailored strategies that address both the cultural and operational dimensions of OKR adoption. *Conclusion:* Our work provides both theoretical and practical implications and supports practitioners in the successful implementation and application of the OKR framework.

Keywords: OKR framework · goal-setting · mixed-method study

1 Introduction

Nowadays, IT organizations need to respond quickly to rapidly changing conditions and market environments. This is not always easy and can lead to conflicting business objectives due to the number of departments or people involved.

D. Taibi and D. Smite (Eds.): SEAA 2025, LNCS 16082, pp. 90–107, 2026.
https://doi.org/10.1007/978-3-032-04200-2_7

These conflicts often stem from lack of communication and transparency regarding business objectives [33]. Moreover, prioritizing operational issues over strategic business objectives can undermine the success of projects and organizations [12]. The Objectives and Key Results (OKR) framework [6] promises a solution to these challenges. OKR represents a framework for goal-setting and performance evaluation that has become increasingly important in recent years [28,30]. Initially developed by Intel in the 1970s and subsequently popularised by companies such as Google, the OKR framework has proven to be an effective means of clearly defining business objectives and measuring their implementation [6]. OKRs provide a structured, yet flexible approach that enables organisations to pursue both long-term strategic goals and short-term operational priorities [28].

The significance of OKRs in contemporary business management is considerable, yet the advantages and potential challenges remain under-researched and under-discussed. Many pioneering technology companies and start-ups have adopted the OKR framework to facilitate the implementation of their business strategies while maintaining agility and adaptability [32]. Implementing OKRs can lead to benefits such as enhanced transparency, improved communication, and a stronger focus on key objectives [20,28,30].

In an increasingly dynamic and competitive business environment, organizations seek solutions to implement their strategies more effectively while remaining flexible in their day-to-day business. OKRs may provide such a solution by harmonising strategic alignment and operational implementation. However, despite these advantages, companies face challenges when introducing OKRs, which can impair both the effectiveness and acceptance of this framework [25]. It is therefore important to analyse the barriers and benefits of OKRs. A deeper understanding of these aspects is essential for better implementation and adaptation of this framework to meet the specific needs of different organisational contexts.

Thus, this paper addresses two research questions to help deepen the understanding and implementation of OKRs:

- **RQ 1:** What is the state of practice of OKRs?
- **RQ 2:** What are the barriers and benefits while implementing OKRs?

Our study makes three key contributions to OKR research and practice. First, it establishes a state-of-practice overview by distinguishing effective approaches, such as alignment with top-level strategic goals and stakeholder involvement across hierarchies, from pitfalls like the misuse of OKRs. Second, it systematically identifies six key barriers and eight benefits of OKR implementation, providing insights into challenges such as inconsistent understanding of objectives within organizations and opportunities like enhanced cross-departmental coordination. Third, it offers actionable strategies for successful OKR implementation, emphasizing the importance of effective communication, role agility, a thorough understanding of the OKR framework, precise planning, and strong leadership. These findings advance the literature and offer practical guidance for organizations seeking to optimize their strategic direction.

This paper is structured as follows: We provide an overview of the related work in Sect. 2. Next, we explain our research design in Sect. 3. We present our study's results, including the answers to the research questions in Sect. 4 and discuss the implications for practice and research in Sect. 5. Before we conclude our findings in Sect. 7, we explain the threats to validity in Sect. 6.

2   Related Work

In this section, we give an overview of the research findings closely related to our study. We considered primary and secondary studies to provide a wide perspective of the related work. However, we focused the literature search on the area of software engineering and agile software development in particular. While we tried to identify scientific publications related to the state of the practice of OKRs, we noticed that OKRs are studied in other fields like education [5, 21]. We found that the literature in our focus area of interest is quite limited. However, we could identify some studies and give a brief overview below.

Butler et al. [4] present insights from their case study from a large global operating software development organization. They focus on the effects on the working environment, including the cultural facet, behaviour, and team practices used. Furthermore, they analyzed upcoming challenges while introducing the OKR framework into a large scale software development context. They found that defining, setting, measuring, and tracking goals in a software development context is complex. However, these findings are not affected by the tools used for the adoption of OKRs. Interestingly, the authors identified a higher maturity of applying the OKR framework in remote operating teams due to the distance to their leadership. Finally, they present five recommendations for optimizing the use of the OKR framework including optimized communication, increasing the transparency of the goal-creation and motivation behind it, or the need for guidance for the process applied in the company.

With a stronger focus on agile software development, Stray et al. [29] analyzed the effects of the combined usage of Slack (from the communication perspective) and OKRs (from the goal-setting perspective) on the coordination in large scale agile teams. The authors identified the positive effects of focusing on the team's outcome while applying OKRs. Also the teams use the OKRs for prioritizing their work, which strengthen the focus on what is important from a goal-oriented perspective. Another study in the area of agile software development, also presented by Stray et al. [30] focuses on how agile teams apply OKRs in practice. They identified increased transparency and knowledge sharing among the teams that applied OKRs. The authors furthermore present four strategies for improving the use of the OKR framework in large scale agile contexts.

The balance between hierarchical and shared leadership is crucial in agile organizations [13]. Weichbrodt et al. [34] found that while shared leadership grows in agile settings, hierarchical leadershipâĂŤespecially transformationalâĂŤremains relevant. Additionally, studies [7, 18] suggested that leaders with an agile mindset are critical for enhancing organizational agility. These insights

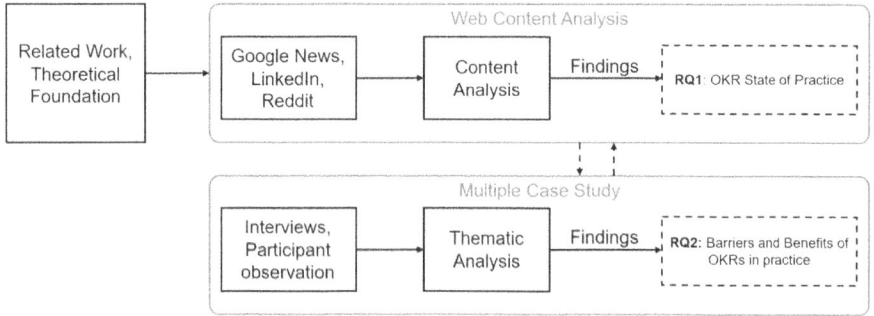

Fig. 1. Visualization of our Research Design

align with our findings on the need for leadership buy-in and engagement at all levels.

While we tried to identify scientific publications related to the state of the practice of OKRs, we noticed that OKR appears frequently as a keyword in publications, but that the number of scientific studies in the context of OKR utilization in teams is low. In particular, the focus on barriers and benefits does not yet appear to have been analyzed to any great extent.

3   Research Design

This study adopts a mixed-method research approach to address the two research questions. Given the exploratory nature of the research and the limited availability of peer-reviewed literature on OKR implementation in practice, we combined a Web Content Analysis (WCA) with a case study. This approach allowed us to capture both the state of practice and the specific barriers and benefits of OKR implementation in two different real-world organizational contexts. Figure 1 provides an overview of the research design, illustrating the connection between the methods and the research questions.

To ensure transparency, reproducibility, and rigor, we developed a comprehensive research protocol that outlines our study's methodology. The protocol is available at Zenodo [22] and is referenced throughout for further details.

3.1   Web Content Analysis

To address the first research question *(RQ 1: What is the state of practice of OKRs?)*, we conducted a Web Content Analysis, synthesizing practitioner insights from Google News, LinkedIn, and Reddit. This approach was informed by the observation that software engineering research often lags behind the state of industry practices (e.g., [8,9,16]). Given the scarcity of peer-reviewed literature on OKR implementation, web content served as our primary source of insights into this topic.

We posit that journalistic content, such as that found via Google News, typically has a shorter publication cycle compared to scientific literature, allowing for more up-to-date insights. Similarly, LinkedIn posts often reflect the experiences of professionals actively engaged in OKR practices. However, both sources are subject to potential biases, such as publication bias or self-reporting bias [10]. For example, professionals publishing under their real names may emphasize success stories or present overly positive narratives, particularly when promoting consulting services. To mitigate this, we included Reddit, which provides abundant software engineering-related content [2] while encouraging anonymous sharing of opinions [1].

Our review methodology adheres to the guidelines for Web Content Analysis [14], systematic literature reviews [15] and reporting secondary studes [17]. Searches were conducted using tailored search strings across the three platforms, resulting in 104 initial results: 52 from Google News, 10 from LinkedIn, and 42 from Reddit. These results were screened using predefined inclusion and exclusion criteria, narrowing the dataset to 22 items: 8 from Google News, 5 from LinkedIn, and 9 from Reddit. Detailed search strings, selection criteria, and the complete content selection protocol are documented in Sect. 1 of our research protocol [22]. The final search runs were performed in April 2024.

To ensure rigor and transparency, we documented the selection process systematically using a spreadsheet. The first and third authors independently conducted the initial selection, with results verified by other researchers in the author group. Notably, no disagreements arose during this process, and no additional resolution measures were required.

For data analysis, we performed applied a web content analysis following Kim and Kuljis [14]. Relevant information from the selected items was systematically extracted and organized using a Miro board. Our coding scheme, detailed in Sect. 1 of [22], guided a cluster-based thematic analysis. Findings were categorized into thematic clusters using color-coded references to distinguish sources (e.g., Reddit posts were marked with green post-it notes). This process allowed us to synthesize practitioner perspectives on OKR implementation systematically and transparently.

3.2 Case Study

We conducted a multiple case study in two companies to answer our second research question *(RQ 2: What are the barriers and benefits while implementing OKRs?)*, building upon the findings from the WCA to inform our data collection approach. Case studies are particularly suitable for investigating contemporary software engineering phenomena in their natural context, especially when the boundaries between the phenomenon and its context are not clearly evident [27, 36]. The first part of our case study was conducted in April and May 2022 (for case Durmstrang) and the second part between April and June 2024 (for case Hogwarts).

Case Study Context

The study was conducted at two German companies. First, we introduce Hogwarts (anonymized), a German insurance company that provides comprehensive insurance services for both private and business customers nationwide. Operating from a single location, Hogwarts employs approximately 1,000 people across various departments. The company maintains an in-house software development department responsible for developing and maintaining its proprietary software systems. The unit of analysis for this study is the implementation process of the OKR framework within Hogwarts, focusing on its alignment with strategic goals, stakeholder involvement, and the challenges and benefits encountered during this transition.

In early 2024, Hogwarts began the process of introducing the OKR framework as part of a broader strategic initiative aimed at improving alignment between its corporate goals and operational activities. At the time of our study, OKRs were still in the early stages of implementation and had not yet been fully adopted across the organization. This timing made Hogwarts particularly suitable for our case study, as it allowed us to examine both the barriers and benefits encountered during OKR introduction in an established company. Furthermore, Hogwarts' position in a highly regulated market, coupled with its ongoing technical challenges such as legacy system replacement and regulatory compliance requirements, provided a rich context for studying OKR implementation.

The second case company is Durmstrang (anonymized), an organization operating in software development focusing on consulting. Durmstrang was founded in 2008, and currently around 50 employees are working for the company. Durmstrang is operating in mainly two business areas: custom software development and agile consulting, e.g., optimization of agile approaches and agile transformation. The employees are operating in teams for different customers and projects.

The OKR adoption at Durmstrang had its origin due to a company-wide retrospective in October 2019 in which employees claimed a more specific focus from the top level management. In the next step, the top-level management created with support from an OKR expert a cision statement and company objectives. Afterwards, the OKR transformation started with a workshop in which the Durmstrang teams discussed and prioritized the objectives aiming to build topic-related OKR teams and define Objectives and Key Results per OKR team. Nowadays, Durmstrang has applied OKRs in its processes and started with specific OKR practices like planning and retrospective meetings as well as roles.

Qualitative Data Collection

Our data collection strategy combined semi-structured interviews and participant observation to ensure comprehensive coverage of the phenomena under study. In sum 13 employees participated in the interviews - 6 from case company Hogwarts, and 7 from case company Durmstrang. This selection represents a cross-section of organizational levels, roles, and departments. All interview participants were directly involved in the OKR implementation process. Table 1 provides an overview of the interviewee profiles.

Below, we give a detailed explanation of the data collection and analysis per case study context.

Table 1. Interviewee profiles

ID	Department/role	Case Company
P01	Organizational development	Hogwarts
P02	Organizational development	Hogwarts
P03	Organizational development	Hogwarts
P04	Department lead	Hogwarts
P05	Department lead	Hogwarts
P06	Department lead	Hogwarts
P07	Sales-Manager	Durmstrang
P08	Project lead & Consultant	Durmstrang
P09	Marketing employee	Durmstrang
P10	Sales employee	Durmstrang
P11	Agile coach & Consultant	Durmstrang
P12	Human resources	Durmstrang
P13	Founder & Manager	Durmstrang

Hogwarts: The interviews were guided by an interview protocol, available at Zenodo [22]. In total, the interview guideline consists of 16 main questions: three warm-up questions aiming to get an understanding of the interviewee's background and 13 questions related to the benefits and barrieres of implementing OKRs.

Conducted virtually via Microsoft Teams in April and May 2024, the interviews were held in German. Five participants (P01, P02, P03, P04, and P06) consented to audio recording, while for the remaining interview (P05), detailed notes were taken in real-time using Microsoft Word. Each interview session ranged from 31:45 to 51:08 min. Two researchers facilitated the interviews: one led the conversation, while the other managed technical aspects, including recording and note-taking. An exception was the interview with P06, which was conducted by a single researcher.

In addition to the interviews, we conducted participant observation to capture the everyday realities of the OKR implementation process. This method allowed us to observe behaviors, interactions, and decision-making in real-time, providing a richer context for understanding how employees navigated challenges and adapted to new practices. Carried out between April and June 2024, the observation period yielded detailed field notes documenting key events, informal dynamics, and organizational responses as they naturally unfolded. These observational insights provided valuable context and served to corroborate and deepen our interview findings.

Durmstrang: As with the Hogwarts case, we created an interview guide that was used to conduct the interviews. The interview guide can be found at Zenodo [22]. In total, the interview guide consists of 21 questions clustered into four categories: 1) warm-up including questions related to the interviewee, 2) the company culture, 3) the OKR framework, and 4) preconditions for an OKR adoption.

The interviews were conducted in person using audio recording. Furthermore, the moderating researcher took field notes.

The methodological triangulation enabled us to cross-validate findings and capture both observable phenomena and participants' perspectives, strengthening the reliability and depth of our data collection.

Qualitative Data Extraction and Analysis

To analyze the qualitative data, we first transcribed recorded interviews from the Hogwarts case using Whisper. The transcriptions were then reviewed and refined by the second and third authors to ensure accuracy and completeness. The transcription for the Durmstrang case was made manually and reviewed by the sixth author. These verified transcripts served as the foundation for thematic analysis, a method for identifying, analyzing, and reporting patterns within qualitative data. We followed Braun and Clarke's approach [3], which comprises five distinct phases followed by reporting: familiarization with the data, initial code generation, theme identification, theme review, and theme definition and naming.

To enhance the reliability and consistency of the coding process, the first three authors independently coded a subset of the data and compared their results with the coding conducted by the last author. Discrepancies in coding were resolved through collaborative discussions, which facilitated a shared understanding of the data and improved the robustness of the thematic framework. This iterative refinement process ensured that the themes were grounded in the data while remaining aligned with the study's objectives.

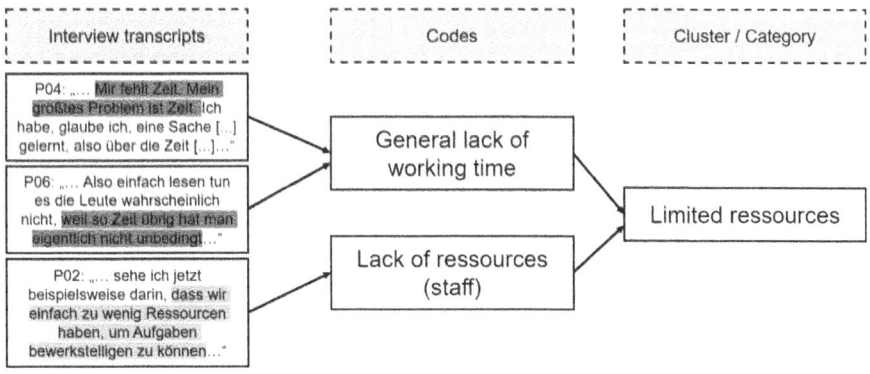

Fig. 2. Example of the coding and clustering process

Thematic analysis resulted in six clusters for barriers and eight clusters for benefits. We documented and visualized these clusters using a Miro Board. Figures 4 and 5 in our research protocol [22] present graphical excerpts of this Miro board. Additionally, Fig. 2 offers a specific example of our coding and clustering process.

4 Results

Throughout the analyses, we found concordance between the existing literature, the state of the practice as reported on the web, as well as the identified benefits and barriers at the two case companies.

4.1 State of the OKR Practice

Based on the results from our WCA, we answer our first research question: *What is the state of practice of OKRs?* First of all, it was not suitable to identify one distinct, universal state of the practice. Instead, we divided our codes into aspects of OKR practice that were reported either as good practice or as bad practice.

Alignment: Being the major motivation for the use of OKR, realising alignment is one major aspect of the OKR framework. Accordingly, good OKR implementations are characterised by OKRs that are derived from top-level strategic company goals. In that regard, leadership plays an important role, ensuring alignment top-down and adequately deriving OKRs for their teams. Complementarily, lack of top-level goals or insufficient ensuring of aligned OKRs were signs of bad OKR implementations.

Buy-In and Involvement Along the Hierarchy: Similarly, the OKR implementation is highly dependent on the level of buy-in along the hierarchy, yet especially from management. To achieve this, good OKR implementations are characterised by a high degree of involvement of all stakeholders, both in top-down and bottom-up approaches. Complementarily, imposing OKRs on a team top-down, without their involvement and consent, diminishes OKRs' advantages. In that regard, Reddit users stated: "OKR needs buy-in from the leaders of the company. If they believe in it, it will be easier to implement, adopt and get the value out of it." (Reddit Post R005) And "Everyone is bought in because you gave everyone a voice." (Reddit Post R007). Too long timeframes were perceived to have a negative effect because of reduced attention to OKRs. In addition, regular meetings to adapt OKRs were reported as a good practice. Not paying attention to horizontal harmonisation and thus setting conflicting OKRs among departments/teams on the same hierarchy level was reported as a bad practice.

Further bad practices were reported which can be summarized as **incorrect use or even misuse of OKRs**. In several cases, the OKR method was simply not understood and thus not used correctly. For example, key results were defined that measure irrelevant metrics. This was in part traced back to overemphasis on metrics, lacking actual objectives to be measured. In other cases, OKRs were reported to be misused, e.g., to instruct other management targets in disguise or even to circumvent actual strategic goals by obscuring them through OKRs.

Finally, certain approaches for OKR implementations were suggested. A frequently made recommendation was to teach the involved stakeholders about the

OKR framework by conducting workshops. However, some of those recommendations likely are to be regarded as self-promotion, especially when seeking external support/consulting is suggested. Other named approaches include piloting the OKR implementation first or, opposingly, following an all-in approach.

4.2   Barriers and Benefits While Implementing OKRs

In this subsection, we answer our second research question: *What are barriers and benefits while using OKRs?* Analyzing our data, we identified six barriers and eight benefits of implementing OKRs in practice. Figure 3 provides an overview of these clusters. Below, we give a detailed explanation per benefit and barrier; starting with the barriers.

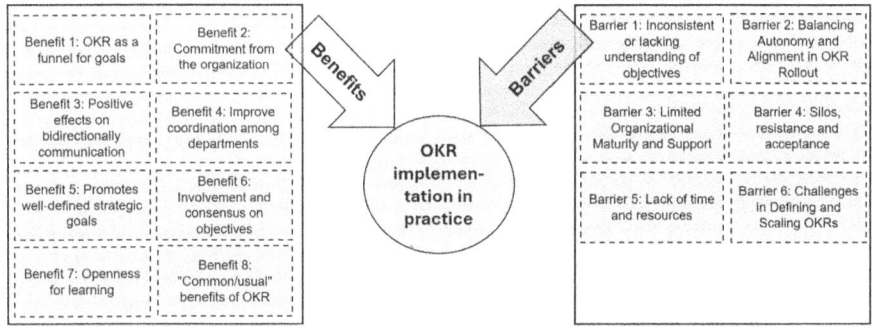

Fig. 3. Overview of the identified Benefits and Barriers of OKR implementation

Barrier 1 - Inconsistent or Lacking Understanding of Objectives: A significant challenge to the implementation of OKRs is the inconsistent or lacking understanding of objectives within the organisation. According to employees, there is sometimes a lack of higher or overarching strategic objectives that are anchored under the OKRs, which leads to a lack of harmonisation between the company's operational and strategic objectives (P08 and P13). A clear distinction between MOALs[1] and objectives used in the company is difficult for several employees. These difficulties result in a more complex and complicated goal setting for the involved employees. Implicit strategy implementation by different management levels (managers, organisational units, employees, group leaders) also make strategy alignment more difficult, as too many players would be involved, and the controllability and measurability of the objectives suffer as a result.

Barrier 2 - Balancing Autonomy and Alignment in OKR Rollout: The OKR methodology necessitates a high degree of personal responsibility and

---

[1] Mid-term goals (also named as MOALS in OKR) are strategic derivations from the vision with a temporal focus on one year [6].

a clear delineation of roles within the teams. This self-responsibility, particularly during the pilot phase of OKR implementation, naturally proves to be less controllable and, according to employees, may not always be optimally result-oriented. Furthermore, the planning of workshops for each team individually is exceedingly time-consuming and may result in an inconsistent understanding of OKRs within the organisation. This makes it challenging to implement the methodology in a coordinated and coherent manner. From a management perspective, balancing autonomy and alignment in a company may often come with a cultural shift (P13).

Barrier 3 - Limited Organizational Maturity and Support: An uneven understanding or an incoherent introduction of the OKR framework represents a further obstacle to the successful implementation of the methodology, as it indicates a lack of maturity within the organisation. For a successful implementation, all employees must fully understand the framework and have a unified level of knowledge. This is often not the case, which leads to difficulties when adapting or changing existing processes (P11, P12). Employees may feel isolated with the new methodology, as there is a lack of continuous guidance and support. The absence of driving forces that promote and support the methodology can result in a considerable decline in acceptance within the organisation.

Barrier 4 - Silos, Resistance, and Acceptance: The existence of silos within the organisation, in which knowledge is shielded by employees, represents a significant obstacle to the joint development and understanding of the OKR methodology. These silos often prevent the necessary transparency and open way of working and in turn strengthen hierarchy (P09, P13). Furthermore, the general OKR specifications can lead to restrictions in the agility of the working method as new specifications emerge. The introduction of a new method is easily met with resistance if there is little understanding for the change. In particular, if the methodology is incompatible with established, conservative reward systems based on individual performance indicators, this resistance makes it considerably more difficult for employees to commit to the new methodology.

Barrier 5 - Lack of Time and Resources: Another significant obstacle to the implementation of OKRs is the lack of time, resources, and personnel. The introduction of OKRs is perceived as an additional burden, as there may be a lack of sufficient resources and, in particular, knowledgeable staff for the methodology. Furthermore, employees often lack the working time required to correctly introduce and maintain OKRs. Smaller operational tasks are difficult to reconcile with the OKR methodology and therefore disrupt the process and continuity of OKR implementation.

Barrier 6 - Challenges in Defining and Scaling OKRs: The definition of objectives and key results is often challenging and in need of improvement, as it requires experience and practice. Large differences in the definition of OKRs between different departments increase complexity, especially in large organisations. The definition of OKRs at the meta-level is particularly challenging. A purely quantitative measurement can result the neglect of challenging goals in favour of a more favourable evaluation.

Benefit 1 - OKR as a Funnel for Objectives; Prioritising, Clarifying, Explicating: The interviews from both case companies showed positively that OKR is used as a funnel for objectives (top-down/bottom-up). This funnel is primarily used for prioritising, clarifying, and explaining the employees' and management's objectives. For this purpose, we divided this benefit two subcategories: (pre-)prioritisation of goals and objectives are made more explicit. For example, prioritisation at a strategic level using MOALS proves to be particularly positive. Furthermore, the use of OKR forces objectives to be made more explicit, comprehensible, and transparent. Examples emphasizing this importance include making objectives visible within the company through alignment. Or that OKR makes it transparent which operational activities are used to achieve the company's objectives. A third example is that OKR enables employees to speak to their stakeholders and make statements.

Benefit 2 - Commitment from the Organisation: The next benefit relates to the commitment from the organisation. In particular, it was shown that (top) management buy-in and support, as well as acceptance from the team/employee level, play a role. For top-level management buy-in and support, the implementation of OKR must start with training at all relevant organizational levels including the management to develop an in-depth understanding of the OKR framework. Another benefit is the support of organizational development (see Sect. 5), which significantly supports the implementation of OKR. In addition, corporate development strengthens the driving and accompanying functions for OKR in the organisation. Acceptance at team/employee level has shown that there is generally a high level of acceptance from the ranks of employees. This can be seen as very positive for the OKR methodology. In addition, the team levels give their final bottom-up commitment to objectives and MOALS and can therefore reach their agreements at the employee level.

Benefit 3 - OKR Effects on Bidirectionally Communication and Feedback: An interesting finding from analysing the interviews is that OKR positively promotes bidirectional effects (P09, P11, P12). This means that benefits for bottom-up feedback and general improvements are possible through a reciprocal approach (top-down/bottom-up). General improvement is understood here as the development of needs/strategies, communication in both directions, and the active involvement of employees in the strategy (initiated by working on the key results at the team level).

Benefit 4 - OKRs Improve Coordination Among Departments (Horizontal Alignment): In contrast to top-down alignment, the benefits of OKR lie primarily in optimising coordination between departments (P10, P11). In particular, the advantages resulting from horizontal alignment should be emphasised. These would be, for example, the strengthening of communication between the teams and improved transparency and resource allocation. In addition, the dialogue between the teams, cross-silo thinking, and cross-functional collaboration is strengthened in such a way that a new model of collaboration is created for the company under investigation. As interviewee P08 stated: "*To set the focus, i.e. to make the company's direction clearer for everyone. And also to* *set a targeted focus in the various iterations so that you don't get bogged down, but also exclude things and reflect on them."*

Benefit 5 - OKR Promotes Well-defined Strategic Goals: The fifth benefit of OKRs is that they promote the development of well-defined strategic goals. For instance, interviewees (P09, P11, P12) highlighted that planning workshops help derive clear and focused strategic objectives. Additionally, they noted that synergies created during the process enhance knowledge sharing and provide valuable insights, which contribute to a better overview when defining strategic goals.

Benefit 6 - Involvement and Consensus on Objectives: When implementing OKR, another benefit that emerges is the involvement of all participants across hierarchical levels and the consensus on goals in OKR. Involvement across hierarchical levels is a fundamental benefit. It was mentioned that the involvement of middle management (derivation managers) has the benefit to translate the strategic objectives into the departments. On a positive note, the agreement on the introduction of OKR and the associated effect on employees was noted. As an interesting anecdote, it was reported that the added value of involvement is that the derivation managers can plan on the one hand and carry out the "doing" at the operational level on the other. This offers the possibility of visibility in the team, or as was mentioned by P05: *"Are we going the right way"*, or *"Where does it pay off?"*. Consensus on objectives offers the benefit in the company analysed that the derivation managers have a consensus on the objectives and also discuss them so that they define the objectives uniformly and also give their approval so that they ultimately have a uniform view of the objectives in their team one level lower.

Benefit 7 - Openness for Learning: The seventh and final core benefit of OKR at Hogwarts is openness for learning. According to this, it is very important for the respondents to create lessons learnt values and to learn from them. Iterative learning, i.e. the creation of values via an OKR cycle for example, and its optimisation, was mentioned repeatedly. Furthermore, the intrinsic motivation and support of the OKR methodology within the organisation through openness to learning were considered beneficial. Finally, the courage to learn to define OKRs was identified as a noteworthy benefit that promotes rhetoric in the methodology.

Benefit 8 - "Common/usual" Benefits of OKR: Alignment, focus, communication - Some benefits and advantages expressed by respondents are very general and therefore cannot be assigned to a cluster that relates to potentials within the organisation. To be more precise, the "common/usual" benefits are those from the literature that OKR is advertised with, which did not quite provide novelty.

5 Implications for Practice and Research

In this section, we discuss the practical and research implications based on our findings aiming to provide specific recommendations for an optimized OKR implementation in practice.

As we explained in Sect. 2, we identified a research gap in OKRs adaption in practice. In turn, the results from our WCA (see Sect. 4.1) show, that the OKR framework is used frequently in practice. Furthermore, we identified specific motivations for the use of the framework in practice, for example, to align the strategic goals of a company into the various organizational levels, including the team level. This aspect is also mentioned by other authors (e.g., [30]).

The first key finding of our study was the strong connection to other change management projects such as the adaption of agile methods like Scrum or Kanban. The agile community is well acquainted with barriers, impediments, or challenges related to agile transitions in practice [11,31] and our identified barriers to the OKR implementation shows various similarities. Here, we focus on one specific aspect of the difference between cultural and technical facets of an OKR implementation, which we know from being vs. doing agile (e.g., [19,23]). We know that the challenges arising from this phenomenon are complex and in particular hard to tackle. However, we already identified specific measures how to deal with such barriers. Practitioners should be aware of the importance of success during an OKR implementation and thus should consider an approach of baby steps aiming to pick low-hanging fruits. In this context, it is important to consider principles such as inspect and adapt. This may motivate the involved employees to move forward and keep up the OKR implementation process. Our second key finding is focussing on the positive aspects of an OKR implementation in organizations. We found that the alignment of strategic goals through the organizational levels is optimized including a better understanding of what is important and what is not. This is in line with existing literature (e.g., [4,29,30]). OKRs can support a better alignment among teams and thus, increase communication and collaboration in an organization. This in turn should help to reduce the risk of knowledge and task silos.

Coming back to the research gap discussed at the beginning of this section, one may assume that the OKR framework is used in various contexts in practice. However, from a research perspective, our knowledge is limited and we thus call on other researchers to tackle this field aiming to analyze this practice-relevant phenomenon. To be more precise, we do not know how (agile) organizations do apply and use OKRs in practice specifically. One may assume that organizations are tailoring the OKR framework to adapt it to their very specific needs, which we know from the area of agile software development [24].

6   Threats to Validity

Every study is subject to specific limitations inherent to the chosen research approach. While we have adhered to established guidelines and meticulously prepared and conducted our study, we emphasize specific limitations and outline the measures taken to mitigate their impact. We used the threats to validity schema according to Wohlin et al. [35] and Runeson and Hoest [27]. A more detailed description of the limitations of our study can be found in Sect. 3 in our research protocol [22].

Construct Validity: Related to the applied WCA, we address especially the quality of the data sources used for construct validity. It is worth mentioning that posts on Reddit and LinkedIn, as well as articles found via Google News, may be shared or reviewed without much scrutiny or regulations for publication [26]. When analyzing the content from the web search, we found that recommendations were often made to counteract barriers to the use of OKRs. However, these recommendations may not be sufficiently evidence-based or may only be based on limited experience. Furthermore, interview participants may have interpreted "benefits" and "barriers" differently or assigned varying meanings to key concepts such as "transparency" and "alignment". To address this, we asked participants for specific examples to clarify their understanding and ensure consistency across responses.

Internal Validity: We took specific actions to follow the same approach in conducting the interviews to mitigate potential bias. First, the interview guidelines was composed of neutral, non-leading questions. Additionally, the interviews were semi-structured, allowing us to explore topics in depth based on the interviewee's responses. Each interview was conducted by at least two researchers, ensuring rigor. Furthermore, we used different data sources to strengthen the internal validity of our findings. However, we have to point to the limitation regarding different data collection approaches in the two case companies due to specifications made by the organizations. This may led to misinterprations during the data analysis procedure. We tried to tackle this challenge by integrating different researchers in the data collection and analysis processes.

External Validity: The results from the interviews are based on the experiences of thirteen employees. Despite the inclusion of employees from different positions, departments, and companies in the survey, it is reasonable to assume that this ratio may have influenced the findings. Also, it is obvious that our findings are strongly related to the case context. As a result, they may not fully generalize to other industries, organizational sizes, or cultural settings. Additionally, since data was collected during the early stages of OKR adoption, the results may evolve as the process stabilizes and matures.

7   Conclusion and Future Work

In our study, we dealt with OKRs in practice and aimed to fill two specific research gaps. First, we created a state of the practice of OKR applying a WCA. The results of our WCA provide valuable insights for both practice and research as we could identify specific aspects, differentiated into good or bad practice. We identified: Alignment with strategic top-level-management goals of an organization, involvement along the hierarchy, and misuse of OKRs. We identified a research gap focusing on the barriers and benefits of implementing OKRs in specific contexts. Thus, the main contribution of the paper are the identified six barriers and eight benefits occuring during OKR implementation in practice, which we derived from a multiple case study. The implementation of OKR comes with numerous challenges for organizations, but these can be effectively managed with the right strategies. Our results show that the successful application of OKR relies on effective communication, team, and role agility, a comprehensive understanding of the OKR approach, precise planning, and strong leadership.

The insights gained from the interviews provided valuable information on specific strategies that can support the use of OKRs. For the future development and optimization of the OKR approach in organizations, it is important to continuously gather feedback and adapt processes based on these insights. Technological tools and software solutions could be more integrated in the future to facilitate and automate OKR management and tracking. From a future research perspective, it is of importance to validate the findings and analyze, if the organization will overcome the barriers. Overall, our study emphasizes that with the right strategies and a clear focus on communication and involvement, commitment throughout the organization, and harmonizing among departments, the introduction of OKR can be successfully managed. This offers organizations the opportunity to achieve their goals more efficiently and continuously optimize their strategic direction.

Acknowledgements. We thank Kim Fabian Skowronek who supported us in the case study data collection and analysis. Furthermore, we want to express our gratitude to the case companies for supporting this study and all teams and interviewees for participating.

Conflict of Interest. The authors declare that they have no conflict of interest.

References

1. Amaya, A., Bach, R., Keusch, F., Kreuter, F.: New data sources in social science research: things to know before working with reddit data. Soc. Sci. Comput. Rev. **39**(5), 943–960 (2021). https://doi.org/10.1177/0894439319893305
2. Bagheri, E., Ensan, F.: Semantic tagging and linking of software engineering social content. Autom. Softw. Eng. **23**(2), 147–190 (2016). https://doi.org/10.1007/s10515-014-0146-2
3. Braun, V., Clarke, V.: Using thematic analysis in psychology. Qual. Res. Psychol. **3**(2), 77–101 (2006). https://doi.org/10.1191/1478088706qp063oa
4. Butler, J.L., Zimmermann, T., Bird, C.: Objectives and key results in software teams: challenges, opportunities and impact on development. In: Proceedings of the International Conference on Software Engineering (2024). https://doi.org/10.1145/3639477.3639747
5. Cao, R.: Research on teaching evaluation system of higher vocational colleges based on OKR and big data. In: Proceedings of the International Conference on Computer Science & Education (2021)
6. Doerr, J.: Measure what matters: How Google, Bono, and the gates foundation rock the world with OKRs. Portfolio/Penguin (2018)
7. Eilers, K., Peters, C., Leimeister, J.M.: Why the agile mindset matters. Technol. Forecast. Soc. Chang. **179**, 121650 (2022). https://doi.org/10.1016/j.techfore.2022.121650

8. Garousi, V., Borg, M., Oivo, M.: Practical relevance of software engineering research: synthesizing the community's voice. Empir. Softw. Eng. **25**(3), 1687–1754 (2020). https://doi.org/10.1007/s10664-020-09803-0

9. Glass, R.L.: The state of the practice of software engineering. IEEE Softw. **20**(6), 20–21 (2003). https://doi.org/10.1109/MS.2003.1241361

10. Héroux-Vaillancourt, M., Beaudry, C., Rietsch, C.: Using web content analysis to create innovation indicators–What do we really measure? Quant. Sci. Stud. **1**(4), 1601–1637 (2020). https://doi.org/10.1162/qss_a_00086

11. Hooshyar, H., et al.: Impact in software engineering activities after one year of Covid-19 restrictions for startups and established companies. IEEE Access **11**, 55178–55203 (2023). https://doi.org/10.1109/ACCESS.2023.3279917

12. Jarzębowicz, A., Ślesiński, W.: Assessing effectiveness of recommendations to requirements-related problems through interviews with experts. In: 2018 Federated Conference on Computer Science and Information Systems (FedCSIS), pp. 959–968. IEEE (2018)

13. Joskowski, A., Przybyłek, A., Marcinkowski, B.: Scaling scrum with a customized nexus framework: a report from a joint industry-academia research project. Softw. Pract. Exp. **53**(7), 1525–1542 (2023). https://doi.org/10.1002/spe.3201

14. Kim, I., Kuljis, J.: Applying content analysis to web-based content. J. Comput. Inf. Technol. **18**(4), 369–375 (2010)

15. Kitchenham, B., Charters, S.: Guidelines for performing systematic literature reviews in software engineering (2007)

16. Kitchenham, B., Madeyski, L., Budgen, D.: How should software engineering secondary studies include grey material? IEEE Trans. Softw. Eng. **49**(2), 872–882 (2023). https://doi.org/10.1109/TSE.2022.3165938

17. Kitchenham, B., Madeyski, L., Budgen, D.: SEGRESS: software engineering guidelines for reporting secondary studies. IEEE Trans. Software Eng. **49**(3), 1273–1298 (2023). https://doi.org/10.1109/TSE.2022.3174092

18. Kucharska, W., Balcerowski, T., Kucharski, M., Jussila, J.: Who is an agile leader? technological vs. non-technological mindset employees' views. In: Proceedings of The 19th European Conference on Management, Leadership and Governance. Academic Conferences International (2024)

19. Kuchel, T., Neumann, M., Diebold, P., Schön, E.M.: Which challenges do exist with agile culture in practice? In: Proceedings of the ACM/SIGAPP Symposium on Applied Computing, pp. 1018–1025 (2023). https://doi.org/10.1145/3555776.3578726

20. Radonic, M.: OKR system as the reference for personal and organizational objectives. Econophysics, Sociophysics Other Multidiscip. Sci. J. **7**(2), 28–37 (2017)

21. Mangipudi, M.R., Prasad, K., W., V.R.: Objectives and key results for higher education institutions - A blended approaches part of post Covid-19 initiatives for keeping the institutions abreast of the industry innovations. Pacific Bus. Rev. International **13**(9), 46–56 (2021)

22. Misslisch, J., Bauer, T., Eibl, F., Spanke, J., Schön, E.M., Przybylek, A., Neumann, M.: Research protocol (2025). https://zenodo.org/records/15851133

23. Neumann, M., Kuchel, T., Diebold, P., Schön, E.M.: Agile culture clash: unveiling challenges in cultivating an agile mindset in organizations. Comput. Sci. Inf. Syst. **21**(3), 1013–1031 (2024). https://doi.org/10.2298/CSIS230715029N

24. Neumann, M.: Towards a taxonomy of agile methods: the tree of agile elements. In: Proceedings of the International Conference in Software Engineering Research and Innovation, pp. 79–87 (2021). https://doi.org/10.1109/CONISOFT52520.2021.00022

25. Niven, P.R., Lamorte, B.: Objectives and Key Results: Driving Focus, Alignment, and Engagement with OKRs. Wiley corporate F&A series, Wiley, Hoboken (2016). https://doi.org/10.1002/9781119255543
26. Proferes, N., Jones, N., Gilbert, S., Fiesler, C., Zimmer, M.: Studying reddit: a systematic overview of disciplines, approaches, methods, and ethics. Social Media + Society **7**(2) (2021). https://doi.org/10.1177/20563051211019004
27. Runeson, P., Höst, M.: Guidelines for conducting and reporting case study research in software engineering. Empir. Softw. Eng. **14**(2), 131–164 (2009). https://doi.org/10.1007/s10664-008-9102-8
28. Silva, R.V., Souza, G.D.S.: Surveying the academic literature on the use of OKR (Objective and Key Results). In: Proceedings of the Brazilian Symposium on Information Systems (2023). https://doi.org/10.1145/3592813.3592934
29. Stray, V., Brede Moe, N., Vedal, H., Berntzen, M.: Objectives and key results (OKRS) and slack: a case study of coordination in large-scale distributed agile. In: Proceedings of the Hawaii International Conference on Systems Science (2022)
30. Stray, V., Gundelsby, J.H., Ulfsnes, R., Brede Moe, N.: How agile teams make objectives and key results (OKRS) work. In: Proceedings of the International Conference on Software and System Processes and International Conference on Global Software Engineering, pp. 104–109 (2022). https://doi.org/10.1145/3529320.3529332
31. Strode, D.E., Sharp, H., Barroca, L., Gregory, P., Taylor, K.: Tensions in organizations transforming to agility. IEEE Trans. Eng. Manage. **69**(6), 3572–3583 (2022). https://doi.org/10.1109/TEM.2022.3160415
32. Troian, T.A., Gori, R.S.L., Lacerda, D.P., Gauss, L., Weber, J.R.: OKRS as a results-focused management model: a systematic literature review. In: Proceedings of the International Joint Conference on Industrial Engineering and Operations Management (2022). https://doi.org/10.14488/IJCIEOM2022_0020_37589
33. Wang, X., Su, M., Sun, X.: Research on implementation strategy of objectives and key results assessment in state-owned enterprises. In: Proceedings of the International Conference on Public Management and Intelligent Society, vol. 8, pp. 718–723. Atlantis Press (Zeger Karssen) (2023). https://doi.org/10.2991/978-94-6463-200-2_74
34. Weichbrodt, J., et al.: Understanding leadership in agile software development teams: Who and how? In: Stray, V., Stol, K.J., Paasivaara, M., Kruchten, P. (eds.) Agile Processes in Software Engineering and Extreme Programming, pp. 99–113. Springer International Publishing, Cham (2022). https://doi.org/10.1007/978-3-031-08169-9_7
35. Wohlin, C., Runeson, P., Höst, M., Ohlsson, M.C., Regnell, B., Wesslén, A.: Experimentation in Software Engineering. Springer, Heidelberg (2012). https://doi.org/10.1007/978-3-642-29044-2
36. Yin, R.K.: Case Study Research: Design and Methods, Applied Social Research Methods Series, vol. 5. Sage, Los Angeles, 4. ed. edn. (2009)

Profiling Processor Usage in Web Applications: Categorization, Usage Patterns, and Experimental Analysis

Gonzalo Sabando-Alonso and Marisol García-Valls(⊠)

Departamento de Comunicaciones, Universitat Politècnica de València,
Valencia 46022, Spain
{gsabalo,mvalls}@dcom.upv.es

Abstract. The determination of the resource consumption patterns of modern web applications is increasingly critical, particularly given stringent non-functional requirements like low-latency user interactions. The increasing population of applications results in high competition for users; and user disatisfaction leads to engaging into some alternative system or app. Despite this, web development has traditionally prioritized functionality over performance, partly due to the perceived abundance of processing power of modern processors. This paper challenges that assumption and advocates for a conscious usage of profiling strategies in web systems that also focuses on the determination of the resource consumption of web application code. This paper explains the importance of determining execution time and its relation to the processor usage in the case of web code. We put forward a set of different strategies and mechanisms to determine the processor usage of web applications. We investigate a number of tools that are of interest for this purpose and provide its usage pattern. We experimentally assess these strategies through a set of experiments and provide a comparative analysis regarding their usability and obtained execution results.

Keywords: Web applications · web component · processor usage · profiling · CPU usage · green computing · performance

1 Introduction

Modern computer systems include web components and applications that are often central players for enabling a wide range of services across heterogeneous domains like finance, healthcare, e-commerce, transportation, or industrial automation. Modern software systems are increasingly architected with web-based components as core elements of their design; such components range from RESTful APIs to full-stack web applications. According to recent surveys, over 90% of software systems deployed in production include at least one web-facing component. The proliferation of microservice-based and cloud-native architectures have increased this trend even further [1]. Additionally, the widespread

© The Author(s), under exclusive license to Springer Nature Switzerland AG 2026
D. Taibi and D. Smite (Eds.): SEAA 2025, LNCS 16082, pp. 108–124, 2026.
https://doi.org/10.1007/978-3-032-04200-2_8

adoption of containerization and orchestration platforms like Docker and Kubernetes has further accelerated the integration of web technologies in both consumer and enterprise systems.

Web components have also reached embedded and critical systems which include medical devices, industrial control systems, automotive platforms, and aerospace systems, among others. Many of these integrate with web servers and/or web front-ends for the purpose of configuration, monitoring, and communication tasks [2]. Also, they are sometimes tightly integrated with remote web services and/or additional backend servers.

Given the mission-critical nature of some of these applications, ensuring that their web components exhibit reliable and performant behavior is key. Monitoring the physical resource usage of these web components is essential to guarantee their performance; precisely, it is most relevant the assessment of their consumption of physical resources like processor, memory, I/O, and network bandwidth. These data are essential not only for maintaining service quality but also for enabling system-level guarantees like real-time behavior, fault tolerance, and energy efficiency. Also, blockchain-based systems ranging from safe blockchain networks like VelogCPS [3] or colaborative digital twin environments [4] make intensive usage of web technologies; these systems need to perform exhaustive profiling of their resource consumption to prove the reduction of the inherent overhead of blockchain software platforms.

The importance of performance evaluation in different domains including IoT platforms [8] or security [9] have been greatly recognized. However, in web-based systems, there remains a significant need for systematic studies that explore and document how web components utilize physical resources under various workloads and deployment scenarios. Existing literature often addresses performance in terms of latency and throughput, but a deeper understanding of the resource footprint of web technologies is essential to guide optimization efforts, inform design trade-offs, and ensure system scalability. Research efforts should thus be directed at developing or consolidating techniques for profiling, monitoring, and analyzing the CPU, memory, and network usage of web servers and applications at runtime. Such studies are especially relevant in hybrid deployments where web components coexist with other time-sensitive processes, and their uncontrolled resource consumption can lead to performance degradation or even critical failures.

In this context, this paper addresses the need of compiling a number of most relevant software tools that are able to determine the resource consumption performed by a web application. We investigate a number of tools that are of interest for this purpose, providing a selected usage pattern each of them through a set of programming structures. These constitute the easiest usage patterns to apply the explained utilities. We carry out a number of experiments to study their behaviour and characteristics, their provided results, and time granularity. We compare the obtained results, analyse and discuss their suitability for different scenarios and their usability.

This paper presents the following structure. Section 2 describes the overall context and related work, explaining the scarcely-populated panorama of works relative to processor usage of web components. Section 3 explains the main concepts about processor profiling and presents how code execution occurs in the domain of web applications. Section 4 describes the main contribution of the paper with a generic classification of strategies for execution time and response time profiling in web, followed by a set of usage patterns to instrument web code for this purpose. Section 5 describes the experiments that have been undertaken to evaluate the presented techniques; also it discusses their suitability for various targets. Section 6 draws some conclusions about the contributed work.

2   Context and Related Work

Web platforms have proliferated greatly over the last decades, mainly those based on JavaScript [5] technology. Web software has been largely applied in a number of execution targets, including embedded systems [7]. As an example, resource-constrained embedded systems were targeted by MicroJS [6], a lightweight virtual execution environment that offered JavaScript runtimes for web.

Monitoring and evaluating the resource consumption of web applications can help assess the existance of potential barriers in their integration with cyber-physical systems and IoT as these have critical targets. The safe integration of web technologies in these systems and in their most critical parts should be done after the evaluation of their performance and resource consumption patterns. Analysing of the obtained performance data is essential also to detect existing threats like anomalous behaviour of some system function.

Resource consumption profiling can be achieved through two main and complementary approaches. The first one consists of using web environments for embedded development and their instrospection capabilities. The second technique is based on the usage of external tools that include libraries that optionally enable the programmer to instrument the developed code.

On the one hand, low-level execution techniques are related to the first type of methods. These are focused on the usage of portable, low-level bytecode formats that achieve improved performance and allow applications to run natively within web browsers. WebAssemly (Wsam) [10] falls in this category and was designed to overcome the limitations of its predecessor *asm* [11], a highly optimizable subset of JavaScript intended for similar purposes. While asm showed near-native performance in the browser through aggressive optimization of JavaScript engines [15], WebAssembly formalised this approach with a binary instruction format enabling faster parsing, smaller file sizes, and more predictable execution [16]. A number of works have benchmarked the improved performance of WebAssembly over asm.js [17,18], especially in applications involving computationally intensive tasks like real-time physics simulation, audio processing, and machine learning inference. Moreover, a number of studies have compared the performance of JavaScript with respect to WebAssembly [12] and other higher-level programming languages for the web [13].

On the other hand, resource profiling can be achieved through external tools like *perf* and *htop* [14], or container-level profilers like *cAdvisor* and *Prometheus* [19] that can track physical resource usage of a system that runs web applications or web services. The provided data can be used to assess real-time behavior, and to detect performance bottlenecks. Analysis of these data may serve to take corrective actions like enforcing limits on resource consumption; that is an essential capability in both cloud-native and embedded deployments where overuse could lead to service degradation or critical failure.

Over the years, some alternatives for performance efficiency in web have appeared like Rust [22]. This is a systems programming language that has increasingly expanded into web development, offering strong performance and memory safety guarantees without a garbage collector. Rust is gaining adoption at the server side through frameworks like Actix-web and Axum, which enable highly efficient, low-latency web services, especially suited for real-time or resource-constrained environments. However, at the client side, Rust compiles to WebAssembly (Wasm), allowing developers to run high-performance Rust code in the browser, often to handle computationally intensive tasks. Also, Rust supports native multithreading at the server and also at the client side via Wasm threads (with proper browser support). For performance analysis, Rust provides tools such as *perf* integration, *flamegraph*, and crates like criterion.rs for statistical benchmarking. These provide fine-grained insights into execution time, processor usage, and memory allocation.

In web-centric environments, it continues to be common practice to focus strictly on the functional aspects of web systems; and the majority of performance studies have focused on virtualization of services for container-based systems. However, little attention has been paid to the execution time determination and analysis of general purpose web software. In this paper, we overcome this part and intend to shed some light into techniques for profiling execution time of web code, providing their usage patterns and analysing them in different scenarios.

3   Web Performance and Execution-Time Profiling

Measuring the execution time of a program, i.e., a process or thread, relates to its CPU usage. Execution time reflects the time that the processor is actively engaged in executing the program instructions. In modern computing systems, where processors typically consist of multiple cores, execution time becomes a function not only of computational complexity but also of how effectively a workload is distributed across available cores. Multi-core execution supports concurrent execution of the different threads or processes which potentially reduces the overall consumed time. Also, multicores enable parallel execution, but this introduces additional factors that affect execution time, including inter-core communication, synchronization overhead, and contention for shared resources such as caches and memory bandwidth. There are situations where threads must frequently synchronize, e.g., through locks, barriers, or message passing. In such cases, the achieved speed of the execution or application response-time can be limited as the execution of one thread can be delayed by the slower progress of another.

Alternatively, tasks that can be executed independently with minimal synchronization scale more effectively across cores. Therefore, the measured execution time of a multi-core workload not only reflects raw computational demand but also the efficiency of parallel execution and the degree of inter-core coordination, making it a key indicator of both performance and CPU utilization.

3.1   Web Execution Environment

Web environments are fundamentally single-threaded, particularly those of standard browser contexts. The core of these browser models is the JavaScript runtime environment, built upon a single main thread responsible for executing all script logic, handling user interactions, rendering updates, and managing communication with web APIs.

Modern browsers use multiple processes internally for their common duties like separating tabs or isolating plugins. However, the execution context of a single web application typically runs in a single-threaded event-driven model. This means that the browser processes tasks such as JavaScript execution, DOM manipulation, and layout rendering in a sequential fashion within one thread. Consequently, long-running computations or blocking operations within this thread can lead to a non-responsive user interface, as no other activity can proceed until the current task completes.

To mitigate the restrictions of this single-threaded model, web environments use a model known as the *event loop* to emulate concurrency. The event loop coordinates the execution of asynchronous tasks by maintaining a queue of callback functions that are scheduled to run after the current call stack is cleared. Activities like handling user input events, resolving promises, or handling timers (e.g., setTimeout) are deferred and executed one at a time in the event loop, creating the illusion of parallelism. The system may execute other activities asynchronously including I/O or network requests that involve operating system support in the end by using background threads managed by the browser or system-level APIs. Nevertheless, the callback functions associated with these operations are always enqueued for execution on the main thread. This mechanism achieves non-blocking behavior and efficient task scheduling, though without true parallelism.

4   Profiling Approach

4.1   Model and Categories

For performance-sensitive web applications, it is essential to understand processor consumption and the associated times as it allows the software engineers to profile bottlenecks, detecting inefficient execution paths, and optimizing overall

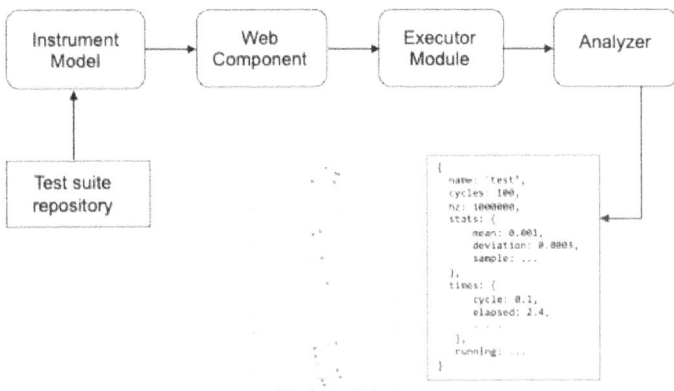

Fig. 1. Model process

throughput. For this important aspect, we propose a model to analyse web code performance through practical tools following the model outlined in Fig. 1.

A number of options exist throught the different web languages landscape to measure time conforming a moderately populated test suite. Surprisingly, most of these are not used by the vast majority of programmers as these are function-oriented. In our model, we acknowledge the importance of analysing all techniques as there are some significant differences between them that make them ideal or discardable in some scenarios. The instrumentation of web code is done differently across available solutions, so the appropriate available instrumentation patterns have to be known and followed in each situation and applied to the single or multiple web components that will be profiled. The experiments have to be defined and executed (executor module) according to the characteristics of the selected option; experiments return a propietary set of measures that need be analyzed (analyzer module), studied, and/or graphed.

In what follows, we explain some of the main concepts related to the temporal aspects and timing of applications as well as its relation to physical resource usage.

Execution time of a program refers to the time taken by the processor to execute its code. It is highly related to the *response time* of the program, that refers to the time elapsed from the start to the end of its execution, i.e., the instant where the program delivers its output. However, this includes not only the time the program spends actively executing on the CPU, but also any other time in which it is blocked or waiting on I/O operations, user interactions, or the higher-priority software like the operating system scheduler.

In contrast, CPU consumption specifically refers to the time a program spends executing instructions in the processor itself; this latter comprises user time (time spent in user-level code) and system time (time spent in the kernel space, such as I/O handling or driver operations).

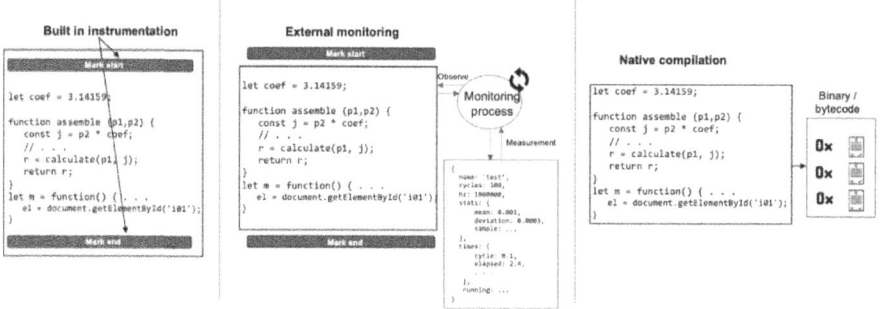

Fig. 2. Strategies for resource-consumption profiling in web software

We propose a classification of program resource consumption monitoring strategies as shown in Fig. 2, based on three sets. These are direct code instrumentation, external supervision of resource consumption, and direct compilation of code. The first one adds little overhead as the additional code belongs to the native programming environment and language (e.g. JavaScript in its vanilla version); the second one does not add to the monitored code but to the overall system; and the last one eliminates instrumentation overhead and makes the code execution more efficient.

Native Instrumentation. This approach is based on adding native code adds to the software code that make use of the native timers of the programming language execution environment. These adds include programming language constructs to embed timing checkpoints directly in the code, before and after the execution of the target code, under the assumption that the function under test does not perform blocking operations or directly neglecting it. This approach introduces controlled overhead, as the inserted instructions are native to the execution environment of the instrumented code. However, the measured execution time may not distinguish between active processor time and time spent waiting on system calls or the event loop; as a result, this technique is less precise in asynchronous or highly concurrent environments. Some examples are in JavaScript environments are `Date` object with its method `now`; `performance` API with its method `now`; or `process` object with its method `hrtime`.

External Profiling (X-probe). This strategy is based on using modules external to (or additional to) the target code that perform active monitoring by operating in parallel with the running application. Some of these tools differenciate between user and system time, providing real-time or aggregated views, and track metrics even when multiple threads or asynchronous processes are active. The target code is not modified. This technique may introduce additional overhead derived from its own need of computational resources to operate, and may require elevated permissions. They can only offer an approximatation to the resource consumption depending on sampling intervals. Some examples are tools like perf, pidusage, or top.

Binary-level Profiling (WASM-probe). The third technique consists of the compilation of the web application software to WebAssembly (Wasm) or another intermediate binary format and executing it inside a profiling-enabled environment [20]. This method leverages the deterministic and low-level nature of Wasm to measure consumed processor cycles with higher accuracy. WASM runtimes like Wasmtime or Wasmer can expose detailed telemetry. The main limitation is the need to translate application logic into WASM and ensure behavioral equivalence between the original and the compiled form, which can be non-trivial for complex or I/O-bound web applications.

To summarize and compare this techniques, we should consider the unique advantages of each strategy and their trade-offs. Native instrumentation is simple and accessible, making it suitable for initial diagnostics and performance checks during development. It provides high flexibility and control over the granularity of the code to be profiled. Nevertheless, given the non-concurrent nature of the web environments, it can be misleading in asynchronous or multithreaded contexts.

X-probe does not interfere directly in the monitored code or application, and provides system-wide visibility; it can, therefore, be suitable for production monitoring, yet it may lack precision due to its sampling nature and may incur setup complexity. Binary-level profiling [21] can offer highest precision and architectural transparency, but it is skills-demanding and limited by its applicability; it requires non-trivial recompilation steps and may not reflect real-world execution conditions of the original codebase or whole server execution context.

Table 1 summarizes a set of profiling options for web software. It focuses on software developed in JavaScript language that is a dominant instrument for web programming nowadays. Those applicable at the client and server sides are signaled with a *both* in column *Client*; if only applicable at the server side, a character ✗ is marked; and ✓ is printed if it is only applicable at the client side.

Table 1. Processor-consumption profiling

Option	Function	Client	Precision
console	`time, timeEnd`	*both*	ms
performance	`now`	*both*	5 µs
performance	`mark, measure`	*both*	ms
performance	`timerify`	✗	ms
microprofiler	`start, measureFrom`	*both*	1 µs
benchmark	`add`	✗	ms

Method `now` returns a `DOMHighResTimeStamp` measured in miliseconds with a precision of 5µs. Performance API provides a way to profile processor usage of individual functions by introducing a wrapper function callee to the target function instead of the original direct call. In situations where a statistical valid profiling is needed, the Microprofiler tool provides a shortcut to obtain the measurement after multiple executions of the target code. Additionally, as the obtained resolution is of microseconds, micro-optimizations can be done. Library *bechmark* for JavaScript provides an environment to run performance tests on code fragments and/or functions that are integrated into suites (**add** function) that are the objects used to run multiple tests over the same context. Tests are run reapeatedly to yield time and behavioral profiling results that are statistically relevant metrics including mean execution time, variance, standard deviation, error margin, and operations per second (Hz), which is a key indicator of function throughput. A detailed explanation of these strategies is provided next.

4.2   Software Patterns

This section compiles and outlines the most relevant profiling strategies; also, a use pattern for each is ellaborated. Additionally, we provide an experimental analysis of these techniques and a comparative analysis derived from the obtained results.

console is a global object that grants access to the debugging console in the browser. Offered methods like **log**, **error**, **time**, or **trace**, among other functions, support the interaction with the client or Node.js server console interface, aiding in program behavior inspection. **time** and **timeEnd** (Listing 8.1) methods provide a lightweight instrumentation mechanism for measuring response time or time elapsed between two points in code execution. It uses the internal timing mechanisms of client or server environments that can, in turn, use the timing facilities of objects like **Date** and system level timers that achieve millisecond precision.

```
console.time('label1');
// Code
console.timeEnd('label1');
```

Listing 8.1. Usage of profiling with **console** object

performance API enables developers to instrument code snippets using functions **mark** and **measure** (see Listing 8.2). **mark** defines named timestamps and **measure** determines durations between them. As a result, an entry is created with the times at which the marks are reached so that they can be later accessed and processed. This strategy supports measuring code pieces of any size as well as individual or multiple functions.

```
performance.mark('start-mark1');
// Code
performance.mark('end-mark1');
performance.measure('function-duration','start-mark1','end-mark2');
```

Listing 8.2. Usage of **mark** and **measure** of performance API

Also, *performance API* contains a timing function **now** (see Listing 8.3) that is provided by the browser or by the server runtime via the **perf_hooks** module in Node.js. While **mark** and **measure** are designed for structured and labeled performance profiling, **now** returns a high-resolution timestamp representing the number of milliseconds (with microsecond precision) elapsed since a fixed time origin; the origin usually is the page load or process start. These can all be used in combination, though now is particularly suited for lightweight and immediate timing needs, whereas mark and measure support more complex performance analysis and reporting.

```
const t1 = performance.now();
// Code
const t2 = performance.now();
```

Listing 8.3. Usage of now in performance API

timerify is a facility of performance API that runs at the server side. In this case, a wrapper (a wrapped version of a given monitored function named func1) is created that serves to run the monitored function code (see Listing 8.4). When the function is called, Node.js environment logs an entry for performance with the function name and its duration.

```
const { performance, PerformanceObserver } = require('perf_hooks');
// Function func1 code
const wrapper = performance.timerify(func1);
const observer = new PerformanceObserver( //callback);

observer.observe({...});
```

Listing 8.4. Usage of timerify in performance API

microprofiler captures high-resolution timestamps often by using method hrtime of process object; or by using method now of performance object at the precise points within the code. This technique supports the embedding of custom markers for profiling start and stop, and it generates detailed temporal statistics across multiple executions. Output includes averages, standard deviation, and outlier detection. It has minimal runtime footprint, so it is suitable for bechnmarking small code portions and micro operations. There are two versions of the pattern available depending on whether it follows the simple structure of start and end time collection (Listing 8.5) or if a start time point is set with some other high resolution mechanism such as performance hooks in a server environment (Listing 8.6).

```
const { Profiler } = require('microprofiler');
const profiler = new Profiler();
profiler.start('label1');
// Code
profiler.end('label1');
profiler.report();
```

Listing 8.5. Microprofiler usage pattern - start, end

```
const { Profiler } = require('microprofiler');
const profiler = new Profiler();
// In server environment, perf_hooks is needed for high-res time
const { performance } = require('perf_hooks');

const start = profiler.performance.now(); // Manual collection of start time
// Code
profiler.measureFrom('label1',start);
profiler.report();
```

Listing 8.6. Microprofiler usage pattern - measureFrom

benchmark library provides high-precision performance measurements facility that delivers statistically relevant information to ensure that provided results reflect consistent performance trends. It is particularly suitable for micro-benchmarking, and for comparing algorithmic implementations or detecting performance regressions in low-latency processor-intensive operations. It leverages high-resolution timers like `performance.now` or `process.hrtime` and achieves accuracies below millisecond. Benchmark performs multiple iterations of a given test, including warm-up cycles. As shown in Listing 8.7, a suite or set of performance tests can be created for different code segments. The tests are included in the suite with function `add`; and they are run multiple times applying statistical analysis with function `run`.

```
const Bench = require('benchmark');
const suite = new Bechmark.Suite();
suite
    .add('label1'), function(){...})
    .add('label2'), function(){...})
    .run( { async: true });
```

Listing 8.7. Benchmark library usage pattern with Suite, add, and run

pidusage (Listing 8.8) is a server side library of the Node environment. It runs cross-platform (Linux, mac, Windows) by internally using platform-specifiy methods like `ps` or `taskList`; or by reading from the virtual file system that exposes kernel and process information and contains real-time system data like process status, memory, processor information and kernel parameters. This library handles all needed activities to call systems level commands and reading operating system specific files to retrieve process stats and return the performance data.

```
const pidusage = require('pidusage');
pidusage(process.pid, () => {
        // Code
    });
const procUse = stats.cpu;
const memUse stats.memory;
const respTime = stats.elapsed;
```

Listing 8.8. Usage pattern for *pidusage* object with cpu, memory, and elapsed

process.cpuUsage (Listing 8.9) determines the processor time consumed by the process separated by user and kernel times, resulting in a returned object with properties `user` and `system` (values in microseconds). It measures only actual processor cycles consumed by the code, excluding idle periods, asynchronous waiting operations like I/O or interference from the event loop overhead. It is suitable for processor intensive tasks like numerical calculations or scenarios where accurate profiling of computation time is needed.

```
const startTime = process.cpuUsage();
// Code
const endTime = process.cpuUsage(startTime);

const userTime   = endTime.user;
const kernelTime = endTime.system;
```

Listing 8.9. Usage pattern for process object with cpuUsage

Table 2. Programmability-oriented classification of performance measurement tools

Variant	Ease	CPU	Memory	Overhead
console	1	1	No	Low
now	1	1	No	Low
mark/measure	2	2	No	Low
timerify	3	3	No	Medium
microprofiler	3	4	No	Medium
benchmark	4	5	No	High
pidusage	2	4	Yes	Low
process.cpuUsage	3	5	Partial	Low

4.3   Usability Discussion

From a programming standpoint, the evaluated tools can be broadly classified by their ease of use into three categories: basic, intermediate, and advanced. Basic tools such as the console object and performance object with now provide the simplest usage patterns, requiring only one or two lines of code with no additional setup. These are ideal for quick, inline performance checks during development. Intermediate strategies include performance API mark and measure, and timerify, that offer more structured profiling but still remain accessible through standard Node.js or browser environments. These require slightly more code and familiarity but provide greater control over measuring specific execution phases.

On the more advanced side, mechanisms like microprofiler, the benchmark library, pidusage, and process object involve extra setup and interpretation. Microprofiler introduces its own API for marking and measuring code, while benchmark provides detailed statistical performance results but requires asynchronous handling. System-level tools like pidusage and process object offer insights into processor and memory usage, but they require understanding of lower-level metrics and additional calculation in some cases. In summary, while basic tools are quick and intuitive for most developers, advanced tools provide deeper insights at the cost of increased integration complexity.

The classification criteria presented in Table 2 are defined to assess the practical usability and diagnostic power of the different performance measurement techniques. Column *ease* provides an overall rating of the programming complexity of each tool, representing 1 the minimal effort and immediate applicability (e.g., a single-line API), and 5 denotes tools requiring additional setup, asynchronous handling, or interpretation of statistical output. Column *CPU* similarly adopts the same scale to reflect the granularity of processor usage information provided, ranging from coarse execution time estimates to fine-grained separation of user and system CPU time. Column *memory* is a binary indicator specifying whether the technique also reports memory usage, which is particularly relevant for profiling memory-intensive workloads. Finally, column *overhead* offers a qualitative assessment of the impact of the technique on the measurement itself,

Table 3. Profiling experiments and measurements

Variant	Light (µs)	Medium (µs)	Heavy (ms)
console time	42	933	131.031
performance API	116	1090	128.999
performance now	9	1017	128.311
performance timerify	48	924	130.226
microprofiler	33	303	127.437
benchmark	0.017	20.1	142.240
pidusage	5	338	133.727
process cpuUsage	17	1033	133.231

acknowledging that some high-overhead tools (e.g., benchmarking frameworks) may introduce distortion into timing results, whereas lightweight tools tend to exert minimal influence on runtime behavior. This classification thus aims to support informed selection of profiling tools based on developer constraints and performance analysis goals.

5 Experimental Analysis and Results

The different strategies have been evaluated in a set of experiments. Different tests have been designed and run multiple times to derive statistically meaningful results.

Table 3 summarizes the execution time of the different techniques over a baseline web code in three different scenarios: running the base code 10 times that we name *light*; a medium load scenario where the code is run for 10^4 repetitions; and execution of the base code for 10^6 iterations (the *heavy* scenario). It can be seen that highest precision is obtained for external tools like the benchmark libraries for the single execution, as opposed to the performance API. However, the situation stabilizes in heavy situations where all techniques exhibit similar times meaning that the effects of initialization cases and initial start up time vanish.

This suggests that finer-resolution timers or purpose-built benchmarking tools like Benchmark library can provide more accurate measurements even in the case of very short executions, while general-purpose instrumentation tools might distort results due to their intrinsic cost.

For the cases of *medium* and *heavy* computations, the differences in overhead start to converge, but important nuances remain. For instance, in the *heavy* case, all methods report durations in the 127–133 ms range, except Benchmark library that returns a larger value of 142.240 ms possibly due to its internal calibration or initialization procedures. Microprofiler consistently exhibits low overhead across all conditions, suggesting its optimization for minimal intrusion. Conversely, techniques like `cpuUsage` and Performance API introduce higher relative cost in *medium*-duration executions, hinting that their usefulness may be limited when high-resolution temporal profiling is needed across many iterations.

For techniques that provide disaggregation of processor usage into user mode and kernel (system) mode like `process.cpuUsage`, results shown in Table 4 reflect that the execution of light and medium workloads appears to occur almost exclusively in user mode; in reality, what occurs is that the system overhead is present but is negligible in this context. As opposed, when the workload increases significantly, user time increases and system time rises more shaply to 95.477 ms. This suggests that in heavy workloads a substantial part of the processor effort shifts to kernel-managed operations potentially due to memory management, context switching, and internal buffering. This highlights the importance of ana- lyzing both execution layers when optimizing performance in JavaScript-based server environments, especially when heavy processor and memory usage oper- ations are performed.

Table 4. Processor consumption dissagretated by user and kernel

Workload	User time	System time
Light	0.066	0.000
Medium	1.330	0.055
Heavy	45.297	95.477

Introducing memory operations in the different scenarios, we observe a clear relationship between the the workload size and the resulting resource consump- tion in terms of processor and memory usage. For smaller workload sizes (light and medium), both processor and memory usage remain virtually unchanged, suggesting negligible system impact. However, as the workload further increases to the heaviest scenario, there is a substantial spike in processor usage (upt to 121.43%) and a significant rise in memory consumption (from 47.89 MB to 252.07 MB). These results indicate that the computational load and memory footprint impact system performance and execution time, highlighting the importance of scalability-aware performance testing.

Table 5. Processor and memory usage under different scenarios

Workload	CPU init.	CPU final	Mem. init.	Mem.final
Light	0.00	0.00	47.67	47.67
Medium	0.00	0.00	47.54	47.79
Heavy	0.00	121.43	47.89	252.07

The results presented in Table 5 offer a comparative view of processor and memory consumption across varying workload intensities when measured using the *pidusage* in a JavaScript execution environment. The memory usage data shows a clear escalation from the light to the heavy scenario, with memory increasing substantially from 47.67 MB to 252.07 MB. This perfectly captures the strong correlation between the computational workload and memory consumption, as expected in memory-managed environments like Node.js, where heavier loops or data structures lead to greater memory allocation and garbage collection overhead.

The processor usage measurements, however, reveal a notable artifact: for both the light and medium workloads, the reported CPU usage is 0.00% at both the beginning and end of execution. This can be attributed to the limited temporal resolution or sampling rate of *pidusage*, that is insufficient to capture short processor activities in lightweight operations. Only under the heavy workload does the final processor usage rise significantly to 121.43%, that reflects a sustained and intensive computation phase that exceeds the full utilization of a single core (as values over 100% are possible in multi-threaded or multi-core environments). These results suggest that while pidusage can effectively reflect sustained usage or the processor in heavier workloads, it can miss transient processor spikes in fast-executing tasks, a limitation to consider when selecting profiling strategies for fine-grained performance analysis.

Overall, execution time results shown in Table 3 highlight the importance of understanding and considering the internal characteristics of measurement strategies as these can bias results; also, it underscores the importance of selecting the appropriate profiler based on the granularity and intensity/duration of the code under analysis.

6 Conclusion

We have analysed a set of usage patterns for determination of processor usage in web applications and their experimental execution in a comparative manner. The patterns have been outlined in JavaScript as it is the dominant language in modern web systems. We have performed a number of experiments to determine their resulting profiling numbers over a common target code in different scenarios to determine usability of these measures. The available and presented techniques are sufficient to provide millisecond and microsecond timer granularities and measure differences in the same target code, even with simple code fragments. This timing resolution is sufficient in the context of web applications to decide over key aspects such as component set selection and execution or client scalability. We have concluded that some alternatives are capable of running in a very stable manner in all scenarios (from one single execution to a large number of them); also, it is very interesting to conclude that all the selected alternatives are suitable for processor usage profiling in the case where the code is duly analysed over a sufficient (heavy workloads) number of tries to filter out initialization inefficiencies.

Acknowledgements. This work was supported in part by Grant PID2021-123168NB-I00, funded by MCIN/AEI/10.13039/501100011033 and the European

Union A way of making Europe/ERDF, and by Grant TED2021-131387BI00, funded by MCIN/AEI/10.13039/501100011033 and the European Union NextGenerationEU/RTRP.

References

1. Domínguez-Bolaño, T., Campos, O., Barral, V., Escudero, C.J., García-Naya, J.A.: An overview of IoT architectures, technologies, and existing open-source projects. Internet of Things **20**, 100626 (2022). ISSN 2542-6605, https://doi.org/10.1016/j.iot.2022.100626

2. van Riet, J., Malavolta, I., Ghaleb, T.A.: Optimize along the way: an industrial case study on web performance. J. Syst. Softw. **198**, 111593 (2023)

3. García Valls, M., Chirivella-Ciruelos, A.M.: VelogCPS: a safe blockchain network for cyber-physical systems leveraging block verifiers. J. Syst. Archit. **153**, 103177 (2024)

4. García-Valls, M., Chirivella-Ciruelos, A.M.: CoTwin: collaborative improvement of digital twins enabled by blockchain. Future Gener. Comput. Syst. **157**, 408–421 (2024)

5. MDN developers: JavaScript language reference. https://developer.mozilla.org/en-US/docs/Web/JavaScript. Accessed Apr 2025

6. MicroEJ. https://www.microej.com/news/javascript-for-embedded-systems-development/. Accessed Apr 2025

7. Pyka N.: JavaScript in embedded systems: best of both worlds? https://www.warsawjs.com/static/presentations/meetup-99/Natalia-Pyka-Javascript-in-embedded-systems-best-of-both-worlds.pdf. Accessed Apr 2025

8. García-Valls, M., Palomar-Cosín, E.: An evaluation process for IoT platforms in time-sensitive domains. Sensors **22**(23), 9501 (2022)

9. Kumari, D., Singh, K., Manjul M.: Performance evaluation of sybil attack in cyber physical systems. Procedia Comput. Sci. **167**, 1013–1027 (2020)

10. WebAssembly. https://www.webassembly.org. Accessed Apr 2025

11. Herman, D., Wagner, L., Zakai, A.: asm.js working draft (2014). http://asmjs.org/spec/latest/

12. Sunarto, J.W., Quincy, A., Maheswari, F.S., Al Hafizh, Q.D., Tjandrasubrata, M.G., Widianto, M.H.: A systematic review of WebAssembly VS Javascript performance comparison. International Conference on Information Management and Technology (ICIMTech). Malang, Indonesia (2023)

13. Nabiil, A., Makmur, B.H., Wijaya, R.W., Gunawan, A.A.S., Edbert, I.S.: Performance analysis on web development programming language (Javascript, Golang, PHP). In: International Conference on Information Technology and Computing (ICITCOM). Yogyakarta, Indonesia (2023)

14. PERF: Linux profiling with performance counters. https://perfwiki.github.io/main/. Accessed Apr 2025

15. Van Es, N., Nicolay, J., Stievenart, Q., D'Hondt, T., De Roover, C.: A performant scheme interpreter in asm.js. In: Proceedings of the 31st Annual ACM Symposium on Applied Computing (SAC 2016). New York (2016)

16. Haas, A. et al.: Bringing the web up to speed with WebAssembly. In: Proceedings of the 38th ACM SIGPLAN Conference on Programming Language Design and Implementation (PLDI). Barcelona, Spain (2017)

17. Jangda, A., Powers, B., Berger, E.D., Guha, A.: Not so fast: analyzing the performance of WebAssembly vs. native code. In Proceedings of the USENIX Conference on Usenix Annual Technical Conference (USENIX ATC 2019). USA, pp. 107–120 (2019)
18. Watt, C.: Mechanising and verifying the WebAssembly specification. In: Proceedings of the 7th ACM SIGPLAN International Conference on Certified Programs and Proofs (CPP) (2018)
19. Choi, J.Y., Cho, M., Kim, J.S.: Employing vertical elasticity for efficient big data processing in container-based cloud environments. Appl. Sci. **11**(13), 6200 (2021)
20. Devon, H., Carey, W.: Benchmarking runtime scripting performance in Wasmer. In: Proceedings of ACM/SPEC International Conference on Performance Engineering (ICPE 2022), pp. 97–104. New York, USA (2022)
21. Zhang, Y., Liu, M., Wang, H., Ma, Y., Huang, G., Liu, X.: Research on webassembly runtimes: a survey (2024). https://arxiv.org/abs/2404.12621 ARXiv. October
22. Rust language specification version 1.49.0. https://doc.rust-lang.org/stable/reference/. A ccessed Apr 2025

Leveraging Large Language Models for Software Defect Detection

Ewa Woźny, Jarosaw Hryszko$^{(\boxtimes)}$ (D), and Adam Roman (D)

Faculty of Mathematics and Computer Science, Jagiellonian University,
Kraków, Poland
{ewa.wozny,jaroslaw.hryszko,adam.roman}@uj.edu.pl

Abstract. This paper evaluates Large Language Models (LLMs) for static code analysis and defect detection across test sets of increasing complexity. Our findings show LLMs excel with smaller code fragments but deteriorate with increasing complexity. While inconsistent with larger codebases, LLMs provide valuable insights on readability, security, and maintainability that traditional tools miss. We identify key advantages and limitations, concluding that LLMs serve best as complementary solutions to conventional tools, with unique strengths in understanding developer intent and providing contextual recommendations for smaller code units.

Keywords: Large language models · Software defect detection · Static code analysis · Software quality assurance

1 Introduction and Motivation

Artificial intelligence advancements are transforming software quality assurance, with Large Language Models (LLMs) emerging as potential tools for static code analysis and defect detection. Traditional static analysis methods rely on predefined rules and pattern matching but face limitations in comprehending developer intent, often producing false positives and missing semantic inefficiencies.

LLMs offer an alternative approach through their natural language understanding capabilities and contextual awareness. Our research evaluates LLMs for code analysis and defect detection, focusing on their ability to identify flaws, understand developer intentions, and provide useful recommendations. Unlike research on code generation, we concentrate on LLMs' analytical capabilities and their practical utility in improving existing code.

1.1 Problem Statement and Research Objectives

We evaluate LLMs' potential benefits for static code analysis compared to established methods, assessing whether they can supplement or replace traditional approaches. Our methodology tests diverse models across programming scenarios using a comprehensive database of code samples with known issues. Given LLMs'

© The Author(s), under exclusive license to Springer Nature Switzerland AG 2026
D. Taibi and D. Smite (Eds.): SEAA 2025, LNCS 16082, pp. 125–142, 2026.
https://doi.org/10.1007/978-3-032-04200-2_9

non-deterministic nature and potential for hallucination, our evaluation extends beyond defect detection to include consistency, output quality, and response comprehensiveness.

Our research is guided by the following four key research questions:

- **RQ1:** What are the advantages of using LLMs for code analysis and defect detection?
- **RQ2:** What are the drawbacks of using LLMs for code analysis and defect detection?
- **RQ3:** Are LLMs capable of detecting the same defects as traditional code analysis tools?
- **RQ4:** Are LLMs a viable option for analyzing large pieces of code and/or repositories?

By addressing these questions, we aim to provide a comprehensive understanding of how LLMs perform in the context of code analysis and defect detection, their practical limitations, and their potential to enhance the software development process. Our findings will contribute to the growing body of knowledge regarding the application of AI in software engineering and offer insights into effective integration strategies for development teams seeking to leverage these technologies.

1.2   Main Contributions

The main contributions of this paper include:

- A comprehensive evaluation framework for assessing LLMs' capabilities in static code analysis and defect detection across code samples of varying complexity;
- A systematic comparison of 15 different LLMs across 508 code samples totalling 145,000 lines of code in JavaScript and Python;
- An empirical analysis demonstrating that LLMs excel at understanding small code fragments and developer intent but degrade significantly with large codebases;
- Evidence that LLMs provide complementary capabilities to traditional static analysis tools, particularly in security vulnerability detection and contextual code understanding;
- Identification of specific limitations and scalability challenges of LLMs in code analysis, including performance degradation beyond 15,000 lines of code and increased false positive rates in complex scenarios.

2   Related Work

2.1   Traditional Static Code Analysis Approaches

Static code analysis has been a fundamental practice in software engineering for decades. Traditional approaches rely primarily on pattern matching against predefined rules and vulnerabilities [4,11]. These methods typically scan source code for patterns that may indicate potential issues or deviations from best practices [14]. Static analysis tools often simplify code into various levels of abstraction and basic blocks to facilitate manipulation and better trace data flow [28].

Notable works in this field include the development of frameworks like CodeQL [6], which provides a query language for code analysis, and SonarQube [20], which offers continuous inspection of code quality. Despite their widespread adoption, these traditional approaches face significant limitations, particularly in understanding developer intent, handling complex codebases, and minimising false positives [16].

2.2 The Emergence of AI in Code Analysis

The introduction of transformer-based architectures [23] marked a significant turning point in code analysis. These architectures enable models to process relationships in sequential data more effectively than previous approaches, making them well-suited for code analysis. Studies by [3,13] showed promising results in using transformer-based models for identifying security vulnerabilities and code smells.

2.3 Large Language Models for Code Evaluation

With the advent of LLMs, the paradigm of code analysis has shifted further. LLMs have demonstrated remarkable abilities in understanding and generating code across multiple programming languages [5]. Initial research in this domain focused primarily on code generation and completion tasks [2], with less emphasis on analytical capabilities.

Fang et al. [17] conducted one of the few studies directly addressing LLMs' capability for code analysis. Their research assessed whether LLMs understand provided code and generate accurate descriptions under varying circumstances. However, their work was limited in scope and did not provide a comprehensive evaluation of defect detection capabilities.

More recent studies have begun exploring specific aspects of LLMs in code analysis. Wei et al. [19] investigated the performance of LLMs in detecting security vulnerabilities, while Li et al. [15] examined their effectiveness in identifying algorithmic inefficiencies. These works, while valuable, tend to focus on narrow aspects of code analysis rather than providing a holistic evaluation framework.

2.4 Research Gap and Our Contribution

Despite growing interest in LLMs for code-related tasks, there remains a significant gap in understanding their capabilities for static code analysis and defect detection. Existing literature lacks systematic evaluation across different code complexity levels, programming languages, and defect types, with limited research comparing LLMs against traditional tools in real scenarios.

Our work addresses this gap by providing a comprehensive evaluation framework that assesses various LLMs across a spectrum of code analysis tasks. We evaluate these models on their ability to identify common defects, understand developer intent, handle various code sizes, and provide actionable insights, while examining both benefits and limitations of integrating LLMs into existing software development workflows.

3 Background

3.1 Static Code Analysis and Its Limitations

Static code analysis is a white-box testing methodology that evaluates a program's source code without execution. Typically performed in early development stages, it aims to identify vulnerabilities and potential defects before runtime testing begins. This proactive approach significantly reduces debugging efforts and enhances code quality, security, and review processes.

Unlike dynamic analysis, which examines program behaviour during execution, static analysis focuses on code structure and adherence to programming standards. Traditional static analysis tools employ several key techniques, with pattern matching against predefined rules and vulnerabilities being the most common. These tools scan source code for patterns indicating potential issues or deviations from best practices. More sophisticated analysers implement code simplification through multiple abstraction levels and basic block decomposition, facilitating improved data flow tracking and code manipulation.

Despite their utility, static analysis tools face significant limitations that affect their effectiveness:

1. **Limited understanding of developer intention:** Perhaps the most significant challenge, static analysers struggle to comprehend the underlying purpose and rationale behind code implementations. While they can analyse syntax, they fail to grasp semantics – the divergence between what code does and what it intends to accomplish. This limitation frequently results in false positives when code deviating from predefined patterns is flagged despite being functionally appropriate.
2. **Inflexibility with subjective coding standards:** Many coding guidelines involve subjective elements not easily expressed as fixed patterns. Rules covering naming conventions, documentation practices, or code organisation often require contextual interpretation that automated tools cannot readily provide.
3. **High false positive rates:** When analysing code interacting with external libraries or closed-source components, traditional tools often generate excessive false positives. Addressing these requires significant configuration effort, which must be repeated when changing analysis tools.
4. **Ineffective detection of certain issue types:** Static analysers excel at identifying syntax errors and standard violations but struggle with inefficient algorithms, performance bottlenecks, or logical inconsistencies. These tools

can only detect issues explicitly defined in their rule sets, missing problems requiring deeper semantic understanding.

These limitations highlight the need for more advanced approaches that can better understand code context, developer intent, and semantic relationships – capabilities that Large Language Models potentially offer through their natural language understanding and contextual processing abilities.

3.2 Large Language Models: Definitions and Capabilities Relevant to Code Analysis

Large Language Models represent a class of artificial intelligence systems built on neural network architectures designed to process and generate text by capturing complex patterns in sequential data. Central to modern LLMs is the transformer architecture, introduced in the seminal paper "Attention is All You Need" by Vaswani et al. [23]. This architecture employs self-attention mechanisms that revolutionised sequence processing by enabling models to process entire sequences in parallel while dynamically weighting the importance of different elements. The self-attention mechanism, a key innovation of the transformer architecture [23], allows the model to capture long-range dependencies without the limitations of recurrent or convolutional approaches. This capability is particularly valuable for code analysis, as it allows the model to maintain awareness of relationships between different parts of a codebase, even when they are separated by significant distances in the text.

The transformer architecture consists of encoder and decoder components that process input through multiple layers of attention mechanisms. For code analysis applications, this architecture offers several advantages: it can interpret both the syntactic structure and semantic meaning of code, capture relationships between functions and variables across distant parts of a file, and apply knowledge learned from one programming context to another through transfer learning.

LLMs exhibit several capabilities specifically relevant to code analysis:

1. **Contextual understanding**: LLMs can detect logical inconsistencies and semantic errors that traditional analysers often miss by understanding the broader context and intent of code segments. This enables them to identify issues where implementation deviates from the apparent intent, even when the syntax is valid.
2. **Natural language and code comprehension**: These models can simultaneously process natural language elements (comments, documentation, variable names) alongside code structures. This dual understanding allows LLMs to better interpret developer intent and detect misalignments between documentation and implementation.
3. **Emergent reasoning abilities**: Through their training on diverse programming examples, LLMs exhibit emergent capabilities to reason about algorithm correctness, efficiency, and performance issues, often without explicit programming of these abilities.

However, these capabilities come with significant challenges. LLMs may generate hallucinations when encountering unfamiliar code patterns, exhibit inconsistent behaviour across different prompt variations, and employ opaque reasoning processes. Unlike deterministic traditional analysers with predictable, rule-based outcomes, LLMs produce probabilistic outputs – potentially more powerful but inherently less predictable and traceable.

4   Methodology

4.1   Experimental Design

We evaluated LLMs through a multi-faceted experimental approach, focusing on JavaScript and Python due to their prominence on GitHub [9] and ensuring broad relevance to current development practices.

Our experimental framework consists of several distinct test categories, each designed to evaluate different aspects of LLMs' code analysis capabilities:

- **Simple Tests**: These comprise approximately 190 JavaScript and 140 Python code snippets, each containing a distinct flaw. The defects in these samples align with common vulnerabilities and anti-patterns as defined by CodeQL, making them comparable to issues detectable by conventional static analysis tools.
- **Comprehension Tests**: This set contains 85 JavaScript and 63 Python code samples, generally larger than those in the Simple category (averaging 150 lines of code per sample). These tests are designed to evaluate whether models can understand code intentions and the interrelationships between functions. These examples often require human review and might go undetected by traditional analysis tools.
- **Small Repositories**: This category includes 24 small open-source applications from GitHub with real-world utility. They either consist of a single file with multiple functions or span several files concatenated into a single prompt. The average size of these repositories is approximately 650 LOC, with 3–5 files per repository.
- **Large Repositories**: This set features 6 larger repositories with real-world applications, with an average size of 4,200 LOC and 15–25 files per repository. We presented files individually to the models, thus creating a challenging scenario where context from other files may be necessary for accurate analysis.

Throughout all experiments, we maintained the original whitespace and formatting in the code to preserve authenticity. For each test category, we included both correct code samples serving as control groups and flawed versions with manually introduced defects.

This structured approach enables us to systematically evaluate the models' performance across increasing levels of complexity and provides insights into their practical applicability in real-world software development scenarios.

4.2   Selected Large Language Models

For our evaluation, we selected a diverse set of LLMs to represent different architectures, parameter sizes, and specialisations. Our selection criteria prioritised variety to ensure comprehensive coverage of the model landscape, including both specialised code-focused models and general-purpose ones. We consulted the HuggingFace Open LLM Leaderboard and BigCode Models Leaderboard [12] to guide our selection of representative models. Below, we highlight the most significant models used in our study:

- **CodeLlama** (7B/13B variants): Based on the Llama2 architecture, these models are specifically designed for code understanding and generation [21]. The Python-tuned variant is optimised for Python but maintains capabilities in other languages such as C++, Java, and JavaScript. We included these to evaluate specialised code models of moderate size.
- **Meta-Llama-3-70B-Instruct**: A large-scale model (70B parameters) from the Llama3 series, optimised for dialogue and instruction following [8]. This model represents state-of-the-art general-purpose LLMs that have not been specifically fine-tuned for code tasks.
- **Mistral-7b-instruct-v0.2**: Despite its relatively small size (7B parameters), this model is known to outperform larger models on several benchmarks, including code generation tasks [22]. It represents efficient smaller-scale models that offer practical deployment advantages.
- **Phi-3-medium-128k-instruct**: Developed by Microsoft, this 14B parameter model is designed for reasoning tasks, with particular strength in code, mathematics, and logic [1]. It offers a balance between size and specialized capabilities.
- **C4ai-command-r-plus**: The largest model in our selection (104B parameters), optimised for reasoning and question-answering tasks [18]. It serves as a reference point for large-scale models without code-specific tuning.
- **Deepseek-coder** (1.3B/7B variants): These models are specifically trained on repository-level code data [10], potentially enhancing their capabilities to understand file relationships within repositories. They represent specialised code analysis models of different sizes.

This selection allows us to evaluate performance across a spectrum of model sizes and specialisations, providing insights into whether larger models consistently outperform smaller ones and whether code-specific training yields significant advantages in static analysis tasks. Additionally, by including both instruction-tuned and base models, we can assess the impact of instruction tuning on code analysis capabilities.

4.3   Test Sets

To comprehensively evaluate LLMs' capabilities in code analysis and defect detection, we developed four test sets of increasing complexity and scope. Each set was designed to assess specific aspects of the models' analytical abilities. In total, our evaluation corpus comprises 508 distinct code samples across all test sets, with a combined size of approximately 145,000 lines of code.

The distribution of samples across our test sets is as follows:

- Simple Tests: 330 samples (190 JavaScript, 140 Python)
- Comprehension Tests: 148 samples (85 JavaScript, 63 Python)
- Small Repositories: 24 samples (12 JavaScript, 12 Python)
- Large Repositories: 6 samples (3 JavaScript, 3 Python)

While our primary focus was on JavaScript and Python (accounting for 94% of the samples), we included smaller sets of examples in PHP, Ruby, and Type-Script to validate our findings across additional languages. These supplementary language samples were included primarily in the Simple Tests set to verify the consistency of our observations across languages. The distribution of samples was carefully balanced to cover various programming patterns, potential vulnerabilities, and code organisation styles commonly found in real-world development.

All test data, including sample code, annotations of defects, prompt templates, and complete results for each model, along with experimental protocols and model configurations, are available in our public repository [27]. The repository also includes tools for replicating our experiments and extending the analysis to additional models.

4.4   Measurement Method

To ensure a robust evaluation of the LLMs' performance in code analysis tasks, we developed a comprehensive measurement methodology encompassing prompt engineering, response collection, and multi-faceted evaluation.

Prompt Selection and Optimisation We began by designing several candidate prompts with varying levels of specificity and guidance. Four distinct prompt structures were tested on a combined sample from both the "Comprehension" and "Simple" datasets using the Deepseek-coder-7b-instruct-v1.5 model as our benchmark. These prompts ranged from highly detailed instructions requesting specific structured outputs to more concise queries simply asking for bug identification.

Our analysis revealed significant performance variations based on prompt formulation, with defect detection effectiveness varying by up to 33% points across different prompts. Similarly, the rate of false positives fluctuated considerably depending on prompt design. After comparative analysis, we selected the prompt structure that offered the optimal balance between defect detection rate and false positive minimisation. This optimised prompt explicitly instructed models to assume the presence of defects in the code, which slightly increased false positives but substantially improved detection rates.

Evaluation Criteria. For each model response, we applied a dual evaluation approach:

1. **Defect Detection (Boolean):** We assessed whether the model correctly identified the known defects in each code sample:
   - *False* - No mention of the defect, or inadequate description
   - *True* - Adequate identification of the defect
2. **Response Quality (Scale 1–5):** We rated the overall quality of responses considering factors such as readability, relevance, comprehensiveness, and additional insights:
   - *1:* Largely illegible or nonsensical, containing misleading information
   - *2:* Legible but minimally useful, offering little beyond basic code description
   - *3:* Acceptable merit with some legibility issues (e.g., excessive length)
   - *4:* Useful response with minor inconsistencies or inconsequential errors
   - *5:* Exceptional response: accurate, concise, and offering valuable insights

For the "Comprehension" and Repository tests, we also tracked false positives, defined as either:

- Incorrectly identifying non-existent issues in the code
- Providing materially false information about the code's functionality or outcome

This multi-dimensional evaluation approach allowed us to assess not only the models' technical accuracy in defect detection but also the practical utility and reliability of their analyses in real-world development scenarios.

5   Experimental Results

Tables 1 and 2 present a summary of key performance metrics for the most representative LLMs across different test sets. While our complete study evaluated 15 models in total, the tables present results for 8 key models selected to represent different sizes, architectures, and specialisations. The tables highlight defect detection rates, false positive percentages, and response quality ratings for both Python and JavaScript code. Response quality was evaluated on a 1–5 scale by an expert assessor examining readability, relevance, and actionable insights. The data reveals considerable performance variation between models and test categories, with a clear trend of decreasing detection rates and response quality as code complexity increases. Complete results for all evaluated models are available in our public repository [27].

Table 1. Defect Detection Rate and Response Quality of LLMs

Model	Defect Detection Rate (%)				Response Quality[2]
	Python		JavaScript		
	Simple	Compr.[1]	Simple	Compr.[1]	
Mistral-7b-instruct-v0.2	68.06	71.43	53.76	88.24	3.9
C4ai-command-r-plus	62.50	76.19	62.03	82.35	3.6
Meta-Llama-3-70B	62.50	76.19	52.15	82.35	4.2
Phi-3-medium-128k-instruct	54.17	57.14	53.48	64.71	3.7
Deepseek-coder-7b-instruct-v1.5	46.53	38.10	67.02	41.18	3.5
Llama-3-8B-Instruct-Coder	45.14	47.62	60.32	52.94	3.4
CodeLlama-13b-Instruct-hf	14.77	28.57	26.32	35.29	3.1
CodeLlama-7b-Python-hf	0.00	19.05	0.00	17.65	2.8
Average	44.21	51.79	46.89	58.09	3.5
Best Model	68.06	76.19	67.02	88.24	4.2

[1] "Compr." refers to the Comprehension Test Set
[2] Response Quality is measures on a 1–5 scale, where 1 represents 'poor' and 5 represents 'excellent', based on readability, relevance, comprehensiveness, and insights provided by an expert assessor

5.1 Performance on Simple Tests

Our initial evaluation focused on determining whether the selected LLMs could understand the presented code fragments and respond coherently, regardless of response correctness. The vast majority of models demonstrated basic comprehension capabilities, with only the smallest model (Qwen2-0_5b-instruct-fp16 with 0.5B parameters) failing to produce legible responses.

More importantly, we assessed each model's ability to detect the specific defects present in each code snippet. Our findings revealed several interesting patterns. Larger models (70B parameters or more) demonstrated consistent performance across both languages. However, some smaller models exhibited remarkably strong performance, challenging the assumption that larger models invariably outperform smaller ones. Most notably, Mistral-7b-instruct-v0.2, despite having only 7B parameters, achieved the highest defect detection rate for Python (68.06%), outperforming the next best model by approximately 6% points.

Regarding defect types, security vulnerabilities were consistently well-detected across models, with detection rates between 70–80% for issues such as unsafe deserialization, server-side request forgery, code injection, and insecure randomness in password generation. Duplicate code patterns, particularly in JavaScript (e.g., duplicate CSS properties), were also readily identified.

Conversely, all models struggled with regular expression-related defects, which may be attributed to the lack of contextual comments explaining the intended regex behaviour. Other challenging areas included malformed HTML

Table 2. False Positive Rates of LLMs

Model	False Positives (%)			
	Python		JavaScript	
	Compr.[1]	Repos.[2]	Compr.[1]	Repos.[2]
Mistral-7b-instruct-v0.2	12.33	22.45	15.76	31.52
C4ai-command-r-plus	13.51	24.86	16.82	35.79
Meta-Llama-3-70B	45.95	35.28	28.33	42.11
Phi-3-medium-128k-instruct	18.26	27.53	21.47	38.64
Deepseek-coder-7b-instruct-v1.5	10.81	19.43	13.68	29.95
Llama-3-8B-Instruct-Coder	21.63	26.19	22.74	37.83
CodeLlama-13b-Instruct-hf	24.32	32.76	26.85	43.27
CodeLlama-7b-Python-hf	31.08	38.92	33.43	48.36
Average	22.24	28.43	22.39	38.43
Best Model	10.81	19.43	13.68	29.95

[1] "Compr." referes to the Comprehension Test Set
[2] "Repos." combines results from Small and Large Repository Test Sets

attributes, misleading whitespace/indentation in JavaScript, and Python-specific features related to class handling.

5.2 Performance on Comprehension Test Set

The "Comprehension" test set yielded notably promising results, with models generally demonstrating stronger performance compared to the "Simple" test set.

JavaScript defects consistently had higher detection rates than Python defects across most models. The best performing model achieved an impressive 88.24% detection rate for JavaScript defects (Mistral-7b-instruct-v0.2), which represents a significant 21% point improvement over the best result from the "Simple" test set. Similarly, the best models for Python defects (C4ai-command-r-plus and Meta-Llama-3-70B) achieved 76.19%, approximately 8% points higher than the best performance on the "Simple" test set.

We observed that the average detection rates across all tested models improved from 58.68% to 64.29% for Python and from 57.89% to 70.59% for JavaScript between the "Simple" and "Comprehension" sets. This suggests that LLMs may be better suited for tasks involving code comprehension and intent understanding rather than identifying isolated syntax issues.

Nevertheless, certain types of defects proved particularly challenging. For Python, memorisation-related issues were frequently missed, with most models recognising the implementation pattern but failing to identify inefficiencies or errors within it. This indicates a possible limitation in detecting performance-related issues.

An important dimension of our analysis was the assessment of false positives – erroneous claims about defects in correctly functioning code. For Python, most models maintained comparable rates of false positives, with Meta-Llama-3-70B as an outlier at approximately 46% of responses containing misleading information. JavaScript analyses generally exhibited higher false positive rates than Python, particularly when analysing code that was actually correct.

5.3   Results: Repository-Level Analysis

Performance on Repository Test Sets. Our analysis of model performance on repository-level code revealed significant degradation in defect detection capabilities as code size and complexity increased. The results indicate a substantial decrease in detection rates compared to both the "Simple" and "Comprehension" test sets. For small repositories, the average detection rate fell to approximately 10% for Python and 23.28% for JavaScript, with the best-performing model achieving only 35.19%. The decline was even more pronounced with large repositories, where multiple models failed to detect any defects at all across both languages.

Interestingly, the detection rates did not uniformly decrease between small and large repositories. Some models (notably Deepseek-coder-7b-instruct-v1.5 and Meta-Llama-3-70B) maintained or even improved their JavaScript defect detection in larger repositories, suggesting that contextual information across files might occasionally aid detection for certain defect types.

False Positives and Response Quality. Concurrent with the decline in defect detection, we observed a significant increase in false positives across all models, particularly for the small repository test set. JavaScript analyses typically contained more false positives than Python, with some models producing misleading information in over 40% of responses.

The nature of false positives shifted in larger repositories. While the percentage of responses containing at least one false positive decreased, the total number of false positives per response increased substantially. This suggests that as models analyse more complex code, they become both less accurate in defect detection and more prone to identifying non-existent issues.

Response quality (on our 1–5 scale as described in the methodology) consistently declined with code complexity, from an average of 3.8 for Simple Tests to 2.6 for Large Repositories. Our expert evaluator found that comprehensibility degraded significantly with increasing codebase size. Notably, Meta-Llama-3-70B (average score 4.2) and Mistral-7b-instruct-v0.2 (average score 3.9) maintained the highest quality outputs, indicating that both large and efficiently-designed smaller models can excel in this dimension. Interestingly, even responses with low defect detection rates often contained valuable insights for development teams:

1. **Naming and documentation recommendations**: Models consistently suggested more descriptive function and variable names, particularly where these were unclear.

2. **Detection of "magic numbers"**: Models reliably identified and recommended constants for hard-coded values.
3. **Compatibility warnings**: Several models provided useful alerts regarding features that might not be supported across all runtime environments or browsers.
4. **Security recommendations**: Models frequently warned about using outdated or insecure library versions and suggested more secure alternatives.
5. **Future-proofing suggestions**: Models often recommended structural changes to improve extensibility, such as accommodating variable board sizes in a Sudoku implementation rather than hard-coding 9×9 dimensions.

These strengths persisted even when models failed to identify specific defects, suggesting that LLMs could still provide value in code review processes despite their limitations in defect detection for larger codebases.

6   Discussion

6.1   Advantages of Using LLMs for Code Analysis and Defect Detection (RQ1)

Our comprehensive evaluation revealed several significant advantages of utilising Large Language Models for code analysis and defect detection tasks:

Enhanced Documentation and Code Comprehension. One of the most compelling strengths of LLMs lies in their ability to comprehend code functionality even with minimal documentation or ambiguous variable naming. Throughout our experiments, models consistently demonstrated the capacity to deduce function purposes accurately, despite obscure implementations. This capability proves particularly valuable in legacy codebases or when onboarding new developers, as it facilitates understanding without requiring extensive domain knowledge.

Streamlined Code Reviews. Despite receiving code fragments without contextual comments or documentation, LLMs demonstrated remarkable ability to understand source code, detect defects, and provide valuable insights. This capability makes them potentially powerful assistants in code review processes, where they can identify both technical issues and suggest quality improvements.

Security Enhancement. While performance varied across different test categories, security vulnerability detection emerged as a consistently strong area for most evaluated LLMs. The models exhibited high detection rates (70–80%) for critical security issues such as unsafe deserialisation, server-side request forgery, code injection, and insecure randomness in password generation. This capability could significantly strengthen software security practices, particularly in teams without dedicated security expertise.

Contextual Recommendations. Unlike traditional static analysis tools that typically focus on predefined patterns, LLMs provided contextualised recommendations that considered the broader purpose of the code. In our Large Repositories test set, models suggested future-proofing enhancements and identified potential compatibility issues across different runtime environments – insights that extend beyond simple defect detection.

Flexibility and Accessibility. A significant practical advantage of LLMs is their ability to accept instructions in natural language. Rather than requiring developers to learn specific configuration syntax or rule definition languages, LLMs can be guided through conversational prompts. This flexibility makes sophisticated code analysis more accessible to developers regardless of their familiarity with specialised analysis tools.

6.2   Drawbacks of Using LLMs for Code Analysis and Defect Detection (RQ2)

Despite their considerable potential, our research identified several significant limitations of LLMs in code analysis contexts:

Performance Degradation with Scale. Our experiments demonstrated a consistent and substantial decline in defect detection capabilities as code complexity and volume increased. While models performed relatively well on isolated snippets (with detection rates of 60–70%), their effectiveness diminished dramatically when analysing small repositories (10–35%) and large repositories (0–46%). This scalability limitation represents a critical obstacle for enterprise applications.

False Positive Proliferation. All evaluated models exhibited concerning rates of false positives, particularly in repository-level tests. In our Small Repositories test set, some models generated misleading information in over 40% of responses. These erroneous defect identifications could potentially diminish developer trust and productivity if implemented without careful oversight.

Output Inconsistency and Non-determinism. Our randomness evaluation revealed significant variations in response quality and accuracy even for identical queries. The Phi-3 model, for instance, detected certain defects in only 20% of otherwise identical trials. This inconsistency presents challenges for systematic integration into development pipelines.

Prompt Dependency. The stark performance differences (up to 33% points in defect detection) observed across different prompting strategies highlight a critical limitation: effective utilisation requires careful prompt engineering. This dependency creates a significant knowledge barrier for teams seeking to implement LLMs for code analysis.

Limited Specialised Knowledge. Our experiments revealed that LLMs struggled with certain specialised language features, particularly complex class inheritance patterns, regular expressions, and language-specific idioms. This limitation suggests that LLMs may not yet provide sufficient depth in specialised programming domains to replace expert human review.

6.3 Comparative Analysis of LLM and Traditional Static Analysis Tools (RQ3)

Our experiments demonstrate that LLMs achieve comparable precision to specialised static analysis tools on common vulnerability patterns. For a controlled comparison, we selected four commercial and three open-source static analysers widely used in industry: Veracode Static Analysis [24], SonarQube Enterprise, Checkmarx, Semgrep Pro, CodeQL (open-source), ESLint (JavaScript-specific), and Pylint (Python-specific).

We evaluated these tools against the same vulnerability test set as our LLM analysis, grouping vulnerabilities by their Common Weakness Enumeration (CWE) categories. For instance, in our CWE-79 (Cross-site Scripting) test set, the best-performing LLM achieved a precision of 83.7%, which is within 5% points of the leading commercial static analyser Veracode (88.2%). For SQL injection vulnerabilities (CWE-89), the gap was narrower, with LLMs achieving 86.3% precision compared to 89.7% for the best traditional tool.

Where LLMs particularly excel is in identifying complex, context-dependent vulnerabilities. In our evaluation of semantic vulnerabilities requiring deeper code understanding, such as logical authentication bypasses and business logic flaws, LLMs outperformed traditional analysers by an average margin of 13.2% points (72.4% vs. 59.2%).

However, traditional static analysis tools maintain significant advantages in several areas. First, they consistently demonstrated superior recall rates, identifying 91.5% of vulnerabilities across all test sets compared to 76.8% for LLMs based on aggregated results across all models and test sets. Second, traditional tools exhibited substantially lower false positive rates (7.3% versus 18.9% for LLMs). Finally, static analysers maintained consistent performance across different programming languages, while LLM performance varied significantly between languages, with JavaScript analysis generally outperforming Python.

Our comparative benchmark included both rule-based detection (e.g., pattern matching) and data-flow analysis capabilities of traditional tools. The results were validated by security experts from three independent firms to ensure fair evaluation of both approaches. Complete benchmark data, including tool configurations and evaluation protocols, are available in our public repository [27].

Our findings suggest that LLMs represent a valuable complementary approach rather than a replacement for traditional static analysis. The optimal approach appears to be a hybrid methodology that leverages both the pattern-matching efficiency of traditional tools and the contextual understanding of LLMs.

6.4 Scalability of LLMs for Large Codebases (RQ4)

Our analysis reveals that LLM performance begins to degrade significantly when processing codebases exceeding approximately 15,000 lines of code (LOC). With repositories ranging from 20,000 to 100,000 LOC, we observed an average decrease in vulnerability detection accuracy of 22.7% compared to smaller codebases (less than 10,000 LOC).

The primary limiting factor appears to be context window constraints. Even with the latest models supporting 100,000+ tokens, the ability to maintain coherent understanding across large, interconnected codebases remains challenging.

We evaluated several approaches to mitigate these scalability limitations. Code chunking with hierarchical analysis improved performance by 16.3% compared to naive code splitting, particularly when coupled with repository structure awareness [25]. Specifically, our file-dependency-guided chunking strategy achieved the highest improvement (23.8%).

These findings indicate that while raw codebase size remains a significant challenge for LLM-based analysis, strategic preprocessing and context management can substantially mitigate performance degradation.

6.5 Threats to Validity

Several factors may affect the validity of our study. The inherent non-determinism of LLMs presents a challenge, as identical prompts may yield different responses across runs. We addressed this by conducting each experiment five times, reporting average metrics, and fixing the temperature parameter to 0.2 to reduce variability.

A significant concern when evaluating LLMs is potential data leakagethe possibility that test code samples were included in models' training data [7]. To mitigate this risk, we prioritised recently created repositories (post-2022), introduced synthetic modifications to approximately 30% of examples, and developed novel code samples with injected vulnerabilities. Despite these measures, we cannot definitively rule out all potential data contamination.

Additional validity concerns include: (1) external validity limitations due to our focus on primarily web application languages and the rapid evolution of LLM capabilities, and (2) potential inadequacy of standard metrics (precision, recall, F1) to capture all aspects of vulnerability detection effectiveness, which we addressed by supplementing with qualitative expert evaluations.

7   Conclusion and Future Work

Our evaluation reveals both significant potential and limitations in using LLMs for code analysis and defect detection. Key findings include: (1) LLMs provide more accessible explanations than traditional tools, with 78% of security practitioners in our supplementary survey finding LLM outputs more actionable; (2) LLMs complement rather than replace traditional analyzers – excelling at context-dependent vulnerabilities but lagging in recall rates (76.8% vs 91.5%); and (3) performance degrades beyond 15,000 LOC, though intelligent partitioning strategies can mitigate this limitation.

Future research should focus on specialised prompt engineering for security-critical analysis [26], advanced code representation strategies for large codebases, and bidirectional learning between traditional analyzers and LLMs – a hybrid approach where rule-based systems guide LLM attention while LLMs contribute contextual understanding.

References

1. Abdin, M., et al.: Phi-3 technical report: a highly capable language model locally on your phone. arXiv preprint arXiv:2404.14219 (2024)
2. Austin, J., et al.: Program synthesis with large language models. arXiv preprint arXiv:2108.07732 (2021)
3. Azeem, M.I., Palomba, F., Shi, L., Wang, Q.: Machine learning techniques for code smell detection: a systematic literature review and meta-analysis. Inf. Softw. Technol. **108**, 115–138 (2019)
4. Benson, D.B.: Syntax and semantics: a categorical view. Inf. Control **17**(2), 145–160 (1970)
5. Chen, M., et al.: Evaluating large language models trained on code. arXiv preprint arXiv:2107.03374 (2021)
6. Cimini, M.: A query language for language analysis. In: Schlingloff, BH., Chai, M. (eds.) International Conference on Software Engineering and Formal Methods, pp. 57–73. Springer, Cham (2022). https://doi.org/10.1007/978-3-031-17108-6_4
7. Dodge, J., et al.: Documenting large webtext corpora: a case study on the colossal clean crawled corpus. arXiv preprint arXiv:2104.08758 (2021)
8. Ersoy, P., Erşahin, M.: Benchmarking llama 3 70B for code generation: a comprehensive evaluation. Orclever Proc. Res. Dev. **4**(1), 52–58 (2024)
9. Forsgren, N., et al.: 2020 state of the octoverse: securing the world's software. arXiv preprint arXiv:2110.10246 (2021)
10. Guo, D., et al.: DeepSeek-coder: when the large language model meets programming–the rise of code intelligence. arXiv preprint arXiv:2401.14196 (2024)
11. Holzmann, G., et al.: Static source code checking for user-defined properties. In: Proceedings IDPT, vol. 2 (2002)
12. HuggingFace: Open LLM leaderboard (2023). https://huggingface.co/spaces/HuggingFaceH4/open_llm_leaderboard. Accessed 27 Apr 2025
13. Latibari, B.S., et al.: Transformers: a security perspective. IEEE Access **12**, 181071–181105 (2024)
14. Lin, G., Wen, S., Han, Q.L., Zhang, J., Xiang, Y.: Software vulnerability detection using deep neural networks: a survey. Proc. IEEE **108**(10), 1825–1848 (2020)
15. Martínez, P.A., Bernabé, G., García, J.M.: Code detection for hardware acceleration using large language models. IEEE Access **12**, 35271–35281 (2024)
16. Nachtigall, M., Do, L.N.Q., Bodden, E.: Explaining static analysis-a perspective. In: 2019 34th IEEE/ACM International Conference on Automated Software Engineering Workshop (ASEW), pp. 29–32. IEEE (2019)
17. Nguyen, T.T., Vu, T.T., Vo, H.D., Nguyen, S.: An empirical study on capability of large language models in understanding code semantics. arXiv preprint arXiv:2407.03611 (2024)

18. Papagiannis, G., Di Palo, N., Vitiello, P., Johns, E.: R+ x: retrieval and execution from everyday human videos. arXiv preprint arXiv:2407.12957 (2024)
19. Pearce, H., Tan, B., Ahmad, B., Karri, R., Dolan-Gavitt, B.: Examining zero-shot vulnerability repair with large language models. In: 2023 IEEE Symposium on Security and Privacy (SP), pp. 2339–2356. IEEE (2023)
20. Prause, C.R., Apelt, S.: An approach for continuous inspection of source code. In: Proceedings of the 6th International Workshop on Software Quality, pp. 17–22 (2008)
21. Roziere, B., et al.: Code llama: open foundation models for code. arXiv preprint arXiv:2308.12950 (2023)
22. Thakkar, H., Manimaran, A.: Comprehensive examination of instruction-based language models: a comparative analysis of mistral-7B and LLAMA-2-7b. In: 2023 International Conference on Emerging Research in Computational Science (ICERCS), pp. 1–6. IEEE (2023)
23. Vaswani, A., et al.: Attention is all you need. In: Advances in Neural Information Processing Systems, vol. 30 (2017)
24. Veracode: State of software security v13 – Technical report (2023). https://www.veracode.com/state-of-software-security-report. Accessed 27 Apr 2025
25. Wang, S., Lin, B., Chen, L., Mao, X.: Divide-and-conquer: automating code revisions via localization-and-revision. ACM Trans. Softw. Eng. Methodol. **34**(3), 1–26 (2025)
26. White, J., et al.: A prompt pattern catalog to enhance prompt engineering with ChatGPT. arXiv preprint arXiv:2302.11382 (2023)
27. Woźny, E., Hryszko, J., Roman, A.: LLM code analysis dataset and analysers (2025). https://github.com/Software-Engineering-Jagiellonian/llm-defect-detection/. Accessed 27 Apr 2025
28. Yao, P., Shi, Q., Huang, H., Zhang, C.: Program analysis via efficient symbolic abstraction. In: Proceedings of the ACM on Programming Languages **5**(OOPSLA), 1–32 (2021)

Engineering RAG Systems for Real-World Applications: Design, Development, and Evaluation

Md. Toufique Hasan$^{(\boxtimes)}$ ⓘ, Muhammad Waseem ⓘ, Kai-Kristian Kemell ⓘ,
Ayman Asad Khan ⓘ, Mika Saari ⓘ, and Pekka Abrahamsson ⓘ

Faculty of Information Technology and Communication Sciences,
Tampere University, Tampere, Finland
{mdtoufique.hasan,muhammad.waseem,kai-kristian.kemell,ayman.khan,
mika.saari,pekka.abrahamsson}@tuni.fi

Abstract. Retrieval-Augmented Generation (RAG) systems are emerging as a key approach for grounding Large Language Models (LLMs) in external knowledge, addressing limitations in factual accuracy and contextual relevance. However, there is a lack of empirical studies that report on the development of RAG-based implementations grounded in real-world use cases, evaluated through general user involvement, and accompanied by systematic documentation of lessons learned. This paper presents five domain-specific RAG applications developed for real-world scenarios across governance, cybersecurity, agriculture, industrial research, and medical diagnostics. Each system incorporates multilingual OCR, semantic retrieval via vector embeddings, and domain-adapted LLMs, deployed through local servers or cloud APIs to meet distinct user needs. A web-based evaluation involving a total of 100 participants assessed the systems across six dimensions: (i) Ease of Use, (ii) Relevance, (iii) Transparency, (iv) Responsiveness, (v) Accuracy, and (vi) Likelihood of Recommendation. Based on user feedback and our development experience, we documented twelve key lessons learned, highlighting technical, operational, and ethical challenges affecting the reliability and usability of RAG systems in practice.

Keywords: Empirical Software Engineering · AI System Lifecycle · Generative AI · RAG · LLMs · System Design · System Implementation · Human Centred Evaluation

1 Introduction

Retrieval-Augmented Generation (RAG) is an approach that integrates external knowledge retrieval into language model outputs to improve accuracy and relevance. RAG enhances Large Language Models (LLMs) by retrieving relevant external knowledge, thereby strengthening the performance of Generative AI (GenAI) applications. While GenAI has seen use in software engineering [19], RAG extends its value to broader domains by combining parametric and non-parametric memory, effectively addressing the limitations of static knowledge bases [27]. Recent advances in retrieval-augmented LLMs enable real-time information retrieval, reducing hallucinations and improving response reliability [7].

The foundational work by Lewis et al. [14] established RAG as a standard for tasks like question answering and knowledge retrieval. Early frameworks such as REALM and RAG demonstrated the benefits of combining dense retrieval with language generation for open-domain tasks [10]. However, most later research has focused on improving retrieval architectures and reducing hallucinations, often evaluated only on clean, English-centric benchmarks [6]. There remains limited exploration of domain-specific, multilingual, or real-world deployments, which this paper addresses through the development and evaluation of RAG systems focused on retrieval quality and system design.

Accurate information access is important in domains like governance, cybersecurity, agriculture, industrial research, and healthcare. As industries adopt AI for complex tasks, traditional search methods often fall short, especially with multilingual, up-to-date, and contextually relevant knowledge. To address this, we developed RAG systems in collaboration with five organizations: the City of Kankaanpää[1], Disarm[2], AgriHubi[3], FEMMa[4], and a clinical diagnostics group[5]. Each collaboration guided the system design to meet distinct operational and information access challenges.

This study investigates how RAG systems can be engineered and evaluated in real-world contexts, focusing on system design, domain-specific applications, user evaluation, and lessons for future practice. Guided by these aims, this paper addresses the following Research Questions (RQs):

– **RQ1:** How can RAG systems be designed and developed to address real-world system needs across diverse application domains, and what are the lessons learned from engineering RAG systems for real-world applications?
– **RQ2:** How do users evaluate domain-specific RAG systems in terms of ease of use, relevance, transparency, responsiveness, and accuracy in real-world applications?

To address these research questions, we developed five domain-specific RAG systems and evaluated them through a web-based user study with 100 participants. The evaluation focused on usability, retrieval relevance, transparency, and other user-centred factors. Full methodological details are provided in Sect. 3.

The contributions of this paper are as follows: end-to-end development and deployment of RAG systems for multilingual, domain-specific applications; user-centred evaluation demonstrating real-world performance across usability and accuracy metrics; practical engineering insights to guide the design of reliable and maintainable RAG pipelines; and system-level considerations for integrating

---

[1] https://www.kankaanpaa.fi/.
[2] https://www.disarm.foundation/framework.
[3] https://maaseutuverkosto.fi/en/agrihubi/.
[4] https://www.tuni.fi/en/research/future-electrified-mobile-machines-femma.
[5] https://tampere.neurocenterfinland.fi/.

RAG into real-world AI-based software, contributing to software engineering practice.

Paper Structure: Section 2 reviews related work. Section 3 outlines the study design. Section 4 details the system implementation. Section 5 presents the evaluation. Section 6 highlights key lessons learned. Section 7 discusses limitations, and Sect. 8 offers conclusions and future directions.

2   Related Work

RAG improves the factual accuracy and contextual relevance of LLMs by incorporating real-time external information, making it especially valuable for complex tasks such as question answering, legal reasoning, and summarization [20]. Recent work has demonstrated RAG's utility in taxonomy-driven dataset design [16], token-efficient document handling [20], and multimodal applications that combine text and images via Vision-Language Models (VLMs) such as VISRAG [29]. Despite these advances, OCR noise remains a limiting factor in retrieval fidelity [32]. Ongoing research addresses this by refining dataset construction [16], tackling architectural scalability [5], improving query-document alignment through prompt engineering [34], and applying speculative retrieval to boost performance in multimodal settings [33].

RAG has been applied in software engineering for code understanding and developer tasks, e.g., StackRAG [1] enhances developer assistance using Stack Overflow, and CodeQA [2] applies LLM agents with retrieval augmentation. Ask-EDA [22] reduces hallucinations in Electronic Design Automation via hybrid retrieval. In industry, Khan et al. [12] address PDF-focused retrieval, while Xiaohua et al. [26] propose re-ranking and repacking for pipeline optimization. In healthcare, MEDGPT [24] extracts structured diagnostic insights, Path-RAG [18] improves pathology image retrieval, Alam et al. [3] introduce multi-agent retrieval for radiology reports, and Guo et al. [9] present LightRAG for graph-based precision retrieval.

RAG continues to expand into domains like energy and finance. Gamage et al. [8] propose a multi-agent chatbot for decision support in net-zero energy systems, while HybridRAG [21] combines knowledge graphs with vector search to enhance financial document analysis. AU-RAG by Jang and Li [11] dynamically selects retrieval sources using metadata, improving adaptability across sectors. To address retrieval noise, Zeng et al. [31] integrate contrastive learning and PCA for better knowledge filtering. Barnett et al. [4] identify core RAG weaknesses, including ranking errors and incomplete integration, underscoring the ongoing need for more reliable retrieval strategies.

The rise of autonomous AI agents has further improved RAG by enabling self-directed reasoning, adaptive retrieval, and memory persistence. Wang et al. [25] survey LLM-driven agent architectures, while Liu et al. [17] benchmark multi-turn reasoning through Agent-bench. Agent-tuning by Zeng et al. [30]

enhances instruction tuning for retrieval-based decisions. Singh et al. [23] categorize Agentic RAG into single-agent, multi-agent, and graph-based designs, highlighting dynamic tool use. On the retrieval side, Yan et al. [28] introduce CRAG to reduce hallucinations using confidence-based filtering, and Li et al. [15] improve precision through contrastive in-context learning and focus-mode filtering, strengthening RAG's reliability in complex scenarios.

Conclusive Summary: While RAG continues to advance, challenges in retrieval accuracy, reliability, and scalability persist [13]. Despite progress in hybrid strategies [21], autonomous agents [23], and correction techniques [15,28,31], domain-specific evaluation remains limited. This paper evaluates five RAG systems and offers practical development and deployment insights.

3 Study Design

Figure 1 provides an overview of the methodological steps, detailing the phased implementation of five domain-specific RAG systems, a user-centred evaluation with 100 participants, and the synthesis of lessons learned across technical, operational, and ethical dimensions.

3.1 Implementing RAG Systems

This section describes how we designed, and built the RAG systems featured in this study. It explains the overall system design, how we selected the case study domains, the unique challenges each domain presented, and the setup used for evaluation.

Domain Selection. We selected the application domains to test RAG systems in real-world, knowledge-heavy environments where accurate information retrieval, contextual understanding, and timely decision-making are important. These domains were chosen because they involve different information and require careful decision-making, providing a solid basis to evaluate how well RAG systems can adapt and perform in different settings.

In this study, we apply RAG across five domains: municipal governance, cybersecurity, agriculture, industrial research, and medical diagnostics, to explore how RAG-based retrieval can address diverse domain-specific information needs and support real-world decision-making processes.

System Design. The design of the RAG systems in this study follows a two-phase approach:

– *Retrieval Phase:* User queries are embedded using pre-trained models (e.g., `text-embedding-ada-002`) and matched with relevant text chunks via similarity search in vector databases.

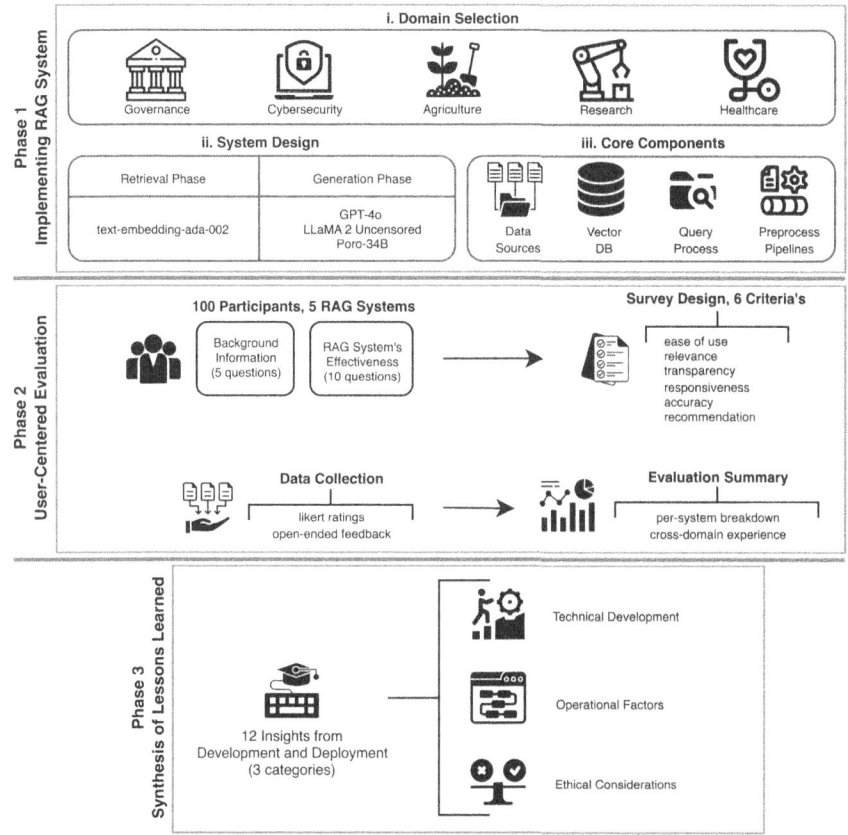

Fig. 1. Overview of the research methodology

- *Generation Phase:* The retrieved text chunks are concatenated with the original user query and passed into a large language model (LLM), such as `GPT-4o`, `LLaMA 2 Uncensored`, or `Poro-34B`, to synthesize contextually relevant responses.

This approach improves factual accuracy, minimizes hallucinations, and delivers insights that are well aligned with domain-specific needs.

Core Components. Each RAG-based system comprises multiple core components:

- *Data Sources:* Knowledge bases include structured and unstructured documents, such as websites, municipal records, cybersecurity reports, agricultural research papers, engineering documents, and clinical guidelines.
- *Vector Database:* The retrieved knowledge is stored as vector embeddings in `FAISS`, `Pinecone`, or `OpenAI's Vector Store`, depending on the system's latency and scalability requirements.

- *Query Processing:* User queries undergo tokenization, embedding generation, and similarity search before being passed to an LLM for the response.
- *Preprocessing Pipelines:* Systems rely on `PyMuPDF` and `Tesseract OCR` to extract text from PDFs and scanned documents, ensuring the inclusion of both text-based and image-based content. Additionally, for web scraping, the pipeline utilizes `BeautifulSoup`, `Scrapy`, and `Selenium` to extract, clean, and structure data from dynamic and static web pages.

These components enable efficient retrieval and context-aware responses in domain-specific RAG systems.

3.2 System Evaluation Method

To understand how the RAG-based systems performed in real usage scenarios, we conducted a structured web-based user study with 100 participants. Each participant was given access to live demo environments and interacted with one or more of the five systems using realistic, domain-specific tasks.

After using the systems, participants completed a standardized survey covering six criteria: Ease of Use, Relevance of Info, Transparency, System Responsiveness, Accuracy of Answers, and Recommendation. The survey included both Likert-scale questions and open-ended feedback. This approach provided both quantitative ratings and qualitative insights into system performance. We reviewed the open-ended feedback to identify common themes in participants' experiences. We also referred to development notes taken throughout the project. These helped us recognize recurring issues and informed the lessons described in Sect. 6.

4 Systems Implementation

This section outlines the implementation of five RAG-based systems for real-world deployment across diverse domains. Figure 2 presents the system architecture, showing user interaction, domain-specific data processing, vector storage, retrieval, and response generation with LLMs.

1. **Kankaanpää City AI**: This system enhances transparency of government records. It processes over 1,000 PDFs from 2023–2024, indexing them in `FAISS` for accurate retrieval of policy documents. The system uses the embedding model `text-embedding-ada-002` to convert documents into vector representations, and `gpt-4o-mini` as the LLM to generate context-aware responses. This setup allows users to search and access municipal decisions, infrastructure projects, and public policies with ease.
2. **Disarm RAG**: It is designed to deliver real-time insights into cyber threats, and forensic investigations. The system uses `LLaMA 2-uncensored` via Ollama to enable open access to cybersecurity knowledge, and is hosted on a secure server at CSC[6] (Finnish IT Center for Science) to ensure full data privacy. The

---

[6] https://research.csc.fi/cloud-computing/.

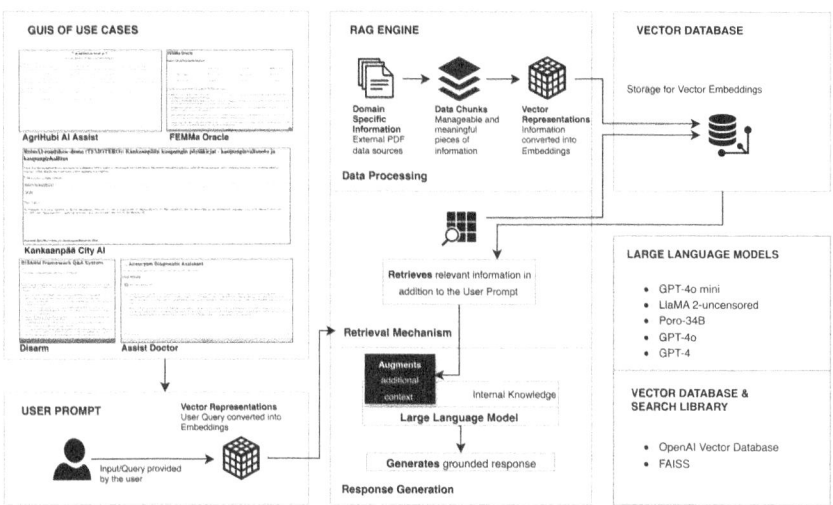

Fig. 2. System architecture of five RAG-based systems, showing data processing, vector storage, retrieval, and LLM-based response generation.

system integrates red team techniques (e.g., phishing, deep-fake disinformation, privilege escalation) and blue team strategies (e.g., bot detection, misinformation control, network forensics), grounded in the `Disarm Framework`. It supports queries such as "How would you create a deep-fake to discredit a public figure?" and "What are the latest techniques for bypassing multi-factor authentication (MFA)?", as well as defensive questions like "How would you detect a disinformation campaign early on?" and "What are effective countermeasures against deep-fake-based phishing attacks?".

3. **AgriHubi AI Assist**: AgriHubi bridges agricultural policy and practice by processing 200+ Finnish-language PDFs using multilingual OCR and embedding the content into a `FAISS` vector database. It leverages the Finnish-optimized `Poro-34B` language model to deliver contextually relevant responses on topics like sustainable farming and soil conservation. The system features a `Streamlit` chat interface, logs interactions via `SQLite`, and includes a feedback mechanism for continuous improvement, making agricultural knowledge more accessible to farmers and researchers.

4. **FEMMa Oracle**: This system optimizes knowledge retrieval for engineering research, particularly in electrified mobile machinery. It processes around 28 PDFs regarding electrified mobile machinery. It integrates `GPT-4o` and `text-embedding-3-large` with `OpenAI's Vector Store` to enable rapid retrieval of structured engineering research documents. The system ensures that researchers can efficiently access validated technical documentation and structured project information, improving efficiency in engineering-related knowledge retrieval.

5. **Assist Doctor**: It is an aneurysm diagnostic RAG based application, developed at `Tampere University` for use by neurologists, radiologists, and vascular surgeons. It retrieves insights from peer-reviewed literature and clinical data using an embedding-based search pipeline and delivers context-aware responses via OpenAI's `GPT-4`. With a `Streamlit` interface, it enables clinicians to access diagnostic criteria, risk stratification models, and treatment comparisons, supporting informed decisions in aneurysm care.

All developed systems comply with *GDPR* and display source references, except *Disarm RAG*, where citations are hidden for security reasons.

5   Systems Evaluation

Understanding the real-world effectiveness of RAG-based systems requires moving beyond technical benchmarks to incorporate user-centred evaluation. We conducted a structured user study across five domain-specific deployments, capturing both system performance metrics and user perceptions of trust, relevance, and usability. This practical feedback offers a grounded view of system behaviour in real settings and highlights opportunities for targeted improvements.

5.1   Participant Demographics and RAG Orientation

To contextualize the system evaluation, we collected detailed background information from the 100 participants involved in the study. Figure 3 illustrates five key dimensions of participant orientation relevant to domain-specific RAG systems: professional role, AI vs. manual search preference, familiarity with RAG, prior usage experience, and comfort with AI-generated outputs.

1. **Role Distribution:** Participants represented five distinct professional categories aligned with our target application domains. Researchers comprised the largest segment (44%), followed by students (20%), domain experts (17%), AI/ML practitioners (16%), and others (3%). This composition reflects a balanced blend of technical stakeholders and domain users, ensuring that the evaluation captures both system-level performance and practical applicability across real-world contexts.
2. **AI-Generated vs. Manual Document Search:** Participants exhibited a task-sensitive perspective on AI assistance. While a substantial majority (83%) preferred AI-generated responses depending on the nature of the task, only (9%) expressed a consistent preference for AI over manual methods. Conversely, (8%) favoured manual search regardless of context. These findings suggest that trust in RAG systems is not absolute but contingent—underscoring the importance of response relevance, transparency, and alignment with user intent.
3. **Familiarity with AI-Based RAG:** Participants demonstrated a strong familiarity with RAG technologies in general, with (75%) identifying as

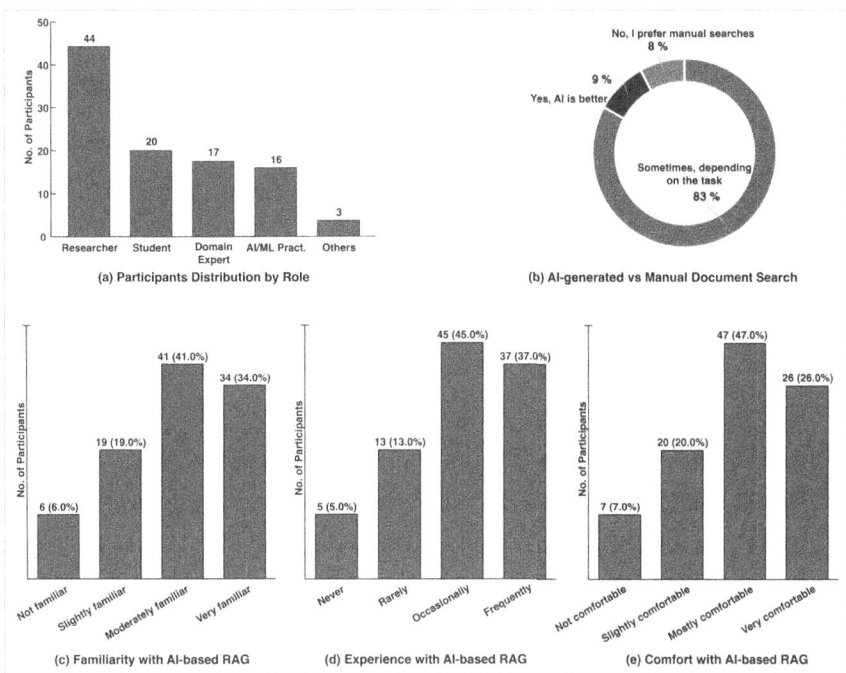

Fig. 3. Participant profiles and interaction with the RAG systems.

either moderately (41%) or very familiar (34%) with AI-based RAG systems. However, since many participants were not domain experts in the specific fields covered by the systems (e.g., healthcare, cybersecurity), their feedback primarily reflects their interaction experience with RAG rather than deep subject-matter validation.

4. **Experience with AI-Based RAG:** Participant engagement with RAG systems was notably high. A majority (82%) reported using such systems either occasionally (45%) or frequently (37%), while only (5%) indicated no prior experience. This distribution reinforces the reliability of the feedback collected, as most evaluations were informed by direct, hands-on interaction rather than hypothetical exposure.

5. **Comfort with AI-Generated Responses:** Overall, participants expressed high confidence in AI-generated outputs. Nearly three-quarters (73%) reported feeling either mostly (47%) or very comfortable (26%) relying on such responses. Only a small minority (7%) expressed discomfort, indicating a strong baseline of user trust and an encouraging signal for broader adoption of generative AI in domain-specific tasks.

5.2   Survey Instrument and Case-Wise Findings

Figure 4 presents the aggregated user ratings across six evaluation criteria for all five RAG systems, offering a comparative perspective on system performance.

To capture both measurable and descriptive insights, we employed a survey combining Likert-scale questions (1–5 scale) with open-ended prompts for qualitative feedback. The evaluation focused on the following six core dimensions:

- *Ease of Use:* How easy was it to use the system?
- *Relevance of Information:* Did the system retrieve relevant and useful information for your queries?
- *Transparency:* Did the system show where the information came from?
- *System Responsiveness:* How would you rate the system's responsiveness in retrieving answers?
- *Accuracy of Answers:* Based on your knowledge, how accurate were the AI-generated answers provided by the system?
- *Recommendation:* Would you recommend this tool to colleagues in your field?

All five RAG systems were evaluated using the same six criteria by a total of 100 participants. The summaries below reflect how each system performed, highlighting key strengths and areas for improvement.

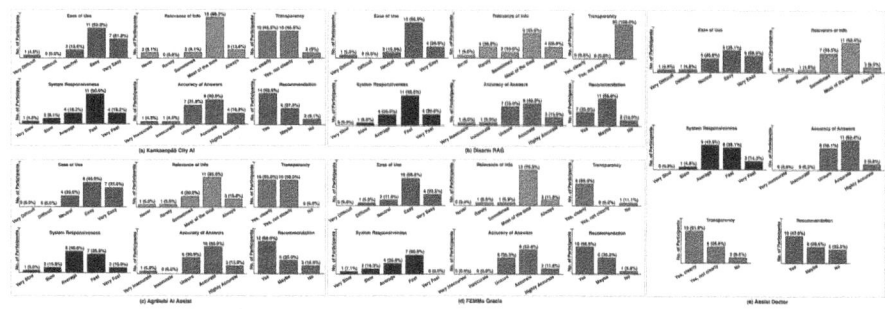

Fig. 4. User ratings of five RAG systems across six evaluation criteria.

1. **Kankaanpää City AI (22 participants):** The system performed well in Ease of Use, with (81.8%) rating it as "easy" or "very easy." Relevance of Info around (82%) and Accuracy of Answers around (91%) were also strong. Transparency was mixed, (45.5%) found it clear, while another (45.5%) found it unclear. (63.6%) said they would recommend the system, suggesting it may be useful in public governance contexts.
2. **Disarm RAG (20 participants):** Participants reported positive ratings for Ease of Use (65%) and System Responsiveness (75%), despite the complexity of the cybersecurity domain. Relevance of Info and Accuracy of Answers received moderate ratings, while Transparency was low due to intentionally hidden sources. Nevertheless, (55%) of participants indicated they would recommend the system.

3. **AgriHubi AI Assist (20 participants):** Tailored for Finnish-language agricultural content, the system received strong ratings for Ease of Use (80%) and Accuracy of Answers (65%). Relevance of Info was generally positive, while System Responsiveness and Transparency showed mixed results. Still, (60%) of users responded positively on the Recommendation dimension.

4. **FEMMa Oracle (17 participants):** The system performed well across all criteria. Accuracy was rated "accurate" or "highly accurate" by (64.7%), and Ease of Use by (82.3%). Relevance of Info was high (88.3%), and (88.9%) found it transparent. Responsiveness was rated "fast" by (50%) and "average" by (28.6%). Overall, (58.8%) said they would recommend it.

5. **Assist Doctor (21 participants):** Participants found the system easy to use, with (66.7%) rating it as "easy" or "very easy." Both Accuracy of Answers and Relevance of Info received favourable ratings, each at approximately (62%). System Responsiveness was positively reviewed by more than half of the users. About (62%) found the system transparent, and (47.6%) said they would recommend it.

Across the five systems, Ease of Use and Accuracy of Answers were consistently rated positively. Transparency and Recommendation showed more variation, sometimes due to design choices. For example, *Disarm RAG* used hidden source information. These differences show that user perception depends on the domain and output presentation.

6   Lessons Learned

While developing and evaluating the five RAG systems, we encountered technical, operational, and ethical challenges. These lessons reflect practical insights drawn from our hands-on engineering work, system deployment in real-world domains, and user-centred feedback. Together, they offer guidance for building reliable, domain-adapted RAG systems that balance performance, compliance, and trustworthiness.

6.1   Technical Development

Building RAG systems for real-world applications surfaced a number of technical hurdles that required hands-on problem solving and thoughtful design decisions.

- *Domain-Specific Models Are Essential*: General-purpose models like GPT-4o struggled with domain-specific and Finnish-language queries. Leveraging Finnish-optimized models like `Poro-34B`, along with compatible embedding models (e.g., `text-embedding-ada-002`), led to more contextually relevant responses.
- *OCR Errors Impact the Pipeline*: Noisy OCR output from agriculture and healthcare PDFs degraded FAISS quality. Using `TesseractOCR`, `easyOCR`, and regex-based cleanup improved extracted text.

– *Chunking Balances Speed and Accuracy*: Token chunk sizes between 200–500 struck a practical balance between retrieval relevance and query latency. Smaller chunks bloated the index, increasing lookup times.
– *FAISS Scalability Hits Limits*: With large corpora (>10k embeddings), FAISS latency increased noticeably. Metadata filtering by document type reduced search time.
– *Manual Environment Management*: Without containerisation, we faced version conflicts across PyTorch, FAISS, OCR libraries, and OpenAI APIs. Strict environment pinning and manual sync across development/production was necessary for stability.

6.2   Operational Factors

Operating RAG systems in real-world settings revealed practical challenges related to data workflows, infrastructure choices, and user interaction management.

– *SQLite for Tracking User Interaction*: We used SQLite to log user questions, responses, and ratings (e.g., in *AgriHubi*). This lightweight store helped identify system failures and understand user behaviour.
– *Scraping Pipelines Are Fragile*: Websites changed often, breaking parsers. Without stable APIs, we relied on semi-structured feeds and regular script maintenance.
– *Self-Hosted Setup for Speed and Compliance*: We hosted LLMs and vector stores on our own servers to reduce GDPR risks and improve speed. This approach balanced control with performance in sensitive domains.
– *Clean Data Boosts Retrieval Quality*: Removing OCR noise and duplicates from source data improved answer relevance without modifying models.
– *User Feedback Drives System Tuning*: User ratings and comments exposed weak spots, guiding adjustments to retrieval settings and chunk sizes.

6.3   Ethical Considerations

While technical and operational aspects were central to system performance, ethical considerations around transparency, and data bias proved equally important during deployment.

– *Source File References Build Trust*: Providing filenames and download links helped users validate AI outputs. In security use cases (e.g., *Disarm RAG*), sources were intentionally hidden to protect sensitive material.
– *Dataset Bias Impacts Retrieval Balance*: Unbalanced source data led to over-representation of some document types. Re-ranking improved diversity and fairness in answers.

Practical and Research Takeaways: Our findings highlight both persistent and emerging challenges in applying RAG systems to real-world, multilingual, and domain-specific settings. While issues like OCR noise, chunk size tuning, and retrieval balancing are well recognized, this study emphasizes the importance of practical strategies such as data cleaning, user feedback mechanisms, and lightweight response validation for improving retrieval quality and system reliability. These lessons extend current research by connecting it to deployment realities and offer value to the software engineering community by addressing concerns related to retrieval infrastructure, stability of data pipelines, and transparency in system outputs. These takeaways help guide the development of adaptable and trustworthy RAG solutions.

7 Study Limitations

This study presents findings grounded in the design, deployment, and evaluation of five domain-specific RAG systems, but several limitations must be acknowledged. First, while our evaluation involved 100 participants across diverse roles including researchers, practitioners, and domain experts, approximately 20% of the sample consisted of students. Although these students had relevant technical or domain experience, their feedback may reflect differing expectations or usage behaviour compared to full-time professionals. This demographic distribution, while broad, could influence the generalizability of findings to strictly industrial settings. Additionally, participants rated the accuracy of system-generated answers, yet only 17% identified as domain experts. Thus, accuracy ratings provided by non-experts might not reliably reflect the factual correctness of the systems' outputs.

Second, participants interacted with one or more systems, and survey responses were collected separately after each system use. Not all 100 participants engaged with every system; the number of responses per system varied based on individual interest and domain familiarity. For instance, feedback on *AgriHubi AI Assist* reflects only the users who selected and interacted with that system. This variation in exposure may affect the comparability of results across different systems, and the limited interaction time restricted analysis of longer-term user engagement.

Third, the lessons learned presented in this paper are based on our development experience and observations during system implementation and evaluation. While they do not result from formal empirical analysis, they reflect recurring challenges and design considerations encountered across multiple domains. Although not statistically validated, these insights can inform future work on the design and implementation of RAG systems in applied settings.

8 Conclusion

In this paper, we presented a tool-assisted approach for designing, implementing, and evaluating RAG-based systems across five real-world domains. Each system was tailored to its specific context–ranging from municipal governance to agriculture and healthcare by integrating multilingual OCR pipelines, semantic retrieval with vector embeddings, and either in-house or cloud-based LLMs. Our user study, involving 100 participants, provided insights into how these systems perform in practice, not just in terms of technical metrics, but also usability, transparency, and user trust.

Through our development work, we identified twelve lessons learned that highlight, in our view, recurring challenges in building practical RAG pipelines. These include balancing chunk size with latency, managing dependencies without containerization, and maintaining retrieval speed at scale. We also found that clean data, user feedback, and clear information presentation are critical for building trust. As industry and research interest in RAG systems grows [10, 13], we hope these insights support future development efforts.

Looking ahead, we see a strong need for more structured evaluation mechanisms that go beyond user ratings. As future work, we propose integrating an *Evaluation Agent Model*, a system-internal module that checks AI-generated responses for accuracy, relevance, and completeness before presenting them to users. Based on our experiences, user feedback alone is often insufficient to catch factual errors or incomplete responses, especially in domains where missing or misleading information could have serious consequences. An automated evaluation agent could trigger second-stage retrievals or prompt reformulations when weaknesses are detected, creating an adaptive feedback loop. We believe that such mechanisms are essential to improving the reliability and trustworthiness of RAG systems in high-stakes, real-world applications.

Acknowledgements. This paper is based on research supported in part by the Synthetica project funded by the Research Council of Finland, the GENT project funded by the European Regional Development Fund, and the AgriHubi initiative supported by Pohjois-Pohjanmaan ELY-keskus (Centre for Economic Development, Transport and the Environment). The authors gratefully acknowledge this support. The authors declare no conflicts of interest related to this work.

References

1. Abrahamyan, D., Fard, F.H.: StackRAG agent: improving developer answers with retrieval-augmented generation. In: 2024 IEEE International Conference on Software Maintenance and Evolution (ICSME), pp. 893–897. IEEE Computer Society, Los Alamitos (2024). https://doi.org/10.1109/ICSME58944.2024.00098. https://doi.ieeecomputersociety.org/10.1109/ICSME58944.2024.00098
2. Ahmed, M., et al.: Codeqa: advanced programming question-answering using llm agent and rag. In: 2024 6th Novel Intelligent and Leading Emerging Sciences Conference (NILES), pp. 494–499 (2024). https://doi.org/10.1109/NILES63360.2024.10753267
3. Alam, H.M.T., Srivastav, D., Kadir, M.A., Sonntag, D.: Towards interpretable radiology report generation via concept bottlenecks using a multi-agentic rag (2025). https://arxiv.org/abs/2412.16086

4. Barnett, S., Kurniawan, S., Thudumu, S., Brannelly, Z., Abdelrazek, M.: Seven failure points when engineering a retrieval augmented generation system. In: Proceedings of the IEEE/ACM 3rd International Conference on AI Engineering - Software Engineering for AI, CAIN '24, pp. 194–199. Association for Computing Machinery, New York (2024). https://doi.org/10.1145/3644815.3644945

5. Chen, J., Xu, D., Fei, J., Feng, C.M., Elhoseiny, M.: Document haystacks: vision-language reasoning over piles of 1000+ documents (2024). https://arxiv.org/abs/2411.16740

6. Chirkova, N., Rau, D., Déjean, H., Formal, T., Clinchant, S., Nikoulina, V.: Retrieval-augmented generation in multilingual settings. In: Li, S., et al. (eds.) Proceedings of the 1st Workshop on Towards Knowledgeable Language Models (KnowLLM 2024), pp. 177–188. Association for Computational Linguistics, Bangkok (2024). https://doi.org/10.18653/v1/2024.knowllm-1.15. https://aclanthology.org/2024.knowllm-1.15/

7. Fan, W., et al.: A survey on rag meeting llms: towards retrieval-augmented large language models. In: Proceedings of the 30th ACM SIGKDD Conference on Knowledge Discovery and Data Mining, KDD '24, pp. 6491–6501. Association for Computing Machinery, New York (2024). https://doi.org/10.1145/3637528.3671470

8. Gamage, G., et al.: Multi-agent rag chatbot architecture for decision support in net-zero emission energy systems. In: 2024 IEEE International Conference on Industrial Technology (ICIT), pp. 1–6 (2024). https://doi.org/10.1109/ICIT58233.2024.10540920

9. Guo, Z., Xia, L., Yu, Y., Ao, T., Huang, C.: Lightrag: simple and fast retrieval-augmented generation (2024). https://arxiv.org/abs/2410.05779

10. Gupta, S., Ranjan, R., Singh, S.N.: A comprehensive survey of retrieval-augmented generation (rag): evolution, current landscape and future directions (2024). https://arxiv.org/abs/2410.12837

11. Jang, J., Li, W.S.: Au-rag: agent-based universal retrieval augmented generation. In: Proceedings of the 2024 Annual International ACM SIGIR Conference on Research and Development in Information Retrieval in the Asia Pacific Region, SIGIR-AP 2024, pp. 2–11. Association for Computing Machinery, New York (2024). https://doi.org/10.1145/3673791.3698416

12. Khan, A.A., Hasan, M.T., Kemell, K.K., Rasku, J., Abrahamsson, P.: Developing retrieval augmented generation (rag) based llm systems from pdfs: an experience report (2024). https://arxiv.org/abs/2410.15944

13. Krishna, S., et al.: Fact, fetch, and reason: a unified evaluation of retrieval-augmented generation (2025). https://arxiv.org/abs/2409.12941

14. Lewis, P., et al.: Retrieval-augmented generation for knowledge-intensive nlp tasks (2021). https://arxiv.org/abs/2005.11401

15. Li, S., Stenzel, L., Eickhoff, C., Bahrainian, S.A.: Enhancing retrieval-augmented generation: a study of best practices. In: Rambow, O., Wanner, L., Apidianaki, M., Al-Khalifa, H., Eugenio, B.D., Schockaert, S. (eds.) Proceedings of the 31st International Conference on Computational Linguistics, pp. 6705–6717. Association for Computational Linguistics, Abu Dhabi (2025). https://aclanthology.org/2025.coling-main.449/

16. de Lima, R.T., et al.: Know your rag: dataset taxonomy and generation strategies for evaluating rag systems (2024). https://arxiv.org/abs/2411.19710

17. Liu, X., et al.: Agentbench: evaluating LLMs as agents. In: The Twelfth International Conference on Learning Representations (2024). https://openreview.net/forum?id=zAdUB0aCTQ

18. Naeem, A., et al.: Path-rag: knowledge-guided key region retrieval for open-ended pathology visual question answering (2024). https://arxiv.org/abs/2411.17073
19. Nguyen-Duc, A., et al.: Generative artificial intelligence for software engineering – a research agenda (2023). https://arxiv.org/abs/2310.18648
20. Pesl, R.D., Mathew, J.G., Mecella, M., Aiello, M.: Advanced system integration: analyzing openapi chunking for retrieval-augmented generation (2024). https://arxiv.org/abs/2411.19804
21. Sarmah, B., Mehta, D., Hall, B., Rao, R., Patel, S., Pasquali, S.: Hybridrag: integrating knowledge graphs and vector retrieval augmented generation for efficient information extraction. In: Proceedings of the 5th ACM International Conference on AI in Finance, ICAIF '24, pp. 608–616. Association for Computing Machinery, New York (2024). https://doi.org/10.1145/3677052.3698671
22. Shi, L., Kazda, M., Sears, B., Shropshire, N., Puri, R.: Ask-eda: a design assistant empowered by llm, hybrid rag and abbreviation de-hallucination. In: 2024 IEEE LLM Aided Design Workshop (LAD), pp. 1–5 (2024). https://doi.org/10.1109/LAD62341.2024.10691824
23. Singh, A., Ehtesham, A., Kumar, S., Khoei, T.T.: Agentic retrieval-augmented generation: a survey on agentic rag (2025). https://arxiv.org/abs/2501.09136
24. Sree, Y.B., Sathvik, A., Hema Akshit, D.S., Kumar, O., Pranav Rao, B.S.: Retrieval-augmented generation based large language model chatbot for improving diagnosis for physical and mental health. In: 2024 6th International Conference on Electrical, Control and Instrumentation Engineering (ICECIE), pp. 1–8 (2024). https://doi.org/10.1109/ICECIE63774.2024.10815693
25. Wang, L., et al.: A survey on large language model based autonomous agents (2024). https://doi.org/10.1007/s11704-024-40231-1
26. Wang, X., et al.: Searching for best practices in retrieval-augmented generation. In: Al-Onaizan, Y., Bansal, M., Chen, Y.N. (eds.) Proceedings of the 2024 Conference on Empirical Methods in Natural Language Processing, pp. 17716–17736. Association for Computational Linguistics, Miami (2024). https://doi.org/10.18653/v1/2024.emnlp-main.981. https://aclanthology.org/2024.emnlp-main.981/
27. Xu, A., et al.: Generative ai and retrieval-augmented generation (rag) systems for enterprise. In: Proceedings of the 33rd ACM International Conference on Information and Knowledge Management, CIKM '24, pp. 5599–5602. Association for Computing Machinery, New York (2024). https://doi.org/10.1145/3627673.3680117
28. Yan, S.Q., Gu, J.C., Zhu, Y., Ling, Z.H.: Corrective retrieval augmented generation (2024). https://arxiv.org/abs/2401.15884
29. Yu, S., et al.: Visrag: vision-based retrieval-augmented generation on multimodality documents (2024). https://arxiv.org/abs/2410.10594
30. Zeng, A., et al.: AgentTuning: enabling generalized agent abilities for LLMs. In: Ku, L.W., Martins, A., Srikumar, V. (eds.) Findings of the Association for Computational Linguistics: ACL 2024, pp. 3053–3077. Association for Computational Linguistics, Bangkok (2024). https://doi.org/10.18653/v1/2024.findings-acl.181
31. Zeng, S., et al.: Towards knowledge checking in retrieval-augmented generation: a representation perspective (2024). https://arxiv.org/abs/2411.14572
32. Zhang, J., et al.: Ocr hinders rag: evaluating the cascading impact of ocr on retrieval-augmented generation (2024). https://arxiv.org/abs/2412.02592
33. Zhao, P., et al.: Retrieval-augmented generation for ai-generated content: a survey (2024). https://arxiv.org/abs/2402.19473
34. Zhao, S., Huang, Y., Song, J., Wang, Z., Wan, C., Ma, L.: Towards understanding retrieval accuracy and prompt quality in rag systems (2024). https://arxiv.org/abs/2411.19463

"Give Software Developers Time": Investigating Perceived Performance and Stress in a Compressed Work Schedule

Michael Neumann[1]([✉]) [ID], Tom Strzelczyk[1], Alex Schwab[1], Daniel Fuchß[1], Quoc Trung Vu[1], Maurice Lotze[1], Joshua Borgmann[1], Justus Donner[1], Melanie Hartkopf[1], Sodaba Hayat[1], Gino Ismaili[1], Lars Wesemann[1], Tim Meiertöns[1], Eva-Maria Schön[2][ID], Lars Baumann[1][ID], and Julia Spanke[3]

[1] University of Applied Sciences Hannover, Hannover, Germany
michael.neumann@hs-hannover.de
[2] University of Applied Sciences Emden/Leer, Emden/Leer, Germany
[3] Mecklenburgische Versicherungs-Gesellschaft a.G., Hannover, Germany

Abstract. *Context:* Compressed work schedules, such as the 4-day work-week, have gained attention due to reported benefits like increased productivity and reduced absenteeism. However, findings on stress-related outcomes remain mixed. *Problem:* Despite growing interest in compressed work schedules, there is limited empirical evidence on how such models affect stress, performance, and team dynamics in software development settings—especially under partial workload compression, as in the 4+ work-week. *Objective:* This study explores the effects of this compressed work schedule on software development teams, focusing on perceived performance, team-level benefits, and stress levels. *Method:* We applied an action research approach in two German organizations and took three software development teams under study. Data collection was conducted in a mixed-method approach combining both questionnaires, field-observations and semi-structured interviews. *Results:* We found that the teams' performance did not decrease. Related to the perceived stress of the team members, the results differ from team to team. In teams with no reduced workload, the stress-level increased over time. The teams under study valued the Plus-Day concept and used the time for process improvements, source code refactoring, or team development workshops and events. *Conclusion:* Our results emphasize the importance of change preparation, fostering team autonomy, and the willingness for organizational learning when transforming to a compressed work schedule. The benefits of a compressed work schedule are obvious: higher job satisfaction and increased motivation of the employees.

Keywords: 4-day work-week · compressed work schedule · stress · performance · action research

© The Author(s), under exclusive license to Springer Nature Switzerland AG 2026
D. Taibi and D. Smite (Eds.): SEAA 2025, LNCS 16082, pp. 159–177, 2026.
https://doi.org/10.1007/978-3-032-04200-2_11

1 Introduction

For software development organizations, demographic change and the resulting shortage of skilled professionals pose an increasing challenge. It is therefore
in the interest of IT organizations to respond flexibly to the needs of employees across different generations. The COVID-19 pandemic has led to profound
changes in how work is organized in companies around the world [13, 26]. How
professional software development is structured and managed today bears little resemblance to pre-pandemic practices [24]. Far-reaching transformations—
such as the widespread adoption of remote and hybrid work models, increased
use of co-working spaces, and the implementation of "work-where-whenever"
principles—have become firmly established in many organizations [14, 27].

Another area that has received increasing attention from organizations in
recent years is adopting alternative and compressed work schedules, such as the
4-day work-week [4, 9]. Pilot programs exploring the implementation of compressed work schedules have been conducted across various countries, industries,
and companies (e.g., [1, 20, 31]). Studies have identified a range of positive effects
associated with the adoption of a 4-day work-week. These include increased productivity, improved employee morale [10], and a reduction in absenteeism. However, findings to health-related factors—particularly stress levels—remain mixed.
For instance, Topp et al. [35] report elevated stress levels among agile software
development teams working within a four-day schedule. In contrast, other studies have found either reduced or unchanged stress levels [9]. It is also important
to note that the concept of compressed work schedules, and the 4-day work-week
specifically, encompasses a variety of implementations. A 4-day work-week may
or may not involve a reduction in total working hours (e.g., four days á 10-h
versus four days á 8-hour a week).

One of the key challenges of implementing a four-day week in practice is its
transformative potential, which can be a barrier for organizations [35]. In the
field of software development, many organizations operate as service providers,
offering their workforce and expertise to external clients—particularly businesses
and public sector institutions. These services are often billed on an hourly basis,
meaning that a 4-day work-week with a reduced number of working hours could
have economic implications. Moreover, such a shift may entail legal consequences,
including the need to amend employment contracts, internal service directives,
or organizational policies. Given these constraints, we chose to explore an alternative form of compressed work schedule: the 4+ work-week, which incorporates
an additional element referred to as the "Plus-Day"[1].

In this study, we aim to investigate how a compressed work model affects
software development teams. Our focus lies particularly on team-oriented outcomes, such as perceived performance and the potential value of the Plus-Day for

---

[1] Definition "Plus-Day": is a regular working day: within a working week on which no
day-to-day business activities are carried out. Examples of these activities can be
team-building or training measures as well as refactoring sessions to reduce technical
debt.

teams. Additionally, we examine the impact on perceived stress levels, as it must be assumed that expectations regarding task completion will remain unchanged despite the reduced number of working days. Thus, the above leads us to our research questions:

- **RQ 1:** How does perceived performance change under a compressed work schedule?
  Perceived performance was assessed using the Individual Work Performance Questionnaire [15] and semi-structured interviews.
- **RQ 2:** How do team members' perceived stress levels change?
  As in RQ1, data was collected using the Perceived Stress Questionnaire [6] and validated with qualitative data.
- **RQ 3:** What are the organizational benefits of the Plus-Day?
  To understand Plus-Day activities, we conducted observations and semi-structured interviews.

This paper is structured as follows: In Sect. 2, we give a brief explanation of the origins of the 4-day work-week concept and further provide an overview of the related work. Section 3 describes our research design. In Sect. 4, we present the results of our study, followed by a discussion to present practical implications in Sect. 5. Before the paper closes with a summary in Sect. 7, we describe this study's limitations in Sect. 6.

2   Background and Related Work

In this section, we first give a brief introduction of the background of the 4-day work-week concept before we present an overview of the identified related work and discuss existing research findings closely related to our study's topic.

2.1   The 4-Day Work-Week Concept

The idea of a 4-day work-week dates back to the 1950s, but it wasn't until the 1970s that the concept gained broader traction—especially in the United States, where both public and private sectors began exploring shorter work weeks more actively [7]. In contrast, Europe explored other unconventional forms of flexible working time models, such as flextime [18]. The 4-day work-week has only recently gained broader international recognition [4]. One contributing factor is the increasing emphasis among younger generations on self-actualization and job satisfaction.

In a meta-analysis conducted by Campbell [4], various 4-day work-week models are examined alongside their organizational and social impacts. The findings suggest that a 4-day work-week can have positive effects on employee satisfaction and well-being.

2.2   Related Work

To contextualize our study, we reviewed primary and secondary literature, including grey literature. We focused the literature search on studies reporting experimental 4-day work-week implementations. However, we found no studies dealing with the 4+ day work-week concept, so our search focused on more established compressed work schedules, especially the 4-day work week.

To determine the effects of the 4-day week, Campbell [4] analyzed the scientific literature chronologically and systematically. Most of the literature points to positive aspects: increased morale, job satisfaction, cost reductions, and reduced staff turnover. Negative aspects include increased performance monitoring and problems with working time planning. The effects on productivity and the environment are also unclear. Topp et al. [35] investigated how working in 4-day weeks and working remotely affect agile software development teams. The authors found that the productivity of the teams studied did not decrease, while the stress level increased due to the 4-day work-week. In addition, it was proven that the job satisfaction of the team members was positively influenced. Paje et al. [28] examined the effects of compressed working time models on job stress, work-life balance, and productivity among 350 participants from Manila working in various industries. Contrary to the findings of Topp et al., this study analyzed the data and found that stress levels decreased as a result of the reduction in working days. It also found that less stress leads to better work-life balance and higher productivity.

Besides peer-reviewed articles, we could identify grey literature dealing with the effects of a 4-day work-week in a broader context. In 2022, two large-scale studies were conducted based on pilot programs initiated by the 4-Day Week Global Foundation. These studies were supported by researchers from the University of Cambridge and Boston College, as well as by local academics. In both studies, working hours were reduced to 32 h over four days per week, with no reduction in pay. The first study [31] began in February/April 2022 and examined the effects in 33 participating companies, primarily located in the United States and Ireland. Among the 969 employees included in the study, perceived stress and work ability—which also encompasses performance capacity—were assessed. The results showed a decrease in perceived stress and a concurrent improvement in work ability. The second study [20] took place between June and December 2022 in the United Kingdom and involved 61 companies with a total of 2,900 employees. In this study, stress was not measured independently but rather analyzed as part of a broader assessment of burnout. Again, the findings indicated a decrease in burnout symptoms and an increase in work ability. The 4-Day Week Global Foundation [1] is continuing to conduct further pilot projects. In May 2023, preliminary results from a pilot program in Australasia—comprising 26 participating companies—were published. Although a full study has not yet been released, early findings similarly suggest reduced burnout symptoms and improved work ability.

3   Research Design

As our study objective relates strongly to a practical phenomenon, we decided to design the study by applying a research approach, which aims to improve a specific organizational setting [8]. In Action Research, researchers and practitioners collaborate regularly. This research approach ensures a regular exchange between research and practice, and thus synergies in which both facets can be considered [2]. Action Research has gained more and more interest in Software Engineering research in recent years (e.g., [12,17,29,30]). For our study, we applied the canonical action research approach according to Susman [34]. Furthermore, we designed our study based on the guidelines by Staron [32,33].

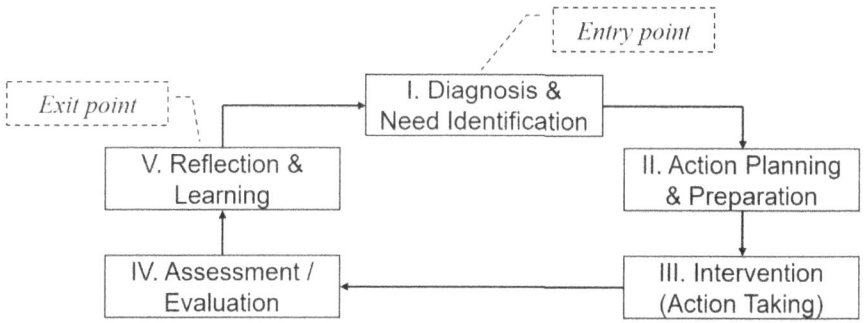

Fig. 1. Action research approach according to [34]

We conducted one Action Research cycle to gain insights into the studied phenomenon. The intervention was prepared and carried out by a steering committee comprising one researcher (first author) and four practitioners—two managers supporting organizational coordination and two team members assisting with data collection. The identified need for intervention and the exit point is explained in Sect. 4.

This study is methodologically grounded by action research, though not all cases followed a full intervention-reflection cycle. All cases involved real organizational change—the experimental introduction of a 4+ work-week—with practitioners and researchers collaborating in planning, implementation, and reflection. We position this as a multi-case study grounded in action research, reflecting varying levels of intervention and co-creation, and contributing to discourse on participatory, practice-based approaches to working time innovation.

3.1   Research Context

The research was conducted in collaboration between the University of Applied Sciences and Arts Hannover (Germany) and two organizations: Nankatsu SC and Toho Academy (both anonymized). Neither organization had applied a compressed work schedule before we began our intervention, and thus, did not have any experience with compressed work schedules gained before. Below, we give a brief introduction of the organizational background and the teams we took under study.

Organization I - Nankatsu SC. Nankatsu SC is a Germany-based insurance company with around 1,000 employees, offering nationwide services for private and business clients and maintaining an in-house software development department. It faces typical industry challenges like legacy system replacement and regulatory compliance. **Team Tsubasa** consists of 10 members responsible for database development, organizing their work using a pull-oriented ticket-based system prioritized by business values or technical aspects. The team manages both project-related tasks and daily support, ensuring continuous availability for production system emergencies. **Team Wakabayashi**, with 6 members, handles maintenance and development of policy administration systems for a specific business line. Tasks include troubleshooting, bug-fixing, optimization, and feature-specific development, operating both service-oriented and project-based.

Organization II - Toho Academy. The second organization is a German state capital's public administration with around 11,000 employees. It provides various urban services, such as childcare, citizen-related processes (e.g., residence notifications, passports), and fire brigade services. A software development department supports digitalizing citizen services. **Team Hyuga**, consisting of 14 employees, develops digitized processes for citizen use, including business registrations, parental allowance applications, and building permits. The team employs a tailored Scrum approach with core agile practices like Sprint Retrospectives, Sprint Planning, Sprint Reviews, and designated Scrum Master and Product Owner roles.

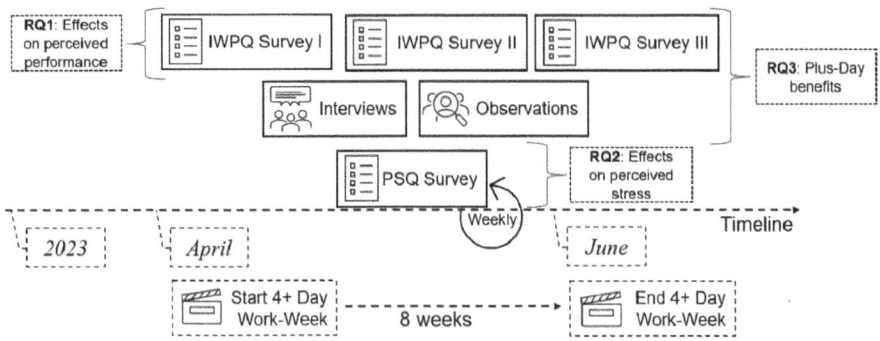

Fig. 2. Timeline of the applied data collection approaches

3.2   Data Collection and Analysis

For our study we applied a mixed-method data collection and analysis approach (see Fig. 2). In total, we applied four different data collection methods from validated questionnaires [16] (e.g., to analyze the perceived stress over the study time) to qualitative methods (such as semi-structured interviews). Below, we explain on detail each data collection method and how we applied it per team as there were different regulations and limitations to consider. Table 1 gives an overview of the applied data collection method per organization and team. The data was collected in both organizations between 07.04.2023 and 02.06.2023. Detailed information about the data collection and analysis can be found in our research protocol [25].

Table 1. Data Collection Methods per Team and Organization

Organization	Team	Data Collection Method
Nankatsu SC	Tsubasa	IWPQ, PSQ, semi-structured interviews, observations
Nankatsu SC	Wakabayashi	IWPQ, PSQ, semi-structured interviews, observations
Toho Academy	Hyuga	PSQ, semi-structured interviews, observations

Individual Work Performance Questionnaire (IWPQ). IWPQ can be used to measure changes in people's work performance [15]. It is designed as a standardized questionnaire and validated in various studies (e.g., [11,21]). In its three-dimensional conceptual framework, IWPQ 1.0 contains a total of 18 elements for measuring performance. The first dimension, Task Performance (TP), represents the competence with which people perform the core content-related or technical tasks central to their job. The second dimension, Contextual Performance (CP), can be defined as behavior that supports the organizational, social, and psychological environment in which the technical core must function. The third dimension, Counter Productive Work Behaviour (CWB), is defined as behavior that affects the well-being of the organization. We applied IWPQ questionnaire by using LimeSurvey for both teams at Nankatsu SC. For team Tsubasa the IWPQ was applied three times: in the first week of our study (n= 4 out of 6), in the middle (n= 5 out of 6), and in the final week (n= 4 out of 6). For team Wakabayashi, we applied the survey twice: in the first (n= 4 out of 4) and the final week of the study (n= 4 out of 4). The link to Limesurvey, including an information message, was sent via email to all the team members. For analyzing the conducted data, we used the guidelines by Koopmans [15].

Perceived Stress Questionnaire (PSQ): Investigating the perceived stress of the team members under study, a total of 8 surveys were conducted over the study period of 8 weeks using the standardized PSQ questionnaire [19]. The PSQ is used to record acute subjective perceived stress. The short version PSQ-20, which contains 20 items, was used for data collection [6]. Table 2 provides an overview of the PSQ sample sizes per team.

Table 2. PSQ scores across 8 weeks for all teams (with sample sizes)

Team	W1	W2	W3	W4	W5	W6	W7	W8
Wakabayashi (n = 6)	3	6	6	4	6	4	3	6
Tsubasa (n = 10)	4	3	4	4	4	5	4	4
Hyuga (n = 14)	14	13	8	10	4	8	7	8

In this questionnaire, stress is defined by four categories: worry, tension, pleasure, and demands. Worry reflects worries, fears about the future, and feelings of frustration, while tension reflects exhaustion, imbalance, and a lack of physical relaxation. Demands represent a lack of time, deadline pressure, and task pressure. We applied the PSQ questionnaire using LimeSurvey for all three teams under study in a weekly data collection approach. The survey link was sent on Friday for the following week, data collection was possible during the whole week for the team members.

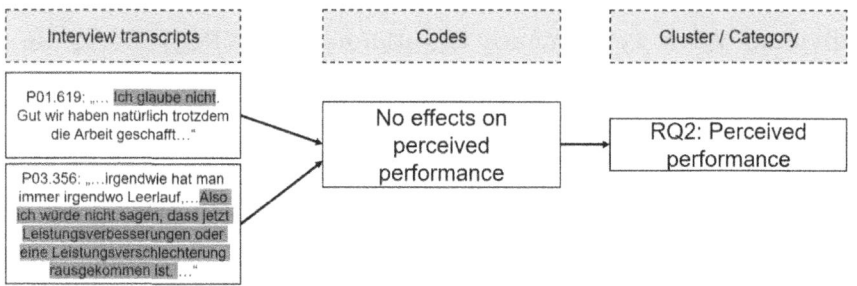

Fig. 3. Coding example of the qualitative data

Semi-Structured Interviews: Besides the surveys explained above, we further conducted qualitative data using semi-structured interviews, which we performed based on an interview guide. For every team, a specific interview guide was used, as the context under study should be taken into account in socio-technical research [5]. Nevertheless, the three interview guides tackled the same themes and meta topics such as the perceived performance and stress. We made the interview guides available in our research protocol [25].

All interview guides were created using the Goal-Question-Metric (GQM) approach [3]. We derived specific research goals based on our research questions and formulated the interview questions per goal [25]. Finally, we defined metric clusters for the later data analysis. All interview guides consist of a warm-up phase, in which the interviewee explains the research objectives and ask the interview partner about demographic information such as job experience and current role in the team/organization. Next, we ask the interview partner the topic-related questions regarding the motivation, effects on stress or performance, or the benefits of the Plus-Day. Finally, we closed the interview with questions regarding the interview itself or if the interview partner wanted to add something.

The interviews in the Wakabayashi team were conducted online with zoom on 9.05.2023, one after the other, between 09:00 and 13:45. The interviews lasted between 22 and 35 min. Participation in the interviews was voluntary. The recorded interviews have been transcribed by using Microsoft Teams or Whisper.

The interviews were systematically analyzed in a similar way for all teams. Mayring's [22] summarizing content analysis was used. The interview-partner identifies the line number and direct statements in the transcript were quoted (pattern example: P_ID.$LINE-NUMBER: QUOTE), the quotes were then paraphrased, generalized, and mapped to the respective research question cluster. The transcripts were organized according to the metrics identified in the GQM and thematically related to the research questions. An example of the coding process including the applied pattern is shown in Fig. 3. Table 3 provides an overview of the interview profiles.

Table 3. Overview of the Interviewee profiles

ID	Team	Role
P01	Tsubasa	Team Lead Database Development
P02	Tsubasa	Database Developer
P03	Tsubasa	Database Developer
P04	Tsubasa	Database Developer
P05	Tsubasa	Database Developer
P06	Tsubasa	Database Developer
P07	Wakabayashi	Team Lead Software Development
P08	Wakabayashi	Software / Database Developer
P09	Wakabayashi	Software Developer
P10	Wakabayashi	Software Developer
P11	Hyuga	Scrum Master
P12	Hyuga	Software Developer
P13	Hyuga	Software Developer

Observations: A template observation protocol was created to facilitate the observations. The protocol contains basic information about the observation, such as the date, location, participants, target/actual duration, research questions, observer, event and context. According to Merklinger [23], the observation protocol contains target questions to help extract relevant information from all observed events. In total, we observed seven events. Table 4 provides on overview of the observed events per team. All events were observed by at least two researchers taking field notes using the prepared observation protocol templates. Detailed information about the events, the data analysis process, and the field notes can be found in our research protocol [25].

Table 4. Observed Events per Team

Organization	Team	Observed Events
Nankatsu SC	Tsubasa	2× Weekly-Meeting, 1× Plus-Day
Nankatsu SC	Wakabayashi	3× Plus-Day
Toho Academy	Hyuga	3× Plus-Day

The observations were analyzed using summarizing content analysis according to Mayring [22]. To achieve this, conversational actions and subjective impressions were quoted alongside the time, and the main statements were generalized and assigned to identified categories.

Methodological triangulation allowed us to rigorously cross-validate our findings and comprehensively capture both observable phenomena and participants' perspectives, significantly enhancing the reliability and depth of our data.

4   Results

In this section, we present the results of our study. This section is structured based on the action research approach phases according to Susman [34]. First, we give a brief explanation of the results from our diagnosing activities with the case organizations and the teams in particular. Afterwards, we present our results and answer the three research questions. Finally, in the next Sect. 5, we discuss our reflections.

4.1   Need Identification and Exit Point

As explained in the previous section, we were in close collaboration with our partners from practice. We held several meetings (between October 2022 and January 2023) with the case organizations to identify the need from the organizational perspective to participate in this study and to discuss the possibilities and usefulness of the planned intervention. Participation in the intervention by the teams involved was voluntary. We also discussed the expectations and needs of the managers in advance with the team leads involved. The potential of compressed work schedules was to be tested in both organizations to investigate their effect on aspects such as employee and team stress, motivation and performance. Another motivation was to address the topic of compressed work schedules without having to consider the significant potential for change associated with a day off in the 4-day work-week aiming to identify opportunities for a smoother transition to a compressed work schedule approach.

However, it was initially agreed to implement a single intervention, leaving open the possibility of additional measures addressing the compressed work schedule in the future. The rationale behind this decision extended beyond mere legal regulations and restrictions, encompassing organizational considerations as well.

4.2 Effects on Perceived Performance

In this subsection, we answer our first research question: *How does perceived performance change under a compressed work schedule?*

The data on perceived team performance draw an ambivalent picture. While the IWPQ results in both the Tsubasa and Wakabayashi teams show that there has been a change in perceived performance (see Table 5), this is not confirmed by the interview data for all three teams including Hyuga.

In the Wakabayashi team, the IWPQ data indicate an increase in effectiveness and efficiency (task performance scale) in relation to the participants' core tasks. There was also a positive development in organizational effectiveness (Contextual Performance Scale) in this team. The Wakabayashi team showed positive changes throughout the intervention on the scale of behaviors that could harm the well-being of the company or employees, although these changes were somewhat relativized throughout the intervention. The data for Team Tsubasa shows a very similar pattern (see Table 5). Although no change was found on the task performance scale, the other scales were more pronounced, meaning that the overall performance of both teams was perceived to have increased.

Table 5. Overview of IWPQ results for Team Tsubasa

Survey Time	Task Performance	Contextual Performance	Counter-productive Work Behavior	Overall Score
Initial Survey	62.2	50.69	22.22	90.67
Final Survey	62.2	54.17	16.7	99.67

In contrast, the interview data reveal no changes related to the perceived performance for any of the three teams. Almost all interviewees noted in the interviews that there was no change in perceived performance (e.g., P01-P05 and P08-P13). Interviewee P04 points out that no more tickets are being processed. Also, P02 notes that performance has remained the same and that there have been no major changes, either negative or positive. However, some interviewees (P01) note that completing tasks in four days instead of five is also a positive change.

4.3   Impact on Perceived Stress

Based on the results from our study, we answer the second research question; RQ2: *How do team members' perceived stress levels change?*

All three teams confirm that the impact of the 4+ day work-week on perceived stress is highly dependent on the context. Figure 4 depicts the PSQ survey data per team and week of data collection. In particular, the adaptation of the workload to the compressed working week is mentioned as a key factor in all teams. If the same amount of work has to be done in fewer regular working days, additional pressure arises - this was indeed observed in team Hyuga (stress increase of 18% with unchanged workload per iteration), and the Tsubasa and Wakabayashi teams also explicitly point out that stress levels increase without workload adjustment. Conversely, these two teams show that the perception of stress can be stabilized or reduced by appropriate compensation (adjustment of priorities, contingency plans for the loss of the Plus-Day, etc.). Another common aspect is the importance of the organization of the Plus-Day: in the Tsubasa and Wakabayashi teams, the content of the Plus-Days plays a role in the perception of stress. Team activities, training, and process improvements were predominantly described as useful and positive for well-being. On the other hand, tasks that are too complex or perceived as 'normal work' can have a stressful effect on the Plus-Day (this was reported mainly by the Tsubasa team). All teams emphasize the importance of ensuring that the Plus-Day does not become an additional burden, but is properly integrated and supported by employees.

As with perceived performance, the results for stress differed somewhat between the teams. Team Hyuga experienced a increase in stress, whereas team Tsubasa experienced a decrease in stress, and team Wakabayashi experienced almost no change in perceived stress (moderate level remained constant). These differences can be partly explained by the organizational context: In Team Hyuga's agile environment, the same project workload had to be completed in less time (sprints were shortened by Plus-Days and holidays), which caused immediate additional stress without corresponding relief. In contrast, in Team Tsubasa, the Plus-Days were used for improvements and team events, and the Plus-Day could be postponed if necessary, providing real relief to the team - the stress level dropped measurably. In the Wakabayashi team, optimisation projects were also carried out on the Plus-Day, but the overall effect was balanced - the additional demands seemed to be compensated by the benefits. The results emphasise that a 4+ day week can reduce stress, but only under favourable conditions - if these are not met, the concept can also be neutral or even counterproductive for the perception of stress.

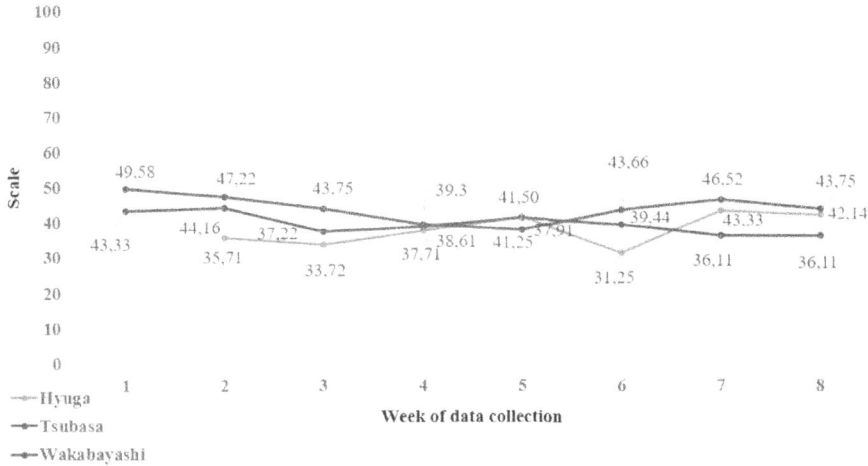

Fig. 4. Vizualization of the PSQ survey results per team

4.4   Benefits of a Plus-Day

In this subsection, we answer our third research question; RQ3: *What are the organizational benefits of the Plus-Day?*

The three teams under study used the Plus-Day in a predominantly positive way, but with different focuses and results: (see Table 6)

Team Tsubasa used the Plus-Day primarily for technical training, process optimization, and the use of new tools. The focus was on joint learning of technical skills and the implementation and optimization of internal workflows. The decision as to which activities should take place was made within the team. This resulted in clearly recognizable benefits, including improved work processes, increased technical expertise among employees, and greater motivation thanks to better team autonomy. However, considerable organizational effort and the need for employees to plan independently were perceived as challenges. In the overall interpretation, the team rated the Plus-Day as clearly positive for productivity and employee motivation, although its organizational implementation remained challenging.

Team Wakabayashi mainly used the Plus-Day for social activities, team building, and occasional specialist training. Planning of the Plus-Day was flexible and internal to the team, which meant that changes could be made at short notice, for example in the event of acute operational needs. Positive effects included a noticeable reduction in stress, improved team spirit, and greater cohesion within the team. However, there were also challenges, particularly when demanding specialist training courses were held or when the Plus-Day had to be canceled due to acute production problems. The overall assessment was clearly positive, although the usability and effectiveness depended heavily on the appropriate framework and the nature of the activities.

Team Hyuga used the Plus-Day primarily for personal development, technical training, and team-building activities. Activities included workshops, technical learning, and internal coordination to continuously improve collaboration. The decision-making process was participatory and digitally supported, for example, using wikis. This approach resulted in higher employee motivation, an improved team atmosphere, and an increase in knowledge transfer. A high initial planning effort and additional organizational burdens were perceived as challenges, particularly due to the compressed working week. Overall, the agile team interpreted the Plus-Day positively in terms of team development and employee motivation, but noted that the planning effort could lead to increased stress.

5   Learnings: Practical Implications

The adoption of compressed work schedules is a major change that comes with various challenges and barriers. The 4+ day work-week may be a good variant for moving towards a compressed work schedule and thus, provides the opportunity for a door-opener to 4-day work-week schedules in organizations, which tend to avoid too much change in a short time. Our findings show, that there is a need for flexible time per week for software development teams to optimize their processes, refactor their source code, perform workshops related to new trends, or conduct team development events. Nevertheless, teams in such a

Table 6. Summary of the utilization and benefits of the Plus-Day across the three teams

Aspect	Team Tsubasa	Team Wakabayashi	Team Hyuga
Primary usage	Technical training, process optimization, utilization of new tools	Team building, social events, occasional training sessions	Personal development, team building, technological skill development
Decision-making processes	Internal team alignment, collaborative research	Internal team planning, flexible adjustments when needed	Participatory, digitally supported (e.g., wiki)
Positive effects (Benefits)	Improved work processes, enhanced technical competencies, increased motivation	Reduced stress, enhanced team cohesion	Increased motivation, improved team atmosphere, knowledge gain
Challenges	Organizational effort, challenges in independent planning	Stress due to demanding training sessions or handling operational emergencies	High initial planning effort, additional organizational burden
Overall interpretation	Clearly positive effects on productivity and motivation, though organizationally demanding	Highly positive for team development and stress reduction, provided activities are suitable	Positive for team development and motivation; however, increased effort might elevate stress

compressed work schedule need a team commitment for a systematic process to prepare, conduct, and review the Plus-day. Thus, the team should consider that the preparation and planning of the Plus-day also takes time. Furthermore, a regular variability in defining when the Plus-day will take place in the workweek is of high importance as every team may need the time of the Plus-day wo tackle upcoming challenges in projects.

However, our findings also show that some team members are tired quickly in finding new ideas for the Plus-day to have an impact on the team, their processes, or projects. Thus, we recommend to indicate an idea pool, which can be used by all the team members to gather ideas day-by-day. To achieve this, and the effectiveness of the 4-Plus-Day, regular and open dialogue within the team is essential. This enables new ideas to be generated and feedback to be used as inspiration for collective activities such as team building or further training. Team-building approaches can include hiking days, for example. Internal and external training opportunities can be used to deepen existing skills and knowledge and to try out new technologies. Implementing these measures improves teamwork, the commitment of team members, and the skills and knowledge of employees. In the long term, this can lead to an increase in performance and a reduction in overall stress levels. From the company's perspective, this offers opportunities to strengthen employee loyalty. Furthermore, research indicates that the stress level of software development team members increase while applying a compressed work schedule (e.g., [35]). Thus, our results are in line with existing literature, and several implications should be taken into account when organizations want to move forward to a compressed work schedule in their day-to-day work. We know, that various types of compressed work schedules exist: From 4-day work-week settings with 40 h per week (10 h a day) to 32 h a week (8 h a day), while keeping in mind that there is a high variety in practice. However, when we know that there is a higher stress level of the team members in such schedules, one should consider enough time for recovering to reduce the stress level in a regularly setting. The Plus-day may also be an opportunity

In summary, we can conclude that the introduction of a 4+ day week also represents a major change for organizations, teams, and employees. Our results show that detailed planning and preparation are important when introducing such a work schedule, and that increased stress among employees must be expected. The respective legal situation and special features of the organizations and teams must also be taken into account during planning. For teams that have to guarantee high availability (e.g., through service level agreements), it must be taken into account that the introduction of a compressed work schedule can often only be compensated for with more employees. Nevertheless, there are many benefits that can be realized within a short period of time. Of the three teams under study, Team Tsubasa still uses the 4+ day week today, and the team has not abolished it since the Action Research study.

6   Threats to Validity

Though we followed a systematically the guidelines for action research interventions [33], some limitations should be taken into account. We discuss the limitations of our study using the threats to validity concept [36], focusing on the measures we took to address the threats to validity below.

Construct Validity: This study deals with abstract constructs such as perceived stress, utilization of the Plus-Day, and subjective benefits. While standardized instruments like the PSQ and semi-structured interviews were employed, the assessment of individual experiences is inherently interpretive and context-dependent. Differences in how each team implemented and experienced the Plus-Day further complicate direct comparisons across cases. Additionally, variations in interview depth and interpretation may have affected consistency in data coding and thematic analysis.

Internal Validity: As the research is based on field experiments without control groups, causality between the intervention (4+ day work-week) and the observed changes in stress or behavior cannot be definitively established. Confounding variables - such as fluctuations in workload, holidays, or internal team dynamics - may have influenced the results. The small sample sizes (n = 5...7) also limit the ability to rule out the effects of outliers or individual influences.

External Validity: All three teams under study were conducted within small, project-oriented teams at two organizations in specific contexts. Therefore, generalizing the findings to other industries, larger or smaller organizations, or different cultural contexts is limited. The relatively high degree of team autonomy and openness to experimentation observed in these cases may not be present in more hierarchical or operationally constrained environments. As such, the observed benefits of the Plus-Day may not transfer without adaptation.

7   Conclusion and Future Work

This studyÂťs results show a differed effect on the stress level per team. While we found a decreased stress level for one team, we identified also an increased stress level in one team. Interestingly, the team with a higher stress level reported as a factor that the workload was not adapted to the compressed work schedule concept, and thus, the team members should achieve a similar workload as before the intervention. Investigating the perceived performance, we found two teams with a similar performance related to the 5-day work-week. However, one team reported an increased performance, especially in terms of optimized effectiveness. The introduced Plus-Day was utilized for a variety of activities. For instance, one team used the additional time to extensively optimize and refactor their source code. Others conducted workshops and training on new topics or focused on team development initiatives.

Our findings are relevant for both research and practice. By introducing and testing a novel concept—the 4+ day work-week—we highlight the potential for a smoother transition toward compressed work schedules. The results emphasize the importance of carefully preparing for the (trial) implementation of such work models. This includes enabling teams to (a) dedicate time to self-selected topics and (b) establish processes that facilitate regular planning and ideation for Plus-Day activities.

Future studies could extend the observation period, incorporate larger and more diverse samples, and ideally include control groups. Moreover, the integration of objective performance and health data (e.g., absenteeism, productivity metrics) could enhance the robustness and generalizability of findings in the context of compressed work schedules.

Disclosure of Interests. The authors have no competing interests to declare that are relevant to the content of this article.

References

1. 4-Day-Week-Global-Foundation: Experimenting with a 4 day week in austral-asia (2023). https://static1.squarespace.com/static/60b956cbe7bf6f2efd86b04e/t/64654696c03e4c1fab3c25ba/1684358809096/4+Day+Week+ANZ+2023+Results.pdf. Accessed 23 Apr 2025
2. Avison, D., Davison, R., Malaurent, J.: Information systems action research: debunking myths and overcoming barriers. Inf. Manag. **55**(2), 177–187 (2018)
3. Basili, V., Caldiera, G., Rombach, D.: The goal question metric approach, pp. 528–532 (1994)
4. Campbell, T.T.: The four-day work week: a chronological, systematic review of the academic literature. Manag. Rev. Q. 1–17 (2023)
5. Dybå, T., Sjøberg, D.I., Cruzes, D.S.: What works for whom, where, when, and why? On the role of context in empirical software engineering. In: Proceedings of the ACM-IEEE International Symposium on Empirical Software Engineering and Measurement, pp. 19–28 (2012). https://doi.org/10.1145/2372251.2372256
6. Fliege, H., Rose, M., Arck, P., Levenstein, S., Klapp, B.F.: Psq - perceived stress questionnaire (2009). https://www.psycharchives.org/en/item/018f244d-58d8-4105-aeb2-b800443c6009. Accessed 23 Apr 2025
7. Hartman, R.L., Weaver, K.M.: Four factors influencing conversion to a four-day work week. IJRB Hum. Res. Manag. **19**(1), 24–27 (1977)
8. Hult, M., Lennung, S.A.: Towards a definition of action research: a note and bibliography. J. Manag. Stud. **17**(2), 241–250 (1980)
9. Jahal, T., Bardoel, E.A., Hopkins, J.: Could the 4-day week work? A scoping review. Asia Pac. J. Hum. Res. **62**(1) (2024)
10. Jain, M.J., Chouliara, N., Blake, H.: From five to four: examining employee perspectives towards the four-day workweek. Adm. Sci. **15**(3) (2025)
11. Jakada, M.B., Kassim, S.I., Hussaini, A., Mohammed, A.I., Rabi'u, A.: Construct validity and reliability of individual work performance questionnaire among academic and non-academic employees. Ilorin J. Hum. Res. Manag. **4**(2), 155–164 (2020)

12. Joskowski, A., Przybylek, A., Marcinkowski, B.: Scaling scrum with a customized nexus framework: a report from a joint industry-academia research project. J. Softw. Evol. Process **53**(7) (2023)
13. Khanna, D., Christensen, E.L., Gosu, S., Wang, X., Paasivaara, M.: Hybrid work meets agile software development: a systematic mapping study. In: Proceedings of the 17th International Conference on Cooperative and Human Aspects of Software Engineering, CHASE '24, pp. 57–67. Association for Computing Machinery (2024)
14. Khanna, D., Edison, H., Nguyen-Duc, A., Kemell, K.K.: Software companies' responses to hybrid working. In: Proceedings of the 50th Euromicro Conference on Software Engineering and Advanced Applications, pp. 244–251 (2024). https://doi.org/10.1109/SEAA64295.2024.00045
15. Koopmans, L., Bernaards, C., Hildebrandt, V., Buuren, S.V., Beek, A.V.d., Vet, H.D.: Improving the individual work performance questionnaire using rasch analysis. J. Appl. Meas. **15**(2), 160–175 (2014)
16. Koopmans, L., Bernaards, C.M., Hildebrandt, V.H., de Vet, H.C.W., van der Beek, A.J.: Construct validity of the individual work performance questionnaire. J. Occup. Environ. Med. **56**(3), 331–337 (2014)
17. Kowalczyk, M., Marcinkowski, B., Przybylek, A.: Scaled agile framework: dealing with software process-related challenges of a financial group with the action research approach. J. Softw. Evol. Process **34**(6) (2022)
18. Kulak, A., Tüzüner, F., Lale, V.: A comparative analysis of flexible working patterns in Germany and Turkey. IJRBS **9**(4), 1–14 (2020)
19. Levenstein, S., et al.: Development of the perceived stress questionnaire: a new tool for psychosomatic research. J. Psychosom. Res. **37**(1), 19–32 (1993)
20. Lewis, K., et al.: The results are in: The uk's four-day week pilot (2023). https://researchrepository.ucd.ie/server/api/core/bitstreams/17e842ef-eb0d-4322-9b6b-dde8e2e74b3a/content. Accessed 21 Apr 2025
21. Lousa, E.P., Alves, M.P., Koopmans, L.: Adaptation and validation of the individual work performance questionnaire into a Portuguese version. Adm. Sci. **14**(7) (2024)
22. Mayring, P.: Einführung in die qualitative Sozialforschung: Eine Anleitung zu qualitativem Denken. Beltz (2016)
23. Merklinger, D.: Beobachtungsprotokolle schreiben: Anforderungen und Stolperstellen, pp. 37–64. Springer Fachmedien Wiesbaden, Wiesbaden (2022)
24. Neumann, M., et al.: What remains from covid-19? Agile software development in hybrid work organization: a single case study. In: 2022 10th International Conference in Software Engineering Research and Innovation (CONISOFT), pp. 29–38 (2022). https://doi.org/10.1109/CONISOFT55708.2022.00015
25. Neumann, M., et al.: Research protocol (2025). https://doi.org/10.5281/zenodo.15446508
26. Ng, Y.Y., Leśniewski, B., Marek, K., Neumann, M., Trzesicki, J.: Unlocking feedback in remote retrospectives: games, anonymity, and continuous reflection in action. In: Marcinkowski, B., et al. (eds.) Harnessing Opportunities: Reshaping ISD in the post-COVID-19 and Generative AI Era. University of Gdańsk (2024). https://doi.org/10.62036/ISD.2024.118
27. Nguyen-Duc, A., et al.: Work-from-home impacts on software project: a global study on software development practices and stakeholder perceptions. Softw. Pract. Exp. **54**(5), 896–926 (2024)
28. Paje, R.C., Escobar, P.B.A., Ruaya, A.M.R., Sulit, P.A.F.: The impact of compressed workweek arrangements on job stress, work-life balance, and work produc-

tivity of rank-and-file employees from different industries in metro manila. J. Phys: Conf. Ser. **3**, 1–7 (2020)

29. Przybylek, A., Albecka, M., Springer, O., Kowalski, W.: Game-based sprint retrospectives: multiple action research. Empir. Softw. Eng. **27**(1) (2022). https://doi.org/10.1007/s10664-021-10043-z

30. Przybyek, A., Belter, D., Conboy, K.: A study of Scrum @ S&P Global in the post-COVID-19 era: Unsuitable for remote work or just flawed implementation? Inf. Softw. Technol. **183**, 107728 (2025)

31. Schor, J., Wen, F., Orla, K., Guolin, G., Bezdenezhnykh, T., Bridson-Hubbard, G.: The four day week: Assessing global trials of reduced work time with no reduction in pay (2022). https://researchrepository.ucd.ie/server/api/core/bitstreams/d3fe0203-cea8-4cd5-8cda-ff2ebbee1bbd/content. Accessed 20 Apr 2025

32. Staron, M.: Action Research in Software Engineering. Springer Nature Switzerland AG (2020)

33. Staron, M.: Guidelines for conducting action research studies in software engineering. e-Informatica Softw. Eng. J. **19**(1) (2025). https://doi.org/10.37190/e-Inf250105

34. Susman, G.: Action research: a sociotechnical systems perspective. In: Beyond Method: Strategies for Social Research, pp. 95–113 (1983)

35. Topp, J., Hille, J.H., Neumann, M., Mötefindt, D.: How a 4-day work week and remote work affect agile software development teams. In: Przybyłek, A., Jarzębowicz, A., Luković, I., Ng, Y.Y. (eds.) LASD 2022. LNBIP, vol. 438, pp. 61–77. Springer, Cham (2022). https://doi.org/10.1007/978-3-030-94238-0_4

36. Wohlin, C., Runeson, P., Höst, M., Ohlsson, M.C., Regnell, B., Wesslén, A.: Experimentation in Software Engineering. Springer, Heidelberg (2012). https://doi.org/10.1007/978-3-642-29044-2

A Multi-agent LLM System for Automated Requirements Analysis: A Study on User Story Generation and Prioritization

Malik Abdul Sami[1]([📧])⬤, Zheying Zhang[1]⬤, Muhammad Waseem[1]⬤,
Kai-Kristian Kemell[1]⬤, Zeeshan Rasheed[1]⬤, Tomas Herda[2]⬤,
Md. Toufique Hasan[1]⬤, Jussi Rasku[1]⬤, and Pekka Abrahamsson[1]⬤

[1] Tampere University, Tampere, Finland
{malik.sami,zheying.zhang,muhammad.waseem,kai-kristian.kemell,
zeeshan.rasheed,mdtoufique.hasan,jussi.rasku,pekka.abrahamsson}@tuni.fi
[2] AI Center of Excellence - Austrian Post, Vienna, Austria
tomas.herda@post.at

Abstract. Manually specifying and prioritizing user stories in software projects is time-consuming and prone to inconsistency. This paper investigates whether Large Language Models (LLMs) can support these activities through a role-based multi-agent system. The proposed system uses four models: GPT-3.5 Turbo, GPT-4o, LLaMA 3.3, and Mistral-Nemo, to generate user stories from a project description and prioritize them using prompts simulating stakeholder roles. Relevance is evaluated using semantic similarity to the project description, and prioritization consistency is assessed using Kendall's Tau distance against expert rankings. Results indicate that all models generate functionally relevant requirements with high semantic similarity, although clarity and conciseness vary. In prioritization, the models show moderate alignment with expert rankings, particularly for mid- and low-priority items, while variability across runs remains a challenge.

Keywords: Requirements generation · Requirements prioritization · Large language model · Multi-agent system

1 Introduction

Agile software projects specify requirements as user stories [1], which describe functionalities from the user's perspective, focusing on their needs and the value provided. This is an iterative process involving close collaboration between users and developers and stories are expressed in non-technical language [8]. Quality user stories are essential for guiding the development process, as they convey user needs. However, poorly specified stories may introduce ambiguities, increase the likelihood of errors and rework in project development [9].

© The Author(s), under exclusive license to Springer Nature Switzerland AG 2026
D. Taibi and D. Smite (Eds.): SEAA 2025, LNCS 16082, pp. 178–187, 2026.
https://doi.org/10.1007/978-3-032-04200-2_12

In Requirements Engineering (RE), Large Language Models (LLMs) have shown potential to support elicitation, specification, and prioritization tasks [12]. Arora *et al.* [4] provide a broader vision for generative AI in RE. LLMs have also been used to address complex software challenges by automating development roles [18]. Earlier studies [17,19] explored multi-agent integration within LLM frameworks to support requirements analysis, design, and code generation. Other studies [10,11,22] showed how LLM agents can enhance user story quality and support role-based collaboration across various stages of the software lifecycle.

This study extends our earlier work by comparing user story generation and prioritization across distinct LLMs within a multi-agent framework [15]. In agile development, requirements prioritization is a collaborative effort involving product owner, developer, and quality assurance, taking into account business value, technical feasibility, and testing [3,16]. Simulating these roles as agents reflects this diversity and allows examination of how role-specific reasoning influences prioritization outcomes. While earlier research has explored LLM use in isolated RE tasks and agent collaboration, limited attention has been given to applying a multi-agent and role-based approach for prioritization and evaluating consistency across models and runs [7]. The following research questions guide the investigation:

- **RQ1:** How relevant are the user stories generated by LLMs from project descriptions using role-specific prompts?
- **RQ2:** To what extent does a multi-agent LLM system produce stable user story prioritizations across multiple runs and models?

To investigate these questions, a system is designed and implemented for automated user story generation, a multi-agent framework is developed to simulate distinct project team roles for user story prioritization, and the outputs are analyzed using quantitative metrics and compared with the human expert's suggestion. In the prioritization task, the agents use the 100-dollar prioritization technique [20] to rank the user stories and support the analysis.

The contributions of this study are twofold: a) we designed and implemented a role-based multi-agent system that leverages LLMs to automatically generate and prioritize user stories from project descriptions. b) We evaluated user story generation and prioritization across four LLMs, i.e. GPT-3.5, GPT-4o, LLaMA 3.3, and Mistral-Nemo, using semantic similarity for functional relevance and Kendall's Tau for prioritization consistency, with results compared to human suggestions.

2 Proposed Approach and System Implementation

Requirements specification and prioritization is an iterative and collaborative process involving multiple stakeholders. User stories, which are commonly used in agile development, describe functionalities from the user's perspective and help communicate needs in a concise format [6]. In typical practice, a product owner gathers and documents feature requests as user stories aligned with project goals. The development team assesses technical feasibility and estimates effort, often in collaboration with architects or quality assurance roles. Prioritization is based on business value, complexity, and team capacity, and feedback cycles may introduce new or updated requirements.

The PO Agent acts as a product owner, maintaining a clear understanding of the product vision and core features. It gathers requirements and generates user stories from the project vision and Minimum Viable Product (MVP) description, describing functionalities from the user's perspective. Once specified, the PO, Developer (Dev), and Quality Assurance (QA) agents prioritize the stories. The PO Agent aligns them with business objectives and customer needs. The Dev Agent, acting as a senior full-stack developer, evaluates technical complexity, dependencies, and feasibility. The QA Agent focuses on quality and testing requirements, identifying usability and performance risks. Each agent allocates scores using the 100-dollar method and provides justifications based on their stakeholder perspective.

The Manager Agent reviews the individual 100-dollar allocations and rankings from all three agents and produces a final prioritization. This balances business goals, technical constraints, and quality risks, reflecting the collaborative decision-making typical of planning sessions. Figure 1 shows the sequence diagram of object interactions and message flow within the system. This multi-agent, role-based design allows the system to produce a balanced prioritization that reflects the perspectives of different roles in a software team.

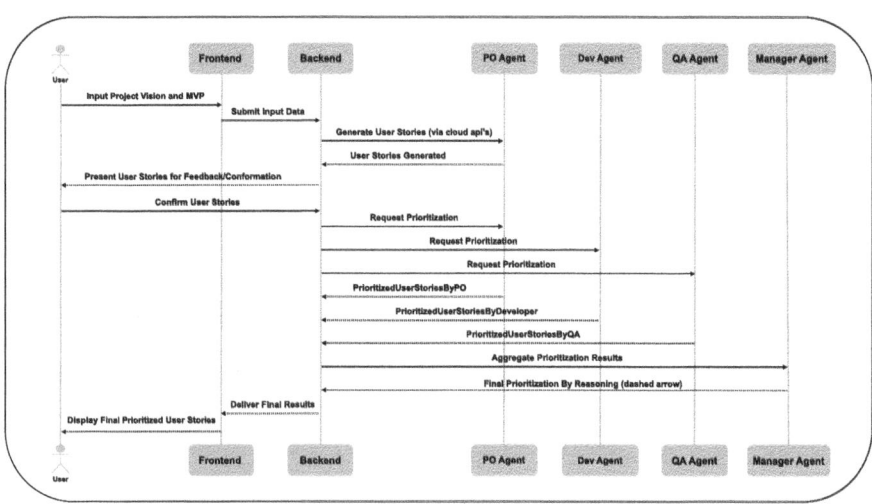

Fig. 1. Sequence diagram of multi-agent system.

2.1   System Design

We implement a web-based multi-agent system to simulate role-based collaboration in requirements analysis. The frontend (HTML, CSS, JavaScript, React) communicates with a Python backend (Starlette) via WebSocket for real-time feedback. User stories are generated using API calls to LLMs (GPT-3.5 Turbo, GPT-4o, LLaMA 3.3, Mistral-Nemo). For prioritization, parallel calls simulate the PO, Dev, and QA agents; their outputs are aggregated by a Manager Agent to produce a final ranked list. This architecture supports coordination logic that reflects common software team decision-making.

Project Description: Mobile Delivery Application (MDA) Vision Statement: For postal delivery workers who need an efficient and accurate way to manage deliveries, the Mobile Delivery Application is a smartphone-enabled tool that streamlines the entire delivery process from preparation to delivery and accounting.

MVP (Excerpt): The Mobile Delivery Application (MDA) is a tool that helps postal delivery workers prepare, deliver, and account for their deliveries. It has three main phases: Preparation, Delivery, and Accounting. In the **Preparation** phase, the user logs in by scanning their user barcode and adding their tour or delivery area number. The user also tags their card to the device. The user then goes to the Preparation menu and scans the items to be ... The user can also print the delivery orders for each list or item by going to the Print menu and selecting the Print orders option. The user is then asked to confirm the pop-up and is returned to the main menu ...

We evaluate the system using a real-world logistics project previously studied in [22], involving a MDA used by postal workers. It supports three workflow phases: Preparation, Delivery, and Accounting. The project vision and MVP documents serve as inputs for story generation, with an excerpt included in the Project Description subsection and a full version with sample inputs available in the repository[1]. To prioritize user stories, we adopt the 100-dollar method [21], where agents distribute scores based on perceived importance. This technique is known for transparency, simplicity, and suitability for LLM-generated content [5].

2.2   Evaluation

We evaluate whether different LLMs can generate relevant user stories and produce consistent prioritizations aligned with expert rankings. The tested models include GPT-3.5 Turbo and GPT-4o LLaMA 3.3 and Mistral-Nemo[2]. Proprietary and open-source models are used to reflect diversity in current tools. Each model runs three independent prioritizations on a shared set of stories, generated from the same project input.

---

[1] https://github.com/GPT-Laboratory/multiagent-prioritization.
[2] https://openrouter.ai/.

User Story Relevance. We assess the semantic relevance of generated user stories using the sentence-transformer model **all-MiniLM-L6-v2** [14]. Each story is compared to the input project description using cosine similarity. The average of the maximum similarity scores across all user stories yields a relevance score:

$$\text{Relevance} = \frac{1}{N} \sum_{i=1}^{N} \max(\text{cos\_sim}(E_i, C)) \qquad (1)$$

where N is the number of stories, E_i is the embedding of the i-th story, and C is the set of sentence embeddings from the Vision and MVP.

Priority Consistency. To measure consistency across runs, we compute Kendall's Tau coefficient τ between priority lists:

$$\tau = \frac{2}{n(n-1)}(C - D) \qquad (2)$$

where C and D are the counts of concordant and discordant pairs, respectively. For each model, we identify the most consistent output by selecting the list with the lowest average Kendall's Tau distance to other runs.

Comparison Against Expert Judgment. The most consistent priority list from each model is compared with a human expert's ranking using Kendall's Tau distance to assess alignment with domain expert suggestions.

3 Results

We implement and experiment with the multi-agent system using GPT-3.5 Turbo and GPT-4o, LLaMA 3.3 and Mistral-Nemo as agents separately. The results are reported based on semantic similarity scores, prioritization rankings, and agreement suggestions by the human expert.

To address **RQ1**, Fig. 2 presents the semantic similarity scores of individual user stories generated by each model with respect to the combined vision and MVP input. GPT-3.5 Turbo generates 10 stories with an average similarity of 0.44, GPT-4o generates 12 stories with an average of 0.47, LLaMA 3.3 generates 17 stories with an average of 0.50, and Mistral-Nemo generates 12 stories with an average of 0.47. Although LLaMA 3.3 achieves the highest average similarity, a manual comparison revealed that the stories generated by GPT-4o, while slightly lower in similarity, provided more comprehensive coverage of the project description; that is to say, capturing relevant requirements from all three phases from the MVP document. In contrast, the outputs from the other three models omitted one or more core feature areas. Based on this coverage and alignment, we selected the 12 user stories generated by GPT-4o for the subsequent prioritization task. The 12 user stories generated by GPT-4o, as shown in Table 2, cover the features described in the MVP: US1US4 belong to the preparation phase,

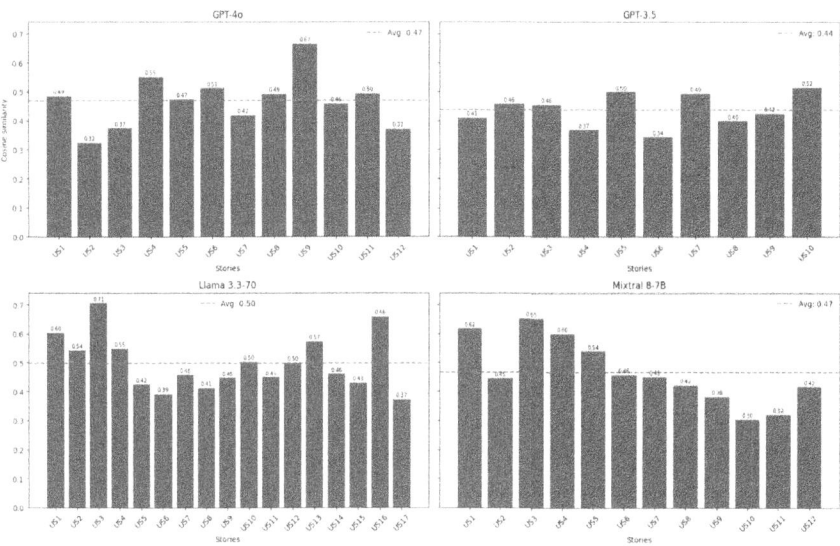

Fig. 2. Semantic similarity of user stories generated by GPT-3.5 Turbo, GPT-4o, Mistral-Nemo and LLaMA 3.3

Table 1. Comparison of Kendall's Tau Distances for GPT-3.5 Turbo, GPT-4o, LLaMA 3.3, and Mistral-Nemo results

GPT-3.5 Turbo	P1&P2	P1&P3	P2&P3	P1	P2	P3
Pairwise Kendall's Tau Distances	0.364	0.333	0.394	–	–	–
Average Kendall's Tau Distance	–	–	–	**0.348**	0.379	0.364
GPT-4o	**P4&P5**	**P4&P6**	**P5&P6**	**P4**	**P5**	**P6**
Pairwise Kendall's Tau Distance	0.606	0.727	0.424	–	–	–
Average Kendall's Tau Distance	–	–	–	0.667	**0.515**	0.576
LLaMA 3.3	**P7&P8**	**P7&P9**	**P8&P9**	**P7**	**P8**	**P9**
Pairwise Kendall's Tau Distance	0.303	0.364	0.364	–	–	–
Average Kendall's Tau Distance	–	–	–	**0.333**	**0.333**	0.364
Mistral-Nemo	**P10&P11**	**P10&P12**	**P11&P12**	**P10**	**P11**	**P12**
Pairwise Kendall's Tau Distance	0.221	0.303	0.282	–	–	–
Average Kendall's Tau Distance	–	–	–	0.312	**0.252**	0.342

US5US10 cover delivery, and US11US12 focus on accounting. We do not include acceptance criteria due to space constraints.

To address **RQ2**, table 1 shows the pairwise Kendall's Tau distances between runs, reflecting each model's internal consistency. P1 (GPT-3.5), P5 (GPT-4o), P7 (LLaMA 3.3), and P11 (Mistral-Nemo) exhibited the highest consistency, i.e., lowest average distance, with P11 achieving the overall lowest at 0.252.

Table 2. User story prioritization by Human, GPT-3.5 Turbo (G3), GPT-4o (G4), LLaMA 3.3 (LL), and Mistral-Nemo (MN) using 100-dollar allocation method. $ = allocation; P = priority rank.

ID	User Story	$-H	P-H	$-G3	P-G3	$-G4	P-G4	$-LL	P-LL	$-MN	P-MN
US1	As a postal worker, I want to scan and organize delivery items into categorized lists so that I can efficiently manage my deliveries	13	1	13	1	17	2	13	1	16	1
US2	As a postal worker, I want to remove items from the list if they are unavailable so that my list stays up to date	4	12	8	7	5	9	5	10	8	6
US3	As a postal worker, I want to create and assign customized STOP and GAS lists so that I can manage grouped deliveries efficiently	7	8	12	2	6	7	10	2	12	2
US4	As a postal worker, I want to log in by scanning my barcode so that I can quickly access the system without manual entry	5	11	6	9	6	8	8	6	8	7
US5	As a postal worker, I want to notify recipients if their item is available for pickup so they can collect it from a designated location	8	5	10	5	5	10	9	4	12	3
US6	As a postal worker, I want to deliver items to a secure location so I can complete deliveries when the recipient is not available	7	9	9	6	7	4	8	7	8	8
US7	As a postal worker, I want to print receipts and notifications for items with special conditions so I can provide proper documentation	8	6	6	10	7	5	5	11	3	9
US8	As a postal worker, I want to assign a delivery status to each item so I can track the progress of the delivery	8	7	8	8	7	6	9	5	12	4
US9	As a postal worker, I want to collect signatures from recipients so I can confirm delivery and maintain accountability	12	2	11	3	18	1	10	3	12	5
US10	As a postal worker, I want to track delivery obstacles so I can report issues like 'Company closed' or 'Refused to accept'	7	10	6	11	5	11	5	12	3	10
US11	As a postal worker, I want to account for cash collected during deliveries so I can reconcile it at the end of the day	11	3	6	12	12	3	6	8	3	11
US12	As a postal worker, I want to deposit undelivered items at a post office so I can complete my accounting for the day	10	4	11	4	5	12	6	9	3	12

These four runs were selected for comparison with the human product owner's suggestion to evaluate both statistical consistency and alignment with human judgment.

Table 2 illustrates prioritization outputs from human product owner, GPT-3.5 Turbo (P1), GPT-4o (P5), LLaMA 3.3 (P7), Mistral-NEMO (P11). The table includes both priority ranks and 100-dollar allocations for each user story, reflecting their relative importance. As shown in Table 2, the human product owner assigns high priority to US1 (organizing delivery items), US9 (recipient signature), US11 (cash reconciliation), and US12 (undelivered item accounting). These imply that the human product owner emphasizes the importance of delivery tracking, validation, and financial reconciliation in postal workflows. GPT-4o (P5) shows the closest to the human view. It keeps the high placement of US1, US9, and US11. The main deviation is that US12's bottom rank, down-weighting end-of-day accounting. Mistral-Nemo (P11) also aligns on US1 and US9 and, like GPT-4o, and values US3 (custom STOP/GAS lists) and US5 (pickup notification). LLaMA 3.3 (P7) values US1, US3, and US5, but lowers US7 (receipt printing) and US10, suggesting less emphasis on documentation and exception reporting than the human. Additionally, the human product owner mentioned that "*The printing user story could be valued higher, however delivery person can use a back-up (paper and pen) to perform his task, even though it could significantly decrease delivery time to implement a user story with printing*". This is significantly different from the priority suggestions by almost all the models. GPT-3.5 Turbo (P1) shows the greatest divergence. It elevates US3 and US12, while lowering US9 and US11, favoring logistical grouping and final accounting over confirmation and cash procedures.

Across the prioritization lists, US6 (secure delivery) and US8 (status tracking) receive similar dollar allocations yet their priority vary from 4th to 9th. This indicates different interpretations of urgency versus effort. US2 (remove unavailable items) and US4 (barcode login) consistently occupy the lower half of every list. In addition, US10 is consistently down-prioritized in all priority lists.

4   Discussion

The semantic similarity scores show that all four models generated stories relevant to the MVP. While LLaMA 3.3 included more UI-level detail, GPT-4o produced concise stories with some content to loss. This suggests that LLMs can extract functional requirements from early project descriptions using role-specific prompts, but clarity and non-redundancy remain important considerations.

We examine the consistency of the prioritization output in three runs for each model using Kendall's Tau and compare selected runs against the human expert rankings. The comparison shows a partial alignment with the prioritization of the human expert. The results indicate that while LLMs consistently recognize the relative importance of individual user stories, none fully replicates the prioritization logic of the product owner familiar with the project. Despite receiving identical prompts and instructions, the models produce divergent rankings and feasibility assessments. This variation is not unexpected. Experienced product owners themselves can prioritize stories differently, depending on how they interpret urgency, strategic value, and project-specific context.

From a research perspective, these findings show that LLM-based multi-agent setups can support the generation and prioritization of user stories. However, complete alignment with expert judgment and rankings remains a challenge. Although the system receives the project description and the defined agent roles, this background information alone is not sufficient. In addition, the dynamic nature of a project can influence requirement priorities. Such context should be considered in future designs. These findings align with recent work highlighting the limitations of large language models in capturing nuanced domain context, expert judgment, and dynamic requirements factors [13]. This can guide future work on hybrid prioritization tools and model calibration methods [2].

For practitioners, the multi-agent system provides recommendations that may differ from human expert judgments but can offer valuable direction and facilitate discussion. However, the outputs should be reviewed and adapted based on domain-specific knowledge. In settings where team alignment or risk management is important, such as agile environments that emphasize collaboration between stakeholders, human oversight remains necessary.

5   Conclusion

In this study, we developed a multi-agent system using role-specific prompts to generate and prioritize user stories from project descriptions. Results show that LLMs can generate relevant user stories, though some outputs were unclear or repetitive. Prioritization was partly consistent with expert rankings, but models followed different reasoning. To improve practical utility, future work will involve multiple experts to examine divergences in model reasoning, adjust model parameters, compare model performance across projects and domains. Also, incorporating real-time expert feedback into agent decisions may help align system outputs with practical needs in dynamic project contexts.

References

1. Abed, O., Nebe, K., Abdellatif, A.B.: Ai-generated user stories supporting human-centred development: an investigation on quality. In: Stephanidis, C., Antona, M., Ntoa, S., Salvendy, G. (eds.) HCI International 2024 Posters, pp. 3–13. Springer, Cham (2024). https://doi.org/10.1007/978-3-031-62110-9_1
2. Agilemania: User story prioritization with ai tools (2024). https://agilemania.com/tutorial/user-story-prioritization-with-ai-tools. Accessed 21 Jan 2025
3. Anwar, R., Bashir, M.B.: A systematic literature review of ai-based software requirements prioritization technique. IEEE Access (2023)
4. Arora, C., Grundy, J., Abdelrazek, M.: Advancing requirements engineering through generative AI: assessing the role of llms. In: Generative AI for Effective Software Development, pp. 129–148. Springer, Heidelberg (2024). https://doi.org/10.1007/978-3-031-55642-5_6
5. Berander, P., Andrews, A.: Requirements prioritization. In: Engineering and Managing Software Requirements, pp. 69–94. Springer, Heidelberg (2005). https://doi.org/10.1007/3-540-28244-0_4

6. Cohn, M.: User Stories Applied: For Agile Software Development. Addison-Wesley Professional, Boston (2004)
7. He, J., Treude, C., Lo, D.: Llm-based multi-agent systems for software engineering: literature review, vision, and the road ahead. ACM Trans. Softw. Eng. Methodol. **34**(5), 1–30 (2025)
8. Herwanto, G.B.: Automating data flow diagram generation from user stories using large language models. In: 7th Workshop on Natural Language Processing for Requirements Engineering (2024)
9. Heyn, H.M., et al.: Requirement engineering challenges for AI-intense systems development. In: 2021 IEEE/ACM 1st Workshop on AI Engineering-Software Engineering for AI (WAIN), pp. 89–96. IEEE (2021)
10. Jin, D., Jin, Z., Chen, X., Wang, C.: Mare: multi-agents collaboration framework for requirements engineering. arXiv preprint arXiv:2405.03256 (2024)
11. Manish, S.: An autonomous multi-agent llm framework for agile software development. Int. J. Trend Sci. Res. Dev. **8**(5), 892–898 (2024)
12. Mehraj, A., Zhang, Z., Systä, K.: A tertiary study on AI for requirements engineering. In: International Working Conference on Requirements Engineering: Foundation for Software Quality, pp. 159–177. Springer, Heidelberg (2024). https://doi.org/10.1007/978-3-031-57327-9_10
13. Norheim, J.J., Rebentisch, E., Xiao, D., Draeger, L., Kerbrat, A., de Weck, O.L.: Challenges in applying large language models to requirements engineering tasks. Des. Sci. **10**, e16 (2024)
14. Reimers, N.: Sentence-bert: sentence embeddings using siamese bert-networks. arXiv preprint arXiv:1908.10084 (2019)
15. Sami, M.A., Waseem, M., Zhang, Z., Rasheed, Z., Systä, K., Abrahamsson, P.: Early results of an ai multiagent system for requirements elicitation and analysis. In: International Conference on Product-Focused Software Process Improvement, pp. 307–316. Springer, Heidelberg (2024). https://doi.org/10.1007/978-3-031-78386-9_20
16. dos Santos, C.A., Bouchard, K., Minetto Napoleão, B.: Automatic user story generation: a comprehensive systematic literature review. Int. J. Data Sci. Anal. 1–24 (2024)
17. Suri, S., Das, S.N., Singi, K., Dey, K., Sharma, V.S., Kaulgud, V.: Software engineering using autonomous agents: are we there yet? In: 2023 38th IEEE/ACM International Conference on Automated Software Engineering (ASE), pp. 1855–1857. IEEE (2023)
18. Waseem, M., et al.: Artificial intelligence procurement assistant: enhancing bid evaluation. In: International Conference on Software Business, pp. 108–114. Springer, Cham (2023). https://doi.org/10.1007/978-3-031-53227-6_8
19. Wei, B.: Requirements are all you need: from requirements to code with llms. In: 2024 IEEE 32nd International Requirements Engineering Conference (RE), pp. 416–422. IEEE (2024)
20. Wiegers, K.E., Beatty, J.: Software Requirements. Pearson Education, Boston (2013)
21. Yaseen, M.: Exploratory study of existing research on software requirements prioritization: a systematic literature review. J. Softw. Evol. Process e2613 (2024)
22. Zhang, Z., Rayhan, M., Herda, T., Goisauf, M., Abrahamsson, P.: Llm-based agents for automating the enhancement of user story quality: an early report. In: International Conference on Agile Software Development, pp. 117–126. Springer, Cham (2024). https://doi.org/10.1007/978-3-031-61154-4_8

Discovering Patterns in Test Code Refactorings: A Preliminary Study

Railana Santana[1]([⊠]) , Luana Martins[2] , Larissa Rocha[3] ,
Carla Ilane Bezerra[4] , Heitor Costa[5] , and Ivan Machado[1]

[1] Federal University of Bahia (UFBA), Salvador, Brazil
{railana.santana,ivan.machado}@ufba.br
[2] University of Salerno (UNISA), Salerno, Italy
lalmeidamartins@unisa.it
[3] State University of Bahia (UNEB), Alagoinhas, Brazil
larissabastos@uneb.br
[4] Federal University of Ceará (UFC), Quixadá, Brazil
carlailane@ufc.br
[5] Federal University of Lavras (UFLA), Lavras, Brazil
heitor@ufla.br

Abstract. Test smells degrade the quality of code and often occur together, indicating the need for combined refactorings to eliminate them. Although existing literature provides evidence of co-occurrences of test smells, little is known about the impact of refactoring such co-occurrences. In this context, it is crucial to understand the potential impact of combining test code refactoring strategies to eliminate multiple instances of test smells. This study reports on the analysis of test code refactoring of an open-source software project. The results indicate some consequences of test code removing concerning test smell co-occurrence: (i) no fixing of test smells; (ii) fixing multiple test smells instances together; and (iii) fixing single test smell instances.

Keywords: Software testing · Test smells · Test code refactoring

1 Introduction

Maintaining a high-quality test code is essential to ensure reliable and maintainable software systems [10,24]. Test smells are poor design choices in test code that can harm the comprehension and maintenance of test code [4,6,21–23,25]. While individual test smells are harmful, their simultaneous occurrence, known as test smell co-occurrence, can amplify their adverse effects. This phenomenon occurs when multiple test smell instances coexist in a test class or method, resulting in a complex and interrelated design issue [20].

Palomba et al. [11] studied the frequent co-occurrence of different test smells. For instance, *Assertion Roulette* often appears along with other smells, and strong correlations have been observed between pairs, such as *Mystery Guest*

D. Taibi and D. Smite (Eds.): SEAA 2025, LNCS 16082, pp. 188–198, 2026.
https://doi.org/10.1007/978-3-032-04200-2_13

and *Resource Optimism, Mystery Guest* and *Indirect pairs Testing*, and *Indirect Testing* and *Test Code Duplication* test smells. These combinations often indicate more severe test code quality issues and are strong candidates for refactoring.

Refactoring involves internal structural changes that preserve the external behavior of the software [1,2,9]. It eliminates antipatterns through targeted transformations, making the code more understandable and easier to maintain [9,17]. Furthermore, refactoring of the test code promotes regression detection and facilitates the evolution of safe systems [10].

Previous research has examined test smells related to code coverage [26], refactoring strategies [12], and their impact on defect proneness and change frequency [20]. However, little has been investigated on how refactorings affect the co-occurrence of smells. Understanding whether refactorings can simultaneously address multiple intertwined smells is critical for improving test quality and guiding maintenance practices. It is especially relevant for practitioners who face ongoing challenges in managing and refactoring test code effectively [7,8,13].

Recent advances in automated refactoring with large language models (LLMs) show promise in simulating manual refactorings. However, these methods can fail when faced with coexisting problems in the test code, as they often do not indicate where to start or how to prioritize refactorings [3]. The order of application can affect the outcome, solving some problems and exacerbating others. Current approaches rely on heuristics or fixed classifications, which often fail to capture the complex interactions inherent in real-world development.

In this study, we investigate whether refactorings in tests with multiple smells effectively eliminate these antipatterns. We analyze a real open-source project, comparing two versions of the test suite to track removed smells. By focusing on removed co-occurrence smells, we identified that refactorings could result in: (i) no fixing of test smells; (ii) fixing of multiple test smells instances; and (iii) fixing of a single test smells instance. Our contributions are threefold: (i) an empirical analysis of test smell co-occurrence before and after refactoring; (ii) a manual inspection of refactored test code to validate behavior preservation; and (iii) insights into how developers address intertwined test smells in practice.

2   Methodology

This study examines the impact of refactoring on co-occurrence test smells in automated test code. Specifically, we examine whether refactoring removes multiple co-occurrence smells while preserving test behavior. Our goal is to provide empirical evidence on the impact of refactoring on clusters of test smells, supporting practitioners and researchers in improving test quality and maintainability.

The main research question (RQ) is: **How does test code refactoring impact test smell co-occurrence?** In this RQ, we seek to understand to what extent refactoring activities address the co-occurrence of test smells and whether they typically result in removing them.

2.1 Context of the Study

We selected the Apache Maven Dependency Plugin (AMDP)[1] project for this study. The project handles artifacts (copying and extracting from local or remote repositories), uses Java and JUnit 4.13.2, and, as of May 2025, has 159 stars, 181 forks, 34 tags, 20 branches, and 75 contributors. Its long history, active community, and significant evolution of the test code make it a great candidate for analyzing refactorings in real tests. We analyzed AMDP's test code by comparing two versions: v_1 ($3.3.0$[2]) and v_0 ($3.1.2$[3]). The nearly two-year gap between them provides enough refactoring data for a broad set of test smells. Tags with shorter intervals before v_1 had too few test code changes for this analysis.

2.2 Study Steps

Detection of Test Smells. We used the RAIDE tool to identify test smells in both versions of the AMDP project, finding 15 types (Table 1) in the JUnit code. The results were exported to CSV files, and the raw data is available online[4].

Tracking of Test Smells. We manually inspected the test classes of both versions to compare the results and identify refactorings (smells present in v_0 and absent in v_1). Smells can change location due to library changes, added or removed methods. Therefore, we classified smells into four statuses: *(i) added* - only in v_1; *(ii) unchanged* - in both versions, same line; *(iii) relocated* - in both, but on different lines; and *(iv) removed* - only in v_0.

Selection of Removed Test Smells Co-occurrence. Since we analyzed the impact of refactoring on multiple smells, we focused only on the smells that were removed together. The 21 smells removed (Table 1) came from methods or classes that also had other smells removed, so we selected all of them.

Inspection of Removed Test Smells Co-occurrence. Next, we analyzed methods that removed co-occurrences of test smells to verify whether the changes preserved the test behavior. If a change had removed a test smell but kept the test behavior, i.e., its sole purpose was to improve the test code, we classified it as a real refactoring effort. Two authors cross-checked this classification to increase reliability and resolve disagreements through discussion.

Data Analysis. We consider test code refactoring as a modification that removes one or more test smells, maintaining the original behavior, following the classic definition [2], with a focus on the quality of the test code. We manually

---

[1] https://maven.apache.org/plugins/maven-dependency-plugin/.

[2] Commit ID: e52bc0248c00dbf5458a0ce080db260148dab4b9.

[3] Commit ID: 4571c8844e5438e6c3514832d071f5e17030c666.

[4] Dataset: https://figshare.com/s/c350afb3b487b0831653.

inspect methods or classes where multiple smells were removed between versions v_0 and v_1, disregarding changes that impacted behavior. This careful classification ensures that our analysis focuses only on deliberate quality improvements in test code rather than incidental or functional changes.

3 Results

Except for the *PS* test smell, present only in v_0, all the others were found in both versions (v_0 and v_1) of the AMDP project. Table 1 shows the number of test smells per version and their status. A total of 1,036 test smells were detected in v_0 and 1,039 in v_1, with *AR* being the most frequent. Comparing the versions, we observed 23 new test smell instances, 384 kept in the same position, 632 repositioned within the method, and only 21 removed. We analyzed the latter to understand the effects of the refactoring in the context of multiple test smells.

Table 1. Details of test smells status.

Test Smell	v_0	v_1	Added	Unchanged	Reallocated	Removed
Assertion Roulette (AR)	455	462	10	207	245	4
Conditional Test Logic (CTL)	68	69	1	26	42	0
Duplicate Assert (DA)	63	62	0	42	20	1
Eager Test (EgT)	51	52	1	18	33	0
Empty Test (EmT)	3	5	2	3	0	0
Exception Catching Throwing (ECT)	19	16	0	4	12	3
Lazy Test (LT)	57	58	3	20	35	2
Magic Number Test (MNT)	94	97	3	13	81	0
Mystery Guest (MG)	92	91	1	16	74	2
Print Statement (PS)	6	0	0	0	0	6
Resource Optimism (RO)	44	43	0	7	36	1
Sensitive Equality (SE)	8	8	0	0	8	0
Sleepy Test (ST)	8	8	0	0	8	0
Unknown Test (UT)	47	48	2	28	18	1
Verbose Test (VT)	21	20	0	0	20	1
Total	**1,036**	**1,039**	**23**	**384**	**632**	**21**

Figure 1 details the removed test smells located in six methods and four test classes. Each instance has been assigned a unique *Id* for reference. For example, Id #01 represents a *MG* on line 52 of the *testEnvironment* method in the *TestBuildClasspathMojo* class. We also indicate whether any refactorings were made. Next, we detail the test class transformations that removed test smell instances.

TestBuildClasspathMojo Test Class. Among the four test classes, the *TestBuildClasspathMojo* class presented the highest number of removed test smells

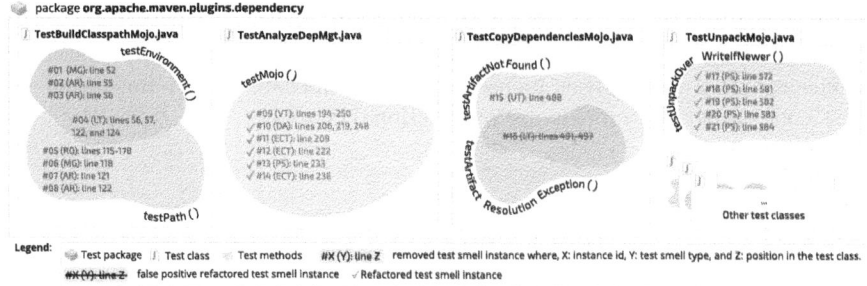

Fig. 1. Overview of the analysis of the removed test smell instances.

(eight instances of four different test smells). Two test methods presented test smells removal: *testEnvironment* and *testPath*. The *testEnvironment* method presented one *MG* test smell instance (Id #01 in Fig. 1) and two *AR* test smell instances (Id #02–03). One *LT* test smell instance occurred in both methods (Id #04). The *testPath* method presented one *RO* test smell instance (Id #05), one *MG* test smell instance (Id #06), and two *AR* test smell instances (Id #07–08). In instance Id #01, there was a call to an external file, and after the changes, the external file was relocated to the *setUp* method. Even after removing the call from the original method, the *MG* test smell remained in the test class, i.e., there was no refactoring. Instances #02 and #03 removed from the original method were found in another method of the same test class in the v_0. In other words, these have been shifted and continue to affect test classes. Instance #04 refers to the call of the *getProject* method in assertions of two different methods. We observed that the changes moved these assertions to the *setUp* method, violating the purpose of that method. Therefore, we could infer that the project changes were not intended to refactor instance #04. As the internal structure of the test class was modified, and the external file used in the *testPath* method was relocated, both the *RO* and *MG* test smell instances (Id #05 and #06, respectively) were relocated in this change. To understand the removed *AR* test smells in the *testPath* test method, we inspected both versions and noticed the *testEnvironment* and *testPath* methods had duplicate code in v_0. Both methods declared an object and made two assertions checking the declared object. Instances #07 and #08 replicate instances #02 and #03. Hence, in addition to these *AR* test smells, the test class had duplication in the test code. The test class transformations caused the removal of that object and its respective assertions from the *testEnvironment* and *testPath* methods to another part of the test class. In other words, no refactoring occurred to remove the *AR* test smell instances between v_0 and v_1. On the other hand, duplicate test code was handled, decreasing the number of assertions without any explanation in the test class. Although eight instances of test smells were removed in this test class, the code was not changed, motivated by refactoring.

TestAnalyzeDepMgt Test Class. We identified six instances of four different removed test smells in the *TestAnalyzeDepMgt* class. All removed test smell instances were in the *testMojo* method. Among the removed test smells, this method presented one *VT* test smell instance (Id #09), one *DA* test smell instance (Id #10), one *PS* test smell instance (Id #13), and three *ECT* test smell instances (Id #11–12 and #14). The *DA* test smell instance (Id #10) occurred due to the three failed checks to the same parameters. In version v_1, the changes took place in the *testMojo* method, and only one fail structure remained, making the test code cleaner and with a single purpose. In addition to the *DA* test smell instance, the changes removed others. We identified three *ECT* test smell instances (Id #11–12 and #14) removed. In version v_0, the method had four *try/catch* structures. After changes, only a *try/catch* structure remained, making the test easier to understand. In line 233 of the *testMojo* method, the changes removed the *System.out.println* statement, resulting in the refactoring of instance #13. Instance #09 (*VT* test smell) occurred in the same method where the *DA*, *ECT*, and *PS* test smell instances were removed. We noted that the transformations in the method reduced four test smells, summing up six test smells instances. As the class had many *try/catch* structures and assertions, the number of lines of that method decreased from 56 to 26 lines of code.

TestCopyDependenciesMojo Test Class. We identified two removed instances of test smells in the *TestCopyDependenciesMojo* class in two test methods: *testArtifactNotFound* and *testArtifactResolutionException*. In version v_0, two test methods had only one statement invoking a helper method with their respective parameters (each invocation with different parameters). However, such parameters were not used in the helper method. In version v_1, the refactoring of the helper method removed the unused parameters. Then, one of the test methods was removed (Id #15), *testArtifactNotFound*. The other test method contains calls for a test method instead of a production method, i.e., there is no refactoring of *UT* test smell (Id #16).

TestUnpackMojo Test Class. We identified five instances of a particular removed test smell in the *TestUnpackMojo* class (Id #17–21). Instances #17–21 occurred in the *testUnpackOverWriteIfNewer* method of the *TestUnpackMojo* class. In version v_1, these instances were refactored by excluding the lines with the *System.out.println* statement. This change did not modify the test result since that statement only tracks the value of objects through the console.

Based on the analysis of test code transformations in the AMDP project, the main findings are:

Summary: One test smell instance was refactored individually (Id #15); 11 were refactored together with others (Id #09–14, #17–21); and eight were resettled within the same test class, without refactoring (Id #01–08).

4   Discussion

In this study, we identified that software engineers might incorrectly modify the test code, resulting in poorly refactored code and, consequently, retaining test smells in the code. For example, one incorrect test code refactoring can unintentionally relocate multiple test smell instances or insert new ones, worsening the code quality of its original version. In addition, when test code undergoes transformations that result in refactoring multiple instances of test smells, it usually proceeds by excluding assertions or test pieces.

The analysis indicates that the *testMojo* and *testUnpackOverWriteIfNewer* methods yield the most significant amount of simultaneous test smell changes. For example, changes refactored six test smells instances from the *testMojo* method (one *DA* test smell, three *ECT* test smells, one *PS* test smell, and one *VT* test smell). In this case, the refactoring was well-successful in removing all instances. For example, we observed that refactoring the *VT* test smell can result in refactoring other test smells.

Additionally, the changes caused the removal of five test smells instances from the *testPath* method (two *AR* test smells, one *LT* test smell, one *MG* test smell, and one *RO* test smell). The result is similar to the *testEnvironment* method because both have duplicated code in version v_0. The *testPath* method differs from the *testEnvironment* method as it has a *RO* test smell instance. Thus, we observed that if reallocation can move test smells together, they also can be refactored through simultaneous transformations.

Although refactoring test smells together is possible, we have noticed that removing some instances of test smells was not well-succeeded. This situation emphasizes the need for guidelines and automated techniques to aid the test code refactoring process. In this context, it might need a set of guidelines to support test code refactoring following a specific order of priority. For example, removing the *MG* test smell before the *RO* test smell can be beneficial as both can be refactored simultaneously.

Thus, some test smells can be refactored before others, reducing the number of changes to a test class and minimizing the side effects of refactoring. Thus, current tools might evolve to refactor test code using guidelines to help practitioners refactor it with test smell co-occurrences faster and safer.

5   Threats Validity

Internal Validity. RAIDE, an extension of a tool previously validated in the literature, was used to detect test smells. Although we performed manual checks, we acknowledge that the choice of tool may have introduced some bias, potentially leading to false positives or negatives. Additionally, some code changes may have occurred for reasons unrelated to the removal of test smells, such as bug fixes or functional adjustments, which were later interpreted as refactorings.

External Validity. Because this is an exploratory study, we selected a design that would be feasible for complete manual and automatic analysis. Although our contributions are novel, we recognize the need for future investigations using a broader dataset to strengthen the generalizability of the results.

Construct Validity. We consider refactoring as the removal of test smells without changing the behavior of the tests. However, this evaluation was done manually, without the systematic execution of automated tests to verify the preservation of the behavior after the observed transformations.

Conclusion Validity. While our study did not perform formal statistical analyses to assess the significance of the results, we conducted a detailed, descriptive qualitative analysis of the 21 removed test smell instances.

6 Related Work

Soares et al. [18] investigated how developers refactor test code to remove test smells. The authors surveyed 73 open-source developers and submitted 50 pull requests to assess developers' preferences and motivation while refactoring the test code. The results showed developers preferred the refactored test code for most test smells. In another work, Soares et al. [19] analyzed refactorings of test code with the JUnit 5 framework to remove test smells in 485 open-source Java projects. The authors sought to understand which new JUnit 5 features can help test developers refactor test code and which features are more common in practice. In contrast, our work focuses on identifying patterns of test smells that developers tend to refactor together, aiming to understand co-refactoring behaviors rather than isolated smell fixes.

In the literature, several tools automate the detection and refactoring of test smells. For instance, RAIDE tool [14–16] automatically detects and refactors two test smells (AR and DA). However, a limitation among these tools, including RAIDE, is that they focus on refactoring one smell type at a time without considering how multiple smells might interact. In practice, test methods often exhibit co-occurrence test smells, and refactoring one in isolation can lead to unintended consequences, such as introducing or exacerbating other test smells. It highlights the need for refactoring strategies that consider the co-existence of test smells. Our work addresses this gap by investigating how to refactor multiple test smells together, providing empirical insights that could guide more holistic and effective automated refactoring approaches.

Martins et al. [5] proposed a machine learning framework to detect test smells and suggest refactorings, showing good detection performance across seven algorithms. In another work, Gao et al. [3] proposed an LLM-based framework for automatic test refactoring in Java projects. It simulates the manual refactoring process through a chain-of-thought approach relying on an external knowledge base with test smell definitions and Domain Specific Language-based refactoring rules. While the LLM-based framework achieved high accuracy, it faced limitations when handling tests with multiple co-existing smells. Although the authors proposed a ranking mechanism to guide the application of refactorings, the sequencing challenge remains a key factor influencing refactoring effectiveness. In this context, our work investigates which test smells are commonly refactored together by developers. The insights derived from these co-refactoring patterns could inform and enhance LLM-based refactoring frameworks, particularly by providing empirical guidance on the sequencing of refactorings, which remains a challenge when multiple smells are present.

7   Conclusion

We studied the impact of refactoring test code on the co-occurrence of test smells. We created a historical view of test smell removal by analyzing two versions of an open-source software, allowing us to examine each refactoring individually. As a result, we noticed that refactoring the test code might yield different results: (i) no fixing of test smells, (ii) fixing multiple test smells instances together, and (iii) fixing single test smell instances. We outlined a methodology for identifying potential test code refactorings based on smell removals between versions. These insights provide a foundation for analyzing the co-occurrence of refactorings and informing the development of guidelines aimed at minimizing code changes while effectively eliminating test smells. As future work, we plan to conduct a longitudinal study using a larger dataset across multiple open-source projects to strengthen the evidence base. The resulting guidelines will be implemented in the RAIDE tool and further validated through empirical evaluation.

Acknowledgments. This study was financed in part by the Coordenação de Aperfeiçoamento de Pessoal de Nível Superior - Brasil (CAPES) - Finance Code 001; CNPq grants 315840/2023-4 and 403361/2023-0; and FAPESB grant PIE0002/2022.

References

1. AlOmar, E.A., Mkaouer, M.W., Newman, C., Ouni, A.: On preserving the behavior in software refactoring: a systematic mapping study. Inf. Softw. Technol. **140** (2021)
2. Fowler, M.: Refactoring: Improving the Design of Existing Code. Addison-Wesley Professional, Boston (2018)
3. Gao, Y., Hu, X., Yang, X., Xia, X.: Automated unit test refactoring. Proc. ACM Softw. Eng. **2**(FSE) (2025)
4. Junior, N.S., Rocha, L., Martins, L.A., Machado, I.: A survey on test practitioners' awareness of test smells. In: Proceedings of the XXIII Iberoamerican Conference on Software Engineering (CIbSE), pp. 462–475 (2020)
5. Martins, L., Bezerra, C., Costa, H., Machado, I.: Smart prediction for refactorings in the software test code. In: Brazilian Symposium on Software Engineering, pp. 115–120 (2021)
6. Martins, L., Campos, D., Santana, R., Junior, J.M., Costa, H., Machado, I.: Hearing the voice of experts: Unveiling stack exchange communities' knowledge of test smells. In: 2023 IEEE/ACM 16th International Conference on Cooperative and Human Aspects of Software Engineering (CHASE), pp. 80–91. IEEE (2023)

7. Martins, L., Ghaleb, T.A., Costa, H., Machado, I.: A comprehensive catalog of refactoring strategies to handle test smells in java-based systems. Softw. Qual. J. **32**(2), 641–679 (2024)
8. Martins, L., Pontillo, V., Costa, H., Ferrucci, F., Palomba, F., Machado, I.: Test code refactoring unveiled: where and how does it affect test code quality and effectiveness? Empir. Softw. Eng. **30**(1), 1–39 (2025)
9. Mens, T., Tourwe, T.: A survey of software refactoring. IEEE Trans. Softw. Eng. **30**(2), 126–139 (2004)
10. Meszaros, G.: xUnit Test Patterns: Refactoring Test Code. Pearson Education, Boston (2007)
11. Palomba, F., Di Nucci, D., Panichella, A., Oliveto, R., De Lucia, A.: On the diffusion of test smells in automatically generated test code: an empirical study. In: Proceedings of the 9th International Workshop on Search-Based Software Testing, SBST '16, pp. 5–14. ACM (2016)
12. Peruma, A., Newman, C.D., Mkaouer, M.W., Ouni, A., Palomba, F.: An exploratory study on the refactoring of unit test files in android applications. In: Proceedings of the IEEE/ACM 42nd International Conference on Software Engineering Workshops, ICSEW'20, pp. 350–357. ACM (2020)
13. Santana, R., Fernandes, D., Campos, D., Soares, L., Maciel, R., Machado, I.: Understanding practitioners' strategies to handle test smells: a multi-method study, pp. 49–53. ACM, New York (2021)
14. Santana, R., et al.: Raide: a tool for assertion roulette and duplicate assert identification and refactoring. In: Proceedings of the 34th Brazilian Symposium on Software Engineering, pp. 374–379 (2020)
15. Santana, R., Martins, L., Virgínio, T., Rocha, L., Costa, H., Machado, I.: An empirical evaluation of raide: a semi-automated approach for test smells detection and refactoring. Sci. Comput. Program. **231**, 103013 (2024)
16. Santana, R., Martins, L., Virgínio, T., Soares, L., Costa, H., Machado, I.: Refactoring assertion roulette and duplicate assert test smells: a controlled experiment. In: Congresso Ibero-Americano em Engenharia de Software (CIbSE), pp. 263–277. SBC (2022)
17. Sellitto, G., et al.: Toward understanding the impact of refactoring on program comprehension. In: 2022 IEEE International Conference on Software Analysis, Evolution and Reengineering (SANER), pp. 731–742 (2022)
18. Soares, E., et al.: Refactoring test smells: a perspective from open-source developers. In: Proceedings of the 5th Brazilian Symposium on Systematic and Automated Software Testing, SAST 20, pp. 50–59. Association for Computing Machinery, New York (2020)
19. Soares, E., Ribeiro, M., Gheyi, R., Amaral, G., Santos, A.M.: Refactoring test smells with junit 5: why should developers keep up-to-date. IEEE Trans. Softw. Eng. (2022)
20. Spadini, D., Palomba, F., Zaidman, A., Bruntink, M., Bacchelli, A.: On the relation of test smells to software code quality. In: 2018 IEEE International Conference on Software Maintenance and Evolution (ICSME), pp. 1–12 (2018)
21. Spadini, D., Schvarcbacher, M., Oprescu, A.M., Bruntink, M., Bacchelli, A.: Investigating severity thresholds for test smells. In: Proceedings of the 17th International Conference on Mining Software Repositories, MSR '20, pp. 311–321. ACM (2020)
22. Tufano, M., Palomba, F., Bavota, G., Di Penta, M., Oliveto, R., De Lucia, A., Poshyvanyk, D.: An empirical investigation into the nature of test smells. In: Proceedings of the 31st IEEE/ACM International Conference on Automated Software Engineering. p. 4–15. ASE 2016, ACM (2016)

23. Van Deursen, A., Moonen, L., Van Den Bergh, A., Kok, G.: Refactoring test code. In: Proceedings of the 2nd International Conference on Extreme Programming and Flexible Processes in Software Engineering (XP2001), pp. 92–95. Citeseer (2001)
24. Virgínio, T., et al.: Jnose: java test smell detector. In: Proceedings of the XXXIV Brazilian Symposium on Software Engineering, pp. 564–569 (2020)
25. Virgínio, T., et al.: On the test smells detection: an empirical study on the jnose test accuracy. J. Softw. Eng. Res. Dev. **9**, 8–1 (2021)
26. Virgínio, T., Santana, R., Martins, L.A., Soares, L.R., Costa, H., Machado, I.: On the influence of test smells on test coverage. In: Proceedings of the XXXIII Brazilian Symposium on Software Engineering, SBES 2019, pp. 467–471. Association for Computing Machinery, New York (2019)

What Makes Customers Reluctant to Deploy Frequent Software Releases? A Case Study from the Telecommunications Domain

Anas Dakkak[1]([⊠])(ID), Piero Daniele[2], Caroline Muzikants[1], and Fredric Ryttegård[1]

[1] Ericsson AB, Stockholm, Sweden
{anas.dakkak,caroline.muzikants,fredric.ryttegard}@ericsson.com
[2] Ericsson SpA, Milan, Italy
piero.daniele@ericsson.com

Abstract. As software-intensive embedded systems adopt more agile development practices, the shift towards frequent software releases has become increasingly prevalent. However, while many companies can deliver software more frequently, customers may hesitate to deploy releases frequently. To understand the factors influencing customers' decisions to deploy frequent releases, we conducted a case study at Ericsson focusing on a large-scale software-intensive embedded system used in mobile telecommunications networks. Based on two years of qualitative and quantitative data, including customer surveys and internal documentation, we identify technical, commercial, and organizational factors influencing customers' decisions to deploy frequent software releases. These factors apply to all customers. Therefore, we segment customers based on their deployment frequency and identify the factors that apply to each category. Based on these findings, we discuss the main activities companies must consider to influence customer decisions to upgrade, providing practical insights for software-intensive embedded systems companies on factors that could motivate customers to deploy frequent releases.

Keywords: Frequent releases · Software-intensive embedded systems · Software deployment

1 Introduction

In recent years, many software companies have shifted their focus towards delivering frequent software releases to their customers. In Meta, for example, the notion of *"release fast, release often"* is central to the engineering culture of the organization [17]. As a result, 97% of code changes are delivered and then deployed to production either continuously or within a short cycle of days or weeks [17]. Similarly, Firefox adopted frequent releases in 2011, which resulted in reducing the cycle time of new software releases to six weeks [19]. Later in

D. Taibi and D. Smite (Eds.): SEAA 2025, LNCS 16082, pp. 199–215, 2026.
https://doi.org/10.1007/978-3-032-04200-2_14

2019, Firefox further reduced the release cycle time to 4 weeks [28]. A similar observation can be drawn from a multitude of other companies across various software industry segments, including gaming [24], automotive [29], and even military aviation [3].

The roots of frequent releases can be found in the Agile Manifesto, which identifies frequent software deliveries to customers with short cycles as the highest software development priority [15]. Besides that, the Manifesto linked the frequent delivery of software to customer satisfaction, implying that the more frequently customers receive a new software version, the more satisfied they will be [15]. However, connecting the frequency of new software delivery with customer satisfaction might apply to web-based software-as-a-service (SaaS) applications, where customers are presented with the content of a new software version without being involved in any of the release, deployment, or operations activities. In addition, deploying new software to production is often a transparent activity to customers, which enables SaaS organizations to continuously release, deploy, experiment, and measure the impact of their changes [14].

On the other hand, frequent releases might not necessarily result in higher customer satisfaction in applications that require customer involvement in the software deployment, such as mobile or personal computer applications. For example, Vitale et al. [39] found that customers often delay deploying a major release of the iOS operating system by 80 days, and Vaniea et al. [38] indicated that customers usually avoid deploying new releases of Windows-based personal computer applications after a negative experience in previous releases.

Similarly, software-intensive embedded systems, such as cars, telecommunication systems, and medical equipment, often require customer involvement when a new software release becomes available [8]. In addition, these systems are usually mass-market products with high geographical distribution. Each product instance is typically owned, used, and operated by customers who decide when to upgrade to a new software release or whether to upgrade at all [23].

While previous research has explored the factors influencing customers' decisions to deploy a new software release, they focused primarily on personal products such as mobile phones and computers. In contrast, studies addressing frequent releases in software-intensive embedded systems, such as [30] and [10] tend to focus on challenges, mitigation strategies, and methods to reduce the release cycle. Thus, it becomes essential to understand the factors that influence customers to deploy frequent releases. By identifying and understanding these factors, software-intensive embedded systems companies can ensure that the software is not only released but also deployed and used by customers.

Therefore, this paper aims to identify the factors that influence customers' decisions to deploy frequent software releases, focusing on software-intensive embedded systems. To achieve this, we present the findings of a case study conducted at Ericsson, one of the largest telecommunications companies in the world. Of the many software-intensive embedded systems that Ericsson develops, we focused on one system that moved from a bi-yearly major release cycle to a quarterly major software release cycle and a bi-weekly incremental minor release cycle.

The contributions are twofold. First, to the author's knowledge, it is one of the few studies that identifies factors influencing customers' decisions to deploy frequent software releases in software-intensive embedded systems. Second, the findings presented in this paper are derived from a system that has had frequent releases for many years, thus providing real-life empirical results from an industrial setting.

This paper is structured as follows: Sect. 2 provides an overview and a literature review of software-intensive embedded systems and cloud computing. Section 3 details the research method used in this study, including data collection, analysis, and threats to validity. Section 4 presents the empirical results of our Delphi study, while Sect. 5 discusses these results. Finally, Sect. 6 concludes the paper.

2 Background

With the increasing dominance of software in traditional embedded systems, it becomes possible to evolve the functionality of these systems through software upgrades [5]. Consequently, companies that develop software-intensive embedded systems have embarked on a journey to evolve their software development practices [30]. A key element of this journey is to mimic the practices adopted by companies developing software-as-a-service products by shortening the software development cycle and offering more frequent releases to customers [4].

2.1 Frequent Releases

While the term *frequent releases* is commonly used in literature and among practitioners, it has different interpretations. For example, according to Greening [16], frequent releases refer to deploying new software more often, resulting in potential customer disruption; however, for Chen et al. [6], it relates to new software being available for download more frequently.

Nevertheless, while there are noticeable differences, the Agile Alliance highlights what most definitions agree upon: providing customers with new software more often [1]. What is meant by "more often" and the means to provide customers with a new software version depends on the software context. For some software applications, such as SaaS, the frequency could be extraordinarily high and involves deployment to production, as deployment is the means of providing the new software to customers. For other software applications, like automotive software, more frequent releases are measured in terms of weeks and months and refer to the delivery of software to customers without deployment [34].

Therefore, the Agile Alliance definition differentiates frequent releases from continuous deployment and continuous delivery in two aspects. First, it is more often, but not necessarily continuously. Second, frequent releases are about providing software to customers without considering whether the release is deployed automatically to production, as in continuous deployment [36], manually to production or staging environments, as in continuous delivery [37], or ignored and not deployed at all by customers.

Furthermore, as software-intensive embedded systems often have high reliability and availability requirements, customers typically need to plan the deployment of new software releases in advance and may also require validation of the release in their own labs or staging environments beforehand, as in the case of medical equipments and telecommunication systems [11, 21].

2.2   Barriers to Deploying Frequent Releases

While empirical studies focusing on software-intensive embedded systems are scarce, some studies have attempted to identify the factors that influence customers' decisions in either IT, personal computers, or smart mobile phone applications.

For example, Min Khoo et al. [27] studied the deployment decision of customers, using Windows Enterprise and SAP software as case studies. The authors depicted the deployment decision as an interaction between motivation and contingency forces. The motivation forces represent internal requirements, such as technology and business needs, while external requirements, such as the expiry of technical support on the older software. Further, the contingency forces represent the availability of resources to execute the upgrade.

Similarly, Kim et al. [20] analyzed the factors that influence new software deployment for on-prem IT systems, such as ERP, using the Analytic Hierarchy Process (AHP). The authors found that managers and users consider software upgrades from different perspectives. For managers, return on investment, upgrade time, and budget were the top three factors influencing their decisions to deploy a new software release. In contrast, for users, the factors were performance improvement, upgrade time, and requirements fulfillment.

Furthermore, based on a literature review of factors influencing the decision to upgrade Information Technology (IT) enterprise systems, Petersen et al. [31] grouped the factors into five categories: supplier, social network, environmental, technological, and organizational.

While the previously mentioned research, in addition to other similar research such as [25], highlights several factors that influence the decisions to deploy software releases, they focused primarily on on-prem IT solutions and mobile applications, not embedded software.

The previously mentioned research focused on the factors influencing the deployment without considering the release frequency. Anderson et al. [2], however, simulated the relation between the release frequency on the one hand and engineering and marketing costs on the other hand. The authors found that a high frequency can lead organizations to overreact to market feedback. Therefore, the authors highlighted that while frequent releases are beneficial, the frequency shall be moderate.

3 Research Method

This paper aims to identify the factors influencing customers' decisions to deploy frequent releases in software-intensive embedded systems. To achieve this objective, we conducted a case study at Ericsson, a large multinational company that produces and delivers various telecommunications equipment and software for all mobile network generations, from 2G to 5G. The company's customers are telecommunications service providers that supply their end-users with various telecommunication services, including mobile broadband, voice, and Internet of Things (IoT) services.

Ericsson has close to one hundred thousand employees, of whom a quarter work in Research and Development (R&D)[1].

We used a case study as a research method for three reasons. First, as discussed in Sect. 2, factors that influence the decision to deploy frequent releases are not solely technical but can also be social and economic. Therefore, as indicated by Runeson et al. [33], case studies are a suitable research method to address multidisciplinary software engineering topics. Second, case studies are applicable to evaluate software engineering practices in an industrial setting where the boundary between the phenomenon and its context is not clear [33,40]. Third, the authors of this paper are employed by Ericsson, providing them with an in-depth understanding of the company's context.

3.1 The Case Study System and Release Strategy

Among the many software-intensive embedded systems Ericsson develops, we focus on a single software-intensive embedded system that plays a key role in 4G and 5G mobile telecommunication networks. The case study system's software is complex, consisting of millions of lines of code. In addition, the software comprises several components, most of which are developed by Ericsson, while others are outsourced from third-party suppliers. On the hardware side, the case study system comprises purpose-built hardware, including multiple electrical units and a specially designed central processor. Therefore, the hardware is specially designed to ensure high performance, besides other non-functional requirements such as reliability and availability. Each customer typically has multiple instances of the case study system within their network, as each instance serves a limited geographical area. Due to the varying characteristics of the areas to be covered (e.g., rural vs. urban) and varying customer needs, each instance of the system is highly configurable and customizable. There are hundreds of software parameters and features to customize, in addition to the various hardware components to select.

Ericsson used to provide two major software releases per year for the case study system. In 2012, the company underwent an agile transformation, resulting in the introduction of cross-functional teams and continuous integration with a single code mainline. From 2017, the company changed the release frequency

---

[1] https://www.ericsson.com/en/about-us/company-facts.

of the case study system's software, doubling the number of major releases to four per year. The company maintains each major release for more than a year, providing frequent fixes and corrections, as depicted in Fig. 1.

Besides the major and maintenance releases, the company introduced biweekly minor releases. These minor releases are branched from the mainline, and their incremental sum is the content of each major release. These minor releases are not maintained as major releases. In addition, the minor releases are only intended to be deployed on a few target systems and are not intended for mass deployment. The main ambition of these releases is to enable faster field feedback and also allow customers to access new content as soon as it becomes available.

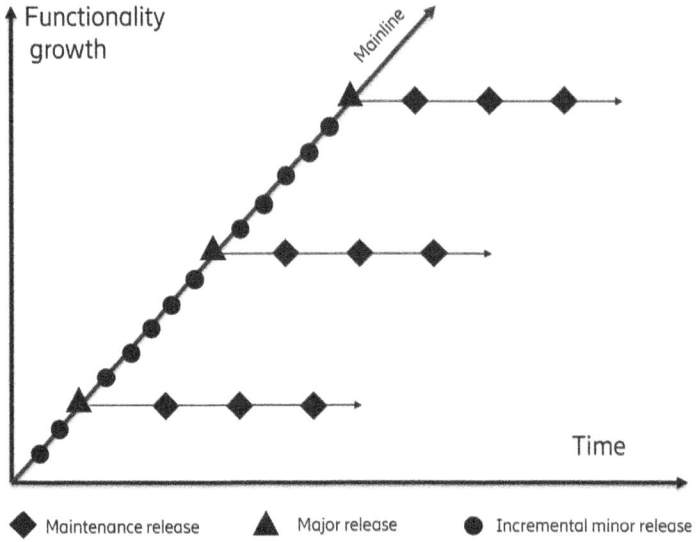

Fig. 1. Case study system releases

3.2   Research Process

After many years of offering four major releases per year, in addition to bi-weekly ones, the company wanted to understand in detail the factors that influence customers' decisions to upgrade to a new release. This initiative was triggered by growing reports that many customers continued to use old software releases despite the availability of more recent ones.

Therefore, a company-wide focus group was established in 2023 and concluded by the end of 2024. The authors of this paper were core members of the focus group due to their direct engagement with customers' post-release activities. During the study time, the first author led a unit responsible for customer support, while the second author led a product introduction unit. The third author led a unit responsible for software quality, while the fourth led a unit responsible for facilitating customer interaction with the R&D organization. In addition to the authors, the focus group involved representatives from various organizations, including sales, technical management, and services.

While the authors initially didn't consider framing their engagement with the focus group as a case study, the idea emerged at the beginning of 2024. At this point, we realized that framing our learnings as a case study would contribute to the literature and provide real-world insights to other embedded systems companies, as we observed the lack of empirical studies focusing on the factors that influence customers' decisions to deploy frequent releases in software-intensive embedded systems. Therefore, from early 2024, we began planning and preparing this case study.

As we have already started collecting data and analyzing from 2023, the case study research process deviated from the guidance of Runeson et al. [33], who proposed a five-step approach for conducting and reporting software engineering case studies. As illustrated in Fig. 2, we began by preparing for data collection and then collecting the data; subsequently, we planned the case study. However, as the focus group was in progress in 2024, we had the opportunity to collect additional data, which helped complement the information collected before conducting the case study.

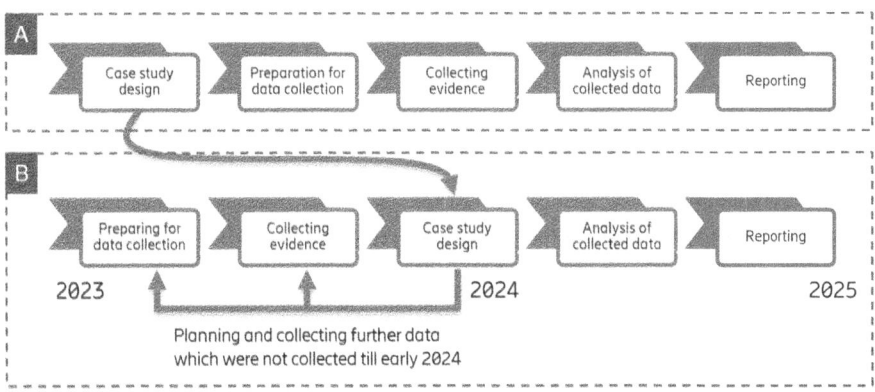

Fig. 2. [A] The five stages case study research process proposed by Runeson et al. [33]. [B] The research process followed in this paper and how it deviates from [A]

The data collected in this study consists of the following:

- Qualitative data: which includes meeting notes, observations, and document reviews. These data were gathered from the numerous meetings and workshops we have participated in during the focus group's lifetime. In addition, we have also read and analyzed more than 30 internal documents during this period, which were either shared with us or of which we were already aware. We also used quantitative data to complement the insights gathered from the qualitative data. Quantitative data were gathered

– Surveys: During our prolonged engagement in the focus group, we participated in drafting and conducting two customer surveys to gain a deeper understanding of the reasons behind customers' upgrade decisions and what would enable them to increase their upgrade frequency. The first survey was conducted at the end of 2023, while the second survey was conducted in the middle of 2024. The survey included several open-ended questions that allowed customers to express their opinions freely.

3.3   Validity Considerations

The authors of this study are familiar with modern software engineering practices, including frequent releases. In addition, each author has many years of experience working at Ericsson and has a deep understanding of the company's context. Furthermore, the data collected in this study come from various resources, both qualitative and quantitative, and were gathered over two years. Therefore, we consider that threats to construct, reliability, and internal validity are minor in this study.

Furthermore, as this study is conducted in a single telecommunications company, we don't claim the generalizability of the results. More studies are required to achieve external validity. However, we believe that the results presented in this study apply to other software-intensive embedded systems industries.

4   Findings

In this study, we have identified several factors that influence customers' decisions to frequently deploy new software releases. We categorize these factors into three categories: technical, commercial, and organizational. We have also found that these factors are not universally applicable to all customers. Some factors are more relevant to customers who deploy the software more frequently, while others are more relevant to customers who deploy the software less often.

Therefore, we segment customers based on their deployment frequency into three segments: (1) *frequent* deployment customers, who deploy at least three, out of the four major releases per year, (2) *moderate* deployment customers, referring to customers who deploy two major releases per year, (3) *low* deployment customers who deploy one major release per year, or less. Based on release deployment data collected from customers, the moderate deployment category is the largest group, as most customers deploy only half of the major releases.

In this section, we describe the three categories and the customer segment to which such factors apply.

4.1   Technical Factors

On the technical side, the first factor is software quality. A software quality issue that impacts the services provided by customers to their users can lead to significant consequences for customers, such as loss of market share, escalations, and even potential penalties due to legal regulations. Therefore, customers often conduct extensive software testing and validation in their labs, followed by field validation and testing, before gradually deploying the software to the instances of the case study system in the mobile network.

However, while many customers' answers in the survey reveal quality concerns, a clear correlation exists between quality concerns and customer category. Customers who deploy frequently or seldom are the least concerned about software quality. In contrast, customers who deploy moderately are the most concerned about quality.

On the other hand, customers who deploy frequently report more software bugs per release than other customers, and the lead time to identify the root causes of the bugs is faster than that of other customers. For example, a customer who mentions that *software quality is good* deploys three out of four major releases per calendar year; however, they report more bugs than a customer who deploys two out of the four major releases per year, while highlighting concerns about software quality as shown in Fig. 3

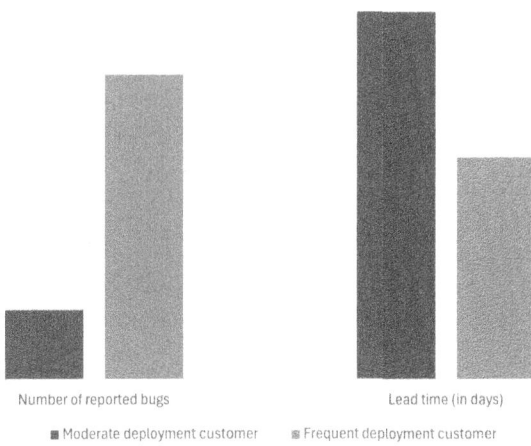

Fig. 3. A comparison between a moderate deployment and a frequent deployment customer. The values on y-axis are omitted for confidentiality

Furthermore, we found that frequent deployment customers not only deploy major releases but also the incremental bi-weekly minor releases to a limited number of system instances in the mobile network. By doing so, these customers take a gradual deployment approach, where a small percentage of system instances in their networks are exposed to the bi-weekly releases, followed by the deployment of the major release to all system instances in the network. As a result, bugs found in minor releases are fixed earlier, often in the next minor release, and are also included in the major release. In addition, as the minor release is deployed to a few system instances, the impact of these bugs, if found, remains limited. Besides, if a serious bug is found, it is easier to roll back the software on a few instances than on all instances in the network. Thus, deploying minor releases reduces the risk associated with deploying major releases to all system instances in the network, while simultaneously increasing confidence in the major release, as its contents are incrementally validated on a limited number of in-service system instances in the network.

Additionally, customers who seldom deploy don't use the latest major release, but rather one of the older releases that are still under maintenance. As these releases are used in many customer networks and have been deployed to different system configurations and customizations, most of the bugs have already been found and corrected. As a result, these customers have a very small risk of encountering a new bug.

The second technical factor is the complexity of the software deployment procedure, which refers to the end-to-end process that involves multiple steps and activities, such as pre-upgrade preparation, lab validation, software installation, upgrade, and post-upgrade validation and monitoring. These activities are not only repetitive, as they are intended to be performed with every software upgrade, but they are also complex and require special competence.

To address the complexity of the upgrade procedure, we find that customers who deploy frequently and moderately rely on three pillars: utilizing automation tools, relying on the vendor to perform the end-to-end deployment procedure, and having in-house competencies that work collaboratively with the vendor during the software deployment process. On the other hand, customers who seldom have a few automotive tools, and the end-to-end deployment procedure is performed manually by internal resources.

The third factor is timing-related, as several activities surrounding the upgrade require a certain amount of time to complete. For example, the pre- and post-upgrade validation and monitoring of the system's performance indicators requires many measurement samples that span over several days to ensure that variations in the system's usage over high and low traffic periods (e.g., day vs. night and weekdays vs. weekends), as well as weekdays and weekends, are captured. Thus, while the analysis of performance measurements can be automated using analytical tools, this analysis requires several days to capture the necessary samples and generate high confidence that the upgrade does not introduce any performance deviations.

Furthermore, in addition to the time required for regression testing and validation of the new release, there is also the time needed to validate new features and introduce them to operations with the new release. For many customers, these are sequential steps, starting with regression validation in the lab and then in the field, followed by testing and validation of new features in both the lab and the field. Thus, considering that both regression and new features require measurement samples to cover seasonality and performance during different load periods, the time span between releases might be challenging.

Similar to the concern about quality, the timing factor is more evident among customers who deploy fewer than 50% of the total number of releases. This is because customers who deploy frequently automate several steps in the deployment activities to save as much time as possible. For example, the analysis of performance deviations is performed using analytical tools once all the measurement points are available, which saves time compared to performing the analysis manually.

Besides using automation tools, customers who deploy more often can run parallel activities on two consecutive releases. For example, while new features of a release N are being validated in production, validation and regression tests are executed in the staging environment on release $N+1$, which is the next available release.

The fourth technical factor is the distribution of features among frequent releases. Based on the survey results, the uneven distribution of features leads customers to avoid deploying releases with little content in favor of releases with more content. To gain a deeper understanding of the distribution of new features in frequent releases, we quantified the contents of releases between 2023 and 2024, which revealed a significant deviation in the included features. As illustrated in Fig. 4, which shows the content of 8 consecutive major releases in 2023 and 2024, the difference between the release that has the fewest new features in 2023 and the release that has the most new features in the same year is almost a factor of 2. Furthermore, concerns about the distribution of new features among frequent releases are raised by moderate and frequent deployment customers, but not by customers who seldom deploy.

The fifth technical factor is the compatibility of the software release with the underlying hardware. While the hardware often has a long life span, it needs to be replaced with newer generations to accommodate new software versions. This concern is evident among customers who seldom deploy, indicating that other customers modernize their hardware to ensure it is ready for frequent releases.

4.2   Commercial Factors

The second category of factors that influence customers' decisions to deploy frequent releases is commercially related. The first factor in this category is the commercial means to acquire software. While software subscriptions where customers pay a recurring fee entitling them to access all major software releases, our findings show that there are deviations. First, there are cases where customers purchase software on a per-license basis, meaning they pay to use a specific release only. These customers who acquire dedicated software deploy new releases seldom.

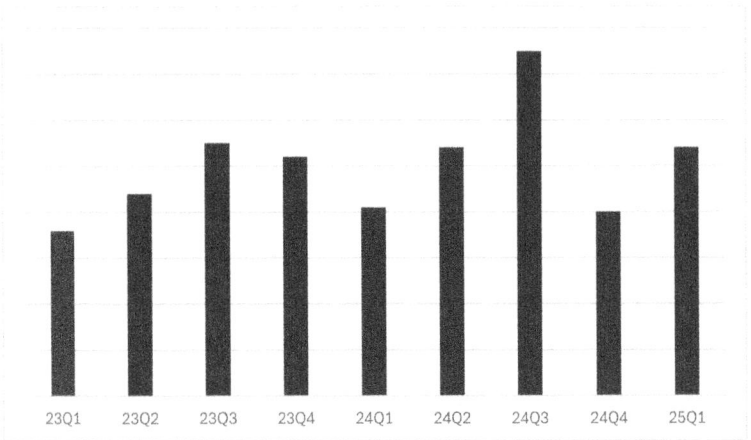

Fig. 4. Number of features in eight consecutive major releases in 2023 and 2024. The release identification on the x-axis represents the year, followed by the quarter, denoted by the letter Q. The values on the y-axis are omitted for confidentiality

Furthermore, while software subscription and software-related services, such as software deployment and support, are offered independently to customers, our survey reveals that they are often bundled together in many cases. When bundled, customers are not only entitled to access the software but also receive deployment services from the case study company to assist with the end-to-end deployment procedure. However, in cases where deployment services are bundled with a software subscription, the case study company limits the deployment services to one or two releases per year. Therefore, while this bundling ensures that at least some releases are deployed and used, customers opt not to deploy more than what is stated in the contract, as they will do so based on their own efforts.

The second factor is the lack of business drivers that interest customers in new software releases. If a new release does not introduce new content that is considered necessary from a business perspective, it becomes more challenging to justify the effort and time required to deploy the new release. This reason is more evident in customers who deploy moderately and infrequently than in those who deploy more frequently.

The third commercial factor is related to the release strategy, which provides an extended support and maintenance window for the released software. This means that new releases are only required for new content, not for fixes and corrections, as customers can acquire these via maintenance releases of the deployed major release.

4.3   Organizational Factors

The third category relates to customers' organizational factors. The first factor is the structure of the customer's operations organization. Customers who deploy frequently have a cross-functional team composed of solution architects, quality assurance, and optimization. This structure limits the number of handovers as the team works together. On the other hand, customers who deploy moderately or seldom have teams structured according to their function, e.g., an optimization team, a deployment team, and a solution architect team. Therefore, once a new release is available, the architects need to check the content and decide which features are of interest. The optimization team proposes customized settings for the features, and then the deployment team starts the validation in the lab and field. Such a waterfall process involves multiple handovers and takes more time. Multiple functions enable the team to work.

Additionally, knowledge-sharing practices also play a significant role. Organizations with a culture of cross-team collaboration and shared documentation are better equipped to handle continuous change. In contrast, those lacking formal knowledge-sharing mechanisms are slower to adopt new versions, as they rely heavily on a few internal experts.

Furthermore, some customers have an operations model that incentivizes network stability. For example, rewarding internal teams for maintaining network stability and performance. As a result, risk aversion becomes institutionalized, with teams preferring to maintain known software versions rather than risk potential instability with new software releases.

5   Discussion

This case study reveals several factors that influence customers' decisions to deploy new software releases frequently. However, these factors do not apply to all customers. In this study, we found that segmenting customers based on their software upgrade frequency reveals significant differences among the factors influencing their deployment decisions. Categorizing customers according to their deployment frequency is used in SaaS applications, e.g., DORA Accelerate state of DevOps report [32], which categorizes customers into four segments: elite, high, medium, and low. Other customer segmentation models might have even more segments, such as the popular innovation of the diffusion model, which has five segments [26]. While our study identified three customer segments, the study highlights that the factors influencing the deployment decisions are not universally applied to all customers.

When it comes to the factors influencing the deployment decision, software quality is the primary consideration. While releasing high-quality software is a key prerequisite for enabling frequent software deployments [11], we find that customers perceive quality differently. This confirms that quality remains a relative concept [18], despite the many parameters available to measure it [7].

Furthermore, to improve the perception of quality, it is evident that combining frequent major releases (e.g., quarterly or monthly) with releases that have a faster frequency (e.g., weekly or daily), but are only deployed to a limited subset of systems in customers' production environments, is beneficial. This combination not only enables customers to deploy the frequent major releases, but also reduces risks by controlling the deployment flow [8]. In addition, it enables customers to stay engaged and enhances collaboration between customers and software development organizations [12]. Such an approach can also be compared to the controlled rollout used by Microsoft, to facilitate continuous experimentation in online applications [41].

Moreover, this study emphasizes the importance of having a business model that not only enables customers to receive frequent releases but also facilitates their deployment. This can be achieved by combining software subscriptions, which are increasingly used as a software sales commercial model, with deployment services to ensure that frequent releases are effectively deployed. As highlighted by Lindstrom et al. [22], a software subscription business model shall also include value-adding services to ensure customer experience. In addition, as many embedded systems companies often offer products and product-related services, such as support and optimization, introducing frequent releases should be carefully aligned with product-related services [9]. However, it is essential to match the number of deployments offered via the service with the frequency of the releases. As seen in this case study, when the number of releases exceeds the capacity of deployment services, it leads to a situation where customers must either perform the deployment themselves or purchase additional deployment services at an extra cost, which increases the customer's reluctance to deploy further releases.

Additionally, this study highlights the importance of customers' organizations and their readiness to handle the deployment of frequent releases. As a result of shortening the time between releases, many previously sequential deployment activities need to be performed in parallel [13]. Consequently, the customer organization must be prepared to deploy frequent releases by having the supporting organization and process, e.g., a cross-functional operations team and processes that facilitate frequent deployment rather than inhibit it. This factor supports what Savor et al. [35], found when comparing two management styles, one supporting more frequent deployments and one prioritizing stability. However, in the case of software-intensive embedded systems, it is the customer's own organization and processes that need to facilitate the deployment of frequent releases, not the software vendor's organization, as in the case of SaaS companies. Therefore, to enable customers to deploy frequently, software vendors shall work closely with customers to transform their organization and operations to facilitate frequent deployments.

6   Conclusion

This case study investigates the factors influencing the decision to deploy new software releases frequently in software-intensive embedded systems. Unlike companies developing SaaS applications, where the deployment of new software releases is transparent to customers, deploying a new software release to a software-intensive system often requires customer involvement. Therefore, understanding the factors that influence the customer's decision to deploy frequently is important to ensure that frequent releases are deployed and eventually used by customers. Therefore, based on a case study at Ericsson, we identified several factors within three categories: technical, commercial, and organizational. Moreover, the case study shows these factors are not universally applied to all customers. Thus, segmenting customers and understanding which factors are relevant for which segment is needed to enable the company to build strategies to influence each segment's decision.

Acknowledgements. We would like to thank our colleagues at Ericsson for the many detailed discussions and the valuable feedback they shared with us during this study.

References

1. Alliance, A.: Agile glossary: Frequent releases. https://www.agilealliance.org/glossary/frequent-releases/. Accessed 14 Mar 2025
2. Anderson, E., Lim, S.Y., Joglekar, N.: Are more frequent releases always better? Dynamics of pivoting, scaling, and the minimum viable product. In: Proceedings of the 50th Hawaii International Conference on System Sciences (2017). https://doi.org/10.24251/HICSS.2017.705
3. Blanchette, S., Jr.: Giant slayer: will you let software be david to your goliath system? J. Aeros. Inf. Syst. **13**(10), 407–417 (2016)
4. Bosch, J.: Continuous software engineering: an introduction. In: Bosch, J. (ed.) Continuous Software Engineering, pp. 3–13. Springer, Cham (2014). https://doi.org/10.1007/978-3-319-11283-1_1
5. Bosch, J., Eklund, U.: Eternal embedded software: towards innovation experiment systems. In: Margaria, T., Steffen, B. (eds.) ISoLA 2012. LNCS, vol. 7609, pp. 19–31. Springer, Heidelberg (2012). https://doi.org/10.1007/978-3-642-34026-0_3
6. Chen, W., Krishnan, V.V., Zhu, K.: "release early, release often"? An empirical analysis of release strategy in open source software co-creation. In: Pacific Asia Conference on Information Systems (2013). https://api.semanticscholar.org/CorpusID:3084971
7. Colakoglu, F.N., Yazici, A., Mishra, A.: Software product quality metrics: a systematic mapping study. IEEE Access **9**, 44647–44670 (2021)
8. Dakkak, A., Bosch, J., Olsson, H.H.: Controlled continuous deployment: a case study from the telecommunications domain. In: Proceedings of the International Conference on Software and System Processes and International Conference on Global Software Engineering, pp. 24–33 (2022)
9. Dakkak, A., Bosch, J., Olsson, H.H.: Devservops: devops for product-oriented product-service systems. arXiv preprint arXiv:2305.08601 (2023)
10. Dakkak, A., Bosch, J., Olsson, H.H., Mattos, D.I.: Continuous deployment in software-intensive system-of-systems. Inf. Softw. Technol. **159**, 107200 (2023)
11. Dakkak, A., Issa Mattos, D., Bosch, J.: Success factors when transitioning to continuous deployment in software-intensive embedded systems. In: 2021 47th Euromicro Conference on Software Engineering and Advanced Applications (SEAA), pp. 129–137. IEEE (2021)
12. Dakkak, A., Mattos, D.I., Bosch, J.: Perceived benefits of continuous deployment in software-intensive embedded systems. In: 2021 IEEE 45th Annual Computers, Software, and Applications Conference (COMPSAC), pp. 934–941. IEEE (2021)

13. Dakkak, A., Munappy, A.R., Bosch, J., Olsson, H.H.: Customer support in the era of continuous deployment: a software-intensive embedded systems case study. In: 2022 IEEE 46th Annual Computers, Software, and Applications Conference (COMPSAC), pp. 914–923. IEEE (2022)

14. Fabijan, A., Arai, B., Dmitriev, P., Vermeer, L.: It takes a flywheel to fly: kick-starting and growing the a/b testing momentum at scale. In: 2021 47th Euromicro Conference on Software Engineering and Advanced Applications (SEAA), pp. 109–118. IEEE (2021)

15. Fowler, M., Highsmith, J., et al.: The agile manifesto. Softw. Dev. **9**(8), 28–35 (2001)

16. Greening, D.R.: Release duration and enterprise agility. In: 2013 46th Hawaii International Conference on System Sciences, pp. 4835–4841 (2013)

17. Grubic, B., et al.: Conveyor:{One-Tool-Fits-All} continuous software deployment at meta. In: 17th USENIX Symposium on Operating Systems Design and Implementation (OSDI 23), pp. 325–342 (2023)

18. Harvey, L., Green, D.: Defining quality. Assess. Eval. High. Educ. **18**(1), 9–34 (1993)

19. Khomh, F., Adams, B., Dhaliwal, T., Zou, Y.: Understanding the impact of rapid releases on software quality: the case of firefox. Empir. Softw. Eng. **20**, 336–373 (2015)

20. Kim, D., Kim, M.: Hybrid analysis of the decision-making factors for software upgrade based on the integration of ahp and dematel. Symmetry **14**(1), 172 (2022)

21. Laukkarinen, T., Kuusinen, K., Mikkonen, T.: Devops in regulated software development: case medical devices. In: 2017 IEEE/ACM 39th International Conference on Software Engineering: New Ideas and Emerging Technologies Results Track (ICSE-NIER), pp. 15–18. IEEE (2017)

22. Lindström, C.W.J., Maleki Vishkaei, B., De Giovanni, P.: Subscription-based business models in the context of tech firms: theory and applications. Int. J. Ind. Eng. Oper. Manag. **6**(3), 256–274 (2024)

23. Lwakatare, L.E., et al.: Towards devops in the embedded systems domain: why is it so hard? In: 2016 49th Hawaii International Conference on System Sciences (HICSS), pp. 5437–5446. IEEE (2016)

24. Maglyas, A., Vanhala, E.: How is release cycle and business model reflecting the success of mobile game? Lappeenrannan teknillinen yliopisto Yliopistopaino p. 7 (2015)

25. Mathur, A., Malkin, N., Harbach, M., Peer, E., Egelman, S.: Quantifying users' beliefs about software updates. arXiv preprint arXiv:1805.04594 (2018)

26. Meade, N., Islam, T.: Modelling and forecasting the diffusion of innovation-a 25-year review. Int. J. Forecast. **22**(3), 519–545 (2006)

27. Min Khoo, H., Robey, D.: Deciding to upgrade packaged software: a comparative case study of motives, contingencies and dependencies. Eur. J. Inf. Syst. **16**(5), 555–567 (2007)

28. Mozilla: Moving firefox to a faster 4-week release cycle (2019). https://hacks.mozilla.org/2019/09/moving-firefox-to-a-faster-4-week-release-cycle/. Accessed 14 Mar 2025

29. Munk, P., Schweizer, M.: Devops and safety? Safeops! towards ensuring safety in feature-driven development with frequent releases. In: International Conference on Computer Safety, Reliability, and Security, pp. 145–157. Springer, Heidelberg (2022). https://doi.org/10.1007/978-3-031-14862-0_11

30. Olsson, H.H., Bosch, J.: Climbing the "Stairway to Heaven": evolving from agile development to continuous deployment of software. In: Bosch, J. (ed.) Continuous Software Engineering, pp. 15–27. Springer, Cham (2014). https://doi.org/10.1007/978-3-319-11283-1_2

31. Petersen, C., Seymour, L.F.: Explaining the network of factors that influence the timing of and decision to upgrade enterprise systems. In: Dennehy, D., Griva, A., Pouloudi, N., Dwivedi, Y.K., Pappas, I., Mäntymäki, M. (eds.) I3E 2021. LNCS, vol. 12896, pp. 506–518. Springer, Cham (2021). https://doi.org/10.1007/978-3-030-85447-8_42

32. Research, D., Assessment (DORA) program, G.C.: Accelerate state of devops report (2024). https://dora.dev/publications/. Accessed 7 May 2025

33. Runeson, P., Höst, M.: Guidelines for conducting and reporting case study research in software engineering. Empir. Softw. Eng. **14**(2), 131 (2009)

34. Şahin, T., Köster, L., Huth, T., Vietor, T.: How to upgrade vehicles? release planning in the automotive industry. In: Bargende, M., Reuss, H.-C., Wagner, A. (eds.) 21. Internationales Stuttgarter Symposium. P, pp. 155–173. Springer, Wiesbaden (2021). https://doi.org/10.1007/978-3-658-33521-2_12

35. Savor, T., Douglas, M., Gentili, M., Williams, L., Beck, K., Stumm, M.: Continuous deployment at facebook and oanda. In: 2016 IEEE/ACM 38th International Conference on Software Engineering Companion (ICSE-C), pp. 21–30. IEEE (2016)

36. Shahin, M., Babar, M.A., Zahedi, M., Zhu, L.: Beyond continuous delivery: an empirical investigation of continuous deployment challenges. In: 2017 ACM/IEEE International Symposium on Empirical Software Engineering and Measurement (ESEM), pp. 111–120. IEEE (2017)

37. Shahin, M., Babar, M.A., Zhu, L.: Continuous integration, delivery and deployment: a systematic review on approaches, tools, challenges and practices. IEEE Access **5**, 3909–3943 (2017)

38. Vaniea, K.E., Rader, E., Wash, R.: Betrayed by updates: how negative experiences affect future security. In: Proceedings of the SIGCHI Conference on Human Factors in Computing Systems, pp. 2671–2674 (2014)

39. Vitale, F., McGrenere, J., Tabard, A., Beaudouin-Lafon, M., Mackay, W.E.: High costs and small benefits: a field study of how users experience operating system upgrades. In: Proceedings of the 2017 CHI Conference on Human Factors in Computing Systems, pp. 4242–4253 (2017)

40. Wohlin, C., Höst, M., Henningsson, K.: Empirical research methods in software engineering. In: Empirical Methods and Studies in Software Engineering, pp. 7–23. Springer, Heidelberg (2003)

41. Xia, T., Bhardwaj, S., Dmitriev, P., Fabijan, A.: Safe velocity: a practical guide to software deployment at scale using controlled rollout. In: 2019 IEEE/ACM 41st International Conference on Software Engineering: Software Engineering in Practice (ICSE-SEIP), pp. 11–20. IEEE (2019)

Systematic Literature Reviews and Mapping Studies in Software Engineering

Regression Testing via Traceability: A Systematic Literature Review

Moldovan Andrada-Mihaela-Nicoleta[✉] [iD]

Babeş-Bolyai University, 400084 Cluj-Napoca, Romania
andrada.moldovan@ubbcluj.ro

Abstract. Regression Testing (RT) ensures that code modifications do not break existing functionality. However, running a full test suite is often costly and time-consuming, making optimization strategies essential. This Systematic Literature Review (SLR) analyzes 67 papers published between 2021âĂŞ2025, focusing on Test Case (TC) Prioritization (TCP), Test Case Minimization (TCM), and Test Case Selection (TCS). Unlike prior reviews, this study places traceability at the center of the analysis, examining how its mechanisms influence these techniques in balancing execution time and fault detection effectiveness. By linking TCs and faults to code changes and requirements, traceability is identified as a key driver in enhancing test selection and prioritization. Additionally, a connectivity-based perspective supports maintainability by ensuring that tests evolve alongside changing software artifacts. The review is structured around four research questions, addressing the types of traceability data used, solution approaches, target systems, and validation practices. It offers practical insights and highlights research gaps. Key challenges such as automation, scalability, and integration with modern development workflows are also discussed.

Keywords: Regression Testing · Systematic Literature Review · Artifacts Traceability

1 Introduction

Software systems are always changing due to bug repairs, improvements, and upgrades. Although these changes are necessary to increase performance and functionality, they also run the risk of causing unexpected flaws in components that were previously stable. This is why software testing [12] takes longer to complete and might be the most costly stage of a software development process.

A crucial quality assurance procedure called Regression Testing [8] is intended to confirm that recent code modifications do not adversely affect already-existing functionality. Regression testing makes sure that software changes do not create new flaws or resurface issues that have already been fixed by methodically running TCs that have already passed. The main objectives of regression testing are

D. Taibi and D. Smite (Eds.): SEAA 2025, LNCS 16082, pp. 219–234, 2026.
https://doi.org/10.1007/978-3-032-04200-2_15

as follows: verification of existing functionality, detection of side effects, preventing software degradation, and facilitating Continuous Integration/Continuous Delivery (CI/CD).

Regression testing can be resource-intensive due to the possibly high number of TCs that need to be rerun after each revision. Several methods [16] have been proposed to optimize the process to overcome this challenge:

– **Retest All**: This method re-executes all existing TCs for thorough validation but is costly and time-consuming.
– **Regression Test Selection**: To maximize testing efforts, this method focuses on running a chosen subset of TCs that are thought to be pertinent to the most recent code changes.
– **TC Prioritization**: To increase the effectiveness of the testing process, TCs are arranged according to certain criteria, such their significance or propensity to find flaws.

An additional regression testing task that is rather overlooked in RT research is Regression Test case Generation, but it requires a different approach and perspective, while TCP, TCM, and TCS assume that a set of TCs are already defined.

Over the past 20 years, the requirements engineering community has conducted an extensive traceability research to date [5]. Implicit relationships are used by certain methods to facilitate the creation, implementation, and assessment of tests, while others use implicit relationships to facilitate RT.

The goal of this SLR is to explore how a unified solution could address both regression testing and maintainability challenges in dynamic environments like Continuous Integration. As requirements, TCs, and code change, maintaining traceability ensures tests remain relevant and aligned. We believe that integrating traceability into regression testing could optimize the related processes, providing a more sustainable approach for evolving systems.

The findings of this study aim to provide a foundation for both practitioners and researchers, offering insights into the feasibility of collecting and processing these artifact traces and links for RT.

The contributions made in this paper are the following:

– Conducting an SLR on traceability in regression testing, covering 67 articles from six publication databases.
– Analyzing findings based on four research questions related to traceability-oriented regression testing. We define this approach, illustrate it with existing studies, and explore its applicability and validation.
– Along with the suggested opportunities and recommendations, the gaps, difficulties, and unresolved concerns are examined.

The paper is structured as follows: Sect. 2 covers related work, Sect. 3 details the methodology, and Sect. 4 outlines the review process. Results (RQ1-RQ4) are outlined in Sect. 5, while Sect. 5.18 discusses findings, gaps, challenges, and recommendations. Threats to validity are provided in Sect. 6, and Sect. 7 concludes the paper.

2   Related Work

Several studies explore regression testing using different methods, with a focus on TCP, TCS, practicability, requirements or ML (Machine Learning)-driven approaches, and in what follows, we outline them.

There are plenty of SLRs [15], surveys [11], and mappings [18] that cover the topic of Regression Testing and its tasks. Similar papers cover specific classes of solution, such as Ontology-based [3], which follows a pattern that we are also trying to populate, but in the context of traceability-oriented approaches for RT.

Another SLR, exploring requirement-based approaches [4], identifies the focus factors (customer priority, fault-proneness, code complexity, and requirement volatility), and discusses metrics, real-world settings, domains of SUT (Software Under Test), validation, and challenges.

Pan et al. [14] explore ML techniques, key features, challenges like data availability and scalability, and future research directions for TCP and TCS, highlighting that while ML shows promise, real-world adoption still faces hurdles.

There is also an investigation into the practicability [2] of such methods, that defines usefulness in practice of 20 types of solutions and 23 metrics, or the performance [18], considering test granularity and the covered programming language. Other recent related work is focused on either TCP [4,11,15,17], or TCS [14]. Researchers categorize solution approaches into various classes, such as meta-heuristic, model-based, generic, ranking, code slicing, and oracle methods [17]; coverage, requirement, risk, search, fault, and history-driven techniques [15]; as well as historical, cost-aware, time-aware, and web-focused strategies [11]. They also analyze key parameters, including selection criteria like cost (divided into seven types [11]], coverage, and fault detection. Additionally, studies explore state-of-the-art advancements, the diversity of considered SUTs, metric trends [15], and employed datasets [17]. While answering such research questions, the strengths, limitations, and strategies are taken into consideration [17].

3   Methodology and Study Design

This section includes information on the methodology, such as review need, research questions, and protocol definition. We follow the well-known guidelines criteria by Kitchenham [6].

3.1   Review Need Identification

This SLR aims to identify existing research that uses traceability in regression testing solutions. By consolidating these studies, we seek to lay the foundation for future traceability-oriented solutions that address both regression testing and software maintainability. Identifying trends, challenges, and gaps in current approaches will guide the development of more effective, integrated solutions for evolving software systems.

3.2   Research Questions Definition

The research questions aim to explore artifact-linking aspects that contribute to effective Regression Testing solutions and investigate types of traceability data, their application, target SUTs, and validation approaches.

> *RQ1: What type of traceability data is used in Regression Testing?*

> *RQ2: What Regression Testing solutions emphasize traceability data?*

> *RQ3: Which System Under Testing (SUT) domains are addressed?*

> *RQ4: How are the techniques validated?*

3.3   Protocol Definition

The following steps outline the SLR protocol proposed by Kitchenham [6]:

- **Selection:** Define inclusion/exclusion for traceability and regression testing.
- **Search & Screen:** Set databases, keywords, and screening.
- **Data Extraction:** Collect key data on traceability in regression testing.
- **Analysis & Synthesis:** Identify trends and answer research questions.
- **Gaps & Challenges:** Outline gaps, challenges, and future work.
- **Recommendations:** Suggest directions for future research and solutions.

Each protocol step is described in depth in the following sections.

4   Conducting the SLR

This section outlines key SLR actions, including database search, selection criteria, and data extraction.

4.1   Search and Selection Process

Following PRISMA 2020 guidelines [13], we identified 850 papers, removed duplicates, and screened for relevance, resulting in 67 studies after excluding non-regression testing and inaccessible works (Fig. 1).

Database Search. To gather the most relevant studies on the subject [6], we performed a structured search across six major academic databases: ACM Digital Library, IEEE Xplore, ScienceDirect, Scopus, Springer, and Web of Science (WOS)[1]. The search, conducted in January 2025, used targeted keywords like regression testing", TC prioritization", TC selection", and TC minimization". Results were retrieved based on keyword match.

---

[1] ACM: https://dl.acm.org, IEEE Xplore: https://ieeexplore.ieee.org, ScienceDirect: https://www.sciencedirect.com, Scopus: https://www.scopus.com, Springer: https://link.springer.com, WOS: https://www.webofscience.com.

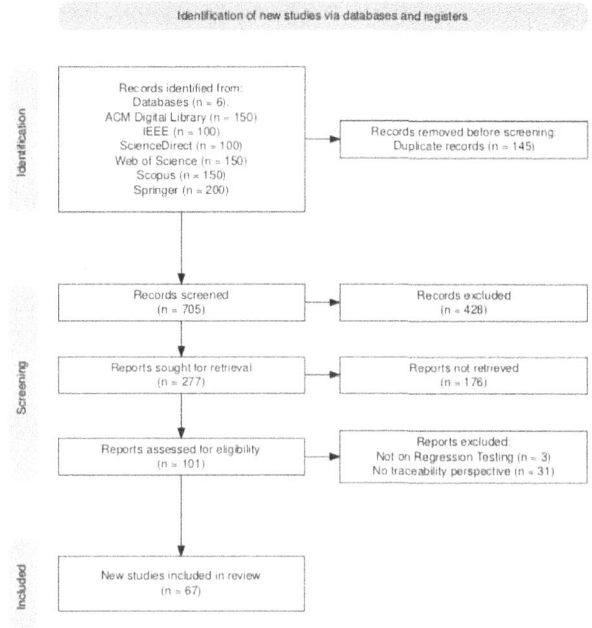

Fig. 1. Scoping Review Flow Diagram complying with PRISMA 2020 statement [13].

Merging, and Duplicates and Impurity Removal. After the searches, citation records were exported in BibTeX format via Zotero[2], and duplicates were automatically removed before analysis.

Application of the Selection Criteria. We initially selected RT studies from 2021âĂŞ2025, later refining them based on traceability focus. This scope ensured a targeted, up-to-date dataset. Studies were included if they met criteria [9]: empirical, peer-reviewed, full-text, in English, and published in reputable sources. Only works directly addressing RT within the time frame were considered.

4.2   Data Extraction

We used a three-stage review to finalize 67 papers. From 277 RT-related articles, keyword-based screening [6] assessed relevance to TCS, TCP, or TCM by checking for key terms in each paper's content, not just references, with occurrences logged in a spreadsheet. The keywords we searched for included *trace**, *connect**, *histori**, *track*, *dependen*, *relat**, *coverage*, *graph*, *link*, *SUT*, and *mapping*. The asterisk (*) served as a wildcard for term variations. We marked keywords only

---

[2] Zotero: https://www.zotero.org.

when explicitly used in the article's approach, not just mentioned or cited—
something hard to automate accurately.

Figure 2 shows the final selection. Traceability-based approaches remain
steady, mainly from Scopus. Peaks occurred in 2022âĂŞ2023, with a decline
likely in 2024âĂŞ2025 due to indexing delays.

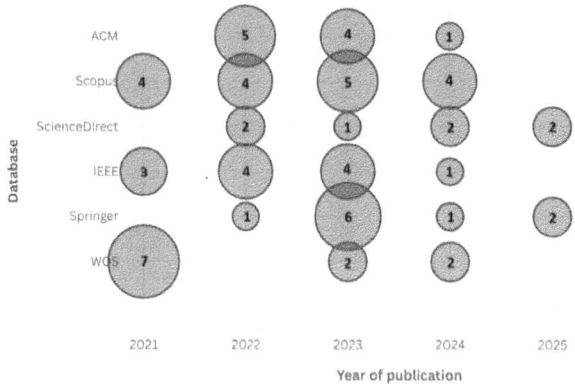

Fig. 2. Selected papers per year for each database.

A replication package with all selected articles is available [10]. Selected
papers are labeled S1 to S67.

Table 1 details database sources from Fig. 1. Most papers came from IEEE,
though many were excluded for thematic mismatch.

Table 1. Table displaying the data for searches and selection across databases.

Source	DB search	Sought for retrieval	Assessed for eligibility	Selected
ACM DigitalLibrary	150	50	24	10
IEEE	100	69	20	12
Science Direct	100	25	7	7
Springer	200	38	14	10
Scopus	150	39	21	17
WOS	150	56	15	11
Total	**850**	**277**	**101**	**67**

5   Results

This section presents findings on traceability in RT (RQ1), related solutions
(RQ2), SUT domains (RQ3), and validation methods (RQ4), with examples
from the literature.

RQ1: What type of traceability data is used in Regression Testing?

Figure 3 shows three main traceability data types in Regression Testing: Test traces, Requirement Traceability, and Test-to-code traceability from NLP (Natural Language Processing), static analysis, and impact analysis. Details and examples follow.

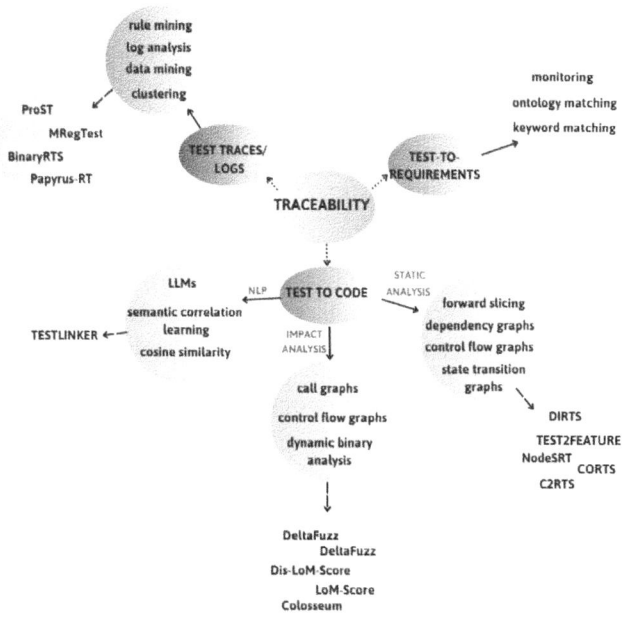

Fig. 3. Traceability types with corresponding methods and tools.

5.1   Test Traces Category

A large set from our paper selection discusses solutions based on logs [*S17, S32, S38, S48, S52, S57*] or test/user traces [*S5, S7, S29, S30, S31, S40, S47, S50, S53, S54, S62, S65, S2*]. Some solutions perform rule mining [*S48, S30*], data mining [*S52, S32*], log analysis [*S38*] or pattern mining [*S17*] on the program traces to identify a mapping that connects it to the modified feature.

Several tools extract runtime features from execution data: ProST [*S53*] uses dynamic instrumentation to capture file interactions; MRegTest [*S65, S50*] selects key executions and detects regressions via MDD tools; BinaryRTS [*S40*] analyzes C++ traces for TCS in CI pipelines. Test traces also aid clustering by execution patterns [*S54*], performance [*S62*], or failure types [*S30*].

5.2   Requirement Traceability Category

Requirement-based regression testing selects and prioritizes TCs by tracing system requirements to tests, ensuring updates for affected or modified functionality [S6, S13, S16, S18, S19, S21, S23, S24, S26, S42, S47, S49, S60, S66]. Vescan et al. [S58] integrate traceability in Agile, linking requirement changes to TC prioritization based on change likelihood. Naheed et al. [S49] reduce redundancy by selecting the highest-priority TC per requirement.

Keyword matching methods detect requirement-artifact relations: Freeda and Rajendran [S18] use weighted keyword tables, Rotaru and Vescan [S60] apply Neural Networks (NN) with feature vectors, and Sakhrawi and Labidi [S6] employ ontology-based semantic traceability.

5.3   Test-to-Code Traceability Category

Various tools link TCs to code using different methods: Duque et al. [S45] detect regressions via object state changes; CATTO [S39] uses call graphs; TREC [S56] ranks tests by commit frequency; Cingil et al. [S34] prioritize TCs by mining past bugs; uRTS [S35] tracks dependencies across tests, code, and configs; RichTest [S14] uses AST analysis; and code change/smell detection [S15] finds design flaws. These illustrate test-to-code traceability approaches via NLP, Static Code Analysis, and Change Impact Analysis.

Natural Language Processing. TESTLINKER [S55] uses semantic correlation with pre-trained code to link TCs and methods. LTM [S46] applies LLMs and similarity measures, while Test2Vec [S59] combines CodeBERT and BiL-STM to embed traces. Della et al. [S57] use a T5-small transformer to generate service invocation sequences.

Static Code Analysis. Static code analysis detects test dependencies without execution by computing method-level dependencies [S43], monitoring parameters [S50], extracting state dependencies [S61], and mapping test-to-code links [S48, S36]. Methods use preprocessing, annotations [S32], slicing, version control [S43, S48], and state graphs [S61], producing graphs, ASTs, CFGs, or trace reports [S32, S36, S48, S61].

Tools include Test2Feature [S36] for TC-feature tracing, NodeSRT [S9] for module imports, DIRTS [S2] for cross-language graphs, and CORTS/C2RTS [S25] for dependency graph generation.

Change Impact Analysis. This technique assesses the consequences of system changes to identify affected artifacts.

BinaryRTS [S40] uses dynamic binary analysis to link execution traces with version control history. DeltaFuzz [S63] detects "change points" via control flow and call graphs. LoM-Score and Dis-LoM-Score [S43] apply similarity analysis to reduce redundant test executions. Colosseum [S1] performs TCP by tracking code element displacement in execution paths.

RQ2: What Regression Testing solutions emphasize traceability data?

The analysis identified RT solutions using traceability, shown in Fig. 4, with requirement and code links equally common. The following sections detail examples and features from selected studies.

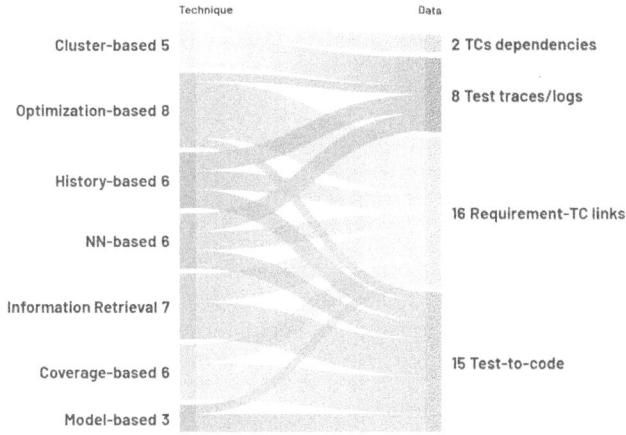

Fig. 4. Connections between traceability data and techniques.

5.4 Model-Based Techniques

Kesserwan et al. [S51] use input templates to link requirements to test data. A metamodel framework [S8] tracks TC-to-rule mappings. LTR-TS [S44] applies EFSMs, mutation testing, and ML for ranking and prioritization.

5.5 Machine Learning-Based Techniques

ML in RT uses traceability to train on code-test links, classify relevance, predict effectiveness, and group tests by changes [S30].

Neural Networks-Based Techniques. NNs enhance ML-based RT ranking [S20, S59, S41, S19]. Traceability data improves TCP training [S30]. Rotaru and Vescan [S60] use NLP to create traceability graphs for ANN-based TCP.

Clustering-Based Techniques. Clustering groups TCs [S26, S28] to find links for TCS or clusters test traces by behavior and logs [S28, S54, S62]. SELogger [S54] uses k-means on runtime features; Tamagnan et al. [S62] consider execution paths and faults. SELogger selects the oldest TC per cluster, Tamagnan et al. sample TCs, and Wang et al. [S26] prioritize by fault detection, adjusting rankings accordingly.

5.6   Optimization-Based Techniques

Greedy, metaheuristic, and optimization methods improve TC selection using graphs and swarms: bipartite graphs [S16], Locust Swarm Optimization and RNNs [S19], Emperor Penguins and Shepherd Optimization with TC links [S21], and MC-TOA with Pareto search [S11].

GA-based methods use TC-requirement links in fitness, prioritizing coverage and cost [S7, S23, S24, S66].

5.7   Coverage-Based Techniques

Coverage-oriented techniques assess requirement and code coverage for thorough testing. **Requirement coverage** verifies features via GA fitness [S23] or keyword matching between TCs and requirements [S18].

Code coverage uses method signatures and code changes to find critical paths [S1, S31], with behavior coverage applied in clustering [S62] and GA fitness [S5].

5.8   History-Based Techniques

History-based methods prioritize TCs using fault detection and change frequency data [S67], combined with code smell [S15] or fault info [S4] to weight NNs [S19] or guide GA TCP [S66]. Historical data is gathered from test logs [S4, S15, S66, S67]; one method converts UML diagrams from past versions into CSV [S19].

5.9   Information Retrieval-Based Techniques

Information retrieval methods enhance RT by using textual and structural similarity. Tools like Smartest [S12], a recommender [S3], QRTest [S10], and FineEkstazi/FineSTARTS [S37] apply vector models and cosine similarity for TCP.

Domain ontologies map TCs to software elements for semantic analysis (Protégé, OWL) [S42]. COSMIC [S6] filters TCs via ontology-driven ranking, and GbWRT [S7] uses ontology-based GA with multi-objective fitness for web RT.

> *RQ3: Which System Under Testing (SUT) domains are addressed?*

Six SUT domains were identified (Fig. 5). The following sections detail examples and features from the selected studies.

5.10   Highly Configurable Systems (HCS)

Mendonça and Vergilio [S32, S36] enhance RT for HCS using feature-based traceability, focusing on TCS linked to affected features. Traceability reports (generated via static analysis) detail code lines, TCs, and exercised lines.

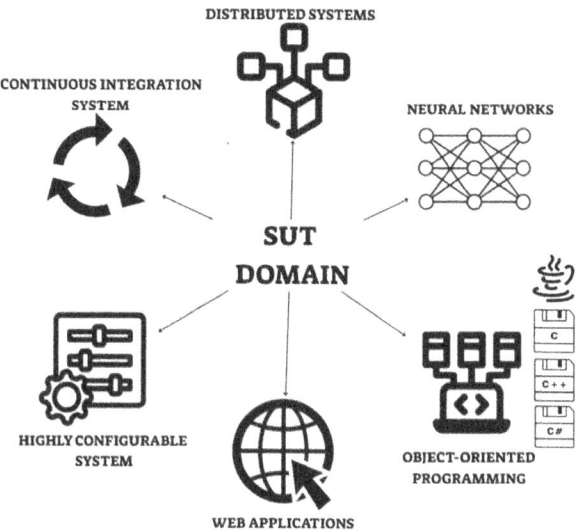

Fig. 5. Target domains of the identified traceability-based approaches.

5.11 Distributed Systems

Most RTS (Regression Test Selection) methods don't fit distributed systems due to single-system analysis. MRegTest [*S50*] generates mutants and replays traces for TCS in distributed systems, while another approach [*S21*] targets TCP for fault detection based on system changes. Traceability-based solutions like MRTS-BP [*S17*] and MicroRTS [*S31*] optimize TC selection in microservices by analyzing service dependencies and change impacts.

5.12 Neural Networks

EFFIMAP [*S64*] is an efficient TCP technique for deep neural networks (DNNs) that uses predictive mutation analysis based on its execution trace, eliminating the need for costly mutant executions.

5.13 Web-Based Applications

Regression testing for web apps handles dynamic, async behavior. NodeSRT [*S9*] optimizes test selection for Node.js, Smartest [*S12*] selects integration tests without file dependencies, [*S52*] uses CI and version control data, and GbWRT [*S7*] applies GAs for adaptive automation.

5.14 Continuous Integration Emphasis

CI/CD automates testing, building, and deployment for fast, reliable releases with minimal errors. Many studies [*S3, S20, S27, S28, S40, S41, S33, S48, S56,*

S58, S60] focus on CI, tackling time constraints and large test data. Elsner et al. [*S52, S29*] optimize RTS using CI and version control metadata. Traceability aids monitoring open-source projects with public logs and trackers [*S13, S67*].

5.15 Object-Oriented Programming

- **Java**: Most of research collected in this review is exclusively performed in the working platform of JAVA [*S2, S14, S15, S19, S21, S31, S33, S35, S37, S38, S39, S41, S43, S48, S53, S56, S59, S60*]. Many Java-based projects, datasets, libraries, and tools are open-source, making them accessible for researchers to study, test, and evaluate different RT techniques.
- **C#**: Other studies have also utilized C# datasets for validation [*S10, S3, S36*], as the tools employed in these approaches offer built-in support for C# (e.g., MineTestLines from Test2Feature), or because there are available open-source projects for assessment (e.g., *nopCommerce, Umbraco*].
- **C/C++**: Traceability aids RT in C/C++ by handling complex dependencies, toolchains, and cross-language links. Solutions like Colosseum [*S1*] and BinaryRTS [*S40*] leverage dynamic analysis, while others focus on build-system-aware RTS [*S29, S32, S36*].

RQ4: How are the techniques validated?

Several strategies for validating methodologies were identified. The following sections present details and examples from selected studies, highlighting their distinct features.

5.16 Validation Approaches

Ekstazi. Ekstazi [1] is a widely used baseline tool for Java regression testing, integrated into Maven Surefire [*S2*]. It tracks per-test execution traces by instrumenting Java bytecode to establish dependencies. Despite criticisms for missing XML dependencies, relying on file checksums, and lacking cross-language support [*S2, S29, S53*], it remains a key benchmark for TCS and TCP techniques [*S25*] and outperforms STARTS, OpenClover, and HyRTS in studies [*S22*]. Many recent solutions build on Ekstazi to improve its features [*S37, S33, S35*].

STARTS. STARTS [7] is a Maven RTS plugin that statically analyzes dependencies using test file checksums and reuses parts of Ekstazi's code [*S12*]. It builds a dependency network linking SUT types like classes and interfaces. Used for benchmarking [*S14, S25*] and optimization [*S37*], STARTS is limited to Java, has JDK/JUnit version constraints, and ignores annotation-based dependencies [*S2*]. Among major RTS tools, only STARTS provides a command-line view of altered files [*S22*].

5.17   Metrics

APFD [16] is the most widely used metric for assessing regression testing [*S20, S28, S38, S43, S48, S44*], with extensions accounting for fault severity, top-k prioritization, and APFDc for enhanced fault detection [*S1, S48, S52*].

Other metrics measure selected classes [*S35*], tested faults [*S15*], safety violation [*S35, S22*], or fault detection ability. Many focus on time efficiency, including time to detect first/last fault, training time, execution time, and overall minimization time [*S20, S22, S28, S46*].

5.18   Datasets

Proposed Datasets. Several datasets have been introduced to support further research on regression testing [*S6, S35, S41, S48*], including real and synthetic ones [*S52, S58, S62*].

Synthetic Datasets. Synthetic traceability datasets, like Zhang et al.'s [*S41*] mutation testing-based dataset, predict failures and mimic RTS. Some extend real datasets, such as Defects4J [*S58*], Ctest [*S35*], and RTPTorrent [*S52*].

Defects4j Validation Dataset. Researchers use Defects4J for validation due to its real-world Java programs with known defects, enabling evaluation of RT techniques in real scenarios [*S15*]. It provides standardized datasets with multiple revisions per project, ideal for testing bug detection methods and comparing metrics like FFR and APFD [*S59, S43*].

This section presents the study's results and offers a variety of viewpoints on the gaps, difficulties, and unresolved problems. The section concludes with a full list of opportunities and recommendations.

5.19   Discussions of Results

We found that trace-based methods are not a distinct solution category but rather a class integrated into other approaches like requirement-based, search-based, and fault-based methods. They follow standard validation and evaluation patterns with no unique metrics, baseline models, or datasets.

Our review highlights increasing diversity in SUTs for traceability-based regression testing, including microservices, HCS, embedded software, and NN. However, repositories like Defects4J and baseline models such as Ekstazi and STARTS remain dominant, primarily for Java-based applications. APFD continues to be the leading evaluation metric for TCP and TCS, with little evidence of novel alternatives.

While this concept has been explored in various studies, it remains an emerging research area. Small-scale efforts show its feasibility but also emphasize the need for further investigation and integration into broader testing frameworks.

5.20   Gaps, Challenges, Open Issues

Despite significant progress in traceability-based regression testing, several gaps, challenges, and open issues persist, requiring further research and development.

- **Domain specificity**. Traceability approaches must adapt to diverse systems, including configurable, mobile, modular, and microservice-based environments, as well as different programming languages. However, most regression testing tools currently focus on Java-based systems.
- **Limitations on adaptability**. Most Java-based RTS methods struggle with cross-language development because of reliance on language-specific analysis. An RTS technique that traces dependencies across languages is crucial for Java tests interacting with C/C++ and non-code artifacts.
- **Costs**. Retrieving traceability information is resource-intensive. Without direct SUT code access, companies rely on attributes like test history and execution time. Even with instrumentation, analyzing binary artifacts is costly, and the dynamic nature of these attributes complicates TCP cost-effectiveness.
- **Open-source tools**. Multiple tools developed for RT are proprietary and often tailored to specific studies, making it unclear whether they were custom-built or just used for validation. There is a notable lack of open-source tools for TCP and TCS tasks, given the unchanging baseline tools used for evaluation across years and studies.
- **Scalability** is key for traceability-based RT, as managing links between test cases, code, and requirements becomes complex in large projects. Few studies address scaling traceability, and while large datasets can assess algorithm efficiency, they may not reflect real-world software complexities.
- **Real-world scenarios**. Many studies focus on libraries, frameworks, or web applications, neglecting real-world systems due to resource constraints. Evaluating actual systems could reveal issues often missed in higher-level abstractions.

5.21   Opportunities and Recommendations

- **Diversity in evaluation criteria**. While the widespread use of APFD provides comparability, a broader set of metrics, including execution time and test suite reduction, is needed for a more comprehensive evaluation of regression testing techniques.
- **Collaboration towards applicability**. To improve traceability, researchers should collaborate with practitioners and open-source communities, developing techniques that strengthen artifact links for more effective regression testing.
- **Maintainability support**. Traceability enhances both regression testing and software maintainability by keeping tests relevant and tracking changes in Continuous Integration, improving test effectiveness and system adaptability.

– **Traceability links**. Practitioners should prioritize defining explicit links between software artifacts (e.g., test-code-requirement) to enhance regression testing processes like TCP and TCS. Maintaining these links ensures that changes in requirements and code are accurately reflected in the relevant test cases.

6 Threats to Validity

Despite careful attention to validity during the survey process, potential threats may still influence the results.

One threat to *external validity* arises from the possibility of overlooking important sources, given the constraints of the reviewer's knowledge regarding all available studies. To minimize this risk, our search strategy focused on using well-established and recognized databases.

Another threat that concerns *construct validity* involves the failure to identify relevant studies due to inconsistencies in terminology or phrasing. To counteract this, we employed and iteratively refined multiple search string combinations to ensure a thorough examination of the literature.

7 Conclusions

This Systematic Literature Review explores traceability-based approaches in regression testing through four research questions, addressing test case prioritization, selection, and minimization using artifact relationships. A systematic search across ACM, IEEE, ScienceDirect, Springer, Scopus, and WoS (2021âĂŞ2025) identified 67 relevant studies through automated queries, manual screening, and quality assessment. The findings provide insights into automating regression testing and emphasize the need for improved traceability links, diverse evaluation metrics, and stronger collaboration to enhance adaptability, scalability, and maintainability, especially in cross-language environments.

Acknowledgements. I would like to express my gratitude to my PhD coordinator for their invaluable guidance and support in the verification and validation of this work.

Disclosure of Interests. There are no relevant conflicts of interest to disclose.

References

1. Gligoric, M., Eloussi, L., Marinov, D.: Practical regression test selection with dynamic file dependencies. In: Proceedings of the 2015 International Symposium on Software Testing and Analysis, pp. 211–222 (2015)
2. Greca, R., Miranda, B., Bertolino, A.: State of practical applicability of regression testing research: a live systematic literature review. ACM Comput. Surv. **55**(13s), 1–36 (2023)

3. Hasnain, M., Ghani, I., Pasha, M.F., Jeong, S.R.: Ontology-based regression testing: a systematic literature review. Appl. Sci. **11**(20), 9709 (2021)
4. Hasnain, M., Pasha, M.F., Ghani, I., Jeong, S.R.: Functional requirement-based test case prioritization in regression testing: a systematic literature review. SN Comput. Sci. **2**(6), 421 (2021)
5. Hussain, T., Eschbach, R.: Automated fault tree generation and risk-based testing of networked automation systems. In: 2010 IEEE 15th Conference on Emerging Technologies & Factory Automation (ETFA 2010), pp. 1–8. IEEE (2010)
6. Kitchenham, B., Charters, S.: Guidelines for performing systematic literature reviews in software engineering, vol. 2 (2007)
7. Legunsen, O., Shi, A., Marinov, D.: Starts: static regression test selection. In: 2017 32nd IEEE/ACM International Conference on Automated Software Engineering (ASE), pp. 949–954. IEEE (2017)
8. Leung, H.K., White, L.: Insights into regression testing (software testing). In: Proceedings. Conference on Software Maintenance-1989, pp. 60–69. IEEE (1989)
9. Meline, T.: Selecting studies for systemic review: inclusion and exclusion criteria. Contemp. Issues Commun. Sci. Disord. **33**(Spring), 21–27 (2006)
10. Moldovan, A.M.N.: Regression testing via traceability: a systematic literature review (2025). https://doi.org/10.6084/m9.figshare.28683719.v1. https://figshare.com/articles/dataset/Publications-SLR_pdf/28683719
11. Mukherjee, R., Patnaik, K.S.: A survey on different approaches for software test case prioritization. J. King Saud Univ.-Comput. Inf. Sci. **33**(9), 1041–1054 (2021)
12. Myers, G.J., Sandler, C., Badgett, T.: The Art of Software Testing. John Wiley & Sons, Hoboken (2011)
13. Page, M.J., et al.: The prisma 2020 statement: an updated guideline for reporting systematic reviews. bmj **372** (2021)
14. Pan, R., Bagherzadeh, M., Ghaleb, T.A., Briand, L.: Test case selection and prioritization using machine learning: a systematic literature review. Empir. Softw. Eng. **27**(2), 29 (2022)
15. Rahmani, A., Ahmad, S., Jalil, I.E.A., Herawan, A.P.: A systematic literature review on regression test case prioritization. Int. J. Adv. Comput. Sci. Appl. **12**(9) (2021)
16. Rothermel, G., Untch, R.H., Chu, C., Harrold, M.J.: Prioritizing test cases for regression testing. IEEE Trans. Softw. Eng. **27**(10), 929–948 (2001)
17. Samad, A., Mahdin, H., Kazmi, R., Ibrahim, R.: Regression test case prioritization: a systematic literature review. Int. J. Adv. Comput. Sci. Appl. **12**(2) (2021)
18. dos Santos, L.B.R., de Souza, É.F., Trubiani, C., Pinciroli, R., Vijaykumar, N.L., et al.: Performance regression testing initiatives: a systematic mapping. Inf. Softw. Technol. 107641 (2024)

On Architectural Tactics
for Resource-Constrained
and Safety-Critical AI-Based Systems

Philipp Straub$^{(\boxtimes)}$ (ID), Christian Decker, and Marco Kuhrmann (ID)

Reutlingen University, Herman Hollerith Center, Böblingen, Germany
{philipp.straub,christian.decker,marco.kuhrmann}@reutlingen-university.de

Abstract. Systems development in resource-constrained, safety-critical areas is significantly impacted by slight discrepancies, such as unknown faults, resulting in system failure. This affects life, the environment, or finances. The rise of Artificial Intelligence (AI), especially through TinyML, encourages the development of AI-based systems for dynamic fault mitigation in safety-critical domains. Architectural tactics are a crucial development practice as they address constraints and quality attributes through low-level design decisions. This paper elaborates on the state-of-the-art by identifying the quality attributes and architectural tactics used by safety-critical, resource-constrained AI-based systems. We conducted a Systematic Mapping Study using a snowballing search procedure, including 217 publications. We inductively identified 150 architectural tactics across 19 categories and provided a detailed overview. Our results show that most publications providing tactics are solution proposals, while few report long-term evaluations. This reveals an immature field. When using ISO/IEC 25059 for quality attribute classification, we found that it lacks twelve relevant attributes. Our research contributes to the development of safe and resource-friendly AI-based systems.

Keywords: Software Architecture · Artificial Intelligence · Architectural Tactics · safety-critical · resource-constrained · Software Development

1 Introduction

During the descent maneuver of the first Israeli Moon mission in 2019, an error indication in the inertial measurement unit reset the probe's computer, resulting in the shutdown of the main engines. So, a small discrepancy lead to fatal results, and the US$100 million-dollar probe was destroyed due to the high-speed impact on the lunar surface [1,10]. Small discrepancies that might result in a disaster pose risks that apply to all application domains in which resource-constrained and safety-critical systems are implemented.

However, since the capabilities of AI-based systems continuously grow, there is an increasing interest in adopting and developing AI-based systems to explore new use cases and mitigate risks—even at a small scale, e.g., through TinyML. This would, for instance, allow for mitigating faults during operation [6]. In this regard, the question for fulfilling *Quality Attributes* (QA) through appropriate *Architectural Tactics* (AT) for developing resource-constrained, safety-critical AI-based systems arises. An architectural tactic *"is a design decision that influences the control of a quality attribute response"* [4] and build the foundation of devising a system architecture at the lowest level. A single tactic does not include a trade-off discussion regarding the quality attributes, as a tactic is only a low-level structure, mechanism, technique, or small development step. Tactics might fulfill several quality attributes and, thus, the selection of tactics and the balancing of attributes are important steps in the architecture design process.

Problem Statement and Objective. The increasing interest in AI in the context of dependable systems raises the question for the applicability of architectural tactics as used in the development of "normal" software-intensive systems. A comprehensive overview of architectural tactics and the associated quality attributes for the domain of resource-constrained, safety-critical AI-based systems is, however, not available. Hence, our objective is to draw a big picture of the current state-of-the-art in applying architectural tactics to this domain with a particular focus on the quality attributes addressed by such tactics.

Contribution. We contribute a *Systematic Mapping Study* on 217 publications that address resource-constrained and safety-critical AI-based systems (short: *constrained systems*) as well as "normal" systems. We extracted 150 architectural tactics, which we clustered into 19 categories. To link the extracted tactics with the quality attributes, we conducted a mapping using the ISO/IEC 25059 [13] standard. We found the attribute *Performance Efficiency* being considered the most relevant for AI-based systems, while 12 quality attributes could not be assigned to the ISO-schema, which indicates potentially new or insufficiently studied quality attributes. However, while only few publications report long-term evaluations, the majority propose solutions, which indicates a still immature, i.e., developing research field. Therefore, our work contributes to the development of safe and resource-friendly AI-based systems.

Related Work. So far, there is no systematic mapping or review on architectural tactics and their relations to quality attributes with a particular focus on resource-constrained, safety-critical AI-systems. Removing this focus, a few related studies can be found. For example, Indykov et al. [11] and Nazir et al. [19] conducted a systematic review on architectural tactics of ML-enabled systems and provided a list of tactics including their impact on quality attributes. Indykov et al. [11] propose a quality model of 42 quality attributes, a list of 16 tactics and an impact analysis of tactics on quality attributes. Nazir et al. [19] complement their review with expert interviews to provide 35 design challenges,

Table 1. Seed Set including the search string and metadata including the paper's reference, the publication year, the application domain, and the classifications regarding the research type facet (RTF; [30]), and the contribution type facet (CTF; [27])

ID	Search String	Ref	Year	Domain	RTF	CTF
1	safety-critical tinyml	[16]	2023	Automotive	Evaluation Research	Solution
2	safety-critical tinyml	[29]	2023	Smart Home	Solution Proposal	Solution
3	CPS tinyml safety-critical	[24]	2021	Automotive	Solution Proposal	Solution
4	iot tinyml safety-critical	[7]	2024	General	Solution Proposal	Framework
5	iot tinyml safety-critical	[2]	2022	Infrastructure	Solution Proposal	Framework
6	safety-critical tinyml architecture	[28]	2023	Healthcare	Evaluation Research	Solution
7	safety-critical tinyml architecture	[34]	2024	Manufacturing	Evaluation Research	Solution
8	safety-critical edge tpu architecture	[18]	2023	General	Experience	Lessons Learned
9	safety-critical edge tpu architecture	[9]	2021	Healthcare	Solution Proposal	Technique
10	safety-critical edge tpu architecture	[33]	2022	General	Experience	Technique
11	safety-critical edge tpu architecture	[6]	2020	Avionics	Experience	Lessons Learned
12	safety-critical Tensorflow Lite software architecture edge	[15]	2022	General	Solution Proposal	Technique
13	resource-constrained safety-critical AI-system	[17]	2024	General	Solution Proposal	Technique

42 best practices and 27 tactics. Considering selected aspects of AI-based systems in the context of safety and resource constraints, a few studies focus on specific application domains, such as Aerospace or Transportation [21,22,25]. Carmo et al. [5] investigate the *task offloading* tactic assisted by a digital twin within a survey to find its impact on selected quality attributes. A more general perspective is taken by [8,20,26] who focus on how AI development under one of the constraints is possible in general, e.g., with limited resources. Therefore, our study fills a gap in research by providing a big picture on architectural tactics and their relations to quality attributes with a particular focus on constrained systems.

Outline. The remainder of the paper is structured as follows: Sect. 2 describes the research design. Section 3 presents our results and Sect. 4 discusses our findings, before we conclude the paper in Sect. 5.

2   Research Design

We describe the research design, including our research questions, the data collection and analysis procedures. Our general approach combines a (backward) snowballing according to Wohlin [31] with aspects of a systematic review [14] to, finally, explore the field using the systematic mapping study instrument as described by Petersen [23].

2.1   Research Objective and Research Questions

Our overall objective is *to identify the state-of-the-art regarding architectural tactics and quality attributes applied to resource-constrained, safety-critical AI-based systems.* In this regard, we pose the following research questions:

RQ1: *What are the quality attributes relevant to resource-constrained, safety-critical AI-based systems?* Constrained systems need to fulfill several quality attributes that need to be addressed by the system architecture. With this research question, we aim to identify the most relevant quality attributes and to structure these based on ISO/IEC 25059 [13].

RQ2: *What are the architectural tactics relevant to resource-constrained, safety-critical AI-based systems?* At its lowest level, the system architecture consists of multiple architectural tactics, each addressing specific quality attributes. With this research question, we aim to identify the most relevant tactics and to structure these using an incremental keywording approach as proposed by Peterson [23].

2.2   Data Collection Procedures

Our data collection procedure consisted of three steps: seed set identification, the actual search, and data collection. We provide details on these steps in the following.

Seed Set Identification. We developed an initial search string based on Wohlin's guidelines [3, 31] to identify a seed set using Google Scholar. The papers found were analyzed to refine the search string(s). To be included in the seed set, a paper must address resource constraints and safety-criticality while including architectural tactics in AI-based systems. These constraints form the key inclusion criterion for the subsequent snowballing procedure (Table 4). The final seed set for backward snowballing is listed in Table 1.

Table 2. Overview of the search steps and the resulting papers

Step	Candidates	Accepted	%
Seed Set		13	
Iteration 1	175	55	31.43
Iteration 2	2,311	149	6.45
Total		**217**	

Search Procedure. Based on the 13 papers in the seed set (Table 1), we conducted two search iterations, which yielded 204 papers. Including the seed set, 217 papers in total were passed to the data extraction. Table 2 provides an overview of the complete search procedure and documents the papers found in the different steps. As the table shows, we already saw a notable drop in the acceptance rate for candidate papers. According to Wohlin [31], it is unlikely to find a significant number of new papers in the third iteration (estimated 0.4%) and, therefore, we decided to stop after the second iteration.

Data Collection. To structure the information of the found papers, we collected the data in a spreadsheet that provides the data structure shown in Table 3.

Table 3. Data structure for data collection and evaluation

Information	Description
Identification number	Unique, running number of the paper
Iteration	Iteration during which the paper appeared
Reference Paper ID	Reference to the paper that has cited this paper
Content	Author, reference link, year, conference/journal
Decision	Decision on the paper's in- or exclusion
Decision Information	Information on the decision, i.e., violated criteria
Context Metadata	Constraints, industry domain, AI task, RTF, CTF
Quality Attributes	Addressed quality attributes (Fig. 1)
Architectural Tactics	Addressed architectural tactics (Fig. 1)

2.3   Data Extraction and Analysis Procedures

The data analysis procedure consisted of the three steps final decision-making, context metadata analysis, and data extraction, which we describe in the following.

Final Decision-Making. The decision-making process connects the data collection and the data analysis steps. The process is guided by the inclusion and exclusion criteria listed in Table 4. A candidate paper identified in the snowballing was screened and could be removed during the screening, but also during the later assessment or extraction steps. The screening was a high-level check whether or not the paper includes architectural tactics. In particular, during the screening, the exclusion criteria EC1–EC14 were checked. For the in-depth assessment, i.e., papers that passed the screening, all exclusion criteria have been checked. If a paper was marked for exclusion, before the actual exclusion, it was checked whether there is a justification for keeping the paper's referred papers, which were only removed from the candidate list if no other paper holds at least one reference. Eventually, the procedure applied ensures that only those papers remained in the result set that fully met IC1.

Context Metadata Analysis. A context metadata analysis was conducted to characterize the result set. For this, based on the papers' abstracts (if necessary the full text), the contribution [27] and research type facets [30], as well as the application domains and the specific AI-related task have been collected.

Data Extraction and Analysis. The actual data extraction was done focussing on the abstracts, introductions, and conclusions of the publications in the result set. These parts were searched for tactics and quality attributes explicitly named by the authors. The main-body text of the paper was used to complete missing information. However, to ensure the tactics and quality attributes were applied by the authors, we ignored the background and related work sections. That is, only tactics and quality attributes that were considered major contributions have been included in the study.

Complementing the data extraction, the first analysis step was conducted to derive the quality attributes. For this, we utilized the ISO/IEC 25059 [13] categorization system with its definitions. This system aims to provide a notion of quality with a particular focus on AI-based systems. However, before using the ISO/IEC 25059, we double-checked it with ISO/IEC 25010 [12] on which the ISO/IEC 25059 is based. In the analysis, we assigned a quality attribute to a ISO/IEC 25059 category if possible. If no acceptable match could be made, we assigned the quality attribute a new category "Other".

For structuring the architectural tactics, other than for quality attributes, there is no standard like the ISO/IEC 25059 available. Therefore, during the data extraction, we inductively developed appropriate categories for tactics using an *incremental keywording approach* as proposed by Peterson [23]. For this purpose, we randomly selected 10% of the publications from the result set and conducted the keywording to create the initial classification system. Another 25% of the papers was analyzed using this initial system and, if necessary, the classification system was evolved. After this step, we reviewed the classification, built initial clusters, which we carefully checked for uniqueness or merging needs. The resulting updated classification system was used to classify the remainder of the result set, followed by another review of the categories and clusters to conclude the final clustering. Note that the classification and/or clustering tasks were executed on the plain extracted data, which remained as extracted. That is, each extracted tactic was assigned to clusters and categories, and a short rationale was provided for why this assignment was done. The final data structure for both quality attributes and architectural tactics is visualized in Fig. 1.

Table 4. Overview of inclusion and exclusion criteria.

IC/EC	Description
IC1	Paper covers/provides architectural tactics for implementation or deployment of AI
EC1	Paper cannot be accessed/only accessed via untrusted provider
EC2	Paper is not in English
EC3	Paper is published before 2014
EC4	Paper is not peer-reviewed or from a independent government agency (e.g., NASA)
EC5	Paper occurred multiple times
EC6	Paper is not a primary study
EC7	Paper is not on development or implementation of AI
EC8	Paper is not on applications, frameworks, libraries, methods, models, tools or guidelines for AI
EC9	The subject of study is hardware design
EC10	Paper is not on quality attributes
EC11	Paper does not name any quality attributes
EC12	The evaluation/proof of concept does not cover quality attributes addressed in the study design
EC13	The subject of study is a mathematical proof
EC14	The subject is only on quality attributes' investigation, confirmation or breaching and does not explain or examine how to achieve quality attributes
EC15	The results, discussion, or conclusion do not explain how the quality attributes addressed in the study design are achieved
EC16	The results, discussion, or conclusion do not describe what low-level single structure, mechanism, technique, or development step has led to the achievement of a single quality attribute addressed in the study design
EC17	The results, discussion, or conclusion only describe how the trade-off between quality attributes has been/can be addressed
EC18	Paper Abstract, Introduction or Conclusion do not provide applied architectural tactics

3 Results

In this section, we present the results of our study. After providing an overview of the final result set in Sect. 3.1, we present the results of our study structured according to the research questions posed in Sect. 2.1.

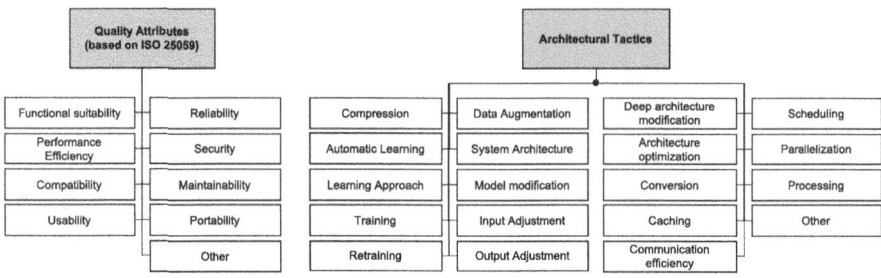

Fig. 1. Overview of the final data structure for the classification of quality attributes and architectural tactics

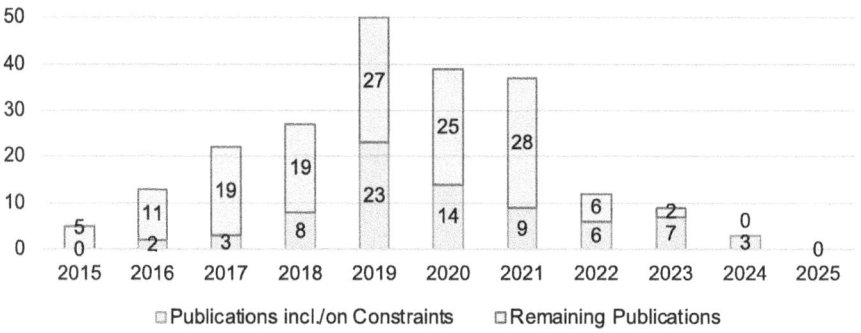

Fig. 2. Publication Frequency of papers on architectural tactics per year (incl. the share of papers addressing constraints in the system design)

3.1   Demographics

We analyzed 217 publications meeting our requirements (Sect. 2.2). Figure 2 provides an overview of the result set in form of their publication frequency. The color coding shows the share of papers that match the aspects "resource-constrained" and/or "safety-critical", and distinguishes these publications from those addressing other related aspects, e.g., privacy. In total, 75 publications address at least one of the major aspects. While the chart shows the topic of our study of certain relevance, the chart also indicates the bandwidth of quality considerations in the context of AI-based systems, which constitute a vibrant field. This observation is supported by the RTF [30] and CTF [27] classification of the result set as shown in Fig. 3. The figure shows that most publications are classified as *Solution Proposal* ($n = 191$, 88.02%). A particular focus is on proposing specific *Techniques* (106 publications). The map also shows that a certain number of *Experiences* ($n = 17$, 7.83%) have been collected, yet, *Evaluation Research* ($n = 4$, 1.84%) is rare. That is, a number of approaches competes for the researchers' and practitioners' favor, but, the field as such must be considered immature and still evolving. Yet, due to this observation, the conclusions drawn

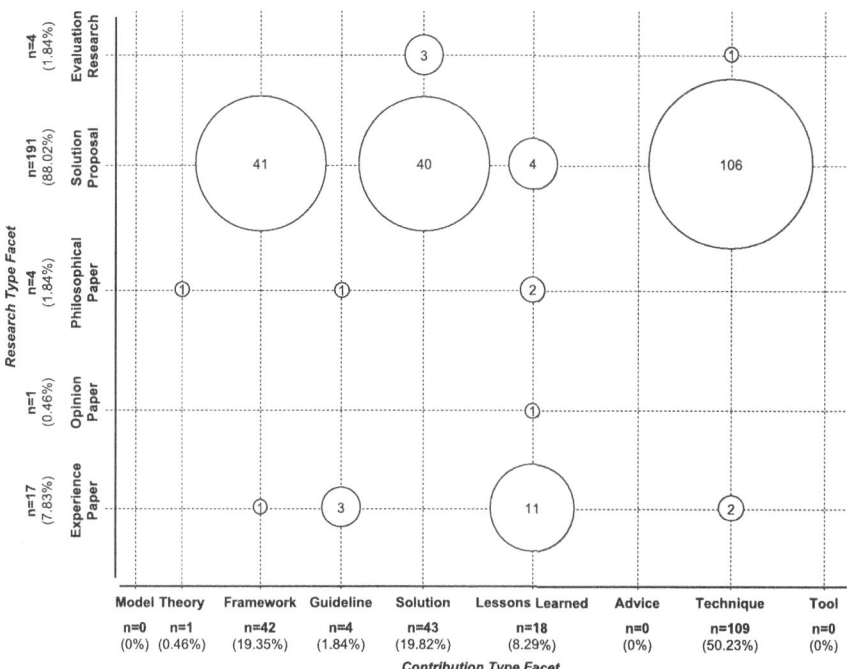

Fig. 3. Classification of the result set according to the research [30] and contribution type facets [27]

in this paper must be considered with care, since the current state-of-the-art presented in the paper at hand is likely a subject to change.

3.2   RQ1: Quality Attributes

The first research question aims to identify quality attributes for resource-constrained, safety-critical AI-based systems. Based on the data extraction and analysis (Sect. 2.3), we categorized the identified quality attributes using the data structure shown in Fig. 1. In total, we extracted 569 quality attributes (mentions) from the 217 publications. It has to be noted that, in some cases, multiple assignments had to be made, as several publications contributed multiple attributes.

Figure 4 connects the top-level ISO/IEC 25059 *Quality Attribute Category* with the contribution and research type facets and, therefore, allows for assessing (i) the focal points, i.e., which category attracts the most attention and (ii) the maturity and actual contribution within these focal points. The map documents three notable focal points: *Performance Efficiency, Functional Suitability*, and *Reliability* are the three most frequently addressed quality attribute categories. The maturity and the actual contributions within these three categories are consistent with the big picture (Fig. 3). The majority of the publications in

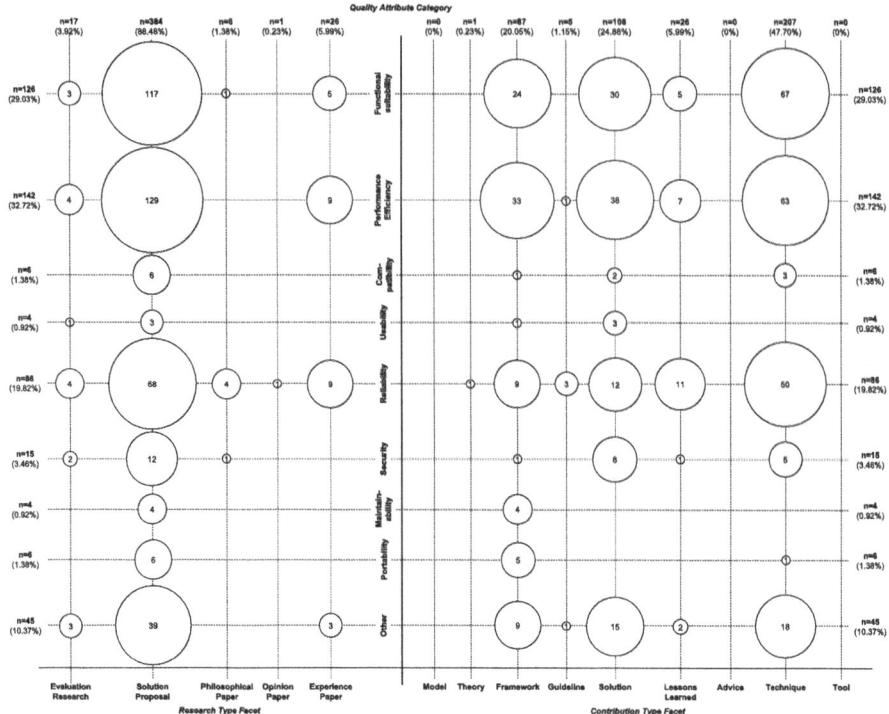

Fig. 4. Mapping of quality attribute categories in relation to the research and contribution type facet (single score within a quality attribute category)

these categories is categorized as a *Solution Proposal*, and most of the publications contribute specific *Techniques*. However, it can also be seen that these three categories account for the majority of publications classified as *Evaluation Research* (11 out of 17), and these three categories also provide the majority of the contributions of type *Framework* (66 out of 87) and of type *Solution* (80 out of 108). It has to be noted that for each of the top-level categories several subcategories do exist. For example, the category *Functional Suitability* contains the sub-category *Functional Correctness*, which is interpreted as *Accuracy* for AI-based systems. The three most frequently addressed categories also reflect the aspects "resource-constrained" and "safety-critical" alongside the assurance of functional correctness (*Accuracy*). Figure 4 also shows that the fourth-largest category is the category *Other*. This indicates a gap in the standard for our specific domain. Specifically, the 12 quality attributes categorized as *Other* that are addressed by at least three publications are: *Safety* ($n = 11$), *Training Efficiency* ($n = 11$), *Resiliency* ($n = 8$), *Flexibility* ($n = 7$), *Autonomy* ($n = 5$), and *Scalability* ($n = 3$). All of these, except *Training Efficiency* and *Autonomy*, are covered in ISO/IEC 25010 [12].

3.3   RQ2: Architectural Tactics

To answer the second research question, we first applied the data structure shown in Fig. 1 and visualized the various architectural tactics in a hierarchy. Figure 5 shows the structured tactics and, at the same time, provides insights regarding the relevance of a specific tactic due to their placements within the hierarchy. In total, we have identified 150 architectural tactics that are classified in 19 categories. A total of 575 mentions of tactics found in the 217 publications defined the order in the figure. Within the hierarchy, the tactics are sorted by their frequency—the higher the tactic in the hierarchy, the more often it was mentioned in the publications.

General Classification. To get a notion of the actual contribution and maturity of the identified tactics, we use the RTF-CTF classification in the same way as for the quality attributes in Sect. 3.2. However, due to the number of identified tactics, we apply a hierarchical mapping starting with the low-level architectural tactics, which are aggregated and passed through the hierarchy to compute the numbers for the top-level categories. In particular, lower-level scores are passed through the hierarchy and generate one point in the mapping if there are more than 0 mentions in the lower-level categories. Figure 6 provides this final top-level perspective as a heat map, based on the data structure from Fig. 1. Figure 6 shows three major clusters illustrating the focal points of architecture activities in the context of AI-based systems. The first cluster lists *Compression, Training*, and *Deep Architecture Modification* as the most relevant ones. Looking into the this cluster, the included contributions mostly apply architectural tactics like *Quantization* or *Pruning* to realize the *Compression* of their solution, *Adversarial Training* or *Finetuning* during the *Training*, and *Width or Depth Adjustment* of the AI network for *Deep Architecture Modification*. This allows the publications to achieve the quality attributes of the previous Sect. 3.2. However, in line with the quality attributes (Sect. 3.2), the majority of the contributions is of type *Technique* that are mostly *Solution Proposals*.

Refined Classification. Due to space limitations, we cannot provide a detailed perspective for all 19 categories. Therefore, we selected the top-ranked category *Compression* from Fig. 6, and we provide a refined perspective of the actual low-level architectural tactics assigned to this category in Fig. 7. At this level, eventually, we see actual tactics, i.e., recommendations, methods, practices, and the like that help architects decide which option to choose when designing an AI-based system. It has to be noted that (i) all tactics that have been mentioned by less than two publications have been assigned to the category *Other* to limit the number of categories. Furthermore, (ii) due to the scoring mechanism, the aggregated numbers from Fig. 7 do not match the ones in Fig. 6, since at the lower-level a mapping of the individual tactics based on their actual frequencies are in the spotlight, while these are ignored at the top-level in favor of the manageable number of categories.

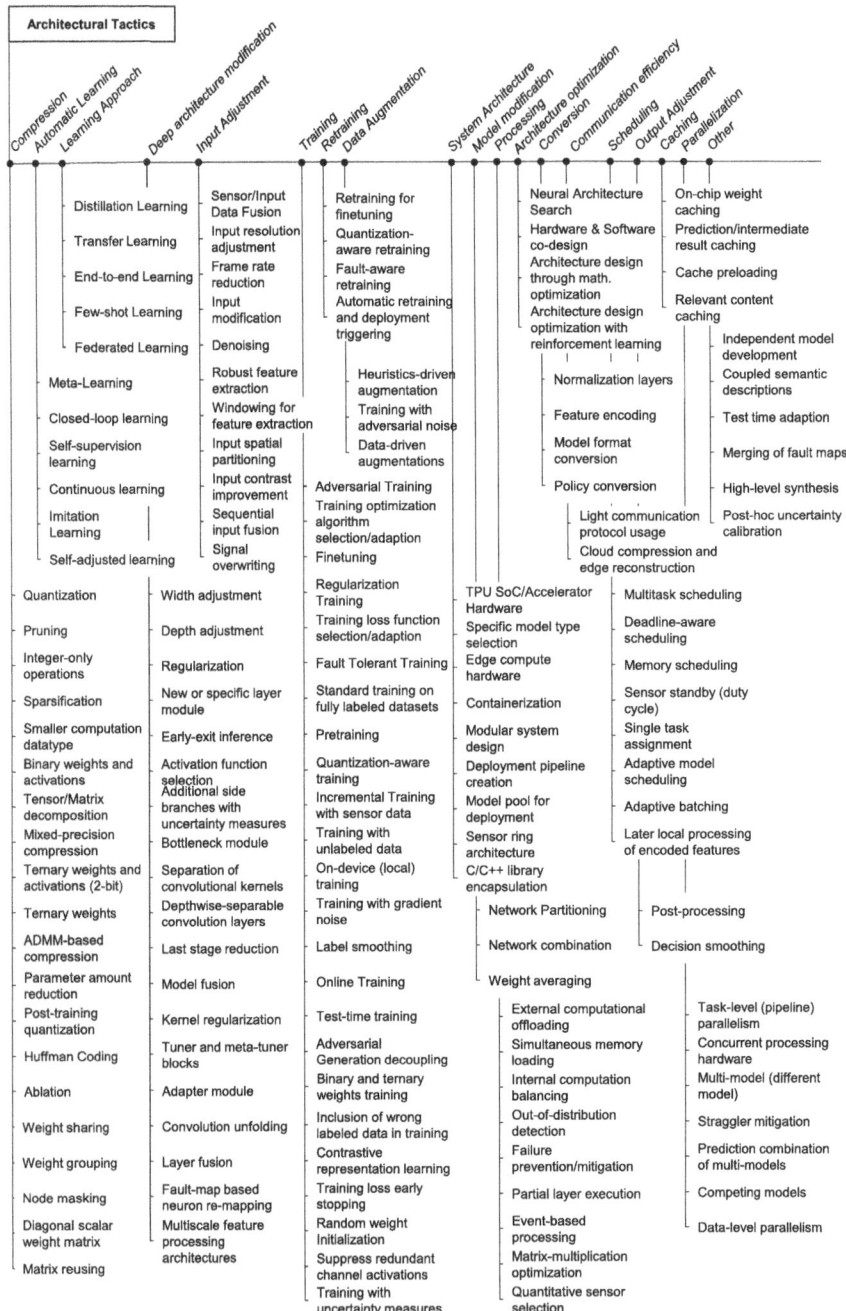

Fig. 5. Overview of the 150 identified architectural tactics within the extracted 19 categories (tactics within the branches are sorted in descending order based on their frequency of mentions)

Architectural Tactic Category	Total	Research Type					Contribution Type Facet								
		Evaluation	Solution	Philosophical	Opinion	Experience	Model	Theory	Framework	Solution	Technique	Guideline	Lessons Learned	Advice	Tool
Compression	84	1	78			5			19	18	44	1	2		
Training	74	1	65	2		6			10	6	50	3	5		
Deep architecture modification	49	1	38	2		8	1		9	11	19	2	7		
Learning Approach	25		25						5	7	13				
Processing	25		24			1			7	8	9		1		
Architecture optimization	23		21		1	1			12	2	8		1		
Parallelization	22		22						10	7	5				
Input Adjustment	21		19			2			4	8	6		3		
Automatic Learning	20		20						6	2	12				
System Architecture	20		17	1		2			8	7	2	1	2		
Data Augmentation	16		14	1	1				3	1	9		3		
Retraining	13		13						1	3	9				
Model modification	13		13						5	4	4				
Scheduling	12	1	11						4	4	4				
Conversion	9		8			1			1	2	5	1			
Caching	6		6						2	1	3				
Communication efficiency	3	1	2						1	1	1				
Output Adjustment	2		2								1			1	
Other	6		6						1	1	4				

Fig. 6. Top-level categorization of the identified architectural tactic groups and their contribution and research type facets (aggregated scores in the sub-categories generate 1 point in the categorization)

Figure 6 shows that the most applied tactic is *Quantization*, while its single framework contribution is the smallest among the top-5 tactics for *Compression*. Note that not all of these tactics can be combined to achieve the optimal *Compression* architecture. Some tactics allow for combination, e.g., *Quantization* and *Pruning*, while others, e.g., *Integer-only Operations* or *Binary Weights and Activations*, do not and exclude each other. The analysis of tactic combinations remains a subject to future investigation.

4   Discussion

We discuss the findings of our study starting with answering our research questions, before we discuss the findings and the threats to validity.

4.1   Answering the Research Questions

The first research question (Sect. 3.2) aimed at the identification of quality attributes of resource-constrained and safety-critical AI-based systems. Based on 217 publications, our results connected the quality attribute categorization from ISO/IEC 25059 with the related RTF and CTF of the publications, as shown in Fig. 4. We found the three most frequently addressed quality attribute categories

Architectural Tactics of the Compression Category	Total	Research Type					Contribution Type Facet								
		Evaluation	Solution	Philosophical	Opinion	Experience	Model	Theory	Framework	Solution	Technique	Guideline	Lessons Learned	Advice	Tool
Quantization	40	1	36			3			1	12	16		2		
Pruning	23	1	21			1			5	5	13				
Integer-only Operations	11		11						5	4	2				
Sparsification	10		9			1			2	2	6				
Smaller Computation Datatype	7		6			1			3	2	1	1			
Binary Weights and Activations	6		6							1	5				
Tensor/Matrix Decomposition	6		6							1	5				
Mixed-Precision Compression	5		5						1		4				
Ternary Weights and Activations (2-bit)	5		5						1	1	3				
Tenary Weights	4		4								4				
ADMM-based Compression	4		4						3		1				
Parameter amount reduction	2		2							1	1				
Other	9		9						3	2	4				

Fig. 7. Refined categorization of architectural tactics inside the category *Compression* and their classification according to the contribution and research type facet (aggregated score per tactic across all papers)

of resource-constrained and safety-critical AI-based systems are *Performance Efficiency* (32.72%), *Functional Suitability* (29.03%), and *Reliability* (19.82%). These categories reflect the aspects "resource-constrained" and "safety-critical" alongside the assurance of functional correctness (*Accuracy*). The fourth rank is the category *Other* (10.37%), which includes 12 quality attributes. This shows a gap in ISO/IEC 25059, while most of these *Other* quality attributes are mentioned in ISO/IEC 25010 [12].

The second research question (Sect. 3.3) aimed at identifying architectural tactics applied in resource-constrained, safety-critical AI-based systems. Drawing from 217 publications, our findings provide a visualized overview of the various architectural tactics within the hierarchy visualized in Fig. 5. As for the first research question, we connected the top-level tactic categories with the RTF and CTF of the publications as a heat map in Fig. 6 to provide a characterization. In total, we identified 150 architectural tactics that are classified in 19 categories. We found the three major architecture activities in the context of AI-based systems being *Compression* (84 out of 443), *Training* (74 out of 443), and *Deep Architecture Modification* (49 out of 443). A detailed perspective for the top-ranked category *Compression* shown in Fig. 6 highlights tactics like *Quantization* or *Pruning* that architects apply when designing an AI-based system.

4.2   Discussion of Findings

This paper identified quality attributes and architectural tactics of safety-critical, resource-constrained AI-based systems to provide an overview of the state-of-the-art in the field. We found 75 out of 217 papers addressing our constraints and non-constrained systems also having an impact on the domain. The map of research and contribution type facets from the received publications in Fig. 3 highlights the focus on *Solution Proposals* (88.02%) in the field, mainly contributing *Techniques* (50.23%). That is, several approaches compete for the researchers' and practitioners' favor, but, the field as such needs to be considered immature and still evolving. Therefore, our conclusions need to be considered with care, since the current state-of-the-art presented in the paper at hand is likely a subject to change. In the first research question, we found that ISO/IEC 25059 acceptably covers the field, however, our results suggest an extension. Such an extension should include both characteristics from ISO/IEC 25010 and the newly identified ones, and this finding is in line with the proposal by Indykov et al. [11].

We found the most significant quality attribute categories to be *Performance Efficiency* (32.72%), *Functional Suitability* (29.03%), and *Reliability* (19.82%). In the second research question, we categorized the architectural tactics in 19 distinguishable categories, in which a total of 150 tactics was categorized. The most significant categories are *Compression* (84 out of 443), *Training* (74 out of 443), and *Deep Architecture Modification* (49 out of 443). Within the top-ranked category, *Compression*, we found the most applied tactic is *Quantization*. Our identified tactics for conducting *Compression* exemplify the importance of tactic selection in the architecture design process. Combining all tactics within a single architecture is impossible, because some tactics, e.g., *Integer-only Operations* or *Binary Weights and Activations*, cannot be combined in a meaningful way. Such a combination of tactics, however, is likely to always generate some sort of trade-off. Yet, such a trade-off discussion requires extra applied research so that industry experience can be included in the development of an effective quality-driven architecture process for AI-based systems.

4.3 Threats to Validity

Our results include numerous findings, yet there is room for improvement. This section discusses the threats to validity according to Wohlin [32]. Literature studies suffer from the incompleteness of results and a general publication bias, i.e., positive results are published more frequently than others, which also affects the study at hand.

The *internal validity* of our study may be influenced by the data collection methods employed. While the selection of the seed set through Google Scholar is endorsed by Wohlin [31], it could still impact our findings. Alternative citation databases, such as the Web of Science, might have provided additional insights. For efficiency, we limited our backward search to two iterations, while a third iteration could have yielded extra, maybe different results. The absence of a forward search may have resulted in missed new findings and evaluation studies. To address these issues, we followed the guidelines by Kitchenham [14], Wohlin [31], and Petersen [23].

The *external validity* is affected by missing knowledge about the generalizability of the results. Our systematic search procedure facilitated the tracing of individual paper outcomes back to their original sources. We identified 315 candidate papers that were cited by multiple studies, which suggests some support to the assumption of generalizability. However, further validation through a forward snowballing procedure in future research is necessary to substantiate this assumption and to provide a supporting evidence, which could also be provided by extra, independent replications.

5   Conclusion

In this paper, we conducted a systematic mapping study using backward snowballing to identify quality attributes and architectural tactics addressed by resource-constrained, safety-critical AI-based systems. The goal was to gain an overview of the state-of-the-art in the field. Based on 217 papers, we found that both constrained and non-constrained AI-based systems have a substantial impact. We found the field's focus to be on *Solution Proposals* (88.02%), mainly contributing *Techniques* (50.23%) and lacking connectivity to industry and long-term evaluation. We applied the ISO/IEC 25059 for quality attribute classification and found it to be incomplete. We extracted 150 architectural tactics in 19 categories. However, this study is only the first step towards a deeper understanding of quality attributes and architectural tactics and, therefore, our study is also a call for action to better understand the development of AI-based systems in industry and conduct long-term evaluation of architectural tactics to allow for an evidence-based design approach. Future work will, among other things, include a solidification of the database by extending the search procedures by a forward snowballing, as well as additional analyses to check on the combinations of architectural tactics and individual impact on quality attributes.

References

1. Aharonson, O., et al.: The science mission of spaceil's beresheet lander. Planet. Space Sci. **194**, 105115 (2020)
2. Antonini, M., Pincheira, M., Vecchio, M., Antonelli, F.: Tiny-MLOps: a framework for orchestrating ml applications at the far edge of IoT systems. In: 2022 IEEE International Conference on Evolving and Adaptive Intelligent Systems (EAIS), pp. 1–8. IEEE (2022)
3. Badampudi, D., Wohlin, C., Petersen, K.: Experiences from using snowballing and database searches in systematic literature studies. In: Proceedings of the 19th International Conference on Evaluation and Assessment in Software Engineering. EASE 2015. Association for Computing Machinery, New York (2015)
4. Bass, L., Clements, P., Kazman, R.: Software Architecture in Practice, 3rd edn. Addison-Wesley Professional (2012)
5. do Carmo, P.R., et al.: Living on the edge: a survey of digital twin-assisted task offloading in safety-critical environments. J. Netw. Comput. Appl. **232**, 104024 (2024)
6. Chichin, S., Brundler, M., Portes, D., Jegu, V.: Capability to embed deep neural networks: study on CPU processor in avionics context. In: 2020 10th European Congress Embedded Real Time Systems (ERTS), pp. 1–10 (2020)

7. Dey, S., Gangopadhyay, B., Dasgupta, P., Dey, S.: Magnets: micro-architectured group neural networks. In: Proceedings of the 23rd International Conference on Autonomous Agents and Multiagent Systems, AAMAS 2024, pp. 2650–2658. International Foundation for Autonomous Agents and Multiagent Systems, Richland, SC (2024)
8. Dutta, D.L., Bharali, S.: TinyML meets IoT: a comprehensive survey. Internet Things **16**, 100461 (2021)
9. Fabarisov, T., Morozov, A., Mamaev, I., Janschek, K.: Deep learning-based error mitigation for assistive exoskeleton with computational-resource-limited platform and edge tensor processing unit. In: Volume 13: Safety Engineering, Risk, and Reliability Analysis; Research Posters. IMECE 2021. American Society of Mechanical Engineers (2021)
10. Gibney, E.: First private moon lander heralds new lunar space race. Nature **566**(7745), 434–436 (2019)
11. Indykov, V., Strüber, D., Wohlrab, R.: Architectural tactics to achieve quality attributes of machine-learning-enabled systems: a systematic literature review. J. Syst. Softw. **223**, 112373 (2025)
12. ISO/IEC: ISO/IEC 25010:2023 Systems and software engineering - Systems and software Quality Requirements and Evaluation (SQuaRE) - Product quality model. Standard, ISO/IEC, Geneva, CH (2023)
13. ISO/IEC: ISO/IEC 25059:2023 Software engineering - Systems and software Quality Requirements and Evaluation (SQuaRE) - Quality model for AI systems. Standard, ISO/IEC, Geneva, CH (2023)
14. Kitchenham, B., Charters, S.: Guidelines for performing systematic literature reviews in software engineering. eBSE Technical Report, EBSE 2007-01, Keele University (2007)
15. Li, P., Wang, X., Huang, K., Huang, Y., Li, S., Iqbal, M.: Multi-model running latency optimization in an edge computing paradigm. Sensors **22**(16), 6097 (2022)
16. Maayah, M., Abunada, A., Al-Janahi, K., Ahmed, M.E., Qadir, J.: LimitAccess: on-device TinyML based robust speech recognition and age classification. Discov. Artif. Intell. **3**(1) (2023)
17. Moskalenko, V., Moskalenko, A., Kudryavtsev, A., Moskalenko, Y.: Resilience-aware MLOps for resource-constrained AI-system. In: International Workshop on Computer Modeling and Intelligent Systems (2024)
18. Mousavi, H., Zoljodi, A., Daneshtalab, M.: Analysing robustness of tiny deep neural networks. In: Abelló, A., et al. (eds.) ADBIS 2023. CCIS, vol. 1850, pp. 150–159. Springer, Cham (2023)
19. Nazir, R., Bucaioni, A., Pelliccione, P.: Architecting ml-enabled systems: challenges, best practices, and design decisions. J. Syst. Softw. **207**, 111860 (2024)
20. Oliveira, F., Costa, D.G., Assis, F., Silva, I.: Internet of intelligent things: a convergence of embedded systems, edge computing and machine learning. Internet Things **26**, 101153 (2024)
21. Ooko, S.O., Karume, S.M.: Application of tiny machine learning in predicative maintenance in industries. J. Comput. Theor. Appl. **2**(1), 131–150 (2024)
22. Perez-Cerrolaza, J., et al.: Artificial intelligence for safety-critical systems in industrial and transportation domains: A survey. ACM Comput. Surv. **56**(7), 1–40 (2024)
23. Petersen, K., Feldt, R., Mujtaba, S., Mattsson, M.: Systematic mapping studies in software engineering. In: Proceedings of the 12th International Conference on Evaluation and Assessment in Software Engineering, EASE 2008, pp. 68–77. BCS Learning & Development Ltd., Swindon, GBR (2008)

24. de Prado, M., Rusci, M., Donze, R., Capotondi, A., Monnerat, S., Benini, L., Pazos, N.: Robustifying the deployment of TinyML models for autonomous mini-vehicles. In: 2021 IEEE International Symposium on Circuits and Systems (ISCAS), pp. 1–5. IEEE (2021)

25. Rech, P.: Artificial neural networks for space and safety-critical applications: reliability issues and potential solutions. IEEE Trans. Nucl. Sci. **71**(4), 377–404 (2024)

26. Schizas, N., Karras, A., Karras, C., Sioutas, S.: TinyML for ultra-low power AI and large scale IoT deployments: a systematic review. Future Internet **14**(12), 363 (2022)

27. Shaw, M.: Writing good software engineering research papers: minitutorial. In: Proceedings of the 25th International Conference on Software Engineering, ICSE 2003, pp. 726–736. IEEE Computer Society (2003)

28. Sun, B., Bayes, S., Abotaleb, A.M., Hassan, M.: The case for TinyML in healthcare: CNNs for real-time on-edge blood pressure estimation. In: Proceedings of the 38th ACM/SIGAPP Symposium on Applied Computing, SAC 2023, pp. 629–638. ACM (2023)

29. Tsoukas, V., Gkogkidis, A., Boumpa, E., Papafotikas, S., Kakarountas, A.: A gas leakage detection device based on the technology of TinyML. Technologies **11**(2), 45 (2023)

30. Wieringa, R., Maiden, N., Mead, N., Rolland, C.: Requirements engineering paper classification and evaluation criteria: a proposal and a discussion. Requirements Eng. **11**(1), 102–107 (2005)

31. Wohlin, C.: Guidelines for snowballing in systematic literature studies and a replication in software engineering. In: Proceedings of the 18th International Conference on Evaluation and Assessment in Software Engineering, EASE 2014, pp. 1–10. ACM (2014)

32. Wohlin, C., Runeson, P., Höst, M., Ohlsson, M.C., Regnell, B., Wesslén, A.: Experimentation in Software Engineering. Springer (2012)

33. Yuhas, M., Xian Ng, D.J., Easwaran, A.: Design methodology for deep out-of-distribution detectors in real-time cyber-physical systems. In: 2022 IEEE 28th International Conference on Embedded and Real-Time Computing Systems and Applications (RTCSA), pp. 180–185. IEEE (2022)

34. Zanghieri, M., et al.: An extreme-edge TCN-based low-latency collision-avoidance safety system for industrial machinery. IEEE Access **12**, 16009–16021 (2024)

Investigating the Use of Snowballing on Q&A Websites

Felipe Gomes[1,2]([⊠]) [iD], Thiago Mendes[2] [iD], Sávio Freire[3] [iD], Rodrigo Spínola[4] [iD],
and Manoel Mendonça[1] [iD]

[1] Federal University of Bahia, Bahia, Brazil
{felipe.gustavo,manoel.mendonca}@ufba.br
[2] Federal Institute of Bahia, Bahia, Brazil
{felipegomes,thiagosouto}@ifba.edu.br
[3] Federal Institute of Ceará, Ceará, Brazil
savio.freire@ifce.edu.br
[4] Virginia Commonwealth University, Richmond, USA
spinolaro@vcu.edu

Abstract. *Background*: The use of grey literature (GL) has grown in software engineering research, especially in studies that consider questions and answers (Q&A) websites, since software development professionals widely use them. Although snowballing (SB) techniques are standard in systematic literature reviews, little is known about how to apply them to GL reviews. *Aims*: This paper investigates how to apply SB approaches on Q&A websites to identify new valid discussions for analysis during the exploration of such sites. *Method*: In previous studies, we compiled and analyzed a set of Stack Exchange Project Management (SEPM) discussions related to software engineering technical debt. Those studies used a data set consisting of 108 valid discussions extracted from SEPM. Based on this start data set, we perform forward and backward SB using two different approaches: link-based and similarity-based SB. We then compare the precision and recall of those two SB approaches against the search-based approach of the original study. *Results*: In just one SB iteration, the approaches yielded 291 new discussions for analysis, 130 of which were considered valid for our study. This represents an approximate 120% increase in recall compared to the original data set. The SB process also yielded a similar rate of valid discussion retrieval when compared to the search-based approach (precision). *Conclusion*: This paper provides guidelines on how to apply two SB approaches to find new valid discussions for review. To our knowledge, this is the first study that analyzes the use of SB on Q&A websites. By applying SB, it is possible to identify new discussions, significantly increasing the relevant data set for a GL review.

Keywords: Snowballing · Grey Literature · Q&A websites · Guideline

D. Taibi and D. Smite (Eds.): SEAA 2025, LNCS 16082, pp. 253–269, 2026.
https://doi.org/10.1007/978-3-032-04200-2_17

1   Introduction

Grey literature (GL) encompasses publications not subject to formal quality control mechanisms, such as peer-review, before its release [2]. Different research areas, such as medicine and nutrition, have been using GL as a valuable source of professional knowledge [4]. GL often describes user-generated web content, like tweets, blogs, and posts on question and answer (Q&A) websites. Recently, the interest in GL has grown in the context of Software Engineering (SE) research, mainly because it is widely used by SE practitioners, especially the Q&A platforms.

In SE, GL is often used to discuss various SE topics, with software professionals sharing their knowledge or asking for advice or solutions on software development issues. SE researchers have noticed that GL is a rich source of SE knowledge, used alone or combined with findings published in the formal white literature (WL) [4].

Q&A platforms, such as Stack Exchange, are part of daily activities of modern software development, and these platforms have raised the interest of software researchers [5]. They are a rich source of information because countless issues are discussed in them, bringing to light the point of view of practitioners on possible solutions for those issues [6]. Moreover, those platforms usually count on a self-moderating system for the discussions and users, making the available information self-regulated and more reliable for practitioners and, by proxy, researchers.

Stack Exchange is composed of different sites, each one focused on a specific topic, such as software development (Stack Overflow) or project management (Stack Exchange Project Management - SEPM). Researchers have analyzed discussions from Stack Exchange regarding topics such as code smells [7], software development trends [8], psychological safety [23], software requirements [22], soft skills [9], and technical debt (TD) [10,16–18,26].

In all those studies, GL reviews have relied on keyword searches to obtain the information they want extracted for analysis. In contrast, systematic literature review (SLR) studies, which are very common in SE, combine database searches and snowballing (SB) as the primary strategy for conducting the searches in these types of studies [11].

In SLR, researchers search different databases using predefined search strings to identify papers [13] and use the SB method to expand the pool of relevant studies [12]. SB recursively traces the references list and citations of initially retrieved papers, also called start set, to identify additional sources that might have been missed [12]. These strategies have been the target of research that seeks to define guidelines for SB [11,12], compare SB to database searches [13], and propose a hybrid approach combining the two approaches [14].

Despite the use of SB techniques being common in SLR studies and the interest of the SE community in GL, to the best of our knowledge, there are no studies analyzing how SB approaches can be translated to Q&A websites, and analyzing the precision and recall of these approaches. This paper investigates how SB techniques can be applied to Stack Exchange websites to discover new and valid discussions for GL reviews.

We have previously analyzed Stack Exchange's SEPM, which encompasses discussions of practitioners interested in project management, to investigate how project managers discusses and experiences TD. This previous work analyzed 108 TD-related discussions, accounting for 547 posts and 882 text comments. This previous work, which did not use SB, is reported in three papers [16–18].

Based on this data set, we performed SB, resulting in a data set with 291 new discussions, composed of 1985 posts and 2532 comments, from SEPM. To evaluate the precision and recall of the SB, we analyzed the 291 discussions quantitatively and qualitatively using the same guidelines from our previous studies [16–18]. Out of 291, we found 130 new valid discussions using backward and forward SB, using two different approaches: link-based SB and similarity-based SB. The amount of new discussions represents an increase of about 120% about the initial data set. Surprisingly, the similarity-based SB yielded good results compared to link-based SB and the original search-based approach.

It is important to point out that the results reported here will not focus on the TD research outcome. Instead, this paper focuses on the SB approach we used, the validity of the discussions we found, and the insights we gained on this process.

The remainder of the paper is organized as follows. Section 2 presents related work. Section 3 describes how we extracted and analyzed the start set from the original studies. Section 4 presents how we adapted the traditional snowballing approach to Stack Exchange Q&A websites. Section 5 presents the results and discussion of the quantitative and qualitative analyses. Section 6 discusses the threats to the study's validity. And lastly, Sect. 7 presents our final remarks.

2   Related Work

SE research widely employs SLR studies. They are commonly used to understand or organize the available knowledge in a research area. When conducting SLR studies, researchers usually use SB in addition to database search to find more relevant papers to their data set. Wohlin *et al.* [12] proposed guidelines to conduct SLR studies using SB. These guidelines were based on the experiences gained over multiple SLR studies. They concluded that using SB, as a first search strategy, may very well be a good alternative to the use of database searches. Wohlin *et al.* [14] also proposed and evaluated a hybrid strategy, combining database search and SB. They concluded that the hybrid strategy is very effective in finding relevant studies. Deepika *et al.* [11] evaluated the precision and reliability of SB as a search strategy in literature studies. By comparing the findings of SB approaches and database search, they concluded that the precision of SB is comparable to that of a database search. Furthermore, they also conclude that SB can be more reliable than a database search. However, the reliability is highly dependent on creating a suitable start data set.

GL reviews have gained increased interest in SE research in recent years. In 2021, Kamei *et al.* [4] published a tertiary study summarizing the last ten years of SE research that uses GL, showing that GL has been essential for bringing practical new perspectives that are scarce in traditional literature. They drew the current use landscape and raised awareness of challenges related to GL reviews.

With the increased interest in GL, SE researchers expanded on how GL should be used in SE literature reviews. Garousi *et al.* [5] proposed multivocal literature review (MLR) guidelines to incorporate GL alongside traditional literature. The authors compared the results of two investigations: one included GL, while the other did not. Their findings highlighted the importance of using GL to cover technical research questions. Raulamo-Jurvanen *et al.* [15] conducted a grey literature review (GLR) aiming to understand how software practitioners choose the right test automation tool. Their findings are mainly derived from practitioners' experiences and opinions. To improve the credibility of their findings, they employed some criteria to assess the evidence of the GL, including, for instance, the number of readers, the number of comments, or the number of hits on Google.

Researchers have also been using (Q&A) platforms to empirically understand how practitioners manage TD, a research topic that is the focus of our original GL-based research [16–18]. Digkas *et al.* [10] conducted an empirical study on the relation between the reusing of code retrieved from Stack Overflow and the TD of the target system. The results provided insights into the potential impact of small-scale code reuse on TD and highlight the benefits of assessing code quality before committing changes to a repository. In another work, Gama *et al.* [26] investigated the point of view of practitioners on Stack Overflow on how developers commonly identify TD items in their projects. They reported that developers commonly discuss TD identification, revealing 29 low-level indicators for recognizing distinct types of TD.

Despite the SE research community's interest in GL, to our knowledge, no previous work has investigated how SB can be applied to Q&A platforms to discover new and valid discussions for GL reviews. This knowledge gap is precisely what this paper addresses.

The inclusion and analysis criteria used in our SB study are the same as those used in the abovementioned studies [16–18]. We will discuss them in the following Section.

3 Start Set and Analysis Process

The basis of every SB procedure is the start set [14]. We use the data set we built in our previous studies on TD [16–18] as our start set. To prepare this data set, we used Stack Exchange data dump (version Sep 07, 2021), which is the raw data dump of all Stack Exchange websites. From this repository, one can access data from any Stack Exchange website, including posts (both questions and answers), comments, and metadata. Due to space limitations we give a brief overview of our analysis, more details are discussed in our previous studies mentioned above.

The discussions in Stack Exchange websites are composed of three main components: the question around which the discussion is centered, the answers to the question, and the comments on both questions and answers. Comments are presented below the post they are related to. Thus, they are part of the discussions.

Besides these main components, the discussions also may have two types of links to other discussions: linked and related. These links appear alongside the discussion. The linked list gathers any links to a specific post the community provides via comments, answers, or questions. In other words, when a user puts a link in the discussion pointing to another discussion in the same forum, a linked link is created. The link is still listed even if the users remove a post or comment.

The related links were introduced in the *'StackExchange 2.0'*. This type of link points to discussions classified as 'related'. To carry out this classification, the Stack Exchange relies on the 'More like this' query provided by Elasticsearch, which is a search engine and analytic tool that provides features like full-text search. The 'More like this' query is based on the Term Frequency - Inverse Document Frequency (TF-IDF) algorithm. The TF-IDF is a numerical statistic that reflects how important a word is to a document in the collection or corpus [19].

The related links are automatically generated by the Stack Exchange platform. It is performed as an adapted TF-IDF using the following criteria: full-text match to tags (+10 weight), full-text match to title (+5 weight), and full-text match to body (+1 weight) [20]. Unfortunately, other details about the related link list generation are closed and subject to change over time. Therefore, we are unable to have a complete understanding of how the algorithm used by Stack Exchange works.

To build the start set [14], we searched the SEPM content for the strings "debt" or "shortcut" in the questions (title, body, and tags), answers' body, and comments' body. The term "debt" catches the different forms of reference to TD, for example, "tech debt" and "code debt". By performing pilot studies, we also detected that the term "shortcut" was used to refer to TD in the discussions. The term "shortcut" catches other references to sub-optimal solutions.

We choose such general terms because of the free nature of discussion forums. The forum user can refer to TD in several ways, and unlike formal literature, there is no standard. Some users refer to TD as "tech debt", "development shortcut", "delivery shortcut", or just "debt". To decide which strings to use, we tested some strings like "technical debt", "code debt" and other terms used in the literature, but the number of returned discussions was very low. Therefore, after the tests, we decided to use the terms "debt" and "shortcut" because they encompassed the discussions found using the other terms and returned a higher number of discussions.

The string-matching phase yielded a total of 263 discussions. Next, we filtered the data as shown in Fig. 1, using the following criteria:

– **Step 1:** *Eliminate incomplete discussions from the data set.* We considered a discussion to be complete when a question was followed by one or more answers, where there was at least one answer whose author differed from the question's author. After applying this criterion, 224 discussions remained out of the initial 263.

- **Step 2:** *Eliminate untrustworthy discussions.* Other studies have found that data from Q&A forums can be affected by noise [24,25], requiring mitigating it using different proxies [26]. We decided to use the discussion score as a filtering proxy. A post score is a Stack Exchange popularity metric in which users, other than the post author, can give an up-vote to the post if they find it useful or a down-vote if they find it not useful. A discussion score is the difference between up-votes and down-votes of all its posts. We decided to filter out discussions with negative scores, since overall they are not considered useful by the SE community. While we did not discard any discussion in this step, we considered it important since it can help to ensure the quality of the discussions.
- **Step 3:** *Qualitative data analysis.* We conducted a qualitative data analysis of the data set. Each of the 224 discussions went through a qualitative analysis process.

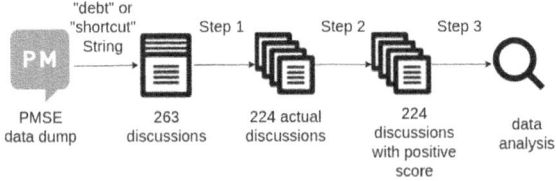

Fig. 1. Data extraction and filtering process.

While going through the information-gathering questions (**Step 1**), we also looked for false positives, taking into consideration the following rules:

- **Rule 1:** *The discussion must be related to TD.* Discussions that, in spite of having the terms *"debt"* or *"shortcut"*, did not discuss TD were marked as false positives.
- **Rule 2:** *The discussed situation must be real.* This work intends to map real problems faced by practitioners, so questions asking for advice without bringing any actual situation from the present or past were flagged as false positives.
- **Rule 3:** *The TD indicators must come from the question's author.* Since the question's author is the one with actual knowledge about the situation, we only considered the author's words concerning TD indicators. TD indicators inferred by other users were considered only if sustained by the question's author in a comment or a post in the same discussion.

The rules defined above allowed us to verify whether a discussion was within the scope of information gathering or was a false positive. After removing all false positives, our final data set was reduced to 108 discussions containing 547 posts and 882 comments. Of those, 81 discussions were related to agile software development (436 posts and 691 comments), and 27 were unrelated to agile software development (111 posts and 191 comments).

We used **step 2** to examine the responses recorded individually in the step 1 and reach a consensus between the researchers. Together, the two researchers checked the information extracted from the discussions and in the case of analysis agreement, they also performed the coding process. Discussions that yielded divergent information were subjected to a second examination in **step 3**, this time with a third researcher. A majority vote among the researchers would define which information should remain for the following analysis step. This process was repeated until all responses were consolidated.

Once again, disagreements in the coding were resolved with the help of the third researcher. This process was performed until no new codes were identified (point of saturation). Then, this encoded data set was added to the results.

After the analysis process, 108 discussions remained and these discussions composed the start set. This start set was then used in the SB processes described in the next sections.

4   Snowballing Study Methodology

This section presents the research questions along with how we adapt the snowballing approach to the Stack Exchange websites.

4.1   Research Questions

As previously stated, this work aims to investigate how SB techniques can be applied in Stack Exchange websites to discover new valid discussions. To this end, we seek answers to the following main research questions (RQs):

- **RQ1:** *How many new discussions does the snowballing find in relation to the original data set?* - This question seeks to identify how many new valid discussions can be discovered in SEPM through SB. This metric is relevant, given that in the WL, SB is widely used to expand the initial pool of papers.
- **RQ2:** *How precise are snowballing techniques in finding new valid discussions?* - This question aims to identify the number of valid discussions in relation to the new discussions discovered in the SEPM through SB. As pointed out by Wohlin [12], one important efficiency measure for SLRs is the number of included papers in relation to the total number of candidate papers examined. Thus, investigating the precision of SB in GL is also relevant.

Regarding the RQs, the following contributions are made:

- A method proposal on how SB can be performed in Q&A websites and an evaluation of the effectiveness of this method. The SB conducted rendered 20% more valid discussion than the original study, and hence it provides an added value to the original study.

– Two strategies of SB are compared, linked SB and related SB. Related SB found more discussions than linked SB, but they are complementary. It is concluded that the full-fledged hybrid search strategy is the best, although it comes at the cost of more work.

The following sections explain how we adapted and applied SB techniques to discussion forums to answer the **RQs**.

4.2   Snowballing Procedure

The basic planning and motivation of a systematic literature study are independent of the search approach. Thus, the basic steps for planning a literature study presented by Keele *et al.* [21] are still relevant even if applying a different approach to the search.

SB is a widely used technique in the WL. It refers to using the reference list of a paper (backward SB) or the citations to a paper (forward SB) to identify additional papers. SB is conducted by first creating a start set, which is a set of articles around a topic of interest, then the two approaches can be applied: Forward Snowballing (FSB) and Backward Snowballing (BSB). Once the start set is decided, it is time to start the BSB and FSB.

In traditional BSB, one use the reference list of the start set to identify new papers to include. On the other hand, FSB refers to identifying new papers based on those papers citing the papers within the start set.

To map the traditional SB approach to discussion forums, we considered the GL discussions as papers and the links between them (related and linked links) as references from one paper to another. We adapted the traditional SB approach to discussion forums by considering these links akin to references or citations between articles. In GL, it is crucial to have inclusion criteria before analyzing and coding the whole discussion.

Regarding the linked links, we tried to obtain them in two ways. Firstly, we mined the links using the Stack Exchange data dump (version April 06, 2024). The links are stored in a specific Stack Exchange table, named PostLinks. It remains recorded even when the post or comment containing that link gets deleted. This table contains two types of links: linked (a post contains a link to another post) and duplicate (a post has a link to itself). The duplicate links were not considered during the analysis since they point to discussions already analyzed. Secondly, we used the Stack Exchange Data Explorer, which is a website where it is possible to run queries against a weekly updated version of the Stack Exchange databases. We executed our queries in the database version of April 14, 2024. Through these queries, we found discussions that pointed to or were pointed to by the discussions at the start.

The BSB consisted of using the extracted links list to identify new discussions to include. The first step was to go through the links list and exclude discussions that do not fulfill the basic criteria such as eliminating incomplete and untrustworthy discussions. The next step was to remove discussions from the list that have already been examined in our previous studies [16–18] either as a false positive or not. As a result, we were able to find 34 new candidate discussions.

The FSB consisted of identifying new discussions based on those with at least a link to a discussion within the start set. Next, we applied the same filters used in the BSB. This step rendered 50 new candidate discussions.

Regarding the related links, they are not available in the Stack Exchange Data Explorer or in the data dump, but they can be obtained through the Stack Exchange API. So, we created scripts to extract these links using the API. Similarly to the linked links extraction, we also found discussions that pointed to or were pointed to by the discussions in the start set by related links.

When applying the related SB, we applied similar steps to the one applied in the linked SB. As a result, we found 687 and 1,132 new candidate discussions for, respectively, BSB and FSB.

A large number of discussions as a result of the related SB was expected since the related links are built automatically by the Stack Exchange platform. The resulting amount of discussions was considered unfeasible to be analyzed in this study. So, we performed one more filtering to reduce the amount of discussions. We extracted from the start set (the originally selected discussions) the average amount of answers and the average score per question. They were, respectively, four answers and a score eight per discussion. Thus, we filtered the related discussions where the number of answers was bigger or equal to four and the score of the question was bigger or equal to eight. After this final filtering, the number of resulting discussions for both BSB and FSB were, respectively, 104 and 156.

At the last step before the analysis, we grouped all the discussions found in two types of SB. During this process, we have counted how many discussions appeared in each combination of different SBs, the numbers are presented in Table 1. As expected the duplications between related BSB and related FSB was the most combination found (37 out of 47 duplications), since related links are built based in the similarities between questions. These duplications indicate that similar discussions point to each other via related links.

After grouping the duplicated discussions, we analyzed them first to avoid duplication of our analysis efforts. The final number of unique discussions for linked BSB, linked FSB, related BSB and related FSB were, respectively, 25, 47, 61, and 111. Including the 47 duplicated discussions, we end up with 291 unique new discussions that were analyzed qualitatively following the same approach discussed in Sect. 3.

In addition to the processes described in this section, we also counted the number of links for each one of the 291 discussions during related BSB and linked BSB. For example, the discussions with IDs 26070 and 28023 have linked links to 26011, and discussion 29724 has a related link pointing to discussion 26011, so 26011 has 3 citations. In the WL, the amount of citations of a paper is one of the metrics used to define the relevance of a paper. So, through this counting, we hope to find clusters of links that can indicate more relevant discussions within the data set.

Table 1. Amount of duplicated discussions among snowballing results.

SB combination	# of duplicated discussions
Related BSB + Related FSB	37
Linked BSB + Related BSB + Related FSB	4
Linked BSB + Related FSB	2
Linked BSB + Linked FSB + Related BSB + Related FSB	1
Linked BSB + Related BSB	1
Linked BSB + Linked FSB	1
Linked FSB + Related FSB	1

Due to space limitations in this paper and our focus on the SB approach, we do not discuss the results of this qualitative analysis in detail. Furthermore, because of the large amount of data that needed to be analyzed, we decided to conduct only one SB iteration. The next section discusses the results of this SB iteration focusing on the validity of the discussions identified by each type of SB.

5   Results and Discussion

This section presents the main results obtained from the discussions analysis. These results are used to answer the proposed research questions.

5.1   RQ1: How Many New Discussions does the Snowballing Find in Relation to the Original Data Set?

After the removal of false positives during the qualitative analysis phase, our final sample of TD-related discussions on SEPM was reduced from 291 to 130 valid discussions. In relation to our previous studies that originated the start set, in which we had 108 valid discussions, it was an increase of 120% of the data set.

None of the 291 discussions discovered through the SB had the terms 'debt' or 'shortcut' in their posts (questions and answers) and comments, nevertheless 130 of them were deemed to be valid. This result shows that the SB approach can be used to find new discussions effectively and expand the original data set.

Moreover, this also means that through the SB approach, we can bring to light new terms that can be considered in future studies. For example, when searching for the term 'motivate' among the valid discussions, we found 19 discussions containing the term, which is 15% of the new data set. By our observation, the term 'motivate' seemed to be associated with team management issues. Thus, by using this term we may find discussions related to process debt. To make more clear our conclusion regarding the term 'motivate', the following are some examples of the titles of valid discussion that included the term:

– "How to deal with a team member who keeps missing deadlines?"
– "How to get burned out team back engaged again?"
– "Advice for dealing with a cowboy programmer in an agile team."
– "Dealing with a coworker who keeps making the same mistakes over and over."
– "Agile team missing commitments regularly and complaining about no trust."
– "How to motivate offshore teams and trust them to deliver?"
– "Help - Technical team does not want to work in agile way."

Regarding the most cited discussions during BSB, the IDs of the top most cited discussions (alongside the number of citations per type of link) were: **8286** (6 related), **11144** (6 related), **718** (4 related), **15505** (3 related) and **16372** (2 linked and 1 related). As we can see, the cluster links were mostly compound per related links, all discussions found via linked BSB had only one linked pointing to it, except for 16372 which had two links. Analyzing the most cited discussions, we can see that they have lots of upvotes, for example, discussion 16372 has alone 91 upvotes scattered between its posts. This means that they were deemed highly useful by the community, being considered more relevant. We can make a parallel between the relevance of a discussion and the relevance of a paper, where in both cases the amount of citations is the key metric for relevance. Finally, all these top-cited discussions were related to process debt and agile, which is a reflection of our data sets that have most discussions related to process debt and agile. These results show that, in a similar way to the WL, highly cited discussions tend to be more relevant.

> **Finding #1**: The SB conducted rendered 20% more valid discussion than the original study, and hence it provides an added value to the original study. Furthermore, we provide evidence suggesting that more cited discussions tend to be more relevant.

5.2 RQ2: How Precise are Snowballing Techniques in Finding New Valid Discussions?

When conducting SB in SLRs, precision is a key metric to evaluate its efficiency. Precision refers to the number of included papers concerning the total number of candidate papers examined [12]. A high precision ensures that the gathered literature remains closely aligned with the topic of interest. This metric is essential for maintaining focus and validity in SLRs. To measure the precision of our study, we used a similar approach to the SLRs, considering discussions as papers and valid discussions as included papers.

As previously discussed, we detected 130 valid discussions in the 291 new discussions found during the SBs, this was a precision of 45% among the SBs. The database search that originated the start set had a precision of 48% (108 valid out of 226 discussions). The SB had a very similar precision to the database search, only a 3% difference, especially when considering that the SB data set was 29% larger. This shows the combined precision of the database search and the SB approach is $(130 + 108)/(291 + 226) = 46\%$.

The detailed numbers for each type of SB, including the duplications in the accounting, are:

- **Linked BSB:** 34 candidates discussions and 15 valid, i.e. precision $= 15/34 = 44\%$.
- **Linked FSB:** 50 candidates discussions and 19 valid, i.e. precision $= 19/50 = 38\%$.
- **Related BSB:** 104 candidates discussions and 59 valid, i.e. precision $= 59/104 = 56\%$.
- **Related FSB:** 156 candidates discussions and 69 valid, i.e. precision $= 69/156 = 44\%$.

The linked SB had an overall precision of $(15 + 19)/(34 + 50) = 40\%$. On the other hand, the related SB had an overall precision of $(59 + 69)/(104 + 156) = 49\%$. The related SB showed to be 9% more precise than the linked SB even with three times more discussions. It appears that discussions found via related links tend to be more effective because related links between discussions are built based on the similarity to the <u>valid discussions</u> from the start set.

It is also worth mentioning the way linked links were used by practitioners. During our qualitative analysis, we detected cases where the SEPM users used these links to point to more theoretical discussions to reinforce their opinions or to link to more detailed discussions about a topic. In Fig. 2, we have an excerpt of a discussion answer from our start set where the user used 8 links (highlighted in blue), where 2 of these links are for blog posts and 6 of them are linked links, and these links are related to various topics such as sprint delivery planning and team velocity management. The links in the scenario shown in Fig. 2 are used to indicate more in-depth materials about the topics, meanwhile, the answer itself is focused in a broader scope with a focus on providing a solution to the TD instance presented in the question. Regarding the precision of the 6 discussions discovered via the linked links presented in Fig. 2, only 2 of them were considered valid (33 % precision). The lower precision of the linked links compared to the related links in the SB can also be attributed to the context and rules of the analysis. Despite being considered false positives, theoretical discussions also have importance, since they show the perspective of practitioners concerning some topics.

Observe that, in a certain way, link-based SB is similar to our use of references in WL review SB. When we are SB over a paper's references, we discard many because they discuss issues not central to the SLR inclusion criteria. Relation-based SB, on the other hand, selects content by global similarity. This process returns more material (better recall) and with a similar precision. From this perspective, our results indicate that researchers interested in systematic literature reviews would also benefit from similarity-based search mechanisms in digital libraries of WL.

A chi-square test [1] revealed no statistically significant difference in the proportion of valid discussions when comparing the two methods. The SB yielded

130 valid objects out of 291 (44.67%), while the string search 2 produced 108 valid objects out of 226 (47.79%). The chi-square test resulted in a test statistic of $\chi^2 = 0.53$ with a p-value of 0.466, which is greater than the conventional significance level of 0.05. This indicates that the observed proportion difference is likely due to random variation rather than a true difference between the methods. Therefore, we can conclude that there is no statistically significant evidence to suggest that the two methods differ in their effectiveness for producing valid discussions.

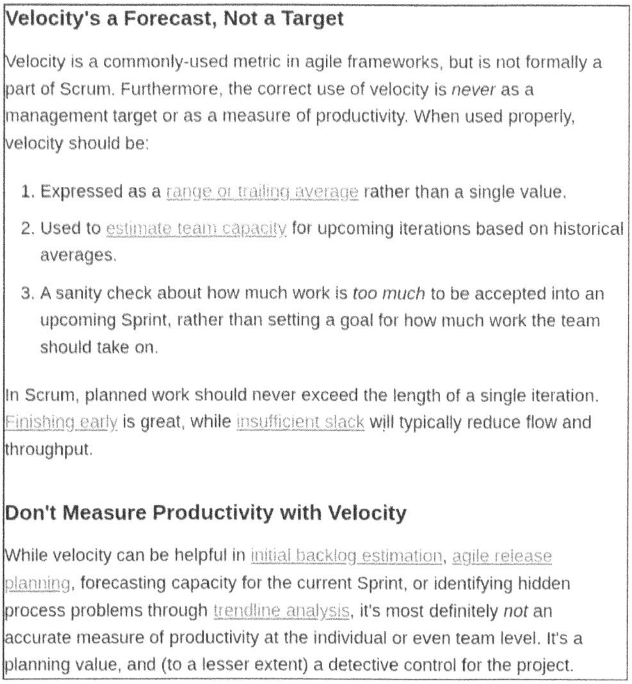

Velocity's a Forecast, Not a Target

Velocity is a commonly-used metric in agile frameworks, but is not formally a part of Scrum. Furthermore, the correct use of velocity is *never* as a management target or as a measure of productivity. When used properly, velocity should be:

1. Expressed as a range or trailing average rather than a single value.

2. Used to estimate team capacity for upcoming iterations based on historical averages.

3. A sanity check about how much work is *too much* to be accepted into an upcoming Sprint, rather than setting a goal for how much work the team should take on.

In Scrum, planned work should never exceed the length of a single iteration. Finishing early is great, while insufficient slack will typically reduce flow and throughput.

Don't Measure Productivity with Velocity

While velocity can be helpful in initial backlog estimation, agile release planning, forecasting capacity for the current Sprint, or identifying hidden process problems through trendline analysis, it's most definitely *not* an accurate measure of productivity at the individual or even team level. It's a planning value, and (to a lesser extent) a detective control for the project.

Fig. 2. Example of linked links usage.

Finding #2: Related SB found more discussions than linked SB, but they are complementary. It is concluded that the full-fledged hybrid search strategy is the best, although it comes at the cost of more work.

---

6   Threats to Validity

Below we present the threats to the validity of our research, following categories defined by Wohlin *et al.* [3].

Construct: One threat is selecting and analyzing the discussions coming from linked links and related links directly from SEPM. This risk was mitigated by using both the discussion evaluation process and the set of discussions from our previous studies [16–18] as the basis for this work. Another threat can be attributed to how the SB procedure was conducted. We mitigate this by following the procedures defined by Wohlin *et al.* [12], adapting some concepts to our context when necessary.

Internal: The process used for analyzing qualitatively the discussions can represent a threat in our study. To reduce this thread, the analysis process was performed by two researchers individually. Besides, a third researcher was inserted to resolve the divergences identified in the consensus phase.

External: Regarding generalizing the conclusions, the study was based on a representative sample of SEPM, a well-known Q&A platform focused on project management discussions, where practitioners discuss day-to-day issues. Although we used SEPM data, we cannot guarantee that all users are practitioners. This is mitigated by the fact that SEPM discussions are contextualized in the software management area. Another threat arises from the risk that the newly selected discussions via SB are unrelated to TD. To mitigate this threat, we qualitatively analyzed the discussions using the same approach from our previous studies [16–18] related to analyzing TD on SEPM. An even more critical threat stems from the fact that SEPM does not represent all Stack Exchange Q&A sites, albeit the fact that it belongs to Stack Exchange, which hosts a large family of software-related Q&A sites. We argue that the resources we used from this platform (direct links and similarity searches) will eventually be available in several Q&A platforms.

Conclusion: Lastly, there is a risk that, even if we applied the same approach to the analysis and interpretation of the discussions, there is the possibility of producing different results. This risk stems from the subjectivity inherent in the process. We mitigated it by the consensus procedures used during the analysis process presented in Sect. 4. Nonetheless, the similarity search algorithm used by the Stack Exchange Platform can evolve and affect the results we have obtained in this study, hopefully providing even better precision and recall of the selected discussions.

7   Conclusion

This work investigates how SB can be conducted on Stack Exchange websites. To the best of our knowledge, this is the first study that defines and analyzes the use of SB in Q&A discussion forums. We also identified two types of links between discussions, linked and related. By performing mining and qualitative analysis of these links in the SEPM forum, we provide a general approach that can be used in any of the Stack Exchange websites, such as Stack Overflow.

This work also shows that SB can be effective and precise in finding new valid discussions. These results indicate that the use of SB can complement the use of text-based searches on the Stack Exchange websites. In addition to new discussions, SB by similarity (related-based) can also bring to light search terms that can be used to expand the initial data set.

Regarding the number of citations of discussions, we also found evidence that often cited discussions tend to be more relevant inside the community. This is aligned with the WL, where highly cited papers are also considered relevant for the research community.

Finally, we share our insights regarding each type of discussion link. We discussed that linked links are used beyond linking similar discussions, they are also used to indicate more theoretical discussions to corroborate the presented opinion or affirmation. This is very similar to how citations are used in the white literature. Analyzing these types of discussions can provide the point of view of the community about some topic. On the other hand, we discussed that related links are more precise and have better recall when searching for valid discussions, since they point toward discussions similar to the ones at the start set. Finally, we commented that despite the differences between them, both types of links should be considered since they drew new valid discussions.

For researchers, our new method can support research efforts in GL. The proposed SB approach can be used to expand any study about discussion analysis on the Stack Exchange websites. For example, we can use SB to expand the study of Gama et al. [26] to enlarge their findings regarding how developers identify TD items on Stack Overflow. Lastly, our findings regarding linked SB and related SB can also motivate new research. For example, a comparison between the Stack Exchange similarity algorithm with other algorithms, or the use of similarity search for SB in systematic literature reviews.

In future work, we intend to (1) perform more SB iterations to expand our study, (2) explore other Stack Exchange websites to verify the SB method we proposed, and (3) investigate the use of other similarity algorithms in comparison to the Stack Exchange in the analysis process.

Artifacts Availability. Our replication package is available at https://zenodo.org/records/11123633. There, the interested reader can find our complete data set.

References

1. Tallarida, R., Murray, R., Tallarida, R., Murray, R.: Chi-square test. In: Manual of Pharmacologic Calculations: With Computer Programs, pp. 140–142 (1987)
2. Petticrew, M., Roberts, H.: Systematic Reviews in the Social Sciences: A Practical Guide. Wiley (2008)
3. Wohlin, C., Runeson, P., Höst, M., Ohlsson, M., Regnell, B., Wesslén, A.: Experimentation in Software Engineering. Springer (2012)
4. Kamei, F., et al.: Grey literature in software engineering: a critical review. Inf. Softw. Technol. **138**, 106609 (2021)

5. Garousi, V., Felderer, M., Mäntylä, M.: Guidelines for including grey literature and conducting multivocal literature reviews in software engineering. Inf. Softw. Technol. **106**, 101–121 (2019)
6. Vasilescu, B., Serebrenik, A., Devanbu, P., Filkov, V.: How social Q&A sites are changing knowledge sharing in open source software communities. In: Proceedings of the 17th ACM Conference on Computer Supported Cooperative Work & Social Computing, pp. 342–354 (2014)
7. Tahir, A., Dietrich, J., Counsell, S., Licorish, S., Yamashita, A.: A large scale study on how developers discuss code smells and anti-pattern in stack exchange sites. Inf. Softw. Technol. **125**, 106333 (2020)
8. Barua, A., Thomas, S., Hassan, A.: What are developers talking about? An analysis of topics and trends in stack overflow. Empir. Softw. Eng. **19**, 619–654 (2014)
9. Montandon, J., Politowski, C., Silva, L., Valente, M., Petrillo, F., Guéhéneuc, Y.: What skills do IT companies look for in new developers? A study with stack overflow jobs. Inf. Softw. Technol. **129**, 106429 (2021)
10. Digkas, G., Nikolaidis, N., Ampatzoglou, A., Chatzigeorgiou, A.: Reusing code from stackoverflow: the effect on technical debt. In: 2019 45th Euromicro Conference on Software Engineering and Advanced Applications (SEAA), pp. 87–91 (2019)
11. Badampudi, D., Wohlin, C., Petersen, K.: Experiences from using snowballing and database searches in systematic literature studies. In: Proceedings of the 19th International Conference on Evaluation and Assessment in Software Engineering, pp. 1–10 (2015)
12. Wohlin, C.: Guidelines for snowballing in systematic literature studies and a replication in software engineering. In: Proceedings of the 18th International Conference on Evaluation and Assessment in Software Engineering, pp. 1–10 (2014)
13. Jalali, S., Wohlin, C.: Systematic literature studies: database searches vs. backward snowballing. In: Proceedings of the ACM-IEEE International Symposium on Empirical Software Engineering and Measurement, pp. 29–38 (2012)
14. Wohlin, C., Kalinowski, M., Felizardo, K., Mendes, E.: Successful combination of database search and snowballing for identification of primary studies in systematic literature studies. Inf. Softw. Technol. **147**, 106908 (2022)
15. Raulamo-Jurvanen, P., Mäntylä, M., Garousi, V.: Choosing the right test automation tool: a grey literature review of practitioner sources. In: Proceedings of the 21st International Conference on Evaluation and Assessment in Software Engineering, pp. 21–30 (2017)
16. Gomes, F., et al.: Investigating the point of view of project management practitioners on technical debt: a preliminary study on stack exchange. In: Proceedings of the International Conference on Technical Debt (2022)
17. Santos, E.P., et al.: Technical debt on agile projects: managers' point of view at stack exchange. In: Proceedings of the XXI Brazilian Symposium on Software Quality (2022)
18. Gomes, F., et al.: Investigating the point of view of project management practitioners on technical debt-a study on stack exchange. J. Softw. Eng. Res. Dev. **11**(1), 12-1 (2023)
19. Salton, G., Buckley, C.: Term-weighting approaches in automatic text retrieval. Inf. Process. Manag. **24**, 513–523 (1988)
20. Atwood, J.: New Linked Posts (2010). https://stackoverflow.blog/2010/04/26/new-linked-posts/?_ga=2.144560373.1554990293.1689726389-150477141.1684451486
21. Keele, S., et al.: Guidelines for performing systematic literature reviews in software engineering. Technical report, ver. 2.3 EBSE technical report. EBSE (2007)

22. Freire, S., et al.: Requirements engineering issues experienced by software practitioners: a study on stack exchange. In: Ferrari, A., Penzenstadler, B. (eds.) REFSQ 2023. LNCS, vol. 13975, pp. 3–20. Springer, Cham (2023). https://doi.org/10.1007/978-3-031-29786-1_1

23. Santana, B., Freire, S., Santos, J., Mendonça, M.: Psychological safety in the software work environment. IEEE Softw. **41**, 86–94 (2024)

24. Ahasanuzzaman, M., Asaduzzaman, M., Roy, C., Schneider, K.: Mining duplicate questions of stack overflow. In: 2016 IEEE/ACM 13th Working MSR, pp. 402–412 (2016)

25. Kavaler, D., Posnett, D., Gibler, C., Chen, H., Devanbu, P., Filkov, V.: Using and asking: APIs used in the android market and asked about in StackOverflow. In: Jatowt, A., et al. (eds.) SocInfo 2013. LNCS, vol. 8238, pp. 405–418. Springer, Cham (2013). https://doi.org/10.1007/978-3-319-03260-3_35

26. Gama, E., Freire, S., Mendonça, M., Spínola, R., Paixao, M., Cortes, M.: Using stack overflow to assess technical debt identification on software projects. In: 34th Brazilian Symposium on Software Engineering (SBES), pp. 730–739 (2020)

Always Evolving: A Systematic Review on Challenges and Needs to Scale RL & FL on Industrial Embedded Systems

Emil Johansson[1]([✉]), Jan Bosch[2,3], and Helena Holmström Olsson[4]

[1] AB Volvo, Gothenburg, Sweden
emil.johansson.2@volvo.com
[2] Chalmers University of Technology, Gothenburg, Sweden
jan.bosch@chalmers.se
[3] Eindhoven University of Technology, Eindhoven, Netherlands
[4] Malmö University, Malmö, Sweden
helena.holmstrom.olsson@mau.se

Abstract. Federated Learning (FL) and Reinforcement Learning (RL) show significant potential for industrial embedded systems, but their application is hindered by challenges like hardware constraints, data heterogeneity, and safety requirements, creating a research-practice gap. This systematic literature review synthesizes the state-of-the-art deployment of FL and RL on such systems, structuring findings across four challenge categories to identify research gaps. Our analysis of 61 studies reveals a dominance of simulation (66%), and FL (62%), with scarce hardware deployments (18%). The key barriers to industrial adoption are a lack of large-scale, real-world validation and unaddressed scalability challenges.

Keywords: SLR · Federated Learning · Reinforcement Learning · edge computing

1 Introduction

Edge computing is transforming the industrial landscape, with federated learning (FL) and reinforcement learning (RL) algorithms showing great potential for deployment on embedded systems. A prominent example showcasing large-scale FL is Google's deployment in GBoard, which enables next-word prediction by learning from millions of users without centralizing raw data, further enhanced by differential privacy [1]. While consumer applications like GBoard demonstrate the power of FL, applying similar algorithms in demanding industrial contexts such as automotive, telecommunications, or smart grids presents challenges such as resource limitations, heterogeneous data and privacy requirements [6,22]. Unique for the industrial context is often more demanding requirements like safety-critical functions, real-time processing guarantees, and complex operational constraints [17,20]. These factors significantly increase the complexity

D. Taibi and D. Smite (Eds.): SEAA 2025, LNCS 16082, pp. 270–279, 2026.
https://doi.org/10.1007/978-3-032-04200-2_18

of deploying FL and RL compared to consumer scenarios. This paper seeks to bridge the gap between theoretical advancements and real-world industrial deployment of adaptive algorithms by identifying and analyzing documented instances of FL and RL deployed on embedded systems. The contribution of this paper is to summarize how existing research handles the complexities of industrial systems and what further steps are needed to enable scalable industrial deployment. The rest of the paper is structured as follows, Sect. 2 shows the background, Sect. 3 highlights the survey structure, including the search strategy. Section 4 reports the findings in a descriptive and thematic synthesis. 5 discusses the research questions.

2 Background

To motivate and illustrate the complexities addressed in this review, the demanding environment of industrial heavy-duty transportation is used as an example. In this sector, maximizing vehicle uptime is critical for operational efficiency and profitability. A primary operational constraint for Battery Electric Vehicles (BEVs) is the limited energy capacity of Energy Storage Systems (ESS), often necessitating charging stops within regulated driving periods [2]. Adding to this is the degradation of the ESS over its lifespan, measured by State of Health (SoH), which progressively reduces range [9]. Ideally, this degradation shouldn't force extra charging stops. However, for long-haul or heavy-payload trucks, significant SoH reduction can lead to unplanned stops, disrupting logistics. Pushing the truck to meet schedules despite low SoH can lead to critical safety issues, the ESS might short-circuit which in worst case can lead to thermal runaway [18] highlighting the importance of reliability and safety considerations industrial deployment.

Current practices often rely on replacing batteries near a generic End of Life threshold around 80% capacity [14]. This generic approach may not be optimal; high-utilization industrial users might benefit from earlier, personalized replacement schedules to maintain consistent performance.

This is where FL and RL offer significant potential, especially when deployed on embedded systems within the trucks. The operational data, driving patterns, charging behavior, payload variations and battery response is highly individualized (non-IID). This heterogeneity is a key aspect of the Data-Related Challenges common in many industrial settings [3]. FL enables collaborative model training directly on each individual embedded system, learning from diverse, real-world usage patterns across the fleet without compromising data privacy. RL agents, potentially trained using FL-aggregated insights, could then learn optimal, personalized battery replacement policies, predicting the future impact of degradation on a specific truck's uptime [21]. While FL and RL make such optimization theoretically possible, their practical deployment within industrial settings introduces complexities that must be addressed.

2.1   Challenges in Current Industrial Systems

The specific problem of ESS degradation in industrial heavy-duty trucks effectively embodies the key challenges that arise when deploying evolving FL and RL algorithms on general industrial embedded systems. Analysis of this problem reveals four core, interconnected challenges critical for successful industrial deployment. These challenges are categorized as follows:

1. **Data-Related Challenges:** Deploying FL/RL on industrial embedded systems faces complex data characteristics. Varied usage (e.g., shift patterns, loads) creates heterogeneous, non-IID data, hindering model generalization. Commercial data sensitivity also requires robust privacy-preserving techniques [19].
2. **Computational and System-Level Challenges:** Industrial embedded hardware (e.g., ECUs) faces significant resource constraints (processing, memory, energy) while managing numerous functions, including safety-critical tasks. This demands computationally efficient algorithms and careful resource management [7].
3. **Operational and Deployment Challenges:** Diverse operational contexts (e.g., varying shifts, maintenance schedules, device availability) complicate practical deployment. This requires flexible mechanisms like asynchronous updates and robust model versioning [16]. Reliable communication protocols and strategies for long-term adaptation are essential due to the extended lifecycle of industrial equipment.
4. **Organizational and Regulatory Challenges:** Beyond technical aspects, deployment is impacted by organizational and regulatory factors. Compliance with data protection laws necessitates clear data governance, while ensuring algorithm safety demands transparency and accountability [11].

3   Methodology

The contribution of this paper is to provide a review of the current state-of-the-art in industrially applied FL and RL on resource-constrained embedded systems. The goal is to see the developments in the key-areas of efficiency, adaptability and scalability while preserving privacy of the user and outputting robust decisions over time. To guide this review and identify key challenges, the research was structured around two primary research questions. First (RQ1), we sought to identify which FL & RL algorithms are currently deployed on industrial resource-constrained embedded systems and how they address the challenges outlined in Sect. 2.1. Second (RQ2), we aimed to understand what challenges these algorithms still experience and what further research is needed for full-scale industrialization.

To answer these questions, a systematic search was conducted on the IEEE Xplore database, chosen for its comprehensive coverage of relevant engineering and computer science literature. A search query was designed to capture studies published between 2018 and 2024. The query combined specific keywords using

'OR' within conceptual categories and 'AND' across them to ensure a focused yet thorough search. The categories and specific terms used, which cover algorithms, hardware, data, industrial domains, and explicit exclusions, are detailed in Table 1.

Table 1. Search Strategy Components

Category	Search Terms
Type of Algorithm	federated learning OR deep reinforcement learning OR FL OR RL OR reinforcement learning
Type of Algorithm (Specific)	Personalization OR Individualization OR User-Centric Optimization OR Adaptive Learning OR Context-Aware Systems OR mass-customization OR privacy-preserving OR privacy
Deployment Hardware	edge computing OR edge AI OR edge intelligence OR embedded system
Data Usage	real-world data OR RWD OR real data
Industrial Domain	autonomous driving OR healthcare OR automotive OR telecom OR field deployment
Application	industrial application OR industry OR application
Exclusion from Query	offloading OR survey OR resource allocation OR blockchain

The subsequent study selection process, visualized in the PRISMA flow chart in Fig. 1, began with 68 records identified from the search. All records were screened, leading to a full-text eligibility assessment where 7 reports were excluded for reasons such as an irrelevant context or a focus on non-applicable technologies. This resulted in a final set of 61 studies. Included studies were peer-reviewed English articles or proceedings that demonstrated or simulated FL/RL on resource-constrained industrial systems. It is important to note that a formal quality assessment was not performed, as the primary goal of this review was to map existing techniques and identify challenges, rather than to synthesize evidence based on study rigor [13].

To systematically analyze the final 61 studies, key details were extracted from each paper to ensure consistency for the thematic analysis. This extracted data included the deployment approach (hardware or simulation), primary contribution type (e.g., algorithm development), the specific algorithms used (FL/RL/Hybrid), data sources utilized, and the industrial domain, providing the foundation for the results presented in Sect. 4 and Table 2.

4   Results

Our analysis of the 61 selected studies provides a clear snapshot of the current research landscape, revealing distinct trends in deployment strategies, algorith-

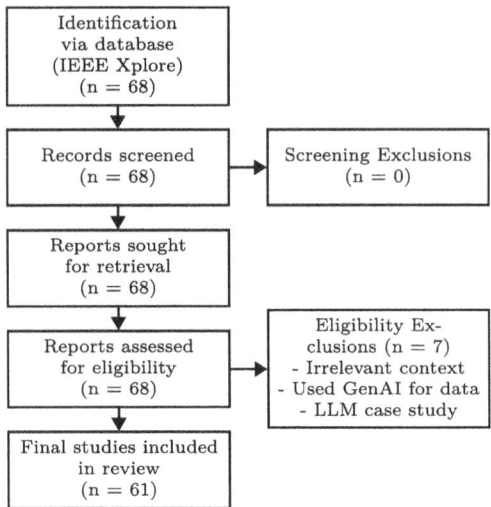

Fig. 1. PRISMA flow chart for included papers in review.

mic focus, and the methods used to address key industrial challenges. A summary of these characteristics is presented in Table 2.

The most striking finding is the significant gap between research and practice, underscored by a heavy reliance on simulation. A substantial majority of studies (66%) were validated in simulated environments, whereas a mere 18% demonstrated deployment on actual hardware. These rare hardware-based studies were consistently small-scale proofs-of-concept, typically utilizing consumer-grade platforms like Raspberry Pi or NVIDIA Jetson rather than industrial-grade ECU's. This indicates that while algorithms are being developed, their practical viability on industrial hardware remains unproven.

In terms of algorithmic focus, FL is the dominant approach, featured in 62% of the papers, while RL is used less frequently (25%). The thematic analysis revealed several key trends in how the literature uses these algorithms to address the challenges outlined in Sect. 2.1:

1. **Data-Related Challenges:** The prevalence of FL is largely driven by its inherent ability to address challenges of data heterogeneity and privacy. The literature shows a strong trend of adapting FL with asynchronous frameworks or meta-learning to handle non-IID data [16]. To tackle privacy concerns, the most common technique supplementing FL's decentralized design is Differential Privacy (DP) [10,24].
2. **Computational and System-Level Challenges:** To meet the constraints of resource-limited devices, the research shows a clear trend towards developing lighter algorithms and employing model compression techniques [12]. This is often complemented by resource-aware frameworks, hardware-specific optimizations [7], and strategies like edge caching to enable real-time processing with Deep RL [25].

3. **Operational and Deployment Challenges:** These challenges are most frequently handled using asynchronous FL protocols, which offer the flexibility needed for diverse device schedules and availability [19]. For the long-term adaptation of models in evolving environments, some research explores Federated Continual Learning (FCL) [23], while reliability is addressed through robust communication and fault-tolerance mechanisms [4].
4. **Organizational and Regulatory Challenges:** While less explicitly targeted, these challenges are implicitly addressed by the use of FL, whose decentralized nature aligns with the principles of data governance and regulations like GDPR. Techniques such as Differential Privacy further strengthen compliance by providing formal privacy guarantees.

Finally, regarding data sources, the reviewed studies showed a roughly equal reliance on standardized benchmarks for comparability and real-world sampled data for practical relevance. However, the use of real-time streaming data, a cornerstone of many industrial applications, was notably infrequent, further highlighting the disconnect between current research and the dynamic nature of live industrial environments.

Table 2. Summary of Usage Characteristics in Reviewed Studies.

Category	Observations
Deployment Reality	Primarily simulation-based (66%), with rare hardware deployments (18%) being small-scale proofs-of-concept
Hardware Platforms	When used, common platforms are Raspberry Pi and NVIDIA Jetson
Dominant Algorithms	FL is the most frequent approach (62%) for privacy and distribution; RL is used for adaptive control (25%)
Key Techniques	FedAvg is a common FL baseline, with asynchronous variants often proposed. For RL, Actor-Critic methods are prevalent
Data Sources	Roughly equal use of standardized benchmarks and real-world sampled data; infrequent use of real-time streaming data

5   Discussion

The pronounced gap between simulation-based research (66%) and scarce hardware deployments (18%) is not accidental but a consequence of fundamental barriers inherent to the industrial domain. Firstly, the high cost and restricted access to operational industrial equipment, make real-world experimentation prohibitively expensive. Secondly, the safety-critical nature of these systems means that deploying unproven algorithms carries significant risk of equipment damage, operational disruption, or physical harm, making simulation a more viable option for validation. Finally, industrial environments are characterized by data heterogeneity, privacy concerns, and complex operational constraints that are difficult to replicate. Simulation offers a controlled environment where algorithms can be tested against these challenges in isolation before attempting to navigate the complexities of a live, large-scale deployment.

5.1   Current Solutions to Key Challenges in Industrial Systems

Addressing RQ1, the review reveals that FL is the most prevalent approach (62%), primarily tackling Data-Related and Organizational challenges through its decentralized nature. While FedAvg is a common baseline, asynchronous variants are increasingly used to manage Operational heterogeneity [16]. Computational constraints are addressed via algorithmic efficiency and model compression [12]. RL, particularly Deep RL, is used less often (25%) but specifically targets adaptive decision-making for control and optimization tasks [17]. However, a critical finding is that most validation occurs in simulation (66%), with limited deployment on actual industrial hardware (18%), indicating a significant gap in demonstrating practical effectiveness [7].

5.2   Persisting Challenges in the Literature

Regarding RQ2, our analysis of the reviewed literature identified five critical and interconnected challenges that currently hinder the large-scale industrialization of FL and RL:

1. **Lack of Real-World Validation and Robustness:** The most critical gap is insufficient validation in large-scale, operational industrial settings. Simulation-based research often overlooks real-world complexities like data drift, network issues, and hardware variability [8].
2. **Scalability Limitations:** Evaluations rarely move beyond simulations or small-scale proofs-of-concept. Demonstrating scalability to hundreds or thousands of heterogeneous devices, typical in industrial fleets, is largely absent but crucial for adoption [15].
3. **Real-time Data Handling on Hardware:** Despite the prevalence of streaming data in industry, few studies (~5%) tackled its processing directly on resource-constrained embedded hardware. Efficiently handling continuous data under strict hardware limitations remains a significant challenge [17].
4. **Algorithm Focus and Adaptation Challenges:** RL's lower usage suggests difficulties that extend beyond its computationally intensive nature. Defining a stable and effective reward function for complex, multi-objective industrial processes is a non-trivial challenge [5]. Furthermore, the inherent sample inefficiency of many RL algorithms makes extensive online exploration—a primary learning mechanism—infeasible in high-stakes environments where each interaction is costly and carries risk. This is compounded by the difficulty of the sim-to-real transfer; policies that perform optimally in simulation may fail on physical hardware due to subtle, unmodeled real-world dynamics.

Consequently, ensuring the safety and predictability of an exploring RL agent poses significant risks, making the validation of safety in simulation a critical but also a barrier for industrial adoption [17,20].

5. **Safety standards for industrial adoption:** Finally, a notable gap in the reviewed literature is the lack of engagement with domain-specific safety standards. For industrial deployment, especially in automotive and manufacturing, compliance with functional safety standards like ISO 26262 and IEC 61508 is mandatory [20]. Future research must bridge this gap by evaluating FL/RL validation, verification, and robustness not just algorithmically, but against the explicit requirements of these critical safety frameworks.

5.3   Future Research Directions

To address these persisting challenges, future research must pivot towards a more integrated and application-grounded approach. A critical direction is the validation of algorithms on industrial-grade hardware, such as automotive ECUs, moving beyond simulation and consumer-grade platforms like Raspberry Pi that dominate current studies. This research should also explore adoption strategies for industrial context, such as a two-phase approach where FL is first deployed for large-scale data analytics and monitoring across a fleet, establishing a foundation of trust and infrastructure. Subsequently, insights aggregated through FL can be used to train more complex, closed-loop RL agents for control and optimization tasks. Throughout this process, research efforts must equally prioritize the integration of robust privacy and safety frameworks. The goal should be to develop trustworthy and transparent systems, shifting the focus from purely optimizing algorithmic accuracy to ensuring verifiability and reliability in safety-critical deployments.

5.4   Limitations of this Review

The literature search was confined to the IEEE Xplore database, and methodologies such as snowballing were not employed, which may have resulted in missing relevant studies from other disciplines. Furthermore, no formal quality assessment of the included studies was performed, as the primary aim was to map existing techniques and identify reported challenges.

6   Conclusions

This review shows that while current research has made algorithmic advancements in addressing the challenges of deploying FL and RL on industrial embedded systems, a critical gap persists between simulation-based studies and the realities of industrial deployment. The key takeaway is that realizing the potential of FL and RL in industry requires a research shift towards real-world validation, scalability, and demonstrable robustness. Future efforts must therefore move beyond consumer-grade platforms and prioritize field trials on industrial-grade hardware like ECUs. This calls for exploring more strategic research paths, such as leveraging FL for data analytics as a foundation for more complex RL control systems. Ultimately, this work shows the need for a new focus where the goal is not only achieving the highest accuracy, but developing verifiably safe, robust, and trustworthy systems that are fit for critical industrial deployment. Pursuing these directions is vital to bridge the gap between current research and the successful, large-scale adoption of FL and RL on industrial embedded systems.

References

1. A scalable approach for partially-local federated learning. https://research.google/blog/a-scalable-approach-for-partially-local-federated-learning/
2. Driving time and rest periods (2025). https://transport.ec.europa.eu/transport-modes/road/social-provisions/driving-time-and-rest-periods_en
3. Bin Syed, M.A., Rhaman, Q., Sushil, S.: Federated learning in manufacturing: a systematic review and pathway to industry 5.0. In: 2023 5th International Conference on Sustainable Technologies for Industry 5.0 (STI), pp. 1–6 (2023). https://doi.org/10.1109/STI59863.2023.10464397
4. Cal, S., Sun, X., Yao, J.: Client selection in fault-tolerant federated reinforcement learning for iot networks. In: ICC 2024 - IEEE International Conference on Communications, pp. 459–464 (2024). https://doi.org/10.1109/ICC51166.2024.10622515
5. Choppara, P., Mangalampalli, S.S.: Resource adaptive automated task scheduling using deep deterministic policy gradient in fog computing. IEEE Access **13**, 25969–25994 (2025). https://doi.org/10.1109/ACCESS.2025.3539606
6. Elkholy, M., Shalash, O., Hamad, M.S., Saraya, M.S.: Empowering the grid: a comprehensive review of artificial intelligence techniques in smart grids. In: 2024 International Telecommunications Conference (ITC-Egypt), pp. 513–518 (2024). https://doi.org/10.1109/ITC-Egypt61547.2024.10620543
7. Kumar, A., Gupta, N., Derawi, M., Pal, R.: Hardware implementation of a reinforcement learning based energy efficient protocol for wireless sensor network. In: 2024 Second International Conference on Microwave, Antenna and Communication (MAC), pp. 1–5 (2024). https://doi.org/10.1109/MAC61551.2024.10837438
8. Lobato, W., Costa, J.B.D.D., Souza, A.MD., Rosário, D., Sommer, C., Villas, L.A.: Flexe: investigating federated learning in connected autonomous vehicle simulations. In: 2022 IEEE 96th Vehicular Technology Conference (VTC2022-Fall), pp. 1–5 (2022). https://doi.org/10.1109/VTC2022-Fall57202.2022.10012905
9. Madani, S.S., et al.: A comprehensive review on lithium-ion battery lifetime prediction and aging mechanism analysis. Batteries **11**(4), 127 (2025)
10. Mariappan, K., Gopal, B., ParthaSarathy, J., Sreekanth, G.R., Nanmaran, R., Jegajothi, B.: Privacy-preserving human activity recognition in smart homes using deep learning and edge computing for real-time processing. In: 2024 International Conference on Sustainable Communication Networks and Application (ICSCNA), pp. 1643–1650 (2024). https://doi.org/10.1109/ICSCNA63714.2024.10864298
11. Nguyen, T.H., Vu, T.G., Tran, H.L., Wong, K.S.: Emerging privacy and trust issues for autonomous vehicle systems. In: 2022 International Conference on Information Networking (ICOIN), pp. 52–57 (2022). https://doi.org/10.1109/ICOIN53446.2022.9687196

12. Odeyomi, O.T., Ajibuwa, O., Roy, K.: A hybrid federated learning architecture with online learning and model compression. IEEE Access **12**, 191046–191058 (2024). https://doi.org/10.1109/ACCESS.2024.3517710

13. Page, M.J., et al.: Prisma 2020 explanation and elaboration: updated guidance and exemplars for reporting systematic reviews. BMJ **372** (2021). https://doi.org/10.1136/bmj.n160. https://www.bmj.com/content/372/bmj.n160

14. Park, S., Lee, J., Heo, S.: Gaussian process regression-based lithium-ion battery end-of-life prediction model under various operating conditions. arXiv preprint arXiv:2410.19886 (2024)

15. Sharma, A., Tripathi, T., Majumdar, A.: Enhancing edge-based cardiovascular diagnosis through federated learning and iot. In: 2024 15th International Conference on Computing Communication and Networking Technologies (ICCCNT), pp. 1–6 (2024). https://doi.org/10.1109/ICCCNT61001.2024.10724661

16. Shiranthika, C., Hadizadeh, H., Saeedi, P., Ivan Bajić, V.: Adaptive asynchronous split federated learning for medical image segmentation. IEEE Access **12**, 182496–182515 (2024). https://doi.org/10.1109/ACCESS.2024.3511430

17. Shirvani, S., Samanta, A., Li, Z., Liu, C.: Duojoule: accurate on-device deep reinforcement learning for energy and timeliness. In: 2024 IEEE Real-Time Systems Symposium (RTSS), pp. 109–122 (2024). https://doi.org/10.1109/RTSS62706.2024.00019

18. Sun, S., Xu, J.: Safety behaviors and degradation mechanisms of aged batteries: a review. Energy Mater. Dev. **2**(4), 9370048 (2024). https://doi.org/10.26599/EMD.2024.9370048. https://www.sciopen.com/article/10.26599/EMD.2024.9370048

19. Tong, C., Zhang, L., Ding, Y., Yue, D.: A heterogeneity-aware adaptive federated learning framework for short-term forecasting in electric iot systems. IEEE Internet Things J. (2025). https://doi.org/10.1109/JIOT.2025.3528545

20. Törngren, M., Thompson, H., Herzog, E., Inam, R., Gross, J., Dán, G.: Industrial edge-based cyber-physical systems - application needs and concerns for realization. In: 2021 IEEE/ACM Symposium on Edge Computing (SEC), pp. 409–415 (2021). https://doi.org/10.1145/3453142.3493507

21. Wang, Y., Zhong, S., Yuan, T.: Grasp control method for robotic manipulator based on federated reinforcement learning. In: 2024 7th International Conference on Advanced Algorithms and Control Engineering (ICAACE), pp. 1513–1519 (2024). https://doi.org/10.1109/ICAACE61206.2024.10549724

22. Xia, Q., Chen, P., Xu, G., Sun, H., Li, L., Yu, G.: Adaptive path-tracking controller embedded with reinforcement learning and preview model for autonomous driving. IEEE Trans. Veh. Technol. 1–15 (2024). https://doi.org/10.1109/TVT.2024.3502640

23. Xu, Z., et al.: Age-aware data selection and aggregator placement for timely federated continual learning in mobile edge computing. IEEE Trans. Comput. **73**(2), 466–480 (2024). https://doi.org/10.1109/TC.2023.3333213

24. Zhao, Y., et al.: Local differential privacy-based federated learning for internet of things. IEEE Internet Things J. **8**(11), 8836–8853 (2021). https://doi.org/10.1109/JIOT.2020.3037194

25. Zhou, X., Liu, Z., Guo, M., Zhao, J., Wang, J.: SACC: a size adaptive content caching algorithm in fog/edge computing using deep reinforcement learning. IEEE Trans. Emerg. Top. Comput. **10**(4), 1810–1820 (2022). https://doi.org/10.1109/TETC.2021.3115793

Explainability in Self-Adaptive Systems: A Systematic Literature Review

Raphael Straub[1]($\boxtimes$)(ID), Florian Sihler[1](ID), Ali Torbati[2](ID), Cong Wang[3](ID),
Raffaela Groner[4](ID), Verena Klös[2](ID), and Matthias Tichy[1](ID)

[1] Ulm University, Ulm, Germany
{raphael.straub,florian.sihler,matthias.tichy}@uni-ulm.de
[2] Carl von Ossietzky Universität Oldenburg, Oldenburg, Germany
{ali.torbati,verena.kloes}@uni-oldenburg.de
[3] LASR Lab, TU Dresden, Dresden, Germany
cong.wang@tu-dresden.de
[4] Chalmers University of Technology and University of Gothenburg,
Gothenburg, Sweden
raffaela@chalmers.se

Abstract. Self-adaptive systems (SAS) dynamically adjust their configuration to changes in environment or internal state. These complex and possibly emergent adaptions require explanations. We conducted a systematic literature review to create an overview over existing research concerning explainability in SASs and identify further research directions. Specifically, we focus on approaches that have been empirically evaluated. We show that there is only a small amount of publications in this area, which, nonetheless, are very diverse concerning their approach and focus. We present our findings along the major parts of the explanation process. However, many of the approaches focus only on some specific aspects. A major finding is a disconnect between the stated explanation objectives and the conducted evaluations, especially, concerning user-centered goals like trust and understanding.

Keywords: SLR · Adaptive-System · Explainability

1 Introduction

Self-Adaptive Systems (SAS) [32] are complex software systems that can modify their behavior in response to changes in their environment or internal state. By incorporating self-adaptation mechanisms, such as feedback loops and autonomous decision-making, these systems can dynamically adjust their configuration, behavior, or structure to meet changing requirements or conditions. This ability to adapt enables SASs to improve their performance, reliability, and overall quality of service, making them increasingly important in a wide range of applications, e.g., from embedded systems [26] to cloud computing [17].

The autonomous nature of SASs requires explainability and transparency in their decision-making. Without clear understanding of how and why a system is adapting, it can be challenging to trust its behavior, identify potential issues, and make informed decisions about its configuration or operation.

D. Taibi and D. Smite (Eds.): SEAA 2025, LNCS 16082, pp. 280–297, 2026.
https://doi.org/10.1007/978-3-032-04200-2_19

Our aim is to synthesize existing research on explainability in SASs in order to derive an overview about the state-of-the-art as well as to identify research gaps. These research gaps define further research directions for the SAS community. We refer the reader to existing systematic literature reviews on explainable AI (XAI) in general (see [15,25] for two tertiary studies).

We conducted a systematic literature review to identify and synthesize existing research on explainability in SASs. First, we performed a search in leading academic databases, followed by snowballing to identify additional studies. We performed thematic analysis to identify key themes, concepts, and findings, providing a comprehensive understanding of the current state of research in this area.

We screened overall 1543 unique papers during the database search as well as the snowballing iterations. We finally included just 12 publications, particularly due to only including publications containing an evaluation. The thematic analysis resulted in seven categories covering the aims of the explanations, their construction as well as the results of the evaluation. With respect to research gaps, we identified four major areas: lack of actionable explanations, adapting the explanations on different persons and roles, improving the consistency between the explanations' aims and the conducted evaluations, and addressing all aspects of SASs [32].

After a discussion of related work in the following section, we detail the research method in Sect. 3. The synthesis of the collected research papers is presented in Sect. 4. After the discussion of research gaps and research directions in Sect. 5, we conclude in Sect. 6.

2   Related Work

While there are many surveys on explainable AI, this is the first survey on the topic of explainable SASs. In the following, we present some related studies. Landuyt et al. investigated notions and operationalization of trust in SASs. They concluded that "communicating the dynamic arguments for trust to stakeholders remains a key challenge in SASs." [30]. Sado et al. survey techniques for explaining goal-driven agents [27], which share with SASs that they autonomously select actions to accomplish their goals. A recent article by Sobrín-Hidalgo et al. presents a systematic literature review on the topic of explainable robots with a focus on which methods are proposed for generating and evaluating explanations [29]. Reinforcement Learning (RL) is often used in modern SASs. Vouros [31] reviews and categorizes methods to explain deepRL algorithms.

3   Research Method

In this section, we describe our research method based on the guidelines by Keele et al. [21] and Kitchenham et al. [23].

3.1   Search Strategy

Figure 2 depicts our selection process.

Search Query. Our search query combines synonyms of "Adaptive System" and "Explainability", as well as related terms like "Adaptive Mechanism":

```
("Adaptive System" OR "Self Adaption" OR "Self Adjusting" OR "Self
Organizing" OR "Autonomous System" OR "Adaptive Algorithm" OR "Adaptive
Mechanism" OR "self reconfiguring" OR "self healing")
AND ("Explainability" OR "Explanation" OR "Interpretability" OR
"Transparency" OR "Understandability" OR "Comprehensibility" OR
"Explicability")
```

Databases. For the initial database search, we used the search query on IEEEXplore and the ACM Digital Library, both known for their relevance in software engineering. For IEEEXplore, we applied the search query to the abstract and all meta-data. For ACM, we applied it only to the abstract and title due to technical limitations by the ACM. The initial search yielded 346 unique results.

Inclusion and Exclusion Criteria. Our inclusion and exclusion criteria are listed in Table 1. As there is a limited number of papers available in the first place, our criteria attempt to be as broad as possible. In addition to the generic exclusion criteria, we exclude publications before 2003. In this year, the paper defining the MAPE-K architecture was published [22]. We finalized this search in 2024, automatically excluding later publications. Furthermore, we only consider publications which include an evaluation of the explainability approach.

Table 1. Inclusion and Exclusion Criteria

Incl./Excl.	Criteria
Inclusion	• Discusses explainability or explanations for SASs
	• Explainability is evaluated
Exclusion	• Publications before 2003 (Pre MAPE-K loop)
	• Publications after 2024
	• Secondary and tertiary studies (SLRs, Surveys)
	• Superseded by an extended version included in the review
	• Not a Conference/Journal Publication
	• The publication was not subject to peer review
	• Not written in English

Selection Process. Papers often do not explicitly describe SASs as self-adaptive, complicating the collection process. Therefore, we were initially permissive in the SAS criteria to maximize collection during snowballing. Two authors independently screened abstracts and full text when necessary. Disputes were resolved by a third author, resulting in 20 selected publications. Two iterations of forward and backward snowballing yielded 8 additional publications, totaling 28 publications. Subsequently, we only selected the publications that align with the SAS definition by Weyns [32], reducing our final selection from 28 to 12.

Temporal Distribution. The papers span 2012–2024. After two early outliers in 2012 and 2016, the topic gains momentum: ten of the twelve studies (83%) appear between 2020 and 2024. 2021 leads with four papers (33%), followed by 2020 and 2023 (two each), 2022 (one) and a fresh contribution in 2024. The trend, visualised in Fig. 1, underscores how explainability for self-adaptive systems has surged only in recent years.

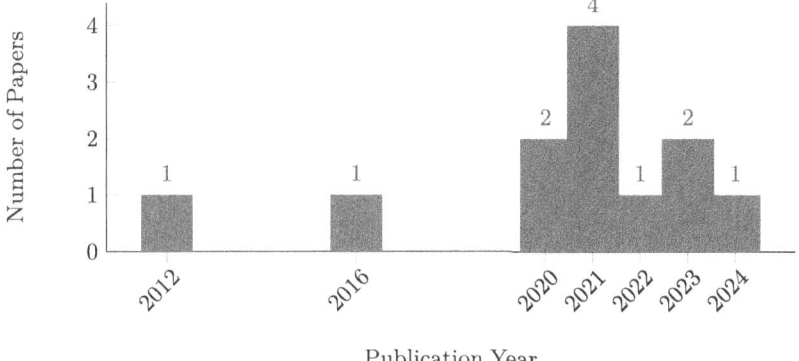

Fig. 1. Temporal distribution of the 12 selected SAS publications.

3.2   Data Extraction

A thematic analysis was used to extract data from the paper. The coding schema was defined based on our research objective and prior research [16]. Given the diversity of the selected papers, each paper was coded by two authors independently. Then, a single author merged the two versions of all paper, ensuring consistency.

3.3   Threats to Validity

We analyze the threats to validity based on the guidelines by Ampatzoglou et al. [13].

The internal validity of this study is threatened by our selection of search terms and misinterpretation when applying the inclusion/exclusion criteria, possibly leading to missed publications. To mitigate this thread, we performed snowballing, systematic voting, and discussions about the applied criteria.

The main threats to data validity are the small sample size and possible mistakes in the data extraction. Our mitigation strategies for the internal validity assure us, that we included the relevant literature. However, excluding publications that do not perform an evaluation might limit this studies generalizability. To avoid mistakes in the data extraction, each paper was coded by two authors independently.

Concerning the research validity, we aim to ensure replicability by transparent documentation of our research process.

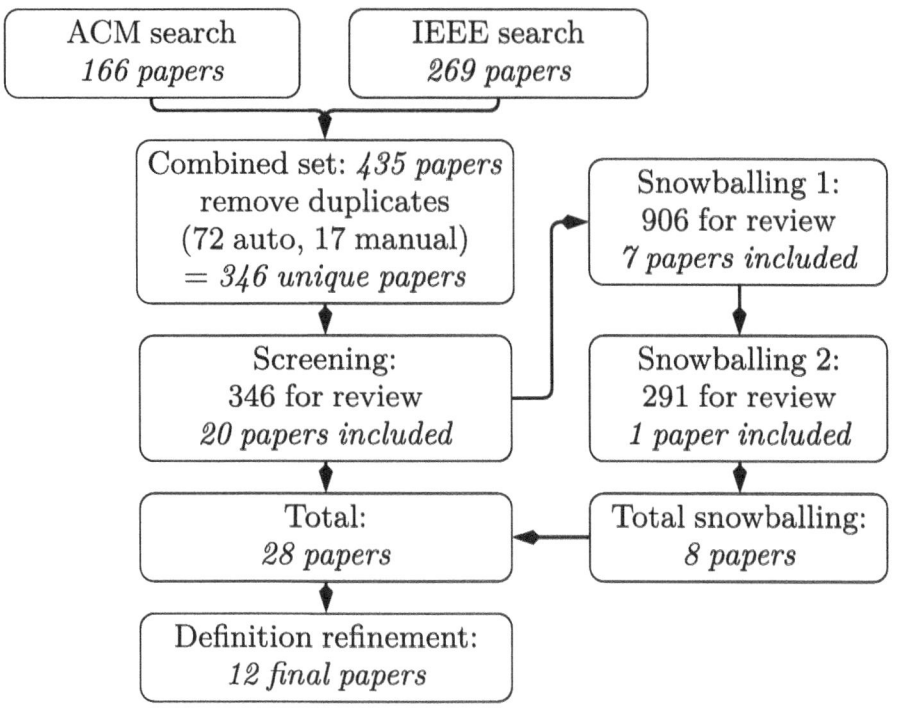

Fig. 2. Overview of the paper collection process

4   Results

In this section, we detail our findings, which are aggregated in Table 2. We structure our findings around the following explanation process: First, the aim and audience of the explanation needs to be defined (Sect. 4.1). Then the target of the explanation needs to be defined (Sect. 4.2), followed by the moment of the explanation (Sect. 4.3). When these aspects are defined the explanation can be constructed accordingly (Sect. 4.4). Once an explanation is constructed, it can be presented to a user (Sect. 4.5). A successful explanation has an effect on the user (Sect. 4.6), which needs to be evaluated afterwards (Sect. 4.7).

4.1   Why is Something Explained?

In this section, we summarize the purposes of explanations that were mentioned in the articles. The purpose differs for different stakeholders and can be categorized into three groups.

In human-on-the-loop(HotL) systems, several works argue that explanations can increase the understanding of adaptation processes and enable *human decision-makers* and *operators* to **supervise and, when necessary, intervene** in questionable decisions [1–5]. It is also suggested that explanations thereby contribute to improving overall system utility in HotL systems [2,4] which is also defined as improving the human-system co-adaptation [6].

A second group of papers targets *system designers/developers* and *service providers*. Here, explanations aim to **support in design and maintenance tasks**, such as the optimization of adaptation processes [1,3,7–10], e.g. by explaining how changes in variables affect adaptation policies [1,7], or **debugging** issues within adaptation processes [9,10]. Additionally, some approaches intend to support *system-/service providers* in **complying with legal and ethical frameworks** by increasing the transparency of decision-making processes [9,10].

Studies that address *system users* mostly focus on **user-centered goals**, e.g. build trust, instill confidence, and increase perceived reliability by making model behavior and predictions more transparent [3,4,8–11], or support system users by improving usability [1,7]. One study targets human-robot collaboration [12] and delivers explanations for tasks to guide users.

4.2   What is Explained?

In the surveyed literature, explanations in SASs generally address the logic of adaptive decisions, clarifying the rationale behind specific decisions or adaptations.

Several studies center on explaining the **decisions made by machine learning components**. For example, why a deep reinforcement learning system selects one adaptation over another (e.g., add web server instead of decrease dimmer) [9,10], and how to interpret the predictions or behavior of a deep learning model using integrated gradients [8].

Other studies emphasize **domain-level rationales for actions**, such as why a system opts for a specific action or transitions to a new state [2], why a small unmanned aerial system behaves in a certain way [4], which rules govern decisions made by a self-driving model [11], and how and why the system achieves the current behavior under the given conditions [3].

Explanations can also focus on the **reasons behind automated planning**, by clarifying how choices in utility functions shape adaptation decisions and reveal underlying tradeoffs among multiple quality attributes [1] or clarifying to human collaborators why they should perform an action and how it is linked to parts of a plan [12].

Some explanations provide insights into **system's global behavior**, such as the overall chain of events occurring in the system's runtime and how that chain influences or correlates with global objectives [7].

4.3   When is it Explained?

In addition to the reason and object of the explanation, we also consider the timing of the explanation. We classify the analysis context (i.e. runtime or design time) and investigate the concrete trigger for the explanation.

The majority of publications focus on explanations at the **runtime** of the system [2–12], only one paper solely considers explanations at the **design time** of the system [1], while some provide explanation at runtime and design time [3, 8,11]. However, this distinction generally is only very briefly discussed.

Most publications place a very **low emphasis** on the trigger of the explanations, or do not discuss this aspect at all. However, [5] even focuses on this aspect. They argue that explanations come with costs like delayed actions, which might even be detrimental to achieving system goals. Using a probabilistic reasoning approach, they aim to provide explanations only when the utility of the system would improve.

The other works that discuss this aspect focus on the human addressee. [6] provide an explanation for every step, however, if the addressee is dissatisfied with the explanation, they continue to provide explanations with changed modality or amount until the user is satisfied. On the other hand, [12] adapt the explanation based on the humans level of expertise. For example, new users gain automatic explanations, while more advanced users may request explanations when they require them.

4.4   How is the Explanation Constructed?

The approaches used to construct explanations can be categorized into machine learning-based, model-based, and other approaches. Also, some works focus on approaches to create user-tailor explanations and do not specify their construction.

Machine learning (ML) techniques, especially clustering, are most frequently mentioned as a means to construct explanations. The work by Wohlrab et al. [1] combines k-means clustering with principal component analysis, multiple correspondence analysis, and expert input to derive decision trees to explain quality attribute tradeoffs. Diallo et al. [8] use a convolutional neural network (CNN) to classify adaptation options and in combination with explainable AI to identify the most important features to explain why an adaption option is picked. Also, the approach from Kim et al. [11] is based on CNNs to visually highlight the causes of actions and train a CNN based on a human-made dataset to generate a textual explanation that combines actions and their causes.

The two publications by Metzger et al. [9,10] rely on XRL-DINE [19], which is a combination of reward decomposition [20] and interestingness elements [28]. Reward decomposition splits a reward function into several functions that express one aspect of a learning goal and interestingness elements determine relevant interactions between an agent and its environment. Due to the combination of these two techniques, XRL-DINE provides insights into the reasons for decisions at certain time steps. Metzger et al. [10] present enhancements of XRL-DINE by using its output as input for an AI chatbot to provide a natural language explanation.

Model-based (MB) approaches leverage models to construct explanations. However, these models do not drive the construction, but they are used as a means to an end [14]. Model-based approaches to construct explanations are reported by Parra-Ullauri et al. [7], Bencomo et al. [3], and Li et al. [2]. Parra-Ullauri et al. [7] propose to mine event graph models based on an event-driven runtime monitoring approach that queries runtime models. Another model-based approach is presented by Bencomo et al. [3]. In this work, the authors use manually created i* [33] goal and claim refinement models to explain a system's behavior. Li et al. [2] propose to create explanations out of a tuple that models the state of the system and its transition. Precisely, they model the preconditions that triggered a transition and the subsequent state.

Finally, Agrawal and Cleland-Huang [4] present **another** approach to construct explanations. Their explanations are based on manually predefined events and how a system can respond to them.

Some publications [2,5,6,12] present approaches to model humans to provide **user-tailored** explanations according to the system users' needs, abilities, or knowledge. However, except for the work by Li et al. [2], these works usually explain their approach to constructing explanations either very superficially or not at all.

4.5   How is the Explanation Presented?

Concerning the presentation of the explanation, we primarily focus on the modality and content.

Most publications [1,4,7–9,11], present explanations in a **visual** form, which might be annotated with additional text. The visualization of [1] and [7] focus on the decision making process, while [8] and [11] highlight the input elements that influence the decision of the models. Alternatively, [4] and [9] provide an **user interface**. For example, the interface of [4] automatically provides an explanation when an event occurs and even allows the user to configure or suspend the autonomous behavior of a drone, allowing for a human-on-the-loop interaction style. The visualizations are provided in various forms, for example, decision trees by [1], line graphs and bar charts by [9], as well as heatmaps by [8] and [11].

[6] and [12] use a **multi-modal** approach that combines multiple modalities like audio, video, and text. However, neither of the two papers describes, for example, how to create a video as explanation or details the content of it. Instead, the two paper focus on reasoning about the ideal modality of the user, where [6] decides this based on personality traits and [12] based on the humans level of expertise.

Only a single paper [10] relies solely on **textual** explanations. However, the main contribution of [10] is the attempt to transfer the explanation technique of prior work [9] to a chat interface based on a large language model. Originally, [9] employs a user interface with visualizations like line graphs and bar charts.

The works of [2,3] and [5] did not detail how an explanation should be presented.

4.6   What is the Effect of the Explanation?

The effects of explanations on human addressees that were observed in the articles and trade-offs that were considered can be categorized into benefits and drawbacks of explanations.

In case of **benefits**, several studies showed that explanations improve *operator* performance by clarifying adaptation decisions and increase their confidence in system correctness [2,5,9]. [6] indicates that considering human psychological traits when designing explanations can enhance *user* performance and human-system utility. Explanations can also alert *operators* to unexpected behaviors that require prompt intervention [2], and positively impact *user* trust [7,9,11] and understandability [7]. In human-robot interactions, explainability has been reported to foster more intuitive interactions, enhancing perceived robot intelligence and adaptability [12]. It is also reported to help *operators* assess whether system responses are suitable, enhancing real-time understanding of system autonomy [4]. Lastly, explanations help *developers* clarify adaptation goals and highlight decision-making anomalies, thus providing valuable debugging insights into RL-based SASs [7,9].

A primary **drawback** of explanations is that they come at a cost, e.g., requiring the *operator* to invest time and effort to understand the information. Thus explanations can slow *human* response times [2,4,6]. If the cost exceeds the advantages, explanations can hinder the satisfaction of system goals [5]. To avoid this, systems might skip the explanations entirely [2]. Moreover, emphasizing explanations can cause issues like information overload, misplaced salience, attentional tunneling, automation bias, and lead *operators* to miss critical autonomous actions [4]. Lastly, [9] have observed difficulties in interpreting visual explanations and dashboards.

However, some papers neglect to mention either the effects of their explanation or the trade-offs that were likely to be involved in their explanation, which is of particular concern [1,3,8,10].

4.7   How is the Explanation Evaluated?

Evaluation approaches for explainability in SASs can be broadly categorized into user studies [4,9,11,12] and demonstrations [1–3,5–8,10] with no direct user-subject testing.

Although most **user studies** [4,9,11] relied only on qualified participants, ensured through a preliminary test, [12] gave no such indication. However, since they analyzed explanations for robots performing a simple task, cooking dinner, no special qualifications are required. Both, [4] and [9], had participants with low expertise and domain experts in their participant pool. Notably, [4] even included participants with no prior experience in the domain.

The majority of publications with **demonstrations** performed an evaluation on a simulated system [1,3,7,8,10]. The other publications with demonstrations [2,5,6], used formal models without a real-world prototype or deployment.

A notable exception to the prior categorization is the approach of [10]. While they did not perform a user study, they compared their approach against the results of a previous user study [9]. This comparison was possible because they analyzed an LLM-based approach which could act as user and answer the questions of the previous user study.

Frequent **limitations** mentioned are the absence of human-subject testing [1, 2,5,6,8] and the lack of evaluations on a physical system [4,5].

The differences in evaluation approaches can partially be explained by the different focus of the papers concerning explainability. For example, [2] is analyzing the best timing to provide an explanation, while [4] and [6] are concerned with the modality of the explanations presentation. On the other hand, [8] uses self-explanation in order to reduce the adaptation space, therefore, not targeting the human at all.

5   Discussion

In this section we discuss our findings of the previous sections, focusing on the purpose of the explanation, the adaptability to the human addressee, the evaluation, and the needs of SASs, aiming to identify future research directions.

5.1   Purpose of the Explanation

In this section, we reflect on the underlying purpose of explanations in SASs and critically assess their broader implications. By analyzing the identified purposes of the explanations in Sect. 4.1 and their content Sect. 4.2, a central question emerges: *Should explanations in SASs be actionable?*

Actionable Explanations enable the addressee of explanations in SASs to take direct, meaningful actions or interventions. Unlike general explanations, actionable explanations are practical, precise, and guide the user towards concrete steps, such as debugging an error, adjusting system parameters, or manually overriding automatic adaptations.

As discussed in Sect. 4.1, explanations in **human-on-the-loop (HotL) systems** aim to enable human decision-makers to supervise and intervene in adaptation decisions [1–5]. Supervision primarily requires situational awareness and understanding of the reasons for and effects of adaptation decisions, as addressed in all these approaches. However, interventions would by definition benefit from actionable explanations. In **maintainability-related goals** (e.g., supporting developers), explanations support developers and providers in tasks such as debugging and adaptation design, e.g. by enhancing the understanding of deep reinforcement learning behavior to help developers to identify faults or compliance issues [10,11], or by highlighting trade-off effects [1]. While these explanations, again, focus on empowering the human by increasing its understanding, embedding actionable elements (e.g., highlighting influential parameters) could streamline better system analysis and refinement. Lastly, for **user-centered goals** (e.g., building trust and confidence) explanations often target intuitive understanding through visual or natural language modalities and rarely intend to trigger user action. In such contexts, actionability is secondary to perceived clarity and reassurance. One exception is an approach that provides actionable explanations to guide a user in a collaborative task setting [12] to improve the perceived quality of interaction.

Our analysis reveals that actionable explanations for SASs are rarely addressed in existing research. However, we believe that actionability is indispensable in HotL SASs, beneficial for maintainability goals, and valuable for

Table 2. Results Overview (—indicates not discussed in the paper)

Paper	Why explained?	What explained?	When explained?	How constructed?	How presented?	What effect?	How evaluated?
[1]	Tradeoff clarity	Policy tradeoffs	—	Machine Learning	Visual (plots, clusters)	Decision clarity	Demonstration (feasibility)
[2]	Understanding	Decision making	When Utility would improve	Model Based	—	Gains in system utility	Demonstration (static PRISM analysis)
[3]	Confidence	Requirements satisfaction	—	Model Based (Goal/claim model)	—	—	Demonstration (simulation)
[4]	Situational Awareness, Automation bias	Autonomy rationale, events	During mission events	Other	Visual (UI)	Heightens bias, reduces awareness	User Study (SAGAT, NASA-RTLX)
[5]	Willingness, Capability	—	When Utility would improve	—	—	Improved Utility for intermediate trained humans	Demonstration (simulation)
[6]	Improve system-human utility	—	Conflict	—	Multi-modal	Utility improvement	Demonstration (simulation)
[7]	Understandability	Global behavior	Post-hoc analysis	Model Based (RTM based event graph)	Visual (event graph)	Global Understanding	Demonstration (feasibility)
[8]	Adaptation Space Reduction	Adaptation options	—	Machine Learning (CNN)	Visual	Improve scalability	Demonstration (analyze packet loss and latency)
[9]	Understanding, debugging	Decision making	Interesting decisions, runtime	Machine Learning (XRL-DINE)	Visual (UI, plots)	Trust, insights, understanding	User Study (TAM metrics)
[10]	Trust, debugging	Decision making	—	Machine Learning (XRL-DINE)	Text (LLM)	—	Demonstration (stability and fidelity)
[11]	Trust in autonomous driving	Decision making	—	Machine Learning (CNN)	Visual (attention maps, text)	Improved trust	User Study (performance, trust)
[12]	Enhance collaboration	Plan tasks	Human knowledge insufficient	—	Multi-modal	Positive acceptance	User Study

achieving some user-centered goals. This leads us to the following research directions:

- How to design actionable explanations for SASs?
- What is the impact of actionable explanations?

5.2   Human-Centered Explanations

In Sect. 4.5, we examined different presentation approaches for explanations. However, different presentations might be required to cater to different types of users. Therefore, in this section, we discuss how the explanations in the selected literature can adapt to the human addressee.

Although explanations are presented in different forms and modalities, most approaches rely solely on the SAS and do not consider the human addressee. Some approaches provide an UI that changes based on the human input. However, that does not constitute an adaptive explanation as it requires the user to initiate changes rather than the explanation adapting autonomously to the user's needs. Furthermore, only the displayed information changes, instead of, for example, the modality.

Only the two multi-modal approaches, of [12] and [6], truly perform a **human-centered adaptation** of the explanation. The adaptation based on human expertise by [12] is motivated by increased efficiency and social acceptability, specifically in the domain of human-robot interaction. It is achieved by dynamically modeling the human's task-specific expertise and adjusting the explanation granularity accordingly. The adaptation proposed by [6] leverages human personality traits to tailor explanations, placing an even stronger emphasis on the addressees characteristics. By modeling personality traits and need for cognition, they select the explanations modality and amount to improve prediction accuracy, explanation satisfaction, and reduce cognitive load.

The motivations of these two approaches are **generic goals** and should apply to all other approaches as well. However, those generally do not consider that aspect, usually just focusing on the content or construction of the explanation. On the other hand, [12] and [6] do not detail how an explanation should be constructed, nor what the content of the explanation should be. For example, [12] state that, in some situations, the explanation should be in video form, but without elaborating how such a video should be generated, or even what the video should contain. The analyzed approaches emphasize either adaptivity to a human addressees, or the creation of the explanation itself, without tackling both problems in the same paper.

We also analyzed the timing of the explanations in Sect. 4.3. [5] mainly focus on the **timing of the explanation** by analyzing the expected utility of adaptation strategies with and without explanations. Similarly, [12] adapt the timing based on the level of the user's expertise. On the other hand, [6] repeat the explanation process when the user is dissatisfied.

Other publications in the surveyed literature [5,9] also recognize the cost associated with providing too much explanations, like a cognitive overhead. To cope with this, however, they do not attempt to change the timing of explanations but focus on a user-centric UI.

The discussion shows, that there is **potential in human-centered explanations** to achieve goals like increased efficiency, satisfaction and reduction in cognitive load. Therefore, other approaches should also consider this aspects when designing and evaluating their explainability mechanism. There should also be a stronger emphasis on evaluating the impact of the adaptability to the human, as this is missing in the literature at hand. This leads us to the following future research directions:

- How to tailor explanations to the human addressee?
- What is the impact of timing, presentation, and addressee on the explanation's effect?

5.3 Evaluation

In this section, we revisit the evaluations summarized in Sect. 4.7 and relate them to the goals of the explanation presented in Sect. 4.1.

The evaluation of performance goals, e.g. the reduction of the adaptation space by [8], is straight forward, as performance metrics can be measured on the system. However, the evaluation of user-centered goals like trust usually requires humans to access related metrics, making the evaluation more challenging and demanding. Therefore, we focus on the **evaluation of user-centered goals** in the remainder of this section.

User-centered goals are also targets of evaluations in the XAI domain, which is why we compare the surveyed literature to the established XAI taxonomy to classify evaluation approaches of explainability by Doshi-Velez and Kim [18]:

With a human-grounded or application-grounded evaluation, i.e. a user study, user-centered goals can be assessed via a questionary, behavioral measures or task performance metrics among other approaches. An example for a functionally-grounded evaluation of explainability by Doshi-Velez and Kim [18] is increasing the precision for an interpretable regression or classification model. As the model is already interpretable, the human understanding does not have to be evaluated again. Therefore, a more precise model implies an improvement in explainability. In this example, the precision works as a proxy for the explainability they want to improve.

We already separated the publications into user studies and demonstrations (cf. Table 2). An application-grounded evaluation requires the participants to perform real tasks in a fully deployed system in a real operational environment. None of the user studies in the selected literature fulfill these criteria, as they rely on a simple exemplar. However,the abstraction level of the study setup between human-grounded and application-grounded evaluations in XAI is usually far more different than in the SAS domain: In XAI, techniques are often evaluated on a simpler setup, like a game. This has the advantage that no prior knowledge is required. Thus, the pool of potential participants is much larger. In contrast, in the selected literature the system domain is the same, but the system is simplified and no real-world application. For example, [9] use the SWIM exemplar [24], which is simple, with only one type of component, but still in the domain of cloud systems. This limits the need for performing an application-grounded evaluation.

All user studies [4,9,11,12] performed an evaluation that adequately addressed their user-centered goals. For the functionally-grounded evaluations, we compare the user-centered goals with the evaluation in Table 3 and analyze if there is a mismatch. Notably, the works of [8] and [6] are excluded, as they do not specify a user-centered goal.

Table 3. Functionally-grounded evaluation

Paper	User-centered Goal	Evaluation	Mismatch?
[1]	Understanding (of tradeoffs)	Demonstrate ML feasibility	No. Analyze information reduction
[2]	Understanding	Static analysis	**Yes**. Only conditions analyzed
[3]	Predictability	Simulation	**Yes**. Analyze performance
[5]	Capability	Demonstration	No. Relate findings to empirical study
[7]	Understandability, Trustworthiness	Demonstrate feasibility	**Yes**. Do not analyze effect of explanation
[10]	Trust	Evaluate stability and fidelity	No. Relate findings to empirical study

The evaluations by [1,6] and [10] do not exhibit a mismatch between user-centered goal and evaluation. These evaluations chose a **proxy task** for their user-centered goal, that we believe to fit the user-centered goals. For example, [10] attempt to increase trust but evaluate stability and fidelity, which inherently does not require human subjects, but also does not generally correlate with increased trust. However, [9] have shown that their approach increases trust, implying that [10], that uses the same explainability technique, also increases trust if stability and fidelity are acceptable.

The other publications [2,3,7] show a **mismatch**. This is due to a focus on other aspects, like the performance by [3], or the feasibility by [7]. This indicates that there is a gap between the evaluation and the desired effect on humans. A human-grounded evaluation would be more suitable to show user-centered goals. However, performing a user study requires more effort, which might not be reasonable. A functionally-grounded evaluation might be preferable, as user studies require more effort. But **meaningful proxy goals** are required to evaluate user-centered goals computationally. Therefore, future research should clearly define proxy metrics to evaluate user-centered goals without a full-fledged user study:

- Which metrics can be used to functionally evaluate explainability in SASs?
- What are the limits of functionally evaluating user-centered goals?

5.4 Explanations Neglect Needs of SASs

In this section, we discuss to what extent the presented approaches to explain SASs align with the external principle and internal principle that define a SAS according to Weyns [32].

The **external principle** states that a SAS reacts autonomously to changes and uncertainties in its environment, itself, and its goals [32].

Our results in Sect. 4.4 show that some works base their explanations on predefined human input. This means that these approaches can only provide explanations for circumstances that were previously known, suggesting that these approaches might not be able to deal with uncertainties. In contrast, the machine learning-based approaches seem to be better suited to deal with uncertainty. However, this depends on the data used for training and whether online machine learning is used to adjust the trained model at runtime. Additionally, our results in Sect. 4.7 show that the works included in our study usually focus on evaluating the quality or usefulness of explanations and ignore their ability to handle uncertainty. Most evaluations rely on simple exemplars where uncertainties remain trivial or isolated, with limited contextual dependencies. On such systems with lower uncertainty, simple explanations might be sufficient, threatening the transferability to larger systems with higher uncertainty. Thus, future research needs to consider uncertainty when evaluating explanations for SASs and evaluate the ability of existing approaches to handle uncertainty.

The **internal principle** states that a SAS consists of a managed system and a managing system. The managed system performs the system's intended tasks. The managing system acts as a feedback loop and handles the adaptation of the managed system [32].

Based on our results presented in Sects. 4.4 and 4.2, we see that current approaches focus on explaining the analysis and plan components of the managing system to explain the behavior of the managed system. Thus, these approaches are based on the assumption that it is sufficient to explain parts of the managing system and neglect that a SAS consists of multiple parts. Future research needs to investigate whether explanations benefit from including insights into other components of a SAS, such as the monitoring or execution component of the managing system.

Based on our discussion, the following two research questions emerge for future research directions:

- How to construct explanations that deal with uncertainty?
- Do addressees benefit from explanations including the monitoring and execution components?

6   Conclusion

By conducting a systematic literature review, we created an overview over the current state of research concerning explainability of SASs. The small amount of publications found show that this still is a niche area of research. Nonetheless, the selected publications demonstrate a great amount of diversity. Not only do they employ very different approaches, they also focus on different aspects of this topic.

Our discussion revealed several further research directions. Explanations should provide actionable insights, and should be tailored to the human addressee. User studies should be conducted to find metrics and measurable objectives to analyze explainability in SASs, enabling functionally-grounded evaluations. Finally, explanations should have a greater focus on the uncertainty condition of SASs.

Acknowledgment. This work was partially funded by the Deutsche Forschungsgemeinschaft (DFG, German Research Foundation) - 453895475, and, as part of Germany's Excellence Strategy - EXC 2050/1 -, Project ID 390696704 - Cluster of Excellence "Centre for Tactile Internet with Human-in-the-Loop" (CeTI) of Technische Universität Dresden, by the Wallenberg AI, Autonomous Systems and Software Program (WASP) funded by the Knut and Alice Wallenberg Foundation.

Disclosure of interests. The authors have no competing interests to declare that are relevant to the content of this article.

References

1. Wohlrab, R., Cámara, J., Garlan, D., Schmerl, B.: Explaining quality attribute tradeoffs in automated planning for self-adaptive systems. J. Syst. Softw. **198**, 111538 (2023). https://doi.org/10.1016/j.jss.2022.111538
2. Li, N., Adepu, S., Kang, E., Garlan, D.: Explanations for human-on-the-loop: a probabilistic model checking approach. In: Proceedings of SEAMS '20, pp. 181–187 (2020). https://doi.org/10.1145/3387939.3391592
3. Bencomo, N., Welsh, K., Sawyer, P., Whittle, J.: Self-explanation in adaptive systems. In: 2012 IEEE 17th International Conference on Engineering of Complex Computer Systems, pp. 157–166 (2012). https://doi.org/10.1109/ICECCS20050.2012.6299211
4. Agrawal, A., Cleland-Huang, J.: Explaining autonomous decisions in swarms of human-on-the-loop small unmanned aerial systems. In: Proceedings of the AAAI Conference on Human Computation and Crowdsourcing, vol.9, no. 1, pp. 15–26 (2021). https://doi.org/10.1609/hcomp.v9i1.18936
5. Li, N., Cámara, J., Garlan, D., Schmerl, B.: Reasoning about when to provide explanation for human-involved self-adaptive systems. In: 2020 IEEE International Conference on Autonomic Computing and Self-Organizing Systems (ACSOS), pp. 195–204 (2020). https://doi.org/10.1109/ACSOS49614.2020.00042
6. Alharbi, M.N., Huang, S., Garlan, D.: A probabilistic model for effective explainability based on personality traits. In: Software Architecture, pp. 205–225. Springer, Cham (2022). https://doi.org/10.1007/978-3-031-15116-3_10
7. Parra-Ullauri, J.M., García-Domínguez, A., Bencomo, N.: From a series of (un)fortunate events to global explainability of runtime model-based self-adaptive systems. In: Proceedings of ACM/IEEE MODELS-C 2021, pp. 807–816 (2021). https://doi.org/10.1109/MODELS-C53483.2021.00127
8. Diallo, A.B., Nakagawa, H., Tsuchiya, T.: Adaptation space reduction using an explainable framework. In: Proceedings of IEEE COMPSAC 2021, pp. 1653–1660 (2021). https://doi.org/10.1109/COMPSAC51774.2021.00247
9. Metzger, A., Laufer, J., Feit, F., Pohl, K.: A user study on explainable online reinforcement learning for adaptive systems. ACM Trans. Auton. Adapt. Syst. **19**(3) (2024). https://doi.org/10.1145/3666005

10. Metzger, A., Bartel, J., Laufer, J.: An ai chatbot for explaining deep reinforcement learning decisions of service-oriented systems. In: Service-Oriented Computing, pp. 323–338. Springer, Heidelberg (2023). https://doi.org/10.1007/978-3-031-48421-6_22

11. Kim, J., et al.: Toward explainable and advisable model for self-driving cars. Appl. AI Lett. **2**(4), e56 (2021). https://doi.org/10.1002/ail2.56

12. Milliez, G., Lallement, R., Fiore, M., Alami, R.: Using human knowledge awareness to adapt collaborative plan generation, explanation and monitoring. In: Proceedings of HRI '16, pp. 43–50 (2016). https://doi.org/10.1109/HRI.2016.7451732

13. Ampatzoglou, A., Bibi, S., Avgeriou, P., Verbeek, M., Chatzigeorgiou, A.: Identifying, categorizing and mitigating threats to validity in software engineering secondary studies. Inf. Softw. Technol. **106**, 201–230 (2019). https://doi.org/10.1016/j.infsof.2018.10.006

14. Brambilla, M., Cabot, J., Wimmer, M.: Model-driven software engineering in practice. Morgan & Claypool Publishers (2017). https://doi.org/10.1007/978-3-031-02549-5

15. Brdnik, S., Sumak, B.: Current trends, challenges and techniques in xai field: a tertiary study. In: Proceedings of 47th MIPRO, pp. 2032–2038. IEEE (2024). https://doi.org/10.1109/MIPRO60963.2024.10569528

16. Chazette, L., Klös, V., Herzog, F., Schneider, K.: Requirements on explanations: a quality framework for explainability. In: 2022 IEEE 30th International Requirements Engineering Conference (RE), pp. 140–152. IEEE (2022). https://doi.org/10.1109/RE54965.2022.00019

17. Chen, T., Bahsoon, R., Yao, X.: A survey and taxonomy of self-aware and self-adaptive cloud autoscaling systems. ACM Comput. Surv. **51**(3) (2018). https://doi.org/10.1145/3190507

18. Doshi-Velez, F., Kim, B.: Towards a rigorous science of interpretable machine learning. arXiv preprint arXiv:1702.08608 (2017). https://doi.org/10.48550/arXiv.1702.08608

19. Feit, F., Metzger, A., Pohl, K.: Explaining online reinforcement learning decisions of self-adaptive systems. In: Proceedings of IEEE ACSOS 2022, pp. 51–60 (2022). https://doi.org/10.1109/ACSOS55765.2022.00023

20. Juozapaitis, Z., Koul, A., Fern, A., Erwig, M., Doshi-Velez, F.: Explainable reinforcement learning via reward decomposition. In: IJCAI/ECAI Workshop on explainable artificial intelligence (2019)

21. Keele, S., et al.: Guidelines for performing systematic literature reviews in software engineering. Technical report, ver. 2.3 ebse technical report. ebse (2007)

22. Kephart, J.O., Chess, D.M.: The vision of autonomic computing. Computer **36**(1), 41–50 (2003). https://doi.org/10.1109/MC.2003.1160055

23. Kitchenham, B., Madeyski, L., Budgen, D.: Segress: software engineering guidelines for reporting secondary studies. IEEE Trans. Softw. Eng. **49**(3), 1273–1298 (2022). https://doi.org/10.1109/TSE.2022.3174092

24. Moreno, G.A., Schmerl, B., Garlan, D.: Swim: an exemplar for evaluation and comparison of self-adaptation approaches for web applications. In: Proceedings of 13th SEAMS, pp. 137–143 (2018). https://doi.org/10.1145/3194133.3194163

25. van Mourik, F., Jutte, A., Berendse, S.E., Bukhsh, F.A., Ahmed, F.: Tertiary review on explainable artificial intelligence: where do we stand? Mach. Learn. Knowl. Extr. **6**(3), 1997–2017 (2024). https://doi.org/10.3390/MAKE6030098

26. Petrovska, A., Kugele, S., Hutzelmann, T., Beffart, T., Bergemann, S., Pretschner, A.: Defining adaptivity and logical architecture for engineering (smart) self-

adaptive cyber-physical systems. Inf. Softw. Technol. **147**, 106866 (2022). https://doi.org/10.1016/j.infsof.2022.106866

27. Sado, F., Loo, C.K., Liew, W.S., Kerzel, M., Wermter, S.: Explainable goal-driven agents and robots - a comprehensive review. ACM Comput. Surv. **55**(10) (2023). https://doi.org/10.1145/3564240

28. Sequeira, P., Gervasio, M.: Interestingness elements for explainable reinforcement learning: understanding agents' capabilities and limitations. Artif. Intell. **288**, 103367 (2020). https://doi.org/10.1016/j.artint.2020.103367

29. Sobrín-Hidalgo, D., Guerrero-Higueras, Á.M., Matellán-Olivera, V.: Generating explanations for autonomous robots: a systematic review. IEEE Access **13**, 20413–20426 (2025). https://doi.org/10.1109/ACCESS.2025.3535097

30. Van Landuyt, D., Halasz, D., Verreydt, S., Weyns, D.: Towards understanding trust in self-adaptive systems. In: Proceedings of 19th International Symposium Software Engineering for Adaptive & Self-Managing Systems (SEAMS 2024), pp. 207–213 (2024). https://doi.org/10.1145/3643915.3644100

31. Vouros, G.A.: Explainable deep reinforcement learning: state of the art and challenges. ACM Comput. Surv. **55**(5) (2022). https://doi.org/10.1145/3527448

32. Weyns, D.: An Introduction to Self-Adaptive Systems: A Contemporary Software Engineering Perspective. John Wiley & Sons, Hoboken (2020). https://doi.org/10.1002/9781119574910

33. Yu, E.: Towards modelling and reasoning support for early-phase requirements engineering. In: Proceedings of ISRE '97: 3rd IEEE International Symposium on Requirements Engineering, pp. 226–235 (1997). https://doi.org/10.1109/ISRE.1997.566873

AI for Better UX in Computer-Aided Engineering: Is Academia Catching Up with Industry Demands? A Multivocal Literature Review

Choro Ulan Uulu[1]([✉]) [iD], Mikhail Kulyabin[1] [iD], Layan Etaiwi[1] [iD],
Nuno Miguel Martins Pacheco[1] [iD], Jan Joosten[1] [iD], Kerstin Röse[1], Filippos Petridis[1],
Jan Bosch[2,3] [iD], and Helena Holmström Olsson[4] [iD]

[1] Siemens AG, Munich, Germany
choro.ulan-uulu@siemens.com
[2] Department of Computer Science and Engineering, Chalmers University of
Technology,Gothenburg, Sweden
j.bosch1@tue.nl
[3] Department of Mathematics and Computer Science, Eindhoven University of Technology,
Eindhoven, Netherlands
[4] Department of Computer Science and Media Technology, Malmö University, Malmö, Sweden
helena.holmstrom.olsson@mau.se

Abstract. Computer-Aided Engineering (CAE) enables simulation experts to optimize complex models, but faces challenges in user experience (UX) that limit efficiency and accessibility. While artificial intelligence (AI) has demonstrated potential to enhance CAE processes, research integrating these fields with a focus on UX remains fragmented. This paper presents a multivocal literature review (MLR) examining how AI enhances UX in CAE software across both academic research and industry implementations. Our analysis reveals significant gaps between academic explorations and industry applications, with companies actively implementing LLMs, adaptive UIs, and recommender systems while academic research focuses primarily on technical capabilities without UX validation. Key findings demonstrate opportunities in AI-powered guidance, adaptive interfaces, and workflow automation that remain underexplored in current research. By mapping the intersection of these domains, this study provides a foundation for future work to address the identified research gaps and advance the integration of AI to improve CAE user experience.

Keywords: Computer-aided engineering · artificial intelligence · user experience · multi vocal literature review · systematic literature review · grey literature review

1 Introduction

Computer-aided engineering (CAE) software employs mathematical models to predict system behavior across engineering domains [15], enabling virtual testing that reduces costs and accelerates development [16]. These tools have become essential in industries

D. Taibi and D. Smite (Eds.): SEAA 2025, LNCS 16082, pp. 298–312, 2026.
https://doi.org/10.1007/978-3-032-04200-2_20

from aerospace to automotive, where engineers simulate everything from aerodynamics to manufacturing quality [34].

Despite their value, simulation tools present significant usability challenges. User experience (UX), defined by [28] as "A person's perceptions and responses resulting from the use and/or anticipated use of a product, system or service", is critical for the effective use of these tools. In the CAE context, effective UX enables engineers to perform complex simulation tasks—such as geometry preparation, mesh generation, physics setup, and results interpretation—with minimal friction, cognitive load, and potential for error. However, many CAE tools struggle in this regard: engineers must often create precise geometric models, accurately specify numerous parameters, and possess extensive domain knowledge—with incorrect settings potentially wasting hours of computation time [15]. These UX challenges limit adoption and effective utilization of powerful simulation capabilities. Artificial intelligence (AI) is transforming simulation workflows through several key interventions [15]. Large language models like AnsysGPT [13] provide around-the-clock technical guidance to engineers, while Siemens' Industrial Copilot [1] enhances interface intuitiveness and reduces cognitive load. Such tools address critical UX barriers by making complex systems more accessible. Beyond assistance, AI accelerates simulation through neural networks trained on previous results, enabling non-specialists to evaluate designs within minutes rather than hours. Ansys SimAI exemplifies this approach, allowing more design alternatives to be tested across development phases [5]. This democratization of simulation capability represents a major UX advancement. Despite AI's demonstrated potential to alleviate CAE's significant UX challenges, a clear, synthesized understanding of how these advancements are currently being implemented and validated—both in academic research and industry practice—is lacking. It remains unclear whether academic explorations align with industry needs, which AI-driven UX enhancements are gaining traction, and what specific research gaps hinder the translation of potential into widespread, effective application. Addressing this knowledge gap is crucial for guiding future research and development efforts aimed at fully leveraging AI to improve CAE user experience.

This paper contributes by: (i) systematically analyzing AI advancements impacting CAE software UX; (ii) identifying gaps between academic research and industry implementation; and (iii) mapping underexplored areas requiring further investigation. To achieve these contributions, this study employs a Multivocal Literature Review (MLR) as its primary methodology. This approach is chosen as it allows for the integration of insights from diverse sources, specifically utilizing a component systematic literature review (SLR) of academic research alongside a component Grey literature review (GLR) of industry practices. Adopting the MLR framework is crucial because, while previous literature has examined CAE and AI integration [15], it often lacks rigorous methodology, comprehensive market analysis, or a specific focus on user experience factors. The MLR overcomes these limitations by systematically analyzing and synthesizing both academic and industry perspectives, providing robust and comprehensive insights into AI-enhanced CAE user experience within this rapidly evolving field.

2 Methodology

This study employed a MLR methodology to investigate the integration of AI for enhancing UX in CAE software and drawing insights from both academic and industry sources. The MLR consists of two complementary components: a SLR examining scholarly research and a GLR analyzing market solutions and industry practices.

A. Research Question (RQ). Bridging the gap between academic research and market solutions requires a well-structured research question that clearly defines the scope of investigation. To achieve this systematically, we applied the PICOC framework [30] during question formulation. This framework helps define the key elements Population, Intervention, Comparison, Outcome, and Context ensuring clarity and focus, an approach suitable within software engineering contexts [20].

RQ: How is AI implemented in CAE software to enhance user experience, and what scientific research approaches remain to be translated into market solutions?

B. Search Strategy. *1) SLR Search:* Based on its coverage and relevance for the topic of AI in CAE software for better UX, we chose *Google Scholar* to find articles [40]. The selected time frame spans from 2010 to March 13th, 2025. This selection ensures a manageable scope for the review process. The study applied the following search string:

("CAE software" OR "engineering simulation") AND ("AI integration" OR "machine learning") AND ("UX" OR "user experience") AND ("industry case study" OR "implementation" OR "adoption challenges")

2) GLR Search: The GLR search strategy adhered to guidelines from [15]. Key companies at the intersection of CAE, Artificial Intelligence (AI), and UX were initially identified via Google. Their websites were subsequently reviewed for relevant literature. Finally, a broad keyword search was conducted until theoretical saturation was achieved [15].

C. Inclusion and Exclusion Criteria. This study formulated the inclusion and exclusion criteria for the SLR part of the MLR based on [20]. Table 1 lists these criteria.

Table 1. Inclusion/exclusion criteria and application results

ID	Criterion		Absence	Exclusions
Note: Application of inclusion criteria resulted in 14 papers for quality assessment				
IC1	Publication date within defined time frame		*EC1*	0
IC2	Primary study (not secondary/tertiary)		*EC2*	38
IC3	Peer-reviewed publication (not GL, blog posts, PhD Thesis, preprints)	*EC3*	57
IC4	Published in English		*EC4*	1
IC5	Not a duplicate of another included study		*EC5*	0
IC6	Explicitly discusses AI integration within CAE software environments		*EC6*	117
IC7	Addresses UX in AI-integrated CAE software OR implies enhanced UX from AI integration	*EC7*	1

For GLR: *(i) Authority of the producer.* Does the author have expertise in the area? (e.g., job title principal software engineer). *(ii) Novelty.* Does it enrich or add something unique to the market? Does it strengthen or refute a current position?

D. Quality Assessment. The 14 selected SLR papers underwent quality assessment (QA) using criteria from [21] with a Likert scale [23]; papers scoring below 60% were excluded. To evaluate the performance of an LLM on this specific QA task, a sequential assessment and comparison process was followed.

First, the QA criteria were provided to the LLM (Claude 3.7). The 14 papers were then uploaded, and the LLM was prompted to assess each paper according to these criteria, generating scores and text-based justifications. Subsequently, the researchers performed an independent manual assessment of the same 14 papers using the identical criteria. Finally, the LLM-generated scores and justifications were compared against the results of the manual assessment. The manual assessment served as the definitive benchmark for accuracy. Final inclusion decisions, based on the 60% quality threshold, were made solely based on the manual assessment scores. Table 2 summarizes the results from both methods; nine papers were included based on the manual evaluation.

Table 2. Number of Studies per Quality Percentile Range

Assessment Method	0–60%	60–70%	70–80%	80–90%	90–100%
Claude 3.7 Assessment	6	3	3	1	1
Manual Assessment	5	3	3	0	3

This comparison revealed crucial inaccuracies in the LLM's assessment compared to the manual benchmark. Our evaluation indicates that while LLMs may aid screening, manual assessment remains essential for ensuring the rigor required in systematic reviews.

E. Data Extraction. Publication details, research field, methods, and outcomes were extracted for the SLR following [14]. The search after quality assessment resulted in 9 papers. The data from those papers was extracted manually. The GLR examination focused on: 1) materials from CAE software manufacturers, 2) identified AI applications enhancing UX in CAE, and 3) results obtained through broad Google searches (Fig. 1).

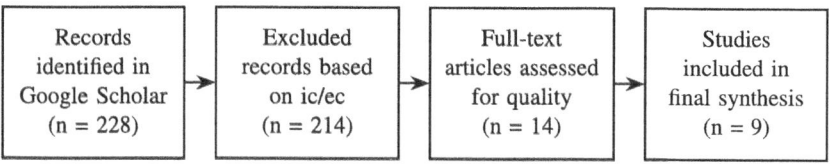

Fig. 1. PRISMA Flow Diagram of SLR Selection Process

Table 3. AI Methods in CAE for Enhanced User Experience: Systematic Literature Review

Classification	AI technique	Paper Title (abbreviated)	Year
Workflow Automation & Efficiency	Conformal mapping	MeshLink: A surface structured mesh generation framework to facilitate automated data linkage	2024
	Procedural Gen., ANN	Enhancing 3D Printing with Procedural Generation and STL Formatting Using Python	2024
Simulation Accel. & Optimization	RL (mPPO, mHPPO)	RL approach with masked agents for chemical process design	2024
	PINN, DL	Physics-Informed DL for cyclone separators	2021
Generative Design & Space Expl.	No direct examples in primary studies		
User Experience	No direct examples in primary studies		
Data-Driven Analysis	ML	Synthetic data generation for autonomous machinery	2023
System-Level Integration	KB (OWL), MAS	OWL ontologies for mixed-reality HRC assembly	2023
	DT, Bayesian Opt.	Nominal digital twin for product design	2023
	DL, GANs	Advanced HCI in digital twins	2023
Manufacturing & QC	ML, DL, Image	ML-Enabled Prediction of 3D-Printed Microneedles	2022
Core AI Research	PINN, RL, DL	Papers listed in categories above	

F. Data Analysis and Synthesis. A qualitative synthesis, suitable for descriptive software reviews [9], was applied. Reciprocal analysis [27] compared SLR and GLR findings to summarize gaps, complemented by descriptive synthesis.

3   Results

This section presents findings from the Multivocal Literature Review (MLR) on AI for enhancing CAE UX, synthesizing Systematic Literature Review (SLR) and Grey Literature Review (GLR) insights. A crucial SLR finding is the lack of published empirical UX evaluation for proposed AI methods, despite frequent claims of benefit. Industry practices, identified via GLR focused on market leaders (Siemens, Ansys, Altair, Dassault, PTC, Autodesk, Hexagon, Comsol) chosen for their influence, show a different emphasis: companies actively market AI features, explicitly articulating how specific capabilities (e.g., LLMs, automation) are designed to improve UX and providing the rationale. However, mirroring the academic gap in published proof, the reviewed grey literature generally lacks formal empirical validation results (like usability metrics) demonstrating these claimed outcomes, potentially due to competitive sensitivity. Growing academic publication volume since 2021 indicates increasing interest. Based on the combined MLR, key impact categories were identified; the following subsections detail SLR findings, GLR findings, and comparisons for each category, referencing summaries in Tables 3, 4, and 5.

Workflow Automation and Efficiency: AI helps to automate tedious tasks that take time and could be automated. This generally leads to better user experience.

Table 4. AI Methods in CAE for Enhanced User Experience: Grey Literature Review

Classification Group	Company	Product	Key AI techniques
Workflow Automation & Efficiency	BETA CAE	Retomo	AI Segmentation
	BETA CAE/Dassault	Ansa, Komvos	ML Toolkit
	ALTAIR	shapeAI	ML
	PTC	Codebeamer Copilot	Generative AI
Simulation Acceleration & Optimization	Ansys	Ansys Suite	Neural Networks
	Ansys	Ansys SimAI	Physics-Informed AI
	Neural Concept	NC Platform	3D Deep learning/LLM
	ALTAIR	PhysicsAI	Geometric Deep Learning
Generative Design & Design Space Expl.	Ansys	Ansys Discovery	HPC & Cloud AI
	Autodesk	Autodesk Forma	Generative AI
	Autodesk	Autodesk Fusion	Generative AI
	Neural Concept	NC	Deep Learning
	SimScale/Nvidia	PhysicsNeMo/SimScale	Physics AI/Eng. AI
	Hexagon	Odysee CAE	AI/ML
User Interaction & Guidance	Ansys	AnsysGPT	Generative AI
	Ansys	Ansys SimAI	NLP
	Autodesk	Autodesk Maya	NLP
	BETA CAE	AI assistant	LLM
	SIEMENS	Simcenter Amesim	LLMs
	SIEMENS	NX	Adaptive UI (ML/AI)
	SIEMENS	Simcenter Amesim	Recommender LLM
Data-Driven Analysis & Knowledge Management	Ansys	Ansys SimAI	Machine Learning
	Autodesk	Autodesk Fusion	Machine Learning
	Comsol	Comsol Multiphysics	LLMs/Supervised ML
System-Level Integration	SIEMENS	Simcenter	Multi-Agent Systems
	Nvidia	Omniverse Blueprint	AI
	Dassault	3D UNIV+RSES	Generative AI
Manufacturing & Quality control	—	—	—
Core AI Methodology Research	—	—	—

SLR Findings: [41] discusses the application of deep learning for generating surface structured meshes, automating a typically manual workflow step and potentially improving UX by reducing user effort. [22] demonstrates the use of procedural generation with AI to create CAD objects, suggesting enhanced UX through the generation of better models for 3D printing with less manual intervention.

GLR Findings: The GLR revealed five relevant industry examples in this area (Table 4). Beta CAE utilizes AI in its RETOMO product for improved segmentation of CT images, enhancing UX by enabling analysis of noisy data [37]. They also offer an AI assistant for documentation navigation and automated CAE model generation from CAD [36]. Altair's ShapeAI employs ML for identifying matching parts [3], PTC developed a Copi-

Table 5. Comparison of Grey vs. Academic Literature by Classified Focus Area

Classification Group	GL Emphasis	Academic literature Emphasis	Overlaps and Gaps
Workflow Automation & Efficiency	High focus: Automating CAD → CAE (BETA CAE), preprocessing (segmentation, part ID), integrating with related domains (software dev).	Present in preprocessing (MeshLink) and design automation (Procedural Generation)	**Overlap:** Automation of preprocessing (meshing/geometry prep) and design tasks. **Gap:** Commercial side addresses broader workflow integration (software dev, direct CAD → CAE automation). Academic focus on specific algorithms/frameworks
Simulation Acceleration & Optimization	Significant focus: Using Physics-Informed AI, Deep Learning/LLMs, NN for faster simulations/predictions or enhanced accuracy. Key value proposition.	Significant focus: Developing/validating methods (PINNs, RL for optimization), demonstrating speed-up/accuracy on specific problems. Often methodological	**Overlap:** Strong interest in Physics-Informed AI/PINNs, ML/DL for prediction/surrogates. **Gap:** Commercial side integrates into platforms; Academic side proves concepts/methods
Generative Design & Design Space Expl.	Strong focus: Using GenAI/AI/DL/ML for design creation/exploration, environmental analysis, optimization (Discovery, Forma, Fusion, NC, SimScale, Hexagon). Aided by ML toolkits (BETA CAE).	Less prominent in this specific academic sample, but exists in wider literature (e.g., topology optimization using AI). Often tied to optimization research	**Overlap:** Use of AI for design exploration/optimization. **Gap:** Commercial side heavily pushing user-facing GenAI tools & integrated toolkits for rapid exploration; Academic has developed algorithms for generating too but was excluded
User Experience & Guidance	High focus: NLP/LLM interfaces (support, interaction, search, code gen, replacing UI elements), Adaptive UI, Recommenders, NLP for scene interaction. Major area for UX improvement	While literature exists on general CAE UX (excluding AI), the reviewed SLR papers showed minimal focus on specifically evaluating the UX impact of AI integration in CAE	**Overlap:** Use of NLP/LLMs. **Gap:** Academic side has literature on LLMs for CAE but they do not mention UX. Commercial focus on LLMs/ML for diverse interaction tasks (support, search, UI replacement, coding, recommendations)
Data-Driven Analysis & Knowledge Management	Present: Predictive modeling (performance, parameters), analysis tools (InfoDrainage), inferring properties (COMSOL viscosity example using ML/LLM)	Present: Prediction (microneedles), synthetic data generation, knowledge representation (Ontology in HRC paper)	**Overlap:** No overlap, different directions. **Gap:** Academic side explores foundational aspects like synthetic data and formal knowledge, software manufacturers focus on inferring viscosity from droplet shape
System-Level Integration	Emerging focus: Digital Twins (Nvidia, Dassault), Agent systems (Siemens, COMSOL ASAs). Positioned as advanced/future capabilities	Clear focus: Developing frameworks/concepts (NDT), enabling interactions (HRC ontology), specific system components (HAR in DT)	**Overlap:** Interest in Digital Twins and Agent concepts. **Gap:** Academic side often develops theoretical foundations for digital twins or models for human robot collaboration
Manufacturing & Quality Control	Less direct focus in the CAE software itself (which is pre-manufacturing), though outputs feed into it	Present: Applying AI directly to manufacturing outcomes (microneedle quality)	**Gap:** This area is more prominent in manufacturing-specific research/tools than typical CAE UX focus, though linked via the design data
Core AI Methodology Research	Not applicable (focus is on application)	Implicit in several papers (PINN development, RL agents, DL architectures for HAR)	N/A - This is primarily the domain of academic research

lot for software development related to physical products [31], and Autodesk utilizes AI to interpret design markups and suggest context-aware actions [8]. These industry applications aim to augment user workflows, reduce redundant actions, and improve access to information, thereby enhancing overall user effectiveness.

Comparison and Gaps: A comparison between the GLR and SLR findings (summarized in Table 5) indicates an overlap in automating preprocessing and design tasks. However, commercial efforts focus more broadly on integrating AI into the end-to-end workflow (e.g., CAD-to-CAE automation), whereas the reviewed academic studies concentrate on developing specific algorithms for tasks like mesh generation and procedural generation. A gap exists in academic research concerning the integration aspects and holistic workflow automation prevalent in industry applications.

Simulation Acceleration and Optimization: AI optimizes parameters and simulation speed with physics, reducing user effort in software optimization.

SLR Findings: Two SLR papers addressed simulation acceleration and optimization. [33] utilized masking techniques with RL agents to enhance the design and optimization of chemical process flowsheets, implying a UX benefit through reduced waiting times. [32] demonstrated the use of physics-informed deep learning (PIDL) for predicting flow fields, claiming a significant UX impact through a model reported to be 200 times faster than traditional CFD simulations, thereby increasing productivity and user satisfaction.

GLR Findings: Industry sources indicate a strong focus on AI for simulation acceleration. Ansys developed SimAI, which facilitates AI-assisted user interaction and predicts design behaviors rapidly based on past simulations [5]. Ansys also published a case study on AI/ML integration for simulation optimization [6]. Neural Concept's NC Platform utilizes 3D deep learning and LLMs for accelerated design and simulation [11]. Altair's PhysicsAI employs geometric deep learning, enabling models to learn from geometry directly without extensive parametrization [2]. These tools aim to empower users with faster results and higher quality insights, enhancing the overall user experience.

Comparison and Gaps: A significant overlap exists between SLR and GLR in the application of AI (particularly PIDL/PINNs and deep learning) for prediction and surrogate modeling. However, a gap lies in the scope of prediction: SLR studies focused on specific phenomena (e.g., flow fields), whereas GLR examples target broader prediction of design behaviors. Furthermore, commercial entities focus on integrating these methods into comprehensive platforms, while academic studies often concentrate on methodological proof-of-concept.

Generative Design and Design Space Exploration and User Experience and Guidance: This combined category considers AI for automatically generating design variations (Generative Design), exploring the design space efficiently (Design Space Exploration), and enhancing user interaction through features like adaptive interfaces or intelligent guidance (User Experience and Guidance).

SLR Findings: The SLR yielded no primary studies specifically focused on Generative Design or AI-driven User Experience/Guidance within the defined scope. While papers generally alluded to improved user experience as an outcome of their proposed methods (e.g., through automation or speed), none provided empirical evaluations of UX or focused directly on AI for interaction design or guidance within CAE. This represents a notable gap in the reviewed academic literature.

GLR Findings: In contrast, there is substantial industry activity in these areas which is shown through GLR findings. Autodesk's Fusion enables real-time 3D model creation and design exploration [8]. Neural Concept's NC platform assists users in product design, claiming AI as a key factor for successful products and improved UX [10]. SimScale and Nvidia collaborated on an AI Foundation Model for rapid exploration of design optimizations [16]. Hexagon developed Odysee for design space exploration and process optimization [17], and Ansys offers Discovery for enhanced scalability and rapid design exploration [4]. For User Experience and Guidance, Ansys provides Ansys-GPT for real-time simulation support [13] and SimAI for interaction assistance. Beta CAE offers an AI assistant for documentation search and code generation [36]. Siemens is actively prototyping AI applications, including generative AI for UX enhancement across user groups [24] and recommender systems [19], aiming to reduce software complexity and improve accessibility.

Comparison and Gaps: A clear disparity exists. A strong industry focus on using AI (especially Generative AI and LLMs) for design creation, exploration, and direct user guidance (support, adaptive UI, recommendations) is demonstrated in GLR results. The academic literature reviewed in the SLR lacks studies addressing the UX implications or evaluations of such systems within CAE environments. While academic research on generative algorithms exists, its integration and UX assessment within CAE tools appear underexplored in the SLR sample. Similarly, the use of LLMs/ML for direct user interaction tasks is prominent in GLR but largely absent from the specific focus of the reviewed SLR papers concerning UX impact.

Data-Driven Analysis and Knowledge Management: AI enables predictions and knowledge management, allowing early parameter adjustments and reducing simulation iterations.

SLR Findings: One SLR paper by [35] highlighted that CAE data can be generated structured, enabling faster data acquisition for developers, which translates to higher productivity and reduced friction, implying a UX benefit.

GLR Findings: Industry examples include Ansys SimAI predicting design performance. Comsol Multiphysics applies ML for inferring material properties, such as viscosity from simulated droplet shapes, using inverse problem techniques [26].

Comparison and Gaps: When comparing the SLR and GLR results (Table 5), its clear that the reviewed academic work emphasized aspects like synthetic data generation for model training and the potential for structured data acquisition. In contrast, the GLR examples focus on applying ML techniques within tools to infer specific properties or predict performance based on existing or simulated data. A gap appears in translating foundational academic work on data generation and formal knowledge representation into practical, user-facing prediction tools within commercial CAE software.

System-Level Integration: AI improves interaction with digital twins and enables multi-agent systems for better UX.

SLR Findings: The SLR included three papers on system-level integration. [12] employed multi-agent systems for human-robot collaboration, suggesting improved UX through enhanced productivity. [42] demonstrated the feasibility and utility of specific digital twin types, potentially reducing user cognitive load by consolidating data. [25] presented advanced Human-Computer Interaction (HCI) techniques, including human pose recognition, to improve interaction within digital twin environments, making systems feel more intuitive.

GLR Findings: Industry efforts focus on integrated platforms. Siemens is developing multi-agent integration within Simcenter Studio [18]. Nvidia's Omniverse Blueprint facilitates real-time CAE digital twins connected with commercial solvers [29]. Dassault integrates generative AI into its virtual twin platform ("3D UNIV+RSES") [39]. These initiatives aim to provide users with more comprehensive, interactive, and data-rich system representations.

Comparison and Gaps: Substantial literature exists in both SLR and GLR concerning AI agents and digital twins. A key difference lies in focus: the academic side often develops theoretical foundations or specific interaction models (e.g., for HRC or specific DT components). Industry concentrates on implementing these concepts within integrated, commercially-oriented platforms. The gap involves bridging foundational academic work with the practical implementation and UX considerations of interacting with these complex, integrated industrial systems.

Manufacturing and Quality Control: AI automates quality assessment of manufactured parts, streamlining the workflow.

SLR Findings: [34] demonstrated the prediction of 3D-printed microneedle quality attributes (e.g., base diameter, height) using deep learning applied to design features. This represents a potential UX improvement by automating a quality control step.

GLR Findings: Autodesk documentation reflects the use of software for predicting manufacturability, integrating CAE with manufacturing considerations [7]. However, specific GLR examples detailing AI integration within CAE for manufacturing quality control were less prominent compared to other categories.

Comparison and Gaps: While manufacturers acknowledge the link between CAE and manufacturing, the academic side provided a specific example of AI predicting quality from design data. The GLR suggests less direct integration of AI for QC within the core CAE UX workflow itself, possibly residing in downstream manufacturing tools. A potential gap exists in tightly coupling AI-driven manufacturability and QC predictions directly into the CAE interface for immediate user feedback during the design phase.

Core AI Methodology Research: Fundamental AI development using engineering problems as test cases to advance user experience.

SLR Findings: Several SLR papers, including those by [32] on PIDL, [33] on RL agents, and [34] on ML for prediction, inherently contribute to this category by developing or applying advanced AI methods within a CAE context.

GLR Findings: The GLR does not typically reflect fundamental AI methodology research, as the focus of commercial software manufacturers is primarily on applying established or adapted AI techniques to deliver user value rather than publishing novel AI methods.

Comparison and Gaps: The comparison highlights the distinct roles: academia focuses on advancing AI methodologies, often validated using CAE problems, while industry concentrates on the application and integration of these methods. GLR empha-sizes applicability and proven solutions, potentially hesitant to adopt untested novel AI approaches in the conservative CAE field. The primary "gap" is the inherent translation challenge in moving cutting-edge academic AI research into robust, scalable commer-cial software.

Based on this comprehensive review, considerable interest exists in leveraging AI to improve the user experience of CAE software. However, significant disparities remain between the focus of academic research and industry implementation. Notably, the eval-uation of UX impacts through established metrics (e.g., usability evaluations, task com-pletion times, adoption rates) appears limited in the reviewed academic literature. Sev-eral factors might explain this discrepancy: the rapid pace of software development, resource limitations hindering rigorous academic UX studies, and competitive sensitiv-ity discouraging the publication of internal industry UX research.

3.1 Mapping Underexplored Areas Requiring Further Investigation

This MLR has identified significant gaps between current industry applications and aca-demic research concerning AI for enhancing UX in CAE. Specifically, the review high-lighted areas where industry utilizes AI (e.g., LLM-based guidance, adaptive interfaces) that lack corresponding rigorous academic investigation or UX validation, alongside foundational academic work not yet fully translated into widespread practice (Sect. 3 and Table 5).

To explore how these identified gaps might be addressed and to map potential future directions, this section leverages findings from broader AI and UX research. Instead of conducting a separate, exhaustive literature search across the vast AI field, a highly relevant systematic literature review by Stige et al. [38] was utilized as a proxy. This peer-reviewed SLR details how AI is leveraged across various stages of the general UX design process (based on 46 research articles).

While not focused specifically on CAE, the AI techniques and UX design princi-ples examined in [38] are often domain-agnostic. Core UX stages like "Understand the context of use," "Specify user requirements," and "Produce design solutions" are uni-versally applicable. AI capabilities such as automation, recommendation, and content generation identified by Stige et al. can potentially be transferred to the specific context of CAE UX, even if implementation details differ. Therefore, [38] provides a robust, systematically derived inventory of established and emerging AI methods relevant to enhancing UX, offering potential solutions for the gaps observed in the current CAE-focused AI literature (both SLR and GLR).

The following analysis involves extracting key AI applications identified as relevant to general UX design in the synthesis by Stige et al. [38]. Our contribution then lies in

Table 6. Potential AI Applications for Enhanced CAE UX, Informed by Methods Identified in Broader AI/UX Research [38]

Classification Group	Potential AI method	Brief description	Potential relevance to CAE UX	Original phase
Workflow Automation & Efficiency	Sketch-to-Wireframe/Code Generation	Using ML/DNNs to convert hand-drawn sketches or low-fidelity mock-ups into digital wireframes or basic UI code	Could potentially speed up early UI/workflow ideation for new CAE features or custom interfaces based on quick sketches from UX designers or even engineers. Its easier to draw a sketch and derive 3D CAD from it and turn it into CAE, then from plain text.	Solution Design/ Development
	Code/GUI Generation from Visual Mockups	Using DL/Computer Vision to reverse engineer UI screenshots or high-fidelity mockups into functional code or GUI skeletons	Although perhaps less common for complex CAE, could potentially automate parts of UI implementation if visual design mockups are created, bridging the design-development gap	Development
Simulation Acceleration & Optimization	Cognitive Modeling/Behavior Simulation	Using AI based on cognitive architectures (like ACT-R) to simulate human behavior and predict performance for different UI designs	Could offer rapid, quantitative feedback on the usability of different CAE workflow designs or UI layouts by simulating how an engineer might interact with them, replacing some testing	Design Evaluation
User Interaction & Guidance	Design Pattern Recommendation	Using supervised ML to recommend appropriate interaction design patterns based on specified design-level requirements.	Could guide CAE developers/designers in selecting proven UI patterns for complex interactions (e.g., managing large parameter sets, visualizing multi-physics results, mesh setup).	Solution Design
	AI for Emotional Design Aspects	Considering AI's role within a design-oriented approach focused on emotional user experience	Could guide the design of interfaces that reduce stress or enhance confidence for engineers using complex tools	Solution Design
Data-Driven Analysis & Knowledge Management	Automated Persona Generation	Using ML and analytics data (e.g., online behavior) to automatically create user personas (AGP)	Could help CAE tool designers better understand different types of engineers using their software, potentially informing UI/feature design through data analysis	Understanding Context of Use
	Predicting Specific Usability Metrics	Using ML/DL to model and predict specific usability aspects like element tappability or interaction effort	Could be adapted to analyze and predict usability challenges in dense CAE interfaces (e.g., discoverability of functions, perceived complexity) based on learned models	Design Evaluation

analyzing the potential relevance and applicability of these broader AI methods specifically to the context of CAE UX, mapping them against the underexplored areas and needs identified in our MLR findings. This provides concrete opportunities for AI/UX experts and researchers to advance the field. The results of this mapping are presented in Table 6.

4   Conclusion

This work presented a systematic multivocal literature review (MLR) examining both academic research and grey literature (GL) on the use of Artificial Intelligence (AI) for enhancing User Experience (UX) in Computer-Aided Engineering (CAE) software.

Key findings reveal a significant disparity between academic focus and industry practice. Primarily, there is a notable lack of empirical UX evaluation in academic studies proposing AI methods for CAE, despite frequent author claims of UX improvement.

Conversely, industry GL indicates active implementation of AI (especially Large Language Models (LLMs) and adaptive UI) aimed directly at enhancing UX, but this work often lacks formal publication detailing methodology or rigorous evaluation, potentially due to the competitive value of such research. Another finding is the limited academic focus on the specific UX implications of generative AI within the CAE manufacturing context. The comparison highlighted these divergences in focus and validation approaches between the two spheres.

The key contributions of this paper are threefold: (i) it provides the first comprehensive MLR specifically analyzing the intersection of AI, UX, and CAE from both academic and industry perspectives; (ii) it systematically identifies and categorizes current applications and research efforts, clearly articulating the critical gaps, particularly the deficit in empirical UX validation within academic publications; and (iii) it proposes concrete avenues for future research by leveraging broader AI/UX research [38] to identify potential AI methods applicable to improving CAE UX (as detailed in Table 6).

By mapping these potential methods against the identified gaps, this work suggests pathways to advance user-centric CAE tool development and bridge the gap between academic potential and industry needs.

4.1 Limitations and Future Work

The search strategy for this review intentionally focused on "CAE AI UX" and publications between 2010 and March 2025 for focused analysis within practical constraints. We acknowledge significant contributions from related areas like "interaction design" and "interface design," but a dedicated search incorporating these broader terms was beyond the current study's scope. Building upon the understanding gained from this review, future research will transition from analysis to creation, developing novel methods and potentially prototype solutions aimed at tangibly improving the user experience of AI capabilities within CAE software. This work will directly address the gaps and leverage opportunities identified herein.

Acknowledgments. The authors gratefully acknowledge the support provided by the Software Center. The authors also thank their colleagues and supervisors within Siemens for valuable discussions and feedback during this research.

References

1. AG, S.: Industrial copilot. https://www.siemens.com/global/en/products/automation/topic-areas/artificial-intelligence-in-industry/industrial-copilot.html. Accessed 26 Feb 2025
2. Altair. Altair physicsai for fast cae predictions using deep learning. https://altair.com/resource/altair-physicsai-for-fast-cae-predictions-using-deep-learning?utm_campaign=CO-Simulation&utm_source=eGuide&utm_medium=pdf&utm_content=eGuide-AI-for-Engineering-Your-Roadmap-to-Getting-Started. Accessed 09 Apr 2025
3. Altair. Automatic fea model build powered by shapeai. https://altair.com/resource/automatic-fea-model-build-powered-by-shapeai. Accessed 09 Apr 2025
4. Ansys. Ansys discovery. https://www.ansys.com/products/3d-design/ansys-discovery. Accessed 04 Apr 2025

5. Ansys. Ansys simai predict at the speed of ai. https://www.ansys.com/products/simai. Accessed 09 Apr 2025
6. Ansys. Artificial intelligence and machine learning applied in computer aided engineering. Accessed 09 Apr 2025
7. Autodesc. Data-driven ai manufacturing is smarter, safer, and more profitable. https://www.autodesk.com/solutions/ai-manufacturing. Accessed 04 Apr 2025
8. Autodesc. Introducing autodesk ai for design and make. https://adsknews.autodesk.com/en/pressrelease/introducing-autodesk-ai/. Accessed 09 Apr 2025
9. Brereton, P., Kitchenham, B.A., Budgen, D., Turner, M., Khalil, M.: Lessons from applying the systematic literature review process within the software engineering domain. J. Syst. Softw. **80**(4), 571–583 (2007).https://doi.org/10.1016/j.jss.2006.07.009 07.009
10. Concept, N.: Ai product design: Benefits and applications. https://www.neuralconcept.com/post/the-future-of-product-design-ais-impact-on-industries#link3. Accessed 03 Apr 2025
11. N. Concept. Set new industry standards with engineering intelligence. https://www.neuralconcept.com/. Accessed 03 Apr 2025
12. David, J., Coatanéa, E., Lobov, A.: Deploying owl ontologies for semantic mediation of mixed-reality interactions for human-robot collaborative assembly. J. Manuf. Syst. **70**, 359–381 (2023). https://doi.org/10.1016/j.jmsy.2023.07.013
13. Dawson, A.: Ansysgpt: Your virtual assistant for simulation queries. https://www.ansys.com/blog/ansysgpt-your-virtual-assistant-simulation-queries. Accessed 26 Feb 2025
14. Dybå, T., Dingsøyr, T.: Empirical studies of agile software development: a systematic review. Inf. Softw. Technol. **50**(9), 833–859 (2008). https://doi.org/10.1016/j.infsof.2008.01.006
15. Garousi, V., Felderer, M., Mäntylä, M.V.: Guidelines for including grey literature and conducting multivocal literature reviews in software engineering. Inf. Softw. Technol. **106**, 101–121 (2019). https://doi.org/10.1016/j.infsof.2018.09.006
16. Heiny, D.: Engineering the future: Launching the first ai foundation model for pump simulation with nvidia. https://www.simscale.com/blog/the-first-ai-foundation-model-for-pump-simulation-with-nvidia/. Accessed 03 Apr 2025
17. Hexagon. Odyssee. https://hexagon.com/products/odyssee. Accessed 03 Apr 2025
18. Kai Liu, A.C., Ghalamzan, C.: Agent studio: A multi-agent system for systems engineering. https://blogs.sw.siemens.com/art-of-the-possible/agent-studio-a-multi-agent-system-for-systems-engineering/#section_4. Accessed 03 Apr 2025
19. Kai Liu, D.B.: Lisa's journey: Embracing simcenter amesim recommender as a new simulation engineer. Accessed 03 Apr 2025
20. Kitchenham, B., Charters, S.: Guidelines for performing systematic literature reviews in software engineering, vol. 2, p. 01 (2007)
21. Kmet, L.M., Lee, R.C., Cook, L.S.: Standard quality assessment criteria for evaluating primary research papers from a variety of fields (2004)
22. Kopowski, J., Mreła, A., Mikołajewski, D., Rojek, I.: Enhancing 3d printing with procedural generation and stl formatting using python. Appl. Sci. **14**(16) (2024). https://doi.org/10.3390/app14167299
23. Likert, R.: A technique for the measurement of attitudes. Arch. Psychol. **22**(140) (1932)
24. Liu, K.: Imagine a world without toolbars or menus. https://blogs.sw.siemens.com/art-of-the-possible/imagine-a-world-without-toolbars-or-menus/. Accessed 03 Apr 2025
25. Lyu, Z., Wu, J., Chen, D., Gander, A.: Advanced Human–Computer Interaction Technology in Digital Twins, pp. 99–123 (2023). https://doi.org/10.1007/978-981-99-4303-67
26. Namy, P.: Using artificial intelligence (ai) within comsol multiphysics to create machine learning tools. Accessed 04 Apr 2025
27. Noblit, G.W., Hare, R.D.: Meta-ethnography: synthesizing qualitative studies (1988)

28. Normalizacyjny, P.P.K., Normalizacyjnych, P.P.K.N.W.W.: Ergonomics of Human-system Interaction - Part 210: Human-centred Design for Interactive Systems (ISO 9241-210:2010). Number Teil 210. Polski Komitet Normalizacyjny (2011)
29. Nvidia. Interactive computer-aided engineering simulations. https://www.nvidia.com/en-us/solutions/cae/. Accessed 04 Apr 2025
30. Petticrew, M., Roberts, H.: Systematic Reviews in the Social Sciences: A Practical Guide, vol. 11 (2006). https://doi.org/10.1002/9780470754887
31. PTC. Ptc partners with microsoft & volkswagen group to develop codebeamer copilot. https://www.ptc.com/en/news/2024/ptc-partners-microsoft-volkswagengroup-codebeamer-generative-ai-copilot. Accessed 09 Apr 2025
32. Queiroz, L., Santos, F., Oliveira, J., Souza, M.: Physics-informed deep learning to predict flow fields in cyclone separators. Dig. Chem. Eng. **1**, 100002 (2021). https://doi.org/10.1016/j.dche.2021.100002
33. Reynoso-Donzelli, S., Ricardez-Sandoval, L.A.: A reinforcement learning approach with masked agents for chemical process flowsheet design. AIChE J. **71**(1), e18584 (2025). https://doi.org/10.1002/aic.18584
34. Sarabi, M.R., Alseed, M.M., Karagoz, A.A., Tasoglu, S.: Machine learning-enabled prediction of 3d-printed microneedle features. Biosensors **12**(7), 491 (2022). https://doi.org/10.1002/aic.18584
35. Schuster, A., Hagmanns, R., Sonji, I., Löcklin, A., Petereit, J., Ebert, C., Weyrich, M.: Synthetic data generation for the continuous development and testing of autonomous construction machinery. at - Automatisierungstechnik **71**(11), 953–968 (2023). https://doi.org/10.1515/auto-2023-0026
36. Simulation Solutions, B.. Beta cae systems announces the release of the v25.0.0 of its software suite. https://www.beta-cae.com/news/20240731_announcement_suite_25.0.0.htm. Accessed 09 Apr 2025
37. Simulation Solutions, B.: Simulation enabling technologies: Introducing artificial intelligence in generating 3d models from ct scans. https://www.beta-cae.com/pdf/ai_in_retomo.pdf. Accessed 09 Apr 2025
38. Stige, A., Zamani, E., Mikalef, P., Zhu, Y.: Artificial intelligence (ai) for user experience (ux) design: a systematic literature review and future research agenda. Inf. Technol. People **37**, 08 (2023). https://doi.org/10.1108/ITP-07-2022-0519
39. Systems, D.: Dassault systèmes reveals "3d univ+rses" and related ai-based services. https://ml-eu.globenewswire.com/Resource/Download/10bebed8-577e-4199-b3b5-992237ae7ee5. Accessed 04 Apr 2025
40. Wohlin, C., Mendes, E., Felizardo, K.R., Kalinowski, M.: Guidelines for the search strategy to update systematic literature reviews in software engineering. Inf. Softw. Technol. **127**, 106366 (2020). https://doi.org/10.1016/j.infsof.2020.106366
41. Zhang, H., Li, H., Li, N.: Meshlink: a surface structured mesh generation framework to facilitate automated data linkage. Adv. Eng. Softw. **194**, 103661 (2024). https://doi.org/10.1016/j.advengsoft.2024.103661
42. Zhang, H., Li, R., Ding, G., Qin, S., Zheng, Q., He, X.: Nominal digital twin for new-generation product design. Int. J. Adv. Manuf. Technol. **128**(3–4), 1317–1335 (2023). https://doi.org/10.1007/s00170-023-11924-x

How have Ethics been Addressed in the Software Development Lifecycle? A Systematic Mapping Study

Otávio Santos Gomes[1], Gláucia Braga e Silva[1], Érica Ferreira de Souza[2(✉)],
Luciana Rebelo[3], Nandamudi L. Vijaykumar[4], and Gabriel Zoéga Fernandes[1]

[1] Federal University of Viçosa (UFV), Florestal, MG, Brazil
{otavio.s.gomes,glaucia,gabriel.z.fernandes}@ufv.br
[2] Federal University of Technology - Paraná (UTFPR), Cornélio Procópio, PR, Brazil
ericasouza@utfpr.edu.br
[3] Gran Sasso Science Institute (GSSI), L'Aquila, Italy
luciana.rebelo@gssi.it
[4] National Institute for Space Research (INPE), São José dos Campos, SP, Brazil
vijay.nl@inpe.br

Abstract. Context: In recent times, there has been increasing interest surrounding ethics within computer science. Ethical issues such as privacy, transparency, and fairness have surfaced, yet their integration into the software development lifecycle (SDLC) remains unclear. There is currently no comprehensive literature review that focuses more broadly on ethics within the SDLC. **Objective:** This paper elucidates the current state of the art of ethics within software development. It seeks to poke into usual ethical dilemmas and examine the stages of the SDLC where they are addressed. **Method:** Employs a Systematic Mapping Study (SMS) to evaluate research published across five databases to address four key research questions. **Results:** Our selection comprised 66 studies. Most studies (47%) concentrated on the software requirements phase within the SDLC. Over 80 distinct ethical issues were identified and organized into seven categories. **Conclusion:** The bulk of the selected studies focus on software requirements. While these studies articulate ethical concerns and transform them into requirements, they often fall short in proposing viable methods to integrate these requirements throughout the entire SDLC.

Keywords: Systematic mapping study · Software development lifecycle · Ethics

1 Introduction

Software systems are now deeply embedded in everyday life, making their societal impact increasingly evident and highlighting the need for ethical considerations throughout the entire software development lifecycle (SDLC), not just in specific

D. Taibi and D. Smite (Eds.): SEAA 2025, LNCS 16082, pp. 313–323, 2026.
https://doi.org/10.1007/978-3-032-04200-2_21

technologies like artificial intelligence. As Gotterbarn [9] notes, software engineering ethics concern the practical decisions engineers make that significantly affect others, with current examples such as biased facial recognition systems illustrating these consequences.

Our tertiary literature review revealed that few comprehensive studies address software ethics [8], and existing research rarely examines the integration of ethics across all development phases, exposing a lack of consensus and practical guidance. While concerns about ethical issues in software design are growing among researchers and affected individuals [7], there remains a need for consolidated reviews and actionable frameworks to effectively embed ethics into software engineering practice.

In this study, we conducted a Systematic Mapping Study (SMS) to elucidate the current state of ethics within the SDLC context. In this SMS, we seek to explore usual ethical dilemmas and examine the phases of the SDLC where they are addressed. Additionally, we evaluated the maturity of the existing literature on this topic.

The structure of this paper is as follows: Sect. 2 details the research method; Sect. 3 presents the results; Sects. 4 and 5 address threats to validity and related work, respectively; and Sect. 6 provides the conclusions.

2   Systematic Mapping Study (SMS)

This study follows the systematic mapping methodology of Kitchenham and Charters [12], structured into three phases: planning (protocol definition), conducting (study selection, quality assessment, and data extraction), and reporting (dissemination of results). To comprehensively analyze how ethics has been addressed in the SDLC, we formulated the following research questions: (RQ1) What are the main ethical issues discussed? (RQ2) Which phase of the SDLC do the studies address? (RQ3) What practical approaches are proposed to deal with ethical issues? and (RQ4) What are the main challenges encountered when addressing ethics?

The search string was iteratively developed to balance inclusivity and precision, combining ethics-related terms with software engineering process terms. We validated its effectiveness using a control group and refined it to minimize irrelevant results. Searches were conducted in the five most prominent computer science databases [6] (ACM Digital Library, IEEE Xplore, ScienceDirect, Scopus, and SpringerLink) to ensure comprehensive coverage.

A preliminary assessment with 28 studies and a Kappa test (coefficient 0.79) confirmed substantial inter-rater agreement and protocol reliability, according to the interpretation provided by Landis and Koch [13]. The search in December 2024 retrieved 2,520 studies; after duplicate removal and two screening phases (titles/abstracts and full-text), 66 studies were included. Figure 1 shows the selection process conducted in this SMS. Furthermore, the process, led by the first author with support from co-authors and regular meetings, is fully documented and available in the replication package at 10.5281/zenodo.15806641. Further clarification of the methodology and results exploration can also be found in this repository.

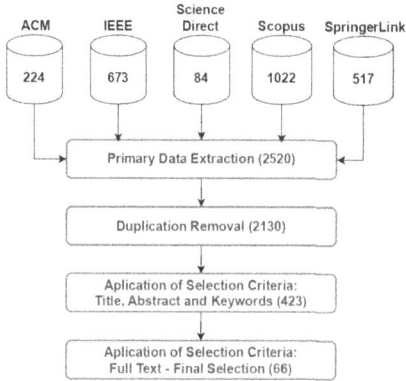

Fig. 1. Studies Selection Process

3   Results

An examination of the selected studies reveals that, although our search covered works up to December 2024, all included publications date from 2001 onward. There has been a notable increase in research addressing ethics in the SDLC since 2018, with the number of studies per year as follows: 1 in 2001, 1 in 2003, 1 in 2004, 1 in 2008, 1 in 2011, 1 in 2012, 1 in 2015, 2 in 2016, 1 in 2017, 3 in 2018, 4 in 2019, 11 in 2020, 7 in 2021, 11 in 2022, and 11 in 2023, and 9 in 2024 indicating a growing and sustained interest in ethical issues within the software engineering community in recent years.

Most studies were published in conferences, workshops, and symposiums (53 out of 66), with only 13 appearing in journals, reflecting the tendency in computer science for researchers to favor conference venues [11]. This pattern is particularly beneficial for our topic, as conference publications foster active discussion within the research community, which represents an important factor given the strong social relevance of ethics in software engineering.

We also analyzed the researchers' affiliations to identify possible geographical concentrations, as shown in Fig. 2, and found that most authors and first authors are based in Finland, the USA, and the Netherlands.

3.1   What are the Main Ethical Issues Discussed? (RQ1)

Using the open coding method [15], we analyzed the studies in two cycles: initially generating codes from the terms employed in the literature, and then grouping these codes into broader categories based on contextual similarity. This process resulted in seven categories of ethical issues (Table 1), which provide practical guidance for developers to consider relevant ethical aspects in various

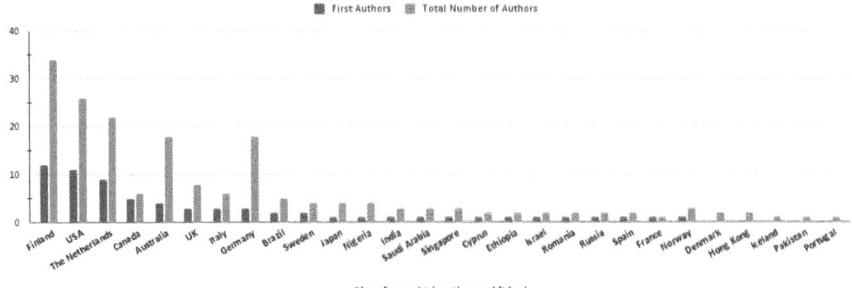

Fig. 2. Authors Affiliation Location

Table 1. Categorization of ethical issues

ID	Categories	Ethical Issues
EIC01	Data Issues	Bias, Data Governance, Data Protection, Encryption, Informed Consent, Lack of Data, Monetization, Openness, Privacy, User Data Collection, Data Quality
EIC02	Governance Issues	Authorship, Autonomy, Beneficence, Business Ethics, Commerce, Compliance, Confidentiality, Conflict of Interest, Context, Dependability, Fairness, Human Agency, Intellectual Property, Oversight, Regulatory Approaches, Responsibility, Trust, Trustworthiness
EIC03	Philosophical Issues	Axiology, Freedom, Self-Conception, Solidarity, Utility
EIC04	Professional Issues	Care, Competence, Professional Ethics, Work Ethics, Communication
EIC05	Social Issues	Access, Accessibility, Common Goods, Dignity, Diversity, Equality, Equity, Humanity, Inclusiveness, Individual Differences, Inequality, Justice, Non-Discrimination, Non-Maleficence, Participation, Plurality, Prevention of Harm, Quality of Life, Respect for Human Autonomy, Retention and Addiction, Social Justice, Sustainability, Unemployment, Welfare, Awareness, Cultural Sensitivity
EIC06	Technical Issues	Accountability, Accuracy, Anonymity, Comprehensibility, Consistency, Contestability, Explainability, Explicability, Integrity, Interpretability, Liability, Reliability, Safety, Security, Speech Issues, Technical Robustness, Traceability, Transparency, Usability
EIC07	Malicious Cases	Computer Abuse, Malicious Use

development contexts. While these categories offer a structured overview, they are not exhaustive, and developers should remain vigilant to additional ethical concerns that may arise.

Table 2 highlights the most frequently discussed ethical issues (cited in at least six studies), emphasizing the concerns most prevalent in software development literature. These issues, mainly categorized as Technical Issues (EIC06), are well-established in software engineering, particularly during the requirements phase as non-functional requirements. Notably, many studies focus on ethics within AI, which shapes the prominence of issues like Transparency, Explainability, and Autonomy. Identifying these concerns helps developers better understand and address the nuanced ethical challenges inherent in their work.

Table 2. Main Ethical Issues Observed

Ethical Issues	Category	Studies	Total
Privacy	EIC01	S6, S7, S11, S13, S14, S16, S17, S19, S22, S23, S24, S25, S33, S30, S31, S34, S39, S40, S41, S42, S43, S44, S51, S53, S59, S61, S66	27
Transparency	EIC06	S13, S14, S15, S16, S17, S18, S24, S25, S26, S30, S31, S34, S35, S37, S39, S40, S43, S45, S51, S54, S59	21
Fairness	EIC02	S3, S6, S7, S8, S9, S13, S15, S17, S23, S25, S26, S30, S40, S42, S43, S51, S54, S58, S59, S66	20
Accountability	EIC06	S13, S15, S16, S17, S19, S23, S25, S26, S30, S34, S37, S39, S40, S43, S45, S52, S59	17
Explainability	EIC06	S8, S19, S23, S25, S26, S30, S31, S40, S45, S54, S59	11
Safety	EIC06	S19, S23, S24, S26, S33, S30, S34, S39, S43, S59	10
Security	EIC06	S19, S24, S25, S26, S30, S34, S41, S53, S66	9
Autonomy	EIC02	S20, S30, S33, S42, S46, S51, S54	7
Sustainability	EIC05	S16, S19, S25, S26, S41, S51, S65	7
Non-Discrimination	EIC05	S7, S9, S17, S13, S14, S43, S58	7
Explicability	EIC06	S9, S19, S20, S43, S46, S54	6
Responsibility	EIC02	S14, S15, S25, S26, S37, S51	6

3.2   Which Phase of the Software Development Cycle does the Study Deal with? (RQ2)

In Table 3, we present the collected studies clustered according to the SWEBOK [4] division of the software lifecycle. Most studies focus on the requirements phase, with a significant number also addressing design. While some propose incorporating ethics beyond initial phases, practical guidance for coding and testing remains scarce. Additionally, several works discuss the SDLC in abstract terms without concrete implementation advice, and one study relates to ethics education, not fitting any specific SDLC phase. This distribution suggests that ethical considerations are often concentrated early in development, with later phases receiving less attention.

Table 3. Studies by software development phase

Phases	Studies	Total
Software Requirements	S3, S17, S18, S19, S20, S22, S24, S25, S26, S27, S29, S30, S31, S38, S34, S43, S45, S46, S47, S48, S50, S51, S53, S54, S57, S59, S60, S62, S64, S65, S66	31
Software Design	S10, S11, S12 S13, S14, S28, S29, S33, S34, S35, S36, S40, S42, S44, S45, S55, S56, S58, S59, S61	20
Software Process	S1, S2, S4, S5, S6, S8 S16, S21, S23, S32, S37, S41	12
Software Testing	S9, S15, S49, S52, S63	5
Software Construction	S13, S17	2
None	S7	1

3.3   What are the Practical Approaches to Deal with Ethical Issues? (RQ3)

While most studies focus on the requirements and design phases, some suggest broader methods, such as models, frameworks, or artifacts that can be integrated throughout development. However, these approaches are generally conceptual and rarely tested in practice, underscoring the need for more robust empirical studies. Table 4 summarizes the main proposals.

Notably, the most cited studies to date (S54) introduces a template and best practices for explainability in AI, while (S9) presents Z-Inspection®, a structured process for assessing AI trustworthiness across ethical, technical, and legal dimensions.

Table 4. Approaches to deal with ethics in the software lifecycle

SDLC Phase	Name/Description of the Approach Proposed	Studies
Requirements	Square of values model, a visual model for decision-making	S50
	AI ethics model to extract AI ethical risks	S39
	Ontology-based Requirements Engineering (ObRE)	S46, S57
	Ethical Guideline	S53
	Template for representing explainability requirements	S54
	Additional phase to requirements elicitation, an ethical analysis	S62
	Framework for capturing sustainability requirements	S65
Requirements/ Design	Focus group with software architects to better understand ethical aspects in architecture	S42
	Method for implementing ethical AI (ECCOLA)	S44, S47, S48
	Factorial survey experiments (FSE)	S45
Design	UML use case diagram adapted to state software purpose	S36
	AWOSE Method	S33
	Modeling of User Stories	S25, S64
	Codebook method	S40
	Fairness in Design Framework	S55
	Deck of game cards (Discrimination by Design)	S56
	FairBalance, fairness in ML software	S58
Process	SAFe agile elements adapted to embed human values in software	S41
	Ethical-Driven Software Development	S32
	Z-Inspection	S9
	A typology of metrics for monitoring ML systems	S63

3.4 What are the Main Challenges when Dealing with Ethics? (RQ4)

As summarized in Table 5, the predominant issues include the lack of established techniques, methods, and processes for implementing ethics across the lifecycle, particularly in practical contexts. Most studies highlight the need for validated approaches, especially beyond the requirements and design phases. Additional challenges involve inadequate strategies for addressing ethical concerns in design, mitigating cognitive bias, and validating ethical requirements during testing. Overall, the field remains largely theoretical, with significant gaps in practical application and guidance.

Table 5. Challenges when dealing with ethics

SLC Phase	Challenge to deal with ethics	No Studies
Requirements	Focus on non-functional requirements instead of functional ones	1
	Lack of a list of relevant ethical issues	1
	Inadequate elicitation of user needs	1
	Identification of ethical requirements	1
	Understanding ethical requirements	1
	Ethical assessments aligned with AI/ML regulatory context	1
	Trust in and trustworthiness of AI systems	1
	Determining and valuing ethical requirements in AI systems	1
Design	Defining strategies to avoid ethical problems	3
	Mitigating cognitive bias	2
	Defining the impact of design decisions	2
	Conciliating all ethical concerns	1
	Translating AI guidelines to practical design	1
	Lack of equalized odds when ground truth labels are not available	1
Testing	Validating/certifying ethical requirements implementation	2
	Validating that functionality satisfies the given ethical conditions	2
Process	Lack of techniques/processes/methods to implement ethics	18
	Lack of studies focusing on implementing ethics	5
	Lack of ethical deliberation in all phases of the lifecycle	1
	Defining what is considered morally good or acceptable	1

4   Threats to Validity

Potential threats to **construct validity** stem from keyword selection; to address this, we used broad terms across major databases and refined the search string through testing, focusing on requirements-related terms only when broader phase terms proved ineffective. **Selection bias** was minimized by applying strict inclusion and exclusion criteria, as well as ensuring substantial inter-rater agreement through kappa testing and regular author meetings. **Misclassification** was mitigated by collaborative review whenever study information was limited. **Conclusion validity** was strengthened by thorough author discussions and drawing only well-supported conclusions. Overall, these measures ensure that our mapping reliably represents empirical research on ethics in the SDLC.

5   Related Work

Only a limited number of secondary studies have focused on ethics in computer science. Most related works discussed in this section were identified from a tertiary literature review [8] that we conducted. Table 6 presents a comprehensive overview of the primary objectives of each study and differentiates them from our research. Other significant distinctions that were not explicitly mentioned include the time frame within which the studies were conducted, as well as the search strings tailored to the specific objectives of each study, developed based on the highlighted research objectives. Notably, our study uniquely focuses on the ethical considerations that cover the entire SDLC rather than confining itself to a particular area, such as AI, or focusing only on specific aspects of the SDLC.

Table 6. Studies objective from each secondary study

Studies	Main Objective
Almazroi [3]	Classify studies on software usability across various facets
Carvalho et al. [5]	Review SBQS Symposium for discussions on ethical issues
Aberkane [1]	Review formal and grey literature to list key ethical issues in CS relevant to Requirements Engineering
Morley et al. [16]	Present tools to help ML developers build ethical systems, bridging theory and practice
Tsamados et al. [18]	Discuss ethical concerns and provide guidance for future development
Stahl et al. [17]	Map and discuss ethical issues and their interrelations
Johnson and Smith [10]	Identify interventions and tools supporting ethical development of data-driven software
Ahmad et al. [2]	Explore existing approaches for modeling ethical issues in AI requirements engineering
Llerena et al. [14]	Review literature and propose an ethical framework to guide software companies
Our SMS	Identify how ethical requirements are defined, modeled, and implemented in the SDLC

6   Conclusion and Future Work

This paper has provided a comprehensive examination of the role of ethics in the SDLC. Through an SMS, we have shed light on the prevailing discourse surrounding ethical considerations in software development. This study has also developed a categorization of ethical issues, presented in Table 1, constituting an initial basis for a taxonomy of ethics in Software Engineering.

Future intentions are: the elaboration of a survey to observe how companies implement and enforce their code of ethics or ethical standards in the development of their software, and the elaboration of directives for software companies to implement the many highlighted aspects of ethics.

Acknowledgements. The 5th author acknowledges FAPESP for their generous support. This paper touches a topic of the IARA-Artificial Intelligence in the Remaking of Spaces Center (FAPESP Grant 2020/09835-1). The authors also acknowledge the support of the MUR (Italy) Department of Excellence 2023–2027 for GSSI, the MUR-PRIN project 20228FT78M DREAM (Design to Reduce uncertainty in Ethics-based cyberphysicAl systeMs), the MUR-PRIN PNRR 2022 project RoboChor: Robot Choreography (grant P2022RSW5W), and the COmmunity-Based Organized Littering (COBOL) national research project (PRIN 2022 PNRR program Contract P20224K9EK).

Disclosure of Interests. The authors have no competing interests to declare that are relevant to the content of this article.

References

1. Aberkane, A.J.: Exploring Ethics in Requirements Engineering. Master's thesis, Utrecht University (2018)
2. Ahmad, K., Bano, M., Abdelrazek, M., Arora, C., Grundy, J.: What's up with requirements engineering for artificial intelligence systems? In: 2021 IEEE 29th International Requirements Engineering Conference (RE), pp. 1–12 (2021). https://doi.org/10.1109/RE51729.2021.00008
3. Almazroi, A.A.: A systematic mapping study of software usability studies. Int. J. Adv. Comput. Sci. Appl. **12**(9) (2021). https://doi.org/10.14569/IJACSA.2021. 0120927
4. Bourque, P., Fairley, R.E., Society, I.C.: Guide to the Software Engineering Body of Knowledge (SWEBOK(R)): Version 3.0, 3rd edn.. IEEE Computer Society Press, Washington, DC (2014)
5. Carvalho, L.P., Suzano, J.A., Pereira, R., Santoro, F.M., Oliveira, J.: Ethics: what is the research scenario in the Brazilian symposium ihc? In: Proceedings of the XX Brazilian Symposium on Human Factors in Computing Systems. IHC '21. Association for Computing Machinery, New York (2021). https://doi.org/10.1145/ 3472301.3484324
6. Dyba, T., Dingsoyr, T., Hanssen, G.K.: Applying systematic reviews to diverse study types: an experience report. In: First International Symposium on Empirical Software Engineering and Measurement (ESEM 2007), pp. 225–234 (2007). https://doi.org/10.1109/ESEM.2007.59
7. Gogoll, J., Zuber, N., Kacianka, S., Greger, T., Pretschner, A., Nida-Rümelin, J.: Ethics in the software development process: from codes of conduct to ethical deliberation. Phil. Technol. (2021). https://doi.org/10.1007/s13347-021-00451-w
8. Gomes, O.S., e Silva, G.B., de Souza,É.F.: Ethics in the software development process: a tertiary literature review. In: Anais do VIII Workshop sobre Aspectos Sociais, Humanos e Econômicos de Software, pp. 71–80. SBC, Porto Alegre (2023). https://doi.org/10.5753/washes.2023.229923
9. Gotterbarn, D.: Software Engineering Ethics. John Wiley & Sons, Hoboken (2002). https://doi.org/10.1002/0471028959.sof314

10. Johnson, B., Smith, J.: Towards ethical data-driven software: filling the gaps in ethics research & practice. In: 2021 IEEE/ACM 2nd International Workshop on Ethics in Software Engineering Research and Practice (SEthics), pp. 18–25 (2021). https://doi.org/10.1109/SEthics52569.2021.00011

11. Kim, J.: Author-based analysis of conference versus journal publication in computer science. J. Am. Soc. Inf. Sci. **70**(1), 71–82 (2019). https://doi.org/10.1002/asi.24079

12. Kitchenham, B.A., Charters, S.: Guidelines for performing systematic literature reviews in software engineering. Technical Report. EBSE 2007-001, Keele University and Durham University Joint Report (2007)

13. Landis, J.R., Koch, G.G.: The measurement of observer agreement for categorical data. Biometrics **33**(1), 159–174 (1977)

14. Llerena, L., Perez, H., Plazarte, J., Castro, J.W., Rodríguez, N.: Ethical framework for the software development process: a systematic mapping study. In: Rocha, A., Adeli, H., Dzemyda, G., Moreira, F., Colla, V. (eds.) Information Systems and Technologies, pp. 144–154. Springer, Cham (2024)

15. Matthew Miles, Michael Hberman, J.S.: Qualitative Data Analysis: A Methods Sourcebook, 3rd edn. Sage, Boca Raton (2014)

16. Morley, J., Floridi, L., Kinsey, L., Elhalal, A.: From what to how: an initial review of publicly available AI ethics tools, methods and research to translate principles into practices. Sci. Eng. Ethics **26**(4), 2141–2168 (2019). https://doi.org/10.1007/s11948-019-00165-5

17. Stahl, B.C., Timmermans, J., Mittelstadt, B.D.: The ethics of computing: a survey of the computing-oriented literature. ACM Comput. Surv. **48**(4) (2016). https://doi.org/10.1145/2871196

18. Tsamados, A., et al.: The ethics of algorithms: key problems and solutions. AI Soc.(2021). https://doi.org/10.1007/s00146-021-01154-8

Computational Solutions for Supporting Systematic Reviews in Software Engineering: a Comprehensive Overview

Maria Fernanda de Abreu Aguiar[1], Érica Ferreira de Souza[1(✉)],
Katia Romero Felizardo[1], and Luciana Rebelo[2]

[1] Federal University of Technology – Paraná, UTFPR, Cornélio Procópio, PR, Brazil
`mariaaguiar@alunos.utfpr.edu.br,`
`{ericasouza,katiascannavino}@utfpr.edu.br`
[2] Gran Sasso Science Institute (GSSI), L'Aquila, Italy
`luciana.rebelo@gssi.it`

Abstract. **Context**: The academic community in Software Engineering (SE) has increasingly embraced Systematic Reviews (SRs) due to their numerous benefits. However, computational support for the SR process still needs improved to minimize the time and effort required for SR conduction. **Objective**: This study aims to identify the main computational solutions designed to support the conduction of SRs in SE. **Method**: A Systematic Mapping was carried out considering studies published from 2007 to May 2024 to answer the four research questions. **Results**: This study identified 38 computational approaches supporting SRs in SE, with the majority focusing on the conduction phase and implemented as tools or algorithms. Although research activity has grown recently, many solutions remain immature, with limited usability and integration. Key challenges include automation bias, search string construction, data management, and the lack of connective tools. **Conclusion**: The findings highlight the need for more integrated computational support across the SRs phases.

Keywords: Systematic Reviews · Systematic Literature Reviews · Systematic Mapping · Computational Solutions · Software Engineering

1 Introduction

Software Engineering (SE) community increasingly relies on Systematic Reviews (SRs), such as Systematic Literature Reviews (SLRs) and Systematic Mappings (SMs), to synthesize evidence from relevant studies and establish the state of the art across various research domains [13]. SRs offer significant advantages, including the ability to consistently and reproducibly synthesize findings, ensure transparency, and support the identification of research gaps and directions for future investigations.

D. Taibi and D. Smite (Eds.): SEAA 2025, LNCS 16082, pp. 324–333, 2026.
https://doi.org/10.1007/978-3-032-04200-2_22

However, despite these benefits, the conduction of SRs remains a complex, time-consuming, and labor-intensive process [24]. Among the reported challenges are: (i) insufficient documentation of the SR process [24]; (ii) primary study quality assessment, particularly qualitative, lacks rigor [24,31]; (iii) defining a research protocol and learning the SR methodology pose significant difficulties for novice researchers [31]; and (iv) accessing and acquiring relevant studies in multiple digital libraries remains a persistent obstacle [31].

In response to these challenges, various tools have been developed to (semi)-automate activities of the SR process [7,10,16,32]. These tools mainly focus on (i) supporting the creation of research protocols; (ii) retrieving relevant studies from digital libraries; (iii) recommending studies for inclusion; (iv) assessing the quality of studies; (v) extracting data from primary studies; (vi) synthesizing evidence; and (vii) reporting the SLR process and its results. Despite their contributions, tools supporting SRs remain limited in scope, often addressing isolated aspects of the SR process rather than offering an integrated, end-to-end solution. Consequently, SR automation in SE still faces significant challenges, highlighting the need for more cohesive, user-friendly, and sustainable approaches to enhance adoption and long-term viability.

Existing secondary studies on SRs tools have overlooked critical factors such as usability, the cognitive burden of learning the tools, and their potential for interoperability. Furthermore, these studies have not explored other types of computational solutions rather than tools, such as algorithms for SR activity automation, Machine Learning (ML) models, or natural language processing (NLP) techniques [19].

In this study, we conducted a SM to identify the main computational solutions designed to support the conduction of SRs in SE. This SM comprehensively summarizes the literature on computational support for SRs, offering insights into existing solutions and their limitations. In this study, we structured our analysis based on the following research questions: (i) What type of studies have been published and when? (ii) What computational approaches are available to support SRs in SE? (iii) How do computational approaches support SRs in SE? and (iv) What challenges have been reported regarding computational approaches to support SRs in SE?

This study was conducted following a systematic approach structured in two main stages, as illustrated in Fig. 1. In the first stage, an automated search was performed in the Scopus database, retrieving 1171 studies. After that, a screening process was then applied based on predefined inclusion and exclusion criteria, leading to the inclusion of 20 primary studies. In the second stage, a forward snowballing technique was employed using the initial set of selected studies. This technique, which analyzes studies that cited the primary set, allowed the identification of 690 additional studies. After applying again the same strategy of stage 1, 18 studies were included following the criteria assessment. As a result, the final selection comprised 38 studies (20 from the database search and 18 from snowballing), ensuring a broader and more robust identification of the literature relevant to the scope of this research. Further details about the SM protocol and methodological procedures, including the search string, selection criteria, assessment, and selection process, are provided in the supplementary material to facilitate reproducibility. The corresponding link is included at the end of this paper.

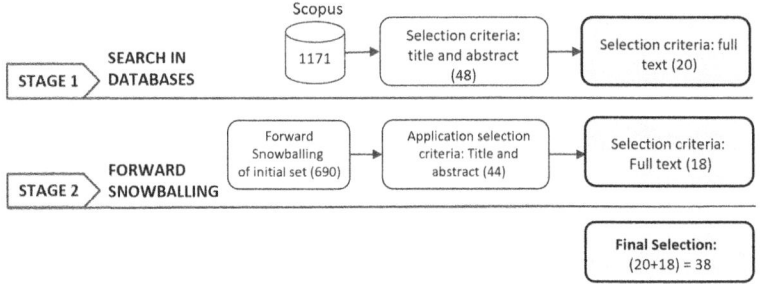

Fig. 1. Search and Selection Process

The remainder of this paper is structured as follows. Section 2 reports the results and discusses the main findings. Related work and threats to validity are presented in Sects. 3 and 4, respectively. Finally, Sect. 5 outlines the conclusion and future research.

2   Results and Discussion

This section presents the results, organized to answer the RQs. Key findings are illustrated with selected studies, referenced by citation and the ID from the replication package.

(RQ1) What type of studies have been published and when? The publication trends in this field have shown periods of fluctuation. In 2015, there was a peak with 7 studies published on computational approaches for supporting the SR process. This was followed by a decline from 2017 to 2019, with an average of one study per year. However, between 2020 and 2022, interest resurged, with 19 studies published, representing (50%) of the total set. While journals accounted for (45%) of these, conferences remained the predominant venue, with (55%) of the publications.

(RQ2) What computational approaches are available to support SR in SE? In this mapping, 38 studies were identified that propose computational approaches to support activities related to the SR process. The goal of RQ2 is to provide an overview of these approaches, detailing their type (e.g., tool, script, algorithm), accessible links, as well as their input and output data. With respect to the type of solution, 19 studies (50%) present tools, 16 (42.1%) describe algorithms, two (5.3%) focus on systems, and one (2.6%) refers to a database,

as illustrated in Fig. 2. Among the tools identified, some appear in more than one study, for example, Visual Text Mining (VTM) is discussed in studies [8] (ID 33) and [21] (ID 27). The VTM tool is designed to support the selection of primary studies using text mining techniques. In contrast, the StArt tool assists in gathering evidence on specific research topics and mapping research areas. Regarding algorithms, eight studies focus specifically on text mining. For example, study [18] (ID 31) proposes a topic modeling method to aid in the selection of studies.

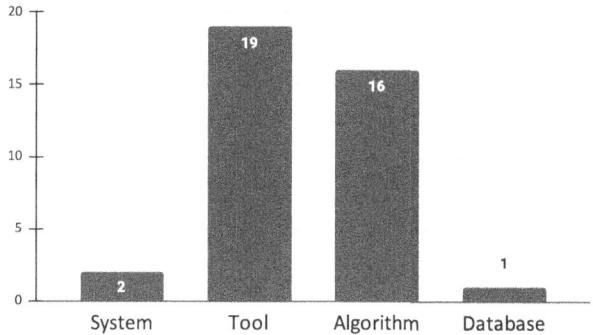

Fig. 2. Type of solution

We evaluated the link availability and update frequency of the 38 approaches analyzed. Among them, 27 provided active access links, while 11 did not. In particular, four of the 27 accessible links were inactive and did not lead to the intended content. Regarding the update history, we observed that four approaches were updated in 2024, three in 2023, and four in 2022.

An analysis of the input and output data types used in the computational solutions identified in the selected studies revealed that textual data was the most common input format, reported in 44.7% of the studies (17 studies). This was followed by PDF files, present in 18.4% of the cases (7 studies). In terms of output, textual data was again the most frequent format, appearing in 52.6% of the studies (20 studies), while CSV files were the second most common, reported in 15.8% of the studies (6 studies).

We have executed each of the 27 computational approaches provided with access links, evaluating them based on several usability criteria: (i) ***Execution Feasibility***: Was the approach executable without significant issues? (ii) ***Availability of documentation***: Does the approach offer an access tutorial or user guide? (iii) ***Graphical User Interface (GUI)***: Is there a user-friendly graphical interface available? (iv) ***Database Integration***: Does the approach include a database for data storage or management? (v) ***Ease of Use***: Is the approach intuitive and straightforward for users? These criteria were selected to assess the practicality and user-friendliness of each approach, providing insights into their usability in the applications.

- (i) Of the 27 identified approaches with accessible links, four were found to be inactive. The remaining 23 were subjected to analysis, but only 10 could be successfully executed. Consequently, the other 11 approaches were not included in the evaluation due to execution failure.
- (ii) Of the 23 approaches analyzed from (i), all offered some explanatory tutorial. Of these, 69.6% (16 studies) are based solely on text-based guidance. Furthermore, 17.4% (4 studies) offer tutorials that combine video and text, while 8.7% (2 studies) adopt an integrated approach using text and images. Finally, 4.3% (1 study) provides video-only tutorials.
- (iii) A Graphical User Interface (GUI) is included in 14 of the proposed approaches to support their execution. A prominent example is the FAST2 system [33] (ID 3), which uses machine learning (ML) techniques to aid in selecting primary studies for SRs. In contrast, nine (9) approaches lack a GUI.
- (iv) Regarding the use of databases, 14 approaches incorporate a database in their solutions. A relevant example is the Google Scholar/IEEE Xplore databases [9] (ID 23), which were used to apply the forward snowballing. However, nine (9) approaches did not include this feature.
- (v) Finally, 10 approaches were positively evaluated based on their **success rate**[1], a usability metric indicating whether users could complete the task. Among these, the SLR-tool [11] (ID 20) is particularly noteworthy, as it was specifically designed to support users in conducting SLRs and prioritizing relevant articles. However, 13 approaches did not meet this metric, as previously mentioned.

(RQ3) How the computational approaches support SR? To address this research question, we examined the activities involved in the various phases of the SR process. Figure 3 presents the number of studies associated with each of the identified SR phases. Within the **planning phase**, three distinct approaches were identified: two focused on constructing the search string and one aimed at supporting the development of the SR protocol, particularly in formulating RQs. A representative example of this phase SeSG study [1] (ID 9), which introduces the Search String Generator (SeSG). This tool takes advantage of a small set of studies as input and employs text mining techniques to generate search strings.

As presented in Table 1, we identified 25 studies that support various activities within the **conduction phase**. A prominent example is the SCAS–AI approach [20] (ID 5), which facilitates the semi-automation of the initial selection of primary studies. SCAS–AI classifies studies into three categories: automatic inclusion (likely relevant), automatic exclusion (likely irrelevant), and manual review (requiring human judgment). The approach utilizes a genetic algorithm to generate a classification coefficient, which is then interpreted by a predefined fuzzy inference system to allow accurate and efficient study classification.

---

[1] https://www.nngroup.com/articles/usability-metrics.

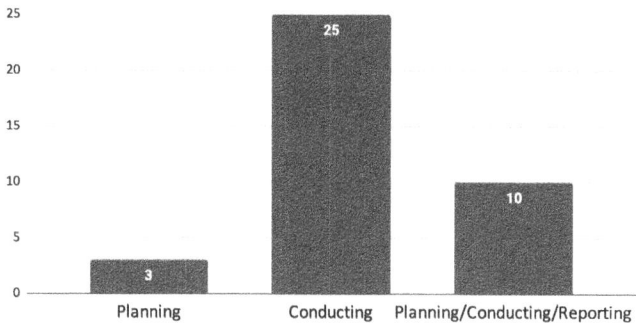

Fig. 3. SR phases

Table 1. Conducting Phase: Activities support

Activity	Number of Studies
Selection of primary studies	19
Data synthesis	3
Snowballing technique	2
Study selection and data extraction	1

Lastly, we have identified 10 approaches to support the SR process as a whole (**Planning, Conducting, and Reporting**). These approaches play a central role in managing each stage of the SR, integrating several activities into a single tool. An example is SLRTool [2] (ID 34), which offers functionalities to support the user in executing an SR. It includes project management, search engine results import, and organizing the articles found, allowing their inclusion or exclusion as needed.

(RQ4) What challenges have been reported regarding computational approaches to support SR? The selected studies addressed various challenges in conducting SRs. One study [33] (ID 3) reported the introduction of selection bias through automated systems like FAST2.

Three studies [5] (ID 6), [16] (ID 29), and [27] (ID 16) examined the complexity of constructing effective search strings, citing inadequate reporting and the lack of standardized guidelines as barriers to reproducibility and transparency. Citation export limitations were also noted by [26] (ID 32), which hinder the efficiency of the SR process.

Challenges in managing large volumes of data were also highlighted by [22] (ID 14), particularly during study selection. Duplicate articles were identified as a complicating factor by [17] (ID 21), as they slow down the process and increase complexity.

[21] (ID 27) proposed strategies to reduce selection effort without compromising quality. Time consumption was another common issue, with [7] (ID 26)

and [2] (ID 34) highlighting the extensive effort needed for selection, extraction, and analysis. [23] (ID 15) discussed the lack of automation in crowd-based SLRs and the absence of a comprehensive framework for large-scale collaboration.

Tool-related limitations were also reported in [14] (ID 22) and [10] (ID 38), that pointed to the lack of integrated tools for managing the SR process, while [11] (ID 20) and [29] (ID 25) noted the reliance on multiple platforms due to partial tool support.

Further issues were reported in data extraction and synthesis. [1] (ID 9) cited insufficient data for generalization, and [6] (ID 12) pointed to the absence of standardized synthesis methods. Finally, two studies [9] (ID 23) and [4] (ID 4) emphasized the need for regular review updates to ensure continued relevance. Together, these findings underscore the persistent challenges faced in performing SRs within SE.

3   Related Work

To identify related work, we applied the same comprehensive search string used in this SM. Of the 1173 initial results, 51 were potential secondary studies, and 43 were confirmed as directly relevant. The complete list of related studies is available as supplementary material.

Guided by the question *"What are the primary objectives of previous studies?"*, we found that 15% of the 43 studies evaluate the effectiveness of specific tools supporting the SR process, such as [28], which assessed active learning for accelerating SLRs. Another 15% aimed to introduce automation tools based on text mining techniques, exemplified by Cairo et al. [3]. In the AI domain, 5% presented ML-based tools. Additionally, 12.5% proposed models or frameworks to improve the SR process, like the Maturity Model developed by Santos and Nakagawa [25].

Only three studies (7.5%) share a similar objective with our work: [30], focused on AI-based tools; [12], which details the SR phases covered by various tools; and [15], a 2013 SM whose findings may now be outdated.

The main distinction of our study is its broader scope: it includes any type of computational solution (tools, algorithms, or scripts) supporting the SR process, and evaluates each identified approach in terms of accessibility, execution, and usability.

4   Threats to Validity

This section discusses potential limitations of our mapping study, following the four groups of threats to validity defined by [34]. To address construct validity, forward snowballing was used to reduce the risk of missing relevant studies. Internal validity was strengthened through a pilot test, kappa agreement analysis, and regular reviewer meetings. External validity may be affected by the exclusion of non-English and gray literature, although this impact is considered minor. To mitigate conclusion validity threats, classification categories were validated in meetings, and all study artifacts were documented to support future replications.

5   Final Remarks and Future Works

This study aimed to identify the main computational approaches that support the execution of SRs in SE. The results reveal fluctuating research activity in computational approaches for supporting SR in SE, with a publication peak in 2015 and renewed growth between 2020 and 2022, mostly in conferences. A total of 38 approaches were identified, primarily tools and algorithms, with emphasis on the conduction phase of SRs and common use of text or PDF files. However, only 23 of the 27 accessible solutions were functional, and just 10 could be executed successfully. Usability remains a challenge, with limited user-friendliness despite some having documentation, GUIs, or database integration. Most approaches focused on aiding study selection and classification, while fewer addressed planning activities such as formulating research questions or search strings. The main challenges identified include bias in automation, search string construction, limited citation export options, data volume management, and a lack of integrated tools. These results highlight the need for more robust, user-friendly, and comprehensive computational support for the entire SR process.

Future research may focus on integrating existing tools and algorithms to create comprehensive solutions that support all SR phases. Additionally, a planned survey aims to identify unpublished approaches.

Supplementary Material

Download all supplementary files included with this article: https://zenodo.org/records/15801576.

Acknowledgements. Maria Fernanda de Abreu Aguiar acknowledges the Institutional Scientific Initiation Scholarship Program (PIBIC–UTFPR) for financial support. Professor Katia Romero Felizardo is funded by a research grant from the Brazilian National Council for Scientific and Technological Development (CNPq), Grant 302339/2022 − 1. The authors acknowledge the support of MUR (Italy) Department of Excellence 2023–2027 for GSSI, the MUR-PRIN project 20228FT78M DREAM (Design to Reduce uncertainty in Ethics-based cyber-physicAl systeMs), the MUR-PRIN PNRR 2022 project RoboChor: Robot Choreography (grant P2022RSW5W), and the COBOL (COmmunity-Based Organized Littering) national research project (PRIN 2022 PNRR Contract P20224K9EK). All authors have contributed to all activities related to the submission.

Disclosure of Interests. The authors have no competing interests to declare that are relevant to the content of this article.

References

1. Alves, L.F., Vasconcellos, F.J., Nogueira, B.M.: SESG: a search string generator for secondary studies with hybrid search strategies using text mining. Empir. Softw. Eng. **27**, 105 (2022)
2. Barn, B.S., Raimondi, F., Athappian, L., Clark, T.: SLRTOOL: a tool to support collaborative systematic literature reviews. In: International Conference on Enterprise Information Systems, vol. 2, pp. 440–447. SCITEPRESS (2014)
3. Cairo, L.S., de Figueiredo Carneiro, G., da Silva, B.C.: Adoption of machine learning techniques to perform secondary studies: a systematic mapping study for the computer science field. In: ICEIS (2), pp. 351–356 (2019)
4. Díaz, O., Contell, J.P.: Developing research questions in conversation with the literature: operationalization&tool support. Empirical Soft. Eng. **27**(7), 174 (2022)
5. Ding, J., et al.: Tell me how to survey: literature review made simple with automatic reading path generation. In: International Conference on Data Engineering (ICDE), pp. 3426–3438. IEEE (2022)
6. Dube, K., McLachlan, S., Daley, B., Hitman, G.A., Fenton, N., Kyrimi, E.: Star approach for supporting analysis and synthesis in collaborative literature reviews
7. Fabbri, S., Silva, C., Hernandes, E., Octaviano, F., Di Thommazo, A., Belgamo, A.: Improvements in the start tool to better support the systematic review process. In: Conference on Evaluation and Assessment in Software Engineering (EASE). ACM DL, Limerick, Ireland (2016)
8. Felizardo, K.R., Barbosa, E.F., Martins, R.M., Valle, P.H.D., Maldonado, J.C.: Visual text mining: ensuring the presence of relevant studies in systematic literature reviews. Int. J. Soft Eng. Knowl. Eng. **25**, 909–928 (2015)
9. Felizardo, K.R., da Silva, A.Y.I., de Souza, É.F., Vijaykumar, N.L., Nakagawa, E.Y.: Evaluating strategies for forward snowballing application to support secondary studies updates: emergent results. In: Proceedings of the XXXII Brazilian Symposium on Software Engineering, pp. 184–189 (2018)
10. Fernández-Sáez, A.M., Genero, M., Romero, F.P.: SLR-tool – a tool for performing systematic literature reviews. In: 5th Conference on Software and Data Technologies (ICSOFT 2010), pp. 157–166. Springer, Athens, Greece (2010)
11. Hinderks, A., Mayo, F., Thomaschewski, J., Escalona, M.: An SLR-tool: search process in practice: a tool to conduct and manage systematic literature review (SLR). In: 42nd Conference on Software Engineering: Companion Proceedings (ICSE-Companion – ICSE 2020), pp. 81–84. IEEE Press, Seoul, Korea (South) (2020)
12. Karakan, B., Wagner, S., Bogner, J.: Tool support for systematic literature reviews: analyzing existing solutions and the potential for automation. Ph.D. thesis, University of Stuttgart (2021)
13. Kitchenham, B., Budgen, D., Brereton, P.: Evidence-Based Software Engineering and Systematic Reviews. Chapman & Hall/CRC (2015)
14. Marchezan, L., Bolfe, G., Rodrigues, E., Bernardino, M., Basso, F.: Thoth: a web-based tool to support systematic reviews. In: Symposium on Empirical Software Engineering and Measurement, pp. 1–6 (2019)
15. Marshall, C., Brereton, O.P.: Tools to support systematic literature reviews in software engineering: a mapping study. In: Symposium on Empirical Software Engineering and Measurement, pp. 296–299 (2013)
16. Mergel, G.D., Silveira, M.S., da Silva, T.S.: A method to support search string building in systematic literature reviews through visual text mining. In: ACM Symposium on Applied Computing (SAC 2015), pp. 1594–160 (2015)

17. Messerschmidt, M., Chan, S., Wen, E., Nanayakkara, S.: Toro: a web-based tool to search, explore, screen, compare and visualize literature (2022)
18. Mo, Y., Kontonatsios, G., Ananiadou, S.: Supporting systematic reviews using LDA-based document representations. Syst. Rev. **4**, 1–12 (2015)
19. Napoleão, B.M., Petrillo, F., Hallé, S.: Automated support for searching and selecting evidence in software engineering: a cross-domain systematic mapping. In: Euromicro Conference on Software Engineering and Advanced Applications (SEAA), pp. 45–53 (2021)
20. Octaviano, F., Felizardo, K.R., Fabbri, S.C., Napoleão, B.M., Petrillo, F., Hallé, S.: SCAS-AI: a strategy to semi-automate the initial selection task in systematic literature reviews. In: 2022 48th Euromicro Conference on Software Engineering and Advanced Applications (SEAA), pp. 483–490. IEEE (2022)
21. Octaviano, F.R., Felizardo, K.R., Maldonado, J.C., Fabbri, S.C.: Semi-automatic selection of primary studies in systematic literature reviews: is it reasonable? Empir. Softw. Eng. **20**, 1898–1917 (2015)
22. Person, T., Ruiz-Rube, I., Mota, J.M., Cobo, M.J., Tselykh, A., Dodero, J.M.: A comprehensive framework to reinforce evidence synthesis features in cloud-based systematic review tools. Appl. Sci. **11**(12), 5527 (2021)
23. Santos, V., Iwazaki, A., Souza, E., Felizardo, K., Vijaykumar, N.: Crowdslr: a tool to support the use of crowdsourcing in systematic literature reviews. In: Brazilian Symposium on Software Engineering, pp. 341–346 (2021)
24. dos Santos, V., Iwazaki, A., Felizardo, K., de Souza, E., Nakagawa, E.Y.: Towards sustainability of systematic literature reviews. In: 15th Symposium on Empirical Software Engineering and Measurement (ESEM 2021). IEEE Press, Bari, Italy (2021)
25. dos Santos, V., Yumi Nakagawa, E.: Towards a maturity model for systematic literature review process. arXiv e-prints, pp. arXiv–2206 (2022)
26. Sellak, H., Ouhbi, B., Frikh, B.: Using rule-based classifiers in systematic reviews: a semantic class association rules approach. In: International Conference on Information Integration and Web-Based Applications & Services, pp. 1–5 (2015)
27. Soundefinednicki, M., Madeyski, L.: Ash: a new tool for automated and full-text search in systematic literature reviews. In: 21nd Conference Computational Science (ICCS 2021), pp. 362–369. Springer, Krakow, Poland (2021)
28. Teijema, J.J., Seuren, S., Anadria, D., Bagheri, A., van de Schoot, R.: Simulation-based active learning for systematic reviews: a systematic review of the literature. PsyArXiv (2023)
29. Tell, P., Cholewa, J.B., Nellemann, P., Kuhrmann, M.: Beyond the spreadsheet: reflections on tool support for literature studies. In: Conference on Evaluation and Assessment in Software Engineering (EASE). IEEE Press, Limerick, Ireland (2016)
30. de la Torre-López, J., Ramírez, A., Romero, J.R.: Artificial intelligence to automate the systematic review of scientific literature. Computing **105**(10), 2171–2194 (2023)
31. Voigt, D., Kopp, O., Wild, K.: Systematic literature tools: are we there yet? In: Central-European Workshop on Services and their Composition, pp. 1–6 (2021)
32. Watanabe, W., Felizardo, K., Candido, A., de Souza, E., Neto, J., Vijaykumar, N.: Reducing efforts of software engineering systematic literature reviews updates using text classification. Inf. Softw. Technol. **128**, 106395 (2020)
33. Yu, Z., Carver, J.C., Rothermel, G., Menzies, T.: Assessing expert system-assisted literature reviews with a case study. Expert Syst. Appl. **200** (2022)
34. Zhou, X., Jin, Y., Zhang, H., Li, S., Huang, X.: A map of threats to validity of systematic literature reviews in software engineering. In: 23rd Asia-Pacific Software Engineering Conference, pp. 153–160 (2016)

MLOps in the Healthcare Domain: a Systematic Literature Review

Giulio Mallardi[(✉)] [iD], Luigi Quaranta[iD], Fabio Calefato[iD],
and Filippo Lanubile[iD]

Department of Computer Science, University of Bari, Bari, Italy
{giulio.mallardi,luigi.quaranta,fabio.calefato,filippo.lanubile}@uniba.it

Abstract. Machine Learning Operations (MLOps) refers to the set of practices and tools designed to streamline and automate machine learning pipelines, enabling the efficient deployment and continuous evolution of ML models in production environments. In the healthcare domain, where machine learning adoption is growing, MLOps plays a crucial role in ensuring reliable, compliant, and maintainable AI systems. This systematic literature review investigates the current use of MLOps in healthcare, focusing on the practices adopted, tools used, workflow stages supported, and medical specialties involved. We conducted a structured search on scholarly databases and selected 14 primary studies published between 2015 and 2024 based on defined inclusion and exclusion criteria. Our findings reveal that while several MLOps practices and tools are being adopted in healthcare, their coverage remains uneven across the ML workflow, with early stages such as data labeling receiving little attention. Regulatory constraints further limit automation, particularly in deployment. Moreover, applications tend to concentrate on a few medical specialties, reflecting the current narrow scope of adoption. Taken together, these insights offer a structured understanding of how MLOps is currently applied in healthcare and point toward opportunities for more reliable, effective, and regulation-aware integration of machine learning in clinical contexts.

Keywords: model deployment · ML pipeline · ML-enabled system · health informatics

1 Introduction

The healthcare domain is experiencing the integration of machine learning (ML) and artificial intelligence (AI) technologies into its practices. However, as these technologies become more prevalent, there is a growing need for efficient management of ML workflows and Machine Learning Operations (MLOps) within the healthcare industry. In order to proceed with this review, we have adopted the following definition of MLOps:

Definition. *MLOps (Machine Learning Operations) is a paradigm, including aspects like best practices, sets of concepts, as well as a development culture when it comes to the end-to-end conceptualization, implementation, monitoring, deployment, and scalability of machine learning products [13].*

© The Author(s), under exclusive license to Springer Nature Switzerland AG 2026
D. Taibi and D. Smite (Eds.): SEAA 2025, LNCS 16082, pp. 334–349, 2026.
https://doi.org/10.1007/978-3-032-04200-2_23

Although the term "MLOps" is still evolving and lacks a standardized definition, its importance in streamlining ML processes cannot be overstated. Despite its potential, the adoption of MLOps in real-world healthcare settings remains limited, primarily due to the relative novelty of the approach. This limitation highlights both the need for further research and the importance of addressing operational challenges in healthcare. This paper aims to investigate the current practices and tools used in MLOps within the healthcare domain. Additionally, we seek to understand the factors influencing MLOps practices and the stages of the ML workflow. In particular, we will explore how regulatory requirements act as bottlenecks for AI-enabled systems in this domain and their impact on MLOps practices. Furthermore, we will examine which medical specialties are involved in experiments utilizing MLOps, providing a comprehensive overview of the current landscape. By doing so, we aim to shed light on the specific areas where MLOps is being applied and the challenges encountered therein. Finally, we examine the domain-specific challenges encountered in healthcare applications of MLOps, identify the affected practices, and explore mitigation strategies. Through this exploration, we aim to contribute to the ongoing discussion on optimizing ML workflows in healthcare and fostering the responsible and effective integration of AI technologies.

2   Background and Related Work

In the context of our research, we draw upon insights from several key studies to frame our understanding of MLOps practices and tools. Kreuzberger et al. [13] offer an in-depth exploration of MLOps, including its definition, architectural principles, and core components. Their contribution provides a conceptual foundation for understanding how MLOps methodologies are structured and implemented.

Amershi et al. [1] present a comprehensive overview of the typical stages in the machine learning workflow. We use this model to map MLOps practices and tools to specific phases of development, deployment, and monitoring, thereby situating MLOps within the broader ML lifecycle.

To support our analysis of MLOps tooling, we refer to the taxonomy proposed by Symeonidis et al. [24], which classifies tools based on their functionalities and the workflow stages they support. This taxonomy enables a structured categorization of the solutions encountered in our systematic literature review.

Toivakka et al. [25] discuss the role of regulatory constraints in software development for highly regulated domains, introducing the concept of RegOps (regulated DevOps). Their work is particularly relevant to the healthcare context, where strict compliance requirements heavily influence the design and deployment of ML systems.

Finally, Haertel et al. [8] conducted a thorough review, focusing on Data Science and its lifecycle while also analyzing the current emphasis of MLOps literature within this context. They explored the automation of Data Science lifecycle activities through MLOps practices and examined various application scenarios, including healthcare. Unlike their study, which covers multiple fields, our research specifically delves into healthcare. Despite this distinction, both studies share a common observation regarding the limited evidence of MLOps adoption, particularly within healthcare, which may be attributed to its novelty. We concur with their assessment that the healthcare sector stands out due to its inherent need for highly reliable and secure systems driven by concerns surrounding risk and security.

3   Methodology

In our study, we conducted a Systematic Literature Review (SLR) to explore the intersection of MLOps, machine learning workflows, and medical specialties within the healthcare domain. Using the "Scopus" scholarly database, we employed a predefined search query to identify relevant research articles. Subsequently, we meticulously analyzed the resulting papers, extracting key excerpts that align with our research objectives. Our primary focus was on elucidating prevalent MLOps practices and tools employed within healthcare settings. Additionally, we aimed to identify the specific stages of the machine learning workflow addressed in each paper, with particular emphasis on understanding the extent to which MLOps facilitates automation across these stages. Furthermore, we documented the medical specialties under examination in each paper, providing valuable insights into the diverse applications of MLOps within various healthcare domains. The following paragraphs describe the process adopted to conduct the SLR, following the Preferred Reporting Items for Systematic Reviews and Meta-Analyses (PRISMA) guidelines to ensure consistency and rigor throughout the review [18].

3.1   Research Questions

To define the scope and objectives of this review, we adopted the PICOC framework [11], a well-established approach in evidence-based software engineering for structuring systematic literature reviews. PICOC, which stands for Population, Intervention, Comparison, Outcome, and Context, provides a structured lens through which to articulate research questions that are both comprehensive and focused.

Applying this framework helped ensure that the review captures not only the technical aspects of MLOps adoption but also the organizational and domain-specific characteristics that influence its application in healthcare. Each element of PICOC was mapped to a specific dimension of our study, as summarized in Table 1. This mapping supported the design of the review protocol and guided both the formulation of the research questions and the selection of relevant literature.

Based on this framework, we formulated the following research questions, aimed at systematically characterizing the adoption of MLOps in healthcare:

Table 1. PICOC elements and their application in this review

Element	Definition	Application
Population	The types of subjects under study	Studies that apply machine learning methods in the healthcare domain
Intervention	The technique, method, or approach being investigated	Use of MLOps practices, tools, or workflows to support ML lifecycle management
Comparison	A baseline or alternative method for comparison	Not applicable (no comparative analysis conducted)
Outcome	The effects or results of the intervention	Identified MLOps practices and tools, supported workflow stages, and involved medical specialties
Context	The environment or domain in which the study takes place	Clinical, medical, health and wellness contexts where ML is deployed

R1. *Which MLOps practices are adopted in healthcare?*
R2. *Which MLOps tools are used in healthcare?*
R3. *Which workflow stages are supported by MLOps in healthcare?*
R4. *Which are the medical specialties covered by MLOps?*

3.2   Search Strategy and Study Selection

To ensure that our results are based on scientific knowledge, we conducted the SLR following the practices described by Kitchenham et al. [11]. After an initial exploratory search, we defined our search query as follows:

$$TITLE\text{-}ABS\text{-}KEY ($$
$$(\text{``}MLOps\text{''} \ OR \ \text{``}CD4ML\text{''} \ OR \ \text{``}Operational \ Machine \ Learning\text{''} \ OR \ (\text{``}CI/CD\text{''}$$
$$AND \ (\text{``}ML\text{''} \ OR \ \text{``}Machine \ Learning\text{''})))$$
$$AND$$
$$(\text{``}healthcare\text{''} \ OR \ \text{``}health\text{''} \ OR \ \text{``}clinical\text{''} \ OR \ \text{``}medicine\text{''} \ OR \ \text{``}medical\text{''} \ OR$$
$$\text{``}wellness\text{''}))$$

This query encompasses the common terminology used in MLOps and healthcare contexts, along with some synonyms, to comprehensively explore the literature. It is noteworthy that we chose not to include the term "DevOps" in our search query to ensure precision and avoid misinterpretation of MLOps, given the lack of consolidated terminology regarding this term.

The search resulted in 34 articles. To ensure relevance, we applied specific inclusion and exclusion criteria. We included studies that reported on the use of MLOps practices and tools within the healthcare domain. Articles were excluded if they were not written in English or published before 2015—the year Sculley et al. published "Hidden Technical Debt in Machine Learning Systems" [21], a seminal work marking the emergence of MLOps for its original focus on the engineering challenges in deploying and maintaining ML systems at scale. We also excluded duplicates and preprints, as well as excerpts that merely mention an MLOps practice or tool without providing evidence of its adoption or usage. A summary of the complete search process is shown in Fig. 1, in compliance with the PRISMA guidelines.

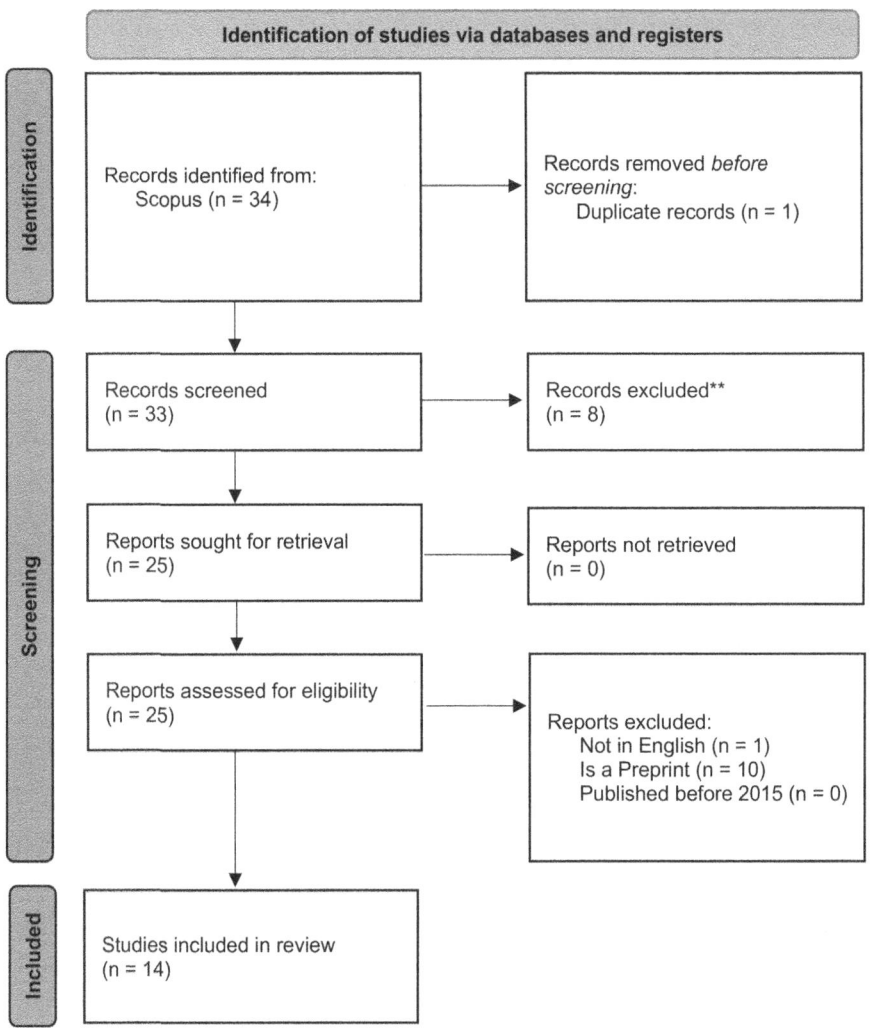

Fig. 1. PRISMA flow diagram for study selection.

3.3   Data Extraction and Synthesis

In our review, we gathered text excerpts based on specific criteria to answer our research questions. We looked for mentions of MLOps practices and tools, focusing on evidence of their adoption or usage in healthcare (RQ1, RQ2). We also noted where these practices or tools were referenced within the machine learning workflow stages (RQ3). To ensure relevance, we excluded mere mentions without evidence. Additionally, we recorded the medical specialties discussed in each paper (RQ4), providing insights into where MLOps is applied in healthcare. We employed a qualitative analysis method based on thematic coding. Codes were applied to relevant excerpts from each included paper—except for those representing medical specialties, which were assigned at the paper level rather than to specific excerpts.

RQ1 Qualitative Analysis Method. The practices were identified using closed coding based on principles outlined by Kreuzberger et al. [13] as follows:

1. CI/CD automation
2. Workflow orchestration
3. Reproducibility
4. Versioning of data, code, model
5. Collaboration
6. Continuous ML training & evaluation
7. ML metadata tracking
8. Continuous monitoring
9. Feedback loops

In modern machine learning (ML) practices, several key practices drive efficiency and effectiveness throughout the development pipeline. (1) *CI/CD automation* involves continuous integration, delivery, and deployment, facilitating fast feedback and increasing productivity. (2) *Workflow orchestration*, guided by directed acyclic graphs (DAGs), coordinates the various tasks within the ML workflow pipeline, ensuring a smooth execution order based on task dependencies and relationships. (3) *Reproducibility* stands as a cornerstone, ensuring that ML experiments can be replicated with precision to obtain identical results. (4) *Versioning of data, code, model* plays a critical role in enabling reproducibility and traceability by maintaining version control of data, models, and code. (5) *Collaboration* is key, facilitating cooperative work on data, models, and code, thereby breaking down silos and fostering a culture of communication and cooperation among different roles. (6) *Continuous ML training and evaluation* involve periodic model retraining based on new feature data, supported by monitoring, feedback loops, and an automated ML workflow pipeline. (7) *ML metadata tracking/logging* ensures the comprehensive traceability of experiment runs by capturing metadata for each task in the ML workflow, including parameters, performance metrics, and model lineage. (8) *Continuous monitoring* is essential for the periodic assessment of model behavior, infrastructure resources, and model serving performance, allowing for the timely detection of potential errors or changes affecting product quality. (9) Finally, *feedback loops* play a crucial role in integrating insights from quality assessments back into the development or engineering process, facilitating continuous improvement and refinement of ML models and workflows. Together, these practices form a cohesive framework for modern ML development, emphasizing efficiency, reproducibility, collaboration, and continuous improvement [13].

RQ2 Qualitative Analysis Method. The tools were identified through open coding, with tool names selected and then clustered according to a taxonomy adapted from Symeonidis et al. [24]:

- Data management tools (Data preprocessing, Data versioning)
- Modeling tools (Hyperparameter optimization, Feature engineering, Experiment tracking)
- Operationalization tools (End-to-end, Model monitoring, Model deployment/serving, CI/CD tools)

(1) *Data management tools*, including data labeling and versioning tools, are essential for effective machine learning (ML) workflows. Data labeling tools annotate various data types and ensure labeling accuracy, contributing to better model performance. Meanwhile, data versioning tools manage dataset versions, providing insights into data evolution and its impact on model performance. (2) *Modeling tools*, such as feature engineering, experiment tracking, and hyperparameter tuning tools, streamline the ML model development process. Feature engineering tools expedite feature extraction, while experiment tracking tools facilitate experiment comparison and analysis. Hyperparameter tuning tools automate the selection of optimal parameters, enhancing model performance. (3) *Operationalization tools* simplify the integration of ML models into production environments. Machine learning model deployment tools simplify deployment processes, while model monitoring tools detect data drifts and anomalies, ensuring sustained model performance. Continuous Integration/Continuous Deployment (CI/CD) tools automate build, test, delivery, and deployment steps, enhancing productivity and providing rapid feedback to developers. End-to-end ML application lifecycle tools provide comprehensive support throughout the ML project lifecycle, optimizing data management, model development, and deployment processes [24].

RQ3 Qualitative Analysis Method. The excerpts referring to MLOps practices and tools were classified using closed coding, aligning with the machine learning workflow stages described by Amershi et al. [1]:

1. Model Requirements
2. Data Collection
3. Data Cleaning
4. Data Labeling

5. Feature Engineering
6. Model Training
7. Model Evaluation
8. Model Deployment
9. Model Monitoring

The machine learning workflow involves nine essential stages, each contributing to the development and deployment of effective models. In the (1) *Model Requirements* stage, designers determine the necessary features and model types for addressing the problem at hand, setting the stage for subsequent steps. Following this, in the (2) *Data Collection* stage, teams gather and compile datasets from various sources, ensuring they accurately represent the problem domain. Once the data is collected, the (3) *Data Cleaning* stage begins, where inaccurate or inconsistent data points are identified and removed to ensure the quality and reliability of the datasets. With clean data in hand, the (4) *Data Labeling* stage assigns ground truth labels to facilitate supervised learning tasks, providing models with essential information to learn from examples. Next, in the (5) *Feature Engineering* stage, relevant features are extracted, transformed, or created from the raw data to enhance model performance. Once features are engineered, the (6) *Model Training* stage commences, where selected machine learning models are trained on the cleaned and labeled datasets, optimizing their parameters for performance. Following training, the (7) *Model Evaluation* stage assesses the performance of trained models using metrics to ensure they generalize well and effectively solve the problem. Successful models then proceed to the (8) *Model Deployment* stage, where they are integrated into target environments and equipped with inference code for making predictions on new data. Throughout this process, the (9) *Feedback Loops* stage plays a crucial role, providing continuous feedback from real-world usage, performance metrics, and user input to refine and improve models iteratively [1].

RQ4 Qualitative Analysis Method. The analyzed papers were classified according to the taxonomy of medical specialties defined in the *ABMS Guide to Medical Specialties* [22]. This classification system delineates recognized specialties and subspecialties based on clinical focus and scope of practice, providing a standardized framework for the categorization of medical domains.

4   Results

In this section, we present the findings of our study, organized by research question. Specifically, we report on the adoption of MLOps practices (RQ1) and the use of MLOps tools (RQ2) in healthcare—with possible references to the specific stages of the ML workflow in which they are applied (RQ3). For the final research query (RQ4), we infer the medical specialty from the case study described in each paper.

4.1 RQ1: Which MLOps Practices are Adopted in Healthcare?

The analysis of the reviewed papers shows comprehensive coverage of MLOps practices, encompassing the full set identified by Kreuzberger et al. [13] (see Table 2).

A prominent insight, which may significantly influence the adoption of MLOps practices, is the common requirement to comply with stringent regulations [7,14,23]. As reported by Granlund et al. [7]: *"When developing a medical device product, it is essential to clearly understand applicable regulatory requirements and determine a regulatory strategy accordingly from the beginning of the project [...] However, such continuous practices are not immediately compatible with regulatory requirements that may need authority involvement."* [7]. Regulatory compliance involves several factors, including the requirement to manage parts of the pipelines within private, on-premises environments, the adherence to strict regulations concerning patient data, and the necessity for stable, explainable, and deterministic models. In particular, to comply with most regulations and ensure the safe use of ML-enabled technologies in this sensitive domain, models must remain stable after deployment, in a so-called "locked state" [7].

Another key insight that emerged from our analysis is the lack of explicit directives from regulatory bodies regarding compliance requirements [7]. Further discussions on these aspects have been elaborated in Sect. 7.

Table 2. Practices and References

Practice	References	Count
CI/CD automation	[2–4, 7, 10, 14, 15, 23]	8
Workflow orchestration	[2–4, 6, 7, 14, 15, 23]	8
Reproducibility	[4, 14–16]	4
Versioning of data, code, model	[7, 12, 16]	3
Collaboration	[7, 10, 23]	3
Continuous ML training & evaluation	[2, 6, 7, 14, 16, 23]	6
ML meta data tracking	[2–4, 6, 7, 14, 15]	7
Continuous monitoring	[4, 7, 14–16, 23]	6
Feedback loops	[4, 7, 10, 23]	4

4.2 RQ2: Which MLOps Tools are Used in Healthcare?

The reviewed studies report the use of a variety of tools, which we organized according to the taxonomy by Symeonidis et al. [24]. MLflow is the most frequently used tool, as evidenced by its adoption in several studies [2,7,15,16]. This underscores its significance in facilitating various aspects of the modeling and operationalization phase. In addition to MLflow, a variety of other tools are also used to facilitate model operationalization (see Table 5).

Despite the abundance of options, it is apparent that the literature lacks significant mention of data preprocessing tools (see Table 3). Furthermore, a notable observation is the absence of hyperparameter optimization and feature engineering tools within the discourse, suggesting potential avenues for further investigation and development in these critical areas (see Table 4).

Table 3. Data management tools

Category	Tools	Count
Data versioning	DVC [7]	1
	Weight and Biases [6]	1
Data preprocessing	-	0

Table 4. Modeling tools

Category	Tools	Count
Experiment Tracking	MLflow Tracking [2,7,15,16]	4
	Weight and Biases [6]	1
	MLweb [2]	1
	ModelDB [2]	1
Hyperparameters Optimization	-	0
Feature Engineering	-	0

Table 5. Operationalization tools

Category	Tools	Count
Model Deployment/Serving	Kubeflow [2]	1
	Kubernetes [2,4,15]	3
	Docker [4,16]	2
	MLflow Registry [2,7,15,16]	4
End-to-End	Google Cloud Platform [15,23]	2
	Microsoft Azure [16]	1
	Edge Impulse Studio [6]	1
	TensorFlow Extended [2]	1
CI/CD Automation	GitHub Actions [15]	1
	TravisCI [15]	1
	JenkinsCI [15]	1

4.3 RQ3: Which Workflow Stages are Supported by MLOps in Healthcare?

The focus of support within the ML workflow stages by MLOps practices and tools primarily centers on phases from Model Training to Model Monitoring (see Table 6). Conversely, fewer papers address the initial stages of the ML workflow, particularly Data Labeling, which is never mentioned.

Table 6. ML Workflow Stages supported by MLOps and References

ML Workflow Stage	References	Count
Model Requirements	[7, 23]	2
Data Collection	[2, 3, 7, 23]	4
Data Cleaning	[4, 7]	2
Data Labeling	-	0
Feature Engineering	[14]	1
Model Training	[2, 4, 6, 7, 12, 14–16, 23]	9
Model Evaluation	[2–4, 6, 7, 14, 15]	7
Model Deployment	[3, 4, 6, 7, 14, 15, 23]	8
Model Monitoring	[4, 7, 10, 14–16, 23]	7

4.4   RQ4: Which are the Medical Specialties Covered by MLOps?

An initial attempt to identify a universally accepted categorization of medical specialties revealed a lack of consensus across international healthcare systems. While multiple national and regional frameworks exist, their classifications often vary significantly in structure and scope. As a result, we adopted the categorization provided by the *American Board of Medical Specialties (ABMS)*, which formally recognizes 40 core specialties and 89 subspecialties within the U.S. medical system [22]. Based on this classification, we identified seven specialties in which MLOps practices are beginning to emerge. These are summarized in Table 7, along with supporting references.

Table 7. Medical Specialties and References

Medical Specialty	Reference	Count
Geriatric Medicine	[6]	1
Internal Medicine	[9, 15, 16]	3
Neurology	[6, 7]	2
Orthopaedics Surgery	[7]	1
Pathology	[3, 4]	2
Preventive Medicine	[20]	1
Radiology	[12]	1

5   Discussion

Our investigation highlights that MLOps practices and tools utilized in healthcare are significantly influenced by regulatory requirements. Specifically, we've observed that practices such as *data versioning, continuous learning and evaluation*, and *CI/CD automation* are particularly affected.

Concerning *data versioning*, due to the sensitive nature of patient data, strict regulations like HIPAA or GDPR require that only authorized personnel access and process this data—typically within secured environments. Data subjected to versioning must comply with these requirements, ensuring auditability and adherence to rigorous processes to maintain traceability and data security—often necessitating on-premises server storage. Common requirements in this context include: (1) the need to keep sensitive healthcare data within approved geographic and access boundaries, (2) the need to track changes to different components (metadata vs. pixel data) within file formats like DICOM, which bundle different types of data, and (3) the need to comprehensively track all events of file creation, modification, movement, and deletion over the entire project life-cycle [19].

As for *continuous learning and evaluation*, Lombardo et al. [14] highlight how this MLOps practice is constrained by data retention policies. The limited availability of patient data prevents retraining on historical information, which hinders the model's ability to consolidate past knowledge. This can lead to *Catastrophic Forgetting*, a phenomenon in which previously learned information is overwritten when models are updated incrementally. To mitigate this phenomenon, one potential solution is to generate synthetic data from batches of historical data, ensuring a consistent amount of information for model retraining experiments.

As for *CI/CD automation* practices, these can be limited by the requirement for updated clinical validation reports before new model deployments [7,23], which can delay clinician approval. To address this issue, it is recommended to develop a pipeline that automatically generates clinical validation reports [7]. Since there are no standards for clinical validation reports for machine learning models, Stirbu et al. [23] proposed using "Model Cards" by Mitchell et al. [17]. Another process that hinders CI/CD automation is the requirement for product validation, meaning that AI-enabled medical devices must be approved by competent authorities (e.g., FDA) for real-world use. This implies that deployment cannot be performed using continuous delivery; instead, new versions of medical devices must be approved by these authorities. To expedite this step, Granlund et al. [7] suggests using "locked" state models since they are usually approved by regulatory bodies and do not change their behavior in a post-market phase.

In addressing RQ2, we found that a major gap in the adoption of MLOps practices in healthcare concerns data labeling. Several factors may contribute to this issue. Firstly, the absence of adequate tools for data labeling may hinder the seamless integration of this MLOps practice into healthcare workflows. Additionally, the necessity to involve human experts in the labeling process to ensure precision adds another layer of complexity. This reliance on human input, while crucial for accuracy, could impede the scalability and efficiency of MLOps implementations. Nevertheless, potential solutions exist to address these challenges.

One promising direction involves the use of *semi-automated annotation methodologies*, which combine algorithmic pre-labeling with expert human validation [5]. These approaches aim to accelerate the annotation process by allowing models to generate initial labels that are then refined or confirmed by domain specialists. Such a hybrid strategy could potentially bridge the gap between traditional labeling practices and the demands of modern MLOps frameworks in healthcare settings.

6 Limitations of the Study

Despite our best efforts to design and execute a comprehensive systematic literature review, it is essential to acknowledge the following key limitations.

First, our findings are based on a relatively small number of primary studies. This is due to the emerging status of the MLOps field, where the novelty of approaches limits the amount of available literature, especially in restricted domains like healthcare. We mitigated this limitation by conducting a comprehensive search using Scopus, a highly regarded and extensive academic database. Additionally, to enhance the rigor and transparency of our source selection process, we employed the PRISMA methodology, which provides a systematic framework for identifying, screening, and including relevant studies. As a result, we are confident in the thoroughness and representativeness of the examined corpus.

Second, the qualitative nature of our analyses may have introduced bias in the interpretation of the reviewed literature. To mitigate this risk, all analyses were conducted collaboratively, with the entire research team thoroughly reviewing both intermediate and final results. This approach helped ensure consistency in the coding activities and reduce individual bias.

7 Conclusion and Future Work

Our systematic literature review reveals common patterns in the adoption of MLOps practices and tools within healthcare applications of machine learning. Across the analyzed studies, MLOps pipelines consistently emphasize support for the stages of model training, deployment, and monitoring. However, real-world case studies underscore the significant impact of regulations on tailoring the MLOps pipeline for the healthcare domain [7,14,23].

A notable gap emerges in the MLOps pipeline's support for data-related stages. Data labeling, in particular, stands out as the least considered stage, potentially due to challenges in automating this process for sensitive healthcare data while ensuring human expert involvement. While the reviewed literature covers a range of medical specialties, our analysis suggests a slight inclination toward applications in internal medicine. This observation aligns with the data-intensive nature of this field and the potential benefits of streamlining machine learning workflows through MLOps.

Overall, our findings highlight the unique challenges and considerations surrounding MLOps adoption in healthcare. Regulatory requirements act as a driving force, shaping practices like data management, continuous integration, and model deployment. Addressing these challenges through tailored MLOps solutions will be crucial for the responsible and effective integration of machine learning technologies in this domain.

For future work, there is a clear opportunity to address the regulatory challenges within MLOps pipelines, drawing inspiration from established practices in other domains. Toivakka et al. [25] introduced the concept of "Regulated DevOps (RegOps)" for regulated continuous software delivery, providing a framework that can be adapted to the healthcare sector. Building upon this, the development of a regulation-compliant RegMLOps pipeline is warranted.

One aspect to explore is the operation of the pipeline partially or fully in a restricted or isolated environment to facilitate data management and model building phases, ensuring compliance with regulatory requirements. Another avenue is the automation of the data labeling phase through the use of Generative AI models, employing a semi-automatic approach that combines computational techniques with human expertise. This approach can enhance efficiency and accuracy while maintaining compliance.

Finally, efforts should be directed toward ensuring continuous deployment by automatically generating validation reports supported by model cards or using a standardized format for reporting. This will streamline the compliance verification process and enable rapid deployment of models into production environments. By addressing these key areas, the development of a regulation-compliant RegMLOps pipeline can significantly advance the integration of machine learning models into healthcare settings while ensuring adherence to regulatory standards and best practices.

Acknowledgements. The authors would like to thank Andrea Basile for assistance with data collection and preliminary analysis. This study has been co-funded by the Complementary National Plan PNC-I.1 - Research initiatives for innovative technologies and pathways in the health and welfare sector - D.D. 931 of 06/06/2022 ("DARE - DigitAl lifelong pRevEntion", code PNC0000002, CUP B53C22006420001) and the NRRP Initiative, Mission 4, Component 2, Investment 1.3 - Partnerships extended to universities, research centres, companies and research D.D. MUR n. 341, 15.03.2022 - Next Generation EU ("FAIR - Future Artificial Intelligence Research", code PE00000013, CUP H97G22000210007).

Disclosure of Interests. The authors have no competing interests to declare that are relevant to the content of this article.

References

1. Amershi, S., et al.: Software engineering for machine learning: a case study. In: 2019 IEEE/ACM 41st International Conference on Software Engineering: Software Engineering in Practice (ICSE-SEIP), pp. 291–300 (2019). https://doi.org/10.1109/ICSE-SEIP.2019.00042

2. Bai, E., Song, S.L., Fraser, H.S.F., Ranney, M.L.: A graphical toolkit for longitudinal dataset maintenance and predictive model training in health care. Appl. Clin. Inform. **13**(01), 056–066 (2022). https://doi.org/10.1055/s-0041-1740923

3. Berezsky, O., Pitsun, O., Melnyk, G., Batko, Y., Liashchynskyi, P., Berezkyy, M.: MLOps approach for automatic segmentation of biomedical images. In: Proceedings of the 6th International Conference on Informatics & Data-Driven Medicine, Bratislava, Slovakia, 17–19 November 2023. CEUR Workshop Proceedings, vol. 3609, pp. 241–248. CEUR-WS (2023)

4. Berezsky, O., Pitsun, O., Melnyk, G., Batko, Y., Derysh, B., Liashchynskyi, P.: Application of MLOps practices for biomedical image classification. In: Proceedings of the 5th International Conference on Informatics & Data-Driven Medicine, Lyon, France, 18–20 November 2022. CEUR Workshop Proceedings, vol. 3302, pp. 69–77. CEUR-WS (2022)

5. Cruz-Sandoval, D., et al.: Semi-automated data labeling for activity recognition in pervasive healthcare. Sensors **19**(14) (2019). https://doi.org/10.3390/s19143035

6. Fergus, P., Chalmers, C., Henderson, W., Roberts, D., Waraich, A.: Pressure ulcer categorization and reporting in domiciliary settings using deep learning and mobile devices: a clinical trial to evaluate end-to-end performance. IEEE Access **11** (2023). https://doi.org/10.1109/ACCESS.2023.3289839

7. Granlund, T., Stirbu, V., Mikkonen, T.: Towards regulatory-compliant MLOps: Oravizio's journey from a machine learning experiment to a deployed certified medical product. SN Comput. Sci. **2**(5), 342 (2021). https://doi.org/10.1007/s42979-021-00726-1

8. Haertel, C., Staegemann, D., Daase, C., Pohl, M., Nahhas, A., Turowski, K.: MLOps in data science projects: a review. In: 2023 IEEE International Conference on Big Data (BigData), pp. 2396–2404. IEEE, Sorrento, Italy (2023). https://doi.org/10.1109/BigData59044.2023.10386139

9. Jain, A., Malviya, A., Bajaj, D., Bhavsar, R., Savyanavar, A.: Brain tumor detection using MLops and hybrid multi-cloud. In: 2022 IEEE International Conference on Blockchain and Distributed Systems Security (ICBDS), pp. 1–6. IEEE, Pune, India (2022). https://doi.org/10.1109/ICBDS53701.2022.9936020

10. Karacsony, T., Loesch-Biffar, A.M., Vollmar, C., Noachtar, S., Cunha, J.P.S.: DeepEpil: towards an epileptologist-friendly AI enabled seizure classification cloud system based on deep learning analysis of 3D videos. In: 2021 IEEE EMBS International Conference on Biomedical and Health Informatics (BHI), pp. 1–5. IEEE, Athens, Greece (2021). https://doi.org/10.1109/BHI50953.2021.9508555

11. Kitchenham, B., Pearl Brereton, O., Budgen, D., Turner, M., Bailey, J., Linkman, S.: Systematic literature reviews in software engineering – a systematic literature review. Inf. Softw. Technol. **51**(1), 7–15 (2009). https://doi.org/10.1016/j.infsof.2008.09.009

12. Koutsopoulos, K., et al.: Federated machine learning through edge ready architectures with privacy preservation as a service. In: 2022 IEEE Future Networks World Forum (FNWF), pp. 347–350. IEEE, Montreal, QC, Canada (2022). https://doi.org/10.1109/FNWF55208.2022.00067

13. Kreuzberger, D., Kühl, N., Hirschl, S.: Machine learning operations (MLOps): overview, definition, and architecture. IEEE Access **11**, 31866–31879 (2023). https://doi.org/10.1109/ACCESS.2023.3262138

14. Lombardo, G., Picone, M., Mamei, M., Mordonini, M., Poggi, A.: Digital twin for continual learning in location based services. Eng. Appl. Artif. Intell. **127**, 107203 (2024). https://doi.org/10.1016/j.engappai.2023.107203

15. Mathew, N., Joseph, C.T.: Applying transfer learning on 3D brain images and an MLOPS study for deployment. In: 2023 9th International Conference on Smart Computing and Communications (ICSCC), pp. 541–547. IEEE, Kochi, Kerala, India (2023). https://doi.org/10.1109/ICSCC59169.2023.10335014

16. Meel, V., Bodepudi, A.: Melatect: a machine learning approach for identifying malignant melanoma in skin growths. In: Osten, W., Nikolaev, D., Zhou, J. (eds.) Fourteenth International Conference on Machine Vision (ICMV 2021), p. 61. SPIE, Rome, Italy (2022). https://doi.org/10.1117/12.2625005

17. Mitchell, M., et al.: Model cards for model reporting. In: Proceedings of the Conference on Fairness, Accountability, and Transparency, FAT* 2019, pp. 220–229. Association for Computing Machinery, New York (2019). https://doi.org/10.1145/3287560.3287596

18. Page, M.J., et al.: The PRISMA 2020 statement: an updated guideline for reporting systematic reviews. BMJ **372** (2021). https://doi.org/10.1136/bmj.n71

19. Ramakrishnan, G., Nori, A., Murfet, H., Cameron, P.: Towards Compliant Data Management Systems for Healthcare ML (2020). https://doi.org/10.48550/arXiv.2011.07555

20. Reddy, M., Dattaprakash, B., Kammath, S., Kn, S., Manokaran, S., Be, R.: Application of MLOps in prediction of lifestyle diseases. ECS Trans. **107**(1), 1191–1198 (2022). https://doi.org/10.1149/10701.1191ecst

21. Sculley, D., et al.: Hidden technical debt in Machine learning systems. In: Proceedings of the 28th International Conference on Neural Information Processing Systems, NIPS 2015, vol. 2, pp. 2503–2511. MIT Press, Cambridge (2015)

22. American Board of Medical Specialties: Guide to Medical Specialties. Technical report, ABMS, USA (2024). https://www.abms.org/abms-guide-to-medical-specialties

23. Stirbu, V., Granlund, T., Mikkonen, T.: Continuous design control for machine learning in certified medical systems. Softw. Qual. J. **31**(2), 307–333 (2023). https://doi.org/10.1007/s11219-022-09601-5

24. Symeonidis, G., Nerantzis, E., Kazakis, A., Papakostas, G.A.: MLOps - definitions, tools and challenges. In: 2022 IEEE 12th Annual Computing and Communication Workshop and Conference (CCWC), pp. 0453–0460 (2022). https://doi.org/10.1109/CCWC54503.2022.9720902

25. Toivakka, H., Granlund, T., Poranen, T., Zhang, Z.: Towards RegOps: a devops pipeline for medical device software. In: Ardito, L., Jedlitschka, A., Morisio, M., Torchiano, M. (eds.) PROFES 2021. LNCS, vol. 13126, pp. 290–306. Springer, Cham (2021). https://doi.org/10.1007/978-3-030-91452-3_20

Agile Management for Machine Learning: A Systematic Mapping Study

Lucas Romao[1]([envelope]) [ID], Hugo Villamizar[2] [ID], Romeu Oliveira[1] [ID], Silvio Alonso[1] [ID], and Marcos Kalinowski[1] [ID]

[1] PUC-Rio, Rio de Janeiro 22451-900, Brazil
{lromao,rferreira,smarques,kalinowski}@inf.puc-rio.br
[2] fortiss GmbH, 80805 Munich, Germany
guarinvillamizar@fortiss.org

Abstract. [Context] The dynamic nature of machine learning (ML) development, characterized by experimental cycles and rapid changes in data, poses challenges to traditional project management. Agile approaches, with their flexibility and incremental delivery, seem well-suited to address this dynamism. However, it is unclear how to effectively apply these methods in the context of ML-enabled systems. [Goal] Our goal is to outline the state of the art in agile management for ML-enabled systems. [Method] We conducted a systematic mapping study using a hybrid search strategy that combines database searches with backward and forward snowballing iterations. [Results] Our study identified 27 papers published between 2008 and 2024. From these, we identified eight approaches, 31 adapted practices, categorized recommendations into eight key themes, and identified main challenges. [Conclusion] This study contributes by mapping the state of the art of agile management for ML.

Keywords: Agile Management · Machine Learning · Mapping Study

1 Introduction

Machine Learning (ML) involves building systems that learn from data using statistical methods, evolving through iterative experimentation [10]. ML's dynamic nature demands flexible development processes to manage uncertainty and rapid changes [21]. Agile management approaches, such as Scrum and Kanban, conceptually align with the iterative exploratory nature of ML.

However, applying agile approaches to ML poses challenges. Time-boxed sprints struggle to accommodate ML's unpredictable experimentation, while sequential dependencies in ML workflows conflict with agile's preference for small independent increments [21]. Bridging this gap requires adaptations of agile practices to address ML-specific complexities, such as evolving data requirements and model uncertainty. Despite growing interest in this area, there remains a lack of consolidated knowledge about how the integration of agile and ML practices is being approached, what challenges persist, and which practices are effective.

D. Taibi and D. Smite (Eds.): SEAA 2025, LNCS 16082, pp. 350–360, 2026.
https://doi.org/10.1007/978-3-032-04200-2_24

To address this need, this paper presents a systematic mapping study (SMS) to synthesize existing research on agile management for ML-enabled systems. Our objective is to characterize the state of the art, by identifying proposed approaches, practices, recommendations, and challenges. The SMS identified 27 peer-reviewed papers published between 2008 and 2024. From this corpus, we identified eight approaches designed to adapt agile management approaches for ML-enabled systems development. Furthermore, by applying thematic synthesis [8], we categorized recommendations into eight key themes.

First, *Iteration Flexibility* enables data processing and model refinement through flexible sprints. Second, *ML-Specific Artifacts*, such as *Model/Data Stories* [34] and *Ethical User Stories* [13], bridge gaps between traditional and ML agile requirements. Third, *Decoupled Ceremonies* detach Scrum rituals from flexible sprint's pace to allow equally paced feedback. Fourth, *Hybrid Approaches* harmonize ML workflows with agile ceremonies to reconcile sequential dependencies and iterative delivery. Fifth, *Demo API* delivers functional models for SE teams, preserving agile deliverables amid ongoing experimentation. Sixth, with *Kanban Adoption* ML teams prioritize Kanban over Scrum as their primary agile approach. Seventh, *Business Alignment* ensures collaboration between technical teams and stakeholders to focus on delivering value. Finally, *Ethical Considerations* for backlog management are provided. Furthermore, we synthesized three challenge themes. First, *Sprint Planning & Effort Estimation*. Second, *Methodological, Training, and Strategic Alignment Deficiencies*. Finally, *Ethical Considerations*, with the foremost being ML effort estimation.

2 Background and Related Work

Agile management is a widely adopted flexible and iterative approach [16], grounded in the Agile Manifesto principles [5], that involves managing projects by focusing on delivering customer value incrementally, quickly adapting to change, and empowering cross-functional teams. Agile approaches seem well suited to address the dynamic nature of ML development, characterized by experimental cycles and rapid changes in data.

However, despite the widespread adoption, their application for managing ML-enabled system projects brings challenges [21]. For instance, the experimental and uncertain nature of ML development complicates effort estimation, making it difficult to guarantee deliverables within sprints. Unpredictable results and variables can derail planned work, while the lack of coherence between ML-enabled and non-ML components often leads to backlog disorganization and development delays [21]. Moreover, gaps in mutual understanding pose significant barriers. ML teams often lack familiarity with Software Engineering (SE) principles, leading to suboptimal coding practices, while developers may struggle to grasp ML concepts, resulting in and communication breakdowns [6].

These challenges underscore the need to better understand how agile project management can be tailored to ML-enabled systems. Although we identified related work concerning a multivocal literature review exploring practices for managing ML products in a more general sense with a focus on operationalizing ML in production environments [2], our mapping study focuses specifically on agile project management and on how agile approaches are adapted to address the unique challenges of ML-enabled system development.

3   Systematic Mapping Protocol

In this section, we present the research goal, questions, search strategy, and inclusion and exclusion criteria of our SMS, which follows the guidelines proposed by Peterson *et al.* [22], widely used in SE research.

3.1   Research Objectives and Questions

The main objective of this SMS is **to outline the state of the art in Agile Management for ML-enabled Systems**. Based on this goal, we propose the following Research Questions (RQ).

RQ1. What agile management approaches have been proposed for ML-enabled systems development? This question aims to uncover agile management approaches used during ML-enabled systems development.

RQ2. How are agile management practices tailored to align with ML-enabled systems development? This question aims to uncover how agile management practices were adapted to fit the demands of ML-enabled systems.

RQ3. What recommendations have been proposed for managing ML-enabled systems development? This question aims to summarize recommendations for managing the development of ML-enabled systems.

RQ4. What are the reported challenges when adapting agile management practices to ML-enabled systems development? This question aims to identify open challenges in agile management for ML-enabled systems.

RQ5. How can the research contributions be classified? This question aims to classify the research type according to the classification scheme proposed by Wieringa *et al.* [36].

RQ6. What empirical methods have been applied to validate the research contributions? This question aims to investigate the empirical methods that have been carried out. Gathering this information provides an initial overview of the applied scientific rigor of the identified studies.

3.2   Search Strategy

In this SMS, we adopted the search strategy proposed by Wohlin *et al.* [37], which has been recommended as effective for identifying relevant primary studies. It combines a structured search in the Scopus[1] digital database using a specific

---

[1] https://www.scopus.com/.

search string to identify a representative seed set to apply iterative backward and forward snowballing.

To perform the initial database search on Scopus, we formulated the search string following the PICO (Population, Intervention, Comparison, Outcomes) strategy [20]. In our study, ML-enabled systems constitute the *population*, and we seek to examine agile management practices for such systems (*intervention*). Since this study does not involve comparing studies, an outcome variable for comparison was not required. Based on this strategy, the final search string to identify the seed set was: (*"machine learning" OR "artificial intelligence") AND (("management" OR "practices") AND ("agile" or "scrum")).*

3.3   Study Selection

We set the timeframe for our search to the end of 2024. The Inclusion Criteria (IC) for our study is to include papers that address agile management practices and approaches used in ML-enabled systems development. The Exclusion Criteria (EC) applied in this study is outlined in Table 1. Details of the IC and EC application process are available in our Zenodo Open Science Repository[2].

Table 1. Exclusion criteria

Criteria	Description
EC1	Papers that do not meet the Inclusion Criteria
EC2	Papers that address ML techniques for Agile Management, given that, is not what we're looking for
EC3	Papers that do not address ML-enabled systems development (e.g., IoT projects, game development, and other software development)
EC4	Papers not written in English
EC5	Short papers (less than four pages)
EC6	Grey literature such as blogs, theses, and papers not reviewed by peers

The selection process is shown in Fig. 1. First, we searched for papers using the defined search string in the Scopus Library, filtering by applying the ECs and specific readings. Of the 1,104 papers initially retrieved, only ten were included. This process was conducted by the first author and peer reviewed.

Secondly, we applied backward and forward snowballing (via Google Scholar) on each selected paper to identify additional relevant studies not captured by the initial Scopus search. Through snowballing, we identified 17 additional papers, totalling 27. The snowballing process is documented online and took six iterations until saturation and involved screened over 1,300 additional papers.

---

[2] https://doi.org/10.5281/zenodo.14105692.

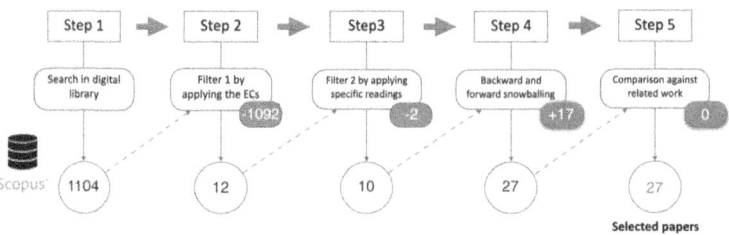

Fig. 1. Paper selection process

3.4   Data Extraction and Classification Scheme

The Data Extraction and Classification Scheme is outlined in Table 2. Given the variety of identified recommendations (RQ3) and challenges (RQ4), we applied thematic synthesis with open coding and summarizing key themes [8]. This entire process, and the extracted data are transparently documented in our repository.

Table 2. Data extraction scheme

Information	Description
Study metadata	Includes the title of the paper and information such as venue, type of venue, and year of publication
Agile approaches (RQ1)	Approaches proposed to suit ML-enabled system management demands
Approaches' practices (RQ2)	Practices created or adapted to suit ML-enabled systems management demands, such as new concepts or new artifacts to manage the backlog
Recommendations (RQ3)	Recommendations from papers that provide insights on how to manage ML-enabled system development using agile approaches
Challenges (RQ4)	Challenges that arise when adopting agile management methodologies in ML-enabled system development
Research type facet (RQ5)	Classification of paper's research type proposed by Wieringa *et al.* [36]: evaluation research, solution proposal, philosophical paper, opinion paper, or experience paper
Empirical Evaluation (RQ6)	Classification of the empirical evaluation strategy

4   Results

Agile management approaches (RQ1) and tailored practices (RQ2). We identified eight agile management approaches to deal with ML-enabled systems development. Moreover, we identified 31 adapted practices to fit the needs of ML-enabled systems. We summarized the approaches and practices, organized per year of their proposal, in Table 3.

Overall recommendations (RQ3). As a result of the thematic synthesis process, eight key themes emerged, which we describe hereafter.

Iteration Flexibility [7,14,15,24–26,29] manifests through capability-based iterations or flexible sprints, addressing the inherent unpredictability of ML experimentation cycles. *ML-Specific Artifacts* [12,13,31,34], such as model stories, data stories, and ethical user stories, introduce new requirements engineering tools aiming at bridging the gap between traditional agile documentation and ML needs. *Decoupled Ceremonies* [25,26,29] reconfigure scrum by detaching rituals from fixed sprint cycles. *Hybrid Approaches* [1,3,10,18,23,27,30,32,33,35], propose an alignment between data mining workflows and agile approaches, to reconcile ML's sequential dependencies to enable continuous value delivery. *Demo API* [3,12,18,34] contributes to the development process by providing small, but functional models that can be used by the SE team to remove bottlenecks from the development process while the ML team continues on their experimentation. *Kanban adoption* [4,24,28,32] points out that the usage of Kanban could be more efficient than scrum due to its absence of sprints. *Business alignment* [9,17,23] aims to ensure that ML teams are aligned with business needs. Finally, *Ethical Considerations* [11,13,19] are important to prevent unethical model behavior.

Reported Challenges (RQ4). We applied thematic synthesis and summarized the challenges into three key themes. First, *Sprint planning* [9,17,18,30] & *Effort estimation* [3,7,15,17,24,26,28,29,31,32]. The inherently sequential and interdependent nature of ML workflows contrasts with the discrete, independent structure of traditional user stories, leading to mismatches in sprint planning. Furthermore, studies highlight difficulties in estimating effort due to the experimental nature of ML workflows. Short sprint cycles struggle to accommodate ML-related activities. Second, *Methodological* [4,14,17,18,25,27,32,33,35], *Training* [7,10,11], and *Strategic Alignment Deficiencies* [23,26,29]. Key challenges include the lack of well-structured guidelines for ML-specific agile practices. Moreover, effective collaboration requires cross-training initiatives, where both ML and SE teams develop mutual competencies [6]. Additional challenges stem from misalignment between stakeholders, with business stakeholders often misunderstanding ML capabilities and data scientists facing difficulties translating technical constraints into actionable business requirements. Finally, the third theme concerns *Ethical Considerations* [11,13,17], with a lack of practical implementation strategies potentially leaving ethical aspects underexplored.

Research contribution types (RQ5) and empirical methods (RQ6). Fig. 2[a] illustrates the annual distribution of research contribution types following the classification framework by Wieringa *et al.* [36]. The distribution reveals that *Solution Proposals* constitute the predominant research type (13 of 27 papers). Furthermore, Fig. 2[b] delineates the distribution of empirical evalu-

Table 3. Agile Management Approaches and Their Adaptations

Year	Approach	Practices
2008	ASD-DM [1]	Speculate-Collaborate-Learn cycle instead Build-Measure-Learn
		Rollback CRISP-DM
		Short iterations (one-two weeks)
2018	Agile-facilitated KD [30]	One CRISP-DM full cycle per sprint (Hybrid-Approach Example)
		An improved model version after each sprint
2019	SKI [26]	Capability-based Iterations
		Decoupled Scrum Ceremonies
		WIP limits
		SKI Master role to manage flow and WIP limits
		Testable Hypothesis alongside each US
2020	ADS [18]	Scrumban + CRISP-DM cycle
		Every phase in the process is rollbackable
	Scrum-DS [3]	Sprint 0 for Data Preparation
		One CRISP-DM full cycle per Sprint
		Four-week Sprint
		Demo API
2021	STAMP4NLP [14]	Development Loop to handle granular model development
		Evolution Loop to handle larger PBIs and CI/CD
		BizDev & CI/CD alignment
2022	Agile4MLS [34]	Model & Data Stories
		Demo API
		One-week Sprints
		Differentiation between ML & non-ML Intensive Product Backlog Items (PBI)
		ML Team Dailies with a rotating SE team member, and vice-versa
		Separate ML and SE teams working in parallel, with ML PBIs planned 2 sprints ahead cover dependencies
		One Weekly with ML & SE teams together
	Data Driven Scrum [25]	Capability-based iterations
		Decoupled scrum ceremonies
		T-Shirt sizing PBI estimation
		Vertical/horizontal slicing
	None [13]	Adapt user stories to address ethical concerns

ation methods. Out of the 27 papers, 17 incorporate empirical evaluations, with *Case Studies* constituting the majority (nine papers).

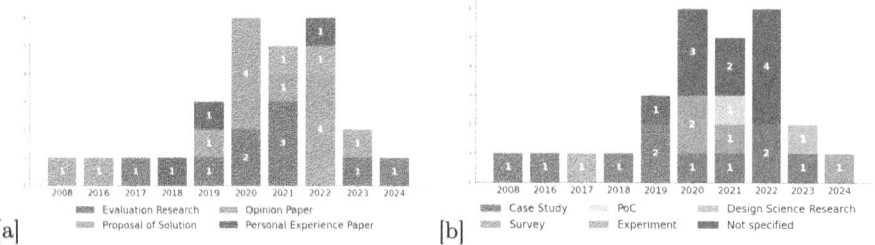

Fig. 2. [a] Distribution of research type per year. [b] Distribution of empirical evaluation type per year

5 Discussion

Several agile management approaches (RQ1) and practices (RQ2) tailored for ML-enabled systems have been proposed, mostly in recent years. The contributions reflect both innovative adaptations and significant challenges that persist in operationalizing the unique demands of ML development. Besides mapping the approaches and practices (*cf.* Table 3), we identified and organized recommendations (RQ3) into themes. Notably, *Hybrid Agile-Lifecycle Integration* emerged as the most prominent recommendation (ten of 27 papers), reflecting efforts to reconcile iterative agile practices with the sequential nature of ML workflows. Regarding the challenges (RQ4), task estimation remains particularly problematic due to the experimental nature of ML tasks and the rigid time-boxing of sprints, underscoring a fundamental tension between agile's predictability and ML's exploratory demands.

Although research contributions of different types emerged in recent years (RQ5), a critical gap lies in their empirical evaluation (RQ6) (*cf.* Fig. 2). We observed an imbalance between solution proposals and empirical evidence. While 17 of 27 papers incorporated some form of evaluation, the predominance of case studies limits their generalizability. Furthermore, 37% of studies completely lacked any empirical evaluation.

Overall, the mapping study reveals a fertile ground for future research. First, there is a need to reconcile the inherently sequential and interdependent nature of machine learning workflows with the iterative cadence of agile approaches. Hence, an important direction is the development of generalizable agile management guidelines tailored for ML-enabled systems. Further, improving collaboration and alignment between ML teams and business stakeholders also remains an important concern. In addition, research could help to answer how to operationalize ethical considerations within agile ML development. Finally, there is an opportunity to advance methods for task prioritization and effort estimation to further support the effective integration of ML into agile approaches.

6   Threats to Validity

In terms of *Internal Validity*, we built the search string for identifying the seed set using the PICO strategy, ensuring its direct alignment with our research goal. Further, we adopted a hybrid search strategy, integrating database search with iterative snowballing techniques. This strategy has shown to be effective for producing an unbiased and representative set of papers for secondary studies [37]. Regarding *External Validity*, to strengthen the generalizability and replicability of our findings, we made an effort to transparently document the steps undertaken and the results obtained. This information is accessible through our Zenodo repository. Finally, *Reliability* concerns center on the potential bias in study selection and thematic synthesis. To mitigate this risk, all steps were peer-reviewed by an independent researchers. Discrepancies were resolved through discussion and consensus involving a third researcher. Furthermore, the open science repository helps to make our research steps auditable.

7   Concluding Remarks

In this paper, we presented an SMS on agile management for ML-enabled systems development. We applied a hybrid search strategy that combines a Scopus database search with iterative backward and forward snowballing. Out of more than 2400 analyzed papers, we identified 27 studies addressing agile practices tailored to the unique challenges of ML development.

We mapped agile management approaches, tailored practices, recommendations, challenges, and the types of research and empirical studies conducted. The findings reveal that hybrid approaches are emerging to bridge the gap between agile approaches and ML workflows. Significant challenges remain in areas like effort estimation and cross-disciplinary collaboration.

The main contributions of this study are twofold: first, providing a comprehensive mapping of the state of the art in agile management for ML-enabled systems, and second, identifying key research gaps that invite further research.

Acknowledgements. We express our gratitude to CNPq (Grant 312275/2023-4), FAPERJ (Grant E-26/204.256/2024), Kunumi, and Stone Co. for their generous support.

References

1. Alnoukari, M., Alzoabi, Z., Hanna, S.: Applying adaptive software development (ASD) agile modeling on predictive data mining applications: ASD-DM methodology. In: International Symposium on Information Technology, vol. 2, pp. 1–6 (2008)
2. Alves, I., Leite, L.A., Meirelles, P., Kon, F., Aguiar, C.S.R.: Practices for managing machine learning products: a multivocal literature review. IEEE Trans. Eng. Manag. **71**, 7425–7455 (2023)

3. Baijens, J., Helms, R., Iren, D.: Applying scrum in data science projects. In: IEEE Conference on Business Informatics (CBI), vol. 1, pp. 30–38 (2020)
4. Baijens, J., Helms, R., Kusters, R.: Data analytics project methodologies: which one to choose? In: International Conference on Big Data in Management, pp. 41–47 (2020)
5. Beck, K., et al.: Manifesto for agile software development (2001)
6. Busquim, G., Villamizar, H., Lima, M.J., Kalinowski, M.: On the interaction between software engineers and data scientists when building machine learning-enabled systems. In: International Conference on Software Quality, pp. 55–75 (2024)
7. Cordeiro, R., Alves, I., Alves, S., Goldman, A.: Being agile in a data science project. In: Kruchten, P., Gregory, P. (eds.) Agile Processes in Software Engineering and Extreme Programming – Workshops (2024)
8. Cruzes, D.S., Dyba, T.: Recommended steps for thematic synthesis in software engineering. In: International Symposium on Empirical Software Engineering and Measurement, pp. 275–284 (2011)
9. Dastgerdi, A.K., Gandomani, T.J.: On the appropriate methodologies for data science projects. In: International Conference on Information Technology (ICIT), pp. 667–673 (2021)
10. Haakman, M., Cruz, L., Huijgens, H., Van Deursen, A.: AI lifecycle models need to be revised: an exploratory study in fintech. Empirical Softw. Eng. **26**(5), 95 (2021)
11. Halme, E., et al.: How to write ethical user stories? Impacts of the ECCOLA method. In: International Conference on Agile Software Development, pp. 36–52 (2021)
12. Jackson, S., Yaqub, M., Li, C.X.: The agile deployment of machine learning models in healthcare. Front. Big Data **1**, 7 (2019)
13. Kemell, K.K., Vakkuri, V., Halme, E.: Utilizing user stories to bring AI ethics into practice in software engineering. In: International Conference on Product-Focused Software Process Improvement, pp. 553–558 (2022)
14. Kohl, P., Schmidts, O., Klöser, L., Werth, H., Kraft, B., Zündorf, A.: Stamp 4 NLP–an agile framework for rapid quality-driven NLP applications development. In: International Conference on the Quality of Information and Communications Technology, pp. 156–166 (2021)
15. Kraut, N., Transchel, F.: On the application of scrum in data science projects. In: International Conference on Big Data Analytics (ICBDA), pp. 1–9 (2022)
16. Kuhrmann, M., Tell, P., Hebig, R., et al.: What makes agile software development agile? IEEE Trans. Softw. Eng. **48**(9), 3523–3539 (2022). https://doi.org/10.1109/TSE.2021.3099532
17. Lahiri, S., Saltz, J.: Evaluating data science project agility by exploring process frameworks used by data science teams (2023)
18. Lei, H., O'Connell, R., Ehwerhemuepha, L., Taraman, S., Feaster, W., Chang, A.: Agile clinical research: a data science approach to scrumban in clinical medicine. Intell.-Based Med. **3**, 100009 (2020)
19. Leijnen, S., Aldewereld, H., van Belkom, R., Bijvank, R., Ossewaarde, R.: An agile framework for trustworthy AI. In: NeHuAI@ ECAI, pp. 75–78 (2020)
20. Leonardo, R.: Pico: model for clinical questions. Evid. Based Med. Pract. **3**(115), 2 (2018)
21. Nahar, N., Zhang, H., Lewis, G., Zhou, S., Kästner, C.: A meta-summary of challenges in building products with ml components–collecting experiences from 4758+ practitioners. In: International Conference on AI Engineering–Software Engineering for AI (CAIN), pp. 171–183 (2023)

22. Petersen, K., Vakkalanka, S., Kuzniarz, L.: Guidelines for conducting systematic mapping studies in software engineering: an update. Inf. Softw. Technol. **64**, 1–18 (2015)
23. Qadadeh, W., Abdallah, S.: An improved agile framework for implementing data science initiatives in the government. In: International Conference on Information and Computer Technologies (ICICT), pp. 24–30 (2020)
24. Saltz, J., Crowston, K., et al.: Comparing data science project management methodologies via a controlled experiment (2017)
25. Saltz, J., Sutherland, A., Hotz, N.: Achieving lean data science agility via data driven scrum (2022)
26. Saltz, J., Suthrland, A.: Ski: an agile framework for data science. In: IEEE International Conference on Big Data (Big Data), pp. 3468–3476 (2019)
27. Saltz, J.S., Hotz, N.: Identifying the most common frameworks data science teams use to structure and coordinate their projects. In: International Conference on Big Data (Big Data), pp. 2038–2042 (2020)
28. Saltz, J.S., Shamshurin, I.: Achieving agile big data science: the evolution of a team's agile process methodology. In: IEEE International Conference on Big Data (Big Data), pp. 3477–3485 (2019)
29. Saltz, J.S., Sutherland, A., Jombart, T.: Identifying and addressing 6 key questions when using data driven scrum. In: International Conference on Big Data (Big Data), pp. 2345–2352 (2021)
30. Schmidt, C., Sun, W.N.: Synthesizing agile and knowledge discovery: case study results. J. Comput. Inf. Syst. **58**(2), 142–150 (2018)
31. Singla, K., Bose, J., Naik, C.: Analysis of software engineering for agile machine learning projects. In: IEEE India Council International Conference (INDICON), pp. 1–5 (2018)
32. Uysal, M.P.: Machine learning and data science project management from an agile perspective: methods and challenges. In: Contemporary Challenges for Agile Project Management, pp. 73–88. IGI Global (2022)
33. Uysal, M.P.: Toward a method engineering framework for project management and machine learning. In: Annual Computers, Software, and Applications Conference (COMPSAC), pp. 1186–1190 (2023)
34. Vaidhyanathan, K., Chandran, A., Muccini, H., Roy, R.: Agile4MLS-leveraging agile practices for developing machine learning-enabled systems: an industrial experience. IEEE Softw. **39**(6), 43–50 (2022)
35. Vial, G., Cameron, A.F., Giannelia, T., Jiang, J.: Managing artificial intelligence projects: key insights from an AI consulting firm. Inf. Syst. J. **33**(3), 669–691 (2023)
36. Wieringa, R., Maiden, N., Mead, N., Rolland, C.: Requirements engineering paper classification and evaluation criteria: a proposal and a discussion. Requirements Eng. **11**, 102–107 (2006)
37. Wohlin, C., Kalinowski, M., Felizardo, K.R., Mendes, E.: Successful combination of database search and snowballing for identification of primary studies in systematic literature studies. Inf. Softw. Technol. **147**, 106908 (2022)

Exploring Perturbation Patterns and Impact in Adversarial Machine Learning: A Systematic Literature Review

Alexandra Sheykina$^{(\boxtimes)}$ ⓘ, Fabio Palomba ⓘ, and Andrea De Lucia ⓘ

Department of Computer Science, SeSa Lab, University of Salerno, Fisciano, Italy
asheykina@unisa.it

Abstract. Adversarial attacks have gained growing attention due to their ability to mislead machine learning models by introducing carefully crafted perturbations. These attacks span a wide variety of domains, from image recognition to graph-based and NLP models. In this context, understanding the nature of such perturbations is crucial for both detecting attacks and designing effective defenses. Despite the abundance of research on adversarial machine learning, little is known about how perturbation types vary based on the category of the targeted feature, or how the amount of perturbation influences the attack's impact. To this aim, we conducted a systematic study to (i) identify and classify the perturbation strategies used in adversarial attacks and (ii) analyze the relationship between the strength of perturbation, the perturbation type, and the impact on model behavior. Our findings show that while many attacks apply minimal but targeted changes, the perturbation type plays a major role in determining the success of the attack. Furthermore, attacks with similar perturbation magnitudes may have vastly different impacts depending on their semantic focus. These insights can support the prioritization of defense mechanisms by focusing on high-impact perturbations, and lay the groundwork for improved adversarial detection systems based on perturbation-level analysis.

Keywords: Adversarial Machine Learning · Software Security · Systematic Literature Reviews

1 Background

Over the past 20 years, Machine Learning (ML) has become integral to many technologies, from virtual assistants like Siri and Alexa to protein folding solutions such as DeepMind's AlphaFold. ML has also transformed sectors like healthcare, agriculture, and transportation. However, as ML systems become more widespread, they face increasing threats from Adversarial Attacks (AAs), which can affect critical infrastructure such as autonomous vehicles and medical devices, raising serious safety, legal, and financial concerns. Given the growing reliance on ML, assessing their robustness against adversarial perturbations is

D. Taibi and D. Smite (Eds.): SEAA 2025, LNCS 16082, pp. 361–370, 2026.
https://doi.org/10.1007/978-3-032-04200-2_25

essential. The study analyzes how various perturbations impact model behavior and security to identify vulnerabilities and guide defense strategies.

Adversarial Machine Learning (AML) has evolved through four research stages. Early work focused on classical ML models (e.g., Random Forest) in domains like cybersecurity and computer vision. Barreno et al. [1] laid foundational concepts, while Liu et al. [2] categorized threats and defenses across the training and testing pipeline. With the rise of Deep Learning (DL), research shifted toward attacks and defenses tailored to neural networks. Akhtar et al. [3,4] surveyed attacks across tasks such as image classification, malware detection, and speech recognition, highlighting attack transferability and robustness of CNNs and RNNs. Biggio et al. [5] focused on the security evaluation of ML algorithms. Later, AML research expanded to broader data: text, audio, video, graphs, and time series [6,7], and applications such as spam filtering, intrusion detection, malware, and face recognition [8–10]. Various attack types, including poisoning, backdoor, evasion, and inference attacks, have been studied [11–14], with corresponding defenses proposed [7,8,11,15–19].

Our Contribution. While prior research in AML has extensively explored attack strategies, defense mechanisms, and even proposed taxonomies of adversarial examples [8,20–23], fewer studies have focused on systematically characterizing how different types of perturbations influence model vulnerability and security outcomes. Our work aims to fill this gap by offering a comprehensive analysis of the relationship between perturbation patterns and their impact on ML model robustness across multiple domains and tasks. We reviewed 162 relevant studies, mostly recent. The *purpose* is to understand how different types of perturbations and their characteristics affect the vulnerability of ML models. We adopt the *perspective* of both researchers, interested in modeling and detecting adversarial behaviors, and practitioners, focused on prioritizing defense strategies and ensuring the reliability of ML models. The *goal* is to examine the relationship between perturbation magnitude, type, and their impact on model security. The study highlights patterns across attack methods, discusses implications for detection and defense prioritization, and identifies open challenges in systematically integrating these insights into robustness evaluation tools for ML systems.

Structure of the Paper. Section 2 describes the research design and research questions of our systematic literature review, while the results are presented in Sect. 3. Finally, Sect. 4 concludes the paper and reports future work.

Online Appendix. All the data collected and the complete analysis conducted in this study are available in the replication package [27].

2   Research Methodology

Our paper investigates the current landscape of AML approaches to characterize the types of perturbations applied in attacks and their impact on model robustness. We aim to answer the following overarching research questions:

–   **RQ$_1$**: *What are the main perturbation patterns that emerge across adversarial attacks?*
–   **RQ$_2$**: *How do the type and perturbation strength influence the security impact on ML models?*

To build the database search string, we extracted keywords from our research questions and validated provisional strings against a set of known relevant studies, following established guidelines. The process concluded when all key studies were captured, the number of results was manageable, and all essential terms were included. We followed Kitchenham et al.'s three-stage approach [24]: (i) formulating the search string, (ii) applying it to selected databases, and (iii) filtering results based on inclusion and exclusion criteria. Furthermore, the search string is based on GQM terms to define the research objective by focusing on purpose, problem, object and point of view. The search query derived from **RQ**s is as follows:

(machine learning ∨ neural network ∨ deep learning) ∧ (adversarial sample* ∨ adversarial perturbation* ∨ adversarial example*) ∧ (misclassif* ∨ robustness ∨ vulnerability) ∧ (attack ∨ defense) ∧ (algorithm ∨ technique)

We applied our search query across three major databases: *Scopus*, *IEEE Xplore*, and *ACM Digital Library*, retrieving a total of 5,314 papers. These were imported into a local database and screened using predefined inclusion and exclusion criteria. The first filtering phase resulted in 2,901 articles. We then applied quality filters using SCIMAGO and CORE rankings, narrowing the list to 1,821 papers. Further manual screening reduced this to 1,525. A scoring system combining citation count, venue rank, and topic relevance helped us select 189 primary studies. A snowballing step using Google Scholar added 40 more, for a total of 229. We assessed study quality based on two criteria: clarity of attack/defense definitions and use of robustness evaluation metrics. We created a checklist for quality assessments, with questions answered as *Yes*, *Partially*, or *No*. Each label was assigned a numerical value: *1* for *Yes*, *0.5* for *Partially*, and *0* for *No*. The overall quality score was the average of these values for the two questions. Only studies scoring at least 0.75 were retained, resulting in 162 high-quality studies. Finally, to answer our research questions, we extracted the main characteristics of ASRs and defense methods by analyzing the documentation and experimental setups reported in the studies. Specifically, for each study, we collected data on the application domain, the addressed task (e.g., image classification, object detection), the input type (e.g., image, text, graph), the dataset used and its nature (in-vitro, synthetic, in-field), the features involved, the model architecture, the type of perturbation pattern applied, the percentage of perturbation, and the impact on the model's performance.

3   Results and Discussion

In the following sections, we present the key findings and insights derived from our analysis. Due to space limitations, the full list of 162 primary studies is not included in this version of the paper; it can be found in the online appendix together with the extended version of the paper [27].

3.1 RQ$_1$: *What are the Main Perturbation Patterns that Emerge Across Adversarial Attacks?*

To systematically examine how adversarial examples affect model robustness, we identify and describe the main perturbation patterns used in AAs across different domains. These patterns represent the characteristic ways in which adversarial modifications are introduced into inputs, models, or their environments. By analyzing 162 studies, we classify perturbations into 14 principal patterns, based on the nature, granularity, and modality of the manipulated data.

Pixel-level perturbation patterns are among the most widely studied forms of AAs, typically involving gradient-based manipulations under different norms L_0, L_1, L_2, L_∞ ranging from imperceptible distortions (e.g., $\epsilon = 0.03$) to more noticeable ones (e.g., $\epsilon = 128/255$) used in style-based attacks. *Structured perturbations*, such as grid-based occlusions and bit-level modifications, as well as *physical perturbations* (e.g., contrast or blur adjustments) have been explored to maintain adversarial effectiveness under real-world conditions. Advanced methods exploit *gradient priors* to concentrate perturbations on sensitive regions. This diversity highlights the complexity and adaptability of adversarial threats.

Packet- and byte-level perturbation refers to attacks that work by modifying specific bytes in a file or communication, without altering the semantic content. This type of attack is often used in contexts where data is represented as sequences of bytes (e.g., PDFs, network packets, executables). The idea is to add or modify a small number of bytes in such a way that the attack evades detection and does not affect the visual behavior or content of the data. Adversarial perturbations typically focus on imperceptible changes involving features like the number of bytes sent and received, the size and count of packets, the number of connections, the average connections per IP, and statistics related to the ratio of bytes exchanged. In the case of documents, they may involve the insertion of bytes without altering the semantic or visual content.

Geometric perturbation pattern acts by directly modifying the spatial arrangement of the image or the represented object. It includes operations such as rotation, translation, scaling, perspective distortion, cropping, and padding. Some of these transformations are applied digitally, and others simulate realistic physical scenarios, including variables such as distances, camera angles, indoor/outdoor settings, and lighting variations. Finally, some experiments employ discrete transformations such as moving some pixels in cardinal directions and specific angular rotations. More sophisticated attacks adopt instance-wise strategies and act on combined transformations to maximize effectiveness while maintaining high stealthiness.

Bytecode-level perturbation pattern directly intervenes on an app's representations (e.g., Android dex files), modifying features such as permissions, APIs, intents, and components to confuse classifiers. The alterations can affect both the structure visible in the manifest (e.g., unused permissions) and the semantic behavior in the bytecode (e.g., never-executed API calls).

Word-level perturbations modify single words or short sequences while preserving meaning, using synonyms, sememes, or morphological changes. In source code tasks, semantics-preserving transformations involve 2–3 identifier renamings (e.g., variables, functions) and structural edits like loop swaps, log insertions, or dead code. Further strategies include operand swaps, operator toggles, and control-flow modifications. Sentence- and document-level perturbations reorder or append sentences to mislead models, while character-level attacks insert, replace, or reorder characters, often using invisible symbols or homoglyphs.

3D Point Clouds perturbation patterns operate directly on the coordinates of points in the point cloud, slightly altering the perceived geometry of the object without changing its macroscopic shape. Some imperceptible perturbations operate in feature space, affecting parameters such as distance, altitude, and azimuth alterations, as well as geometric transformations such as rotation, scaling, and translation.

Node- and edge-level perturbations can be classified into two types: those that alter node or edge features without modifying the graph structure, and those that manipulate the structure itself. These modifications are often minimal but strategically crafted to mislead the model during classification or inference.

Patch-level perturbation pattern involves inserting modified and localized patches into real images, designed to remain "natural" and not obvious to the human eye. Perturbations are often generated via GANs or guided optimizations and can be physically printed as stickers or posters to be applied to real-world objects (e.g., road signs). These patches are designed to withstand variations in distance, angle, light conditions, and motion. Graffiti-style stickers represent a particularly dangerous form of attack because they combine stealth with real-world effectiveness.

Waveform-level perturbations involve the addition of ambient noise or sudden sounds to the audio signal. They can be natural (traffic, rain, voice) or synthetic. Perturbations, both physical and digital, have been studied across various real-world settings such as homes, offices, airports, and malls. Another critical aspect involves manipulating the volume and distance of the adversary signal, with measurements in dB SPL. Even at low intensity, these noises can cause significant degradation in speech recognition or command systems, especially when the model is sensitive to acoustic or semantic context.

Frame-level: perturbations are applied to individual frames or their fragments while preserving the main content. Temporal masks and optimization based on L_1, L_2 norms are used to ensure spatiotemporal efficiency. Attacks can be dispersed over time or concentrated within specific windows, and may also target blocks within a frame for precise and less noticeable manipulation.

Trojan trigger perturbations involve visible or invisible modifications introduced during training to activate malicious behavior in the model. The trigger acts as a "switch" that causes the model to produce an attacker-chosen output, without affecting performance on clean data. Triggers vary in shape, size, position, and transparency, and include image overlays, patch insertions, semantic patterns, or audio signals (e.g., bird chirps, engine noise). TrojanNet embeds auxiliary modules that activate backdoor behavior only when a specific pattern is present, overriding predictions without degrading accuracy on legitimate inputs.

Feature-level perturbation pattern involves the direct manipulation of the numerical data that serve as inputs to machine learning models. One example is the perturbation of time series data points, where the perturbation is progressively increased, resulting in a significant degradation of performance in models. Another scenario concerns the creation of adversarial users, where the objective is to determine the minimal perturbation vector that, when added to the feature vector of a sample, causes a classifier to misclassify it without raising suspicion. A further example is adversarial feature injection, in which perturbations are applied to dynamic features, treating each network flow or connection as a numerical vector, much like an image is represented by a pixel matrix.

Parameter and hyperparameter perturbations target the model's internal structure, manipulating layers, feature maps, or neuron counts to influence behavior. Techniques include backdoor injections via weight manipulation, malicious architectural changes (e.g., added nodes or connections), and deliberate tuning of hyperparameters like learning rate or optimizer to induce vulnerabilities or divergent outputs.

Query-based perturbation pattern includes attacks that indirectly manipulate the model through a strategic sequence of queries. The goal is to infer information about the internal structure, weights, or training data of the model or data. Attackers can build surrogate models, reconstruct sensitive inputs via model inversion, or violate privacy by detecting whether an example belongs to the training set (membership inference). The attack is particularly dangerous in black-box environments, where the only access channel is the model response.

3.2   RQ$_2$: *What is the Relationship Between the Amount and Type of Perturbation and Their Impact?*

Upon thoroughly examining the existing literature concerning the impact of AAs on machine learning systems, to assess our RQ_2, our attention has shifted towards identifying the specific areas in which the impact manifests most critically. We aim to gain insight into the consequences and vulnerabilities exposed by these attacks, highlighting the dimensions where their effect is most profound. The main impact dimensions have been grouped into three categories:

Model performance degradation varies significantly depending on the type of perturbation. *Pixel-level* and *waveform-level* perturbations demonstrate a nonlinear relationship between the amount of perturbation and the performance degradation: even small changes (e.g., subtle changes in a single pixel or a slight audio noise) can cause a large performance degradation, with $L_0 = 2$ achieve an ASR of up to 100%, reducing key metrics such as AUC from 0.87 to 0.52, with particularly severe impacts in medical imaging models, computer vision, and speech recognition models. In NLP, semantics-preserving perturbations also cause significant performance drops. Models like CodeGPT, PLBART, and CodeT5 show CodeBLEU reductions. Importantly, models that rely heavily on contextual information, such as LSTM- or Transformer-based architectures, exhibit greater susceptibility compared to models incorporating structural information. In the physical context, slight *geometric transformations* are enough to achieve *ASR* up to 100%. Imperceptible perturbations applied to waveform patterns have been shown to achieve an *ASR* of 99.5%. While physically applied patch-level perturbations, such as camouflaged sticker attacks, have demonstrated a 100% *ASR*. Physical or digital *triggers*, even invisible ones, can activate unwanted behaviors while maintaining high performance on clean data, as demonstrated in TrojanNet. In the *binary-level* perturbations, the insertion of sequences from 500 to 20,000 bytes can generate *ASR*s between 74% and 99.5%. *Bytecode* or *feature* attacks significantly degrade the performance of malware detection systems: alterations affecting only 0.0004% of the features lead to errors in 63% of malicious samples. At the *3D point-level*, small perturbations or the addition of some spoofed points drastically reduce *accuracy* with an *ASR* of ≈75%, especially on models pre-trained on complex datasets such as ModelNet40. In graphs, tree structural changes significantly compromise performance. *Query-based* perturbations do not directly degrade performance during the attack, but allow the construction of equivalent models for malicious uses.

Security and Robustness Threats. Several mitigation techniques have been proposed in the scientific literature, aiming to reduce the impact of adversarial perturbations and improve the robustness of models. These strategies include approaches based on adversarial training, dynamic perturbation detection, model distillation, randomization, and feature squeezing techniques, all designed to mitigate the effects of attacks and ensure more stable performance. However, despite the progress made, many defenses such as denoising, super-resolution, and adversarial training show only partial effectiveness, often at the expense of predictive quality. In graphs, simple structural changes outperform non-optimized defenses, while approaches such as RGCN and Pro-GNN offer improvements. Geometric transformations represent a concrete threat to visual models, with high transferability between architectures, even if trained with defensive techniques (FGSM, PGD, C&W). Bytecode-level perturbations have less impact on standard performance metrics, but can significantly alter the model's ability to distinguish between benign and malicious code, causing critical errors in security contexts. Invisible backdoors, activated by realistic inputs, can elude even advanced techniques, showing high transferability and confirmed effectiveness on real devices. Defenses such as data augmentation or spectral analysis are not effective. Trojan attacks represent a serious threat, with minimal alterations difficult to detect even with advanced structural analysis. Model extraction, inversion, and membership inference attacks undermine intellectual property and privacy, facilitating future manipulation.

Severity and Exploitability Factors. The severity of an adversarial attack is determined by the potential damage it can cause to the application or the end user, while exploitability reflects the ease with which the attack can be executed, taking into account the necessary knowledge, the required computational resources, and the type of access to the model. The severity assessment considers several factors: complexity of the attack, level of access required, available mitigations, and impact on data integrity, confidentiality, and availability. In AML contexts, it is also essential to consider transferability. Attacks characterized by very small perturbation values are particularly insidious, especially in areas such as autonomous driving, where they can hide critical elements such as pedestrians with invisible noise, seriously compromising safety. In the audio domain, threats countered by AntiFake demonstrate the severity of real-world vulnerabilities: financial fraud, sensitive data theft, and bypassing voice authentication systems can be performed simply by using public or stolen audio. Stealth attacks with high transferability are among the most dangerous because they work on different models without the need for internal access, are effective even on complex models in production, and are difficult to detect, especially when localized in physical patches rather than distributed across the entire input.

4   Conclusion and Future Work

In this systematic literature review, we analyzed 162 studies to provide a structured synthesis of AML research. Our contributions include: (i) a comprehensive categorization of attacks and defenses across domains; (ii) an analysis of perturbation patterns and their influence on attack success; (iii) an evaluation of how perturbation type and strength affect model robustness; and (iv) the publication of an online appendix with all study references and materials [27]. There are some threats to validity in our study, these were addressed through established practices [25, 26]. To mitigate *descriptive validity* threats, we collaboratively designed the data collection form. *Theoretical validity* was ensured via a systematic search and snowballing on Scopus, IEEE, and ACM. *Interpretive validity* was addressed by involving experienced researchers. For *constructive validity*, two reviewers independently assigned scores, resolving disagreements through discussion; although no inter-rater metric was computed, shared guidelines supported consistency. To ensure *repeatability*, the process was documented and data are available in the replication package [27]. Future work includes developing a vulnerability assessment framework based on our taxonomy and leveraging perturbation impact to prioritize risks in ML security evaluations.

Acknowledgements. This work has been partially supported by the EMELIOT national research project, which has been funded by the MUR under the PRIN 2020 program (Contract 2020W3A5FY), by project SERICS (PE00000014) under the NRRP

MUR program funded by the EU - NGEU, and by project FAIR (PE0000013) under the NRRP MUR program funded by the EU - NGEU.

Disclosure of Interests. The authors have no competing interests to declare that are relevant to the content of this article.

References

1. Barreno, M., Nelson, B., Sears, R., Joseph, A.D., Tygar, J.D.: Can machine learning be secure? In: Proceedings of the ACM Symposium on Information, Computer and Communications Security, pp. 16–25. ACM, New York (2006)
2. Liu, Q., Li, P., Zhao, W., Cai, W., Yu, S., Leung, V.C.M.: A survey on security threats and defensive techniques of machine learning: a data driven view. IEEE Access **6**, 12103–12117 (2018)
3. Akhtar, N., Mian, A.: Threat of adversarial attacks on deep learning in computer vision: a survey. IEEE Access **6**, 14410–14430 (2018)
4. Akhtar, N., Mian, A., Kardan, N., Shah, M.: Advances in adversarial attacks and defenses in computer vision: a survey. IEEE Access **9**, 155161–155196 (2021)
5. Biggio, B., Roli, F.: Wild patterns: ten years after the rise of adversarial machine learning. In: Proceedings of the ACM SIGSAC Conference on Computer and Communications Security, pp. 2154–2156. ACM, New York (2018)
6. Xu, H., et al.: Adversarial attacks and defenses in images, graphs and text: a review. Int. J. Autom. Comput. **17**, 151–178 (2020)
7. Jin, W., et al.: Adversarial attacks and defenses on graphs. ACM SIGKDD Explor. Newsl. **22**(2) (2021)
8. Vakhshiteh, F., Nickabadi, A., Ramachandra, R.: Adversarial attacks against face recognition: a comprehensive study. IEEE Access **9**, 92735–92756 (2021)
9. Aryal, K., Gupta, M., Abdelsalam, M.: A survey on adversarial attacks for malware analysis. arXiv preprint arXiv:2111.08223 (2021)
10. Pitropakis, N., Panaousis, E., Giannetsos, T., Anastasiadis, E., Loukas, G.: A taxonomy and survey of attacks against machine learning. Comput. Sci. Rev. **34**, 100199 (2019)
11. Wang, Z., Ma, J., Wang, X., Hu, J., Qin, Z., Ren, K.: Threats to training: a survey of poisoning attacks and defenses on machine learning systems. ACM Comput. Surv. **55**(7) (2022)
12. Xue, M., Yuan, C., Wu, H., Zhang, Y., Liu, W.: Machine learning security: threats, countermeasures, and evaluations. IEEE Access **8**, 74720–74742 (2020)
13. Aldahdooh, A., Hamidouche, W., Fezza, S.A., Déforges, O.: Adversarial example detection for DNN models: a review and experimental comparison. Artif. Intell. Rev. 1–60 (2022). https://doi.org/10.1007/s10462-021-10125-w
14. Cinà, A.E., Grosse, K., Demontis, A., Biggio, B., Roli, F., Pelillo, M.: Machine learning security against data poisoning: are we there yet? arXiv preprint arXiv:2204.05986 (2022)
15. Ilahi, I., et al.: Challenges and countermeasures for adversarial attacks on deep reinforcement learning. IEEE Trans. Artif. Intell. **3**(2) (2021)
16. Liu, Y., Tantithamthavorn, C., Li, L., Liu, Y.: Deep learning for Android malware defenses: a systematic literature review. ACM Comput. Surv. **55**(8) (2022)
17. Cinà, A.E., et al.: Wild patterns reloaded: a survey of machine learning security against training data poisoning. ACM Comput. Surv. **55**(13s) (2023)

18. Dong, H., Dong, J., Yuan, S., Guan, Z.: Adversarial attack and defense on natural language processing in deep learning: a survey and perspective. In: Proceedings of the International Conference on Machine Learning for Cyber Security, pp. 409–424 (2022)

19. Ling, X., et al.: Adversarial attacks against Windows PE malware detection: a survey of the state-of-the-art. Comput. Secur. 103134 (2023)

20. Yuan, X., He, P., Zhu, Q., Li, X.: Adversarial examples: attacks and defenses for deep learning. IEEE Trans. Neural Netw. Learn. Syst. **30**(9) (2019)

21. Silva, S.H., Najafirad, P.: Opportunities and challenges in deep learning adversarial robustness: a survey. arXiv preprint arXiv:2007.00753 (2020)

22. Chakraborty, A., Alam, M., Dey, V., Chattopadhyay, A., Mukhopadhyay, D.: A survey on adversarial attacks and defences. CAAI Trans. Intell. Technol. **6**(1) (2021)

23. Serban, A., Poll, E., Visser, J.: Adversarial examples on object recognition: a comprehensive survey. ACM Comput. Surv. **53**(3) (2020)

24. Kitchenham, B.: Procedures for performing systematic reviews. Technical report 33, Keele University (2004)

25. Kitchenham, B., Brereton, O.P., Budgen, D., Turner, M., Bailey, J., Linkman, S.: Systematic literature reviews in software engineering-a systematic literature review. Inf. Softw. Technol. **51**(1), 7–15 (2009)

26. Petersen, K., Feldt, R., Mujtaba, S., Mattsson, M.: Systematic mapping studies in software engineering. In: 12th International Conference on Evaluation and Assessment in Software Engineering, pp. 1–10. BCS, Swinton (2008)

27. Sheykina, A.: Replication package for Exploring Perturbation Patterns and Impact in AML. https://github.com/sashasheykina/Adversarial-Machine-Lerning-SRL

Mapping the Landscape of Requirements Completeness: Definitions, Techniques, Tools, and the Emerging Role of AI

Mohamad Kassab[1]([⊠])[iD] and Marwan AbdElhameed[2]

[1] Boston University, Boston, MA 02215, USA
mkassab@bu.edu
[2] New York University Abu Dhabi, Abu Dhabi, UAE
mwa7459@nyu.edu

Abstract. Requirements completeness is crucial yet challenging in software engineering, significantly impacting project success. This paper systematically reviews existing research from 2000 to 2024 to consolidate definitions, detection methods, completeness metrics, improvement frameworks, and supporting tools, emphasizing emerging AI-based solutions. Our synthesis identifies the multi-dimensional nature of completeness and reveals opportunities to integrate AI and automation more deeply into the requirements engineering process. We highlight gaps and propose future directions to achieve systematic and scalable completeness checking, emphasizing the transformative potential of Large Language Models (LLMs) in enhancing requirements quality.

Keywords: Requirements Completeness · Software Requirements Engineering · Requirements Quality Metrics · Large Language Models (LLMs)

1 Introduction

Requirements completeness refers to the degree to which a Software Requirements Specification (SRS) fully captures all necessary information about the system and its context [6,30]. Gaps in requirements spawn not only costly downstream errors [18] but also contribute to around 78% of project failures [36]. Ensuring completeness is therefore indispensable for project success.

In practice, achieving complete requirements is difficult. Natural language remains the dominant format for writing requirements (increased from 61% in 2013 to 69% in 2020 [22]), which can make omissions hard to detect. In addition, completeness itself has multiple facets. According to the ISO/IEEE 29148 standard [1], a complete requirements set should address all inputs and outputs, cover all required behaviors and constraints, and make no implicit assumptions. Lindland *et al.* [30] describe completeness as one of the fundamental qualities of requirements, meaning no relevant information is omitted from the specification. Zowghi and Gervasi [45] further distinguish between internal completeness (each individual requirement is fully stated with no placeholders like "TBD") and external completeness (the set of requirements covers all stakeholder goals and system contexts). However, the literature shows variability in how completeness is interpreted and evaluated.

Although critical, requirements completeness lacks a comprehensive synthesis—existing work remains fragmented across early definitions [6,30], individual metrics (e.g., [12,34]), and isolated tools prototyping (e.g., [18,36]). To address this, we conducted an AI-supported systematic literature review (SLR) on requirements completeness in software systems, driven by six research questions:

- **RQ1:** How is requirements completeness defined in software-systems research?
- **RQ2:** Which methods detect incompleteness in software requirements?
- **RQ3:** Which metrics quantify completeness in software specifications?
- **RQ4:** Which approaches improve completeness once gaps are identified?
- **RQ5:** Which tools support assessment or enhancement of completeness?
- **RQ6:** What role do AI and LLMs play in addressing requirements completeness?

By answering these RQs, we map existing approaches, pinpoint research gaps, and outline practical strategies for improving requirement quality and reducing costly rework.

The remainder of this paper is structured as follows: Sect. 2 details our SLR methodology; Sect. 3 presents the findings for RQ1–RQ6; Sect. 4 examines the key insights and their practical implications; Sect. 5 outlines threats to validity, while Sect. 6 concludes the paper by exploring future work (including a vision for a multi-LLM-based completeness tool that is currently under development by the authors).

2   Methodology

2.1   Review Process

Our review followed established SLR guidelines [23,24,41] and the ACM SIG-SOFT empirical standards [39]. We defined a detailed protocol in advance and documented every step for reproducibility (the extraction questions, the prompt, all extracted data, and the mapped data to their corresponding categories per research questions are available in an online repository: (https://shorturl.at/NAwVV). We searched three major bibliographic databases IEEE Xplore, ACM Digital Library, and Scopus. The search was executed in September 2024 using the following Boolean expression:

```
("Completeness" OR "Complete" OR "Missing" OR
"Incompleteness" OR "Incomplete" OR "coverage" OR "omission")
AND ("Requirements") AND ( "Assessment" OR "Evaluation" OR
"Measurement" OR "Criteria" OR "Framework" OR "Method" OR
"Technique")
```

The search was limited to English-language, peer-reviewed articles from January 2000 through May 2024. We selected 2000 as our start year because, prior to that, completeness was discussed only at a conceptual level (e.g., early models by Boehm and Papaccio [6] and Lindland *et al.* [30]), whereas the turn of the millennium saw the first rigorous metrics and prototype tools for assessing completeness. In addition, the 830-1998 - IEEE Recommended Practice for Software Requirements Specifications formally codified completeness as a key quality attribute [14], laying the groundwork for systematic, tool-supported approaches in the new millennium.

To streamline study selection, screening, and data extraction, we utilized the Covidence tool[1]. The initial search yielded 292 records, from which 6 duplicates were removed, resulting in 286 unique records for further screening.

We applied explicit inclusion and exclusion criteria across two screening rounds.

Inclusion Criteria. To be included, studies had to meet all of the following:

- be peer-reviewed,
- be written in English,
- be published in or after the year 2000,
- explicitly address software requirements completeness (e.g., by defining completeness, proposing metrics, or presenting evaluation methods) within a software engineering context.

Exclusion Criteria. Studies were excluded if they met any of the following:

- did not focus on software or requirements engineering,
- were not written in English,
- were not peer-reviewed (e.g., theses, reports, or other gray literature),
- lacked a substantial focus on the concept of completeness.

2.2   Screening and Quality Control

The study selection was carried out in two stages. First, title and abstract screening was performed on all retrieved records. The two authors independently screened each title/abstract against the inclusion criteria; papers clearly not related to requirements completeness were filtered out. In cases of disagreement, the reviewers discussed to reach consensus (or consulted a third reviewer). We excluded 217 papers based on title/abstract screening (for not meeting the inclusion criteria). Next, we obtained the full texts of the remaining 69 papers and conducted a full-text screening. Each paper was carefully reviewed to ensure that it addressed requirements completeness in sufficient depth and met the inclusion and exclusion criteria. We excluded 8 papers that fell outside the study

---

[1] Covidence is a paid tool; researchers without access may use free alternatives such as Rayyan to replicate this process.

scope—most commonly because they referred to completeness only in passing, lacked original insights, or focused on data completeness in databases rather than requirements completeness. While we assessed study quality (e.g., clarity of context and methodological rigor) to support our interpretation of results, no studies were excluded solely on the basis of quality as long as they were relevant to our research focus.

As illustrated in the PRISMA figure (Fig. 1), the search and selection process yielded 61 primary studies for data extraction and analysis. These studies span publication years from the early 2000s to 2024. The temporal distribution is as follows: 3 studies from 2000–2004, 5 from 2005–2009, 19 from 2010–2014, 15 from 2015–2019, and 19 from 2020–2024. This pattern suggests a marked increase in interest and research activity on requirements completeness starting in the early 2010s, with continued momentum into the most recent years, indicating its growing relevance in contemporary software engineering research. The primary studies set represents a mix of journal articles (21) and conference papers (40) in requirements engineering and software engineering venues.

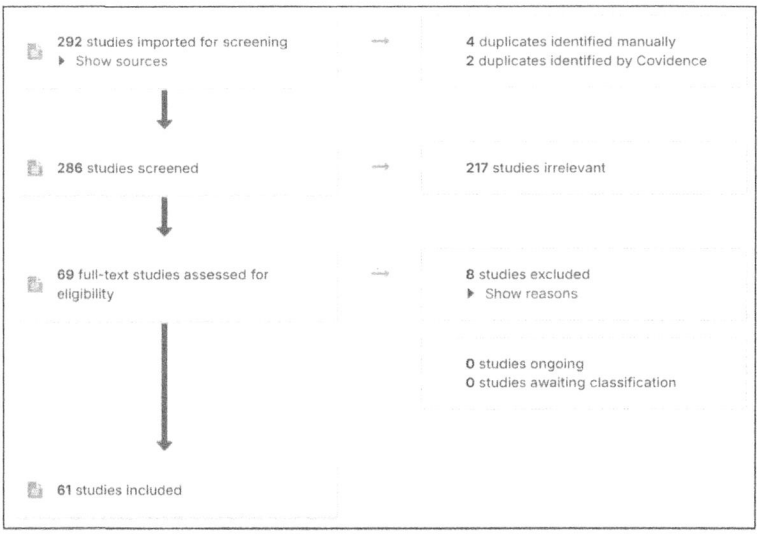

Fig. 1. Papers Selection Process.

2.3   Data Extraction

For each of the 61 primary studies, we used a structured data extraction form of 17 questions grouped into 7 sections to record information relevant to our research questions (The extraction form is available in the online repository).

The data extraction process was conducted in September 2024. To streamline the extraction process and ensure consistency, we employed the Claude 3.5 Sonnet LLM through prompt engineering. Claude 3.5 Sonnet was selected based on its demonstrated strength in structured information extraction and its ability to handle long textual contexts. Compared to other LLMs, Sonnet exhibits superior prompt adherence and tends to produce concise, non-speculative responses—qualities essential for maintaining fidelity to SLR protocols. Prior comparative evaluations (e.g., [4,28,32]) have highlighted Sonnet's strong alignment, domain-specific reliability, and reduced hallucination rates, making it particularly well-suited for evidence synthesis tasks.

The prompt used for extraction was carefully designed to reflect our defined extraction questions and was validated through an iterative and systematic process. As part of the validation process, Claude's output from the initial prompt was manually reviewed for 6 studies, approximately 10% of the dataset, by both authors. We iteratively refined prompts based on a proxy inter-rater agreement $\kappa > 0.8$, validated with a random sample of studies. This process was repeated until the final prompt version was agreed on. This approach is also aligned with recent evidence showing that LLMs can effectively support data extraction and conceptual coding in systematic reviews when combined with human oversight [13,26]. The final version of the prompt used is available in the online repository.

Following prompt calibration, the validated prompt was applied to all 61 primary studies. Extracted results were stored and organized using the Covidence platform. All data were manually reviewed by both authors to ensure correctness and consistency through cross-checking with the original study texts. In cases where Claude's output was ambiguous, encountered in 8 studies, a full manual extraction was conducted for that study. This human-in-the-loop approach reflects best practices in AI-assisted SLRs.

2.4 Analysis

Our synthesis comprised both quantitative aggregation and qualitative thematic analysis to provide a comprehensive understanding of the literature.

First, we organized the extracted data by research question (RQ1–RQ6), clustering studies that addressed each question in comparable ways. For RQ1, we catalogued every unique definition of requirements completeness, annotating each with its source and contextual framing (e.g., internal vs. external completeness).

For RQ2–RQ6, we performed an inductive thematic analysis. Extraction outputs were open-coded to identify recurring concepts, which were then grouped into higher-order themes (for example, NLP-based detection methods, template-matching techniques, model-checking approaches, and stakeholder-driven reviews). Using the constant-comparison method, we refined these themes, establishing precise definitions, inclusion criteria, and boundaries for each category. Following theme development, we conducted frequency counts for each category to quantify their prevalence.

Throughout this process, we preserved a strict chain of evidence by linking each synthesized theme back to the original extraction item. In the Results section, we present illustrative examples to substantiate our findings.

To validate the reliability of our synthesis, two independent external researchers reviewed and cross-checked the thematic categorizations and interpretations. Any discrepancies were resolved through collaborative re-examination of the source studies.

3   Synthesis of Findings on Requirements Completeness

This section synthesizes the results of our SLR, organized around the six RQs that address how requirements completeness is defined, evaluated, improved, and supported by tools and AI-based techniques.

3.1   RQ1: Definitions of Requirements Completeness

Among the 61 primary studies in our review, 34 provide an explicit definition of what it means for a requirements specification to be *complete* (see the online repository). While there is broad agreement that completeness entails capturing every necessary requirement or piece of information in the SRS, authors frame this concept in subtly different ways.

A frequent starting point is established standards or seminal models. For example, IEEE 29148–2018 mandates that a complete requirements set "addresses all inputs, outputs, and behaviors with no implicit assumptions" [1]. Likewise, Lindland *et al.* characterize completeness as having "no relevant information missing" from the requirements document [30]. In practice, these definitions imply that every functionality, constraint, or interface must be explicitly specified.

Many studies further distinguish between two complementary views: *internal completeness*, which requires each requirement statement to be self-contained (no blank sections or "TBD" markers), and *external completeness*, which demands that the requirements set as a whole exhaustively covers stakeholder needs and the system's environment. Zowghi and Gervasi illustrate this distinction by showing how an SRS can be internally complete yet still omit entire requirements domains if they were never elicited [45].

To better organize the diversity of definitions, we further cluster them into three broad families:

1. **General Definitions**, grounded in standards and foundational works, which emphasize the absence of omissions at both the statement and document levels;
2. **Stakeholder-Centered Definitions**, which tie completeness to formal stakeholder consensus (e.g., a specification is complete only when all key parties approve it [7]);

3. **Context-Specific Definitions**, which tailor completeness criteria to partic-ular domains or artifact types—for instance, Yu *et al.* define *event complete-ness* in event-driven systems as covering every possible event in a scenario to avoid costly defects [43].

Across all these perspectives, two core dimensions consistently emerge:

- *No Missing Pieces*: Ensuring every required detail is documented with no "TBD" placeholders (internal completeness).
- *Coverage of Intended Scope*: Verifying that the specification addresses all relevant stakeholder needs and domain concerns (external completeness).

Achieving true requirements completeness thus requires satisfying both internal consistency and external coverage. In practice, teams blend general standards, stakeholder sign-off processes, and domain-specific checklists to operationalize completeness in their unique project contexts.

3.2 RQ2: Methods and Techniques Used to Detect Requirements Incompleteness

Across our 61 primary studies, 59 propose at least one method for uncover-ing missing or incomplete requirements. We group these into eight thematic categories—ranging from manual inspections to AI-driven analyses (Table 1). Many studies employ multiple approaches, so the total count in the table exceeds 59. We provide the complete mapping of the studies to these categories in the online repository.

Formal methods and model checking (9 studies) detect omissions by prov-ing or refuting completeness properties. For example, Alrajeh *et al.* generate "obstacle" scenarios via formal specifications to expose unhandled conditions [3], and Zowghi & Gervasi link evolution proof obligations to the discovery of newly missing requirements [45]. In parallel, semi-formal model-based techniques (11 studies) employ information models or directed graphs—Menzel *et al.* map each requirement to model elements to count gaps [35], and Moketar *et al.* derive abstract test cases from use cases to pinpoint requirements lacking test coverage [37].

Given the predominance of natural-language specifications, a dozen stud-ies adopt NLP and ML. Xiang *et al.* use semantic role labeling to flag policy statements missing key roles [42], while Eckhardt *et al.* apply linguistic patterns to performance requirements to identify absent parameters [9]. Recent BERT-based approaches mask tokens to predict and highlight missing terminology [33]. Knowledge-based and ontology-driven methods (5 studies) further enrich this by mapping requirements to domain ontologies—Kaiya *et al.* flag unmapped con-cepts as gaps [19], and Kravari *et al.* execute SPARQL queries to uncover missing relationships [27].

Simpler, pattern-based and checklist techniques remain popular (13 stud-ies), using templates (e.g., user-story or IEEE 830 outlines) to highlight empty sections as omissions. Manual reviews (5 studies) leverage guided walkthroughs and stakeholder workshops to catch what automated tools might miss. Finally, metrics-driven evaluations (5 studies) quantify completeness via scores or ratios, such as the `degFEC` functional encapsulation metric [11].

In practice, these methods often serve as aides to analysts: automated tools scale and reveal subtle gaps, while manual inspections provide essential domain context. Notably, most approaches emphasize functional coverage, with less explicit focus on non-functional requirements [21]. Ultimately, detection techniques highlight potential omissions, but expert judgment remains crucial to confirm and remedy them.

Table 1. RQ2: Methods for detecting requirements incompleteness

Category	Short Description	# Studies
Manual Review	Guided walkthroughs and stakeholder workshops	5
Pattern-Based	Templates or checklists to flag empty sections	13
NLP/ML	Semantic parsing, token prediction, and classification	12
Formal Modeling & Verification	Proof obligations and model checking to expose gaps	9
Model-Based	Information models, graphs, and traceability analyses	11
Goal-Oriented	KAOS refinements and obstacle analysis	5
Knowledge-Based & Ontology	Ontology mapping and SPARQL queries	5
Metrics-Driven	Numeric completeness scores and ratios	5

3.3   RQ3: Metrics and Quantification of Completeness

While most research on requirements completeness remains qualitative, 41 of our 61 primary studies propose explicit metrics, which we classify into seven categories (Table 2). We provide the complete mapping of the studies to these categories in the online repository. *Recall-based metrics* (13 studies) dominate the field by measuring the percentage of expected requirements recovered against a reference set [16,35]. Closely following are *traceability-based metrics* (9 studies), which quantify how thoroughly requirements map to related artifacts such as design models or test cases [19,43]. Together, these two families underscore a prevailing emphasis on coverage—confirming that all "modeled" or "anticipated" elements appear in the specification.

Complementing coverage, *pattern/template metrics* (6 studies) assess structural completeness by verifying that all sections of SRS templates or sentence patterns (e.g., performance requirement slots) are populated [8,40]. In contrast, the lone *attribute-based metric* [15] and finer-grained measures like Ferrari *et al.*'s sentence-level completeness score [12] probe the internal coherence of individual requirements. Less common are *goal-model metrics* (3 studies), *defect/TBD counters* (3 studies), and various *other indicators* (6 studies) such as expert Likert-scale scoring [2].

This uneven distribution has practical consequences: teams can benchmark coverage easily but lack robust instruments for evaluating requirement clarity, consistency, and semantic depth. As a result, expert judgment remains indispensable. To advance practice, future work should develop *hybrid metrics* that integrate coverage, structural checks, and semantic analysis into a unified, data-driven framework—transforming completeness from a qualitative ideal into a measurable engineering discipline.

Table 2. RQ3: Metric categories for quantifying requirements completeness

Category	Short Description	# Studies
Recall-based metrics	Coverage of a reference set	13
Goal-model-based metrics	Refinement of high-level objectives	3
Pattern/template coverage	Filling all template slots	6
Attribute-based metrics	Proportion of filled requirement fields	1
Traceability-based metrics	Mapping artifacts to requirements	9
Defect/TBD counters	Counting explicit omissions (defects/TBDs)	3
Other indicators	Miscellaneous proxy/expert measures	6

3.4 RQ4: Methods for Improving Requirements Completeness

Although detection dominates the literature, 42 of our 61 studies go further by proposing systematic remedies for the gaps they uncover. These methods, organized into seven categories (Table 3), span from intelligent tool support to process-embedded guidelines, yet all share the aim of translating diagnostic insights into concrete additions that render specifications complete. We provide the complete mapping in the online repository. Since some studies employ more than one approach, the total count in the table exceeds 42.

At the process level, *checklist-based reviews & guidelines* embed completeness verification at every phase: Carson *et al.* advocate iterative completeness checks—from elicitation through validation—using stakeholder feedback and checklists to ensure each revision addresses prior omissions [7]. Complementing this, *templates & patterns* leverage structured SRS outlines (e.g. Volere or IEEE) to force analysts to populate every section; empty fields in such templates become explicit prompts for action, as demonstrated by Menzel *et al.* [35].

On the tool side, *automated suggestion tools* harness AI or rule engines to recommend missing content: Ferrari's CAR tool mines domain documents for omitted terms [12], Ko's recommender fills absent use-case steps [25], and Luitel *et al.* employ a BERT-based model to generate candidate requirements in natural language [33]. In parallel, *ontology & knowledge-based* techniques compare the SRS against domain ontologies—Kaiya's ORE maps requirements to ontology concepts to flag unmapped entities [19], while Ong's meta-requirement repository suggests additions based on prior projects [38].

Finally, model-centered approaches guide refinement via *goal-based refinement* and *obstacle resolution*. Espada's PLGWA metric drives the addition of missing goal assignments in KAOS models [10], and Jurkiewicz *et al.* apply a HAZOP-inspired framework to uncover and add alternate flows in use cases [18]. Alrajeh *et al.* extend this by generating "obstacles" through model checking, which are then translated into new requirements to mitigate each identified risk [3]. Across all categories, *iterative correction processes* (e.g. TestMEReq's detect–correct–verify loop [37]) reinforce that completeness is best achieved through continual refinement rather than one-off edits.

Despite these diverse strategies, most studies stop short of fully integrating detection with guided remediation, leaving refinement largely to practitioner judgment. This gap suggests fertile ground for future work on end-to-end environments that both highlight omissions and actively steer engineers in formulating and validating the new requirements needed to achieve truly complete specifications.

3.5   RQ5: Tool Support for Requirements Completeness

A substantial portion of the literature (40 out of 61 studies) reports on tools— either novel prototypes or adaptations of existing platforms—designed to assess or enhance requirements completeness (full tools catalogue in the online repository). These tools vary in scope and implementation, yet they share the goal of automating aspects of completeness evaluation:

- **SMACK (Simple Model Automatic Consistency Checker)** uses propositional model checking to ensure that every specified condition and behavior is captured in the requirements [45].
- **QuARS (Quality Analyzer for Requirements Specifications)** applies NLP techniques to flag undefined terms, missing sections, and other linguistic indicators of incompleteness in industrial requirements documents [29].

Table 3. RQ4: Methods for correcting requirements incompleteness (RQ4)

Category	Short Description	# Studies
Automated Suggestion Tools	AI or rule engines recommend missing requirements	11
Templates & Patterns	Structured forms force all template slots to be filled	7
Ontology & Knowledge-Based	Domain models suggest semantic additions	3
Checklist-Based Reviews & Guidelines	Process checklists ensure systematic coverage	10
Goal-Based Refinement	Decompose high-level goals into detailed requirements	4
Obstacle Resolution	Generate and mitigate failure scenarios	2
Iterative Correction Processes	Continuous detect–correct–verify cycles	8

- **USQA (User Story Quality Analyzer)** enforces the agile "As a ... I want ... so that ..." template, automatically verifying that each user story includes role, action, and purpose [17].
- **RASS (Requirements Analysis and Specification System)** integrates a knowledge base with automated checks to detect both completeness and consistency issues during authoring [44].
- **OREW (Ontology Reconstruction Environment for the Web)** combines web-mined domain concepts with ontologies to recommend missing requirements elements [20].
- **Service Requirements Completeness Analyzer** (telecom domain) compares documented service features against a master catalogue to identify unaddressed functionality [31].

While most of these tools remain at the prototype stage, a few have been validated in real projects: SMACK's case studies uncovered omissions that human reviewers missed [45], and QuARS has been trialed in industrial quality-assurance workflows [29]. Technically, they draw on a range of methods—formal logic (SMACK), NLP and pattern matching (QuARS, USQA), and ontology- or ML-driven inference (OREW)—yet each tends to be developed in isolation. This lack of standardization and tool reuse may explain why requirements completeness checking remains predominantly manual in industrial practice.

3.6   RQ6: AI and LLMs in Addressing Requirements Completeness

The use of AI—and in particular modern LLMs—to support requirements completeness is nascent, appearing explicitly in only 8 of our 61 primary studies. These early explorations fall roughly into two categories:

– **LLM-assisted requirement generation:** Luitel *et al.* [33] prompt GPT-3.5 with an incomplete requirements set and ask it to propose additional requirements. Their evaluation shows that the model can suggest plausible items, some of which align with human-identified gaps, suggesting that LLMs can act as a "second pair of eyes" to surface unstated needs.
– **ML/NLP-based completeness checking:** Xiang *et al.* [42] apply a semantic role labeling model to privacy policy sentences, flagging any that omit critical roles (agent, action, object). Although not framed as an LLM application, this approach exemplifies how pretrained language models can automate parts of the RQ2 detection methods.

Beyond these, any RQ2 technique that leverages statistical or transformer-based NLP (e.g., BERT-mask prediction [33], fine-tuned classifiers in privacy domains [5]) can be viewed as an AI-driven completeness method, even if the authors did not highlight LLMs by name. Moreover, recent advances outside the requirements-engineering community—such as LLM-powered document summarization and large-scale data extraction [28,32]—point to future possibilities: handling very large SRS documents, mining extensive corpora of past requirements for lessons learned, and integrating continuous learning from new project data. Taken together, these early studies demonstrate the promise of AI/LLMs to both detect and generate missing requirements, but they also underscore that the field is in its infancy and ripe for more systematic, large-scale investigations.

4   Discussion and Implications

Our SLR has brought to light a comprehensive picture of how requirements completeness is understood and addressed in current research. A first key finding is the multi-faceted nature of completeness definitions (RQ1). The fact that completeness must sometimes be tailored to context implies that practitioners should explicitly define what completeness means for their project at the outset. For example, on a safety-critical project, completeness might entail covering all hazards and failure modes; on a business app, it might mean including all user workflows. Recognizing this, teams can develop project-specific completeness criteria or checklists. The variety of definitions also suggests a need for better standardization or taxonomy: researchers and standards bodies could collaborate to provide a reference framework of completeness (somewhat like ISO/IEC 25010 does for quality characteristics, but more specific to completeness). This would help ensure when we talk about completeness, we cover both internal (no placeholders, all sections done) and external (no stakeholder needs missed) completeness.

From RQ2 and RQ4 (detection and correction methods), a major implication is that automation is increasingly feasible for what was once a purely manual task. Tools and techniques now exist to assist requirements engineers in uncovering missing requirements. This can significantly reduce the risk of late-discovered requirements. For practitioners, adopting these techniques (even simple ones like pattern comparisons or checklists augmented with AI suggestions) can improve requirements quality with relatively low overhead. For instance, using a pattern catalogue for a domain can systematically ensure common functionalities aren't forgotten. One lesson learned is that complementary methods yield the best results. No single technique captures everything: NLP might catch missing domain terms, formal models catch missing alternate behaviors, and human insight catches contextual gaps. Therefore, an organization aiming for high completeness might implement a hybrid completeness assurance process where, say, an NLP tool runs first, then a manual HAZOP session, then a metrics check, etc. The research provides building blocks for such a process.

Our review of metrics (RQ3) highlights the old adage: "You can't improve what you can't measure". By defining metrics like RCoI or completeness ratios, projects can put completeness on their quality dashboard. An implication is that organizations should track requirements completeness as a key quality indicator during requirements engineering. If an iterative process is used, each iteration could measure completeness and aim to improve it. However, we caution that metrics are proxies and must be interpreted with care. Also, the existence of many different metrics (goals vs functional vs structural) indicates that measuring completeness is complex. Future research should validate standardized metrics to ensure they reliably predict outcomes, addressing current anecdotal limitations.

From RQ5 (tools), it's clear that tool support is essential for scalability. Manually checking completeness in a 500-page requirements document is impractical; tool support like SMACK or quality analyzers can drastically cut down the effort. The implication is that practitioners should leverage available tools (or prototypes) when possible. For instance, even using general text analysis tools or writing one's own simple scripts to find "TBD" or check term consistency can help. For the research community, one implication is the importance of moving prototypes to plugins or open-source tools that practitioners can actually use. The knowledge exists, but if the tools remain confined to papers, industry uptake will lag. Encouragingly, some commercial requirements management platforms are starting to include AI-driven analytics, so we might see wider adoption soon.

On RQ6 (AI/LLMs), the main implication is that AI holds promise to finally tackle completeness in a more holistic way, but current efforts are just the beginning. LLMs like GPT-4 could potentially reason about requirements and ask intelligent questions like a human analyst would. If integrated properly, they could serve as an ever-vigilant reviewer for completeness. For researchers, it opens many questions: How do we effectively prompt LLMs for finding requirements gaps? How do we ensure the AI's suggestions are correct and not hallucinations? And importantly, how do we integrate such suggestions into the workflow so that engineers trust and verify them? Our findings show only limited use of AI so far, suggesting a gap that is a ripe opportunity. This is indeed part of our motivation for future work (discussed below).

Another general implication revolves around project stages and completeness. Many methods we reviewed assume a fairly defined set of requirements (perhaps at end of elicitation) that we then check for completeness. In agile methodologies, however, requirements (user stories) evolve continuously. Ensuring completeness is different there – it might mean by the time you release, you haven't missed any critical stories. The methods (especially AI ones) could be applied continuously to backlogs or wikis. A lesson is that completeness checking shouldn't be a one-time gate; it can be integrated into iterative development. For example, every sprint review could include running a completeness tool on the current backlog to see if any obvious features are missing. This aligns with the incremental approaches suggested by some studies.

5   Threats to Validity

As with any systematic literature review, our findings must be interpreted in light of several potential validity threats:

- **Selection Bias.** Despite constructing a broad search string—including synonyms like "omissions" and "coverage"—and querying IEEE Xplore, ACM DL, and Scopus, we may have overlooked relevant studies, particularly in gray literature or non-software-engineering venues.
- **Publication Bias.** Our analysis likely overrepresents successful or positive results, since industry failures and negative evaluations of completeness techniques are rarely published. We partially mitigated this by including industrial case studies that candidly discuss tool limitations.
- **Extraction and Interpretation Bias.** Qualitative coding inherently involves subjective judgment. To reduce this risk, two reviewers independently extracted and cross-checked the data, and we preserved direct quotations of key definitions to minimize misinterpretation.
- **Temporal Validity.** Our review covers publications up to September 2024. Given the rapid evolution of AI and LLM technologies, novel completeness approaches—especially multi-LLM integrations—emerging after our cutoff will not be reflected.
- **Construct Validity.** We focused our six research questions on technical facets of completeness (definitions, detection, metrics, correction, tools, AI). As a result, broader human, organizational, or cognitive factors influencing completeness may be under-represented.

Nevertheless, adherence to a pre-registered protocol, the involvement of multiple reviewers, and the maintenance of transparent audit trails all serve to bolster our confidence in the rigor and reliability of this synthesis.

6 Conclusion and Future Work

This systematic review provides a consolidated understanding of how requirements completeness is defined, detected, quantified, and improved. Our findings reveal that while definitions of completeness are multifaceted—ranging from internal syntactic checks to external stakeholder alignment—there is little consensus or standardization across the literature. Detection techniques have matured, with a growing shift toward semi-automated and AI-supported approaches. However, structured remediation methods and integrated toolchains remain underdeveloped.

We also observe that while completeness metrics exist, they often emphasize coverage over semantic depth, and very few are validated across diverse domains. Tools for assessing completeness are increasing in number but vary widely in scope and maturity. Importantly, the role of AI—particularly Large Language Models (LLMs)—is only beginning to emerge, offering new avenues for both detection and correction.

Building on these insights, we developed a prototype that orchestrates three complementary LLMs—DeepSeek Chat, GPT-o4 mini, and Claude 3.7 Sonnet—to support domain modeling, gap detection, and requirement refinement. The tool enables an iterative detect–correct–verify cycle through an interactive interface, using ensemble techniques such as majority voting and meta-analysis.

As next steps, we plan to (1) evaluate the tool's performance on real-world datasets, (2) address scalability challenges through intelligent chunking and summarization, (3) incorporate a conversational LLM for interactive requirement elicitation, and (4) release a benchmark suite of requirement documents with seeded omissions. By combining methodological rigor with LLM-driven assistance, we aim to make the process of ensuring requirements completeness more scalable, systematic, and accessible—moving closer to the ideal of "no requirement left behind".

References

1. ISO/IEC/IEEE 29148:2018 – Systems and Software Engineering – Life Cycle Processes – Requirements Engineering (2018). https://shorturl.at/XCAYR
2. Ahmad, S., Anuar, U., Emran, N.: A tool-based boilerplate technique to improve SRS quality: an evaluation. J. Telecommun. Electron. Comput. Eng. (JTEC) **10**(2-7), 111–114 (2018)
3. Alrajeh, D., Kramer, J., Van Lamsweerde, A., Russo, A., Uchitel, S.: Generating obstacle conditions for requirements completeness. In: 2012 34th International Conference on Software Engineering (ICSE), pp. 705–715. IEEE (2012)
4. Anthropic: Model card and evaluations for Claude models. Technical report, Anthropic (2023). https://shorturl.at/HqAfR. Accessed 03 May 2025
5. Azeem, M.I., Abualhaija, S.: A multi-solution study on GDPR AI-enabled completeness checking of DPAs. Empir. Softw. Eng. **29**(4), 96 (2024)
6. Boehm, B.W.: Software engineering economics. IEEE Trans. Softw. Eng. **1**, 4–21 (1984)

7. Carson, R.S., et al.: Requirements completeness. In: INCOSE International Symposium, vol. 14, pp. 930–944. International Council on Systems Engineering, Toulouse (2004). http://bit.ly/3U9TQyF

8. Chattopadhyay, A., Malla, G., Niu, N., Bhowmik, T., Savolainen, J.: Completeness of natural language requirements: a comparative study of user stories and feature descriptions. In: 2023 IEEE 24th International Conference on Information Reuse and Integration for Data Science (IRI), pp. 52–57. IEEE (2023)

9. Eckhardt, J., Vogelsang, A., Femmer, H., Mager, P.: Challenging incompleteness of performance requirements by sentence patterns. In: 2016 IEEE 24th International Requirements Engineering Conference (RE), pp. 46–55. IEEE (2016)

10. Espada, P., Goulão, M., Araújo, J.: A framework to evaluate complexity and completeness of KAOS goal models. In: Salinesi, C., Norrie, M.C., Pastor, Ó. (eds.) CAiSE 2013. LNCS, vol. 7908, pp. 562–577. Springer, Heidelberg (2013). https://doi.org/10.1007/978-3-642-38709-8_36

11. España, S., Condori-Fernandez, N., González, A., Pastor, Ó.: An empirical comparative evaluation of requirements engineering methods. J. Braz. Comput. Soc. **16**(1), 3–19 (2010). https://doi.org/10.1007/s13173-010-0003-5

12. Ferrari, A., dell'Orletta, F., Spagnolo, G.O., Gnesi, S.: Measuring and improving the completeness of natural language requirements. In: Salinesi, C., van de Weerd, I. (eds.) REFSQ 2014. LNCS, vol. 8396, pp. 23–38. Springer, Cham (2014). https://doi.org/10.1007/978-3-319-05843-6_3

13. Gartlehner, G., et al.: Data extraction for evidence synthesis using a large language model: a proof-of-concept study. Res. Synthesis Methods **15**(4), 576–589 (2024)

14. IEEE Computer Society Software Engineering Standards Committee: IEEE recommended practice for software requirements specifications. Technical report IEEE Std 830-1998, Institute of Electrical and Electronics Engineers (1998). https://rb.gy/1sc4td

15. Iqbal, S., Khan, M.N.A.: Yet another set of requirement metrics for software projects. Int. J. Softw. Eng. Appl. **6**(1), 19–28 (2012)

16. Issa, A.A., Al-Ali, A.: Use case patterns driven requirements engineering. In: 2010 Second International Conference on Computer Research and Development, pp. 307–313. IEEE (2010)

17. Jiménez, S., Alanis, A., Beltrán, C., Juárez-Ramírez, R., Ramírez-Noriega, A., Tona, C.: USQA: a user story quality analyzer prototype for supporting software engineering students. Comput. Appl. Eng. Educ. **31**(4), 1014–1024 (2023)

18. Jurkiewicz, J., Nawrocki, J., Ochodek, M., Głowacki, T.: Hazop-based identification of events in use cases: an empirical study. Empir. Softw. Eng. **20**, 82–109 (2015)

19. Kaiya, H., Ohnishi, A.: Improving software quality requirements specifications using spectrum analysis. In: 2012 IEEE 36th Annual Computer Software and Applications Conference Workshops, pp. 379–384. IEEE (2012)

20. Kaiya, H., Shimizu, Y., Yasui, H., Kaijiri, K., Saeki, M.: Enhancing domain knowledge for requirements elicitation with web mining. In: 2010 Asia Pacific Software Engineering Conference, pp. 3–12. IEEE (2010)

21. Kassab, M.: An integrated approach of AHP and NFRs framework. In: IEEE 7th International Conference on Research Challenges in Information Science (RCIS), pp. 1–8. IEEE (2013)

22. Kassab, M., Laplante, P.: The current and evolving landscape of requirements engineering in practice. IEEE Softw. **39**(5), 76–83 (2022)

23. Kitchenham: Guidelines for performing systematic literature reviews in software engineering. Technical report, ver. 2.3 EBSE technical report. EBSE (2007)

24. Kitchenham, B., Brereton, O.P., Budgen, D., Turner, M., Bailey, J., Linkman, S.: Systematic literature reviews in software engineering-a systematic literature review. Inf. Softw. Technol. **51**(1), 7–15 (2009)

25. Ko, D., Kim, S., Park, S.: Automatic recommendation to omitted steps in use case specification. Requirements Eng. **24**, 431–458 (2019)

26. Konet, A., et al.: Performance of two large language models for data extraction in evidence synthesis. Res. Synthesis Methods **15**(5), 818–824 (2024)

27. Kravari, K., Antoniou, C., Bassiliades, N.: SENSE: a flow-down semantics-based requirements engineering framework. Algorithms **14**(10), 298 (2021)

28. Laban, P., Fabbri, A.R., Xiong, C., Wu, C.S.: Summary of a haystack: a challenge to long-context LLMs and rag systems. arXiv preprint arXiv:2407.01370 (2024)

29. Lami, G., Gnesi, S., Fabbrini, F., Fusani, M., Trentanni, G.: An automatic tool for the analysis of natural language requirements. Informe técnico, CNR Information Science and Technology Institute, Pisa, Italia, Setiembre (2004)

30. Lindland, O.I., Sindre, G., Solvberg, A.: Understanding quality in conceptual modeling. IEEE Softw. **11**(2), 42–49 (1994)

31. Liu, W., He, C., Zhang, K.: Domain component-based service requirements modeling and analysis. In: 2009 International Conference on Computational Intelligence and Software Engineering, pp. 1–5. IEEE (2009)

32. Lu, Y., et al.: Beyond believability: accurate human behavior simulation with fine-tuned LLMs. arXiv preprint arXiv:2503.20749 (2025)

33. Luitel, D., Hassani, S., Sabetzadeh, M.: Improving requirements completeness: automated assistance through large language models. Requirements Eng. **29**(1), 73–95 (2024)

34. Meincke, W.: Requirements in the loop: a computer-aided analysis of consistency, completeness, and correctness of requirements. In: 2020 IEEE 28th International Requirements Engineering Conference (RE), pp. 396–399. IEEE (2020)

35. Menzel, I., Mueller, M., Gross, A., Doerr, J.: An experimental comparison regarding the completeness of functional requirements specifications. In: 2010 18th IEEE International Requirements Engineering Conference, pp. 15–24. IEEE (2010)

36. Mirabelli, V., Eckman, H.: Scale up your requirements management practices. Blueprint, Info-Tech Research Group (2024). https://shorturl.at/SWn3D. Accessed 26 Sept 2024

37. Moketar, N.A., Kamalrudin, M., Sidek, S., Robinson, M., Grundy, J.: TestMEReq: generating abstract tests for requirements validation. In: Proceedings of the 3rd International Workshop on Software Engineering Research and Industrial Practice, pp. 39–45 (2016)

38. Ong, M.I.U., Ameeden, M.A.: A meta-requirement approach to validate user requirement specification: threshold definition. In: 2023 IEEE 8th International Conference on Software Engineering and Computer Systems (ICSECS), pp. 5–10. IEEE (2023)

39. Ralph, P., et al.: Empirical standards for software engineering research. arXiv preprint arXiv:2010.03525 (2020)

40. Stephen, E., Mit, E.: Framework for measuring the quality of software specification. J. Telecommun. Electron. Comput. Eng. (JTEC) **9**(2-10), 79–84 (2017)

41. Wohlin, C., et al.: Experimentation in Software Engineering, vol. 236. Springer (2012)

42. Xiang, A., Pei, W., Yue, C.: PolicyChecker: analyzing the GDPR completeness of mobile apps' privacy policies. In: Proceedings of the 2023 ACM SIGSAC Conference on Computer and Communications Security, pp. 3373–3387 (2023)

43. Yu, L., Su, S., Luo, S., Su, Y.: Completeness and consistency analysis on requirements of distributed event-driven systems. In: 2008 2nd IFIP/IEEE International Symposium on Theoretical Aspects of Software Engineering, pp. 241–244. IEEE (2008)
44. Zhu, H., Jin, L.: Automating scenario-driven structured requirements engineering. In: Proceedings 24th Annual International Computer Software and Applications Conference, COMPSAC2000, pp. 311–316. IEEE (2000)
45. Zowghi, D., Gervasi, V.: On the interplay between consistency, completeness, and correctness in requirements evolution. Inf. Softw. Technol. 45(14), 993–1009 (2003)

What Do We Know About Software Analytics Research? A Critical Review of Secondary Studies

Muhammad Laiq[1]([✉]), Nauman bin Ali[1], Jürgen Börstler[1],
and Emelie Engström[2]

[1] Blekinge Institute of Technology, Karlskrona, Sweden
{muhammad.laiq,nauman.ali,jurgen.borstler}@bth.se
[2] Lund University, Lund, Sweden
emelie.engstrom@cs.lth.se

Abstract. Software analytics (SA) is often proposed as a tool to support software engineering (SE) tasks. Several secondary studies on SA have been published, some published within the same calendar year. This presents an opportunity to take a meta-perspective and examine how the field of SA has been conceptualized and synthesized so far. By analyzing how SA is defined, which topics are emphasized, what search strategies are employed, and to what extent primary studies overlap, we aim to identify gaps, trends, and redundancies in the current body of secondary studies. Such insights can inform the design and focus of future secondary studies.

We identified five secondary studies on SA published from 2015 to 2023 that cover primary research from 2000 to 2021. Despite similarities in objectives and overlapping search timeframes, the secondary studies have negligible overlap in their included primary studies. Each secondary study presents a distinct perspective, and collectively, the five secondary studies offer a fragmented rather than cohesive view of the research landscape.

We present a structured overview of the identified secondary studies in terms of their objectives, research quality, and findings. This overview helps readers navigate and leverage existing research. The analysis also indicates that there is potential for further secondary research to build a more cohesive and comprehensive understanding of the SA literature.

Keywords: Software engineering · Software analytics · Tertiary review · Tertiary study · Literature review · Critical appraisal

1 Introduction

Throughout the software life cycle, a large amount of data is produced, embedded in, for example, bug reports, test cases, test executions, version control systems, and source code. These data can be used to support practitioners in decision-making processes regarding their daily activities. However, such insights are not directly available from the data. Software analytics (SA) has emerged as a systematic approach to utilize data embedded in software engineering (SE) artifacts to generate insights for supporting practitioners in decision-making processes [19]. SA has been proposed in various areas of SE to support different practitioner roles, such as testers [14], developers [17], and managers [13].

Several secondary studies (e.g., [1,4]) have been conducted to provide an overview of the use of SA. The publication years of these studies are close to each other, and they cover overlapping topics. This presents an opportunity to investigate them together and compare and contrast their definition of SA, search and selection approach for identifying relevant literature, and their conclusions.

While several tertiary studies (e.g., [2,3]) have been conducted in SE, to our knowledge, there is no tertiary review focusing on SA.

By comparing the findings of the secondary studies on SA, a tertiary review can identify potential gaps, overlaps, or inconsistencies in the literature. Beyond mapping the current state of research, it can offer strategic guidance for future secondary and primary studies.

In this paper, we present a tertiary review to analyze existing secondary studies on the use of SA. Specifically, we investigate how SA is conceptualized, which topics have been the focus of past reviews, what search strategies have been employed, and the extent to which the primary studies included in those reviews overlap. To this end, we address the following research questions:

- *RQ1: How is SA conceptualized in existing secondary studies?*
- *RQ2: What topics have been the focus of these secondary studies?*
- *RQ3: What search strategies and inclusion criteria have been employed in these studies?*
- *RQ4: To what extent do the secondary studies rely on overlapping sets of primary studies?*

2   Research Method

In this study, we conducted a tertiary review [12] of secondary studies on software analytics. Figure 1 presents an overview of our search and selection process.

2.1   Search Process

Table 1 shows our search string in selected databases to find relevant literature on SA. Our search string is focused on secondary studies that explicitly discuss SA. To find papers that use phrasings such as analytics for software development, or analytics for software testing, or software development analytics, we utilized the proximity operators supported by Scopus, IEEE Xplore, and Web of Science. For example, in Scopus, 'software w/1 analytics' will cover the occurrence of 'software' and 'analytics' with at most one word between them, regardless of

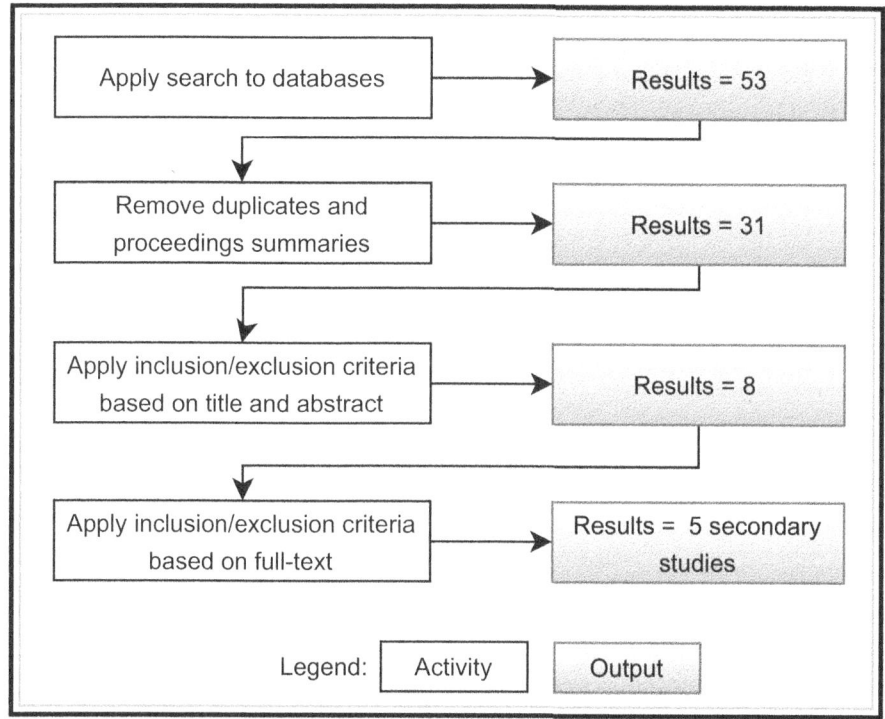

Fig. 1. Overview of our search and selection process

their order. We increased the proximity from 1 to 3, but could not find any additional relevant papers. Thus, we decided to keep the proximity at 1.

Table 2 shows the number of search results in each database. As shown in Table 2, our search, performed on April 2, 2023, found 53 documents in selected databases. Five secondary studies of the 53 were selected after applying the selection criteria (see Sect. 2.2).

2.2 Study Selection

We selected papers based on title, abstract reading, and full-text reading. We performed full-text reading only when we could not decide whether to include or exclude a paper based on the title and abstract reading. The following inclusion criteria were followed for study selection. A paper was included if it met all inclusion criteria; otherwise, it was excluded.

I1: The paper is peer-reviewed.
I2: The paper is a secondary study.
I3: The paper is positioned explicitly as an SA review, i.e., it explicitly reports that the review has been performed on SA-based work.

Table 1. Search strings in selected databases

Database/search engine	Search string
Scopus	*TITLE-ABS-KEY ((software w/1 analytics) AND ("literature review" OR "systematic review" OR "systematic map" OR "systematic mapping" OR "systematic scoping"))*
IEEE Xplore	Full-text search was performed using the command feature of IEEE Xplore: *((software NEAR/1 analytics) AND ("literature review" OR "systematic review" OR "systematic map" OR "systematic mapping" OR "systematic scoping"))*
ACM	Search was performed on title, abstract, and keywords and combined using the OR operator utilizing the query editor feature of ACM: (("software analytics" OR "software development analytics") AND ("literature review" OR "systematic review" OR "systematic map" OR "systematic mapping" OR "systematic scoping"))
Web of Science	Search was performed on title, abstract, and keywords and combined using the OR operator: *((software NEAR/1 analytics) AND ("literature review" OR "systematic review" OR "systematic map" OR "systematic mapping" OR "systematic scoping"))*

Table 2. Databases used and documents found

Database	Documents found		
	total	selected	*unique
Scopus	23	5	9
IEEE Xplore	15	2	10
ACM	1	1	0
Web of Science	14	5	3
Total	53	5	22

*The papers that were uniquely found in one specific database.

Figure 1 shows the number of included and excluded[1] papers at each stage. As shown in Fig. 1, full-text reading was performed on eight papers. Of these eight papers, five were selected, and three were excluded. Of those three excluded, two papers did not explicitly discuss SA, and one did not provide the list of primary studies.

Two reviewers were involved in the selection process at each stage. The pilot was carried out before the actual study selection process to ensure mutual understanding. During the selection process, we had disagreements on seven papers, which we resolved through discussion and reconsideration. We discussed and

---

[1] https://tinyurl.com/yxmcz7pd.

agreed to include only those papers that explicitly talk about SA and an SE context.

2.3 Data Extraction

We use the following data extraction template to extract data from the selected secondary studies on SA.
#1: Definition of SA.
#2: Topic of secondary study, e.g., SA.
#3: Study publication year.
#4: Search strategy and inclusion criteria used.
#5: Databases used for identifying literature on SA.
#6: Timeline covered by search.
#7: A list of the included primary studies on SA.

2.4 Synthesis and Analysis Approach

The extracted information was tabulated and visualized using graphs. For example, the total number of primary studies in each secondary study and the frequency of publications over time. We also visualized the timeline covered by the selected secondary studies. Furthermore, we identified an overlap between the primary studies of the secondary studies.

2.5 Quality Assessment

We adopted the quality assessment criteria provided by the York University Centre for Reviews and Dissemination (CRD) guide for reviews [9] to assess the selected secondary studies. To answer the five CRD/DARE questions, we used the criteria proposed by Budgen et al. [7]. The first author performed the quality assessment on the five selected secondary studies. Not having multiple authors perform this assessment is not a major validity threat as the criteria proposed by Budgen et al. [7] are very objective and do not require subjective judgment as some other assessment instruments like QAISER [18].

2.6 Validity Threats

Missing Relevant Secondary Studies. One potential threat to this review could be that our search string misses the relevant secondary studies. We mitigated this by carefully developing our search string based on the aim of the review, i.e., our search string searches for secondary studies that report a review of SA literature. In addition, we have used two indexing (i.e., Scopus and Web of Science) and two publisher-specific databases (i.e., IEEE Xplore and ACM) without restricting our search to papers from specific years to have sufficient coverage. These databases sufficiently cover SE literature [12,18].

Bias in Paper Selection. Another threat to this review is bias during the paper selection process. We mitigate this risk by ensuring that every paper is reviewed by two reviewers. We also performed piloting before the actual study selection process. We had good agreements during the selection process. Disagreements were discussed and resolved as described in Sect. 2.2.

3   Results

Sections 3.1, 3.2, 3.3 and 3.4 present the results of our research questions.

We selected five secondary studies (see details in Table 3) following the selection criteria described in Sect. 2.2. An overview/map of these studies is shown in Fig. 3. In Fig. 2, we show the timeline of the primary research covered by these studies and the count of the included primary studies in each secondary study.

Table 3. Selected secondary studies on SA

Id	Pub. Year	Title	Venue	Ref.
SS1	2015	Software Analytics to Software Practice: A Systematic Literature Review	International Workshop on Big Data Software Engineering	[1]
SS2	2021	Big Data analytics in Agile software development: A systematic mapping study	Information and Software Technology	[5]
SS3	2023	Software Development Analytics in Practice: A Systematic Literature Review	Archives of Computational Methods in Engineering	[8]
SS4	2017	Software analytics for web usability: A systematic mapping	Computational Science and Its Applications	[15]
SS5	2017	Towards greener software engineering using software analytics: A systematic mapping	Euromicro Conference on Software Engineering and Advanced Applications	[4]

In Table 4, we show the summary of the quality assessment of the selected secondary studies. Table 4 shows that all studies have reported inclusion/exclusion criteria (C1). These studies have provided sufficient details of the selected primary studies (C5) and have used, to some extent, an adequate search strategy (C2). Both systematic literature reviews have assessed the quality of the included primary studies (C4).

Among the included studies, except for C3, all other criteria are adequately covered in most of the secondary studies, particularly C1, C2, and C5. This indicates that the identified literature in these studies could be sufficient to provide a map of the existing literature on the topic, provided that a sufficient timeline is covered in these studies. Furthermore, it is evident that there is generally a lack of synthesis of the evidence in these studies.

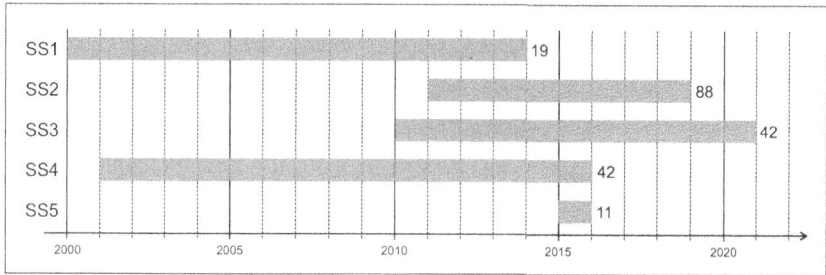

Fig. 2. Timeline of the primary research covered by secondary studies on SA with the count of their primary studies

3.1 RQ1: How is SA Conceptualized in Existing Secondary Studies?

The selected secondary studies define SA as cited below:

- **SS1:** Abdellatif et al. [1]: *"Software analytics (SA) represents a branch of big data analytics. SA is concerned with the analysis of all software artifacts, not only source code. Its importance comes from the need to extract support insights and facts from the available software artifacts to facilitate decision making."*
- **SS2:** Biesialska et al. [5] did not explicitly define SA in their paper. However, they relate it to big data and data analytics, i.e., *"Software analytics or data analytics belong to a common category. In order to provide non-obvious insights and improve the decision-making process, they need to employ ML, DL, or AI methods in some shape or form. Those methods require a significant amount of data (often complex or unstructured) to train models."*
- **SS3:** Caldeira et al. [8]: (i) *"The term 'software analytics' (SA) emerged naturally expressing the work of several research groups aiming to expand the traditional scope on analyzing software artifacts by means of mining software repositories. These groups conducted cutting-edge research and technology innovation in an interdisciplinary area that spans big data, machine learning, systems, and software engineering. This approach led software practitioners to perform data exploration and analysis in order to obtain insightful and actionable information for completing various tasks around software systems, software users, and software development processes."*, and (ii) *"Software Development Analytics (SDA), the adoption of analytics methods with the focus on the management of software development projects."*
- **SS4:** Pellizon et al. [15]: *"The software analytics area is concerned with collecting, exploring and analyzing this large amount of data aiming to transform it into actions to improve the product and its usability."*
- **SS5:** Anwar et al. [4] did not explicitly describe SA in their paper; instead, they define the usefulness of SA: *"Software analytics could support practitioners with actionable and timely information as it combines information from different software artifacts and converts it into useful information."*

Table 4. Quality assessment of the identified secondary studies

Criterion and interpretation	Study score (Y: 1; P: 0.5; N: 0)				
	SS1***	SS2**	SS3***	SS4**	SS5**
C1: "Were inclusion/exclusion criteria reported?" **Y:** The criteria are clearly defined **P:** The criteria are implicitly defined **N:** The criteria are not defined and can not be inferred readily	1	1	1	1	1
C2: "Was the search adequate?" **Y:** The authors have searched four or more digital libraries and included additional search strategies OR identified and referenced all journals addressing the topic of interest **P:** Searched three or four digital libraries with no extra search strategies OR searched a defined but restricted set of journals and conference proceedings **N:** Searched up to two digital libraries or an extremely restricted set of journals	0	1	0.5	0.5	0.5
C3: "Were the included studies synthesized?" **C3a:** "Was the evidence actually synthesized and aggregated, or merely summarized?" **Y:** The authors have performed a meta-analysis or used another form of synthesis for all the data of the study **P:** Synthesis has been performed for some of the data from some of the primary studies **N:** There is no real/explicit synthesis (as in a mapping study)	0	*	0	*	*
C3b: "Was the quality of individual studies taken into account in the synthesis?" **Y:** To some extent, yes **N:** No	0	*	0	*	*
C4: "Was the quality of the included studies assessed?" **Y:** The authors have explicitly defined quality criteria and extracted them from each primary study **P:** The research question involved quality issues that are addressed by the study **N:** There is no explicit quality assessment for individual studies	1	*	1	*	*
C5: "Are sufficient details about the individual included studies presented?" **Y:** Information for each study has been provided **P:** Information has been provided in a summarized form only **N:** The results of individual studies have not been specified	1	1	1	0.5	0.5
Total score =	3/6	3/3	3.5/6	2/3	2/3

*We do not apply this criterion to systematic mapping studies. **Systematic mapping study. ***Systematic literature review.

3.2 RQ2: What Topics Have Been the Focus of These Secondary Studies?

We found that the selected secondary studies have targeted different areas of SE when identifying the usage of SA (see overview in Table 3). Two secondary studies generally focused on aggregating research on SA [SS1, SS3]. The remaining three focused on SA in different areas of SE, that is, exploring SA usage for web usability [SS4], agile software development [SS2], and green SE [SS5].

Id	Year	Paper type	Focused area	Count of PSs	Timeline of PSs	Aim	Quality assessment score and limitations	Main results	Future directions. Future work should:
SS1	2015	Workshop	SA	19	2000-2014	• To identify which practitioners are targeted by SA. • To identify which domains are covered by existing work. • To identify the types of software artifacts extracted and whether and how different artifacts are interconnected.	3.0/6.0. Inadequate search strategy and lack of data synthesis.	• SA research primarily caters to developers' needs. • Most of the existing research uses just a single artifact. • A lack of relevant and mature research in the field of SA.	• include a broader range of artifacts and additional datasets to improve the robustness and reliability of results. • address the research gap in higher-level business decision-making areas like portfolio management, marketing strategy, and sales direction.
SS2	2021	Journal	SA for Agile development	88	2011-2019	• To provide a comprehensive understanding of data-driven agile software development. • To explore the integration of agile software development with big data analytics.	3.0/3.0. None.	• SA is applied across the Agile software development lifecycle. • Existing work mainly focuses on code repository analytics, defects/bug fixing, testing, project management analytics, and application usage analytics.	• focus on generalizable and representative empirical studies, especially in industrial settings. • investigate data from customer feedback and experimentation across diverse domains beyond mobile applications. • review gray literature for valuable insights.
SS3	2023	Journal	SA	42	2010-2021	• To provide an aggregate view of the existing work on SA, emphasizing its application in practical settings. • To identify and aggregate information such as techniques used, types of analytics, SE tasks, and data sources.	3.5/6.0. Inadequate data synthesis and partially fulfilled search strategy.	• SA research mainly caters to developers' needs, followed by testers and product managers. • Source code repositories are the main source of data. • Mining methods are evolving quickly, with descriptive statistics being the most widely used approach, followed by correlation analysis.	• diversify repositories with non-trivial sources like IDEs and fine-grained development event archives. • address the needs of broader stakeholders, including requirements engineers, project managers, and executives. • support operational aspects of development to ensure insights impact ongoing projects. • focus on process mining, project time and cost analysis, and holistic security and risk management approaches.
SS4	2017	Conference	SA for web usability	42	2001-2016	• To provide an overview of research on SA for web-based software usability. • To identify and aggregate techniques and tools commonly used to capture and analyze navigation behavior and usage data.	2.0/3.0. Partially fulfilled search strategy and lack of details about PSs.	• Most experimental studies are conducted in academic settings. • Over half of the papers focus on tools for capturing navigation data. • Data collection methods include JavaScript, proxy/server loggers, and browser plugins.	• focus on developing mechanisms for visualizing collected data. • focus on the relationship between capture technologies and data visualization.
SS5	2017	Conference	SA for green SE	11	2015-2016	• To provide an overview of the existing work on SA for green SE. • To identify contribution types, research types, research methods, future research potentials, and the role of SA in green SE.	2.0/3.0. Partially fulfilled search strategy and lack of details about PSs.	• There are many validation studies but hardly any evaluation and experience papers in the domain of green SE.	• focus on developing new/improved automated SA tools for practitioners and metrics explaining the correlation between energy usage and other quality attributes associated with green SE.

Fig. 3. Overview/Map of the identified secondary studies on SA. Primary studies (PSs)

Table 5. Analysis of the definitions of SA used in the selected SSs

Id	Technology/Methods	Aims/Outcomes	Data sources	Stakeholders
SS1	Big data	Facilitate decision-making, provide insights and facts	Available software artifacts	Practitioners*
SS2	Big data, data analytics, AI, ML, deep learning (DL)	Improve decision-making, provide non-obvious insights	Large data, complex data, unstructured data	Practitioners*
SS3	Mining software repositories, big data, ML	Enable data exploration and data analysis, provide insightful and actionable information, management of software development projects	Software artifacts	Practitioners
SS4	-	Actions to improve product and its usability	Large amount of data	Practitioners*
SS5	-	Actionable information, timely information, useful information	Use different software artifacts	Practitioners

* Indicates that the practitioner as a target stakeholder is implied in the definition.

3.3   RQ3: What Search Strategies and Inclusion Criteria Have Been Employed in These Studies?

Table 6 shows the search and inclusion criteria used in each selected secondary study. The search strings in SS1 and SS3 are targeted at work that is explicitly SA-based. However, SS3 is also limited to studies that use techniques such as data mining and big data, as well as research methods such as experimental and empirical studies. SS2 used a manual search strategy in selected venues and focused on SA for agile software development. SS4 focuses on web usability, and SS5 focuses on green SE.

Table 7 shows the targeted databases in each selected secondary study. The publisher-specific databases IEEE Xplore and ACM seem to be commonly used and have been targeted in 3 out of 5 studies with other databases, such as Scopus and Web of Science. SS1 has only used IEEE Xplore and ACM, which could be considered a limitation of their search coverage. These two databases do not provide full coverage of SE literature. Systematic literature review guidelines [10,11] in SE also recommend using at least one indexing database, such as Scopus, along with publisher-specific databases.

3.4   RQ4: To What Extent Do the Secondary Studies Rely on Overlapping Sets of Primary Studies?

In the selected secondary studies, we found only two common papers between SS1 and SS2, one between SS1 and SS3, and no other overlaps (see Table 8 for an overview).

As shown in Table 8, the total overlap between secondary studies is 0.4%, which is very low, up to <6%, the overlap is considered as "slight.' The small

Table 6. Search strings/strategies and inclusion criteria used in the selected secondary studies

Id	Search string/strategy and inclusion criteria (IC)
SS1	*"Software analytics" OR "Software analytic" OR "Software development analytics" OR "Software development analytic"* IC: (1) SA concepts were applied to extract insights from software project artifacts. (2) Research was relevant to software project lifecycle phases. (3) Research was directly related to the software industry and stakeholders. (4) For duplicate publications of the same study, the newest and most complete one was selected
SS2	*Manual search in a pre-selected list of venues (e.g., Information and Software Technology Journal, International Conference on Software Engineering, and Software Quality Journal), and backward and forward snowballing* IC: (1) Studies related to big data analytics and agile software development. (2) Studies published from 2011 until 2019 (inclusive). (3) Primary studies. (4) Studies published in selected publishing venues
SS3	*("software analytics" OR "software development analytics") AND ("process mining" OR "data mining" OR "big data" OR "data science") AND ("study" OR "empirical" OR "evidence based" OR "experimental" OR "in vivo")* IC: (1) Publications should be journal, conference, or workshop papers, or books. (2) Works that put validated analytical methods into practice with the goal of understanding and/or improving the software development process. (3) Articles that clearly addressed any of the analytics depth and provided benefits for the software development lifecycle
SS4	*(capture OR collect OR analyze) AND (user behavior OR usability OR user experience) AND (web)* IC: (1) Peer-reviewed studies. (2) Addresses web analytics and usability. (3) Means for capturing navigation behaviour. (4) Technologies for capturing usage data.
SS5	*("Software engineering") AND (green* OR sustain* OR "energy consumption" OR "energy-aware" "energy-efficient" OR "resource optimization") AND NOT (feedback OR domestic OR electric* OR mechanic* OR industrial OR chemical* OR bio* OR hardware OR net*)* IC: (1) The papers related to the field of green SE. (2) The latest version of a paper was included when different versions were published in various online repositories

Table 7. Databases used in the selected secondary studies

Database/ Search engine	SS1	SS2	SS3	SS4	SS5
IEEE Xplore	✓		✓		✓
ACM	✓		✓		✓
Scopus			✓	✓	
Web of Science			✓		✓
Google Scholar			✓		
Wiley Online			✓		✓
ScienceDirect			✓		✓
SpringerLink			✓		✓
Selected Venues		✓			

overlaps between existing secondary studies could ·be the result of insufficient/different search strategies and databases used in these secondary studies (see details of the search strategy used in these studies in Sect. 3.3).

Table 8. Overlap of primary studies between selected secondary studies (measured in CCA*)

	SS1 (2015)	SS2 (2021)	SS3 (2023)	SS4 (2017)	SS5 (2017)
SS1 (2015)	NA	1.9%	1.66%	0	0
SS2 (2021)	1.9%	NA	0	0	0
SS3 (2023)	1.66%	0	NA	0	0
SS4 (2017)	0	0	0	NA	0
SS5 (2017)	0	0	0	0	NA
Total overlap = 0.4%					

*The corrected covered area (CCA) indicates the total overlap of primary studies for all included secondary studies [6]. 0 = no overlap and NA = not applicable.

4   Analysis

4.1   Definition of SA

Table 5 shows an analysis of the definitions of SA in the selected secondary studies. The diversity in defining SA makes defining the boundaries of what we should consider SA research problematic.

In Table 5, we show the main themes we noticed in the statements describing SA and its purpose in the included secondary studies. Below, we analyze these further using the six interrogative words as proposed by Petersen et al. [16].

Why is a solution required? To facilitate decision-making regarding the software processes, products, or their usability

What is the solution? Big data analytics, AI, ML, or DL to derive actionable and non-obvious insights.

How does the solution work? By using any available large data (structured or unstructured), or various other software artifacts in software repositories.

Where in the process is the solution required? Entire software lifecycle.

Who are the users of the solution? Various practitioners. Here, we see that SA is primarily focused on software practitioners and not researchers. This is again obvious in the following aspect of timing.

When refers to timing. Timely information, i.e., the information should be readily available when relevant decisions in the software development lifecycle arise. So, the feedback time for the solution is bound by the frequency and urgency of the practical decisions.

Based on the above analysis of the definitions of SA in the selected secondary studies, we define SA as follows:

> *"Software Analytics is concerned with **collecting, exploring and analyzing a large amount of data and software artifacts** using AI (e.g., ML and DL) and other big data and data analytics techniques to support **software practitioners** in **decision making** related to software development by providing **non-obvious, timely, insights and actionable information.**"*

The above definition can help distinguish SA-based studies from others by considering the following four perspectives.

1. **Practitioners:** The target user for which support is provided in the study should be a practitioner, for example, a manager, developer, or tester.
2. **Activity:** The activities may include, but are not limited to, data analysis and exploration, summarization, and forecasting.
3. **Scale of data/analysis:** The scale of analysis/data should generally be large. However, there may be some exceptions.
4. **Techniques:** The techniques may include AI (e.g., ML and DL) and other big data and data analytics techniques.

4.2 Co-citations Among Secondary Studies on SA

Among the included five studies, only SS2 and SS3 have cited SS1. SS2 reported that none of the previously published related studies extensively cover the topic by addressing research questions similar to ours. SS3 reported that their goal is to expand the existing knowledge on SA by adapting and extending the data perspectives, dimensions, and concerns identified and used in the related work. The studies (SS4 and SS5) published in 2017 have not discussed the study (SS1) published in 2015. Similarly, the studies published in 2021 (SS2) and 2023 (SS3) have not discussed the two secondary studies published in 2017. Lastly, the 2023 publication (SS3) does not discuss the studies published in 2017 or 2021. This tertiary study improves the visibility of the existing secondary studies in the area by identifying these secondary studies. Thus, it reduces the likelihood of unintended duplication of effort and enables further research to capitalize on these studies. The absence of discussion of previous related studies in this set of papers also highlights the importance of establishing the need for a review (see the quality assessment instrument, QAISER, for further details [18]).

4.3 Broader Conclusions from Secondary Studies on SA

Figure 3 shows an overview/map of the identified secondary studies on SA. Given the lack of overlap between the studies, we cannot check the consistency of conclusions. However, a comparison of the findings of these studies with a consideration of their aims and approach reveals the following themes:

- SS1, SS2, and SS3 highlight that SA research mainly caters to the needs of developers and that future work on SA should target the needs of other stakeholders, too, and make use of data sources beyond the source code repository. Given that these had similar aims, with SS2 having a narrower scope of Agile software development, one can be confident that the above trend has not changed between periods 2000–2014 and 2010–2021.
- SS1, SS4, and SS5 highlight that there is a lack of mature or industrial validation-based research in the field of SA. This indicates that secondary studies found a lack of evaluation research in general in the SA literature and also in the areas of green SE and web usability.

– SS4 and SS5 suggest the development of new and improved methods and tools for visualization and green SE. SS2 highlights that visualization that supports the decision-making process is very important. The need for visualization and green SE tools was not highlighted in any other studies.

5 Discussion

The timeline covered by the primary studies included in the five selected secondary studies ranges from 2000 to 2021. Despite the overlapping timelines of the selected secondary studies (see Fig. 2), there is a negligible overlap of primary studies between the secondary studies. Thus, each of these studies provides an isolated view, and together, they provide a fragmented view, i.e., there is no "common picture" of the area as these studies have used distinct classification schemes. For example, SS1 and SS3 classify the included primary studies in the following categories (C) or areas. **SS1** – C1: Maintainability and reverse engineering; C2: Team collaboration and dashboard; C3: Incident management and defect prediction; C4: Software analytics platform; C5: Software effort estimation. **SS3** – C1: Implementation; C2: Maintenance; C3: Testing; C4: Debugging; C5: Operations. Thus, there is a need to structure the existing work using a single classification scheme in a consistent map.

SS1 and SS3 have a broad scope and have generally focused on aggregating research on SA. These two studies cover primary research from 2000 to 2021. Given this focus and timeline, it could be expected that these two studies should have a significant overlap of the primary studies included in these secondary studies and those found in SS2, SS4, and SS5 since the latter three have a narrow focus on the use of SA. However, our findings indicate that this is not the case.

One possible explanation for the lack of overlap between primary studies of these secondary studies could be the different search strategies used in the secondary studies. For example, SS1 and SS3 focused on generally aggregating research on SA. However, their search string differs. SS1 search string searches for literature that uses the terms "software analytics" or "software development analytics." SS3 has these terms with additional criteria that include terms such as "big data" and "data mining" and type of study, e.g., "empirical" and "evidence-based". Similarly, the search strategies for SS2, SS4, and SS5 have their own criteria.

Considering the different areas, the number of included primary studies, and the timeline covered by the selected secondary studies, an overview study combining the primary studies included in these secondary studies could be adequate to provide a comprehensive overview of the usage of SA.

In summary, the above-mentioned findings indicate that the existing secondary studies on the usage of SA do not provide a comprehensive and consistent map, which has the following limitations: (a) for researchers, it limits the possibilities of identifying future research directions, while (b) for practitioners, there is no extensive collection of what potentially relevant SA solutions exist. Consequently, there is a need for an overview study that combines the primary studies included in these secondary studies to provide a consistent and comprehensive map of the usage of SA.

6 Conclusion and Future Work

In this study, we analyzed existing secondary studies on the usage of SA. We found five secondary studies on the topic covering the primary research from 2000 to 2021. Despite the overlapping objectives and search timeframes of these secondary studies, there is a negligible overlap of primary studies between these secondary studies. This has resulted in a fragmented view of the literature on the topic. In addition, these studies have used distinct classification schemes. Thus, there is a need for an overview study that combines these studies to provide a more comprehensive overview of the topic using a consistent mapping scheme.

In the future, we aim to conduct a comprehensive overview study to provide a map of the existing literature on SA by collectively analyzing primary studies from the identified secondary studies. Furthermore, future work should use the SA definition synthesized in this paper to guide the search and selection criteria for a secondary study. The use of this definition will help avoid missing relevant research that does not explicitly position itself as an SA study.

Acknowledgements. This work has been supported by ELLIIT; the Strategic Research Area within IT and Mobile Communications, funded by the Swedish Government, and by a research grant for the GIST project (reference number 20220235) from the Knowledge Foundation in Sweden.

Disclosure of Interests. The authors declare that they have no known competing financial interests or personal relationships that could have appeared to influence the work reported in this paper.

References

1. Abdellatif, T.M., Capretz, L.F., Ho, D.: Software analytics to software practice: a systematic literature review. In: International Workshop on Big Data Software Engineering, pp. 30–36. IEEE (2015)
2. Amable, M., Dávila, A.: Knowledge sharing in software development: a tertiary study. In: Mejía, J., Muñoz, M., Rocha, A., Hernández Pérez, Y., Avila-George, H. (eds) New Perspectives in Software Engineering. Studies in Computational Intelligence, vol. 1135, pp. 175–187. Springer, Cham (2024). https://doi.org/10.1007/978-3-031-50590-4_11
3. Angeloni, M.P.C., Duque, R., de Oliveira, K.M., Strugeon, E.G.L., Tirnauca, C.: A tertiary study on quality in use evaluation of smart environment applications. In: Araújo, J., de la Vara, J.L., Santos, M.Y., Assar, S. (eds.) RCIS 2024. LNBIP, vol. 513, pp. 115–130. Springer, Cham (2024). https://doi.org/10.1007/978-3-031-59465-6_8

4. Anwar, H., Pfahl, D.: Towards greener software engineering using software analytics: a systematic mapping. In: Euromicro Conference on Software Engineering and Advanced Applications, pp. 157–166. IEEE (2017)

5. Biesialska, K., Franch, X., Muntés-Mulero, V.: Big data analytics in agile software development: a systematic mapping study. Inf. Softw. Technol. **132**, 106448 (2021)

6. Börstler, J., bin Ali, N., Petersen, K.: Double-counting in software engineering tertiary studies—an overlooked threat to validity. Inf. Softw. Technol. **158**, 107174 (2023)

7. Budgen, D., Brereton, P., Williams, N., Drummond, S.: What support do systematic reviews provide for evidence-informed teaching about software engineering practice? E-Inform. Softw. Eng. J. **14**(1), 7–60 (2020)

8. Caldeira, J., Brito e Abreu, F., Cardoso, J., Simões, R., Oliveira, T., Pereira dos Reis, J.: Software development analytics in practice: a systematic literature review. Arch. Comput. Methods Eng. 1–40 (2023)

9. Dissemination, C.: Systematic reviews: CRD's guidance for undertaking reviews in healthcare. University of York NHS Centre for Reviews & Dissemination, York (2009)

10. Dyba, T., Dingsoyr, T., Hanssen, G.K.: Applying systematic reviews to diverse study types: an experience report. In: International Symposium on Empirical Software Engineering and Measurement, pp. 225–234. IEEE (2007)

11. Kitchenham, B., Brereton, P.: A systematic review of systematic review process research in software engineering. Inf. Softw. Technol. **55**(12), 2049–2075 (2013)

12. Kitchenham, B.A., Budgen, D., Brereton, P.: Evidence-Based Software Engineering and Systematic Reviews. CRC Press (2015)

13. Laiq, M., Ali, N.b., Börstler, J., Engström, E.: Industrial adoption of machine learning techniques for early identification of invalid bug reports. Empir. Softw. Eng. **29**(5), 130 (2024)

14. Marijan, D., Gotlieb, A., Sen, S.: Test case prioritization for continuous regression testing: an industrial case study. In: International Conference on Software Maintenance, pp. 540–543. IEEE (2013)

15. Pellizon, L.H., Choma, J., da Silva, T.S., Guerra, E., Zaina, L.: Software analytics for web usability: a systematic mapping. In: Gervasi, O., et al. (eds.) ICCSA 2017. LNCS, vol. 10409, pp. 246–261. Springer, Cham (2017). https://doi.org/10.1007/978-3-319-62407-5_17

16. Petersen, K., Börstler, J., Ali, N.B., Engström, E.: Revisiting the construct and assessment of industrial relevance in software engineering research. In: International Workshop on Methodological Issues with Empirical Studies in Software Engineering, pp. 17–20 (2024)

17. Rakha, M.S., Bezemer, C.-P., Hassan, A.E.: Revisiting the performance of automated approaches for the retrieval of duplicate reports in issue tracking systems that perform just-in-time duplicate retrieval. Empir. Softw. Eng. **23**(5), 2597–2621 (2018). https://doi.org/10.1007/s10664-017-9590-5

18. Usman, M., Ali, N.B., Wohlin, C.: A quality assessment instrument for systematic literature reviews in software engineering. e-Inform. Softw. Eng. J. **17**(1), 230105 (2023). https://doi.org/10.37190/E-INF230105

19. Zhang, D., Han, S., Dang, Y., Lou, J.G., Zhang, H., Xie, T.: Software analytics in practice. IEEE softw. **30**(5), 30–37 (2013)

Achieving Energy Efficiency
in Microservice-Based Cloud Applications:
A Systematic Study

César Perdigão Batista[1]([✉])[iD], Glauber Barros[2][iD], Thais Batista[2][iD],
Sophie Chabridon[1][iD], and Denis Conan[1][iD]

[1] SAMOVAR, Télécom SudParis, Institut Polytechnique de Paris,
91120 Palaiseau, France
{cesar-augusto.perdigao_batista,sophie.chabridon,
denis.conan}@telecom-sudparis.eu
[2] Universidade Federal do Rio Grande do Norte, Natal, Rio Grande do Norte, Brazil
glauber.mendes.112@ufrn.edu.br,thais.batista@ufrn.br

Abstract. The growth of Cloud computing has enabled scalable and
accessible services, while also intensifying concerns over energy consumption, carbon emissions, and both the environmental and financial
sustainability of data centers. Microservice architectures offer promising opportunities for granular resource optimization and energy savings,
though it can also introduce complexities. It is crucial to investigate
how microservice-based Cloud applications address energy efficiency. For
this purpose, we conducted a systematic literature review (SLR) aiming to establish an overview of the state-of-the-art on energy-efficient
microservice-based Cloud applications. The research questions of the
SLR focus on revealing: (i) strategies to mitigate energy inefficiencies
in microservice-based Cloud applications; (ii) experimental methodologies used to assess the effectiveness of the proposed strategy, and (iii)
mechanisms for measuring energy consumption. As a result, 25 studies were selected and synthesized to provide a comprehensive overview
about the topic. This paper also presents a taxonomy and raises important challenges and potential directions for future research.

Keywords: Energy Efficiency · Microservices · Cloud Applications ·
Systematic Literature Review

1 Introduction

In the last decade, Cloud computing has emerged as the standard approach
for organizations to manage and operate their computing resources, systems,
and applications. The widespread adoption of the Cloud paradigm has led to
increased data center energy consumption, raising environmental and economic
concerns.

From this perspective, regulatory and governmental mandates for sustainable
practices have pushed research efforts towards energy efficiency. Organizations

D. Taibi and D. Smite (Eds.): SEAA 2025, LNCS 16082, pp. 405–424, 2026.
https://doi.org/10.1007/978-3-032-04200-2_28

adopt a myriad of Cloud service architectures to adhere to regulations and mitigate their operational carbon footprint understanding that improving energy efficiency in Cloud infrastructures is not only essential for reducing costs but also for achieving sustainability goals [3]. Extensive research and component evolution have significantly improved Cloud data center energy efficiency, leading to Cloud computing's recognition as a cost-effective solution [5]. Energy efficiency, which involves resource optimization and consolidation, can impact performance. Early Cloud deployments focused on performance, often neglecting energy consumption in their design and operations [7]. Balancing these conflicting requirements requires careful architectural decisions.

Cloud-native deployments, which commonly adopt a microservices architecture, are employed in 89% of organizations to enable fine-grained software evolution and deployment units [10]. Therefore, there is a pressing need to map and classify energy-efficiency strategies tailored to this paradigm. However, existing research on Cloud energy efficiency focus primarily on monolithic or VM-level strategies, for example, dynamic voltage/frequency scaling at the host, virtual machine consolidation, and coarse-grained scheduling, to reduce aggregate power draw. These approaches overlook two critical sets of characteristics of microservice architectures: (i) fine granularity with ephemerality and (ii) prolific inter-service communication coupled with resilience patterns. This characterizes a dynamic environment in which short-lived and low-granularity services may continuously spawn and die faster than host-level controllers can adapt, making per-service energy measurement and control infeasible without new instrumentation. In addition, practices like retries, circuit breakers, and distributed tracing improve reliability but may increase network and CPU overhead, and thus energy consumption, if applied without energy-aware tuning. These patterns, although not exclusive to microservices, are prevalent and often more intensively used due to the distributed nature of this architecture.

The adoption of microservices architecture is a promising approach to enhance energy efficiency in Cloud environments. This paradigm enables more granular control over resource allocation and usage, providing a new perspective on this issue. Typically deployed in resource-efficient containers, such services can be horizontally scaled and load-balanced. Despite the advancements, the energy efficiency of microservice architectures remains complex, with significant challenges in fully realizing their energy-saving potential. A key issue is the complexity of managing and orchestrating numerous small services, which can lead to overhead that reduces energy benefits. Efficient communication among microservices is essential to avoid excessive network usage and latency, maintaining both performance and energy efficiency [21]. While microservice architectures offer a promising path toward more energy-efficient Cloud data centers, achieving optimal energy savings requires an approach that includes effective resource management, advanced scheduling, and continuous monitoring.

Although the importance of this subject is widely recognized, there is a lack of a comprehensive state-of-the-art overview, hindering researchers' understanding the existing knowledge on the area. To tackle this problem, we conducted a

Systematic Literature Review (SLR) focused on exploring recent research strategies for supporting energy efficiency of microservice-based applications in the Cloud, evaluation mechanisms, and measurement approaches. The outcome of this SLR includes outlining the current research landscape, classifying the existing literature by defining a taxonomy, and revealing open challenges for further investigation.

The remainder of this paper is organized as follows. Section 2 describes the methodology employed to conduct the SLR. Section 3 synthesizes the findings by answering the posed research questions. Section 4 presents a taxonomy to understand the research landscape related to this SLR. Section 5 discusses the current challenges and perspectives for further development. Section 6 summarizes some threats to the study's validity. Section 7 discusses related work. Section 8 presents the final remarks.

2   Research Methodology

The SLR carried out by the authors of this work adhered to established literature guidelines [19], using the support of the Parsif.al online tool. It consisted of three main steps: (i) *planning*, which involves protocol creation with research questions, search strategy, selection criteria, and data extraction and synthesis methods; (ii) *execution*, which entails the identification, selection, and analysis of studies; and (iii) *reporting*, which aggregates the information extracted from relevant studies in relation to the research questions, synthesizing the findings to draw conclusions.

Goals. The research goal is defined as follows: to establish an overview of the state-of-the-art on energy-efficient microservice-based Cloud applications.

Data Availability. The list of study data can be found on page 16 and in the replication package available online at https://zenodo.org/records/15514643.

Research Questions. Three research questions (RQs) were proposed aiming at finding primary studies to understand and summarize evidence on energy-efficient microservice-based Cloud applications.

> RQ1. Which strategies are used to support energy efficiency of microservice-based applications in the Cloud?

RQ1 Rationale: Microservice architectures, while offering benefits, also introduce complexities that can impact energy consumption: e.g. inter-service communication overhead, resource allocation inefficiencies, and the potential for over-provisioning. Understanding the specific strategies employed to mitigate these energy inefficiencies is the first step for developing practical guidelines. This RQ aims to identify and categorize these strategies. Additionally, it highlights whether strategies are tailored to microservices' modularity (per-service scaling) or merely adapted from monolithic systems, ensuring that solutions address microservices-specific complexities.

RQ2. What kind of experimentation was conducted in the work?

RQ2 Rationale: Different experimental methodologies offer varying levels of rigor and provide different types of insights. This RQ aims to identify the types of experiments conducted in the reviewed literature, focusing on the methodologies used, the metrics measured, and the overall experimental design. The relevance of this RQ lies in providing an understanding of how energy efficiency strategies are evaluated.

RQ3. Which mechanisms are used for measuring energy consumption?

RQ3 Rationale: Various measurement mechanisms offer different levels of accuracy and granularity, and the choice of the mechanism may impact the results of an evaluation. This research question aims to identify the specific mechanisms used to measure energy consumption in the reviewed literature. RQ3 addresses the tools, metrics, and methodologies used to measure energy consumption for microservice-based applications in the Cloud. Its relevance lies in revealing and cataloging measurement mechanisms.

Search Strategy. An automated search process was carried out over four electronic publication databases to retrieve relevant studies to answer the posed RQs. The employed databases were: ACM Digital Library, IEEEXplore, Scopus, and Springer Link. These sources are among the most popular publication databases in Computer Science and Engineering, and have good coverage of the literature.

Based on the defined RQs, four main terms were initially identified, namely Cloud, Energy Efficient, Evaluation and Microservice. The following search string was built considering synonyms and alternative terms to increase coverage of the literature search until the end of 2024:

```
("cloud" OR "cloud-based") AND ("microservice" OR "microservices") AND
("energy efficient" OR "energy efficiency" OR "power efficiency" OR
"power efficient") AND ("evaluation" OR "performance evaluation") AND
NOT ("edge" OR "edge computing" OR "fog" OR "fog computing")
```

Selection Criteria. Selection criteria were used to assess the relevance of each primary study to answer the established RQs. Inclusion criteria define circumstances that make a study relevant, whereas exclusion criteria exclude studies that are unrelated to the RQs. Table 1 lists inclusion criteria (ICs) and exclusion criteria (ECs) of this SLR.

A given primary study was regarded as relevant if it did not meet any EC and met at least one IC.

Selection Process. The process is divided into four phases: (i) exclude duplicates, (ii) select based on titles, (iii) select based on abstracts, and (iv) select based on full text. Figure 1 depicts the process for selecting the primary studies.

Table 1. Inclusion and Exclusion Criteria

Inclusion Criteria
1) The study describes a software architecture
2) It focuses on Cloud and microservices applications
3) It focuses on power efficiency

Exclusion Criteria
1) The study does not concern software architectures
2) It does not focus on Cloud and microservices applications
3) It does not focus on power efficiency
4) It does not present an abstract or its full text is not available
5) It does not present sufficient technical information
6) It is not written in English

The automated search retrieved 475 results. After the removal of duplicates, 456 studies remain. In Phase 2, which begins to apply the selection criteria (ICs and ECs), 101 studies were excluded based on title, resulting in 355 studies remaining. Next, in Phase 3, we excluded based on reading the abstract, remaining 92 studies. Finally, in Phase 4, we fully read the studies to select those that address any RQ. This resulted in a final set of 25 studies relevant to this work, identified as S1 to S25 in references.

3 Results and Discussion

3.1 Overview of the Selected Studies

Distribution of the Studies over the Years. Over the period 2018âĂŞ2024, we observed an average of approximately 3.6 studies published per year (median = 4). The years of 2019, 2022 and 2023 had the highest number of selected studies, with 5 studies each.

Publication Venues. The primary selected studies were published in 18 different venues, showing that there is no specific reference point for publications on energy-efficient microservice-based Cloud applications. Among these venues, the IEEE/ACM International Symposium on Microarchitecture stood out with 3 studies. It can be observed that a higher number of primary selected studies were published in journals: 10 (40%) studies were published in journals, 8 (32%) in conferences, 6 (24%) in symposia and 1 (4%) in book chapter.

3.2 Strategies to Support Energy Efficiency (RQ1)

To synthesize the strategies identified in the systematic review, we organize them into recurring patterns observed in the key techniques employed across the study corpus. As most studies employ multiple strategies, they can be mentioned more

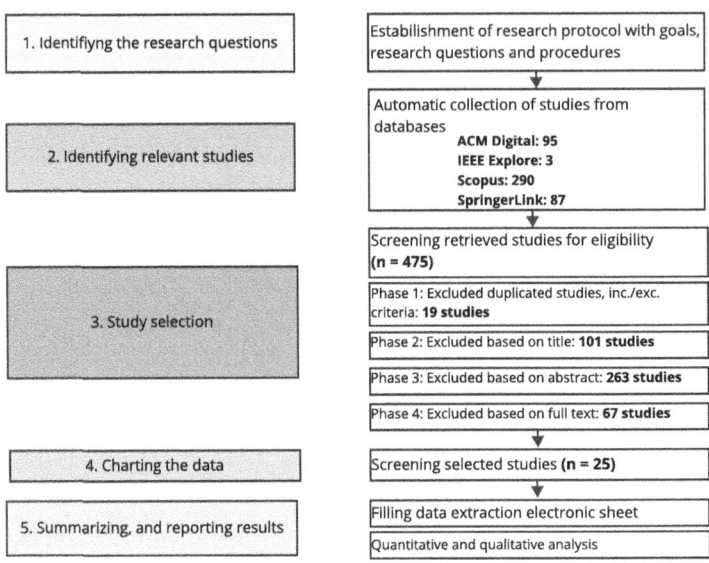

Fig. 1. Process for selecting and analyzing the relevant primary studies.

than once, thus they are not mutually exclusive. In this section, we provide a perspective on how these strategies are applied, both conceptually and in practical implementations. Furthermore, we acknowledge that certain studies employ well-known strategies, while others either present extensions or introduce novel techniques beyond conventional energy-efficiency methods.

Resource Allocation and Optimization. Resource Allocation and Optimization aims to minimize energy waste while meeting performance goals by using algorithmic techniques and hardware-software co-design. **S25** and **S7** apply fine- and medium-grained power management strategies to reduce CPU energy usage. **S11** utilizes fuzzy Q-learning for dynamic microservice placement based on CPU utilization, addressing resource fragmentation. Power management approaches vary in granularity, with **S4** focusing on package-level control and **S5** on core-level cache and PLL retention. Hybrid methods like those in **S20** combine genetic algorithms with architectural redesign for improved energy efficiency. **S6** introduces a decentralized scheduling algorithm using a four-dimensional resource model to optimize microservice placement and address scalability in geodistributed systems.

Consolidation and Scheduling. Consolidation and Scheduling strategies aim to group workloads or containers to reduce overhead and improve resource usage. This approach is central in microservices applications, where lightweight containers often operate at suboptimal usage levels. **S24** demonstrates how consolidating containers within fewer VMs reduces energy waste by minimizing hypervisor overhead. **S13** uses interval graph models to schedule container reservations, avoiding resource contention and idle periods. **S19** employs Binary Particle Swarm Optimization (BPSO) heuristic mapping to assign microservices to containers, ensuring balanced loads across physical machines. These techniques mitigate the energy costs of distributed microservice orchestration, particularly in environments with fluctuating workloads. Further analysis reveals distinctions in consolidation methodologies. For example, **S3** advocates for container state reclamation (pause/stop/disconnect) to reclaim idle resources, achieving 15% energy savings in idle-heavy scenarios. In contrast, **S14** prioritizes proactive scaling to align container counts with predicted demand, reducing cold-start penalties in serverless functions. The interplay between consolidation and prediction is evident in **S2**, which integrates VM consolidation with brownout policies that postpones uncritical services only to be spawned when renewable energy is available. These studies collectively underscore that effective consolidation requires both static grouping and dynamic adaptation to address the transient nature of microservices.

Architectural Optimization. Architectural Optimization involves redesigning system structures or communication patterns to reduce energy-intensive operations. This approach targets the high communication overhead typical of microservice architectures. **S23** batches similar requests into streamlined instruction flows, reducing redundant processing. **S17** evaluates sharding and local proxies to minimize inter-service communication energy. **S16** ranks microservices by interaction intensity, co-locating high-affinity services to cut network energy use. These strategies highlight how architectural redesigns can decouple performance from energy consumption in distributed systems. Additionally, our synthesis reveals that refining inter-service protocols can have long-term energy implications. The studies emphasize that, while architectural optimization may require upfront design modifications, the resulting efficiency gains, such as those observed in **S23**, can significantly lower operational costs. This reorganization is particularly vital in microservices, where a high volume of small, interdependent services can otherwise lead to considerable communication overhead.

Dynamic Adaptation. Dynamic Adaptation enables runtime adjustments to resource usage based on workload or environmental conditions. This approach is essential for microservices, where unpredictable traffic patterns demand flexibility. **S18** vertically scales container resources in response to carbon-intensity data, aligning energy use with renewable availability. **S12** and **S8** deactivate optional microservices during overloads, preserving energy for critical tasks. These methods exemplify how adaptive mechanisms can balance energy efficiency with QoS in volatile environments. The granularity of adaptation varies across studies. **S10** employs predictive load adaptation at the function level, whereas **S7** adjusts power budgets at the hardware-register level. **S2** combines VM consolidation with brownout, showcasing that multi-layered adaptation (infrastructure + application) can maximize energy savings.

Workload Prediction and Management. Workload Prediction and Management leverages forecasting to preemptively allocate resources, avoiding energy spikes from reactive scaling. This approach is particularly effective for microservices with cyclical or bursty traffic, where anticipating peak loads and idle periods allows for more precise energy control. Multi-criteria forecasting is present in many technniques, with the central goal of reducing the energy penalty for over-provisioning while maintaining responsiveness. **S14** combines proactive and reactive scaling, leveraging workload predictions to minimize idle containers. **S10** employs predictive load adaptation to adjust container counts based on anticipated demand, mitigating resource underutilization. **S2** integrates renewable energy forecasts with VM consolidation and brownout, optimizing energy use across temporal scales. Furthermore, the analytical models, ranging from statistical measures to machine learning (ML) algorithms, used in these studies underscore the importance of integrating predictive insights into dynamic resource management. Techniques reported in **S14** and **S2** demonstrate that proactive management not only improves energy efficiency but also enhances overall service reliability.

Energy-Aware Monitoring. Energy-Aware Monitoring provides granular insights into energy consumption, enabling data-driven optimizations. This approach addresses the opacity of energy usage in distributed microservices. **S1** attributes energy consumption to individual microservices using extended Berkeley Packet Filter (eBPF) and Intel's RAPL, enabling targeted optimizations. **S21** compares low-overhead tools to minimize measurement overhead. These tools empower developers to identify energy hotspots and refine resource allocation policies.

The trade-off between measurement granularity and system overhead is a key concern in energy monitoring. **S1** employs eBPF agents with RAPL to measure energy at the thread level, offering precision but introducing CPU overhead. Similarly, **S21** shows that higher-frequency and more detailed data collection improves accuracy but increases energy and performance costs. These studies emphasize the need to balance accuracy, energy consumption, and system impact, especially when designing monitoring frameworks for microservice-based Cloud applications.

Design-Time Sustainability. Design-time sustainability integrates energy efficiency into application architecture from the outset, embedding sustainability metadata and annotations to address energy concerns early. **S22** and **S16** present frameworks that incorporate sustainability through structured design methodologies. This early integration leads to long-term energy savings by influencing deployment and resource management. For example, **S22** proposes energy-aware annotations for specifying consumption profiles, QoS constraints, and low-power alternatives. Additionally, **S16** shows that such design-time strategies enhance adaptability to runtime energy conditions, underscoring the value of embedding energy considerations throughout the software lifecycle, especially in microservices-based systems.

> **Main Findings (RQ1).** The analysis reveals seven dominant strategies to energy efficiency in Cloud-based microservices, each addressing distinct challenges of the paradigm. While *Dynamic Adaptation* and *Resource Allocation and Optimization* are the most prevalent, emerging strategies like *Architectural Optimization* and *Design-Time Sustainability* highlight a shift towards application-level energy management. Although few studies combine multiple approaches, hybrid solutions emerge as a promising research direction.

3.3   Experimentation Conducted (RQ2)

The reviewed studies reveal a spectrum of experimental methodologies, each tailored to distinct objectives, from theoretical validation under controlled conditions to real-world applicability in heterogeneous environments. In this context, the following criteria are relevant to assess the maturity of the experimentation scenario: (i) deployment categories, (ii) key metrics, and (iii) reproducibility.

Simulated approaches are used in studies prioritizing scalability or theoretical evaluation, enabling systematic parameter variation and sensitivity analysis. For instance, **S13** employs synthetic workloads and mathematical models to simulate container placement strategies, measuring performance per watt and communication costs. **S11** employs ContainerCloudSim with Google Cluster traces to simulate its fuzzy Q-learning algorithm, systematically varying resource availability and workload intensities. While such simulations offer repeatability and scalability, they often rely on idealized assumptions (e.g., static power models), limiting fidelity to hardware-level dynamics like voltage-frequency scaling or cache contention.

Real-world testbed experiments are widely used to ensure ecological validity, especially in hardware-level and orchestration evaluations. **S25** uses Intel Xeon servers to assess core energy consumption with nanosecond precision, though its fixed setup limits generalizability. Brownout strategies are validated in realistic settings: **S12** employs the Grid'5000 testbed with physical power meters, while **S8** integrates container- and host-level controls to evaluate energy and availability trade-offs. **S2** combines OpenStack/Docker Swarm with renewable energy forecasts and physical measurements via Eaton ePDUs. These studies highlight the importance of empirical validation for robust and scalable energy-efficient solutions.

Hybrid methodologies bridge simulation and physical deployment to balance granularity and scalability. **S14** extensively evaluates its approach leveraging a real system scenario (limited to 160-core custer) with simulations (11k-core cluster) to explore scalability, examining proactive scaling policies, isolating variables like request arrival rates and function invocation probabilities. In a similar way,

S18 validates migration strategies in simulated environment and on CloudLab testbed, compatible with model-based power monitoring (PowerAPI) to account for energy consumption and external APIs to monitor carbon intensity of servers. While hybrid designs mitigate the trade-off between granularity and realism, they face challenges in synchronizing assumptions across layers. Metric selection and measurement frameworks further differentiate studies, reflecting divergent priorities, which are not mutually exclusive. **S6** uses simulations to prioritize algorithmic metrics (e.g., energy savings vs. baselines), while real-world studies, such as **S21**, emphasize physical rigor, employing Watts Up Pro meters (1-second sampling) and SAR profiling to prioritize system monitoring capabilities. The main metrics are energy consumption measured in 88% of the studies, with latency and SLA violations addressed in nearly half and one-quarter of the studies, respectively. The studies that do not focus on energy itself focus on carbon emission instead.

Among the studies, there is also variation in reproducibility. *High reproducibility* is assigned when the study provides complete, detailed hardware and software configuration information or employs standardized tools, indicating that experiments can be replicated. *Medium reproducibility* is given when sufficient details are available but some key parameters or data (e.g., synthetic or proprietary datasets) are only partially disclosed, leading to potential disparity in replication. *Low reproducibility* is defined by a lack of essential experimental details, with missing or proprietary data and configurations that prevent independent replication of the experiments. For example, **S17** detailed configuration and experiment data are provided, whereas studies like **S2** have a similar experiment rigor but lacks artifact availability, underscoring general inconsistencies in reporting standards for the field. Collectively, the abovementioned methodologies reflect a field dealing with the tension of theoretical innovation and operational viability. Simulation studies enable parameter exploration and model validation (e.g., Google trace replays in **S19** and **S11**), while testbeds like CloudLab and Grid'5000 validate techniques under infrastructural heterogeneity. Hybrid approaches, though promising, require harmonization of assumptions and metrics to properly extend or transplant real-world behaviors into simulation or vice-versa. Standardizing benchmarks and artifact sharing would enhance cross-study comparability, ensuring that energy efficiency strategies are both theoretically sound and practically robust.

Main Findings (RQ2). Experimental methodologies show a diverse spectrum in terms of deployment categories, metrics and reproducibility. Real-world experiments using platforms like CloudLab and Grid'5000 combined with intermediary reproducibility directions are common approaches, but not prevalent. Such observation indicates that the field is in an evolving phase, with a lack of standardized methodologies. This can be viewed as a consequence from the plethora of techniques described in RQ1. This scenario emphasizes the need for specialized guidelines and benchmarks.

3.4   Mechanism for Energy Consumption Measurement (RQ3)

RQ3 explores the mechanisms, metrics, and methodologies employed to measure energy consumption and identify inconsistencies in measurement approaches. We divided these mechanisms into two major groups: *physical* and *logical-level measurement mechanisms*. *Physical mechanisms* involves collecting data directly from the physical infrastructure of the data center or computing environment. For example, rack Power Distribution Units (PDU) and physical power meters are considered energy measurement mechanisms at the physical hardware level. *Logical-level measurement mechanisms* estimate energy consumption using consumption profiles and operating system metrics such as CPU, memory, disk, and network usage. The choice of a physical or a logical mechanism depends on the required level of granularity. For coarse granularity and precise hardware-level measurements, PDUs are more reliable. In contrast, for independent software-level energy measurement in virtualized and containerized application services, tools like PowerAPI are more appropriate. Due to fine granularity, this mechanism allows measurement of energy consumption at a specific service container. In the selected studies of this SLR, we classified twenty studies that use a logical-level energy consumption measurement mechanism. We further subdivided this group into approaches that model energy consumption through mathematical models (**S6, S9, S11, S13, S15, S16, S18, S19, S20** and **S23**) and software-based power meters (**S1, S4, S5, S7, S8, S10, S11, S12, S14, S17** and **S25**). A remarkable case is the study **S1** that employs a multitude of measuring mechanisms at different granularities, so it was categorized in the most suitable group. In physical-level measurement mechanism, we classified four selected studies and these major group was subdivided in racks PDU and physical power meters. **S2** and **S3** use PDU as an energy consumption measurement mechanism, which not only functions as a power distributor for all connected devices but can also be used to monitor their energy consumption. **S21** and **S24** use physical power meters as an energy measurement mechanism. Despite being a physical measurement method, this type of mechanism can measure energy consumption at a more granular level than PDUs, including individual devices or components such as CPUs and GPUs. Finally, only one study (**S22**) does not specify a way to measure energy consumption.

Main Findings (RQ3). Most of the studies adopted a logical-level mechanism approach. These studies uses energy profiles from mathematical models and software-defined power meters to measure the energy consumption of the proposals.

---

4   Proposed Taxonomy

After the analysis of the selected studies (strategies, experimentation approaches, and measurement mechanisms), this work introduces a taxonomy, illustrated in Fig. 2, aimed at capturing key aspects related to the RQs. The proposed taxonomy goes beyond merely summarizing the stat-of-the-art on this topic. It also offers a framework to classify existing approaches and understand their characteristics, serving as a foundation for reasoning about this field. It is hierarchically displayed in isolated tree forms to facilitate the analysis and comprehension of the nuances answered by research questions RQ1, RQ2 and RQ3 (each starting from a separate root), which are major activities that researchers and practitioners have to contemplate prior to designing their contributions and applications.

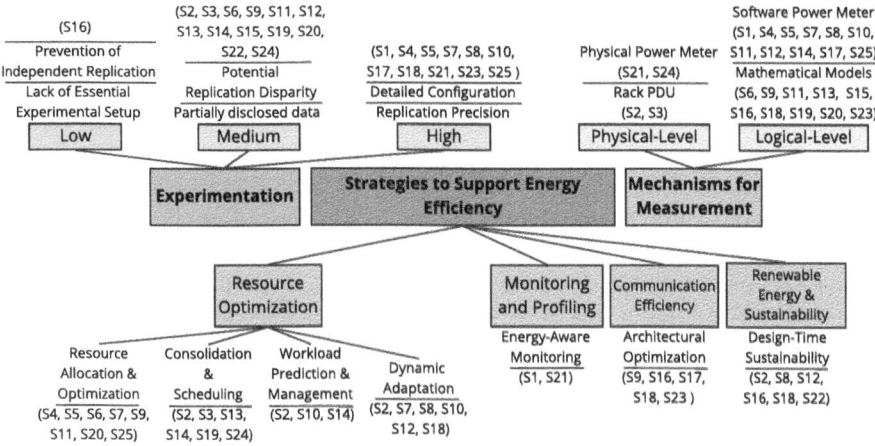

Fig. 2. Taxonomy.

The central root, related to RQ1, organizes the strategies to support energy efficiency in microservice-based Cloud applications. They are categorized across four primary dimensions, each encompassing one or more strategies of techniques explored in Sect. 3.2. These categories are built upon [1], where the authors propose a sustainability framework that categorizes Cloud-related decisions into two levels: *Cloud architecture (CA)*, focusing on infrastructural provider-side choices or concepts, and *Cloud-based architecture (CB)*, concerning application-level functionality and delivery of services using Cloud infrastructure. On the one hand, concerning CA decisions, there is one main category named *Resource Optimization* that groups strategies related to low-abstraction Cloud service layers. On the other hand, concerning CB decisions, the categories *Monitoring and Profiling, Communication Efficiency,* and *Renewable Energy and Sustainability* address strategies for higher-level abstraction. This category partitioning enhances reader understanding and addresses their stated objectives.

The leftmost root explores part of RQ2, delineating the levels of the reproducibility criteria represented along a continuum of Low, Medium, and High. The Low level typically indicates a reliance on purely theoretical or simulation-based methods with only partial configuration details, limiting their ecological validity. By contrast, the High level denotes fully fledged testbed experiments that capture real hardware dynamics, ensuring near-complete replicability when all hardware and software parameters, and all the software artefacts are disclosed.

The rightmost root explores RQ3 focusing on the mechanisms employed to measure energy consumption. It distinguishes between physical-level approaches that use hardware data, and logical-level methods that estimate energy use via software metrics and mathematical models, highlighting the trade-offs in granularity and measurement overhead.

The proposed taxonomy clarifies the spectrum of energy-efficient strategies, while integrating experimental reproducibility and measurement approaches into a cohesive framework. The convenience of this taxonomy is in providing a systematic basis for comparing implementable approaches and identifying best practices. Ultimately, it offers a systematic, actionable pathway for aligning experimental rigor with broader energy efficiency objectives in Cloud.

5   Challenges and Perspectives

This SLR findings reveal reliance on complex observability (**S21**) to enable energy-aware optimizations, such as granular monitoring (**S1**) and adaptive resource control (**S2**). Nevertheless, gaps persist in harmonizing application-specific insights with infrastructure dynamics. The synthesis in this work signals a shift from past research that targeted infrastructure-level decisions (CA), to recent publications raising awareness towards the opportunities of the CB category. This trend suggests application-level interventions emphasizing strategies that address particular energy inefficiencies imposed by microservices.

Achieving optimal balance between monitoring granularity, responsiveness and measurement overhead is a recurrent challenge in a dynamic environment. This becomes more critical when resilience patterns are applied without considering their energy impact. Future studies should address this balance through lightweight monitoring tools, capable of delivering detailed energy insights without imposing significant performance penalties.

From the user's viewpoint, energy transparency, such as per-application energy budgets to meet user-defined energy constraints, is increasingly relevant. Studies like **S22** showcase how design-time annotations (e.g., energy profiles or optional components) empower users to align deployments with sustainability goals. These efforts are in line with proposals such as [24], which advocate for user-facing dashboards and Cloud-native architectural tactics to visualize energy footprint. In this scenario, user decision can be subsidized by data from different levels that compose Cloud applications. Traditional server or VM measurements, coupled with energy estimations per microservice or individual requests would enrich models with runtime data to be leveraged by techniques applied to resource optimization, for instance.

Experimental approaches with higher accuracy that correlate energy data across variable tiers from Cloud systems would create a cohesive feedback loop between application and infrastructure layers. Fostering the synergy of CA and CB strategies, the field can advance towards systems where energy efficiency is both measurable and actionable across the Cloud stack.

6   Threats to Validity

Threats to validity are associated with the rigor of the SLR design and execution. To minimize them, we adhered to well-established guidelines for systematic studies, following a precise protocol. External validity (EV) refers to the generalizability of findings. A potential threat to EV in this SLR is the risk of missing relevant studies. To mitigate this, we applied a search strategy across 4 different databases. Some limitations persist: (i) technical constraints inherent to search engines may have hindered retrieving some studies; (ii) our database selection was robust, but it was not exhaustive, and additional studies may still exist; (iii) no grey literature was included; (iv) no snowballing techniques were applied. Selection validity could be affected by insufficient search strategies, selection bias, or overlooked studies, though this was mitigated via consensus meetings. Data validity, potentially impacted by bias or inaccuracies, was ensured through rigorous review and discussion.

7   Related Work

Energy efficiency in Cloud has gained considerable attention from researchers in the last decade. Table 2 summarizes secondary studies related to our SLR. All papers focus on Cloud and energy, and a minority of them involve microservices. The table also briefly describes the content of each article. Most works are inserted within the context of improving energy efficiency of data center resources across the many layers of the hardware and software stack that compose such infrastructure. The concept of microservices is not prominently featured within the analyzed works. In [13], the authors discuss scheduling and resource provisioning for workflows in multi-tenant platforms, mentioning techniques that can be pertinent to microservices architectures such as data locality awareness, task dependency analysis, clustering, and allocation. However, microservices are not the main subject. Another work linking microservices and energy consumption is [26] that investigates ML-based container orchestration approaches. Some microservices-related techniques have the potential for enhancing the orchestration of containers: (i) *workload distribution characterization* to model and predict the request arrival rates and resource usage patterns across microservice units, and (ii) *microservice dependency analysis* to identify critical microservice units and address the relationship between the status of individual microservices with the overall application performance. However, its main contribution is the taxonomy regarding ML techniques.

In [22], the authors conducted a SLR to map microservice design and architectural patterns to various quality attributes, such as maintainability, reliability, security, and performance efficiency. Although it is not primarily targeted at improving energy efficiency, it appears as a secondary observation rather than the core, leaving a gap in detailed methodologies or optimization strategies for reducing energy consumption.

Despite the growing interest in microservices and energy efficiency, to the best of our knowledge, only one literature review integrates them. Authors of [4]

Table 2. Comparison of This Work with Existing Surveys Based on Key Criteria

Ref.	Year	Cloud	Energy	µS	Context
[17]	2014	Yes	Yes	No	Energy efficiency of computing and network resources
[16]	2014	Yes	Yes	No	Data center infrastructure energy efficiency
[9]	2015	Yes	Yes	No	Energy consumption modeling and prediction for data centers
[15]	2015	Yes	Yes	No	Software-oriented energy efficiency techniques within data centers
[11]	2016	Yes	Yes	No	Energy-efficient cloud service resource allocation
[20]	2017	Yes	Yes	No	Greening IT technologies (Cloud, Mobile, IoT, Big Data, Networking)
[2]	2018	Yes	Yes	No	Energy monitoring of large-scale systems at multiple granularities
[25]	2019	Yes	Yes	No	Brownout for adaptive resource and application management
[22]	2019	Yes	Yes	Yes	Quality attributes in microservice architecture patterns
[13]	2020	Yes	Yes*	Yes*	Scheduling and resource provisioning for scientific workflows
[12]	2021	Yes	Yes	No	Data center consolidation in cloud computing
[18]	2022	Yes	Yes	No	Virtual and physical machine consolidation strategies
[6]	2022	Yes	Yes	No	Environmental impact of energy consumption in cloud data centers
[26]	2022	Yes	Yes*	Yes*	Machine learning-based container orchestration approaches
[14]	2023	Yes	Yes	No	Layer-by-layer soft. modeling of green data centers
[8]	2023	Yes	Yes	No	Integrated management of data center resources and workloads
[23]	2023	Yes	Yes*	No	Sustainable software engineering
[1]	2024	Yes	Yes	No	Sustainability in cloud software architecture
[4]	2024	Yes	Yes	Yes	Overview on energy consumption within microservices
This study	2025	Yes	Yes	Yes	Implementable strategies for energy-efficient microservices applications

Cases where the criteria was considered, but not as the primary focus of the study.

present a SLR about energy consumption in microservices architectures whose primary focus is on outlining the current research landscape, identifying trends and research gaps. The 37 selected studies are evaluated based on criteria such as metrics, evaluation methodologies, architectural topologies, orchestrating tools, and deployment models. Similarly, our work also aims to highlight the advancements and emerging technologies in energy-efficient microservices applications, showing a comparison of different approaches. However, the scope of their study is relatively broad, and it does not address techniques for improving energy efficiency tailored for microservices. The strategies are centered on optimizing infrastructure-level operations and resource management within data centers to enhance energy efficiency. While these methods are the basis, they largely focus on the low-level resource management, lacking application-level guidance.

Unlike previous efforts, our work aims to identify the strategies used to support energy efficiency of microservice-based applications in the Cloud, the experimentation methodologies, and the energy consumption measurement mechanisms. Furthermore, the SLR findings were synthesized into a taxonomy, providing a concise overview of the domain covered by the SLR.

8   Final Remarks

This paper presented the results of a SLR to investigate the state-of-the-art on energy efficiency in microservice-based Cloud applications. We analyzed a corpus of 25 studies aiming to: (i) provide an overview of the strategies for energy efficiency in microservice Cloud applications; (ii) unveil experimental methodologies employed to evaluate the proposed strategies; (iii) describe mechanisms used to measure energy consumption; (iv) define a taxonomy that categorizes the SLR findings. Our analysis reveals that current approaches leverage granular resource management, runtime optimization, energy monitoring and architectural tactics, targeting energy savings and sustainability. Our synthesis indicates that unexplored avenues for research remain to overcome inherent complexities introduced by microservices, particularly in balancing the trade-off between observability and energy overhead, providing user-centric information, refining inter-service communication patterns and establishing standardized evaluation methodologies.

Acknowledgements. This research was produced within the framework of Energy4Climate Interdisciplinary Center (E4C) of IP Paris and Ecole des Ponts Paris-Tech. This research was supported by 3rd Programme d'Investissements d'Avenir [ANR-18-EUR-0006-02]. This work received funding from the France 2030 program, managed by the French National Research Agency under grant agreement No. ANR-23-PECL-0003.

Disclosure of Interests. The authors have no competing interests to declare that are relevant to the content of this article.

References Selected by the SLR

S1   R. Brondolin *et al.*: A black-box monitoring approach to measure microservices runtime performance. ACM Transactions on Architecture and Code Optimization 17(4), 1–26 (2020)

S2   M. Xu *et al.*: A Self-Adaptive Approach for Managing Applications and Harnessing Renewable Energy for Sustainable Cloud Computing. IEEE Transactions on Sustainable Computing 6(4), 544–558 (2021)

S3   Ö.E. Demirkol *et al.*: A study on application container resource efficiency. Turkish Journal of Electrical Engineering and Computer Sciences 27(2), 1041–1051 (2019)

S4   G. Antoniou *et al.*: AgilePkgC: An Agile System Idle State Architecture for Energy Proportional Datacenter Servers. In: 2022 55th IEEE/ACM International Symposium on Microarchitecture (MICRO), pp. 851–867 (2022)

S5   J.H. Yahya *et al.*: AgileWatts: An Energy-Efficient CPU Core Idle-State Architecture for Latency-Sensitive Server Applications. In: 2022 55th IEEE/ACM International Symposium on Microarchitecture (MICRO), pp. 835–850 (2022)

S6   H.H.A. Valera *et al.*: An energy saving approach: understanding microservices as multidimensional entities in p2p networks. In. SAC '21, pp. 69–78. ACM, Virtual Event, Republic of Korea (2021)

S7   X. Hou *et al.*: ANT-Man: Towards Agile Power Management in the Microservice Era. In: SC20: International Conference for High Performance Computing, Networking, Storage and Analysis, pp. 1–14 (2020)

S8   M. Xu *et al.*: BrownoutCon: A software system based on brownout and containers for energy-efficient cloud computing. J. Syst. Softw. 155(C), 91–103 (2019)

S9   A. Saboor *et al.*: Enabling rank-based distribution of microservices among containers for green cloud computing environment. Peer-to-Peer Networking and Applications 15 (2022)

S10 Gunasekaran, J.R. et al.: Fifer: Tackling Underutilization in the Serverless Era (2020)

S11 C.T. Joseph *et al.*: Fuzzy Reinforcement Learning based Microservice Allocation in Cloud Computing Environments. In: TENCON 2019 - 2019 IEEE Region 10 Conference (TENCON), pp. 1559–1563 (2019)

S12 M. Xu *et al.*: iBrownout: An Integrated Approach for Managing Energy and Brownout in Container-Based Clouds. IEEE Transactions on Sustainable Computing 4(1), 53–66 (2019)

S13 Y.S. Patel *et al.*: Interval graph multi-coloring-based resource reservation for energy-efficient containerized cloud data centers. The Journal of Supercomputing 77, 4484–4532 (2021)

S14 V.M. Bhasi *et al.*: Kraken: Adaptive Container Provisioning for Deploying Dynamic DAGs in Serverless Platforms. In: Proceedings of the ACM Symposium on Cloud Computing. SoCC '21, pp. 153–167. ACM, Seattle, WA, USA (2021)

S15 H.H. lvarez Valera *et al.*: The Architecture of Kaligreen V2: A Middleware Aware of Hardware Opportunities to Save Energy. In: 2019 Sixth International Conference on Internet of Things: Systems, Management and Security (IOTSMS), pp. 79–86 (2019)

S16 M. Vitali: Towards greener applications: enabling sustainable-aware cloud native applications design. In: Proc. of the International Conference on Advanced Information Systems Engineering, pp. 93–108 (2022)

S17 F. Khomh *et al.*: Understanding the Impact of Cloud Patterns on Performance and Energy Consumption. Journal of Systems and Software 141 (2018)

S18 J. Thiede *et al.*: Carbon Containers: A System-level Facility for Managing Application-level Carbon Emissions. In: Proceedings of the ACM Symposium on Cloud Computing. SoCC '23, pp. 17–31. ACM, Santa Cruz, CA, USA (2023)

S19 D. Kumar *et al.*: "Containerized Deployment of Microservices in Cloud Computing". In: Sept. 2023, pp. 35–59.

S20 Z. Fang *et al.*: Energy-Efficient and Communication-Aware Resource Allocation in Container-Based Cloud with Group Genetic Algorithm. In: F. Monti *et al.* Service-Oriented Computing, pp. 212–226. Springer Nature Switzerland, Cham (2023)

S21 M. Dinga *et al.*: An empirical evaluation of the energy and performance overhead of monitoring tools on docker-based systems. In: Proc. of the Int. Conf. on Service-Oriented Computing, pp. 181–196 (2023)

S22 M. Vitali *et al.*: Enriching Cloud-native Applications with Sustainability Features. In: Proc. of the International Conference on Cloud Engineering, pp. 21–31 (2023)

S23 M. Khairy *et al.*: SIMR: Single Instruction Multiple Request Processing for Energy-Efficient Data Center Microservices. In: 2022 55th IEEE/ACM Interna-tional Symposium on Microarchitecture (MICRO), pp. 441–463 (2022)

S24 B. Bermejo *et al.*: The Goodness of Nesting Containers in Virtual Machines for Server Consolidation: The Goodness of Nesting Containers in Virtual Machines for Server Consolidation. J. Grid Comput. 22 (2024)

S25 G. Antoniou *et al.*: Agile C-states: A Core C-state Architecture for Latency Critical Applications Optimizing both Transition and Cold-Start Latency. ACM Trans. Archit. Code Optim. 21(4) (2024)

References

1. Ahmadisakha, S., et al.: Architecting for sustainability of and in the cloud: a systematic literature review. Inf. Softw. Technol. (2024)
2. Almeida, F., et al.: Energy monitoring as an essential building block towards sustainable ultrascale systems. Sustain. Comput.: Inform. Syst. **17**, 27–42 (2018)

3. Andrikopoulos, V., Lago, P.: Software sustainability in the age of everything as a service. In: Aiello, M., Bouguettaya, A., Tamburri, D.A., van den Heuvel, W.-J. (eds.) Next-Gen Digital Services. A Retrospective and Roadmap for Service Computing of the Future. LNCS, vol. 12521, pp. 35–47. Springer, Cham (2021). https://doi.org/10.1007/978-3-030-73203-5_3

4. Araújo, G., et al.: Energy consumption in microservices architectures: a systematic literature review. IEEE Access **12**, 186710–186729 (2024)

5. Berl, A., et al.: Energy-efficient cloud computing. Comput. J. **53**(7) (2010)

6. Bharany, S., et al.: A systematic survey on energy-efficient techniques in sustainable cloud computing. Sustainability **14**(10), 6256 (2022)

7. Buyya, R., et al.: A manifesto for future generation cloud computing: research directions for the next decade. ACM Comput. Surv. **51**(5) (2018)

8. Buyya, R., et al.: Energy-efficiency and sustainability in new generation cloud computing: a vision and directions for integrated management of data centre resources and workloads. Softw.: Pract. Exp. **54**(1), 24–38 (2024)

9. Dayarathna, M., et al.: Data center energy consumption modeling: a survey. IEEE Commun. Surv. Tutor. **18**(1), 732–794 (2015)

10. Foundation, C.N.C.: Cloud Native 2024: Approaching a Decade of Code, Cloud, and Change (2025). https://www.cncf.io/reports/cncf-annual-survey-2024/. Accessed July 2025

11. Hameed, A., et al.: A survey and taxonomy on energy efficient resource allocation techniques for cloud computing systems. Computing **98**, 751–774 (2016)

12. Helali, L., et al.: A survey of data center consolidation in cloud computing systems. Comput. Sci. Rev. **39**, 100366 (2021)

13. Hilman, M., et al.: Multiple workflows scheduling in multi-tenant distributed systems: a taxonomy and future directions. ACM Comput. Surv. **53**(1), 1–39 (2020)

14. Katal, A., et al.: Energy efficiency in cloud computing data centers: a survey on software technologies. Cluster Comput. **26**(3), 1845–1875 (2023)

15. Kaur, T., et al.: Energy efficiency techniques in cloud computing: a survey and taxonomy. ACM Comput. Surv. **48**(2), 1–46 (2015)

16. Mastelic, T., et al.: Cloud computing: survey on energy efficiency. ACM Comput. Surv. **47**(2), 1–36 (2014)

17. Orgerie, A.-C., et al.: A survey on techniques for improving the energy efficiency of large-scale distributed systems. ACM Comput. Surv. **46**(4), 1–31 (2014)

18. Panwar, S.S., et al.: A systematic review on effective energy utilization management strategies in cloud data centers. J. Cloud Comput. **11**(1), 95 (2022)

19. Petersen, K., et al.: Guidelines for conducting systematic mapping studies in software engineering: an update. Inf. Softw. Technol. **64**, 1–18 (2015)

20. Shuja, J., et al.: Greening emerging IT technologies: techniques and practices. J. Internet Serv. Appl. **8**, 1–11 (2017)

21. Sriraman, A., et al.: μ suite: a benchmark suite for microservices. In: Proceedings of the IEEE International Symposium on Workload Characterization, pp. 1–12 (2018)

22. Valdivia, J., et al.: Quality attributes in patterns related to microservice architecture: a Systematic Literature Review. In: 2019 7th International Conference in Software Engineering Research and Innovation, pp. 181–190 (2019)

23. Venters, C., et al.: Sustainable software engineering: reflections on advances in research and practice. Inf. Softw. Technol. (2023)

24. Vos, S., et al.: Architectural tactics to optimize software for energy efficiency in the public cloud. In: International Conference on ICT for Sustainability (ICT4S) (2022)

25. Xu, M., Buyya, R.: Brownout approach for adaptive management of resources and applications in cloud computing systems: a taxonomy and future directions. ACM Comput. Surv. **52**(1), 1–27 (2019)
26. Zhong, Z., et al: Machine learning-based orchestration of containers: a taxonomy and future directions. ACM Comput. Surv. **54**, 1–35 (2022)

Domain Knowledge in Requirements Engineering: A Systematic Mapping Study

Marina Araújo[(✉)] , Júlia Araújo , Romeu Oliveira , Lucas Romao ,
and Marcos Kalinowski

Pontifical Catholic University of Rio de Janeiro (PUC-Rio), Rio de Janeiro, Brazil
{maraujo,jcaraujo,rferreira,lromao,kalinowski}@inf.puc-rio.br

Abstract. Domain knowledge is recognized as a key component for the
success of Requirements Engineering (RE), as it provides the conceptual support needed to understand the system context, ensure alignment
with stakeholder needs, and reduce ambiguity in requirements specification. Despite its relevance, the scientific literature still lacks a systematic consolidation of how domain knowledge can be effectively used and
operationalized in RE. [Goal] This paper addresses this gap by offering a comprehensive overview of existing contributions, including methods, techniques, and tools to incorporate domain knowledge into RE
practices. [Method] We conducted a systematic mapping study using
a hybrid search strategy that combines database searches with iterative backward and forward snowballing. [Results] In total, we found
75 papers that met our inclusion criteria. The analysis highlights the
main types of requirements addressed, the most frequently considered
quality attributes, and recurring challenges in the formalization, acquisition, and long-term maintenance of domain knowledge. The results provide support for researchers and practitioners in identifying established
approaches and unresolved issues. The study also outlines promising
directions for future research, emphasizing the development of scalable,
automated, and sustainable solutions to integrate domain knowledge into
RE processes. [Conclusion] The study contributes by providing a comprehensive overview that helps to build a conceptual and methodological
foundation for knowledge-driven requirements engineering.

Keywords: Domain knowledge · Requirements engineering ·
Systematic mapping

1 Introduction

Domain knowledge plays a fundamental role in Requirements Engineering (RE),
as it provides the context for understanding, eliciting, and validating requirements [29]. In the context of software development, domain knowledge refers
to the specialized understanding of the field in which a system operates. This
knowledge is essential to ensure that the software meets the user's needs and is

© The Author(s), under exclusive license to Springer Nature Switzerland AG 2026
D. Taibi and D. Smite (Eds.): SEAA 2025, LNCS 16082, pp. 425–441, 2026.
https://doi.org/10.1007/978-3-032-04200-2_29

aligned with their objectives. However, capturing and integrating domain knowledge into the requirements process presents significant challenges, particularly in complex and evolving domains [6], given that domain knowledge is often tacit, residing in human expertise and embedded within organizational processes [19].

The relation between domain knowledge and requirements engineering (RE) has been extensively studied. Studies have demonstrated that domain knowledge enhances the quality of requirements by reducing ambiguity and increasing specificity. In this context, research indicates that understanding the domain is as crucial as understanding the technical aspects of software development. Without adequate domain knowledge, RE activities risk becoming superficial, leading to requirements that fail to fully address stakeholder needs [16].

Over the years, several solution proposals to enhance domain knowledge integration emerged in RE. Techniques such as knowledge-based requirements engineering, domain ontologies, and model-driven approaches have been proposed to formalize and structure domain knowledge within the RE process [22]. Additionally, artificial intelligence (AI) and machine learning (ML) are being explored as tools for extracting domain knowledge from existing data sources [13].

Recognizing the importance of domain knowledge in RE, we contribute a systematic analysis of existing research on this topic. Our objective is to characterize the role of domain knowledge in RE in terms of its impact on requirements quality, challenges in capturing and utilizing it, and the methodologies employed to enhance domain knowledge integration in RE processes. Therefore, we conducted a systematic mapping study, strictly following the search strategy recommended by Wohlin *et al.* [27]. We identified 75 articles that present contributions related to domain knowledge to support RE.

Our findings indicate that several studies have applied domain knowledge-based solutions to support key RE activities, such as requirements elicitation, analysis, and validation. Furthermore, we identify key challenges such as knowledge transfer between domain experts and software engineers, evolving domain landscapes, and the need for structured knowledge representation. Addressing these challenges is essential for ensuring that RE practices effectively leverage domain knowledge to produce high-quality software systems.

The remainder of this paper is structured as follows. Section 2 outlines the background and provides an overview of the related work. Section 3 details the mapping study protocol and its implementation. Section 4 presents the results of the mapping study. Section 5 discusses the findings. Section 6 discusses potential threats to the validity of our study. Lastly, Sect. 7 offers the concluding remarks.

2   Background and Related Work

Effective RE is fundamentally intertwined with a deep understanding of the problem domain. Domain knowledge, encompassing the concepts, relationships, and constraints specific to a particular field, is crucial for eliciting, analyzing, specifying, and validating requirements that are both accurate and relevant [29].

This section lays the background for a deeper understanding of the role and management of domain knowledge within the RE process.

An important aspect of RE is the need for stakeholders to have sufficient expertise to effectively communicate their needs and expectations. Without a solid grasp of the domain, stakeholders may have difficulty articulating requirements precisely, leading to ambiguity, incompleteness, and, ultimately, to a system that fails to meet its intended purpose. This is particularly relevant in complex or specialized domains [3,5,9,20,29]. Furthermore, requirement validation is highly dependent on domain knowledge. Ensuring that requirements are consistent, complete, and feasible requires a thorough understanding of their constraints, limitations, and potential risks [14,21], as well as the implicit need for feasibility assessment [7].

The selection and application of appropriate RE techniques, as well as effective management of evolving requirements, also depend on domain expertise [2,8,11]. It is important that all terminology used in RE be related to the reality of the environment in which the system will be used. Zave and Jackson [29] emphasized the importance of avoiding vague or abstract terms, which can lead to erroneous interpretations and ambiguities. To ensure clarity, each term employed in RE should be precisely defined, connecting it to concrete, real-world concepts. The work by Parnas and Madey [17] and van Schouwen et al. [23] presents a methodology and a set of tools for documenting software requirements, emphasizing the importance of clear and precise specifications. Their approach highlights the need for a shared understanding of the domain between stakeholders and developers, which is facilitated by the use of structured documentation and formal methods [3,9,20,29].

The aforementioned studies recognize and reinforce the role of domain knowledge in RE. However, we did not identify research specifically focused on investigating and synthesizing the state of the art of approaches based on the acquisition and management of domain knowledge to support RE activities.

3 Systematic Mapping Protocol

Systematic Mapping (SM) studies are designed to provide a broad overview of a research area, identify the existence of evidence on a topic, and indicate the quantity of such evidence. The SM study was conducted following the guidelines proposed by Kitchenham and Charters [10], as well as the SM-specific guidelines by Petersen et al. [18]. After identifying the need for the review, we defined the research questions, search strategy, and inclusion/exclusion criteria.

3.1 Goal and Research Questions

The main goal of this systematic mapping is to identify and analyze research that leverages domain knowledge to support RE activities. To support this objective, the following research questions were defined.

RQ1. What domain knowledge contributions have emerged to support RE? This question aims to provide an overview of the contributions related to domain knowledge that support the execution of RE activities.

RQ2. What types of domain knowledge are addressed by the identified contributions? The goal of this question is to identify the different types of domain knowledge considered (tacit, explicit knowledge, or both), helping to understand its role in the elicitation and specification of requirements.

RQ3. What types of requirements were most addressed by the domain knowledge-related contributions? Here, the aim is to investigate whether the identified contributions focus on functional or non-functional requirements.

RQ4. What quality attributes or non-functional requirements (NFRs) were most addressed in domain knowledge-related research? According to the ISO 25010 [1], domain knowledge can impact different quality characteristics (*e.g.*, performance, maintainability, and usability). This question aims to identify which quality attributes were most addressed.

RQ5. What are the main research challenges reported at the intersection of domain knowledge and RE? This question seeks to identify unresolved issues and obstacles in integrating domain knowledge into RE, highlighting gaps that hinder progress in this field.

RQ6. What are the main research directions reported at the intersection of domain knowledge and RE? This question aims to identify opportunities for future research, helping to guide new studies and investigations.

RQ7. What types of research were identified in the contributions? The goal of this question is to classify the studies according to their research type facets, adopting the taxonomy by Wieringa et al. [25]. This will help understand the nature of the contributions.

RQ8. What types of empirical evaluations were conducted to assess the contributions? This question aims to identify the empirical methods used (experiments, comparative studies, case studies), providing insight into the scientific rigor and maturity of the evidence in the field.

While questions RQ1-RQ4 aim at structuring the publication landscape in a conceptual manner, RQ5 and RQ6 focus on identifying challenges and future research directions, finally RQ7 and RQ8 provide insights into the nature of the current reported evidence.

3.2 Search Strategy

The mapping study used a hybrid search strategy [27], which involved performing a database search with a search string on a particular digital library (Scopus) to identify a representative seed set and then applying iterative backward and forward snowballing (using Google Scholar). We chose this hybrid strategy as it has shown to be effective to identify relevant primary studies [27]. We selected the more comprehensive iterative snowballing technique to maximize recall, even though it would mean analyzing a greater number of papers [15]. Iterative backward and forward snowballing entails applying both backward and forward snowballing on every newly included paper.

To begin the database search on Scopus, we crafted the search string using the PICO (Population, Intervention, Comparison, Outcome) criteria [12]. Our study focuses on RE (population) and investigates the contribution of domain knowledge (intervention) to this field. Since this is a mapping study, there was no need for specific comparisons or limiting the outcomes, so we only required keywords related to RE and domain knowledge. The defined search string, to be applied on titles, abstracts and keywords was: *"Requirements Engineering" AND "Domain Knowledge"*. It is noteworthy that this search string is only used to retrieve and filter a representative initial seed set, which is then complemented by applying detailed iterative backward and forward snowballing procedures.

3.3   Study Selection

The primary inclusion criterion focused on studies presenting contributions related to domain knowledge that support RE (IC1). If multiple papers reported the same study, only the most recent one was included.

To ensure the quality and relevance of the selected papers, we applied specific exclusion criteria. RE is a research area with a high volume of publications and numerous contributions from different perspectives. Given this extensive body of work, it was essential to apply a filtering strategy to focus on the most impactful studies. Therefore, we restricted our selection to papers published in the top 20 venues in software engineering (SE) and the top 5 venues in RE, as ranked by Google Scholar. This approach ensured that our dataset consisted only of rigorously peer-reviewed research from the most authoritative sources while keeping the study manageable. Additionally, we excluded papers that do not include, in the title, abstract, or keywords, at least the terms 'Requirements' or 'Domain', in order to retain only studies with a direct connection to the topic under investigation. Finally we excluded grey literature and short papers. The selection criteria applied for filtering the papers are shown in Table 1.

Table 1. Selection criteria.

Criteria	Description
IC1	Articles that present contributions related to domain knowledge that have emerged to support RE
EC1	Papers that are not full papers published in the main venues of the SE field or in the leading venues specifically focused on RE
EC2	Papers that not include, in the title, abstract, or keywords, terms such as 'Requirements' or 'Domain'
EC3	Theses and dissertations, book chapters, calls for papers, basic teaching materials, and short papers (less than 6 pages)

The selected SE venues were the Google Scholar top-ranked venues in the area at the time of writing this article[1]: *International Conference on Software Engineering*; *IEEE Transactions on Software Engineering*; *Journal of Systems and Software*; *Proceedings of the ACM on Programming Languages*; *Information and Software Technology*; *Empirical Software Engineering*; *International Symposium on Foundations of Software Engineering*; *International Conference on Automated Software Engineering*, *ACM SIGPLAN Conference on Programming Language Design and Implementation*; *ACM Transactions on Software Engineering and Methodology*; *Mining Software Repositories*; *International Symposium on Software Testing and Analysis*; *IEEE Software*; *Software: Practice and Experience*; *Software and Systems Modeling*; *Symposium on Operating Systems Principles*; *International Conference on Software Analysis, Evolution, and Reengineering*; *International Conference on Tools and Algorithms for the Construction and Analysis of Systems*; *Symposium on Principles and Practice of Parallel Programming*; and the *International Conference on Software Maintenance and Evolution*.

For RE, we specifically included the *IEEE International Requirements Engineering Conference (RE Conference)*, the *Requirements Engineering Journal (RE Journal)*, the *International Working Conference on Requirements Engineering: Foundation for Software Quality (REFSQ)*, the *International Conference on Advanced Information Systems Engineering (CAiSE)*, and *ACM Symposium on Applied Computing âĂŞ Requirements Engineering Track (ACM SAC - RE Track)*. CAiSE and ACM SAC were included because they have a dedicated RE track, making them relevant for research in the field.

Given that the selection criteria already imposed strict restrictions regarding the source of the publications (only full papers from high-quality journals and conferences), we assume methodological quality and scientific relevance in the included studies. Therefore, no additional quality assessment criteria were applied in this review.

Figure 1 illustrates the steps carried out in the paper selection process. The first step consisted of conducting a search using the search string in the digital library selected for this study. The search string was applied to titles, abstracts, and keywords in Scopus, in February 2025, resulting in 289 papers. Exclusion criterion EC1 was then applied, removing papers that were not published in the selected venues, reducing the set to 66 papers. Next, exclusion criterion EC2 was applied, eliminating all papers that did not contain the terms 'domain' or 'requirements' in the title, abstract, or keywords. Finally, EC3 excluded grey literature and short papers. As a result, 11 papers were included.

In the following stage, carried out during the months of March and April, the iterative backward and forward snowballing process was applied, following the guidelines established by [26]. A total of five backward snowballing (BS) and five forward snowballing (FS) iterations were conducted until the final set of studies was consolidated (*i.e.*, no more cited or citing studies to be included

---

[1] Google Scholar - Category Software Systems https://scholar.google.com/citations?view_op=top_venues&hl=en&vq=eng_softwaresystems.

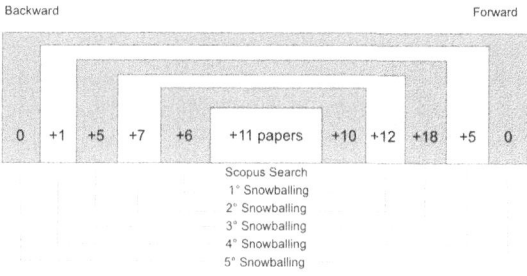

Fig. 1. Papers selection process.

were found). The ten snowballing iterations (BS and FS) resulted in analyzing 1.687 papers that passed the exclusion criterion EC1 (*i.e.*, that were published in the selected venues).

After removing duplicates, applying the inclusion criterion and the exclusion criteria EC2 and EC3, 64 papers were selected to compose the final set obtained through snowballing. Therefore, the study included a total of 75 papers: 11 from the Scopus search and 64 from the snowballing process. The detailed filtering process, including all papers analyzed from Scopus and from each snowballing iteration, as well as the application of the criteria to each paper, is transparently available in our open science repository [4].

3.4   Data Extraction and Classification Scheme

The data and information collected from the selected papers, along with the classification schemes outlining the various categories, are presented in Table 2. The full set of extracted data is also accessible in our online open science repository [4].

Table 2. Data Extraction Form.

Information	Description
Domain Knowledge Contributions (RQ1)	Contributions related to domain knowledge that emerged to support RE
Types of Domain Knowledge (RQ2)	Types of domain knowledge that were addressed by the identified contributions
Requirement Types (RQ3)	Types of requirements that were most addressed by the contributions related to domain knowledge
Quality Attributes/Non-Functional Requirements (RQ4)	Quality attributes or non-functional requirements (NFRs) that were most addressed in research related to domain knowledge
Research Challenges (RQ5)	Major research challenges reported at the intersection of domain knowledge and RE
Research Directions (RQ6)	Main research directions reported at the intersection of domain knowledge and RE
Research Type Facet (RQ7)	The classification of research types: evaluation research, solution proposal, philosophical paper, opinion paper, or experience paper, as outlined by Wieringa *et al.* [25]
Empirical Evaluation (RQ8)	Classification of the empirical strategy [28], including categories such as experiment and case study

4   Systematic Mapping Results

This section presents the results of the systematic mapping study on Domain Knowledge for RE. The selected studies were analyzed based on predefined classification criteria, aiming to provide a structured overview of how domain knowledge has been addressed in the context of RE. Due to space constraints, we had to move the references of the 75 included studies (P1–P75) to an online supplement in our open science repository [4]. The results are detailed hereafter.

4.1   RQ.1 What Domain Knowledge Contributions Have Emerged to Support RE?

The literature review indicates that contributions related to the use of domain knowledge in RE are predominantly grouped into three categories: methods, techniques, and tools, as presented in Table 3.

Table 3. Identified Contributions.

Category	ID	Examples
Method (3)	P3, P11, P69	Some studies propose structured methods for using domain knowledge. One transforms textual requirements into production rules [P3], another uses conceptual modeling for complex domains [P11], and a third applies logic-based structures to formalize semantics [P69]
Method and Technique (11)	P1, P10, P14, P16, P17, P19, P21, P22, P57, P61, P68	Several works combine formal modeling with semantic techniques. Some align models with domain terms [P1], reuse prior requirements via similarity [P10], or integrate automated extraction with structured modeling [P14, P16, P21, P22]
Method and Tool (4)	P35, P38, P39, P59	Some methods are implemented with tool support. Examples include semantic visualizations [P35], interactive categorization [P38, P39] and automated validation [P59]
Technique and Tool (7)	P4, P25, P36, P37, P42, P65, P67	These studies merge techniques like clustering and NLP with tools for elicitation and analysis. Applications include collaborative modeling [P4], similarity detection [P25, P36], and semantic mapping [P42, P67]
Method, Technique and Tool (46)	P2, P5, P6, P7, P9, P12, P13, P15, P18, P20, P23, P24, P26, P27, P28, P29, P30, P32, P33, P34, P40, P41, P44, P45, P46, P47, P49, P50, P51, P52, P53, P54, P55, P56, P58, P60, P62, P63, P64, P66, P70, P71, P72, P73, P74, P75	This is the most common category. Examples include Domain Theory combining ontologies and tools [P2], automated extraction using embeddings [P5], semantic reasoning in critical systems [P6], and hybrid frameworks for intelligent elicitation [P13]. Many others follow similar patterns
Other (4)	P8, P31, P43, P48	Some works offer theoretical reflections, methodologies and frameworks. One discusses tacit knowledge challenges [P8], another highlights gaps in formalization [P43], and a third critiques traditional elicitation in agile settings [P48]

These contributions aim to formalize and operationalize knowledge derived from experts or structured sources, with the objective of enhancing key processes such as requirements elicitation, analysis, and validation. The category analysis reveals that 3 articles were identified in the exclusive method category, the method and technique combination includes 11 articles, method and tool accounts for 4 articles, technique and tool includes 7 articles and the most comprehensive combination, method, technique, and tool, comprises 46 articles. Finally, the other category, which includes methodology, framework, and evaluation, encompasses 4 articles. Notably, no study was classified solely as a technique or a tool without being integrated with other approaches.

4.2 RQ.2 What Types of Domain Knowledge are Addressed by the Identified Contributions?

The vast majority of the selected papers address explicit domain knowledge (68 out of 75), emphasizing formalization, representation, and computational manipulation. A smaller number of contributions explore tacit knowledge (2 papers), often related to expert judgment or experiential insights. Additionally, 5 studies propose hybrid approaches, combining both explicit and tacit elements to enrich the elicitation and modeling of requirements. These results highlight a predominant focus on knowledge that can be structured and encoded, with limited attention to more experiential or informal dimensions.

4.3 RQ.3 What Types of Requirements Were Most Addressed by the Domain Knowledge-Related Contributions?

An analysis of the selected studies reveals distinct emphases regarding the types of requirements addressed through domain knowledge. Among the 75 contributions reviewed, the majority focused on functional requirements (34 papers), indicating a prevailing concern with specifying system behaviors and functionalities grounded in domain expertise. In addition, 24 studies addressed nonfunctional requirements, and 17 contributions considered both types simultaneously. This distribution highlights the predominant attention given to functional aspects, while also evidencing a meaningful, though less frequent, effort to use domain knowledge to address quality-related attributes in the RE process.

4.4 RQ.4 What Quality Attributes Were Most Addressed in Domain Knowledge-Related Research?

The analysis of the contributions enabled the identification of a variety of quality requirements, also referred to as non-functional requirements (NFRs), addressed in the selected studies. Table 4 presents the frequency with which these quality characteristics are considered across the papers. The definition and categorization of these quality criteria are based on the ISO 25010 [1]. It is possible to observe that domain knowledge has been mainly considered to support reliability, compliance, usability, and security-related issues.

4.5 RQ.5 What Are the Main Research Challenges Reported at the Intersection of Domain Knowledge and RE?

The integration of domain knowledge into RE presents a range of challenges, which have been consistently reported across the literature. Based on the analysis

Table 4. Frequency of quality characteristics.

Characteristic	Frequency	Characteristic	Frequency
Adaptability	5	Usability	23
Portability	0	Compatibility	3
Security	20	Performance	8
Reliability	28	Maintainability	9
Compliance	23	–	–

of the 75 selected papers, the challenges can be grouped into three themes: technical, acquisition, and management challenges.

Technical Challenges: This was the most frequently reported category in the analysis. Common issues include the complexity of integrating domain knowledge into modeling and reasoning tools [P2, P5, P12], limitations in the scalability of formal representations [P1, P27, P33], and the lack of tool support for semantic or rule-based processing [P3, P6, P13, P42, P46]. Other studies pointed to the need for advanced mechanisms to maintain traceability and consistency during the application of domain knowledge [P36, P44, P52, P64].

Acquisition Challenges: Refer to the difficulties in capturing, formalizing, and structuring domain knowledge. Many papers highlighted the lack of accessible documentation or expert availability, especially in complex or regulated domains [P7, P9, P14, P28, P53]. Others emphasized the need for automated or semi-automated extraction methods [P26, P34, P38, P51, P61], as well as barriers to generalizing tacit knowledge into reusable forms [P13, P25, P29].

Management Challenges: This was the least reported category, these challenges revolve around the governance, evolution, and standardization of domain knowledge over time. For instance, papers such as P10, P16, and P20 mentioned difficulties in maintaining knowledge consistency across system updates or organizational changes. Others [P22, P27, P31, P54] discussed the lack of versioning strategies, reuse policies, and the need for institutional frameworks to support the long-term management of knowledge assets.

4.6 RQ.6 What Are the Main Research Directions Reported at the Intersection of Domain Knowledge and RE?

The analysis of research directions reported in the selected articles reveals a consensus on the need for continuous advancements on multiple fronts, which can be grouped into seven themes.

First, **Enhancement of Techniques and Methods** proposes the development and refinement using AI approaches through the application of advancements in Natural Language Processing (NLP), Large Language Models (LLMs), and machine learning (ML) [P5, P6, P32, P50]. Future research seeks to improve the extraction, representation (*e.g.*, via ontologies and knowledge graphs [P2, P29]), and reasoning about domain knowledge to identify, analyze, and validate requirements more accurately, addressing challenges such as ambiguity [P7, P71], variability [P35, P43], and tacit requirements [P35]. Increasing the explainability and interpretability of applied AI models is also a concern [P49, P59].

Second, **Generalization, Scalability, and Applicability** point to the need to adapt and validate techniques new domains (e.g., healthcare, finance, building and infrastructure industry, critical systems) [P3, P14, P15], deal with different languages and requirements formats [P16, P73], and ensure that approaches are scalable for large-scale systems [P9, P28].

Third, **Automation and Tool Support** aims to reduce manual effort and increase the efficiency of requirements engineers. Directions include the development of more sophisticated tools to partially or fully automate the construction of domain models [P5, P12], the extraction and annotation of requirements [P13, P42], the generation of artifacts [P39, P53], and integration with development environments [P2, P23].

Fourth, **User Focus, Collaboration, and Interaction** recognizes the importance of the human factor. Future research aims to improve the involvement of experts and stakeholders in the RE lifecycle [P1, P31], develop mechanisms for collecting and incorporating user feedback [P24, P26, P36], support negotiation and collaborative conflict resolution [P28, P69], and explore the personalization of RE approaches [P57].

Fifth, **Integration and Interoperability** seeks creating more holistic solutions. This includes the integration of different logics and modeling paradigms [P1, P33], the combination of symbolic and learning-based techniques [P52], and a stronger connection with other SE artifacts and processes, such as architectural design and defect analysis [P35, P45, P56].

Sixth **Validation and Empirical Evaluation** future directions include conducting more case studies in real industrial contexts [P3, P61], controlled experiments, usability studies with requirements engineers [P6, P9], and the development of benchmarks and metrics for comparative evaluation of approaches [P19, P59].

Finally, **Knowledge Management, Evolution, and Quality** are important directions to ensure the long-term relevance and utility of domain knowledge in RE. This involves research on how to maintain and evolve domain models and ontologies [P8, P21, P38], ensure traceability and consistency of requirements [P31, P45], manage volatility, and identify missing or inconsistent requirements [P8, P51, P75].

4.7 RQ.7 What Types of Research Were Identified in the Contributions?

To structure the data regarding the type of research in the analyzed papers, we initially considered the primary intent of each study. For example, if a given paper proposed a method, technique, or tool, it was classified as a "Solution

Proposal", even if it included some empirical study. In such cases, the evaluation or validation of the proposal was regarded as a secondary intent, serving as methodological support to empirically substantiate the proposed approach. By considering this, most of the analyzed papers were classified as "Solution Proposal", totaling 69 studies. Research with a primary intent related to evaluation accounted for 5 papers. Additionally, 1 paper was identified as an "Opinion Paper". Considering the primary focus, no validation research, philosophical papers, or personal experience papers were identified. Table 5 presents a quantitative summary of the articles grouped by research type.

Table 5. Research Types.

Information	Description
Research type	Highlights/ Examples
Solution proposal (69)	Development of new methods, techniques, or tools, often accompanied by some form of empirical study. For example, in paper P2, the authors propose a solution evaluated with the support of RE experts, including cognitive studies (such as card sorting) and application in real-world scenarios. In P5, the proposal is scenario-based and supported by a tool designed to collect software requirements specific to the building and infrastructure industry. In paper P7, the authors present a method for detecting and interpreting syntactic ambiguity, which is rigorously evaluated using quantitative metrics (precision, recall, and accuracy), comparisons with the Stanford Parser and a generic corpus, as well as validation across seven distinct industrial domains
Evaluation research (5)	Evaluations conducted in case studies or industrial settings. Some conducted evaluations were not necessarily empirical. For instance, P8 involved the support of experts for the application and evaluation of the card sorting method as a knowledge elicitation technique in requirements. Additionally, P31 evaluates a methodology for analyzing security and privacy requirements regarding compliance with legislation (HIPAA), using a case study that involves mapping, refinement, and traceability of existing requirements
Opinion paper (1)	Literature review and theoretical development of a conceptual framework. There is no proposal for a technical solution or systematic empirical evaluation, but rather a structured reflection on existing approaches and future directions [P43]

We also highlight the strong intersections between solution proposals (primary intent) and some form of empirical study, as many papers proposed a strategy and have already undertaken some form of evaluation and/or validation. As shown in Fig. 2, only three papers proposed a solution without conducting empirical studies for its evaluation and/or validation. Conversely, 17 papers performed both empirical evaluations and validations of the proposed solution. In the responses to RQ8, we provide a more detailed discussion regarding the types of empirical studies applied.

4.8   RQ.8 What Types of Empirical Evaluations Were Conducted to Assess the Contributions?

Among the 75 papers included in this mapping, the majority conducted some type of empirical study, totaling 70 papers. It is also worth noting that several of these articles applied more than one type of empirical study (Fig. 3). For

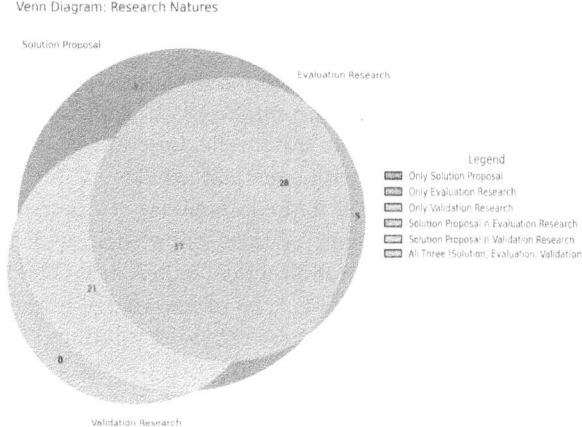

Fig. 2. Quantitative summary of the types of research identified and their intersections.

example, some works combined case studies and comparative studies in their research. It was possible to observe that a portion of the studies empirically supported their approaches using only experimental studies, totaling 26 papers, while 25 papers used only case studies. Finally, only 5 papers did not include any type of empirical study.

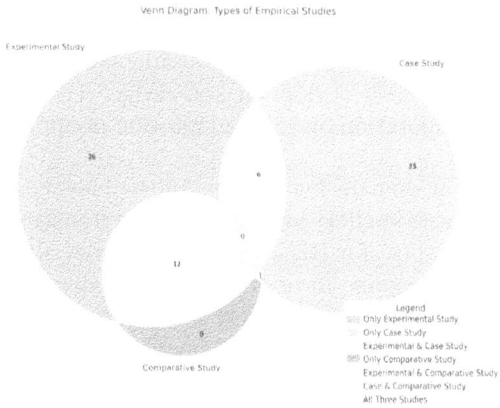

Fig. 3. Quantitative summary of the types of empirical studies identified and their intersections.

5   Discussion

The results indicate a significant amount of research that involves the application of domain knowledge in RE, with an emphasis on approaches that integrate methods, techniques, and tools. This trend reflects a pursuit of more structured and automated solutions aligned with practical needs.

We also observed that there is a predominance of approaches focused on explicit knowledge, to the detriment of tacit knowledge, which is essential in complex domains that rely heavily on practical experience. The lack of effective strategies to capture and integrate this type of knowledge reveals an important gap and highlights the need for more robust hybrid solutions capable of articulating different forms of knowledge.

Although non-functional requirements (NFRs) such as reliability, security, and usability are critical for software quality, especially in regulated or high-risk environments, this study reveals a predominant focus on functional requirements. Among the 75 analyzed papers, 34 addressed only functional requirements, compared to 24 that focused on NFRs and 17 that considered both. This imbalance reflects a common issue in software engineering, where NFRs are often postponed or neglected, a practice that can lead to rework, financial loss, and compliance failures [24].

On the other hand, technical challenges remain, such as difficulties in scaling formal representations, integrating tools, and efficiently maintaining traceability. In addition, barriers persist in knowledge acquisition, whether due to the lack of proper documentation or limited access to experts. Management aspects, such as updating and reusing knowledge over time, are also still underexplored.

Future research directions indicate increasing interest in the use of artificial intelligence, machine learning, and natural language processing to support the extraction and application of domain knowledge. There is also a growing emphasis on expert collaboration and the adaptation of approaches to different organizational contexts.

The predominance of domain knowledge studies classified as solution proposals may reflect a proactive effort by researchers to translate theoretical foundations into practical support for RE activities. However, although most of the analyzed proposals include some form of empirical evaluation, there is still an opportunity to deepen these investigations in industrial settings and with greater methodological rigor. Broader and more replicable studies supported by standardized metrics can play an important role in consolidating existing practices and strengthening the practical impact of the contributions in RE.

6   Threats to Validity

This section outlines potential threats to the validity of our systematic mapping study and describes the measures adopted to mitigate them.

With respect to **internal validity**, a common threat for systematic mapping studies concerns the application of the search strategy. We designed the search string based on the PICO strategy to ensure direct alignment with our research goals. Furthermore, we employed a hybrid search strategy that combined database searches with iterative backward and forward snowballing. This approach has been recognized as effective in secondary studies, contributing to a representative selection of relevant papers [27]. The search strategy was systematically applied and thoroughly documented in our open science repository [4], with details on each snowballing iteration and the screening of the papers.

Regarding **external validity**, we used a search strategy recognized as a suitable approach for secondary studies. Despite these efforts, it is not possible to completely rule out the possibility that some relevant studies might have been missed. However, no additional publications matching our inclusion criteria were identified through manual searches, which reinforces our confidence in having a representative dataset. The conclusions presented in this work are based exclusively on the evidence reported in the included primary studies. Although all selected studies were peer-reviewed and published in the most influential venues in the field, we did not conduct a formal assessment of methodological quality. This step, while relevant, is generally not part of the scope of mapping studies and may be incorporated in a future systematic review.

Finally, concerning **reliability**, to reduce potential bias in study selection, screening, data extraction, and coding were independently conducted by two researchers with peer review. A third researcher mediated any disagreements, which were resolved by consensus, ensuring the consistency and reliability of the results. All methodological details, including the search protocol, data extraction procedures, and coding criteria, are transparently documented and publicly available and auditable in our open science repository [4].

7   Concluding Remarks

This paper presents the results of a systematic mapping study on domain knowledge-based research aimed at supporting RE activities. We applied a hybrid search strategy, combining a structured search on the Scopus database with iterative backward and forward snowballing using Google Scholar. This approach enabled the identification of a total of 75 primary studies.

We summarized and classified the identified contributions into categories such as methods, techniques, tools, or their combinations. These studies address both functional and non-functional requirements, with particular emphasis on quality attributes like reliability, usability, and security. We also analyzed the types of domain knowledge considered (explicit, tacit, and hybrid), the nature of the research (*e.g.*, solution proposals and evaluation studies), and the empirical strategies adopted for validation. Our analysis revealed recurring technical, acquisition, and management challenges, as well as a wide range of promising research directions. These include the application of AI techniques, improvements in tool support, enhanced user collaboration, and more rigorous empirical validation in industrial contexts.

To the best of our knowledge, this is the first systematic mapping study to consolidate evidence on how domain knowledge has been used to support RE processes. Hence, the main contributions of this study are twofold: (i) providing a structured map of current contributions that integrate domain knowledge into RE practices, a topic of growing importance but that was still lacking systematization; and (ii) identifying critical research gaps and future research opportunities that can inform and guide subsequent investigations.

Acknowledgment. We express our gratitude to CNPq (Grant 312275/2023-4), FAPERJ (Grant E-26/204.256/2024), Kunumi, and Stone Co. for their generous support.

References

1. ISO/IEC 25010:2023 Systems and software engineering—Systems and software Quality Requirements and Evaluation (SQuaRE)—Product quality model, Std. (2023). https://www.iso.org/standard/78176.html
2. Agrawal, R., Imieliński, T., Swami, A.: Mining association rules between sets of items in large databases. In: ACM SIGMOD International Conference on Management of Data, pp. 207–216 (1993)
3. Aranda, A.M., Dieste, O., Juristo, N.: Effect of domain knowledge on elicitation effectiveness: an internally replicated controlled experiment. IEEE Trans. Softw. Eng. **42**(5), 427–451 (2015)
4. Araújo, M., Araújo, J., Oliveira, R., Romao, L., Kalinowski, M.: Artifacts - domain knowledge in requirements engineering: a systematic mapping study (2025). https://doi.org/10.5281/zenodo.15491047
5. Callele, D., Neufeld, E., Schneider, K.: Requirements engineering and the creative process in the video game industry. In: IEEE International Conference on Requirements Engineering, pp. 240–250 (2005)
6. Cao, L., Ramesh, B.: Agile requirements engineering practices: an empirical study. IEEE Softw. **25**(1), 60–67 (2008)
7. Chen, B., et al.: On the use of GPT-4 for creating goal models: an exploratory study. In: International Requirements Engineering Conference Workshops, pp. 262–271 (2023)
8. Guo, J.L., Monaikul, N., Cleland-Huang, J.: Domain knowledge discovery guided by software trace links. In: International Workshop on Artificial Intelligence for Requirements Engineering, pp. 1–7 (2018)
9. Hadar, I., Soffer, P., Kenzi, K.: The role of domain knowledge in requirements elicitation via interviews: an exploratory study. Requirements Eng. **19**, 143–159 (2014)
10. Keele, S., et al.: Guidelines for performing systematic literature reviews in software engineering. EBSE Technical report, Keele University, ver. 2.3 (2007)
11. Kim, M., Dey, S., Lee, S.-W.: Ontology-driven security requirements recommendation for apt attack. In: International Requirements Engineering Conference Workshops (REW), pp. 150–156 (2019)
12. Leonardo, R.: PICO: model for clinical questions. Evid. Based Med. Pract. **3**(115), 2 (2018)
13. Li, T., Zhang, X., Wang, Y., Zhou, Q., Wang, Y., Dong, F.: Machine learning for requirements engineering (ML4RE): a systematic literature review complemented by practitioners' voices from stack overflow. Inf. Softw. Technol. 107477 (2024)

14. Machanavajjhala, A., Kifer, D., Gehrke, J., Venkitasubramaniam, M.: l-diversity: privacy beyond k-anonymity. ACM Trans. Knowl. Discov. Data (TKDD) **1**(1), 3-es (2007)
15. Mourão, E., Pimentel, J.F., Murta, L., Kalinowski, M., Mendes, E., Wohlin, C.: On the performance of hybrid search strategies for systematic literature reviews in software engineering. Inf. Softw. Technol. **123**, 106294 (2020)
16. Niknafs, A., Berry, D.M.: The impact of domain knowledge on the effectiveness of requirements idea generation during requirements elicitation. In: IEEE International Requirements Engineering Conference (RE), pp. 181–190 (2012)
17. Parnas, D.L., Madey, J.: Functional documents for computer systems. Sci. Comput. Program. **25**(1), 41–61 (1995)
18. Petersen, K., Vakkalanka, S., Kuzniarz, L.: Guidelines for conducting systematic mapping studies in software engineering: an update. Inf. Softw. Technol. **64**, 1–18 (2015)
19. Ryan, S., O'Connor, R.V.: Acquiring and sharing tacit knowledge in software development teams: an empirical study. Inf. Softw. Technol. **55**(9), 1614–1624 (2013)
20. Siqueira, F.L., Silva, P.S.M.: Transforming an enterprise model into a use case model in business process systems. J. Syst. Softw. **96**, 152–171 (2014)
21. Sweeney, L.: k-anonymity: a model for protecting privacy. Internat. J. Uncertain. Fuzziness Knowl.-Based Syst. **10**(05), 557–570 (2002)
22. Umar, M.A., Lano, K., Abubakar, A.K.: Automated requirements engineering framework for agile model-driven development. Front. Comput. Sci. **7**, 1537100 (2025)
23. van Schouwen, A.J., Parnas, D.L., Madey, J.: Documentation of requirements for computer systems. In: IEEE International Symposium on Requirements Engineering, pp. 198–207. IEEE (1993)
24. Viviani, L., Guerra, E., Melegati, J., Wang, X.: An empirical study about the instability and uncertainty of non-functional requirements. In: Stettina, C.J., Garbajosa, J., Kruchten, P. (eds.) XP 2023. LNBIP, vol. 475, pp. 77–93. Springer, Cham (2023). https://doi.org/10.1007/978-3-031-33976-9_6
25. Wieringa, R., Maiden, N., Mead, N., Rolland, C.: Requirements engineering paper classification and evaluation criteria: a proposal and a discussion. Requirements Eng. **11**, 102–107 (2006)
26. Wohlin, C.: Guidelines for snowballing in systematic literature studies and a replication in software engineering. In: International Conference on Evaluation and Assessment in Software Engineering, pp. 1–10 (2014)
27. Wohlin, C., Kalinowski, M., Felizardo, K.R., Mendes, E.: Successful combination of database search and snowballing for identification of primary studies in systematic literature studies. Inf. Softw. Technol. **147**, 106908 (2022)
28. Wohlin, C., Runeson, P., Höst, M., Ohlsson, M.C., Regnell, B., Wesslén, A., et al.: Experimentation in Software Engineering, vol. 236. Springer (2024)
29. Zave, P., Jackson, M.: Four dark corners of requirements engineering. ACM Trans. Softw. Eng. Methodol. (TOSEM) **6**(1), 1–30 (1997)

Author Index

The manufacturer's authorised representative in the EU is Springer
Nature Customer Service Centre GmbH, Europaplatz 3, 69115 Heidelberg,
Germany. If you have any concerns regarding our products, please
contact ProductSafety@springernature.com

Printed and bound by CPI Group (UK) Ltd, Croydon, CR0 4YY
28/04/2026
02098524-0010